Special
Relationships

BOOKS BY HENRY BRANDON

Special Relationships

A FOREIGN CORRESPONDENT'S MEMOIRS

FROM ROOSEVELT TO REAGAN

Henry Brandon

MACMILLAN
LONDON

First published in the United States of America 1988 by Macmillan Publishing Company, New York.

First published in the United Kingdom 1989 by
MACMILLAN LONDON LIMITED
4 Little Essex Street London WC2R 3LF
and Basingstoke

Associated companies in Auckland, Delhi, Dublin, Gaborone, Hamburg, Harare, Hong Kong, Johannesburg, Kuala Lumpur, Lagos, Manzini, Melbourne, Mexico City, Nairobi, New York, Singapore and Tokyo

ISBN 0-333-49920-4

A CIP catalogue record for this book is available from the British Library.

Designed by Jack Meserole

PRINTED IN THE UNITED STATES OF AMERICA

Special Relationships

A FOREIGN CORRESPONDENT'S MEMOIRS

FROM ROOSEVELT TO REAGAN

Henry Brandon

MACMILLAN
LONDON

First published in the United States of America 1988 by Macmillan Publishing Company, New York.

First published in the United Kingdom 1989 by
MACMILLAN LONDON LIMITED
4 Little Essex Street London WC2R 3LF
and Basingstoke

Associated companies in Auckland, Delhi, Dublin, Gaborone, Hamburg, Harare, Hong Kong, Johannesburg, Kuala Lumpur, Lagos, Manzini, Melbourne, Mexico City, Nairobi, New York, Singapore and Tokyo

ISBN 0-333-49920-4

A CIP catalogue record for this book is available from the British Library.

Designed by Jack Meserole

PRINTED IN THE UNITED STATES OF AMERICA

PREFACE

These memoirs reflect two aspects of my life as a journalist, my passion for reporting history in the making and my fascination with people. In my more than thirty-five years of reporting from Washington on the conduct of American politics with sidelong glances at Anglo-American and Soviet-American relations, I had, as the American correspondent of *The Sunday Times* of London, the rare opportunity to witness the dawn of the American Century, the United States rise to superpower status, and the decline of American hegemony, all in a lifetime; during that time span I met almost every great American who played a part in forging the Pax Americana.

By a lucky coincidence I arrived in the United States on my first brief assignment to the United States shortly before the Japanese attack on Pearl Harbor and Hitler's declaration of war. It was the time when the United States began to shed its innocence and suddenly found itself thrust into the mainstream of world history. It also helped to prolong what for me had originally been a three-month assignment. I returned to England in 1942 to become a war correspondent in North Africa and Western Europe and settled down as Paris correspondent after the liberation of Paris. In 1947 I asked to be assigned to the United Nations, which brought me back to the United States, and when that ceased to be a full-time job, I moved to Washington in 1949 to become chief American correspondent. In those days, according to a secret analysis of Anglo-American relations by the British Foreign Office, the US was seen as "having been thrust into a position of world leadership before she had developed fully the experience and political and economic philosophy necessary for the role." The document concluded that "Britain therefore must seek to remain the United States principal partner in world affairs, prevent an American retreat into isolationism or an accommodation with the Soviet Union which would leave Western Europe exposed to Russian pressures and at the mercy of world forces outside her control." Britain's chosen task, at least in the early postwar years; the formidable challenges to Western civilization the United States had to meet and at a speed altogether unprecedented in human history; the mind-boggling inventions, such as nuclear weapons and their impact on warfare and military strategy; the penetration of space; television which brought the world into the living room; and the speed of communications, all contributed to make the assignment to Washington the most desirable, the most exciting, and the most important in the world.

I have reported on nine presidents, from Franklin D. Roosevelt to Ronald Reagan, and I enjoyed many special relationships with some of the leading players on the Washington and world scene. Secretary of State John Foster Dulles once quipped during the Suez crisis, while the British government was in the doghouse, that I had become the last remnant of the "special relationship" with Britain. "Journalism is the only job that robs routine of its monotony," Sir Wilmot Lewis, one of the greatest among British foreign correspondents (he represented the *Times* of London in Washington for over twenty-five years and it was at his knee that I learned my first lessons in how to cover American politics when I arrived here in 1941), used to say, and reporting from Washington is one of the most convincing examples. But if there is anything missing in Washington, it was and is monotony. Part of the challenge to presidents and reporters is the system of political institutions designed to restrain the powers of virtually all of them. Operating the American government therefore is a constant struggle, an endless drama with the outcome more often than not in doubt. It is the greatest political gambling casino in the world, where not even the president—and least of all reporters —can ever take anything for granted or count his winnings in advance.

Anglo-American affinity, similarity of language, and shared interests of national security may suggest that it is easy to understand how the world looks from an American vantage point and to explain how American democracy works, especially in such a wide open society. But I would not be surprised if you think differently by the time you reach the end of this memoir.

We West Europeans have been brought up to respect government, which is not exactly what Americans are taught early on at school. My attitude to the American government was therefore more tolerant than that of my American colleagues, whose adversarial attitude (though it existed between government and the press from the beginning of the Republic) has become intensely antagonistic for various understandable reasons. Under the British political system this clash is not so much between a prime minister and the press as between a prime minister and Parliament where he or she has to answer questions twice a week. Most of the time these questions are not as inquisitive and personal as at a presidential press conference. But, over all, a prime minister is much less shielded from being tested in public than a president. What matters is whether he or she can keep the opposition rather than the press within bounds. Americans, accustomed to a political system of carefully devised checks and balances, are instinctively concerned that the news media have acquired too much unchecked power. That does not prevent them from expressing their appreciation of the critical and investigative role which is the news media's contribution to American democracy. In the absence of divided government in Britain, the press does not have that kind of leverage.

If I enjoyed relatively good contacts in almost every administration of whatever coloration, it was probably thanks to a certain ideological detachment with which I could look over the political battlefields, to my efforts at fairminded reporting, and to my judging any administration not by its political objectives but by how well it governed in the national and international interest. I have approached reporting as a traditionalist, which I am by instinct; as an optimist, which I am by temperament; and as a moderate, for such is my outlook on the world. Though I became gradually convinced that in the interest of a more potent Europe, Britain had to join and take a strong hand in steering the European community, I have remained—and still remain—a strong believer in a close Anglo-American relationship. For me it will always be very special indeed.

ACKNOWLEDGMENTS

The editors of *The Sunday Times* of London gave me an unusual opportunity to live through and report on the United States' rise from a sleeping giant to a superpower. In all I spent some forty-two years in this country, plus some months as a British war correspondent attached, for a period, to the American forces in Europe. It is this experience, unique in so many ways, that has led me to write what are largely my professional memoirs mixed in with some of my personal history.

The diaries I myself kept since 1944 and the scrapbooks compiled with great care by my successive secretaries of everything I have written and published were of enormous help. So were a good many people who played their part in the making of American history and were willing to spend a great deal of time helping me in the sifting of events: Mrs. Dean Acheson, Doak Barnett, Lucius Battle, Sir Isaiah Berlin, Benjamin Bradlee, Zbigniew Brzezinski, Patrick Buchanan, McGeorge Bundy, William P. Bundy, Lord Caccia, Joe Canzeri, Liz Carpenter, Clark Clifford, Lord Franks, Leslie Gelb, Hays Gorey, Harry Harding, Averell Harriman, Richard Helms, Sir Nicholas Henderson, Stephen Hess, Richard Holbrooke, Frank Holman, Lord Hunt, William Hyland, William Kaufmann, Henry Kissinger, Lord Leaver of Manchester, Harold Macmillan, Murray Marder, Robert McNamara, Harry McPherson, Sir Derek Mitchell, Sir Michael Palliser, Richard Perle, Walter Pincus, Jody Powell, William B. Quant, Sir Peter Ramsbotham, James Reston, Chalmers Roberts, Dean Rusk, William Safire, Nathaniel Samuel, Richard M. Scammon, Arthur Schlesinger, Jr., Lord Sherfield, Hugh Sidey, Richard Solomon, John Steinbrunner, Sir Michael Stewart, Jerry terHorst, Sir John Thompson, Bob Woodward, and many others. They were so numerous and cover so many years that I can only thank them in general for their friendship, their patience, and their help.

The main players in my life, of course—at least until I got married in 1970 and until the birth of my daughter, Fiona, in 1971, who was greeted by three baby-sitters; my stepchildren, John, Elizabeth, and Alexandra—have been the editors of *The Sunday Times*. They were not only remarkably gifted journalists, but gentlemen, with whom it was a constant pleasure to work. Apart from the late Iain Lang and the late W. W. Hadley, who gave me my start with *The Sunday Times,* I owe a deep debt of friendship to Sir Denis Hamilton, who knew how to delegate and to lead, and who turned *The Sunday Times* into the most successful among the so-called quality newspapers without lowering its standards—in fact, raising them in many ways. It was he who encouraged me to write three of my earlier books and whose personal interest in my life went well beyond professional boundaries. Professor Richard Neustadt, the late Bromley Smith, General Andrew Goodpaster, Richard Helms, Lloyd Cutler, Robert Bowie, William Bundy, William Safire, Arthur Schlesinger, Jr., and others were especially helpful in reading parts of the manuscript to make sure that I did not indulge in improving on history which they themselves had lived through. But more than anybody, it is Oscar Turnill who deserves my deepest gratitude for helping me not only with this but two earlier books. His constructive intelligence in assisting in the organization of the book, his penetrating editorial judgment, his stylistic artistry, and his remarkable awareness of American life and affairs all made a crucial contribution to the birth of this book. Having also applied his editorial skills to Henry Kissinger's and Harold Evans's memoirs, he is without a doubt one of the finest among book editors. I also very much appreciated Pat Knopf's editorial touches and Tom Stewart's thoughtful and sensitive comments to the completed typescript.

I am deeply indebted to Bruce MacLaury, the president of the Brookings Institution, for extending visiting scholarship privileges to me, which enabled me to draw for advice and information on many of Brookings' outstanding scholars. For three diligent and most helpful researchers, Susan Bettencourt, Laura Schiedel, and Harold Schlicht, my thanks go to the Cooperative Education Program of American University.

Finally, Muffie, my wife, deserves my most deep-felt thanks for her patience, her encouragement, and her counsel.

Special
Relationships

I

The Start of a Love Affair

IT WAS early November. We were fortunate for the first days of the voyage, enjoying sunshine and a calm sea. It was plainly too good to last, and we ran into a biting gale. Huge waves broke across our decks and the engines struggled audibly against the angry, menacing sea, which kept me forcibly in my bunk for much of the time. Life was harder for those on smaller ships, and for the convoy commander, a retired Royal Naval admiral who had volunteered to return to active service and now found himself riding herd on this floating League of Nations. Each morning at daybreak we learned that we had lost one or two stragglers: we never found out whether they made it safely to New York or had become victims of the armed underwater predators.

We on our 14,000-ton tanker—considered pretty big in those days—felt relatively safe, though the old-fashioned artillery piece on the fo'c'sle struck me as slightly ridiculous in terms of armament. Our actual defense was provided by one British destroyer and four corvettes, which darted around the perimeter of our convoy like mother hens chasing up their chicks. Still, we felt a little queasy apprehension when the tanker's Norwegian captain, a taciturn but confidence-inspiring old sea dog, told us that these escort ships usually turned back in mid-Atlantic: the main danger zone had been passed, they were needed elsewhere, and we had to take, well, a certain risk . . .

Our apprehension quickly abated, however, one morning when word spread that American warships—yes, American warships—would take over the protection of our convoy from the Atlantic halfway mark and shepherd us to New York Harbor. Under a secret agreement, unknown to us and the British and American public generally, President Franklin Roosevelt's partisan neutrality had American warships patrolling the American "half" of the Atlantic; in practice, as we soon learned to our relief, the US warships were not just cruising aimlessly around—they were doing exactly the same kind of escort work that the Royal Navy was doing.

The storm had now abated, and the sun again shone brilliantly out of an ice-blue sky when the captain sent word to the passengers to join him on the bridge to watch the changing of the guard. There, lined up on the skyline, lay eight full-size American destroyers, with the British vessels—looking, it has to be admitted, puny by comparison—facing them in line abreast as they exchanged naval courtesies. I shall never forget the sight of those American warships. In our own, narrow concerns, they promised a safer voyage, but they also provided for me the first solid testimony of American participation in the war. *The Sunday Times* had sent me on this trip primarily to report on America's growing commitment, its defense collaboration to provide Britain with the "tools," as Churchill called them, with which to finish the job. The day before I left London the editor, W. W. Hadley, a short, frail looking septuagenarian—he was referred to as "W.W."—asked me to come to his inner sanctum, to give me my final marching orders. "We need to tell our readers what the Americans are doing to help our war effort. 'Bundles for Britain,' wrapped by well-meaning American ladies, is all right, but not enough. Three months should give you enough time to tell the story. Keep everything short, we're now down to eight pages and with newsprint getting shorter, we may have to cut to six." As he got up from his chair to wish me a safe crossing, I dared an unexpected question: ". . . and what if the Japanese enter the war on Hitler's side? Would that prolong my assignment?" I was fishing for a possible extension. "We'll decide if and when it happens," was the short and noncommittal answer.

Watching this thrilling naval rendezvous, my companions on the bridge, the American photographer Bill Vandivert and his wife (Bill took some of the most audacious and dramatic pictures of the London blitz for *Life* magazine), shared my hopes that the United States' entry into the war could not be far off. My fingers itched to send off my first dispatch and describe this inspiring scene, but we ran into more bad weather and it was another five days before we reached New York. *The Sunday Times* carried a two-column headline—much the biggest display used in those days—over my story: AMERICAN TAKE-OVER IN MID-ATLANTIC, and, below, a second deck of heading: CHANGING OF THE GUARD ON ATLANTIC CONVOY. It was a lucky start to my very first foreign assignment.

Only two years and eight months earlier I had arrived in England from my native Czechoslovakia. It was on the day that Hitler's soldiers occupied it that I made up my mind to flee to England. Luckily I had foreseen the inevitable, and had already equipped myself with a letter from relatives in England that guaranteed me work as a horticulturist. It was a job for which I had no training —mine was in economics—but the letter and its assurance of work would allow me to enter England without a visa. My father, a bank and later industrial manager, had died some years earlier. My mother, though she herself did not want to leave, gave every support to my escape plans. She died of heart failure two years later. I traveled first to Vienna, which was easy, and then crossed Nazi Germany by train, which was risky, to the Dutch frontier. The mean-looking Nazi passport control officer hesitated for an unconscionably long time over whether to recognize my Czechoslovak passport as still valid or to confiscate it as that country was now under German occupation. Fortunately for me, it seemed that there was no specific order about how to deal with Czech passports, so, after all sorts of questioning, he let me pass, with my two small suitcases containing clothes into whose shoulder pads my mother had sewn some of her most precious jewelry.

The British in those days opened their hearts and embraced the refugees from Hitlerism with a solicitude that was touching and reassuring. From Lady Rowntree of the British Refugee Committee, who sat at a simple wooden table at Venlo, the Dutch frontier town, vetting arriving refugees, to the caseworkers in London and to the ordinary working people, everyone was eager to help. Americans had by then long become used to dealing with an influx of immigrants, but for the insular British it was a new experience. Public opinion by then was well ahead of Neville Chamberlain's government, clamoring for more support in meeting the human emergency created by the ogre Hitler and the bungling at Munich.

Fortunately, relatives on my mother's side and personal friends of my father's helped me in making London my home. First I began to exploit an old hobby of mine, drawing cartoons for a racing paper called the *Greyhound Express*. In addition I worked as a clerk for a few months in a factory making brier pipes. I made a living of sorts. My real objective was to go into journalism as soon as I had perfected my English. I already had some experience in journalism as a sports writer for the *Prager Tagblatt*, Prague's and one of Europe's leading German newspapers, and *l'Auto*, a French sports paper. Thanks to an English cousin who was a barrister, I met Iain Lang, the foreign editor of *The Sunday Times*, an elegant, ascetic-looking Scotsman with a sardonic tongue, a compassionate heart, and a passion for jazz, who took a professional interest in my human predicament, and soon my knowledge of Central Europe was proving an invaluable asset to me and to his paper. I made contacts among the Czechoslovak government-in-exile, which had remarkably reliable intelligence channels into Central Europe, and with other refugee governments, including the Norwegian one, which later offered me a free passage across the Atlantic, thereby contributing to my being given the assignment to the United States by *The Sunday Times.* (Newspapers in those days were particularly short of funds.) Gradually, I established myself as an authority on developments from inside Hitler's Reich. I reported the first seismic rumblings of Hitler's invasion of Russia, and my accurate prediction of its launching established my reputation with the editors of *The Sunday Times.* Quite soon I was being given a good deal of space not only in *The Sunday Times,* but also on the editorial pages of the *Daily Telegraph* and the *News Chronicle.* W. W. Hadley had supported Chamberlain's policy of appeasement in *The Sunday Times,* and even gone to the extent of writing an enthusiastic book about the Munich agreement. Afterwards, I wondered often whether the support he gave me had been some kind of unspoken expiation for his earlier errors, but although I kept up a correspondence with him long after his retirement, until he died at the age of ninety-three, I never knew for certain. But it was thanks to him, Valentine Heywood—the managing editor, also once a strong believer in appeasing Hitler—and, above all, Iain Lang, an ardent opponent of Chamberlain's policies, that I found myself approaching New York and an experience that was to have an unexpectedly lasting impact on the rest of my life.

We arrived at Hoboken, New Jersey, at night, and for someone coming from blacked-out Britain the New York panorama was stunning. Looking at this brazenly lit-up city I felt as if I were making landfall on a different planet. My second impression was a shock of a different kind: the rudeness of Immigration and Customs officers, who seemed to treat everybody like undesirable aliens. Then I met my first New York taxi driver. This was even worse as, after my baggage had already been stored away in the trunk, he insisted on negotiating in advance what I fearfully suspected was an outrageously high fare (it was). Unfamiliar with the distances, relieved if not thankful to have found a taxi at all, I meekly agreed, seeing nobody but intimidating hoboes and toughs around me. Like other Europeans, I had learned my America at the movies.

I asked to be taken to the Taft Hotel on Times Square, which the pilot who boarded our tanker outside the harbor had recommended. He thought it would fit my two requirements, to be relatively inexpensive and centrally located so that, ironically, I would not have to spend too much on taxi fares. In those days the Bank of England restricted every visitor to the United States to twenty dollars a day to cover food and board and transport. It virtually made a beggar of every Briton. A *New Yorker* cartoon of about that time showed a street holdup, a man with handkerchief over mouth and nose, pointing a gun at a passerby: "Sorry, old boy" (the caption ran, or words to this effect) "but I'm English, and I need the dollars."

My third impression—all within a few hours of my arrival—was of a different kind and, in retrospect at least, amusing. I checked into the Taft, where the reception clerk commiserated with me over my having had to spend nine days crossing the Atlantic, and the bellboy guided me to my room. I had hardly begun to enjoy the comfort of a warm soak in the tub when there was a knock at my door, first gentle, then more insistent. I got out of the bath, wrapped a towel around me, and cautiously opened the door just a chink. In the hallway was a girl; no uniform, street clothes, and just a little too much makeup. "Are you Mr. Brown?" she asked. No, I said, I wasn't Mr. Brown, and then noticed that she had stuck her foot in the door in a very determined way. Whatever she radiated, it wasn't innocence. Now I had heard about girls in New York who wheedled their way into strangers' hotel rooms and then quickly lost their clothing before screaming for help or hush money, so I slammed the door shut. I was a bit brusque, but she did get her foot out just in time. Apart from anything else, I was pretty sure that neither the Bank of England nor my employer would be keen on bankrolling that kind of embarrassment. Next evening I was at a dinner party at the apartment of Content Peckham, foreign editor of *Time* magazine, and told the tale in detail. Everybody had a good laugh and it was explained to me that whatever else, I had probably robbed the sympathetic bellboy of the pleasure of making my first evening in New York even more memorable, plus his chance of a little commission on the side.

What shook me much more than these initial impressions, however, was the almost total lack of interest in what was going on in Britain and the war. Only those people with relatives in Europe, or an international outlook anyway, seemed to care. A few kind souls whose consciences told them that the British were fighting with their backs to the wall to preserve Western civilization joined in the gift scheme of Bundles for Britain. Among the courageous exceptions were such Anglophiles as Stewart Alsop, the columnist (later on, my very good friend and neighbor), who felt compelled to volunteer for the British services and help fight the war. There were others, but they were few. Senator Gerald Prentice Nye of North Dakota and Charles Lindbergh, heading the America First Committee, had proclaimed that they would oppose Roosevelt and the interventionists in the next elections. Some factories were strikebound, and the so-called defense program about which I was to report was behind schedule. Most people expected the United States to remain sheltered by the Atlantic and Pacific oceans and the Royal Navy. The mood reminded me very much of that which prevailed in London in August 1939. There, by contrast, people had now begun to realize that without direct American participation victory was a remote hope.

Pearl Harbor and the "day that will live in infamy," as President Roosevelt called it, changed everything. Yet not immediately: the news was at first simply beyond belief. On Sunday evening December 7 I went the rounds of some Manhattan bars with Mary Johnson (now Tweedy), whom I had met at Content Peckham's party. To Mary's utter embarrassment, as we eavesdropped on conversations over brass rails and at fast-food places, we found that only a few people seemed to have taken in what had happened. Most of the talk was still about that afternoon's ball game. It was clear to me that without the Japanese perfidy Roosevelt, however much he might personally have wished to take the United States into the war on Britain's side, would have been unable to overcome the unwillingness in the Congress and among the American people. What if Japan had not attacked? It is a devastating speculation, which I for one prefer not to try to think through. Slowly, though, the realization that things had changed did sink in. The New York *Daily News,* the notoriously isolationist newspaper which only the day before Pearl Harbor had attacked the administration for its "war-mongering" policies, carried an editorial saying ". . . the time has come for us all to stand by the President"; and its Chicago cousin, the *Tribune,* sounded the same note: "Recriminations are useless and we doubt whether they will be indulged in, certainly not by us . . ." Even Lindbergh raised his voice in Roosevelt's support.

I had planned to spend two weeks in New York to get acclimatized to my new surroundings before moving to Washington and starting my assignment in earnest, but that had become impossible now. So, after keeping an appointment with the then mayor of New York City, Fiorello La Guardia, who boasted with disarming candor that personally he had always felt himself at war with Hitler, I hurried to the nation's capital.

Coming from New York to Washington was like coming from a huge and busy railroad terminal to a country church. There were no skyscrapers, no ear-splitting traffic noise, no sense that I was some kind of cogwheel in an overpowering machine. Here were wide, tree-lined streets, with long and broad vistas, slower and thinner traffic, and above all, literally and figuratively, a visible canopy of blue sky. People in the streets seemed then, and still do, less in a hurry, more ready to tell a stranger how to find an address, more at ease with one another. I shall write of Washington the city at greater length in a later chapter, but on this first visit I was immediately aware of Washington's pride in its monuments; the Georgian charm of its private homes; the pseudo-classical style of its public architecture, marble surfaces gleaming in the sun. What impressed me most on this first visit was the colonial grace of the White House—deceptively small when seen from Pennsylvania Avenue—for its striking contrast to American hankering for the big and ostentatious.

I had little time to get to know the city; I was too busy trying to procure my journalistic accreditations and to collect enough information on what was going on. People seemed highly confused by events and how to react to them. My new American colleagues were enormously helpful in explaining the intricacies of the power game to me, introducing me to the rules and liberties of covering the news, and assisting me with appointments. I had introductions to Raymond Clapper, a liberal columnist close to the president, to Arthur Krock, the conservative head of the *New York Times* Washington bureau, and to Richard Rendell of the cocky Chicago *Sun,* who all in their own ways opened doors and vistas for me. Most of the resident British correspondents covered the US from New York. Only the *Times,* the *Daily Telegraph,* and the *News Chronicle* had their own Washington correspondents. I remember an argument Robert Waithman, the thoughtful, well-informed, and witty *News Chronicle* man, had with the robust but endearing C. V. R. Thompson of the *Daily Express,* over the brass rail of the National Press Club bar, about which city it was better to cover the war from. Waithman argued that Washington had now become the "front line." Thompson replied that his adored New York was still the center: "Even though the guns may be fired in Washington, the shells still explode in New York."

The biggest news story after Pearl Harbor was Winston Churchill's visit to Washington to see Roosevelt. The shrewd prime minister knew that he must act immediately to forge the Anglo-American military alliance so as to ensure that the US gave priority to the war in Europe. The anger of many Americans, and particularly those living in the West, was understandably directed primarily against Japan. I myself doubt whether Roosevelt could have ordered the priorities in the way Churchill wanted, and carried the country with him, if Hitler had not declared war on the United States almost immediately after Pearl Harbor. Roosevelt knew that victory in that theater of conflict was essential for the survival of civilization. Hitler made it easier for him to follow his instincts. The Fuehrer's declaration of war was one of his greatest mistakes.

Still, such were the divisions in American public opinion that Roosevelt needed Churchill to strengthen his hand with the Congress and with the American people. There was no other foreigner who could even remotely hold such sway with both of them. His voice sounded like a rallying cry, simultaneously choking off the anti-British feelings that many American hearts still held at that time, and arousing in them instead a certain fighting spirit. His visit electrified Washington, and Roosevelt, in a gesture that gave the occasion a special meaning, significant for the nascent Anglo-American relationship, invited him to stay at the White House. This led to a famous encounter, which like others may or may not be apocryphal. Roosevelt, entering the guest room, found Churchill emerging stark naked from his bath, and apologized for having barged in at the wrong moment. "The Prime Minister of Great Britain," came the ringing reply, "has nothing to conceal from the President of the United States."

The joint press conference they gave on December 23, 1941 was my very first, and it remains the most memorable I have ever attended. In those days a presidential press conference was a relatively intimate, friendly affair, not the confrontation it has become today. There were far fewer correspondents, which enabled the president to hold it in the Oval Office, with the reporters clustering round his desk. They met twice a week, once in the morning and once in the afternoon, to keep both morning and evening editions sweet.

Roosevelt as president still thought in terms of keeping the press happy. There was frequent good-natured banter, as well as a fair amount of needling, and Roosevelt could give as good as he got, sometimes with malice aforethought —he once gave John O'Donnell, a columnist who often viciously attacked him, a Nazi Iron Cross in its original velvet-covered box.

At the joint Churchill-Roosevelt conference, however, everything was new to me. It was also unusual. As we were ushered into the Oval Office one by one we passed an impressive phalanx of British and American guards, mostly secret service men, who subjected us to extremely close scrutiny. Over a hundred of us crowded into what was barely adequate space for such a number, and by the time I entered a human wall had formed around the president's desk. Fortunately for me, Richard Strout of the *Christian Science Monitor* and Richard Rendell of the Chicago *Sun* took me under their wing. They explained to several of their colleagues ahead of us that I was a British correspondent, and here for the first time. Moses could not have divided those human waves more efficiently. I was allowed to edge myself forward to the very front row. There I stood, with my stomach pressed against the president's huge mahogany desk, little more than an arm's length from the man who for years had been my idol and was now the ultimate hope for victory in the war.

There was the man who had loomed so large in my imagination. More than a whole generation felt that it had been let down by the blindness, the weakness, and the irresponsibilities of its leaders. In this emptiness Franklin D. Roosevelt shone like a prophet, a visionary, almost a god. He exuded strength and confidence backed by the latent powers of the United States, the last great hope of what was left of the democratic world. In contrast to the brutalities and miseries that led to another bloody war, he incorporated to me humanism, vision, and an intellectual quality that had died out in Europe. Here was a man endowed with a special political sense, a craftsman, who, it seemed to me, could achieve anything he wanted. Of course, it did not take long for me to learn that his powers were far more circumscribed than I had expected, that despite his skills, his grand manner, his sense of the world, he was considered by many of his American enemies as a traitor to his class and a frustrated dictator. Roosevelt presided over the potentially most powerful country in the world, and his statesmanship and vision stood high above that of every other American. Even before the war he had advocated the imposition of a "quarantine" against Nazi Germany, and, as we now know, in January 1938 had sent to Prime Minister Neville Chamberlain a secret message warning of Hitler's and Mussolini's aggressive intentions, and offering to address an appeal to the world for new disarmament measures, better access to raw materials, and the preservation of treaties, in exchange for guarantees of the integrity of the smaller, threatened nations. But Chamberlain trusted Hitler and Mussolini, and feared that Roosevelt's ideas would offend them. Roosevelt had his prejudices about British colonialism, but what was that in comparison to the service he already and would in future perform for mankind.

Well, there was FDR in the flesh, with his broad, fetching smile, his cigarette in its famous long holder cockily held in the corner of his mouth, the embodiment of self-confidence, urbanity, joy of life, and American power. No one, if anyone existed who did not already know, would have guessed that he was an invalid who had to get about in a wheelchair. Churchill, sitting next to him, looked curiously impassive, like an actor thinking through his lines just before curtain. He looked the bulldog rather than the cherub, in spite of his plump, rosy countenance.

In those days the signal for the start of the conference came not from the press secretary but from the secret service man at the door who, raising his voice slightly, announced, "All in." After a few minor announcements relating to domestic matters, the president moved to put the prime minister center stage. He had first suggested, he said, that Mr. Churchill might care just to make a statement, and thereby spare himself interrogation by the reporters, who were "wolves compared with the British lambs"; but the premier, with his great parliamentary experience, had courteously declined: "Like myself, Winston enjoys a new experience." Roosevelt smiled, and then, the gracious host, turned the meeting over to his guest.

Reporters at the back shouted that they could not see him. With remarkable dexterity for a pudgy man he climbed on his chair, and stood there smiling. Everybody exploded into applause. He raised his hand in the famous V-sign, and cheering overtook the clapping. It was without precedent, I was told, for this detached, studiedly cynical body of men to behave with such spontaneous emotion. Roosevelt too joined in the applause. Churchill, seemingly unconscious of the slightly undignified and precarious position which he had chosen on the spur of the moment, beamed his enjoyment. In that moment I—and, I am sure, everyone in the room—suddenly realized the legendary power of the man, began to grasp what it was that made him a hero.

The questioning—in spite of the presidential forebodings—was good-natured, its handling deft. To the proverbial American optimism of "How soon, Mr. Prime Minister, do you expect we will win the war?" came the blithe "If we manage it well, it will only take half as long as if we manage it badly." Everybody laughed. Then somebody wondered whether this meeting with President Roosevelt would be included in his list of "climactic points" in the war. He framed his answer in a sheepish smile and an attempt at a Southern accent: "Ah shuah do!" This time the laughter became a roar. He was also asked some serious questions—about the future of Singapore, for instance, and the significance of the latest Russian victories over the Germans (or, as he called them, "the Huns").

By the end of the conference Churchill had secured a most important beachhead in the United States and taken an important body of prisoners, the White House press corps. For everyone there it had been a moving experience, one that provided a window onto the first making of the Anglo-American "special relationship" and also its ultimate personification. For me in particular it was of added moment, for it brought the world of great journalism sharply into focus. I felt exhilarated and, frankly, scared by the challenge.

When Churchill later addressed the Congress, he swept its members too off their feet with the same gravelly, resonant, and commanding tones that had lifted the spirit of the entire British nation at its darkest hour. Later Senator Arthur Vandenberg of Michigan, who had been one of the isolationists, told me the oration had converted him to internationalism, and showed me the notes he had made after it: "It was the breezy, self-confident statesman-of-the-world who . . . put on the greatest show on earth when he descended on Washington. But there is vastly more than that to it. There was the insight into a vivid, dynamic personality so powerful that it led the United States to its own salvation at a moment of all-out disaster and perhaps thus saved the world." With his tall, powerful build, his white mane, and his own theatrical eloquence, Vandenberg looked more like an actor chosen for the role by Hollywood Central Casting than a real senator. The extent of his conversion emerged from the things he went on to tell me—they were, indeed, the glimmerings of an almost sentimental notion of the special fraternity between the two nations. "You Europeans like to remind us that this war was a consequence of the reluctance of the United States Congress to join the League of Nations. But this is not so. There were other reasons. We, here, were only too well aware that the idea of the League of Nations would be a futile undertaking, and that it should never be revived. A world federation is nothing but a fantasy in which neither the British nor the Americans believe. Britain will never resign her Empire, and we don't want to give up our existence as a nation, not even to a union with Britain." Vandenberg spoke with a flourish, and almost a Churchillian intonation himself, as if he were addressing the entire Senate, and not a single lowly foreign correspondent.

Then, exhibiting his delight in history and his respect for the prime minister's powers as a seer, he went on to tell me of a speculative article that Churchill had written for *Scribner's* magazine in December 1932—what might have happened, he had asked, if Lee and the Confederacy had won at Gettysburg? And how would it have affected relations between Britain and the Union? "Few Americans have had a better grasp of this decisive week in the story of our rebellion," Vandenberg declared. "Few other writers would have dared to undertake such an experiment." He read me excerpts from the article, at the end of which Churchill wrote how Britain would be linked to the whole enterprise by her own interests and a Covenant of the English-Speaking Association. This Union he dubbed the "Re-United States." It altered no institutions and required no elaborate machinery, Vandenberg pointed out; it only created a higher loyalty and a wider sentiment. Except for the idea of common citizenship he liked the Churchillian concept, which made a deep and lasting impression on him: years later, after the death of his first wife, he carried the idea into practice in his personal life, and married an Englishwoman.

In February 1942 I moved to the West Coast in anticipation of a Japanese attack on the US mainland, and found myself making news instead. On my arrival in Los Angeles I was interviewed by a reporter from the Los Angeles *Times*. This was a new experience. I mentioned in passing my experience with the convoy, and next morning the headlines were over three columns, as well as being someone else's: BRITISH WRITER SAYS U.S. NAVY ON CONVOY DUTY IN ATLANTIC. The copy led off with, "To the question on the lips of many Americans, what's the Navy doing? . . ." and went on to credit me with a partial answer. Looking after convoys in the Atlantic was not, of course, what people on the Pacific coast believed was the right thing for the Navy to be doing —especially because the Pacific fleet had been caught at Pearl Harbor so disastrously unprepared.

I felt strangely guilty writing "front-line" dispatches from California, with on one side the gray-blue Pacific waves breaking over soft, sandy beaches, teeming with surfers and sun worshipers, and on the other the snow-capped mountains with their thousands of campers at weekends. I had to be careful about my choice of subject. As my London news editor was at pains to remind me, the people who bought *The Sunday Times* were not expecting to read about Hollywood or the other pleasures of California. So I concentrated on war-related matters: shipyards that were cutting down the production time for merchant ships from 185 days to 75; aircraft factories that were spewing out planes; coastal defenses that included Maginot Line–type gun equipment; visits to various military bases. The last included a US-Canadian unit that was being prepared for fighting in almost any conditions: I came across it again two years later as a war correspondent on the Anzio beachhead in Italy, only to find it laboring away at routine infantry tasks, its personnel's hard-earned versatility wasted. I conducted interviews with a variety of officers, of whom one commanding general talked to me of offensive action against Japan from Alaska, which he regarded as the most important strategic area in the world. The action never materialized.

I also found in my scrapbooks the clipping of a dispatch mentioning a meeting with an Army Lieutenant Ronald Reagan. He was stationed at Fort Mason as a liaison officer attached to an embarkation unit in San Francisco Harbor, and his main task, it seemed to me, was to fend off inquiring reporters with facile excuses and little in the way of stories. Still, he had a charming twinkle and in an easygoing way made it appear that he was being as helpful as was possible in the circumstances of wartime. I think he was genuinely unhappy about the strict secrecy regulations that applied to all troop movements and which he had to defend. "I would like to see those boys who are shipped off across the seas given a proper farewell with music, flowers, and waving girls," he told me. "We cannot conceal the embarkation, so why not give the boys a true American send-off?" His upbeat style has not changed; it is deeply embedded in the man. It did indeed make little sense to deny the boys a rousing send-off, because by simply standing on one of San Francisco's seven hills it was possible to observe all the ship movements in and out of the harbor. But regulations were regulations, and for Lieutenant Reagan (a "former Hollywood film star," as I described him), in his apparently tailor-made uniform, they provided a task he fulfilled with admirable diplomacy.

Having lived through those nights when the Germans tried to set London on fire and having escaped the destruction of the Café de Paris when the Luftwaffe scored a direct hit on it (thanks to the fact that all tables had already been booked that night), I had little fear that San Francisco would be a target for enemy action, except perhaps for sporadic attacks from the air. Apart from a few false air-raid alarms the war had made very little impact on California, or indeed on the entire United States.

"Traveling through America, looking at it from the window of a Pullman car," I reported, "it is hard to believe that this country is engaged in total warfare. The countryside looks undisturbed, traffic has hardly diminished, people are as well dressed as ever and nobody looks worried. There are uniforms to be seen on the trains, but there are still plenty of people in mufti (civilian clothes). Restrictions are few and the established habits of American life have hardly changed. The stores are full, the nightclubs are packed, the theaters are sold out, and everything is available in abundance."

But these were superficial conclusions; it was the vastness of the country that made the war so little apparent. In the Pacific coastal cities one began to feel some proximity to the war, for every port was an embarkation port, every factory a defense plant, and the cities swarmed with soldiers and defense workers. The workers in Detroit or Chicago did not see the warships or the hospital transports bringing back the wounded, nor did they feel that the Japanese could bomb them from the Aleutian Islands. And then one day I sat next to a sergeant of the Marine Corps on a train journey to Pittsburgh, his hometown. "I always loathed this place," he said. "I thought it dirty and ugly and unfriendly, a mass of factories . . ." Then he looked out of the window as the chimneys of the big steel mills, the pillars of America's industrial might, slid past, and he added: "Look. They never seemed beautiful until today."

As my assignment was coming to an end and I was getting ready to return to England, I asked for an appointment with the First Lady, Mrs. Eleanor Roosevelt. In truth I would have liked to meet the president himself, but I supposed that he would not have the time to see a departing foreign correspondent. Along with my request I gave a brief outline of my assignment and mentioned that in Seattle I had been fortunate enough, thanks to a letter of introduction from columnist Ray Clapper, to stay briefly with the Boettigers —the editor of the city's leading newspaper, the Seattle *Intelligencer*, and his wife, Anna, the Roosevelts' daughter. Still slightly to my surprise, I got an invitation to lunch at the White House within a week.

Excited, I asked my American colleagues what I should wear, and was advised that a suit, either white or dark, was *de rigueur*. Alas I had never acquired a white suit, nor would my stringent finances allow me to invest in one now; I had only the formless white seersucker which was the Washington summer uniform in those days, and that would not do. I did, however, have a dark suit, black, with a pinstripe. It was made of the heaviest British woolen cloth, and was fully lined. I was very proud of it—it was my first tailor-made suit. Thus my choice was made easy for me. I would wear my black suit.

Fate decreed that on the great day Washington was suffering one of its suffocating heat waves. I arrived, correctly dark-suited, in a taxi, which was motioned into the White House grounds as soon as I flashed my invitation to lunch with Mrs. Roosevelt. We drove to the front steps of the main entrance, where a man in a black suit gestured me up the stairs and into the large entrance hall (I noted later in my diary that this was the door that Winston Churchill had used, and I had never expected to find myself crossing the same threshold). Now a man, dressed in an informal cream suit, showed me over red carpets and into the Red Room—a waiting room, though it seemed to me more a salon. Several people had already arrived, so I made the rounds of them, shaking hands and introducing myself to Henry Morgenthau, secretary of the treasury, and Mrs. Morgenthau; Norman Davis, head of the American Red Cross and former chief-of-mission to the London Disarmament Conference in 1937, and Mrs. Davis; Harry Hopkins, the president's chief trouble-shooter, and Mrs. Hopkins; and Miss Mildred McAfee, in uniform as commander in chief of the WAVES.

In those days, few rooms in the White House were air-conditioned, and the Red Room, alas, was not one of them. Perspiration poured from me as I sat on a dainty chair covered with red brocade. I wondered how I would get through the lunch without constantly mopping my brow. Then in swept Mrs. Roosevelt, extending her unusually long arm to shake hands with her guests. Naturally I jumped to my feet as she entered—and then I noticed with horror that the back of my chair had taken on the color of my suit. Panic-stricken, I managed to stay rooted in front of it, contriving to be the last to leave the room so that none could discover my wretched despoliation of that beautiful red brocade. As I followed, I prayed that the damage would not be discovered until after my departure at the end of the lunch.

Mrs. Roosevelt looked to me unexpectedly old in her face, but everything else about her was youthful. She had the mobility of a girl, eyes that seemed full of expectation, and a temperament of electricity. She also had a commanding presence, knowing how to take charge and how to keep control of a situation. She wore a dark blue dress with white spots which somehow went oddly with her ungainly body and her large feet. By now I had caught up, and as we approached the table she asked me to sit on her left; Mr. Morgenthau took the chair on her right (Harry Hopkins was not considered a guest, as he and his wife and daughter lived at the White House, to be always at hand).

Mr. Morgenthau spoke about the problems he encountered on his farm, Mr. Davis complained about the Japanese not wanting to let food into the Philippines, and Miss McAfee on my left reported that women were flocking into the services. Many, she said, had to be turned down because there were not enough places for them—and only a few years ago American women had found it shocking that women in Russia did men's jobs in factories and armies. Mrs. Roosevelt told us about the mail she was getting (mostly complaints from wives of servicemen), and the impressions she had brought back from a trip to the Middle East. Then suddenly she turned to me and, lowering her voice, said, "Mr. Brandon, the reason I invited you was to seek some advice from you." She went on to say that Lady Reading, the chairman of Women's Voluntary Services for Civil Defence, had invited her to visit England, but she did not want to preempt transport facilities from more important people, eat rations that should go to the needy, or attract too much attention and occupy the time of people who were busy with the war. Spontaneously—for of course I had had no warning of what was on her mind—I suggested that she should make the trip not as the president's wife, but informally as a writer, since she had her own syndicated column. I tried to reassure her that such a visit not only would be welcome but would help reinforce the close bond that tied Britain and the US together in the war.

As the other guests departed, taking the elevator downstairs, she asked me to stay behind for another five minutes. She took me by the hand and said, "Come now," indicating that with the lunch over we could discuss more interesting things. She wanted to talk about the problems of peace, what the United States should then do to help restore Europe, and what would happen to the women who had taken the place of men in so many professions. "Post-war decisions are so difficult," she said. "One does not know how long the war will last, or how many men will die . . . Or how best to pay for postwar reconstruction." My admiration for her rose to new heights. She not only exuded absolute confidence in victory, but she had already begun to think far ahead about the role the United States would have to play when the killing was over and the human condition was once again the problem that govern-ments would have to face. This "earth mother" was an idealist, yet her questions were realistic—practical, searching, imaginative. She had great sensitivity without sentimentality, outwardly at least. Her voice was soft, and she was often anxious to give credit to others when in reality it was due to her. She exuded strength, drive, curiosity—and combined them with the ability to decide and to act. She had an exuberant belief that progress was there to be achieved, if only one worked hard enough.

I decided to spend the last few days before my return to England on Capitol Hill, talking to senators and congressmen across the political spectrum. There is a decided difference between walking the endless corridors of the US Congress, which bustle with activity, and those of the Houses of Parliament, where people who do not seem to be in any hurry, lower their voices, and everything is muffled. Tourists in Washington want to say hello to their state's representatives, introduce their children, and have photographs taken with them. Members of Congress take all this in their stride—they have to keep in this kind of personal touch with their constituents much more than do British MPs, so there is a constant flow of visitors to their offices. Yet the corridors of congressional power, with their high ceilings, their bland walls and marble floors, are long and drab. The buildings are substantially of the same mid-nineteenth-century date (Westminster Hall apart) as their British counterparts, yet—despite a few marble statues—one does not get on Capitol Hill the sense of history that lurks in the Palace of Westminster, where every inch seems to carry some fading glitter of history.

I decided to begin at one extreme, and went to see first the noted isolationist Senator Nye. The cartoons on the walls of his outer office were all testimony to his creed. I looked in vain for another, more important newspaper document. This was the note that a reporter had handed to him while he was making a speech on December 7, 1941, informing him of Pearl Harbor—news which he at first dismissed as Roosevelt propaganda. He had an unnaturally red nose and a rasping voice. During our talk he admitted, however reluctantly, that he had somewhat changed his views because the war had "given us allies and with them we must lay the kind of foundation that would lessen the risk of recurrence of world conflict." But that was about all he was ready to concede.

I then went to see Senator Vandenberg, who again spoke of how his admiration for Churchill had influenced his thinking. Years later, perhaps in an attempt to realize the Churchillian vision in a form adapted to modern needs, he launched what became known as the Vandenberg Resolution, which was designed to bury the American aversion to "entangling alliances" and which opened the door to the creation of NATO. Vandenberg is not given the credit he deserves in the American and British history books. It was he who gave the lead to a bipartisan foreign policy after brilliant coaching by Secretary of State Dean Acheson, a Democrat with whom he forged a personal alliance that laid the foundation stone, on Capitol Hill at least, for the Pax Americana.

Some months earlier Henry Luce, the powerful and power-seeking publisher of *Time, Life,* and *Fortune* magazines, had advocated a convergence of the two ideologies that alternately dominated the American outlook on the world—the liberal one that had been converted to the uses of power by the threat of Nazism and Fascism, and the conservative one whose reaction was fostered by the mounting threat of Soviet communism. In January 1942 he had published a five-page editorial in which he proclaimed the advent of the "American Century," proposed a de facto partnership with Britain, and denounced

isolationism as a manifestation of Americans' inability to accommodate themselves to having become the world's most powerful and vital nation. Luce saw
himself as the authentic megaphone of American national interests, a builder
of a bridge between the Christian-liberal-humanistic tradition based on unconditional individual liberty, and the national interest deriving from America's
newly acquired position of power in the world. It is the persistent conflict
between these two ideologies that has robbed American foreign policy of true
consistency and purpose. Luce in fact wrote with a great deal of foresight. His
grandiloquence, however, aroused widespread criticism. In his view it was "for
Americans and Americans alone to determine whether . . . an economic order
compatible with freedom and progress shall or shall not prevail in this century." America had become "the principal guarantor of the freedom of the
seas, the dynamic leader of world trade . . . the Good Samaritan of the entire
world." To liberals and conservatives alike this smacked of imperialism, and
thus went against the American grain.

   The memory of the critical storm that her husband's editorial unleashed
was still very much alive in his widow, Clare Boothe Luce, when years later
I asked her about the meaning of the phrase "American Century." "Did he
say that everybody should adopt our form of government?" she asked rhetorically, and then answered: "No." After a pause, she continued: "Did he say that
the United States should take over the world?" Again "No." Then: "What he
said was no more than that we should be the city on the hill, that we should
be generous with our knowledge and our wealth. As the son of a missionary,
he was always generous with his own wealth and gave far more for charity than
he did for his own family. All he wanted to say in this editorial was that the
United States should be strong and great."

   There were other Americans, less moralistic than Henry Luce, who too
signaled the advent of a new epoch for the United States. Walter Lippmann
was one. He spoke of the American awakening to a unique power position in
three lectures he called "The American Destiny." His basic argument was that
the United States had become heir to regulating the world balance of power.
Other influential communicators—such as Dorothy Thompson, the columnist;
Hamilton Fish Armstrong, the founder of the magazine *Foreign Affairs*: Professor Max Lerner—helped to offset appeasers such as Joseph P. Kennedy, the
US ambassador to the Court of St. James's, and former President Herbert
Hoover. Gradually the objectors came to realize that the US had been forced
into an interventionist policy, and in fact had no alternative but to assume
responsibility for the protection and preservation of the non-Communist
world.

   It was an indelible experience for me to watch America awakening to its
new challenge, slowly and reluctantly. By the time I boarded a Norwegian
meat refrigeration ship at Halifax, Nova Scotia, for the long voyage home,
war-mindedness had penetrated virtually every corner of the North American
continent. The United States, faced with a two-ocean conflict, was discovering

its powers and learning to apply them. I was deeply impressed by the élan and inventiveness with which this was achieved—impressed too by the self-confidence with which Franklin Roosevelt deployed the powers vested in the presidency. All was done without the pressures of total war that enforced discipline in Britain. The pulling together of this loose confederation of United States—looser than I had ever imagined, for "United" is in many ways an exaggeration—was awe-inspiring. The ready acceptance of Roosevelt's decision to give priority to the war in Europe over that in Asia was helped partly by the European origins of so many American immigrants, but the superb reporting from Europe of American war correspondents and photographers also had tremendous impact. Men and women like Ed Murrow, Quentin Reynolds, Ned Russel, Helen Kirkpatrick, Robert Capa, and others brought the faraway war and the Nazi menace across the ocean and into the homes of Americans. And now I was on my way back to rejoin them. Little did I suspect that this was only the prologue to a love affair that was to lead to marriage for a lifetime.

2

Squaring a Circle

WHEN as a *Sunday Times* war correspondent, attached to the American Third Army, I found myself only some fifty miles from the gates of Prague, the city I had left almost exactly six years earlier, it seemed like some magic squaring of a circle in my life. Not surprisingly, I waited eagerly and anxiously near a town inside Czechoslovakia called Rokycany for General Eisenhower's order to the Second US Infantry Division to advance and liberate Prague. It never came. From General Walter M. Robertson down everybody was heartbroken. I would have felt it poetic justice had I been able to see and report on Allied troops entering the city. But it was not to be.

The idea of covering the war became an obsession with me on my return from the United States. The assignment as a diplomatic correspondent I had been given offered little satisfaction, and so I made my own proposal for covering the war. There was something to be said, I suggested, for having a war correspondent on hand who could also report, whenever appropriate, on political situations as they were developing behind the front lines or in liberated capitals. (Prague was one I had in mind.) Iain Lang liked the idea and proposed it to Hadley, who had been pleased with my reporting from the United States. He readily agreed. With *The Sunday Times* backing, it did not take long for me to obtain my British military credentials and, given a broad pragmatic brief, I flew off in a Lancaster bomber to my first destination, Cairo, to combine covering the desert war, the uneasy political situation in Egypt, and those Yugoslav and Greek officials exiled there.

Later, I reported on General de Gaulle's activities in Algiers and Marshal Badoglio's in Naples. I covered the costly stalemate siege at Monte Cassino, and the even costlier landing at Anzio. Between the two I watched the massive eruption of Vesuvius and shared in the relief that the Germans were not inspired to harness nature as a weapon and bomb the crater to release the lava ... After a stint with the American PT boats off Corsica I landed in the south of France and so came eventually to witness the liberation of Paris, the greatest festival I have ever experienced, a day of singing, dancing, kissing, and of total, unadulterated triumph. To crown all, there was Charles de Gaulle, who had almost refused to address the French nation over the BBC on the eve of the invasion, walking proud, erect, and fearless down the Champs Elysées as if he had himself commanded the victorious advance all the way from Normandy. Now he was a hero to the majority of the French, and from the start proved a formidable leader. But for him, the Communists would have made an unholy mess of the city's liberation.

We war correspondents were billeted at the Scribe Hotel, which then housed some of the most famous among American writers and war reporters —William Saroyan, Edgar Snow, Charles Collingwood, Irwin Shaw, George Stevens, Robert Capa among them. Ernest Hemingway, although he stayed at the Ritz, spent much time in the evenings at our hotel bar swapping stories. Their poker games, lasting until the early hours and with thousands of dollars changing hands, were themselves the stuff of legend. One evening, after the Battle of Bastogne, Ernest Hemingway came to our table in the dining room and read aloud to us a letter from a reader of *Collier's* magazine, for which he wrote. "Dear Mr. Hemingway," it went, "I have been a great admirer of yours and I have read every novel and every short story of yours and I have read them over and over again. I therefore think that you would want to know that somebody is writing in *Collier's* magazine using your name." Hemingway himself had felt that his war writing was not his best, and clearly took the letter seriously. He ended up by saying abruptly, "I'm going back to Cuba next week." And he did. At the same hotel I got an SOS call one day from Ruth Cowan, an Associated Press reporter who had just arrived in France. She demanded to know what the contraption in her bathroom was that she had never seen before. After I had given her an introduction to its use, stopping short of an actual demonstration, she exclaimed with delight, "I have the title for my next book: 'From D-day to Bidet'!"

Many battles later I found myself close to Prague and yet still so far—utterly frustrated, with the Americans not going in, and the Russians about to do so. We had been moving toward Prague virtually without opposition when we were ordered to stop some seventy-five kilometers from the capital of Czechoslovakia. We had all expected to liberate the city, but instead we were now idling along the line Karlové Vary-Plzeň-Budějovice chewing our nails. There was nothing for me to do but to take matters into my own hands—so an Australian colleague and I got into our jeep, and drove off into the city on May 8. By that time the rout of the Germans from the east had assumed such proportions that all they could think of was how to reach the American lines as quickly as possible to escape capture by the Russians. They passed us in their armored vehicles and jeeps and motorcars but not one attempted to stop us, and some even waved us on. In Prague again nobody stopped us. We checked into one of the better hotels, called Steiner, and without any hesitation went on a sightseeing tour in our jeep with the American insignia on it. The city had suffered comparatively little destruction. Much of its baroque architectural splendor remained untouched, except for the old Town Hall which had been burned down by the occupying Germans in reprisal for a Czech partisan uprising; the famous old clock, with its Apostles parading every hour, had been destroyed with it. The fourteenth-century Charles bridge remained one of the main arteries and Hradčany Castle and St. Vitus Cathedral still looked proud and protective over the city, good for another thousand years. Not even the barbaric Nazis, architects of ruin, had been able to rid Prague of its air of timelessness. Yet however untouched its facades, there was abroad in the city a drabness of spirit, an inescapable sense that this monument to Western culture, which had inspired some of the greatest writers, musicians, churchmen, humanists, teachers, and architects, whether Czech or German or Jew, had lost its soul. And now fate was decreeing that it would become a mere outpost of the Soviet empire, and after their sufferings under the Nazis its people were to be condemned to live within yet another alien culture. I felt sorrow for them, but within myself I knew that the umbilical cord to my youth and origins had been severed. I had no relatives left here, no friends; my emotional attachments had withered. I also realized that I had made a deep commitment to a new life, to putting down new roots in the Anglo-Saxon world. I had to learn and absorb all those things that were implicit in the British outlook—for how else could I interpret affairs and write about them for a British audience? I had to learn about British history, politics, and habits. My friends were now primarily British and American, and it was to their mores, their intellectual life, their feelings that I must adjust myself. It was with them that I felt myself in full and rich human and intellectual contact. I had driven past thousands of the skeletons of what had been the cities and houses of Germany, and had at last come to a city virtually untouched by the war, its glorious past preserved; to see such a thing was in itself a heartening relief. But it was no longer my home; I felt myself to be a stranger here.

However, once Eduard Beneš, as president, had resumed residence at Hradčany Castle I asked to see him. I had got to know him in London during the exile in which he kept the Czechoslovak flame burning and its flag flying. After the British government had helped him to do so, it was quite annoyed when he made it clear that he had decided to base his country's postwar policies on a "close understanding and alliance with Russia." His foreign minister, Jan Masaryk (son of Thomas G. Masaryk, founder of Czechoslovakia), did not share this view. He saw it as a sharp deviation from the country's prewar orientation, which had been to the West, and toward which his heart unwaveringly took him—he tried later to bring Czechoslovakia into the Marshall Plan, an attempt which was aborted when it was vetoed by the Soviets. Beneš' view also irked Anthony Eden, Britain's foreign secretary. Eden intervened with Moscow in the first place and succeeded in persuading them not to conclude a bilateral treaty with Prague. Beneš, however, subsequently succeeded in negotiating one anyway. If his hope in doing so was that he might at one stroke protect his back and restore Czechoslovakia to its previous role as the bridge between East and West, then it was a hope that was to be bitterly disappointed.

I saw him again two years later. He was still the same short, dry, and pedantic man, though perhaps by then he no longer reposed such utter confidence in his own judgment. "The ultimate future of world peace," he told me then, "rests with the United States and Russia. Russia needs economic aid, but if necessary she can do without it. Without it, it will take her probably fifteen years to regain her full strength; with it, probably only ten; but strong she will be again sooner or later. If nothing is done to create mutual confidence in the meantime, the whole world will continue to live in tension. On the other hand," he went on as if to forestall whatever premonition had begun to haunt him, "Russia will surely avoid certain political mistakes which could engender suspicion in the West. We accept that our own security is dependent on Russia; Britain's to a certain degree is dependent on the United States, but she is the most suitable power today to cement peace between East and West." (It was Jan Masaryk who once said to me, speaking of prewar Czechoslovakia, "It is hard to serve as a bridge, because everybody will trample on you.") Beneš also foresaw the de facto division of Germany and realized that it threatened Czechoslovakia's ability "to remain culturally a country of the West yet maintaining close contact with the Soviet Union." Winding up the interview, he walked me to a window overlooking the city. It was a beautifully sunny day. Prague with its many knobbly spires and gleaming rooftops stretched below us in all its ancient magnificence and beauty. The president's eyes were now noticeably moist, and he spoke in a whisper: "I wonder how long I will be able to enjoy this view." In less than a year the Communists forced him to resign.

Did General Eisenhower make a historic mistake in allowing the Russians to occupy Berlin and Prague? His decision caused a profound disagreement between him and Churchill and has remained a controversy ever since, with the British saying emphatically yes and most Americans that it would not have made a great deal of difference. Eisenhower gave "logistical reasons" as his explanation for his refusal to allow the Third Army under General Patton to advance beyond the line of the towns of Budějovice-Plzeň-Karlové Vary, and offered Churchill three reasons for his refusal: first, that a further advance eastward could lead to a clash with the Red Army; second, that American intelligence had warned him that Hitler was preparing for a last stand in what proved to be a phantom "national redoubt" in Bavaria and West Austria (there was ample intelligence firmly contradicting this prediction); and, third, a race for Berlin, according to General Omar Bradley, might have cost as many as 100,000 casualties. Basically, what influenced Ike was his principal objective, victory, and to end the war as quickly as possible and get out of Europe. Nothing was to complicate or delay it. In this case, as in others, Americans found it difficult to project their thinking further ahead, and to combine military or intelligence operations with political aims. They also suspected Churchill of wanting to suck them into a confrontation with the Soviet Union —one of those wellings up of old prejudices which, on both sides, from time to time marred the wartime relationship.

There is no reason to believe that Churchill wanted to prolong hostilities into a war against the Soviet Union. On the contrary, there was a strong tendency, especially in the Foreign Office, toward believing that a British alliance with the Soviet Union was negotiable. What he was very conscious of was the need for the Allies to place themselves into a position from which they would be able to negotiate from strength at the peace conference. Stalin, like Churchill, had his postwar objectives. Such calculations did not suit the American mind. Americans are relatively single-minded, less conscious than Europeans of the longer-term political objectives. In his autobiography, *A Soldier's Tale,* Bradley later admitted: "We looked naively on the British inclination to complicate the war with political foresight and non-military objectives."

I doubt whether Eisenhower could have snatched Berlin away from the advancing Soviet forces. But I can testify that the divisions of the Third Army in southwestern Czechoslovakia could have danced into Prague. The Russians were held up by German resistance, most likely to enable as many of the German troops as possible to surrender to the Americans. In fact, on May 4 Eisenhower was prepared to give Patton the go-ahead into Prague well ahead of the Russians. The Czechs I talked to in Prague were ready to tear out their hair in despair when they heard that the Americans were under orders to let the Russians occupy the city. How the Allies might have used their presence in Prague is very difficult to speculate on. But there is no doubt in my mind that Eisenhower was naive in thinking that he could establish close cooperation with the Russians' chiefs of staff and that any trade-offs were possible. But the idea, expressed by his grandson David Eisenhower in his *Eisenhower: At War 1943–45,* that to take Prague would have cost Patton "heavy casualties" is simply based on a misleading assessment. There was some piquancy in the Eisenhower administration's pretension later on of wishing to repudiate "all secret commitments aimed at Communist enslavement" (such as Yalta). The promise was in its party platform, but it never did so formally.

Six weeks after my first return visit to Czechoslovakia I entered Berlin with the American forces to cover the Potsdam summit, the follow-up conference to Yalta. It brought me my first encounter with a Russian officer and Soviet occupation troops. The night after our arrival at the press camp in the suburb of Zehlendorf I went with Erika Mann—daughter of the novelist Thomas Mann and sister of Klaus Mann—to the Deutsches Theater in the Soviet zone. We had no difficulty in crossing over. There were as yet no official dividing lines—all the political decisions concerning Germany were expected to be taken at Potsdam. We saw a play by Friedrich Schiller, the great *Sturm und Drang* dramatist with whose plays I was generally familiar, though not this one, *The Parasites.* In the interval we went backstage to greet the leading actor, who was an old friend of Erika's. He told us how he had managed to get through the war relatively easily, how Goering had once saved him from having to appear in a Goebbels propaganda film playing Churchill (to whom he bore an uncanny likeness, bodily and facially), and how he had evaded joining the Nazi Party. Erika asked about the fate of her former husband, Gustav Gruedgens, also an actor, and was told that the Russians had arrested him and taken him to a labor camp at Fuerstenwald. Erika said nothing until we had resumed our seats, and then commented with lighthearted sarcasm in her voice that it was the "best news I have had for a long time." It clearly made her evening. She did not mind anymore having sat through a second-rate Schiller. I did not ask any questions, but I could imagine how she felt having been married to a man who, she was convinced, had surrendered to the Nazis. Gruedgens did not spend much time in Fuerstenwald. Very soon he once again became one of Germany's leading actors and directors. Years later, his life story was made into a film based on a book written by Klaus Mann. It was called *Mephisto* after the part in Goethe's *Faust* that had made him famous. The film said at great length what Erika summed up in one sentence.

At an interview with the mayor of Berlin, an obvious sycophant installed by the Soviets, I met Major Lipnicki, his Red Army aide. After the interview he invited me to his office. Tea, sandwiches, and *zakusky* were wheeled in, and after a few exchanges about the occupation of Berlin, the engaging English-speaking Russian turned the conversation to English literature, which, he told me, he had been teaching at the University of Kiev before he was called up. We talked for about four hours, and forgot all about the war. When I mentioned that at our press camp at Zehlendorf we had all the London newspapers, including the Communist *Daily Worker,* he declined to believe me. So to convince him I suggested he come and visit us there—never expecting that he would.

Three days later, however, there he was on my doorstep, in full uniform, wanting to see the *Daily Worker.* After I had proved my point, and given him a little more insight into how the press operated in the West, he said his good-byes, adding, a little mysteriously, that I should visit him next day in his office, as he would then have some news for me. Full of curiosity I made my way next morning to City Hall to see him. He began the conversation by saying that he wanted to tell me about some of the decisions of the Potsdam Conference. Since the press was being kept on a short leash—at our headquarters we were being briefed only on what Stalin, Churchill, and Truman were having for their meals—his offer seemed too good to be true, but I was careful not to let my skepticism show. He began explaining to me what the great men had decided about how Germany was to be administered and politically organized. He even drew me a chart demonstrating the various levels of administration, to make quite sure that I fully understood what he was trying to explain to me.

When I departed I was left wondering what to do with this unverifiable scoop—even whether to use it at all. He seemed such an honest, almost naive man about news and reporting, and if he was not, or was being used in some way, I could not for the life of me see what advantage the Russians might hope to gain from having the story leaked. I decided to risk it, and filed the story to my London office. Luckily—and I dare say once again to my relief—it proved to be correct. When we next met I asked the major what had prompted his generosity. He said that he had wanted to show his gratitude for having had so enjoyable a conversation with me about English literature, the first opportunity of the kind that he had had since joining the army. When in 1947 I was sent to Moscow to cover a meeting of the Council of Foreign Ministers, I asked the authorities for permission to visit Kiev, in the private hope of finding him at the university there. But permission was refused, and I never saw him again.

The unfolding political situation in France, as de Gaulle grasped the reins of power with extraordinary firmness, kept me tied to Paris more than I wished, for there were still some crucial battles ahead. However, such major diplomatic events as the Yalta Conference and the French reaction to it began to overshadow the war itself. Yalta, first hailed as a great achievement, had since become a battleground of controversy—the right-wing revisionists accusing Roosevelt of deceit either for having gone at all or for having failed to walk out on Stalin, their left-wing counterparts blaming it as the source of the cold war. Certainly Roosevelt held misconceptions about what he could achieve in man-to-man talks with Stalin. On more than one occasion, according to Averell Harriman, he talked openly to Stalin about Churchill's old-fashioned attachment to the British Empire—either letting his anticolonialism run away with him, or maybe just trying to endear himself to "Uncle Joe." But the harsh reality of the time was that the Red Army was already in full control of Poland. As Harriman put it: "If Stalin was determined to have his way, he was bound to break or bend the agreements, even if they had been sewn up more tightly." Churchill had no illusions about Stalin's reliability and tried his best to save what could be saved in such unfavorable circumstances. "Our hopeful assumptions were soon to be falsified," he wrote in *Triumph and Tragedy*. "Still, they were the only ones possible at the time." What is forgotten or overlooked now, and what may have strengthened Stalin's negotiating hand, is that Roosevelt wanted to commit Stalin to joining the war against Japan. Moreover, public opinion back home wanted to see the war coming to an end: neither Roosevelt nor Churchill could have risked a showdown with Stalin and a breakdown of the conference. Admittedly, both Western statesmen made mistakes—in agreeing to the handing over of Russian prisoners to those who proved to be their executioners; and in letting ambiguities creep in to the agreements. But the modern tendency to rewrite history on the basis of what might have been, and what sounds politically expedient today, is unjust to those who spoke for the West at Yalta. The people of Eastern Europe suffer today not because of Yalta but because they have to live under Soviet domination. Stalin never offered a basis for a postwar consensus, except the one that was based on a divided Europe and a Poland that could never again be used as a corridor for an attack against Russia.

There was only one man on the American side who argued that the United States should have refused to bargain with the Russians at Yalta—George Kennan, then minister at the American Embassy in Moscow under Ambassador Harriman. He believed that the rational course was to divide Europe into two spheres of influence: whatever the Russians then chose to do in theirs would be their own responsibility—and in any case the US and Britain lacked sufficient strength to influence it. In hindsight, this approach was the essence of realpolitik, but at a time when many still cherished hopes of cooperation with the Soviet Union it stood to be regarded as little better than defeatism. What Yalta taught—still teaches—is that the Russians must be treated with great circumspection and their strength must be matched with equal strength.

As I was made very well aware in Paris, the French were hopping mad at not having been invited to Yalta; even their share in the postwar control of Germany had been granted only on Churchill's insistence. All three Allied leaders, though, took the view that the French had done too little fighting to be at the conference table. Once the Yalta decisions had been made public I went to see de Gaulle's foreign minister, Georges Bidault, to get his reaction. Bidault was a member of the Christian Socialist Party, a former university professor who had been a leader of the underground during the Occupation. By this time he had become a friend. He was a man of natural modesty, somewhat skeptical of his sudden rise to power and unsure how his political ideas would mesh with the general's. With almost childish pride Bidault conducted me through the private floor of the Quai d'Orsay, the French Foreign Ministry, where he had an apartment filled with fine antique furniture. All his personal effects at that time were in the bedroom: one suit, two shirts, one pair of shoes. We got along well. I lunched often with him in his private dining room and was flattered to note that while according to his secretary he normally ate virtually nothing in the middle of the day, merely taking two or more glasses of wine, in my company he took a full meal, clearly a healthier diet than alcohol alone for this small and highly strung intellectual. When he collapsed during his first speech before the provisional Chamber of Deputies the newspapers printed the official explanation, that he had the grippe and a high fever. Only the puckish satirical weekly, *Le Canard Enchaine,* offered the truth, and in one line: "In Bidault veritas."

Bidault was a weak man who wanted to be taken for a strong one—in the shadow of de Gaulle, a formidable task. When he first gave me an interview he was reprimanded by the general: only de Gaulle, he was told, could speak for France. I enjoyed listening to Bidault's ideas on the future of Europe, his conciliatory approach to relations with Germany, expressed in such elegant French. He was a brilliant impromptu talker, and a memorable one. On Britain: *La Manche est un credit ouvert par la geographie à l'histoire, et l'Angleterre estime toujours qu'elle n'a pas l'avoir encore complètement épuisé* ("The English Channel is a line of credit opened by geography to history, and England always considers that she has still not completely exhausted it"). Or on prewar Germany: *C'était des tentations de désespoir et les coups d'état de servitude* ("It lived by the temptations of despair and revolts against subjection"). Or: *Les frontiers sont les cicatrices de l'histoire* ("Frontiers are the seams of history"). One day he called in his private secretary, a charming, pretty, and vivacious woman who had worked for him in the underground, and showed her a report he had had from the Deuxième Bureau, the secret service, listing exact dates when she and I had met. At first, she told me later, she was a little taken aback, but then could not help laughing because, as she told the minister, the Deuxième Bureau was not really all that efficient—we had seen each other more often than that. Bidault smiled, and later let the Bureau agent know that she had been seeing me on his own orders.

When he and I met in his office just after Yalta he made no bones about his anger with de Gaulle for rejecting his advice to accept Roosevelt's invitation to a meeting on the cruiser *Quincy* off Algiers. "Charles le Grand" was sulking in his tent because of his exclusion from the summit meeting and in no mood to accept consolation prizes. The invitation and its refusal were not yet public knowledge, so I remained with bated breath all that week, praying that the scoop Bidault had handed me on Tuesday would hold until Sunday. As the days passed without the story breaking I realized to my surprise, and great relief, that I was sitting on my first-ever world scoop. Then I began to worry: if I broke the story, would it risk serious hurt to Roosevelt's triumphant return to Washington? On Friday, therefore, before filing my story to the office, I went to see the American ambassador, Jefferson Caffrey, a dryly taciturn and highly competent professional, and asked his opinion. Today, the idea of a reporter making such a solicitous inquiry seems naively unprofessional. But it was my first big political scoop and I still considered myself an inexperienced political correspondent. Caffrey was as furious as Bidault because he too had failed to persuade de Gaulle to accept the president's offer. "It's news," he told me laconically, "and it's your story." I filed. On April 12 Roosevelt was dead, and the high point of a resplendent memorial service for him in Notre Dame

Cathedral came when General de Gaulle knelt in uniform before the altar, head bowed, for what seemed minutes on end. I could not help thinking that this proud man was now regretting his lost rendezvous, if for nothing more than the opportunity of a last farewell.

Coming face to face with the general was always an intimidating experience. At the start of one personal interview he looked at me calmly and coldly, with me unsure whether I was expected to break the silence. Then, after what seemed minutes on end, he spoke: *J'écoute* ("I am listening"), sounding to me almost like a military command. It took me long seconds before I managed to come out with my first question. At times his anti-British views surfaced. When, for instance, after he had talked persuasively about the vast changes the invention of the atomic bomb would have on diplomacy, I asked whether it had also changed his own ideas—about, say, the separation of the Rhineland from Germany, one of his crucial ideas for the future—the military philosopher suddenly saw only a British correspondent before him, and caustically and defensively demanded, ". . . and what about Gibraltar and Suez and strategic bases?"

In Washington he asked for American economic aid, support for the Rhineland proposal, for an expansion of the French zone in Germany, and for the French occupation of Indochina. He got most of the loans he asked for, but President Truman made clear that he considered the Potsdam decisions sacrosanct, and so would not support the internationalization of the Ruhr or the separation of the Rhineland.

So, as the war came to an end, and each Ally sought to provide for its own long-term security, old and new differences bubbled to the surface and obscured the future. Within the Foreign Office there was a division between those who believed that it was necessary to plan for war with Russia, possibly with Germany as an ally (a prospect that also preoccupied the British chiefs of staff), and the Policy Planning Committee under Sir Gladwyn Jebb, who strongly advocated continued reliance on the tripartite alliance. In their heated debates, the FO and the military could agree on only one assumption: that the United States could not be relied upon to support Britain's imperial interests. In addition, a powerful group in the Foreign Office, led by Anthony Eden, was distrustful of American intentions and skeptical of reliance on them to maintain a commitment to Western Europe, arguing that instead it might be safer to seek an alliance with the Russians or the French. Sir Oliver Harvey, an undersecretary, the prototype of a Foreign Office official of the old school— a wall of reserve, and at the time probably the strongest influence in the Foreign Office among permanent officials—shared Eden's preference for a British-led security bloc in Western Europe, but one that would have no role for Germany. Stalin would be welcome to form a similar one in Eastern Europe, said Harvey, "provided we always think in terms of the Anglo-Soviet alliance and not, as the Chiefs of Staff would have it, in terms of 'Russia the next enemy.' " Britain's ambassador to Moscow, Sir Archibald Clark-Kerr (later Lord Inverchapel), was asked to present this concept of an Anglo-Soviet alliance, but there is no evidence that he ever received an answer. Harvey had little confidence in postwar cooperation with the Americans: "We must regard the United States," he wrote in a Foreign Office memo, "as a bonus, not as a dividend in making our plans." Sir Pierson Dixon, then Eden's private secretary, was also among those who regarded the Americans as unreliable allies, and the notion of Britain's becoming a junior partner in an alliance as humiliating.

The British were rightly wary of the anticolonialism that lies at the very heart of the United States' existence. In a dispatch in mid-1944, for instance, the then British ambassador, Lord Halifax, had reported from Washington: "Attacks on the Empire reveal conflicting tendencies. On the one hand there has been an increasing realization of America's own interest in the perpetuation of the Empire for strategic reasons. . . . On the other hand from an economic standpoint the belief has gained strength that British and American interests conflict all along the line." Harold Macmillan noted in his diary in May of the same year that the Americans "either wish to revert to isolation combined with suspicion of British imperialism, or to intervene in a pathetic desire to solve in a few months problems which have baffled statesmen for many centuries."

Churchill tried formally at Potsdam to interest President Truman in the idea of a permanent Anglo-American alliance, but got no reply, for the reason that the State Department favored the termination of the special relationship. Cordell Hull, the secretary of state, ordered the cancellation of various combined boards and insisted that nobody be given special privileges. At the same time the Foreign Office produced a trenchant memorandum summing up the prevailing American state of mind: "The Americans are mercurial people, unduly swayed by sentiment and prejudice rather than by reason or even by consideration of their own long-term interests. Their Government is handicapped by an archaic Constitution, sometimes to the point of impotence, and their policy is to an exceptional degree at the mercy of both electoral changes and of violent economic fluctuations . . ."

All of this gravely misjudged the Americans' ability to shed their isolationist instincts and grow into a new role in the world as successive administrations and the American public reacted to the Soviet threat, the true morticians of isolationism. Those who ruled Britain after the war also gravely misjudged Britain's ability, after the massive lacerations of the war, to preserve its prestige as a Great Power by creating and leading a new Western Europe. The French too, as Bidault told me more than once, were convinced that Western Europe could not rely on the United States in case of another war. Distrust also grew between Paris and London when Ernest Bevin, who followed Eden at the Foreign Office, showed little interest in France's demands on Germany. But,

above all, it was British and French distrust of the Americans that still dominated their policy calculations for the future.

American disillusionment with the Russians developed gradually. Curiously enough, one of the tip-offs that Soviet-American relations were heading
downhill came from Maxim Maximovich Litvinov, who had been Soviet foreign commissar in the days of the League of Nations—when he became an
advocate of "collective security"—and ambassador to the United States at the
time of Pearl Harbor. Averell Harriman told me in late 1951 that he ran into
Litvinov in November 1945 in Moscow during an opera at the Bolshoi Theater
when the Russian had whispered that "things are getting bad." To Harriman's
question what could be done about it, he replied only: "Nothing." Harriman
persisted: "Can I or we Americans do anything?" and Litvinov replied again:
"No, nothing," and hurried away. Harriman took it as a tip-off that any senior
official friendly to the West was in trouble and hence relations with the West
were in trouble too. I had myself met Litvinov in the spring of 1942 at the Soviet
embassy in Washington. I was entranced by his temperamental charm and his
fast-talking agitator-type manner, with arms gesticulating to underline what
he wanted to emphasize like a salesman in a bazaar. What he wanted was for
the Allies to open up a second front in Europe against the Germans immediately to help relieve the pressure on the Russians. Watching his almost feverish
performance also made me understand why he had been so successful in
creating a favorable attitude toward the Soviet Union in the West. It did not
protect him, though, from falling into disgrace after Munich, when it became
obvious that his pro-Western policy had failed and was dismissed, or again,
late in the Second World War, when his usefulness as an ambassador to the
United States had run out and his survival hung on a thread.

The first to ring what became the most effective alarm bell was George
Kennan, then minister at the American Embassy in Moscow, with his famous
"long telegram" drafted as an interpretation of a speech by Stalin in February
1946. It had a tremendous impact on American policymakers. Averell Harriman, who was at that time the American ambassador to the Soviet Union,
told me years later that Kennan had badly wanted to send a long series of
warnings about Soviet Union's new expansionist tendencies, but that he, Harriman, had prevented it because he did not want to "stir up trouble." However
when Harriman left Moscow, his farewell remark, as he told me himself, was
"George, you're now on your own, you are now chargé d'affaires"; and,
Harriman added, "Sure enough out came those telegrams." They advocated
the containment—which became a winged word—of the Soviet Union.

Winston Churchill tried to drive the same lesson home when, out of office,
he traveled on a special train with President Truman (spending some time
playing a mild poker game with the president) to Fulton, Missouri, to deliver
his famous, carefully planned speech on March 4, 1946, in which he warned that

from "Stettin in the Baltic to Trieste in the Adriatic, an iron curtain has descended across the continent." It continued to reverberate in people's minds and ears for years afterwards. Even the columnist Walter Lippmann, who believed that it was not through conflict but diplomacy—the classic combination of power and compromise—that civilization could be preserved, began to accept the argument, however passingly, that the Kremlin was intent on various forms of military expansionism. Such were the many political conflicts that divided the policymakers, the Great Power illusions of Britain and the disillusionments that set in even among men of goodwill, in those first postwar years. The British though, even if they admitted to themselves that they could not alone preserve the Pax Britannica, believed they could preserve their Great Power status. It meant hanging on to the Commonwealth, hopefully, with sympathetic American support in the interests of world stability, for, they said to themselves, the Americans, with their comparatively minimal experience, had no understanding of how to preserve a worldwide network of bases. Churchill remained convinced that only a firm Anglo-American alliance could safeguard the peace in the face of a mounting threat from the Soviet Union; others saw good relations with the US as the hopeful means of tempering American anticolonialism and gaining support to preserve a modernized Empire and Commonwealth. With the military triumphs over, the Allies found themselves in a new and different, largely incalculable world, and the Americans perhaps most of all, under their new and inexperienced President Harry S. Truman, were groping around for how to cope with the leadership role that they had not sought, but events had thrust upon them.

Individuals, too, had their decisions to make. I cannot remember accurately now whether it was on my return from Washington in 1942 or shortly after I had become Paris correspondent at the end of my service as a war correspondent that I suggested to W.W. Hadley that, were some kind of League of Nations organization to be established after the war, then I would like to cover it. I thought that my cosmopolitan background and my knowledge of languages, combined with the desire to be somehow at the center of peacemaking, would make this the ideal job for me, and me the ideal man for the job. Just after the founding conference of the United Nations in San Francisco, the editor reminded me of what I had said and asked if I was still keen on such an assignment. I replied with alacrity, expressing the hope that after the lessons of the League this new body would become an effective center of world diplomacy, and saying that yes, I would be only too glad to be assigned to it. And so on November 11, 1945, I left Paris.

Before saying good-bye to France, however, I went for a holiday at the Hôtel du Cap at Antibes, which was still under American military control, with a whole floor reserved by General Eisenhower for his own use. When Ike heard that Churchill, having been defeated in the general election in the middle of the Potsdam Conference, had retreated to his favorite watering place, Monte

Carlo, he invited the ex-premier to dinner with some of his staff officers. For some reason which now escapes me, at the last minute Eisenhower himself could not attend, but the dinner nevertheless went ahead.

During dinner it soon became clear that the defeated prime minister suffered from an encircling gloom. He was full of forebodings. Time and again he repeated that he could not understand how, after he had led Britain to victory in the war, the British people had not trusted him to lead them in peace, as he had firmly expected to do. It was a catastrophe, he declared, that neither he nor Roosevelt had been present up to the conclusion of Potsdam, for it was they who had laid the plans for Europe's future. "Neither Attlee nor Truman," he said, "could match Stalin at the green baize table." He said that the Russians now had too many cards in their hand; the future of the West, he predicted, would depend upon the skill of American diplomacy and the maintenance of American military power. When asked whom he would choose as the next American president, he answered without hesitation: "General Eisenhower."

On November 24 the United Nations Preparatory Commission met in London and so my new assignment began. The decision to base the international organization in the United States had not yet been taken; I therefore did not realize at the time that this assignment would carry me once more across the Atlantic. But I was very happy that after having covered the war, I would now be a part of the peacemaking.

3

Pax Anti-Sovietica

I T W A S Andrei Gromyko, of all people, who helped me give my editor
the best proof that I was on my toes in my new job as United Nations
correspondent. The dour-visaged Soviet diplomat, whose personality
and presence were to constitute for the next forty years a *leitmotiv* in the
lives of all of us, was at a UN Security Council meeting that had been called
to get occupying Russian troops withdrawn from Azerbaijan, the northern-
most province of Iran—a concession that the Soviets were doggedly, and
characteristically, declining to make. The UN was then temporarily housed in
Hunter College, New York City. US Secretary of State James F. Byrnes, a man
too clever for his own good, had recently been on a mission to Moscow, trying
to get the matter sorted out with Foreign Minister Molotov. All his efforts had
succeeded in doing, however, was to bring fire down on himself from some
members of Congress. So he was good and ready for the Soviet delegate to the
UN, daily escalating his attacks in the face of Gromyko's stubborn refusal to
make any concession. Finally—and I must have sensed somehow that the
Russian had had enough, for I was already running from the press gallery
toward the delegates' entrance—Gromyko jumped from his seat as if bitten by
a tarantula and stalked from the chamber. I reached the entrance just in time
to catch him before he escaped into his limousine, which with remarkably
quick reactions on the part of the driver was already waiting (or—who knows?
—maybe it was always there, with its engine running). Naturally, what I

wanted to find out was whether this was just a temporary demonstration of pique or an indefinite walkout. Gromyko, after I shot my question at him, looked past me, hurrying toward his waiting limousine, and answered with nothing more than an indefinable grunt. If my foray left me empty-handed in terms of substance, I got my reward from the battery of photographers who had by this time arrived and into whose clutches Gromyko and I stepped. The resulting picture appeared on virtually every front page around the world. Probably not *Pravda* or *Izvestia,* it's true: but it was certainly seen in my office back in London, and so my editor knew that I was where the news was. A year later, I asked Andrei Gromyko if he would sign a copy of the photograph for me. He replied, somewhat pompously, I thought, "It was an important occasion." But then he did sign the picture.

James Byrnes left those Security Council meetings to warm applause on the Hill and in the press. "If you appeal to the moral sense of the American people," one of his friends told him later, "they will always support you." In the end the Russians did bow to all the pressures and gave up Azerbaijan, but their attempt to annex it was a strand in the web of fear that lay over those first few years of peace. It seemed to me unbelievable, when all the killing and sacrifice were still so fresh in people's minds, that there should again be talk of war. Yet, however irrational, the fear was real enough, and Stalin seemed to encourage it. There was his determination to ignore the Yalta agreements and bring all of Eastern Europe under his control. There was his speech in February 1946 when he implied that future wars were inevitable until the world economic system was reformed, with communism replacing capitalism. There was Azerbaijan. There was that curious remark to Averell Harriman at Potsdam: after the US ambassador had remarked how gratifying it must be for the Soviet leader to be in Berlin after all the struggle and tragedy, Stalin replied, "Czar Alexander got to Paris." There was the nerve-racking Berlin blockade, and there was Europe's sense of being economically prostrate and militarily exhausted, while America was bent on getting its armies home and demobilizing them. The Western Allies found themselves wondering whether the Soviet Union under Stalin could really be trusted to cooperate in systems such as the United Nations or the Council of Foreign Ministers, whether it could ever be restrained from its expansionist aims.

And however united they had been during the war, in peace they were soon clearly divided. On the British side there was disagreement as to whether the greater threat in future would come from Russia or Germany; and whether it was better to seek a direct agreement with Moscow than to form an alliance with the "unreliable" Americans. There were de Gaulle's overtures to the Russians, about which he kept the British and the Americans in the dark; and there was Roosevelt's attempt to sidestep Churchill at Yalta in the belief that it would be possible to ensure a peaceful postwar world by direct Soviet-American cooperation. According to his closest aide, Clark Clifford, President Truman after Potsdam felt very much as FDR had done: "With Hitler and

Japan defeated, and much impressed by Stalin, he thought that the United States and the Soviet Union could work together to build a permanent peace for the world. But that belief began to erode when the Russians imposed their control, one by one, over their Eastern European neighbors." The British Foreign Office, as we now know from a memorandum by Sir Pierson Dixon, had suspected that Harriman was seeking to make a deal with Molotov behind their backs—and, as Harriman has since confessed to me, that was his instruction from President Roosevelt. Byrnes's attempt to open negotiations with Molotov—incidentally, done without the knowledge of President Truman— renewed those British suspicions.

But to come back to George Kennan's famous long telegram: I can think of no other dispatch in modern diplomatic history which has had a comparable effect on governmental thinking. Kennan complained some years later that his telegram had been misinterpreted, but at the time nobody doubted that he meant it to be read as a clarion call to alert American policymakers to the Soviet threat and to give a powerful impetus to policies that would fortify other countries and enable them to resist Communist attempts at overthrow. He achieved with a vengeance what he had intended. His telegram became compulsory reading in the government and the foreign policy establishment. And it fell on very receptive ears. However, when Kennan allowed an edited version to be published in the quarterly *Foreign Affairs* under the signature "Mr. X," Walter Lippmann was among the few who attacked it, arguing that "a free and undirected economy like our own cannot be used by diplomatic planners to wage a diplomatic war against a planned economy at a series of constantly shifting geographical and political points."

Kennan was a tall, lean-looking man, bald-headed in the best egghead fashion, whose every movement betrayed his inner nervous intensity and an intellect that was working overtime. His quizzical blue eyes could look at one with tolerant patience one moment and with scornful agitation the next. But however cool and detached outwardly, he had deep wells of passion in him. He seemed to me a complex bundle of weary experience and precarious innocence. However much he resented the idea that he had laid the psychological cornerstone for the Pax Anti-Sovietica, he did, and in that sense has played a far more important role in American diplomatic history than he is willing to own up to. The political cornerstone was laid when the United States agreed to take over from the British responsibility for aid to Greece and Turkey, key bastions of the eastern Mediterranean which the West was anxious not to lose. In Britain there was an abortive attempt to get the Labour government to rescind its decision, but thereafter Washington did not take long to announce a new aid program to the two countries which came to be known as the Truman Doctrine. For Britain the plan meant the start of the reduction in her international commitments. For the United States it meant involvement in the defense of Europe, and so was intended also to reinforce American understanding, after all the flirtation with them, of how dangerous the Russians really were to the security of the West and to Western civilization in general.

In 1947 my United Nations asssignment was broadened to include all important international conferences, and this in turn led, in early March, to my first visit to Moscow. The purpose of the trip was to cover a now-forgotten meeting of the Council of Foreign Ministers to draft a peace treaty with Germany that never came to pass. But it remains memorable for me as a rail trip right across Europe, from Calais to Moscow, that in its uniqueness easily outdid the now revived Orient Express.

I had Ernest Bevin's heart to thank for the experience. Because of its condition, the foreign secretary's doctors did not want him to fly, and so by courtesy of the French government the British delegation set out on the journey in five well-equipped though shabby wagon-lits and five baggage cars. The Foreign Office, careful and self-reliant as ever, filled those baggage cars with food and liquor reserves and a million cigarettes, as well as office furniture and filing cabinets without number. Thus equipped, we traversed a Europe in which—until the point where we changed to the wider Russian gauge track —frontiers hardly existed. Inside our train we were warm and provided with adequate food. But beyond the windows a cold silence hovered over the grisly silhouettes of destruction. Snow lay over all, as if trying to hide the suffering of the homeless and the hungry. Hour after hour, day after day, we traveled through the landscapes of war and saw nothing but devastation.

Bevin had his own suite, and was accompanied by a contingent of top civil servants, and then there was the press. After tedious negotiations the Russians had agreed to allow each of the other participating countries twenty correspondents. A few American and French were traveling with us, rather than flying with their own delegations, for the uniqueness—as they correctly guessed— of the journey. I shared a compartment with the correspondent of my own paper's principal competitor, the *Observer*. This was Edward Crankshaw, one of the most knowledgeable among Sovietologists, a fine writer and a good companion. During the war he had spent some time as a military attaché in the British Embassy in Moscow. Somehow the *Observer* specialized in placing its most brilliant writers opposite me: George Orwell for part of the time I was stationed in Paris; Alastair Buchan (who later founded the influential Institute of International Studies, a nongovernmental "think tank"), Godfrey Hodson, and Patrick O'Donovan in Washington; and Crankshaw on this occasion.

Our first stop was in a small Belgian town, where we picked up Bevin— he had been in Dunkirk signing an Anglo-French treaty of friendship. This pause was just long enough for us to have a quick beer in a local bar. The Belgians we saw looked shabby but well-fed. A gendarme, getting into high gear, raised his glass and praised his country because *"On mange et on gagne des sous."* A French correspondent, raising his glass, countered that the *sous* had little value nowadays: what mattered was dollars. The Belgian would not agree: *"Les dollars,"* he retorted, *"sont pour les intellectuels."* Our next stop was Berlin, where we got off the train long enough for a bath and tea at the Hotel am Zoo. Superficially the city seemed hardly to have changed since 1945, except that the Germans no longer seemed embarrassingly servile. We did not stop again until Brest-Litovsk, and the wider Russian gauge. Curiously enough, Brest-Litovsk had the first restored railway station we had seen on our entire journey thus far. Probably it had been done on orders from Moscow to impress us with an example of Soviet reconstruction in progress.

We waited for a long time until Russian passport control officers had passed through the train and, with utter politeness, stamped our passports and tagged our baggage. Without these tags the porters, who resembled penguins in their black uniforms and white aprons, refused to transfer our possessions to the train that would take us on to Moscow. This train had been shifted for our benefit from its regular run between the capital and Leningrad and consisted of wagons-lits Russian-style. Everything looked very Victorian: red carpets, green blinds, yellow lampshades, a combination of Café Royal and *salon privé*. Dinner was smoked salmon, beef stew, Crimean apples, and—a special luxury anywhere in Europe, but especially here—white bread. A woman barber was on the train, in a special compartment that looked like a theater dressing room and had a proper barber chair.

In the evening some of us among the correspondents had a heated, almost surrealistic debate about what to expect from the future. No subject was deemed too extravagant. Did we detect signs of the coming end of the world? Would communism overwhelm Christianity? A majority seemed convinced that communism was the religion of the future, and none was even a crypto-Communist—certainly not Alex Clifford of the London *Daily Mail* or Helen Kirkpatrick of the Chicago *Daily News* or George Backer of the New York *Post*. But communism in those days loomed large over Europe, especially in France and Italy, while the Soviet Union controlled half of the continent and did not have to persuade its allies into cohesion. These things raised apprehensions—military, political, social—throughout the West.

Moscow was cold and bleak, but after all the devastation seen on our route past Minsk and Pinsk it was a relief and a surprise to see how little the city had suffered. And there was the fortress of the Kremlin, in all its power and glory, untouched by the war, right in front of our window at the new Moskva Hotel. The Muscovites seemed proud that their city had been chosen for the meeting, and the government made every effort amid the pervasive austerity to provide us with such reasonable comforts as heat in all rooms, clean laundry in two days, a suit press within the hour.

The star of the conference was the newly appointed Secretary of State George Marshall, whom friends described as a man of "many opinions but few prejudices." It was rumored that Stalin liked him because of his early advocacy of a second front in Europe to ease the German pressure on the Red Army. Field Marshal Montgomery, after dining in the Kremlin, had quoted Stalin as commenting on Marshall, "Military men of experience make good politicians." Some had hoped that Stalin's proximity would speed up the decision-making process, but nothing of the kind happened. The conference became a dreary diplomatic tug-o'-war in which I for one was glad of the time-out provided by two sightseeing visits to Stalingrad and Leningrad. In Stalingrad there was an impressive contrast between the stillness enfolding the skeletal buildings for which 90,000 Russians and 147,000 Germans had died, and the incandescence against the night sky of the furnaces of the Red October steel plant, which was already working around the clock—an impressive symbol of the prostrate country trying to pull itself up by its industrial bootstraps. As a special favor the visiting foreign correspondents were given a tour of the Kremlin, which in those days was still closed to the public. For all the beauty among the old icons, the sense of isolation from the rest of the world, the air of operatic opulence fit for a production of *Boris Godunov* cheek by jowl with the long, bleak corridors of bureaucracy, one could not help thinking of the centuries-old savage history of the place, and however impressive the tour, it was a great relief to be outside those high walls once again.

When the conference finally adjourned after six long weeks the foreign ministers toasted each other at a festive banquet in the Kremlin, but the best that could be said of it was said by Bevin, with a touch of sarcasm: "Four Power unity has been maintained both in agreement and disagreement." Ian Fleming, *The Sunday Times* foreign manager, as he called himself, even then enjoyed putting Bond-like touches of imagination into his instructions to keep his team of correspondents on their toes. In the middle of the conference he sent a cable asking me to get reactions to the conference from people on the streets of Moscow: he might just as well have asked me to arrange for Stalin to take a lie-detector test. Then he suggested that I travel to Washington via Vladivostok—presumably so that I would then know everything there was to know about the Soviet Union, having traversed it from end to end. It took no time at all, as I expected, for the Russians to say no, everybody had to return westwards. So I chose what I thought might anyway be a more fruitful route for me, via Czechoslovakia.

My fellow passengers in the DC-3 aircraft to Prague included a dozen or so Czechoslovak colonels—and one general—all on their way home after thirteen months attending the Marshal Voroshilov War College, where they had shared Russian officers' advanced studies in military strategy; it was the Soviet Union's highest such establishment. They were all dropouts, as we would say now, because they had cut off their two-year course eleven months early. What they were being taught, they already knew; but what they wanted to escape by leaving was a long course in Marxism and Leninism. One of them said that the most embarrassing feature of their stay had been the practice in the officers' mess of putting generals at one table, colonels at another, lieutenant colonels at a third. There were hors d'oeuvres for the generals, but not for the colonels; the generals had mixed vegetable soup followed by chicken; the colonels were given barley soup and mutton. After the Czech general explained that in their army such separation was unusual, the rest of the officers were allowed to sit together. The general, though, had to dine in another room.

The growing Russian shadow over the Czechs was also evident in my meetings with President Beneš—which I have already described—and my good friend Jan Masaryk, the foreign minister. The latter was in bed with influenza, but greeted me cheerily enough with the question, "No war?" With cocky disregard for the microphones which must have been hidden about his bedroom, he said that if the Russians decided to annex Czechoslovakia, or if it came to war again, "I would run." He was still paying rent for his London apartment, he told me, but with his pound savings running low, he might soon have to give it up. I offered to lend him whatever he needed, but he laughed it off.

Masaryk was an amusing raconteur. One of his best tales was how he silenced lady table companions if he found them boring. He would first ask the one on his right whether she was married. Provided she said no, he would then ask, "And how many children do you have?" That would shut her up. Then, turning to the one on his left, he would ask the same first question. If she was married he would ask how many children she had. She might reply "Two," and he would ask, "By whom?" And if the lady across the table proved to be married with no children, his line was, "And how did you manage that?"— which ended that conversation. Despite all this he was very much a ladies' man, but they had to be good company, and good-looking.

Jan Masaryk was torn between love of his country and the realization that the new Czechoslovakia was a far cry from the democracy his father had founded after the First World War. Jan refused to be called an eastern or a central or a western European. Filling out an American visa form which asked whether the applicant was white or black, he put down "Human." He wanted to be a free man, one who, as he put it himself, could say with impunity in a streetcar, "I don't think much of our present government." He wanted Czechoslovakia out of the limelight, not sharing Beneš's aim to be an East-West bridge.

Masaryk made a last desperate attempt to keep his country closely tied to the West by attending the abortive Marshall Plan conference in Paris in June, but the Russians made it thoroughly clear that they would regard such a step as Czechoslovakia's allowing itself "to be used as a tool against the Soviet Union," and he had no alternative but to withdraw. Some historians believe that the Russian refusal to participate in the Marshall Plan conference, which implied an offer to continue the wartime partnership, and the order to Masaryk to cancel Czechoslovakia's attendance, marked the beginning of the cold war.

I saw him for the last time a few months later, in November. We were in New York, and the end of Czechoslovakia's democracy looked ominously inevitable. Masaryk, who enjoyed laughing and making other people laugh, looked drawn and tense. He did not say much, another sign that his mind was elsewhere. At a meeting of the Comintern in Poland, he told me, designed to coordinate the policies of all Communist parties, the Czech representatives had been given orders to liquidate their political opposition, as had already been done in Poland, Hungary, and Romania. His own position had by then become so precarious that, as he told me, he could no longer use the official code to communicate with Beneš. The Czech Communists distrusted him, he knew he was surrounded by their agents, but if nothing else, he thought, the name Masaryk was an invisible protective shield. I begged him, in vain, not to return to Prague, but he was unwavering. He said that he could not leave Beneš to cope alone. More likely, I thought, it was the memory of his own father that would not allow him to desert his cause, his monument. There were others who tried to keep him from returning to Prague. But he was adamant. Two months after our conversation Beneš's government was overthrown by the Communists and two months after that, on March 10, 1948, Masaryk was found dead in the courtyard beneath his bedroom window. Whether he was "defenestrated"—thrown from the window like those earlier victims of insurrection at Hradčany Castle in 1618—or had committed suicide remains unresolved. In an article in the *Saturday Evening Post* I gave a detailed account of all the available evidence given to me by Masaryk's personal doctor, who had managed to get out of Czechoslovakia within days of what he considered to have been Masaryk's murder. No new evidence has since been unearthed.

Few had expected the Russians to attend the Marshall Plan conference. The White House worried that if they were to become beneficiaries of the plan then Congress would refuse to endorse it, but the Russians obliged with a policy blunder on the grand scale, by flaying the whole idea. It was one more proof to the world how impossible it was to cooperate with the Soviets, and it more or less assured congressional approval. Some influential men like Bernard M. Baruch, the Wall Street financier who enjoyed dispensing his wisdom from a bench in Lafayette Park, across the road from the White House, opposed the plan. Baruch argued that it would build Europe into too powerful a competitor with the United States, but he became a voice in the wilderness: communism was feared, competition was not.

George F. Kennan, the specialist in Russian affairs, formulated the American riposte to the Soviet threat and drafted the original memorandum out of which the Marshall Plan grew. He also became directly involved in laying the basis for a new Atlantic pact. Kennan describes in his own memoirs the shock his long telegram had caused. He felt like someone who had "inadvertently loosened a large boulder from the top of a cliff and now helplessly witnesses its path of destruction in the valley below, shuddering and wincing at each successive glimpse of disaster." He complained some years later that although his essay had serious "deficiencies" and lent itself to misinterpretation, its entire thrust had been misunderstood, because he had meant containment of the Soviets not by *military* means but only by *political* efforts. He had not meant to imply, he said, that the Russians aspired to invade other areas and that the task of American policy was to prevent their doing so, and thus that war between the two powers was inevitable.

Eighteen months after he had stirred Washington with that telegram I had my first long background talk with him. Many more such talks followed—he agreed to see me once in three months or so, on the strict understanding that nothing he said could be used as a news story. He was the most interesting personality in the State Department to talk to because he liked letting his mind roam and also letting me rummage around in it. He enjoyed tossing out ideas against my European outlook, but we both understood that that was what they were—ideas, often in a raw form, and were I to publish them, no reliable guide to the future course of American foreign policy. When he stretched out on his office couch, staring at the ceiling, I knew that he was in a relaxed mood and ready to talk for an hour or more. I sat there in the pose, if not the role, of a psychiatrist listening to a patient spilling his mind. When he stayed in his chair, tipping it back casually as he looked at me, I knew that he was in a more challenging mood, and that the discussion would assume a more give-and-take form. Sometimes he would react accommodatingly to my questions or arguments; sometimes he would be blunt and irritable, particularly when I disagreed with one of his ideas. Most of the time, though, he was a sympathetic interlocutor. As head of the State Department Policy Planning Staff, and later in his two ambassadorial posts in Moscow and Belgrade, he kept his instincts under control; once out of office, and in the academic world, his stance changed, and power gave him nausea.

In his "Mr. X" article he had maintained that by remaining firm, the industrial democracies could unify the West and so aid the speedy recovery of Western Europe that Russian influence would gradually recede. As he saw his theory succeeding in practice he began to feel concern that if the Russians felt their sphere of influence contracting too quickly, then out of weakness or fear they would resort to force. Tito's revolt in Yugoslavia, the purges in the Communist parties of the satellite countries, economic progress in the West as opposed to deterioration in the East, Russia's failure to gain complete control over Berlin (the key, he thought, to dominance over Germany), the possibility that the Kremlin was in fact opting for a divided Germany as a "protective psychological wall" against the spread of Western influence—all these things helped bolster his concern. "If the Russians believe," he said, "that we not only want to push their influence back but replace it by American, then they are wrong. The trouble is that they judge others by themselves and therefore assume *a priori* that we are out to deceive them." He complained of the difficulty of persuading the Soviet Union that the US wanted a neutralized Europe which would act as a buffer between them both.

There was of course good reason for the Russians' doubts: while that was Kennan's aim, it was not the direction in which US policy was heading. By the spring of 1948 preparations for the Atlantic Pact were underway, but according to Sir Nicholas Henderson (who was also involved in them, and thirty-two years later became ambassador to the United States), both Kennan and his friend and fellow Sovietologist Charles "Chip" Bohlen opposed the idea. They wondered especially (Henderson wrote in *The Birth of NATO*) whether such a pact would not "cause undue provocation to the Soviets." What they would have preferred the US to do was simply to say that it was prepared to supply the countries of Western Europe with war material, delivery of which, however, would have to await congressional approval in the following year. Henderson fell short of concluding that Kennan and Bohlen tried to sabotage the treaty. "But," he wrote diplomatically, "for many months they were not sure in their own minds what the most desirable outcome should be. . . . Kennan had to be satisfied that what was agreed . . . would not obstruct or deflect the peaceful flow of history. He therefore tried to look at the subject through the wrong end of the telescope of time and from very far away."

History, of which some understanding is vital to the policy planner, can also mislead. In Kennan's case it taught him that a divided Germany was inherently dangerous. He therefore searched for a solution that, by neutralization, would defuse the risks of a united Germany. I found it surprising that he believed a country of the size and power of Germany could be neutralized, or that a Soviet withdrawal from Eastern Europe could be made enduring. It surprised me even more when in 1957 he advanced the same concept in the prestigious Reith Lectures over the BBC. Kennan was taken aback by the wave of criticism that followed. Virtually every European and American statesman condemned his theories. He later admitted, in his self-critical and fair-minded way, that his comments had been "rash and out of place for that time and situation." The respect Kennan enjoyed in Europe was based on his Russian expertise and, less appealing to Americans, his belief in a balance-of-power concept. It remained unclear whether he accepted the logic of the inevitable need to acquire the weapons, nuclear or nonnuclear, necessary to establish "mutual deterrence" and preserve that balance.

In mid-April 1949, shortly before he resigned from the State Department, I again sought his views on Germany. He sounded bitter and disillusioned, arguing that the US had done "almost irreparable damage" with its policies in Germany. "The victors are never up to the demands of peace. We have made every mistake of Versailles and more. We have engendered nationalism, and ignored the liberal element." He thought that the Russians had more to offer the Germans, and we had only an even chance of winning the game. It was not wholly surprising that Secretary of State Dean Acheson ignored the recommendations that came from Kennan's planning staff, or that West German Chancellor Konrad Adenauer called him an "enemy of the German people."

He was rarely less than controversial. His most amazing blunder came when, as ambassador to Moscow, he gave a press conference in Berlin en route to a NATO conference in London in September 1952. Did Americans in Moscow enjoy many social contacts, someone asked. Kennan replied: "I was

interned here in Germany for several months during the last war. The treatment we receive in Moscow is just about like the treatment we internees
received then, except that in Moscow we are at liberty to go out and walk the
streets under guard." Within two weeks the Russians declared him persona
non grata, and obliged him to leave his post. He admitted later that he had
been "too highly strung emotionally, too imaginative, too sensitive, too impressed with the importance of my own opinions" for the job. After he had
left government office, his interest in Soviet affairs unabated, he spoke up more
and more, and with eloquence, in favor of détente and arms control. In
domestic affairs he spoke—as a man familiar with communism and its dangers
—against McCarthyism; a decade later, in the 1960s, he was critical of the
unruliness of the young and of the lack of discipline that rent the country, and
wondered aloud whether representative democracy was still a tenable form of
government. He denounced materialism and anti-intellectualism and intoler-
ance at a time when his was often a lone voice.

Where Kennan went wrong, I believe, is in having assumed Soviet willingness to withdraw from Eastern Europe if the United States took *its* forces home
—an uneven deal in Russia's favor, since in an emergency American forces
would have to come all the way back across the Atlantic. He did not fully
comprehend the fierceness of the desire of Germany's neighbors to ensure that
never again would that country dominate Europe, and he underestimated the
Soviet Union's capacity to become a superpower. This did not mean that he
was to be discounted. He wrote brilliantly and spoke eloquently, and became
—in a country where, in the last two generations at least, passions usually flare
at the extremes of the political spectrum—that rare species, the passionate
moderate. He remained unsure about the uses of power, and whether US
leadership was a blessing for the rest of the world. He once said that Washington was divided into mechanics and gardeners. The mechanics thought that
foreign policy could be assembled like an automobile. The gardeners were
more modest: they knew that they had to till the soil, and could only cultivate
growth in a certain direction. Kennan in office belonged among the gardeners.

Kennan's containment idea, as generally perceived, made a lot of sense to
George Marshall. He had looked Stalin in the eye and sat across the table from
Molotov, his Soviet counterpart, for days on end, and had concluded that there
was little hope of coming to terms with them on a German peace treaty. So
he and his aides decided to translate Kennan's theories into practice. The
Potsdam agreements were in jeopardy because the Russians were imposing
their own system on Eastern Europe; American and British taxpayers had
come to realize that reparations had become a liability for them rather than
a punishment for the Germans; and economic aid to Western Europe had
become imperative to prevent the communists from gaining the upper hand
in France and Italy. Even the French began to accept that their own and the
West's security depended on German recovery. At the same time it was

becoming fairly clear that the United Nations would not become a real force in world affairs: the Russians had turned down the idea of a UN military force, and so many decisions of policy that were bound to affect the future stability of the world were being taken outside its conference chambers. It fell to Marshall to take the crucial decisions leading to acceptance of the division of Europe.

At that time he was an unusual appointee as secretary of state. That is, he was not a lawyer, and he was a soldier. In Britain in peacetime a senior officer of the armed forces could not become foreign secretary without leaving the services and entering Parliament, normally by election to the House of Commons (Lord Carrington's tenure as foreign secretary while in the House of Lords was unusual in modern times). There seems also to have been something of an unwritten rule about not putting a lawyer into the Foreign Office—lawyers are seen as fellows who can adjust their outlook to the case that they are hired to plead, who by training concentrate on the small print rather than the big picture, are quibblers about detail who tend to be too clever by half. Selwyn Lloyd, foreign secretary at the time of Suez, was the first lawyer in modern times to be given the job, and did nothing to overturn the accepted view.

For Americans it is different, probably because of their history and experience. The lawlessness that accompanied the westward advance of the frontier put the burden on lawyers to bring order to their country. Lincoln Steffens said that "you cannot reform government, you've got to get the scoundrels on your side—they know how to operate it." And to do that you need lawyers too. They have become the pillars and buttresses of American society, and from their ranks come, often, the most educated, the most articulate, those most desirable as leaders in the community, on corporate boards, and above all in politics. To study the law offers Americans the broadest scaffolding on which to build a livelihood. I once asked a black maid who looked after my house what she would like her then six-year-old son to become. "A lawyer," she replied unhesitatingly. I asked why, and she said: "Because you can't cheat a lawyer." Most Americans feel the same way about the selection of a secretary of state. They feel safer with somebody in the job who is good at reading the fine print.

In mid-1947 I had the opportunity to gauge the difference between two archtypes of the military and legal approaches: Secretary of State Marshall and John Foster Dulles, the Wall Street lawyer who had established himself as the Republicans' supreme foreign policy expert. Marshall never expected to be called on to take over the State Department; Dulles consciously and conscientiously trained himself for the job. In appointing Marshall, President Truman breached the rule of excluding the military from State, because he needed a man widely respected and of unchallengeable integrity. Marshall was at the other extreme from generals like MacArthur and Patton: he abhorred all flamboyance or showmanship. He was a spruce, cool, modest, and thoughtful man whose knowledge of foreign affairs lacked depth but whose instincts and sense of command were right for the role. He combined the sober acceptance of American ideals with the sober assessment of America's vital national interests. Power, he saw, was essential, and not in itself either good or evil; Americans had to be brought to recognize and use theirs in a responsible way. His decisions seemed to come from some inner certainty—as when he had given up the supreme command in Europe to Eisenhower, knowing that he himself was needed at the Pentagon to direct the military buildup for victory; and at the State Department, where he had to rely for detail on his experts, but set the direction for the big decisions himself. In his presence I felt awed by the Olympian modesty of his countenance, and the evident fact that he did not care about flattery, or even whether you liked him. General Eisenhower was a diplomat first and a soldier second, relying a great deal on his charm and his ability to develop a consensus. Marshall was always the soldier first, ready to face the difficult decision head on. Truman knew where he was with him, as he did not with Eisenhower: he knew Marshall would be both loyal and politically neutral.

One difference between Dulles and Marshall that struck me was how the former misjudged the future role of the United Nations while the latter assessed it with down-to-earth realism. Dulles expected the UN's General Assembly to become its most important organ, to develop into "a world House of Commons where governments of the world would be taken to task before the bar of world public opinion," as he put to me more than once, while the Security Council would be reduced to what he called "scenery," incapable of action because of the Soviet use of the veto. Instinctively anticolonialist, Dulles yet failed to see how the end of the colonial era would transform the Assembly into an anti-American forum. He thought the threat of war relatively remote: what worried him was the spread of communism. Marshall told a group of journalists of whom I was one that he did not regard the United Nations as a preserver of the peace, and he rejected talk of weakening the power of the veto. There could come a time, he predicted, when such countries as India and Pakistan, Burma, Indonesia, and others might exercise their newly found freedom by choosing to follow Soviet policies, and then the Russians would find the General Assembly more useful than would the United States. He was quite clear that there was no common ground, political, economic or ideological, with the Soviets.

As American policymakers began to dip their toes in world affairs there were wide differences about how best they should deal with them. It had been relatively simple to handle mainly military power during the war, but power in peacetime, power to be used with caution and responsibility, that was a totally new experience. When Truman ordered the demobilization of American troops, he quickly found out that he had deprived himself of an important tool; and when, later on, he threatened to use the atomic bomb in Korea, he had failed to understand that the means of ending World War Two did not lend itself easily to being an instrument of diplomacy. Though Eisenhower and Dulles believed that the implied threat of a nuclear response brought the Chinese to the negotiating table, they recognized soon that nuclear blackmail was of little political utility. (Eisenhower, as president, went about things differently, letting the Chinese know secretly that the A-bomb was under consideration as a last resort to end the Korean War. But Richard K. Betts, in his carefully researched book *Nuclear Blackmail and Nuclear Balance,* Brookings 1987, reached the conclusion that "the evidence does not permit precise conclusions about the coercive efficacy of the nuclear signal. The inherently delicate nature of such an initiative makes it unlikely that clear evidence would exist. Those who made the threats, however, attributed great significance to them—at least after they happened." The most specific evidence is John Foster Dulles's record of conversation with Prime Minister Nehru in May 1953 which refers to a warning "that if the armistice negotiations collapsed, the United States would probably make a stronger rather than a lesser military exertion, and that this might well extend the area of conflict." Dulles later claimed that the Chinese two weeks later began negotiating more earnestly.)

Another reason why Americans found it difficult to set limits to the uses of power was that the national interest had not been defined. It still needs definition even today. In the forties it seemed simple because of the direct confrontation in Europe. It was this: to contain Soviet power. But as the Pax Britannica faded and the Pax Americana rose on the horizon, a more complex definition was necessary. Marshall saw that the days of innocence had gone, and the US could not afford to return to isolationism: "War is not to be counted out unless we are prepared to withdraw into our hemisphere and give the Russians the rest of the world by default." Marshall had concluded that America must not lose the initiative it had gained in Europe. This was probably one reason why he decided to break up the Council of Foreign Ministers' abortive discussions in London. He had come to suspect that the Russians wanted to tap the productive power of the Ruhr to help rebuild their own industrial base, and he feared that unless the US assumed leadership in the West a united Germany would become an appendix of Moscow, tipping the balance of power in favor of the Soviet Union.

On the same day of the meeting with Marshall I happened to see two Soviet journalists sitting in the United Nations cafeteria. They asked me to join them, and very soon they were complaining about the "negative and superficial" reaction to a speech by the Russian delegate, Andrei Vishinsky, which had amounted to a full-blown attack on the Marshall Plan. One of them, called Izakov, remarked that curiously enough a very important point in the speech had been totally overlooked—a reference to atomic manufacture "of which the US thinks she holds the monopoly at present." He added that a major announcement with reference to this remark would be forthcoming in two to three days. *Pravda* and *Izvestia* correspondents are very often briefed as well as or better than Soviet diplomats. I therefore took his pointer seriously—the more so since he added, with obvious satisfaction, that this event would induce a major change in American foreign policy. I filed the story, furnished with what seemed at the time a few prudent reservations, predicting the Soviet Union's announcement of its possession of the atomic bomb. Izakov of course proved to be correct.

When I returned to London that December 1947, I found a very self-preoccupied Britain. From Lord Kemsley, press baron owner of *The Sunday Times* and a string of London and regional newspapers, down to the shopkeepers who sold them for him, people complained bitterly about food shortages, the high cost of living, financial restrictions . . . With Britain in the economic doldrums, all were gloomy about the future, wondering (if they were young) whether they should emigrate to Canada or Australia, or (if politically conscious) whether Britain would not be better off to cut the cost of her ambitions to suit the cloth —for example, abandoning a "blue water" naval policy now that India had her independence. A "poor man's policy" would have been in tune with the spirit of the day, expressed to me by one man as "We continue to exist, but we don't live. People go about their business, they go to their pubs and cinemas, they occasionally smile and joke, but the stiff upper lip and sense of humor we were so proud of during the war years has gone." After a costly, hard-won victory, the liberator seemed as badly off as the liberated: a deep disappointment was abroad. Little love was lost for the US, whose Communist "scare" was feared, more than Soviet hostility, as the possible genesis of another conflict: "We have gone through two bloody wars," was the refrain, "we can't go through another one." Eleanor Roosevelt was alert to these fears, commenting at a Geneva conference on human rights that while Communist witch-hunting had become one of the most exciting of Washington pastimes, it left Europeans unsure whether Americans knew how to make democracy work. It is a question Europeans are still asking.

It was a special honor when Lord Kemsley invited me to attend my first Tuesday conference at *The Sunday Times,* which he presided over as editor in chief and which his editors approached weekly with some trepidation. We were about ten: the leading editorial staff, the managerial group, sitting in a semicircle around the huge mahogany desk of the god of the machine. "K," as he was referred to when not present, smiled patronizingly most of the time, leading the discussion and pointing out the good and bad pages of the previous Sunday's edition. Finally he turned to me, to congratulate me on my appointment as consultant to the forthcoming UN Conference on the Freedom of Information, which seemed to please him as a compliment to his papers in general at a time when some of them (not mine) had been under fire for their customary lack of ethics. This personal interest may have led to another breakthrough the following Sunday with my first signed article ("Can the UN

Survive?") on the editorial page, a position usually reserved for leading establishment figures—churchmen, politicians, high-ranking military—preferably titled ones.

Before leaving for Geneva and the Freedom of Information conference I took a little "memory lane" trip to the brier-pipe factory where I had been a progress clerk after first arriving in England. The old proprietor, a grandfatherly type with a gentle sense of humor, was still running the place, and he and a few of the older foremen remembered me and gave me a warm welcome, though they were all surprised that I should have wanted to come back. There was nothing memorable about the conference, but it did bring about another return trip. This was a visit to Vevey, a cheerful little town on Lake Geneva, just outside which, at Gilamont, I had gone to a private school at the age of fourteen. A woman friend in the American delegation came with me, and once we were off the boat I had no difficulty finding the road I used to walk whenever I went to the beach club. I recognized the old tennis courts but, to my distress, I could not find the school building. Bewildered, I asked an elderly woman about it. She replied with a sympathetic smile, "I know the school you mean. It doesn't exist anymore. They razed it, it was such an old building." Then, looking at my companion, she added, "So many of the old students come here to show their wives where they went to school . . ." On a more recent visit to Vevey I found the old school playground buried under a four-lane highway.

The conference was doomed by the fact of the cold war and was primarily designed, anyway, to expose what the Soviet dictatorship meant for the freedom of the press. Yet it still made quite a difference to my life. First of all I got to know Hector McNeil, the minister of state who headed the British delegation. It was the start of a very special friendship. His trust in me was such that he would invite me to breakfast with other delegates to discuss policy and conference tactics. Although Dulles used to say that he had to switch into the French simultaneous translation when McNeil spoke, because he could not follow his Scots accent, his speeches were among the most effective contributions to UN debates. His personal speechwriter was Guy Burgess. McNeil kept him on in spite of his often irascible behavior and drinking habits because, he said, Burgess had all the important Stalin and Lenin quotes at his fingertips. Burgess came to dislike our friendship: he considered me too prejudiced against the Soviet Union. Once at a small dinner in McNeil's flat in London Burgess attacked me personally in such an abusive manner that next day the minister of state sent me a note of apology; none came from Burgess. A lighter note recalled from the conference concerns the millionaire Senator Bill Benton, who headed the American delegation. Benton had made his money in advertising, and among other properties owned the *Encyclopaedia Britannica,* as well as Muzak. He was the epitome of the salesman with intellectual ambitions. "Henry," he counseled me one day, "to become a millionaire is easy. All you have to have is *one* good idea. Mine was sanitary towels."

There was an unreality about this long (four months) conference, for the world outside our ivory tower was preoccupied with more immediate events. The situation of Berlin had become precarious as the Soviets tightened the blockade. Masaryk died a violent death. Congress passed the Marshall Plan and the Senate was about to adopt the so-called Vandenberg Resolution, a historic breakaway from American wariness of foreign "entanglements" that allowed the US to enter into collective security pacts. Freedom of information may have been one of the deep-rooted problems of East-West relations, with the Russians claiming that a responsible press must be under government control and the West that a press so controlled could not be free, and both sides claiming that the other's system was aggravating the cold war. In the end both sides agreed to a resolution against "warmongering" to which everybody could subscribe and which everybody ignored.

On my way back to the United States I stopped briefly in London, where, over lunch arranged by Bill Clark, a columnist of the *Observer* and a longtime friend, its editor and publisher, David Astor, asked whether in principle I would be interested in becoming his paper's correspondent in Washington. It was a tempting thought, particularly since Ian Fleming had asked me to take a salary cut as part of one of those waves of financial stringency that overtake all newspapers from time to time. But however much thrift had to be practiced in Kemsley House, it would have seemed to me ungrateful and disloyal to turn my back on *The Sunday Times* after all the opportunities I had been given there. So I took up Fleming's suggestion that, with the debate about the Baruch Plan droning on at the UN, I should instead spend a little time immersing myself in American politics and spend a few days on President Truman's whistle-stop train on his election tour.

Before the instant ubiquity afforded by television and jet plane, the candidate's whistle-stop tour, appealing from the back platform of a train to the people in small towns and farm communities, as well as industrial centers, in a vast country where the emphasis was on mass production, mass consumption, mass merchandising, was an eccentric and uniquely American form of political retailing, a reaching out to the forgotten individual. Truman's vehicle was the Ferdinand Magellan, a private rail car with armored walls originally built by the Association of American Railroads for Franklin Roosevelt. As it rolled out of Washington's Union station on June 3 at the tail end of a sixteen-car Presidential Special, hardly anybody thought this would make much difference to Truman's discouraging electoral prospects. But it was still a special event, and with the White House press corps accompanying the president wherever he went, in accordance with tradition, it was a good story, and an unusual way of seeing the country.

Next to the president's car was a parlor car, used as a "holding tank," so to speak, for the local bigwigs who would join the train for one or two stops, to be seen in the presence of the president while the cavalcade moved through their home territory. Then came the carriage for the White House staff with their living and sleeping accommodations, and then the press car, which had had all its seats taken out to make room for several long tables to put our typewriters on. The itinerary was to extend to more than eight thousand miles, from Washington D.C. to Seattle to Los Angeles and back to Washington, more than twice the distance between, say, London and Tehran.

Truman was delightfully informal in his dealings with the press. He treated reporters very much like comrades-in-arms, joking and laughing with them, occasionally cursing them. In the mornings in Washington they joined with him for his brisk walk around the White House, and in the evenings he played poker with some of them. Some of the publishers, however, he despised. Frank Holeman of the New York *Daily News* remembers that Truman called his paper, which belonged to the true-blue Republican McCormick and Patterson axis, "shit paper"—but there was never the slightest attempt at discrimination against a reporter who worked for such a paper.

We had on board forty-two newspaper and magazine reporters, four photographers, five radio correspondents, four newsreel men, four television technicians, and a bevy of Western Union employees, the foot soldiers of communications who made sure that our copy was safely transmitted from railroad stations that we passed, while we speeded on. I mention the composition of the press corps because of its contrast with today's television circus of competing national and international networks. In those days the men of print were still the princes among the media. Newsreel men and television technicians led separate, subordinate lives.

There was something wonderfully serene about this campaigning on a human scale. People came from hundreds of miles just to get a glimpse of the president on the back platform, even though the halts were sometimes for scarcely ten minutes. For Truman it was an opportunity to make the folksy most of getting close to the people: "They say a lot of things about me that are not true," he would tell them. "Here I am. Look me over and decide for yourself." And people would laugh and applaud. There were ample indications, as we moved along, that people liked the man and most of the time liked what he said, whatever might be the current wisdom of political punditry. We watched the president, and mingled with his audiences to learn their reactions. We followed his performance with growing admiration for his perseverance, good humor, and optimism when not one of the polls gave him an outside chance of winning. Even when some of the larger halls, at Fort Wayne, or Chicago, were more than half empty, or when he dedicated an airport to the wrong person, he remained unabashed and, on the contrary, gave every impression of enjoying his mobile rendezvous with the American people.

On the third day I was invited to visit the president in his car. After a hearty handshake and a few warm words of welcome, asking if I was enjoying myself, he directed one of his aides to show me his looseleaf political "Baedeker." This was his black-covered portfolio, briefing him about what he should emphasize at each stop. There were the names of local officials who were working hard for the Democrats, local projects to which the federal government had contributed, the names of the "favorite sons" of whichever state we were passing through, those who had made their contribution to the greatness of the United States—all this in no more than three or four paragraphs. For myself, I had become enchanted by Truman's bubbling humanity, his daunting vitality, his pugnacity, and his puckishness. He did not mind getting his hands dirty fighting in the political underbrush, yet he still managed to convey that he was above the battle, that he knew what it meant to be president. After all, he had come into office totally unprepared, because Roosevelt had never taken him into his confidence or allowed him into the councils of state. Yet he had shown great courage in developing an entirely new American foreign policy.

Once off the Truman train, however, the intoxication of this intensive short course in American politics did not long survive my return to the United Nations, where the debate about the so-called Baruch Plan was moving toward a climax. Bernard Baruch belonged to an American species that has never quite died out. Throughout his life he had relied on only one person, himself. His self-confidence knew no limit. His tall and handsome appearance and aristocratic bearing provided a facade for an ambitious, ruthless, autocratic man who became the center of attention wherever he went. Like a king, or some gangster chieftain, he was always surrounded by an impressive entourage whose duty it was to protect and promote the Baruch cause of the moment, whatever it might be, and to see that he got maximum and favorable publicity. Money was no object. When Truman asked Baruch to take over the so-called Acheson-Lilienthal Report—commissioned to shape an international agency that would control virtually all atomic energy activities under the aegis of the UN, including worldwide supplies of uranium—he soon got into a bitter hassle with the original authors and developed his own "Baruch Report." His two crucial contributions were to propose that there should be no punishment for violators of the treaty, nor any veto in matters concerned with atomic energy. These were so extreme that one could only suppose him to be more interested in perfection and the political safe ground than a negotiable position. In any event, the Russians were by then, thanks to the betrayal of secrets by scientists from the West, well on the way to their own first nuclear explosion; they were not about to surrender their atomic rights and let the US keep its A-weapons. On June 22, Gromyko used the twenty-sixth Soviet veto in the Security Council to block the Baruch plan.

Soon after this the General Assembly met for the first—and last—time in Europe, specifically in Paris. I sailed in the *Mauretania,* slightly smaller than the *Queens* and less impersonal, leaving on August 29, one of the hottest days of the summer. My cabin temperature was 98 degrees, in spite of a fan and an open porthole. Many people preferred to sleep on deck, and one middle-aged lady told me the next morning, slightly horrified, that she had been awakened in the middle of the night by a voice saying, "Get up, sweetheart!" It belonged to a sailor who was cleaning the deck with a hose. The passengers included the British actor Charles Laughton, but to the disappointment of the captain Laughton declined to join the captain's table. He also refused to put on a dinner jacket, his greatest sartorial concession being to wear a tie. The captain still held hopes that he could persuade the star to perform for him and his guests on Captain's Night, but once again his hopes were dashed, and he was told it was out of the question. That night, however, just after we had finished dinner and I had settled down in one of the salons with a book, my steward rushed in and whispered in my ear for me to accompany him. He took me down by elevator into the bowels of the *Mauretania* and the crew's mess room. There was Laughton, sitting on one of the workaday dining tables, giving the boys a recital—the Gettysburg Address.

The most flamboyant recitalist at the UN, Andrei Vishinsky, also chose to keep the Paris General Assembly date in low key: vituperation was out, probably to try to emphasize to European Communists the sweet reasonableness of the Soviets in general and their chief delegate in particular. Anyway, the event was a damp squib, never to be repeated. In October, when the Security Council came to debate the Berlin blockade, Vishinsky was in quite different voice, using all his verbal acrobatics to argue that no blockade existed and even if one did it would represent an issue outside the Council's competence. But soon it was clear that the calm and no less legalistic American delegate, Dr. Philip Jessup, was getting the better of the argument.

However much we were distracted by the astonishing feat of Truman in overturning all predictions and winning his own term in the White House, it was the Berlin blockade that was our daily stuff of crisis. Truman had taken the sensible decision to supply Berlin by air rather than by an armed convoy running the gauntlet of East Germany, with its greater risk of war, a decision much in line with the thinking of the British government. As one of a group of correspondents invited to look at the operation from the sharp end I flew first to Wiesbaden, where the briefing given us left no doubt in our minds of the seriousness of the operation and the dangers involved. But here for the first time was an example of Western technological superiority being used for diplomatic ends. The desirable minimum of 4,000 tons of supplies a day had been squeezed down to a practical 3,500 by the foul weather—senior Western officers regarded this as a more significant factor than the occasional buzzing of airlift planes by Soviet fighters, which they put down to the indiscipline and overzealousness of youth.

Each correspondent traveled in a different aircraft from the Rhein-Main base. Waiting in a queue on the runway, with planes going at five-minute intervals, it suddenly felt like a throwback to wartime. The pilot pointed out the Russian air base of Dessau, with several Yak fighters visible on the ground, but none moving. In the end it was an uneventful flight, if an odd one—the plane was filled with very smelly cheeses—and even the landing at Tempelhof, a small field for such an operation, proved easy. In the streets of Berlin everything seemed serene. In the evening I went to a restaurant in the Russian sector—movement between sectors was uninhibited then—but when I tried to pay in rubles the waiter regretted that only dollars or sterling was acceptable. Even in time of crisis, the world was still turning around the hard currencies of the West. Our return flight was made in thick rain clouds, and it was an uncomfortable thought, however competently routine this operation had become, that we were part of a flying caravan of planes at only five-minute intervals traveling along a narrow corridor. At one point I heard the control tower at Rheinmegen warn us that we were at exactly the same altitude as another plane; we hurriedly climbed an extra 5,000 feet. Seeing how these planes created a bridge in the air in defiance of all Russian threats gave one an enormous confidence in Western strength and determination. The Russians finally lifted the blockade on May 12, 1949. Berlin remained a fitful barometer for East-West relations until the Russians concluded that it was too much of a tinderbox and needed to be defused through a four-power agreement.

Christmas Eve 1948 was one of those perfectly serene days when nothing startling should happen. I was in France, stretched out in a deck chair on the terrace of the Trois Dauphins hotel at Alpe d'Huez, enjoying the view of the snow-covered peaks after a good day's skiing along with Porter and Susan McKeever (he was press officer to the American delegation to the UN). Suddenly the *patronne* of the hotel arrived to announce breathlessly that I had a call from London. A little concerned, I wondered who would want to reach me that urgently, and hurried down to the telephone. Before I could even ask who was calling I heard the familiar voice of Ian Fleming: "The editor and I would be very pleased if you would accept the appointment as *The Sunday Times* correspondent in Washington."

I could hardly believe my ears. All I could do was to stammer, "What a marvelous Christmas present!" This was the assignment I had dreamed about but had not allowed myself to believe would be entrusted to me. Traditionally Paris had been the plum appointment for a foreign correspondent from London, but now the focus was admitted—everywhere else, at least—to have moved to Washington; before the Second World War my paper had seen no need to have a correspondent in the American capital, not even a "stringer." Fleming, who liked to play the tough guy, could also be thoroughly human, though he hated to admit it. He knew that this job was my dearest wish, and had planned things so that he could give me the news as a Christmas surprise. Later, in London, I learned that it had taken him almost all day to get through to Alpe d'Huez, but he would not be put off.

After almost three years of a gypsy existence as a roving diplomatic correspondent I could look forward to hanging my hat in a permanent home and taking my books along. When Fleming suggested that I start in Washington on April 1, All Fools' Day, the sudden fear clutched at my heart that after all it was some kind of joke, but he gaily reassured me that no, it was the real thing. I must be ready to start filing on April 10.

I was not sorry to be leaving the UN (though it was to remain part of my assignment), for the high hopes I had had of it when first asked to go there had been transmuted by experience into a deep sense of disappointment. It had been hobbled from infancy by the safeguards and reservations imposed on its Charter by the big powers, and by 1947 it was clear that it would never be able to exert really effective peacekeeping powers. More and more it had become obvious that the crucial problems were dealt with by the permanent members of the Security Council *outside* the UN. Peace in the world would still have to depend on some kind of balance of power, and humanity would be condemned to live in anxiety more or less indefinitely. And so on March 10, 1949, I packed what little I owned in my Olds convertible, and left New York to take up residence in Washington.

4

Social Snorkeling

I HAVE PLIED my trade as a political reporter all over the world —in London, Paris, Berlin, Moscow, Beijing, Tokyo, Saigon, Cairo, New Delhi, Rome, Rio de Janeiro—turning my passport into a kind of world gazetteer. But for forty years I have returned to the same place —yet never *quite* the same place. For just as Washington changed, in my eyes at least, between my first fleeting sight of it on my original visit to the United States and my arrival, years later, as a fully fledged Washington correspondent, so now, another forty years on, it has become a vastly different place. No capital has changed faster. It is the city where I made my career, where I got married to an American from Cambridge, Massachusetts, where my daughter, Fiona, was born, where I have made more friends than anywhere else. It has become home, though I remain a British citizen.

When I first searched for an apartment in 1949 nothing seemed less probable than all this, so anxiously uncertain was I about whether I could live up to my editors' expectations. They did not help by omitting to offer me a contract or a time frame within which they would decide whether to keep me in Washington or not. I knew that Washington was considered a taxing assignment, the plum job for a foreign correspondent and a place in which time is not meant to be wasted.

I hoped to find a place to live in Georgetown, not only because it was the most civilized part of the town but because what mattered for a reporter, I was told, was to establish "connections" with the mighty, and the best way to do that was to live near them in Georgetown. It was clearly the most pleasant place to live. To walk along the leafy privacy of the secluded residential streets, past the trim whitewashed and red-brick row houses interspersed with austere federal-style houses (or sooty derelict shacks with big-eyed black children playing on the threshold) was a relief from New York's skyscrapers and its prosaic, dirty streets.

Thanks to a committee of concerned Georgetown citizens, this little district with its staid maples, elms, and linden trees, often frivolously bright yellow- or pink-painted cottages, looking more like dolls' houses next to the stilted Dutch colonial dwellings or the ivy-covered old English cottages, was and still is perhaps one of the most charming enclaves of unspoiled human dimension of any big city.

Unspoiled—but expensive. It did not take me long to find out that housing in Georgetown was beyond my means, and so, keeping in mind my insecurities about whether I would be able to live up to my editor's expectations, I moved into an efficiency apartment at the pleasantly old-fashioned if slightly seedy Hotel Fairfax on the fringe of Georgetown as my first base until I found a reasonably priced two-room apartment around the corner on 21st Street. The idea of renting office space did not even occur to the editors and I did not raise the matter, knowing they would think me dangerously extravagant. Instead, in a corner in my bedroom I put a telephone, a typewriter, and a cardboard box to house my newspaper clipping file. The era of the telemachine had not yet arrived, transmission was by ITT cable, and stories had to be written in "cablese," a special kind of shorthand that helped to reduce the cost of the wordage.

Building up one's special relationships, or as they are called in Washington, "contacts," with government officials, politicians, and secretaries of state, defense, and others, and finding out who are the best informed, the most willing to talk, and the most reliable is a gradual, painstaking process. Intimate knowledge about where power resides and how decisions are made is a special science, a high-priced commodity that baffles not only foreigners but Americans too.

What made my start in Washington easier was the relationships I had established with many important American officials and American correspondents while covering various international conferences and the United Nations. The US usually fielded the same experts at these conferences and so I got to know them well and they got to know my reporting and gradually I thus built up a reservoir of sources. It also helped that the press is more lionized in Washington than in any other capital. And so did my being a bachelor, because the "spare man" was a vital commodity on the dinner party circuit. One invitation led to another, so widening my circle of acquaintances, some of which led to friendships.

Building up special relationships is indeed one of the most crucial ingredients of the métier of a foreign correspondent. They are the key to the gathering of information, to learning to understand a country and its people, to the gradual absorption of the essence of a nation. Knowledge of history, reading the great novels of American life, crisscrossing by train or car the vast continent of the United States—all these help. To be able to establish special relationships is somehow the essence of living whether professionally or privately. Access to the men at the top, whether presidents or secretaries of state, defense, or the treasury, matters when it comes to predicting the likely outcome of crucial decisions or when editors request a character sketch; for to be able to analyze the man it is necessary to take into consideration not only his record, but also one's own sense of him. And that needs "eyeball to eyeball" encounters, impressions of the man's behavior at private occasions outside his office. Editors, too, like to know that their correspondent has access to the top so that they themselves can expect to meet anybody they want on a visit. Frank Giles, for instance, the longtime foreign editor of *The Sunday Times* and later editor, used to send me, six weeks in advance of his visit, long lists of the people, from the president down, he wanted to meet. What matters no less in the daily life of a foreign correspondent are the people at the switches, the people at the middle level. They are the most knowledgeable, they are the ones who prepare the position papers or the documents on the basis of which decisions are carried out. Among them are also the private or appointment secretaries, who have their own kind of power in the Washington game of access. It is they who have the power to arrange or delay an appointment. Special relations with one's American colleagues are also very important. They can be very helpful. They are the best informed, they often attend briefings foreign correspondents are excluded from, but, above all, they are very good company—perhaps the best and most entertaining in Washington. Special relations lead to friendships that make life worth living, that lead to the sharing of memories of wonderful times spent together, to consolation in times of stress, to satisfactions and affections that can linger on for a lifetime, even— as in my own case—to a still deeper alliance—marriage.

Washington in the late forties was a truly provincial, sleepy town with no fashionable dining places, no luxury hotels, no gaudy nightclubs or bars. There was not a trace of Bohemianism. Evenings, especially in Georgetown, were spent in the little back gardens or in the winter in front of old-fashioned fireplaces discussing the endless complexities of American politics or the latest moves on the international scene with an earnestness and intensity that was unique to Washington society. In those early days Georgetown was free of the Weltschmerz of London's Chelsea or of the Paris Left Bank. Georgetowners were supposedly divided sociologically into three categories: the "cave dwellers," the old local aristocracy; the "governmental aristocracy," which included those in the cabinet, members of Congress, Supreme Court justices, top officials of the Central Intelligence Agency, and diplomats; and, thirdly, what was referred to as "les gens du monde," the nouveaux riches, their fellow travelers, and a sprinkling of newspapermen who could live in style, such as Joseph Alsop and Drew Pearson.

A cave dweller, I was told by a tall, overpowering, chain-smoking lady in her early sixties who claimed that her seventh great-grandfather had had two land grants in Georgetown, was an old fogy who would not poke his head out of his cave for fear of getting robbed in unruly, crime-infested eighteenth-century Washington. Later, though, they became the gentry of what they considered the heart of the city, they gave it firm roots in the past. Among them were the Blairs, for instance, who presented to the government their charming house on Pennsylvania Avenue, which since then has become the official presidential guest house. Now there are few of the tribe left, and whatever influence they retained was lost as they were pushed into the background by the Democrats who flocked into Washington in Franklin D. Roosevelt's days and who gave it its reputation as a power center of the Eastern Establishment.

This term "Eastern Establishment" is a journalistic catchword that is hard to define. It irritates most of those who are considered part of it, just as it delights those seeking to deprecate, ridicule, or allocate blame. I saw its members, though, as a group of broadly like-minded men and women who believed in certain basic values, who had a shared outlook on their own country and the world, who enjoyed a fairly high level of education, and who believed in good government and public service undertaken either because they had private means or because they were incorrigibly public-spirited.

The Eastern Establishment's concepts of the Marshall Plan and the Western alliance, and their outlook on international commerce, appealed to me. I admired their sense of initiative, their courageous willingness to break with the past if need be, and their conceptual view of the world. This made it easy for me in my early days to write with wholehearted sympathy about the policies of the Truman administration. I went perhaps further in my enthusiasm than many Americans, who are brought up to distrust government while we Europeans are taught to support it. Americans favor diversity and individualism, Europeans order and discipline. My European upbringing certainly influenced my reporting, which did not mean necessarily that I was wholly uncritical. But I wanted President Truman and his administration to succeed.

When I came to feel secure enough in my job to invest in a house, Georgetown real estate prices remained far beyond my means, so I bought a small house in Cleveland Park, a good second best to Georgetown. The few true-blue members of the Eastern Establishment who lived there did so because they either had too many children for Georgetown's smallish houses or also could not afford Georgetown real estate prices. William Bundy, older brother to McGeorge Bundy, lived there and so did Stewart Alsop, who was my neighbor and wrote an influential column together with his brother Joe, who lived in greater splendor in Georgetown. (When the younger Bundy came to serve in the Kennedy White House, he too chose Georgetown.)

One of my new neighbors was James Rowe, a lawyer who became one of Lyndon Johnson's closest friends. Rowe enjoyed nothing more than twisting the tail of Establishmentarians, many of whom were his friends. He came from Montana, and believed that power resides with the Middle West and the West and that leadership should be in the hands of the elected, not the self-appointed. Being a man who could keep his tongue in his cheek, he used to say he considered the law too precious to be pursued by Washington lawyers, whose main purpose was to find ways around it. His cynicism hid a deep romance with politics. He taught me more about American politics, which he loved the way a gardener loves tending his roses, than perhaps any other American. As a young lawyer he worked in the Department of Justice under Roosevelt and got his first kudos by advising the president to ignore an accurate and dangerous breach of security when the Chicago *Tribune,* shortly after Pearl Harbor, claimed that the United States had broken the Japanese secret code. The president followed his advice, despite clamors from others to prosecute the *Trib.* To everybody's surprise, the Japanese overlooked the report and did not change their code.

Rowe often talked to me with nostalgia about the days of the Roosevelt and Truman administrations, when it was still possible to solve governmental problems by talking to two or three people, preferably on their way to or from the office: "But later, as the bureaucracies ballooned," he lamented in his rasping voice, "one had to twist the arms of twenty or more and by the time one got to the last two, the first two had died." To get something done in Washington, he meant to say, became an arduous, complex business, for as the bureaucracies grew so grew the number of lobbyists to deal with them.

Social life in Washington is so deeply intertwined with political life that it is hard to keep the two apart—in fact, nobody tries, for one serves the other. It accounted for the role of the political salons when Washington was still a more homogeneous place and everybody knew everybody who mattered. They were journalistic gold mines, because Americans are freer than most people in expressing their views and because they live for their expectations: they talk either about the present or the future.

In Britain country-house weekend parties used to be where the influential decided how to play their political cards. In Washington it happened over dinner at the political salons. For a visiting VIP an evening at one of the salons was like political snorkeling. It gave him a quick view of what was going on under the surface. For the residents it was more an exercise in scuba diving, watching the important political fish making waves.

The leading political salons were those of columnists Walter Lippmann and Joseph Alsop. Intellectually and politically perhaps the most interesting parties were the Lippmanns'. As the solon among columnists, his standing and influence, built up over a lifetime, were unique. His reputation worldwide as a foreign policy oracle and his impact on editorial writers in the United States were second to none. Foreign heads of government treated him like a statesman, and American presidents made great efforts to solicit his support. Whenever Walter traveled to Europe, he stopped off in Paris to see General de Gaulle, who admired him for his prescience because he was one of the very few who defended de Gaulle when President Roosevelt and Secretary of State Hull refused to support him. Once, though, he came back without having requested to see the general, because, he said, "we're so much in disagreement these days that I did not think it would have been wise for me to see him." De Gaulle, on hearing that Lippmann had been to Paris, sent a message to the French ambassador in Washington instructing him to inquire of Lippmann why he had failed to get in touch with him. Over the years Lippmann became to me more than a mentor and teacher; he was a dearly loved friend.

At the Lippmann evenings you were judged not by what you knew about this one-man town, but whether you could also discuss literature—French or Russian, if you wanted to be in Helen's good books—or what was going on in Whitehall or at the Elysée in Paris, to get Walter's attention. Discretion too was an essential quality. Everybody present always assumed that the walls had no ears, and no one ever would tell a society reporter that he had been at the Lippmanns' for dinner and who else was there. Consequently conversation was remarkably free and candid and at times sounded like a cabinet meeting.

On one such night in 1956, just before the Suez crisis, when Nasser was already causing a great deal of annoyance, Cy Sulzberger, the *New York Times* chief foreign correspondent, asked Allen Dulles, then director of the Central Intelligence Agency, whether he had given any thought to the idea of doing away with Nasser. It seemed to him an obvious solution to an increasingly urgent problem, he said, a task ripe for CIA consideration. Riveted, we all looked at Dulles as he began puffing at his pipe and gazing into the gray-blue smoke that screened his thoughts. Seconds passed as he continued to puff and not even Walter came to his aid by changing the subject. "Of course, we have considered the idea," Dulles finally replied, and a faint, slightly amused smile scurried over his face, "but the trouble is that we have no fanatics on our side and to undertake such an operation, you have to find a man willing to take his life instantly if caught."

The Lippmanns and the Alsops were hardly on speaking terms. Walter believed that diplomacy could resolve most conflicts, or at best keep them from developing into wars. He shuddered at the thought of the use of force as an arm of diplomacy. Joe Alsop, on the contrary, was a strong believer in at least threatening the use of force; he had little faith in diplomacy as such.

Dinners at the Lippmanns' were staid compared to the fireworks that often cascaded across the dinner table at Joe and Susan Mary Alsop's. Lippmann's nature was to pour oil on troubled waters, Joe Alsop enjoyed churning them up. Lippmann was always correct and sought to avoid personal unpleasantness. Joe was provocative, didactic, assertive, occasionally even rude to his guests, which did not prevent him from inviting them again or them from accepting his next invitation. Joe's tantrums were always excused as part of his eccentricity, and although Americans have little tolerance for eccentrics, in his case, being an influential columnist, brilliant in his own ways, he was easily forgiven. Once, for instance, he greeted Senator Stuart Symington, who was one of his favorites, but who, as secretary of air, had come close to advocating preventive war, by saying: "You're the best-dressed senator and you have many fine suits, but all are turncoats."

Joe considered Lippmann an appeaser, Walter saw Joe as a warmonger. Joe was blunt, emotional, cantankerous, magisterial; Lippmann calm, detached, analytical. Joe and Susan Mary surrounded themselves in their house with an exquisitely elegant French ambience; the Lippmanns preferred a more unobtrusive, more conventional style. Joe and his brother Stewart looked for exclusive information from the horse's mouth; Lippmann relied on his own personal interpretation—he considered himself an authority in his own right. These were three great journalists who raised the profession to heights it is unlikely to attain again.

Another serious salon that made culture, not politics, its attraction was the occasional literary Sunday evening in the modest home of Edith Hamilton, the great teacher and historian of Greek antiquities. Her evenings helped me to keep in touch with the literary scene. Mrs. Hamilton, a ramrod of a lady with a commanding voice and a gadget of Walkman-size hanging down her neck to help her overcome her deafness, was close to ninety when I first met her. She was slightly intimidating in her schoolmarm manner and her directness. Perhaps the most memorable evening I remember at her house on Massachusetts Avenue was when Robert Frost, the poet, had come to visit her. The others present were Huntington Cairns, the erudite treasurer of the National Gallery, a philosopher in his own right, and Robert Richman, who was a poet and a kind of literary impresario organizing lectures and readings by famous authors for a small group of literature-conscious Washingtonians.

It did not take long for Mrs. Hamilton, as the inveterate education-minded teacher, to ask Mr. Frost, with the voice of an inquisitor, whether he had studied Greek or Latin. A long, embarrassed silence followed, after which Mr. Frost meekly replied that he had studied Latin. Mrs. Hamilton, sensing his embarrassment, persisted: "Why, Mr. Frost, why not Greek?" Frost, not sure whether to laugh or to blush, replied: "Because I thought it would be easier." Perhaps to reconcile her, he then added that he was never happy at the way he was taught Latin, that he was never allowed to translate, always asked to "construct." For this and other reasons, he said, his great wish was to say at a commencement address: "I have none of this knowledge of yours, the only thing I can say is that I have the right feelings about it."

The two were in complete agreement that modern poetry without rhyme and rhythm was not poetry, and hence very difficult to learn by heart. Even at ninety Mrs. Hamilton still could recite much of the poetry she had learned many years before. Frost, delighted to find himself in agreement with her, complained that modern poetry was "turgid, rotten, and hollow." He also got quite hot under the collar denouncing Freud as "visceral" because he found the psychiatrist's way of talking about oneself vulgar. The only delicate way to talk about oneself, he proclaimed, was through poetry. My question as to how people who can't write poetry should talk about themselves was hardly given a hearing.

As the evening wore on the discussion had other turbulent moments—for instance, when Frost said that he preferred the *Odyssey* to the *Iliad*—but they were in harmony about the English language not lending itself to poetry as well as Latin or Greek. Cairns, who apart from having written about philosophy and art history—and a popularizer at both—also had had the dubious honor of acting as censor of pornographic literature for the U.S. Treasury Department, when asked what his duties were, said: "To make sure the customs officers know the difference between a Botticelli painting and a French postcard."

To the question about the secret of her longevity Mrs. H. replied with one simple word, and she pronounced it with delight: "Enjoyment." There was nothing more enjoyable, apart from Greek history, than being able to teach the young. And both were her life's main occupations. Frost agreed with her definition and raised his glass of straight Scotch to longevity—I believe he was eighty-three at the time. Later, when the two parted, his last words at the door were: "On to a hundred." It was one of those evenings when the usual Washington nourishment, politics, was banished and when two forceful personalities made one realize that there were higher and more enduring things in life than the passing political scene.

Some of the most congenial and most enjoyable parties I remember were those given by the William Bundys, who became close friends. Both had in them the gift of friendship, Bill in his outwardly unemotional solidity and Mary in her emotional, generous, and sensitive ways. She had survived a pneumothorax operation after a dangerous bout with pneumonia—she therefore knew what it meant to have an encounter with fate. It was then that her father, Dean Acheson, already secretary of state, wrote to her daily to reinforce her in meeting this test. It was also at their house that I met him for the first time.

5

How Dean Acheson Cast the Tables of American Foreign Policy

DEAN ACHESON was the most impressive, most fascinating, most powerful personality in the Truman administration. President Truman has been given the credit for the towering achievement in foreign affairs—and deservedly so, since it was he who had to make the ultimate decisions and take the final responsibility. But it was Acheson who, in my view, created the intellectual concepts that informed those decisions, who had an unwavering sense of direction and the willpower to translate them into practice. He was the prime mover and chief negotiator first as undersecretary and later as secretary of state. He gave the Western alliance its postwar shape. He gave backbone and reality to the North Atlantic pact.

Truman's choosing him was all the more creditable because he looked and behaved more like some cavalier out of a portrait by Frans Hals than an American. Imbued with all the virtues and principles of the New England upper class, he came as close to being an aristocrat as any American I have known. He was always impeccably dressed, almost too much so, the only irregularity being the way his carefully matched tie would bulge from his vest. His steel blue eyes could smile benevolently or sardonically, but not laugh. He held himself stiffly erect, warning of his mental stubbornness and willpower. And behind his jaunty-looking mustache, always perfectly trimmed, was a stiff upper lip any Englishman could have envied. He was ultimately to need that stiff upper lip when his high standards and combativeness turned him finally into a tragic figure.

I was very fortunate that I got to know not only the official but also the private Acheson. He was not an easy man to get to know or to converse with. Both his height and his intellect, which at times he enjoyed flaunting aggressively, made him intimidating, if not overpowering. Any conversation with him was a challenge because he demanded from others the same intellectual rigor he demanded of himself. Thus most of the time others (including myself) felt uncomfortably on the defensive. It was at press conferences, unfortunately, that he made it most obvious that he did not tolerate fools gladly. If a reporter, for instance, asked a fuzzy question, Acheson could become very condescending. He would first reply by saying that he had not quite understood the question and would (helpfully, of course) rephrase it. After he had done this, he would ask whether he had correctly expressed what the reporter had meant to ask. Having cleared the air, with the reporter meekly agreeing that he had interpreted him properly, Acheson would then proceed: "Now that we have the question right, I can answer it." Obviously that did not go down too well with the press. It was at a press conference that he made the biggest political mistake of his life, but I will come back to that later.

The first time I met him privately was when Bill and Mary Bundy took me to a traditional event in the Acheson household—a Christmas caroling party. It was a gathering of family and close friends. After a glass or two of eggnog and seasonal chat—any discussion of foreign affairs was frowned upon —Mrs. Acheson would sit down at the piano to signal that the singing was to begin. Acheson threw himself to lead the chorus with gusto. He seemed completely absorbed in his singing. Throughout the evening he remained the gracious, smiling, teasing host.

I was given the occasional opportunity to see him in his office on business and I was included in the very short list of the official "leaker," as we called him—Bromley Smith, a rather shy, cautious foreign service official, whose unusual task was to give a few correspondents representing influential newspapers or magazines an unattributable briefing about sensitive information. Acheson's orders to Smith, sardonic to the hilt, were: "Read everything, including what I don't read. And if a leak occurs I will say that I am outraged how things leak here. But you will go on seeing those guys." John Foster Dulles, when he became secretary of state, continued to employ secret leakers, except that he chose men of means, such as Bill Scranton (later governor of Pennsylvania and a candidate for the presidency), who could afford to be fired instantly if they embarrassed the secretary of state and he wanted to prove how conscientious he was about preventing leaks. The confidential relationship between the press and government that existed then grew out of the war, when the press was, so to say, part of the exercise, and nobody complained that the press was being "used." We were more interested in those days in actually knowing the background to problems than in just amassing factual information, and we tended to stay off discussions of personalities or what happened inside delegations, say, on the National Security Council. There was no collusion between government and press, only a mutual feeling that it was easier for both sides if there existed an understanding between them. Nowadays, especially since the many deceptions perpetrated by government on the press during the Vietnam war and the Watergate affair, the relationship has changed drastically. The news media have come to believe that it makes for better government and freer information if the two preserve the deepest suspicion of each other. Neither trusts the other anymore.

By early 1950 Dean Acheson had already burned the stamp of his own personality and his own thinking on American foreign policy and had won President Truman's total trust. If he was a statesman, he was also a shrewd constitutional lawyer, for unlike Jimmy Byrnes, he always deferred to the president. Acheson kept him scrupulously informed, gave him the feeling that it was he who was in the driver's seat and that the State Department was a tool on which he could rely. Acheson as a result was given the same free hand as his opposite number in the British government, Ernest Bevin. Prime Minister Attlee allowed Bevin to run British foreign policy as he thought best: Attlee explained it to his able biographer, Kenneth Harris, by saying, "You don't keep a good dog and bark yourself—and Ernie was a very good dog."

Acheson, a pedigree hound, admired strong-minded men. He admired Truman for this quality and he cherished it in Bevin, who sustained him in some of the most difficult decisions. He saw in Bevin a working-class John Bull who knew what was in Britain's best interest not by intellect but by instinct and experience as a trade-union leader. "He could lead and learn at the same time," Acheson said of him. Bevin's attention span was short, but while it lasted it was worth engaging it. Sir Oliver Franks, the British ambassador to the United States at the time, once confided that if he wanted to make sure that Ernie would read his telegrams, he kept them to two paragraphs. (John Kenneth Galbraith, then U.S. ambassador to India, used to say in a lighter vein that whenever he wanted President Kennedy to read his telegrams, he included two or three four-letter words.) Franks saw Acheson's relationship with Truman as one between the office of the secretary of state and the office of the presidency. Not being a yes-man and yet being trustworthy is the best recipe, in my view, for being seen as a reliable friend by the Americans. Bevin was not by any means a yes-man, but Acheson felt that he could rely on him in the clinches. This helped Bevin to secure American support for Europe's recovery through the Marshall Plan and for its security through NATO.

In spite of their almost fathomless contrast in class, style, and intellect, Acheson and Truman added up to a remarkably congenial pair. Truman never went to college, but acquired an extraordinary fund of knowledge by reading the *Encyclopaedia Britannica* from cover to cover while his schoolmates were indulging in sports he could not because of his poor eyesight. He tried to make a living as a farm hand and bank clerk, set himself up as a haberdasher but went broke, and was finally catapulted into politics and the Senate by a man called Pendergast, whose Democratic Party machine was known to play favorites in exchange for loyalty to his political interests. Truman's politics and his thinking were relatively simple and progressive, in Roosevelt's New Deal mode. He was proud of coming from the heartland, secure in himself despite his many failures, and a devoted family man. In foreign policy, while Truman was the conductor of the orchestra, Acheson was both the first violinist and the composer of the music.

Truman did not always understand all the tonal variations in Acheson's scores. This weakness on Truman's part at times surfaced at his press conferences. Acheson, relaxed after a family party at Mary Bundy's house, once sat watching a toy dog I had given his grandson, Michael, for his birthday. This animal shook itself and sort of squirmed when wound up. Acheson said it reminded him of the way he sometimes reacted to Truman's off-the-cuff shots at his press conferences. These slipups or malapropisms offered a temptation to White House correspondents to throw political banana peels for the president to step on, and so come out with unguarded remarks that would make startling headlines. Once he claimed, for instance, to have delivered an ultimatum to Stalin in 1946 to get Soviet troops out of Iran by a certain date, a contention that a White House spokesman had to deny half an hour later. Acheson enjoyed regaling his friends with stories about Truman's bloopers and how often he blurted out information he had been told to keep to himself. When one guest suggested that what he found so attractive about Truman was his spontaneity, Acheson, with a bittersweet smile, pointed at his gray hair and said: "That's Truman's spontaneity for me."

An answer that echoed around the world and brought Prime Minister Attlee flying posthaste to Washington occurred in 1950 when Truman allowed himself to be goaded by New York *Daily News* reporter Jack Doherty into saying that the use of the atom bomb in Korea was under "active consideration." This was shortly after the Chinese had intervened and forced the UN army to retreat in 1950. Truman had been relatively unknown even to Americans when he succeeded to the presidency, and to Europeans he was a total unknown. "Harry who?" persisted until he decided to drop the atomic bomb on Japan. This brought him to life for British public opinion and made it credible that he could decide to drop another lot on Korea. What heightened the scare was that he added that General MacArthur, who had a reputation for insubordination and hawkishness, "will have charge of the use of weapons."

Attlee, under pressure from his own Parliament, and brushing aside all attempts by Washington to keep him away, arrived on December 4, just as the crisis in Korea began to worsen. There was open talk about evacuating the United Nations troops (mostly American) and, indeed, secret discussions among American policymakers about the possibility of protecting the evacua-

tion with a few A-bombs. Paul Nitze, Kennan's successor as chairman of the
State Department Policy Planning Staff and a highly competent man, had
asked General Herbert B. Loper for an assessment of the wisdom of their use
on Chinese troops in North Korea. Nitze's final report, however, advised
against, because it could lead to Soviet intervention in the war and damage
American interests in Asia. John Allison, the director of the office of Northeast
Asian affairs, denounced this verdict as a "policy of appeasement." This acrimonious infighting behind the scenes added to the uncertainties.

After a day-long meeting with the president and his aides, Prime Minister
Attlee met with the British correspondents at the British Embassy, as was the
habit on prime ministerial visits. He did not strike me as a forceful man,
capable of impressing his deep concerns convincingly on the Americans. What
he did not tell us was that in his face-to-face talk with Truman, his attempt
to obtain a British veto on the use of the A-bomb had failed, as had his efforts
to convince the Americans to take the long view and seek a negotiated solution.
To do so, it was objected, would be to reward aggression. The visit was one
of the least effective encounters between the Americans and a British premier.
Much later Acheson told me that Truman actually conceded the veto to Attlee,
but his secretary of state persuaded him to rescind it on the obvious ground
that as president of the United States he could not allow a foreign power to
impose limits on his powers for action. All Attlee took home were private
assurances that Truman's A-bomb blast was based on an "unfortunate choice
of words" and that he was not in fact contemplating use of the atomic bomb
in Korea.

There was a cosy, chintzy simplicity and a rural calm about Acheson's little
farmhouse in Sandy Springs, Maryland, which made everybody, but especially
the secretary of state, at ease with the world. There was a flower and vegetable
garden where he pottered with his wife Alice, and a remarkably well-equipped
carpentry shop where he built stylish furniture. To see Dean standing en-
grossed over a lathe, using his hands with great skill rather than his mind, was
almost mind-boggling. This pastime was not inspired by any kind of inverted
snobbery; it was genuine diversion from the burdens of everyday life. "The
great thing about this hobby," he said with infinite satisfaction, "is that when
I have finished a table or a chair and I put it down, it either stands or falls.
It's not like foreign policy, you don't have to wait for twenty years to see
whether it works." The enthusiasm, the persistence with which he pursued this
hobby, and the satisfaction it gave him offered a new perspective on the hidden
aspects of his personality.

Dean did not use the tennis court on the farm, but he liked a swim in the
pool before lunch and before his martini. The making and drinking of martinis
was akin to a religious ceremony with him. It took him five minutes to make
one exactly the way he wanted it and it got him into his best storytelling mood.
Bruce MacLaury, the president of the Brookings Institution, the oldest and

highly respected Washington think tank, told me that when Acheson once came to give a lecture at lunchtime, the first thing he asked for on arrival was a martini. There was great embarrassment because of a rule that no liquor be served. "No martini, no lecture," Dean said tartly, and within minutes the rule was broken.

I enjoyed listening to Acheson's anecdotes because he was such an amusing storyteller. On one occasion at lunch on the farm Dean entertained us with the story of a dinner he had given for President Dutra of Brazil. He was seated on one side of the president, Mrs. Acheson on the other. Both he and Mrs. Acheson tried their best to entertain the president in conversation, but he said not one word either on his own initiative or in reply. Finally, Mr. Acheson, turning his attention elsewhere, spotted an attractive blonde at another table. He leaned over Dutra's shoulder to his wife and asked whether she knew who the blonde was. That, for the first time, loosened Dutra's tongue, and he said, "Do you always ask your wife for such information?"

Despite his savoir faire, Acheson confessed with a certain gleeful delight that he felt a little unsure of how to deal with British royalty. In 1952, he recalled, he had an audience with Queen Elizabeth. Anthony Eden, the foreign minister, was present. Remembering how much King George VI had praised Winston Churchill for keeping him fully informed about everything, he decided to follow his example. Therefore when the Queen started off by saying that she hoped everything had gone well between him and Eden, he, a little mischievously, shook his head as if to indicate that perhaps not everything had gone as well as it might have done. Both the Queen and Prince Philip suddenly got really interested and both began asking questions, while Eden fingered his tie nervously. Twice her private secretary opened the door slightly, but the Queen asked that whoever was next for audience be asked to wait. When she went so far as to ask Acheson about Eden's views, he said he was sure Eden would best explain those to her directly. But the Queen persisted, saying that she could talk to Eden at any time. And so, with Acheson impressed by the Queen's interest and knowledge of foreign affairs, the audience lasted well beyond the appointed time. Later, Acheson recalled, Eden seemed annoyed because he had told the Queen too much.

Acheson took a puckish delight in telling the story, and enjoyed having made a hit with British royalty at the expense of Eden, whom he considered a man of veneer rather than substance. It has often been written that the two had too much in common, a certain haughtiness, a sartorial elegance, each believing that he knew more about foreign affairs than the other. But according to Lucius "Luke" Battle, Dean Acheson's devoted private secretary, Acheson did not think highly of Eden's understanding of the function of military power in diplomacy. He considered Eden a weakling. Acheson believed that it was power that mattered in diplomacy; Eden saw it more as an exercise in negotiating skills. The first time Dean met Anthony was in the home of a British diplomat in Washington. Eden, then out of office, was leaning back in an easy chair, virtually on his shoulder blades, languidly drooping his arms and wrists, making insipid conversation. Dean's first impression therefore was of a limp character, an impression that was only reinforced by Eden's performance in office. Curiously, much later in life, when both had come to feel that the world did not appreciate them, they became friends; they even visited South Africa together with their wives.

To understand Acheson it is important to know about his relationship with Felix Frankfurter, with whom he walked to his office every morning. Frankfurter held strong views about everything and everybody, and since Acheson had a profound respect for him, Frankfurter had a major influence on his thinking. He too enjoyed listening to Dean's stories. One Saturday evening at the Achesons' Georgetown house, all the guests had left except the justice of the Supreme Court, his wife, Marion, and myself. Turning to Frankfurter— I sat between the two on a settee—Acheson began in an ostentatiously indiscreet way to talk about a telephone call he had had that morning from Sir Oliver Franks, who, he explained, had asked him, at Anthony Eden's behest, to postpone the new instructions to Korea. He embroidered his account with some remarks about Eden and why he had become fed up with these continuing delays by the British and then, quoting himself, said: "and I told Oliver to tell Eden to stop stalling, that I wanted to go ahead," etc., etc. He clearly enjoyed—and so did Frankfurter—tantalizing me with information that would have made a nice exclusive story for tomorrow's *Sunday Times,* but which, he knew, I could not use since it was past my London deadline.

Frankfurter was titillated by Acheson's out-of-school tales for, as someone once said, "he was a journalist by nature and a jurist by perversity." He was indeed one of the best-informed men in Washington not only because of his friendship with Acheson but because he had been for so long an éminence grise of Washington—first with President Roosevelt, then Secretary of Defense Henry Stimson, and now President Truman and a number of prominent members of Congress. He played a part, Mrs. Acheson told me later, in Truman's selection of Acheson over Averell Harriman or Robert Lovett as secretary of state.

Felix Frankfurter was born in Vienna, Austria, and came to the United States at the age of twelve, knowing no English. He rose to the highest judicial authority in the country via the Harvard Law School, and some of the greatest justices—such as Holmes, Cardozo, and Brandeis—became his close friends. Dean Acheson, who had been his student at Harvard, became his best friend —and after the justice's death, Acheson financially supported his widow, whose Supreme Court pension amounted to a pittance of $5,000 a year.

About once a month I got an invitation from the justice to lunch at his book-lined chambers. After a glass of sherry the meal was served on a folding table which one of the clerks carried in. Its quality did not matter, for the nourishment was intellectual. He was a man full of passions: for his wife, for

Franklin D. Roosevelt, for the law, for Oxford University where he taught, for British culture (he was the most Anglophile American I ever met), for political gossip. He did not lose his gift for enjoying what he considered life's excitements even after he suffered a stroke. From time to time I got handwritten notes—they were more than scribbles—either praising something I had written or questioning it. He enjoyed sending out those missives; it was one of his many ways of keeping in touch with his friends and with the world. Occasionally, I teased him about his attaching too much importance to the press and of exaggerating its power and influence. "The press," he once replied, "should stop the dishonesty of disparaging its omnipotence."

He never ceased to be a great teacher, and he taught me a good deal about the American constitutional processes and American institutions. His definition of the role of the Supreme Court in relation to the US Constitution impressed me so much that I put it down in my diary: "Of all forms of a national community, a federal system is the most complicated. It demands the greatest flexibility and imagination to harmonize national and local interests. The Constitution of the U.S. is thus not a historic parchment in a glass case. It is a continuous process of delicate governmental adjustments. And its judicial application is not a mechanical exercise, but a profound task of statecraft, exercised by judges set apart from the turbulence of politics." No one who has to write about the tortuous processes of American government could fail to be helped to understand them by such clear exposition.

One of Frankfurter's favorite games of one-upmanship was to demonstrate the intense interest with which he followed British affairs. He would ask me, for instance, at those lunches whether I had read the prime minister's remark in Parliament in the latest *Hansard* (the British equivalent to the *Congressional Record*) or a letter in the *Times* (of London, of course) by so-and-so, and too often I had to admit my ignorance. After he confided to me that whenever he went to a dinner party he prepared himself in advance for a subject he would bring up for discussion, I began to prepare myself in a similar way for our causeries over lunch, for his curiosity about British affairs, whether in Whitehall or Fleet Street or the Oxford common rooms, was insatiable.

He was either a devoted friend forever or a passionate hater. He knew how to blend humor and venom. Walter Lippmann, for instance, and Arthur Krock, the *New York Times* columnist, were high on his enemy list and when, occasionally, I mentioned a Lippmann column that I admired, his prince-nez would begin to tremble, I would be cut off in mid-sentence, and no more was to be said on the matter. There was one subject, according to Mrs. Acheson, that was absolutely taboo even between him and Dean, and that was Zionism. Frankfurter was an ardent believer, Acheson was not. For a while—before 1948—Frankfurter tried to convert Acheson but failed, and from then on it became an unmentionable subject. Sometimes it took Acheson, according to Luke Battle, hours after he had reached the office to digest his morning conversations with Felix, and sometimes they went on gossiping again late in the evening over the phone. Frankfurter's vitality, his zest for battle, his biting repartee, and his flights into scholarship were relief to Acheson from the daily chores.

The two shared a hate for cheap or slovenly journalism. Any editorial or any indiscretion that hurt one of his friends sent Frankfurter into a tirade of indignation. As an example of how badly ethics had deteriorated in the newspaper business, and what exemplary discretion existed during World War II, Frankfurter recalled a story about a dinner party for Winston Churchill at the British Embassy, given by Lord Halifax, the ambassador, shortly before the American elections in 1944. There were seven Britons and seven Americans present, including Eugene Meyer, father of Katherine Graham and then publisher of the Washington *Post,* and a Republican senator. Churchill, for everybody to hear, said that he counted on Roosevelt's being reelected. When someone expressed doubts about FDR's victory, Churchill was obviously taken aback, jumped to his feet, and made an impassioned little speech, saying: "If that happened I would have to get up in the House of Commons and tell it that this is a calamity of the gravest sort." If that peroration had leaked out, it could have swung the elections against Roosevelt—but discretion prevailed.

An example of Frankfurter's irrepressible cockiness, in which he delighted, was an encounter with General Eisenhower at a dinner party at the Danish Embassy. When he found himself sitting next to the general, who had just then accepted the presidency of Columbia University, he said to Ike that he felt the urge to tell him to his face what he had been saying behind his back: "It speaks for you to have accepted the presidency of Columbia University in spite of the many more lucrative positions you have been offered, and it speaks against the trustees of the university to have offered it to you." To his surprise, Ike heartily agreed and thus took the sting out of Frankfurter's remark. Ike was not a man to argue with the justice.

Frankfurter's penchant for taking on the opposition or defending controversial causes often got him into hot water. "Few questions bother me from time to time more than what it is that makes people cowardly . . ." He detested those who refused to take moral risks, especially those who were financially and socially independent, because he believed that was how Hitler and Mussolini and Huey Long and Senator Joseph McCarthy were allowed to grow into monsters. He therefore admired the reply Acheson gave at his fateful press conference on January 25, 1950, when asked about his attitude to Alger Hiss and, by implication, he claimed some credit for it. In fact, Luke Battle has reason to believe that Frankfurter egged Acheson on to make it, though, not doubt, Acheson had also concluded that his conscience demanded that he declare his position on Hiss.

"Mr. Secretary, have you any comment on the Alger Hiss case?" was the innocent sounding yet fatal question. Hiss that day had been convicted of perjury and sentenced to five years in prison. I held my breath. His head high, either to accept with pride the applause from the gallery for his courage or to offer his head on the platter to the political executioners, Acheson made three points: first, that he would not discuss the law while the case was before the court; second, that regardless of the ultimate verdict, he did not intend "to turn his back on Alger Hiss"; third, that the gospel of St. Matthew defined his own standards and principles. It was a high-minded statement given in political surroundings that were anything but high-minded. As I noted in my diary: "High-mindedness is not a plus in American politics." I was both admiring and fearful on his behalf as I left the press conference. All of us there felt that he was taking a huge gamble, putting personal principle before the responsibilities of a secretary of state.

There had been no need to go as far as saying that "he would not turn his back on Alger Hiss." It was self-assurance gone overboard and poor political judgment, for it gave his enemies ammunition unnecessarily. It also showed that even a trained lawyer, who has carefully considered his reply in advance, can be carried away by a sudden burst of emotion. The New York *Herald Tribune* alone commented favorably, saying editorially that the statement was "as courageous as it was Christian." Politically, it proved a massive mistake. From then on he was like a man with a knife in his back that was no threat to his life but kept hurting, a pain he bore heroically. He had discussed his statement in advance with Luke Battle, Paul Nitze, and another aide, Carl Hummelsine, and all three were opposed to his making it. But he felt he could not keep silent, as did John Foster Dulles, who, when he sponsored Hiss for the chairmanship of the Carnegie Endowment for International Peace, had committed himself far more to vouching for Hiss's integrity than Acheson, yet did not do so once the Hiss case went to court. (Acheson, unlike Dulles, had only a purely professional relationship with him. It was his brother, Donald Hiss, who was a personal friend of the Acheson family.) But the country had been made fearful of Communist infiltration in the wake of the discovery of Communist spy rings in the United States and Canada and had become so hysterical that President Truman went so far as to order an FBI loyalty probe of all federal employees which lasted from 1947 to 1951.

"My goodness, what a controversial figure I had become," Acheson wrote to his daughter Mary, whose letters from her sickbed at that time gave him enormous psychological support. It seemed the *cri de coeur* of a wounded man. His refusal "to turn his back on Alger Hiss" came to haunt him for the rest of his public career, for the Hiss case did not turn out to be another Dreyfus case, as he had expected. Only very rarely did he show how it continued to upset him emotionally—as, for instance, after a meeting with his undersecretary of state James Webb, whose insensitivity came increasingly to irritate him. It reached a climax when, after the Democrats had lost the elections in 1952, Webb came to his office to tell him that Speaker Sam Rayburn had said that he did not believe Acheson was to blame. "What does he think this makes me feel?" Acheson complained bitterly to Luke Battle. Webb had evidently thought that it would comfort Acheson to learn that not *everybody* thought he had lost the elections for the Democratic Party. Not surprisingly, the charges that he was a "traitor to his class," that Senator McCarthy called him the Red Dean, that no Democrat in Congress rose to defend him, deeply upset him. And yet, despite what he called "a somber time," his strength of character, his belief in the tasks he had set himself, and the continued support he received from President Truman enabled him to keep his mind on the making of a foreign policy that stood the test of time. There was a granite foundation to his character which shone through something he once wrote: "Much in life cannot be affected or mitigated, and hence must be borne without complaint because complaint undermines the serenity essential to endurance."

Acheson to us Europeans was an attractive figure not only because, at least superficially, he looked and acted like a European, but because he was a "Europe First-er." It was his profound conviction that the preservation of Europe was the key to the future of Western civilization, that the Soviet Union and communism were a serious threat to it; and, however much he viewed Europe's economic rehabilitation as the essential basis, he had also concluded that this was not enough and that Europe would have to be helped to defend itself against Soviet imperialist tendencies by an American military presence. Soviet aggressiveness and pigheadedness, as demonstrated by the Communist coup in Czechoslovakia, the Berlin blockade, the pretensions to a major role in West Germany, the defection of Tito, and finally the invasion of South Korea, confirmed in him the belief that containment had to be globalized. He laid down the basic guidelines with his speech of February 8, 1950, when he proclaimed the policy of seeking "situations of strength." The public was readily receptive; according to a public opinion poll in July 1949, 80 percent of the respondents had said "yes" to the question whether the United States should stay in Berlin, "even if it means war with Russia." Americans were in no mood to make concessions to the Soviets. They also, clearly, assumed that the cold war was not so much a prelude to a hot one as it was a game of power politics in which the United States would have to play the role of leader of the Western world for a long time.

The British not only shared Acheson's views on Europe and the Communist threat, but they were the only non-Americans with whom he could have a congenial intellectual discourse. He once said to Paul Nitze: "We must talk to people outside the United States to clarify our own mind, and only the British are intellectually close enough to us to fulfill this function." Moreover, Britain in the early postwar years, if no longer actually a big power with worldwide interests, still enjoyed big-power habits of mind and even status. A majority in Britain considered themselves Atlanticists, especially members of the Labour Party. They saw the US as being close to a classless society, while the Conservatives, especially in the fifties, saw it as in competition with British interests. The Labour governments viewed the "special relationship" primarily as an instrument to regain Britain's own stature as a great power.

In Ernest Bevin and Oliver Franks, Britain was lucky to have found two men superbly fitted to meet this aim, for both, in their very own ways, held extraordinary personal appeal for Dean Acheson. Civil services, especially Britain's, like to believe that training and experience matter most, but personal empathy can transcend both. Certainly in Washington it can make an enormous difference if an ambassador can establish a close personal relationship either with the secretary of state or with the president. Lord Inverchapel, Sir Oliver's predecessor, was a good example of the wrong choice. He arrived from Moscow with the reputation of being a brilliant diplomat. But he came to Washington for the wrong reasons, one of which was that he assumed it might persuade his estranged wife to remarry him (which, indeed, she did) and another that he wanted to crown his career there. He came to dislike Washington and told friends that he got along better with Stalin because with him he could exchange dirty jokes and, between laughter, conduct business with him. In answer to the obvious follow-up question, how he was getting along with the State Department, he said: "Not so good. The trouble is that they lack a sense of humor, they don't like dirty stories."

Oliver Franks was the kind of serious intellectual whose austere charm made one wonder whether he would know a dirty story if he heard one. I never put him to the test; I would not have dared. The relationship that he developed with Dean Acheson was remarkable because they were able to have both an official and a very private relationship and the one never interfered with the other. Franks was tall and lanky, a beanstalk of a man, outwardly shy but intellectually secure, securer perhaps than anyone else in public office I have met. To some it was a forbidding intellect; to me it was something to enjoy watching and listening to. One of the delights of a session with him was that he would relax in his chair, sometimes hang one leg over the arm support, and then begin by saying: "If I look into my crystal ball, this is what I see for the next three months . . ." And usually his crystal ball proved a good guide for the future. He had the capacity to home in on the essentials of a problem. On the face of it, it seemed incongruous to have a former professor of moral philosophy from the University of Glasgow engaged in the business of diplomacy, but it was his training in clear thinking, his ability to speak his mind in simple, direct and morally honest ways, and having a vision of the future that was closely tied to existing realities that made him such an outstanding ambassador. For he had vision, even if he was not what we usually think of as a visionary.

All these qualities made a deep impression on Dean Acheson. He saw in Franks not only an equal intellectually—an unusual concession on his part—but a man who could mentally dissociate himself from his own interests, put himself into Acheson's shoes and provide him with detached advice on almost any problem, however remote from Anglo-American affairs.

Acheson once talked to me about his friendship with Franks, how he admired not only his intellect but his nature, and how, unknown to virtually anybody, they met fairly regularly at the end of the day, to mull over any problem that occupied their minds. "I consult Oliver on problems that have nothing to do with Anglo-American relations," he confided, "and if you write this, I'll cut your throat." His steel blue eyes rolled in delight at the thought. No other British ambassador was able to establish this kind of intimate relationship with the American secretary of state.

Franks was a very private man, but he was also an extraordinary public performer. He was the only ambassador in my memory who was asked to speak before one of the most influential of American audiences, the annual convention of American Society of Newspaper Editors. After Franks had mounted the rostrum and taken off his wristwatch—it was on Saturday evening, usually reserved for the most prestigious speaker—he began by saying that since virtually all the key members of the Truman administration had spoken before this audience on virtually every conceivable subject, he would therefore talk about what he meant by "Western civilization."

He spoke for about half an hour without a note, analyzing the spiritual and material aspects of Western civilization, how consideration of one without the other led to dictatorship and to a lack of regard for human factors, and how the two must interact. Some of what he said may have been above the heads of his audience, who probably had never before listened to a professor of moral philosophy. But everybody nevertheless left with the tingling feeling that they had been somehow privileged to be present at such an event. When a few days later I asked Sir Oliver whether he had not put Western civilization on too high a pedestal—after all, there were other great civilizations still around which might feel slighted, such as the Chinese or Arab or Indian—he replied firmly: "Western civilization has achieved so much during the last centuries in consolidating the world without force that we need not be apologetic about it." What puzzled him was why Western civilization had lost out in Russia and why the Russians had adopted a doctrine born in the West, which they hated.

The intimate relationship between Acheson and Franks certainly was an unusual bonus to the special relationship, which rested then on such firm pillars as the common stand against communism; the practical part Britain played in the Berlin airlift, in the collection of intelligence, and in maintaining its military establishment; and the global usefulness of the Commonwealth. A sense of common destiny still provided the psychological glue, even though by then Americans saw Britain as a junior partner to an American enterprise. The special relationship meant that the British had access to most of the information, even if not always as quickly as Americans did, and often participated in the making of policy, right in Dean Acheson's office. British military participated in the planning of American strategy, especially in the Far East, where no consultative institution such as NATO existed. It helped that almost the same men who had been working together during the war were now discussing what to do about the vulnerable points in the Pacific and Indian oceans.

Only in the field of exchange of nuclear information, which the Congress cut off when Britain's participation was of no more particular use, did the special relationship suffer a setback. Negotiations to resume those exchanges made progress with Acheson pressing the British case, but they came to a dead stop after the British scientist Dr. Klaus Fuchs, who worked at Los Alamos, was caught "red-handed" passing information to the Russians. When the news broke, Britain's chief negotiator, who happened to be in Sir Oliver's library at the British Embassy, was literally sick.

Franks had no difficulty in seeing President Truman any time he needed to. The first time he did, it was to complain that the Israelis were shelling British troops at a vital crossroad in Gaza and thereby interfering with British communications. Franks had been instructed to ask the President to intervene with the Israelis. To Franks' utter surprise Truman turned to a map in his Oval Office and told Franks that since the Israelis were using 25-pounders they could not reach the road with their shells. Having been an artillery man in World War I, he said, he knew what he was talking about, and that was the end of Franks' first call on the president. The veteran artillery man visibly enjoyed applying his own expertise.

Although Nitze's NSC 68 did not have the same dramatic repercussions on American policymakers as did Kennan's long telegram and his "Mr. X" article, both intellectually had similar roots, a deep mistrust of the aims of Soviet leaders because the Russians, as Kennan put it, were "committed fanatically to the belief that with the US there can be no permanent modus vivendi." Nitze took Kennan's containment theories one step further; he put flesh on them in what became known as NSC 68. The memo began with an analysis of the conflicting aims and purposes of the two superpowers and defining those of the Soviet Union as "world domination." It then recommended drastic ways for bolstering American military capabilities to be up to America's international commitments. Acheson was mentally willing to use force if challenged or as a demonstration of American power—he was not deterred by pangs of morality, he advocated the use of force in Korea, Vietnam (at least until 1968), and Cuba. He felt the United States had the responsibility and duty to preserve Western civilization. But he was much more troubled by the existence and possible use of nuclear weapons than was the Eisenhower administration. He feared that excessive reliance on the atomic bomb would lead to the neglect of conventional forces and a downgrading of essential alliances, for he felt the United States could not "go it alone."

By then Kennan, in his thinking, had gone in almost the opposite direction. He began to advocate the American disengagement from Europe as the best way to avoid a continued and direct confrontation with the Russians that could lead to war. Nitze had convinced himself that the road to peace was military superiority. Kennan and Nitze were two of the most impressive among American public servants I ever met. In many ways they represented two very different strands in the American attitude toward the Soviet Union, toward American security, toward morality. Kennan was emotional and hence intellectually reactive and at heart a poet and humanitarian. Nitze was a tough-minded analyst who relied on numbers and facts, not on hunches. In terms of American strategy toward the Soviet Union the two were in harmony at the end of World War II. On Kennan's part it was an emotional reaction to what he perceived as Franklin Roosevelt's gullibility and soft-headedness toward the Russians, a lack of knowledge of history; in Nitze's case it was a cool assessment of Soviet strength in stark figures, a very rational analysis of the Soviet Union's geopolitical position and the yearning for something close to absolute security that influenced him. When Kennan realized what it would mean to gear up the United States to meet the Soviet threat as he had described it, he concluded that he had gone too far and, emotionally upset, claimed that he had been misinterpreted, and that he never meant to inspire the kind of power buildup akin to the NSC 68 memo. Nitze had the inclination to think in terms of worst case scenarios that overestimated reality and made more sense as an exercise in advocacy. As Acheson put it in his memoirs, *Present at the Creation,* its purpose was "to bludgeon the mass mind of top-government." It represents a perfect example of the "oversell," the method American presidents or secretaries of state have to resort to when they want to make sure of congressional and public approval for a policy that is hard to swallow. But this is, alas, the way of the American policymaking system—the system has to be whipped into a frenzy to make it work. Too often Americans need to be scared out of their wits to shoulder the burdens of their destiny, which is unfortunate because later, after the sobering has set in, such tactics have often led to mistrust and post-facto investigations by Congress or the press, which undermine confidence in government and jar in people's ears abroad. Unlike Britain, where people, having elected a government, leave it to decide what is best for them, in the United States policy must reflect to a large degree the reactions of the ordinary American citizens to the political hurricanes which hit their shore.

Kennan reminded me of Rodin's statue *The Thinker,* with his penetrating, restless eyes, more the thought-provoking pedagogue than the diplomat, very conscious of the importance of the peripheral vision; while Nitze, like Acheson, thought in absolutes very much like the early Robert McNamara, who later revealed himself as being not simply a cold calculating machine, but a highly emotional Irishman who had kept his deeper feelings under tight control. Nitze, who later became McNamara's deputy, was a man with a strong handsome face, framed by a white shock of hair, and a permanent banker's suntan. Kennan impressed by the elegance of his style and sophistication, Nitze by the facts at his fingertips and his doggedness in playing the long game. When Kennan backed off from the views he had expressed in his "Mr. X" article, he lost Acheson's confidence and was replaced as chairman of the Policy Planning Staff by none other than Paul Nitze, the true disciple of Mr. X. Kennan retreated to the ivory tower of Princeton University and became a leading historian of our time. The two became powerful intellectual antagonists.

If Nitze and Kennan tried to determine the thrust of American policy toward the Soviet Union, Chip Bohlen was the most listened to interpreter of Soviet policies, Soviet intentions, and Soviet psychology. Bohlen, for instance, did not think that the decision to attack South Korea was indicative of Soviet expansionism (he attributed it to speeches given by Acheson on January 12, 1950 and earlier by General Douglas MacArthur, because they both omitted mention of Korea as being within the American defense perimeter), and he disputed American intelligence estimates about the scale of Soviet weapons production and the contention that the Russians believed that this was the last chance to administer a military defeat to the United States and its allies. He therefore opposed NSC 68.

From my days as international conference correspondent, I had known Bohlen as the Soviet expert in the American delegation. He was a handsome man with a strong jaw and penetrating blue eyes. He exuded utter self-confidence, for he knew that there was no American with more experience than he in dealing with the Russians. He began as President Roosevelt's Russian interpreter at Yalta and he claimed that he knew "Soviet man" (who, he also asserted, did not really exist). He enjoyed fraternizing with the press and in a delightfully wry way explaining the Russian character and habits—he said that Marxism-Leninism was but a fig leaf of their respectability—through anecdotal vignettes, usually with some sexual allusions. To illustrate how difficult dealing with the Russians was, how hard to get anything out of them, and how occasionally patience was rewarded, he told the apocryphal story about a man who came to New York and wanted to know how to find a girl for the night. He was told to stand at the corner of 42d Street and Broadway and to ask every girl that passed by whether she would come with him to spend the night. "But don't you get a lot of black eyes that way?" the first man asked. "Yes," he replied, "I get some black eyes, but I also get some girls to spend the night with." Bohlen had no patience with people who pretended to know something about the Soviet Union without ever having been there. "To explain the Russian people to someone who has never been to the Soviet Union," he used to say, "is like explaining intercourse to a virgin." Secretary of State James Byrnes once introduced him to the deputy minister of foreign affairs, Andrei Gromyko, as "our Russian expert, Mr. Bohlen." Whereupon Gromyko replied—having known about Bohlen for a long time—"You mean your anti-Russian expert."

The British mistrusted Bohlen because they suspected him—not without reason—of sympathizing with the Rooseveltian idea of a world organized on a bilateral basis between the Soviet Union and the United States. Ambassador Sir Frank Roberts, for instance, in August 1953 sent a highly secret message to the British Foreign Office from Moscow that Bohlen, then American ambassador to the Soviet Union, talking at a private party, suggested that "it would not surprise him if during his term of office in Moscow he would receive instructions to open negotiations with Mr. Molotov [Gromyko's predecessor] on these lines." He then blamed Stalin for "foolishly" rejecting the outstretched American hand in 1945 because he wrongly thought there would be an industrial recession in the United States and that he could get better terms later on. I mention this dispatch as an illustration of the persistent suspicions about differences over policy toward the Soviet Union that plagued Anglo-American relations from time to time.

Sir Frank was right that Bohlen was not a believer in the Anglo-American alliance or in the idea of a North Atlantic treaty. He hankered for a United States that kept its hands free for an eventual deal with the Russians as the most promising road to the avoidance of war. This was neither Nitze's nor Acheson's view. Their minds were focused on the Soviet threat and how to build up Western strength to resist it.

So very much against Bohlen's and Kennan's advice, NSC 68 laid down the vast needs for what Nitze (and Acheson) believed was necessary to allow the Pax Americana "to flourish." The two Sovietologists argued that the Kremlin had no intention of risking war with the United States and was guided primarily by national interests, not the ambition to create a world revolution. I was fascinated and duly confused hearing Kennan arguing that the emphasis on military power would undermine the prospects for achieving a negotiated end to the cold war and Bohlen that it would improve them.

These policy conflicts did not make it easy for either diplomats or the press to report on American policy toward the Soviet Union, for each party tried to influence the public thrust of the debate. Truman approved NSC 68 only in principle, for there loomed in the background General Marshall's opposition and that of his economic counselors. Its costs were never seriously calculated and I very much doubt whether, without the Korean War, which somewhat vindicated NSC 68, it would have become policy. But for the Russians giving the go-ahead for the attack on South Korea, the consequent military buildup would not have taken place.

Just as Kennan was not suited temperamentally to service in government, so Nitze was not suited temperamentally to be out of government. While Kennan enjoyed writing history, Nitze's métier was drafting policy papers. But writing history in an ivory tower was a quiet, peaceful occupation, drafting policy papers was a nerve-wracking occupation, more so perhaps in the field of arms control, Nitze's speciality, because of the basic clash between those in government and Congress who were for and those who were against it. Nitze, at different intervals, was viewed with suspicion by both sides. The liberal establishment considered him a dangerous hardliner after he authored the NSC 68 memorandum, and the hardliners suspected him of being a closet problem-solver and a man, who after a career full of frustrations, wanted to score a major success. His opportunity to score came when, after fourteen years in government, he did a yeoman's job in helping to clinch the ABM Treaty of 1972. It cheered the liberals and confirmed the hardliners' suspicions. But it did not take long until his fears that Nixon and Kissinger, in their eagerness for a breakthrough in the SALT II talks, would concede nuclear superiority to the Russians made him resign and return to private life. He became the spear carrier for the Committee on the Present Danger to crusade against Kissinger's and later President Carter's handling of SALT II. He scored a negative triumph: the Treaty was never ratified. Nobody should underrate the force of his convictions nor his deep-seated hurt feelings. Neither Kissinger nor Carter offered him the job he thought he deserved. It was not until Reagan came to power that he became the driving force in arms control negotiations. He deserves a great deal of credit for the INF Treaty that the Senate ratified, though Kissinger gave him a taste of the verbal whiplashing he once received from Nitze. But Kissinger's convictions were tempered by his concern that another failure to ratify an arms control treaty would cause untold damage to the United States as a world power. And so Nitze's contribution to arms control, the INF Treaty, got the Senate's seal of approval, while Kissinger's SALT II Treaty never did. Kissinger set the pace for arms control negotiations and when Nitze followed in his footsteps seeking ways to get acceptance for what came to be called the Grand Compromise—restraints on SDI against substantial reductions in Soviet offensive weaponry—to reach a "Start" agreement which involved a 50 percent reduction in long-range strategic missiles (an idea Kennan had once put forward), Nitze, the one-time hardliner, learned what it meant to struggle against hardliners. By then, however, he had concluded that American nuclear superiority was unattainable and that it therefore made more sense to seek equitable arms reduction agreements.

Thus by a very circuitous route Nitze and Kennan had no problem when they faced each other at a celebration of Kennan's eightieth birthday. Nitze, looking younger and stronger than the more fragile-looking Kennan, toasted his life-long antagonist as a man with regard for "the opinion of mankind," and Kennan, in reply, admitted his respect for Nitze, who, unlike him, soldiered on as a public servant, which gave him a better chance "to make things you believe in come out right." And so these two exceptional men, who exerted an inordinate influence on governmental thinking, after fighting each other almost for a lifetime, had virtually come full circle.

Some political historians dispute the necessity of postwar European rearmament and claim, not without reason, that it undermined some of the economic reconstruction of the Marshall Plan. But it is my belief that, in the absence of an armed military alliance, the Western coalition would have disintegrated and the Soviet Union would have been a much more unpleasant neighbor for the West. Acheson, however, afraid of weakening support for his policy, went too far in his refusal to countenance any approaches "from the free world [to the Soviet Union], however imaginative, to help resolve our mutual problems."

The American aversion to negotiating with the Soviets became an unsettling factor among the Western allies, who don't like the two superadversaries just to glare at each other. American administrations on the other hand are much more comfortable with the status quo than with what they consider the slippery slope of negotiations. They tend to fear that they will get the short end of the bargain, as Roosevelt did at Yalta, and that any easing of tension will make it much more difficult to get Congress to support various aid requests. That applied to the Johnson and Reagan administrations and led to the Kennedy, Nixon, Ford, and Carter administrations' being accused of having bargained away "the store." Another factor is that the American governmental processes are so complex, and require such arduous negotiations among the various duchies involved, that by the time an interagency agreement has been reached, the American position has become too rigid for an ally to weigh in with modifications or for the American negotiator to show flexibility at the conference table. Acheson once asked Harold Ickes, who had been President Roosevelt's secretary of the interior, how he felt about being out of government. Ickes replied: "Outside government I worry to death. Inside, I used to be scared to death." Acheson then confessed that it was the same with him: "Half the time I am worried, half the time I am scared." And Acheson was still in office!

Little in their history prepared Americans for the role they were assuming or for the problems they were facing and the policies required to cope with them. Considering the dislocation, the insecurities, the economic needs, and the general confusion that pervaded the world the United States had inherited, it was a daunting task Americans had assumed. They had neither the tradition, knowledge, or training in diplomacy or intelligence. The confidence in American superior strength, based on the possession of the A-bomb, did not last much beyond the birth of the Soviet A-bomb. The obvious comparison is with British naval power and the place of its rise and fall in Britain's role as a world power, but that takes one back beyond the Battle of Waterloo. Considering how few years Americans had had to lay out the practical political, economic, and military bases for a new Weltanschauung, and adjust to it, the accomplishments of Truman and Acheson were awe-inspiring.

I had become used to celebrating Thanksgiving Day as Americans do with a turkey dinner that takes all day to eat and even longer to digest, but on that day of 1949 its sanctity was interrupted by a sudden summons from Field Marshal Viscount Montgomery of Alamein, whom I had first met as a war correspondent in the North African desert, to the house of General Sir William

Morgan, head of the British Joint Military Mission in Washington. I was looking forward to seeing again the crusty curmudgeon who, I suspected, having been used to seeing his name in the headlines, found it hard to live without them. Monty greeted me with the exuberance that was his trademark. He first wanted to know whether I had an answer to the British dollar problem and whether the much-advertised export drive could effect the necessary difference. He shared my doubts and did not like the idea of Britain joining an economic union either with the United States or with Western Europe because it would mean Britain would lose her independence. Instead he argued that Britain needed a "master plan" for the development of its colonies which would, within five to ten years, lead to more promising results. It was the kind of totally unrealistic statement only someone out of power could make.

I soon realized that the main reason for his invitation was to discuss West German rearmament, which he believed had to come about because, as he put it in his sharp-edged, high-pitched voice, "if we wanted to hold the Germans to our bosom, we must give them an army. The Germans might prefer to be overrun by the Russians, but we must do everything to make them fight with us." He then asked me how the idea would go down with American audiences if he took the initiative in advocating German rearmament. I suggested that the American public, like the British, was not yet quite ready for German rearmament. But it soon became clear to me that he had already made up his mind to speak out. He had thought about it crossing the Atlantic, he said, and decided then and there that this would be his mission. Monty, indeed, in a speech the following week before a packed audience at the National Press Club presented a German contribution toward a general European defense effort as the only plausible cure for Western security. It did not shatter too much crockery, but judging by some of the criticism, the idea would have had a better reception had it come from a civilian. Americans don't trust military men at the podium. But, whatever the reactions, Monty showed foresight, as he did some ten years later in advocating American recognition of Communist China, which advocacy earned him censure in Congress.

Monty had recently had an interview with Stalin, and I asked him about it. He said he was very much impressed by Stalin's personality and his shrewdness. When Monty asked him, for instance, what in his view was the difference between a Socialist and Communist state, a question often in American minds, Stalin replied: "In a Socialist state you earn according to your work, in a Communist state you earn according to your needs." Then he added: "Therefore only rich states can become Communist, and that is why Britain cannot become one and the United States can." So much for Stalin's outlook on the future of the United States and his complete misapprehension of capitalism. It may explain some of the miscalculations he made after the war.

I doubt whether Monty knew at the time that Dean Acheson had already convinced himself in September 1949, after the Russians had exploded their first A-bomb, that West German rearmament was a necessary corollary to the American balance-of-power, and to achieve it, he therefore made it a condition for the sending of American troops to Europe a year later.

On March 8, 1950, Sir Oliver Franks sent Bevin one of those secret and personal letters: ". . . it would be difficult and embarrassing [Franks pleaded] if either of my guests [Dean Acheson and Lew Douglas, the American ambassador to Britain] had occasion to suppose their conversation had been reported to London." The letter outlined Acheson's deep conern about growing Soviet strength, the deterioration of the common positions in the West, his searching of his mind for "major new policies" to reverse this trend, and his invitation to Britain to help formulate these policies. Franks, a little skeptical about Acheson's worries, commented that "I'm sure it is true now as so often that the Americans are looking at time and events in smaller compartments than we naturally do . . ." and, more forcefully, criticized as absurd Acheson's assumption that Britain's legitimate ambition to play a part as a world power could be achieved without continuous reference to its economic position. "The power which we could exert in the world depended on the level at which we could exist." Five months later Franks again emphasized the need for Britain not to lose sight of its means: "One difficulty in this is the dichotomy between the American view of Britain they have held in the last five years and the Britain they knew in each of the two world wars."

British statesmen were bedeviled by the clash between their desire to maintain the role and influence of a great power and the rapidly declining economic and financial means to back it up. For their part, the Americans wanted Britain both to submerge its power in that of Europe and to be a special partner in the American responsibilities of maintaining order in the world.

By September 1950 Acheson's major new policies had jelled and he presented Bevin and France's foreign minister, Robert Schuman, with his proposal for a first step in the rearmament of West Germany. The idea had originated with the Pentagon, and Acheson, after Truman had approved it, was asked to sell it to the two allied foreign ministers in a package with an extremely tempting offer, the indefinite presence of American troops on the European continent.

To my surprise, I got an invitation for a drink before Acheson dined with the two foreign ministers at the Acheson suite in the Waldorf Tower. There were the secretary of state, Mrs. Acheson, and daughter Mary Bundy. Dean seemed in fine form, looking forward to meeting with two men whom he liked and respected, but also well aware that his was a very difficult task. However, reveling in difficult problems, he was looking forward to this test of diplomatic persuasion.

Acheson admired Bevin greatly. What appealed to him most was that there was a man brought up in the docks, yet steeped in British traditions like Lord Grey and feeling all the time that he had to live up to them. "I've had some stormy sessions with Ernie," Acheson said. "I'll probably have one tomorrow, but nothing ever transpired about our bouts and in the end we got along very well."

I once asked Harold Wilson how he compared his own government with Attlee's, to which he replied: "I never had the kind of strong anchor Bevin provided. Neither Callaghan nor Brown gave it to me."

Under pressure from the "China lobby," Acheson had serious bouts with the British over the recognition of Communist China. The China lobby blamed him for not putting enough pressure on the British. Another wrangle was over the nationalization of the Anglo-Iranian oil company, which created a lot of bad blood because the Americans, with good reason, treated it as one of the worst vestiges of colonialism; and accusations that the sterling balances undermined the value of the dollar and trade policies also led to controversies. But German rearmament became the most divisive issue because the idea was politically explosive in Britain and France. Too many wounds were still too fresh. However the prospect of American troop reinforcements in Europe, as promised by Truman, and the prospect of getting General Dwight D. Eisenhower as supreme commander of a unified force, convinced Bevin to run the political risks. He telegraphed the prime minister, summing up this momentous step the Americans were willing to take: "The U.S. has taken a historic decision to commit itself to station forces in Europe as part of a combined European force so that the U.S. would be in the fighting in Europe from the first day. It would however be impossible for the U.S. to undertake such a commitment without some assurances that the common effort was likely to be a successful one. The U.S. Government could see no prospect of achieving this aim without German participation in the European defense force. I propose to give general concurrence."

Bevin and the prime minister had the foresight to understand what a historic breakthrough the American offer represented. The French did not. Eight months later French President Vincent Auriol pleaded with Acheson to abandon his insistence on German rearmament, to which Acheson replied that he would if offered any good alternative. Auriol answered that an arrangement with Russia of some kind would be his alternative. That was totally unacceptable to Acheson. Curiously, German Chancellor Konrad Adenauer was in Paris at the same time and came to see Acheson the next day to find out whether he was not playing the Germans along until the time was ripe for making an arrangement with Russia and throwing Germany into the bargaining pot. Acheson, who made no mention of this meeting in his book *Present at the Creation,* reassured him that he had no such intentions, but it made him realize how suspicious and how well-informed Adenauer was about the thinking of the French.

When I arrived in Bonn in July 1951 in the expectation of getting an interview with Adenauer, German rearmament was still an issue to be resolved. I had with me a letter of introduction from an extraordinary American, Danny Heinemann, who was the chancellor's closest friend. The two had met first when Heinemann, then an engineer for General Electric, later a shrewd entrepreneur, built the electric power station in Cologne where Adenauer (before Hitler) was mayor. Heinemann, a short, distinguished-looking man who enjoyed accumulating money as much as listening to classical music, became one of those millionaires who almost obsessively avoid all publicity. During the war, when Adenauer lived with his family in obscurity, Heinemann maintained him financially through illegal channels by way of Spain. I had put in a written request in advance, but when I called Adenauer's office, his secretary said that he had a very busy schedule and would probably not be able to see me. I then mentioned that I had a letter of introduction from Mr. Heinemann. Suddenly the chancellor switched himself into the conversation and said that he would be delighted to see me at twelve thirty.

The Chancellery, the old Schaumburg Palace, had been completely renovated—all the furniture was modern, all the secretaries were curiously dressed in a single style of suit. Only a few old paintings looked like holdovers from the past. Adenauer, seated behind a huge desk, looked me up and down. He was very suspicious of the British because they had at first kept him under lock and key; it was the Americans who chose him for the chancellorship. He was excessively polite, a bit haughty and sanctimonious, and eager to prove that he was a man who knew the world. He was convinced that the Russians wanted to unify Germany in order to neutralize it and then bring it into their orbit. For this reason it was to him exceedingly important, even urgent, that Germany be integrated firmly into the West through the Schuman plan and the European army plan. With Germany, he argued, the Western alliance would grow strong and, like a big magnet, would gradually pull East Germany to the West. It sounded persuasive, but he underrated the Russian ability to keep Eastern Europe under its control. "What is Europe?" he suddenly asked rhetorically. "Britain," he said, "is economically weak and aloof from Europe, France is politically badly divided, and the Benelux countries [Belgium, the Netherlands, and Luxembourg] don't exist . . . well, who is left?" he asked. "The Federal Republic of Germany, of course. That is what counts in Europe today."

A few years later, thanks to my friendship with Danny Heinemann's son Jimmy, I was asked to a dinner his father was giving for Dr. Adenauer at his Westchester home. We were twelve, including Rudolf Serkin, who played the piano after dinner. There was hardly any political talk. The evening really belonged to Serkin, who began with the Hammerklavier Sonata and then took requests from the audience—one of those great luxuries few people can afford and fewer people think of. Adenauer was not an easy conversationalist at the dinner table. All I remember is that Jimmy's wife told the chancellor how pleased she was to meet him, and he, to her surprise, asked "Why?" To which she replied: "Because you're such a good friend of my father-in-law." This was not the answer he had expected, but the general laughter which followed helped to get him over this embarrassment.

Danny Heinemann was about three years younger than Adenauer, and there was a kind of unspoken competition between them as to who would live longer. Adenauer did. The last time I saw him in Washington he confessed that he always assumed that the Americans would withdraw from Europe in his lifetime, hence his eagerness to create a strong Western Europe; it was reassuring to him that the Americans had stayed on but it worried him that there was still no strong Europe, not even a strong Federal Republic of Germany.

The next test for the staying power of the United States and its readiness to live up to its commitment of containing communism did not occur in Europe and it came out of the blue. The entry in my diary for June 27, 1950, begins: "Today was a great day in US history. President Truman decided to use American air and naval forces to preserve the integrity of South Korea. There was no declaration of war but action in the name of the United Nations. Only a few days ago, it was looking for someone to rescue it from the paralysis caused by a Russian boycott, but overnight the United Nations had taken on a new meaning made possible by a Russian boycott. If a Russian delegate had been present, he, no doubt, would have vetoed the resolution which allowed the United States to wrap its forces in the blue flag of the United Nations."

Korea's division was one of those hardly noted decisions taken at Potsdam on the assumption that unification and independence would follow "in due course." But the temporary expedient of a dividing line, the 38th parallel, became a heavily defended border; in the North the Russians, with their puppet Kim Il Sung, imposed their system, and in the South political chaos was rampant. And so the 38th parallel soon became the equivalent of a fire hazard. With four hundred Soviet-built tanks as the spearhead of the North Korean onslaught, the invasion of the South unquestionably was a carefully prepared attack.

President Truman was in Independence, Missouri, when the tanks crossed. He later told a friend that he had made up his mind immediately that such an aggression must be resisted at all cost, and Dean Acheson later talked about the "unblinking courage and clear-sightedness" that Truman displayed at the crucial cabinet meeting that took the decision to intervene. Truman committed troops in Korea without consulting Congress, ordered the protection of Formosa (Taiwan), and promised more arms for Indochina. He began calling up more men and ordered the army to take over a strike-bound railroad, all within three days. And there was hardly a murmur of dissent on Capitol Hill.

The American people, it was overwhelmingly clear, supported him to the hilt. Simplicity was still Truman's dominant quality, but there was also a moral righteousness, a deep-seated conviction and fearless courage behind that simplicity. The legends of the haberdasher who went bankrupt, the politician who owed his election to the notorious Pendergast machine, the poker player who

Special Relationships

enjoyed showing off in curious hats, were all more or less true. Nevertheless, he had the stuff of leadership in him. Never did he pretend to be a genius or a great statesman. He was, at least to Americans, a kind of everyman. They could mirror themselves in him. He lacked the grand manner of presidents but everyone understood what, in his simple language, he meant to say. He did not whip up great emotions among the public, but his fundamental approach to world affairs gave him a new kind of elemental greatness.

With the United Nations having become the diplomatic battleground in the Korean War, I had to move back and forth between Washington and Lake Success, Long Island, the temporary headquarters of the United Nations. The Russians, in the person of Yacov Malik, had opened a second Korean front to defeat the UN on its home ground as an armed peacemaker. He fought with all his rhetorical guns blazing to win the struggle for the soul of Asia, and, more specifically, that of India, and to split the Anglo-American front. Sir Gladwyn Jebb, the new British UN delegate, had been a backroom boy at the Foreign Office. Tall, handsome as a matinee idol, he soon proved that he was the most effective speaker on the Western side. He wielded the rapier with supple skill, and since the entire proceedings in the Security Council were carried on television, he soon became something of a star. The *New York Times* praised his performance as proof that the British "have not practiced the gentle art of verbal homicide at Oxford all these years for nothing." One morning, driving to Lake Success, I was stopped by a policeman for speeding. Asked for my driver's license, I found to my distress that I did not have it on me. Asked for some other identification I pulled out my UN press pass. When he saw that I represented the London *Sunday Times* he asked: "British?" I nodded, expecting the worst from this Irish cop. "Do you know that British guy, what's his name, Jebb?" he then asked. I said yes, that indeed I knew him very well. "Okay, then, tell him that I think he is a great guy . . . and don't speed again." I gave Jebb a sumptuous lunch the next day.

Those were dramatic days at the UN, with some three thousand people lined up daily for the galleries, the best ticket in town. However successful the Western diplomats were at the UN front, or their soldiers on the Korean battlefield, it soon became obvious that it would be a hard road to peace or victory. But nobody expected that this American intervention, which had been praised throughout the Western world as a statesmanlike act, would turn gradually into an unmitigated disaster for the Truman administration.

General MacArthur, in command of the United Nations forces, had brilliantly forced the North Koreans into retreat with his strategic master stroke, the Inchon landing behind enemy lines; but after he had pushed the enemy back across the 38th parallel, the Truman administration lost its head, intoxicated by success. Luke Battle remembers when Dean Rusk, the assistant secretary for Far Eastern Affairs, rushed to New York with the memo of instructions that the Joint Chiefs of Staff and the secretary of defense had drafted for Acheson to sign before it was submitted to the president. Battle, after reading the memo, argued that it was a mistake to give MacArthur so much of a free hand, but the secretary of state gave him a steely look and asked: "How old are you, Luke?" And he replied: "Thirty." "And you are willing to pit your judgment against the entire JCS?" The instructions reflected public pressures that had been building up in support of the hero of Inchon in the expectation of his being able to finish the war in blazing glory for the United States. In his memoirs, Acheson confessed: "None of us, myself prominently included, served him [the president] as he was entitled to be served." When the UN forces recovered the ground to the 38th parallel, doubts were widespread in Washington that peace and security could be restored in Korea by going no farther than that 38th parallel. The recommendation by George Kennan and Chip Bohlen was against crossing the parallel and moving to the Yalu River. So was the initial advice from the State Department Policy Planning Staff under Paul Nitze. They feared Chinese and/or Russian intervention. However, emotions, political expediency, and the possibility of scoring a smashing victory in what was, in fact, an East-West confrontation, combined to give General MacArthur a free hand to defeat the North Koreans, wherever, south or north of the 38th parallel.

A nightmarish time began to set in, for when irrationality grabs American lawmakers, it is hard to keep cool nerves and remain patient until the storm waves subside; they always do, as the American political system, designed to prevent extremes in either direction from occurring, asserts itself. But until it does so, things can become frightening. At the hard core of the irrationalists was the China lobby, whose passionate belief in the Nationalist Chinese regime surpassed their American patriotism. They wanted to broaden the Korean conflict into a war against Communist China and, if necessary, the Soviet Union, not realizing that the United States in fact was quite unprepared for such a war or wars, as proven partly by the poor fighting qualities of some of the American units in Korea. Even General Eisenhower, then still president of Columbia University, said that it would be difficult to pacify Korea without crossing the 38th parallel. In the circumstances, the small band of experts warning against the crossing, and the allies, such as the British, were helpless. The most specific warnings against moving toward the Yalu River came from Beijing via the Indian prime minister, Pandit Nehru, and the Indian ambassador to China, K. M. Panikkar. Both were distrusted in Washington and their advice discounted. On top of all, Senator Joseph McCarthy was riding high with his accusations of Communists under every governmental chair. However, when the Chinese showed that theirs had not been an empty threat and their forces, in overwhelming numbers, crossed into North Korea, the United Nations forces were abruptly thrown back. What followed was slightly reminiscent of the retreat from Moscow. The American Napoleon, Douglas MacArthur, formerly hell-bent on starting a full-scale war with China, was now faced with a strategic defeat. To save his skin and that of the UN forces, he first asked for permission to bomb Chinese bases in homeland Manchuria, then for the so-called "hot pursuit" of enemy aircraft into China, and finally for the power to use A-bombs. A military study of whether A-bombs made military sense in this situation came up with a negative, which put an end to that mad idea. It was a tragic setback for the United Nations and for a great soldier, whose political ambitions combined with false intelligence from his own staff led him into disaster, into a forced dismissal by President Truman for insubordination, and ultimately into a surprisingly quiet retreat into retirement.

Once the Joint Chiefs of Staff recognized that MacArthur's attempt to mount a white horse could lead to a backlash against the military, they backed President Truman and helped to deflate MacArthur's swollen head. They knew they had to prevent him from broadening a war which could suck in the Soviet Union, because they did not have the means to fight one on that scale. Furthermore, the Western allies were in no mood to fight a general war over Korea. The brilliant rescue operation of General Matthew Ridgway, one of the finest among operational commanders, helped to restore the 38th parallel to its former status as the dividing line between South and North Korea. But it was not a victory. Had Ridgway been listened to later on, the United States would have saved itself another military failure, the Vietnam war. As to General MacArthur, he will go down in history not so much for his military achievements as for his post–World War II diplomatic triumph in turning Japan into a functioning democracy.

To Acheson the Korean experience meant that the risks of war in the world had escalated, that building up the defenses in Europe had become even more important. It also convinced Congress of the need to make NATO into a serious military bulwark by the end of 1952. Above all, the Korean experience changed the sweep of American history. The United States assumed far greater and more long-range responsibilities in Asia; it reinforced its commitment to Taiwan, turning a country which the Joint Chiefs of Staff had considered a strategic liability into a major military commitment. And it convinced Americans that the Soviet Union and Communist China had aggressive designs they were willing to pursue with arms. It also diverted public attention, at least for the time being, from the fact that the real East-West confrontation was in Europe.

The real winners in Korea were the Russians. At virtually no cost beyond the weapons they supplied to the North Koreans, they obtained twenty years of Sino-American hostility. Americans felt that for sixty years they had done the right thing by China, and they were angered by their rejection. When I visited China in November 1975, and was entertained at lunch by the commander of the Ninety-second Infantry Division, whose mission was to defend Beijing, he mentioned that he had participated in the Korean War. Asked whether he thought that Russian prodding led to China's intervention in

Korea, he looked at me with surprise as if the thought had never occurred to him. "Of course not," he replied. "Our government took the decision because we considered the American advance to our borders a threat to China." Another winner in the Korean War was Eisenhower, who as presidential candidate promised to end it.

The evolution of American foreign policy after World War II superficially consisted of a number of empirical decisions, often improvised in haste, to meet each crisis as it occurred. Nevertheless there was a remarkable pattern to it. It evolved on the basis of the realization that, first, communism was and would be a continuing threat; second, that the United States had to assume responsibility for containing that threat; third, that economic aid was not enough, and military strength was necessary to achieve deterrence; and, fourth, that there had to be an organized coalition to give it cohesion. The viewpoint of the lawyers coincided with that of the soldiers. It was the civilians who turned the Pax Americana into practical politics.

Recognizing that the United States could not shoulder the Pax Americana alone, American policymakers began to judge their allies according to their actual and potential contribution to the American world role rather than against the measure of desirable international and internal behavior. While this certainly helped to raise the importance of Britain above that of any other ally, and pleased and flattered successive British governments, it also contributed heavily to Britain's economic decline, which proved more decisive than her military strength to her standing as a great power.

In retrospect the overstraining of Britain's economic resources was one of the major mistakes of British governments, whether Tory or Labour; but in view of those political leaders and leading civil servants I have questioned about this, British governments of those days had no choice. First, they wanted to make certain that the United States remained fully engaged in protecting the security of Western Europe, which it may have tired of as a lone guardian; second, British governments, in fact, overrated Britain's economic strength (Lord Franks told me when I saw him at his Oxford home thirty-three years later that he himself was one of those who had overrated Britain's economic resilience); and, third, both Conservative and Labour governments could not have downgraded Britain as a great power without losing popular support at the polls. The British people wanted Britain to be in the "big league," which meant having a special relationship with the United States, not joining Europe. For this reason the British rejected the so-called Schuman plan for the creation of the Coal and Steel community, a rejection that Acheson in his memoirs called "Britain's great mistake of the postwar period." Dean Rusk, who shared Acheson's view, teased me, telling me how he saw the English reacting to the American strenuous efforts to persuade Europe to integrate: "A girl was dreaming in her bed when suddenly a hulk of a man entered the room through the window. The girl, frightened, pulled her blanket over her eyes and asked the man: 'What are you going to do to me?' To which he replied: 'That's for you to decide, it's your dream.' "

One of my last diary entries for 1950 reads: "The United States and the Soviet Union, each in their own language, have been attacking British imperialism. Now the United States finds itself in a situation when, for security reasons, it is compelled to pursue an imperialist policy without having as yet succeeded in finding a term or ideology to make it acceptable to the world." It was not acceptable even to many Americans, such as Walter Lippmann, the columnist and coiner of the phrase Atlantic Community, who wrote: "In place of a national doctrine of American security we have the Truman doctrine . . . when the Free American doctrine—both in defense and offense—is to recognize the limitations, and to exploit the advantages, of our island character —our inferiority in manpower, our superiority in technology and in production, the oceans of sea and air around us which offer us the means of flexible defense and of a highly mobile defense." Overimpressed by the isolationist outcry, he predicted that if the globalism of the Truman-Acheson policy was not deflated, "armed isolation" would be the new direction. Acheson, at a press conference, rejected "armed isolation" because it would mean disaster for the security of the United States, which, he said, needed Europe just as much as Europe needed the United States. The idea of the Pax Americana stirred up deep convulsions in the American soul.

With Senator Vandenberg ailing and Senator Robert Taft lusting after the presidency, the old serviceable bipartisanism in foreign affairs was gone. It made everything much more difficult for Acheson, who had known Robert Taft for forty years and thought that he was now out of his mind, having seen himself virtually on the doorstep of the White House when suddenly Eisenhower became the political deus ex machina. After a lunch on the Hill with Tom Connally, the Democratic majority leader in the Senate, Acheson reported that Connally had said to him: "Dean, you're making the goddamnest mistakes. But don't think I'm trying to be offensive." He already had too many scars to feel this pinprick. The only bipartisan support he could enlist was through John Foster Dulles, whom he despised, and to whom, very reluctantly, he had entrusted the negotiations for a Japanese peace treaty.

Dulles had been given a vacant seat in the Senate by Governor Thomas E. Dewey of New York in 1949—there are no by-elections under the American political system, it is up to the state governor to appoint a successor—but when Herbert Lehman defeated him in the 1950 elections, Dulles had his friend the reporter Carl McCardle telephone Luke Battle to find out whether Dulles could not become once again Republican adviser to Dean Acheson. Both Truman and Acheson were horrified at the thought because they had come to distrust and dislike Dulles, especially after he had attacked Democratic Party politics in the election campaign. But, realizing that they were in dire need of

Republican support in Congress, they reluctantly agreed, and Dulles again became secretary-of-state-in-waiting. He was, no doubt, an exceedingly knowledgeable man about foreign affairs, an able corporation lawyer with a gloomy, forbidding presence and a melodramatic *gravitas,* even out of office. But he had some of those legal qualities which have kept lawyers out of the British Foreign Office, almost as a tradition, including too much concentration on the fine print. Two British ambassadors, Sir Roger Makins and Sir Harold Caccia, who served in Washington while Dulles was secretary of state under President Eisenhower, had to keep notes when they saw him because he sometimes brazenly denied having said something; they therefore needed to have something to prove the contrary. His strongest suit was as a negotiator and the best example of his negotiating skills was the Japanese peace treaty which he clinched single-handedly and then shepherded easily through Congress.

Though outwardly dull, rather long-winded and humorless, he did have a sense of the theatrical. I remember vividly, because it caught me totally off guard, how I went to see him before a Council of Foreign Ministers meeting to find out what he thought of the policies that had been prepared, under Acheson's guidance, for the occasion. He first looked at me with a smirk, then his eyes began to twitch, which, I knew, meant that he would either come out with an indiscretion or something to which he attached great importance. Instead of answering, he grabbed a large stack of "position papers" from his desk and tossed them high into the air. As they fluttered to the ground, he pointed to them and, clearly enjoying the melodrama of his gesture, said with a voice of studied despair: "Words, nothing but words!" When the time came in 1952 for him to act as Eisenhower's foreign policy adviser in the election campaign, he called Luke Battle to his office to show him a draft of a parting statement, in which he gave as reason for his leaving that he had completed the task he had been given, the Japanese peace treaty. "The statement has one flaw," Battle said after he had read it. "It is not true because you participated in many other negotiations, as you well know." But Dulles wanted to dissociate himself from all other policies of the administration in case his bipartisan role could come to embarrass him, and refused to change his statement.

When Winston Churchill, back in power, walked down the gangplank of his airplane on January 2, 1952, he looked very old. He did not seem firm on his feet and needed help. For a moment I felt sad seeing age grinding down a man whose bulldog vigor had been one of his shining qualities. But the moment he stepped with President Truman before the waiting microphone, his face muscles tightened, his famous jaw jutted forward and, suddenly, he looked in his old fighting trim. He was filled with nostalgia for the old wartime relationship and hoped to blow new life into it; his visit therefore was bound to be a disappointment to him. Dealing with Truman, who relied on his advisers, was quite different from dealing with Roosevelt, who relied on himself. Indeed, the disagreements over policy toward China, toward a European army, toward the

Soviet Union, toward Iran, all remained unresolved. Furthermore, Eden and Acheson were each too proud and too self-confident to have an easy relationship with one another. It did not help matters that Eden, at their first meeting in Paris the year before, immediately started calling Acheson "dear Dean," and so did again in Washington. When Luke Battle asked him after the meeting how he felt about this, he simply said: "On balance, I prefer 'me boy' [as Bevin used to call him] to 'dear Dean.' " When even such a relatively trivial disagreement as whether the American or British new automatic rifle should be adopted by NATO could not be resolved, Field Marshal "Bill" Slim said sarcastically, "I suppose what we shall do is to compromise on an inferior bastard rifle which is half American, half British." To this, Churchill raised his voice gravely and said: "Field Marshal, moderate your language, remember that I myself am half British and half American."

Next day, looking contemplative and sad, Churchill listened to Truman delivering the State of the Union message. A few days later, Churchill mounted the same rostrum in Congress to deliver his own address, the third, before that august audience. Since his exuberant press conference with President Roosevelt a drastic change in Britain's world position had occurred, but the great old performer sounded almost as confident as ever. The packed chamber was in awe and veneration as it listened to the world's greatest parliamentarian. His voice still had its rolling resonance, but his words sounded more like distant thunder. The only specific initiative he proposed, a token force of American troops to be sent to the Suez Canal, fell absolutely flat.

The next day at a luncheon given by the press and attended by seven hundred, his was another bravura performance. I can't help giving some of the flavor of the give-and-take that had the press in rapture. They had come not in the expectation of a story that would make headlines, but to watch a hero, a drama, and somehow to touch glorious history. In an American election year, a question about the American elections of course was inevitable: "In the United States they come according to schedule, in Britain the government has the right to pounce, which makes for awareness. No doubt, elections do a lot of harm," he added to general laughter, "but not as much as having none." To the chairman of the occasion, Paul Wootten of the National Press Club, who awkwardly characterized the current state of affairs between the United States and Britain as the United States having the might and Britain the prestige, Churchill curtly replied: "I don't feel on uneven terms with your might and my prestige." In what was meant to be a provocative question, since most Americans in those days did not see much difference between socialism and communism, he was asked how much further he would allow socialism to go in Britain. With surprising benevolence, he replied: "These fellows fought with us in the war, they were my faithful colleagues, this binds me to them. They only adhere to the fallacy that the state can produce better than the individual. We have to abuse one another at elections, but there is a great deal of humanism left in England. We have a close bond with the Socialists—they are even more in the front line against communism than we Conservatives."

Two months later during a long talk Sir Oliver offered some of his own conclusions about American foreign policy. He was concerned about the Americans' new emphasis on military rather than economic aid. He considered this switch a "great mistake." "Americans are inclined to think through the moral and ethical principles first," Franks suggested, "and then they try to fit the facts to them. They get excited, say, about a European army, although this is only priority number five, and then everything is concentrated on marshaling support for No. 5. This leads to overselling and overpressures and if the results are not on schedule, a crisis occurs which then makes Americans think that the Europeans are uncooperative, while the Europeans feel that they are chafing under American domination. To me this is not so much a form of applying political pressures as a form of imperialistic behavior." Franks obviously had his reservations about the management of the Pax Americana. But when I asked him in the 1980s what he was particularly proud of when he thought back to his Washington days, he said that what gave him particular satisfaction was the quality of his relations with Americans. "It was like having made a marriage work," he said, and his face reflected pleasure and contentment, the kind often associated with a golden wedding anniversary.

What makes the life of America's own ambassadors difficult is the unpredictability of Congress. As John McCloy, the High Commissioner in West Germany, said—"To be successful in one's mission of interpreting the United States abroad and in developing unity among the free nations, American representatives must possess the vision of a statesman, the insight of a philosopher and the healing powers of a doctor."

Therefore when Marshall Shulman, Dean Acheson's speech writer, asked me what sort of a speech Acheson should deliver at the annual convention of the American Society of Newspaper Editors, I suggested that he enumerate the reasons that were then leading to a relaxation of international tension for which Acheson could claim credit. Shulman replied that Acheson could not afford to admit that such relaxation existed as yet. The defense and military aid appropriations still had to pass Congress, the House had already cut almost five billion out of the defense budget, and no one was quite sure how the Russians would react to the actual integration of West Germany into the West. His reaction was a good example of the reluctance on the part of the State Department to admit that its policies had, at least partially, been successful.

In contrast, Adlai Stevenson, speaking in San Francisco as the Democratic presidential candidate, said: "We have little discussion of the conditions of coexistence and will probably get little during the campaign. Unless and until Americans are prepared by prolonged public consideration of what it will be necessary to concede, negotiations may make little progress . . . There has been so much emphasis on keeping Congress quiet, getting appropriations approved, and showing a stern, tough face to the Russians that there has been little useful discussion of the bargaining alternatives. But we cannot accept as everlasting this era of staggering taxes, towering budgets, and falling dollars. We cannot allow America to become a permanent armed camp forever under the dark shadow of catastrophic war." It was not surprising that Stevenson became popular abroad but lost the election at home, albeit against an almost unbeatable hero rather than a true Republican. Americans find it difficult to follow Disraeli's maxim that "Next to knowing when to seize an opportunity, the most important thing in life is to know when to forgo an advantage." On the other hand Acheson, in his efforts to give leadership to the Western alliance, preferred another of Disraeli's maxims: "What is the usefulness of power if you don't make people do what they don't like?"

What seems even more amazing in retrospect is that Acheson, with his power (and Truman's) declining as Eisenhower entered the presidential race, with Adlai Stevenson challenging him, and the Taft wing and some Democrats trying to force him out of office, still managed to keep a clear head and steady hand. Walter Lippmann too called for his resignation. Acheson self-mockingly called this clamor "my immolation." It is hard to imagine the fears that pervaded the government in those days, the terror that struck everyone mentioned by the run-amok Senator McCarthy, and the panic he created in distant Communist "hideouts" like Hollywood. (He called Acheson "this pompous diplomat in striped pants with a phony British accent," and accused him of being responsible for keeping known Communists in the State Department.)

As the election campaign in 1952 entered the bitter and anguished last lap, Stevenson surprised everybody by the high standards he maintained in his speeches, while Eisenhower disappointed many by his refusal to defend General Marshall from McCarthy's attacks. But the crowds paid little attention to what Ike actually said. They considered him the man with experience as a general and a statesman. They assumed he knew everything that was needed about the world and that he was the better man to end the bloody, costly, and unhappy war in Korea. Truman, who felt betrayed by him, laid into Eisenhower far more vehemently than did Stevenson. After all, he had not only appointed Ike to command NATO, but had even considered him as a possible Democratic presidential candidate. He accused him of lacking in moral courage when he failed to defend General Marshall, whom he had to thank for his meteoric career. General Goodpaster, Ike's close friend, told me years later that Ike could never forgive himself for having failed to stand up for his great benefactor.

It was a bitter disappointment for Truman when Eisenhower won. I remember standing with a huge crowd of people in front of the White House, in Lafayette Park, about a week after the elections, watching Eisenhower arriving for a visit and a briefing with Truman. When he stepped out and into his car people cheered and waved. Truman stayed inside. On Inauguration Day, when the two, sitting in the same limousine in the old tradition symbolizing the changing of the "guard," drove up to Capitol Hill, they did not exchange a word. Truman's enmity went deep. After the ceremonies Acheson gave Truman a last lunch at his Georgetown home. According to Robert Donovan's fine biography, Truman looked out of the window over Georgetown and commented: "Two hours ago I could have said five words and been quoted in fifteen minutes in every capital of the world. Now I could talk for two hours and nobody would give a damn." Such is the fate of American presidents, who, under the American political system, have no platform, no role to play, once the White House gate has closed behind them. Only the never-despairing Nixon has succeeded in papering over the reasons for his demise by reasserting himself as a foreign affairs expert and elder statesman.

Later in the afternoon Truman was driven to Union Station, where a special train was waiting to take him back to Independence, Missouri. It is hard to believe today that he left under a thick, dark cloud: the rising casualties in Korea, the cease-fire negotiations in Panmunjom deadlocked, and the accusations of trivial corruption known as "Truman's mess in Washington." Truman looked gaunt, himself for the last time on parade, but if he felt depressed, he did not show it. A crowd of loyalists, even much of the diplomatic corps, came to the station for a last, emotional farewell. Truman, obviously moved, cheerfully shook hands and smiled, elated and exhilarated, as if he knew that history would treat him more kindly than his contemporaries.

For Dean Acheson, used to making difficult decisions for so long, life suddenly became very empty. A certain bitterness surfaced because, as time went on, he was not asked for advice on anything. He heard that Eisenhower had said privately how much he respected him, but he did not hear from him directly. He returned to his old law firm, yet even there he found little to do. The role of the elder statesman did not fit his character; he yearned for active duty. Mary, his thoughtful and perceptive daughter, once beautifully described her parents as "a lion and a gazelle," Dean proud, active, and the lord of the jungle, Alice, his wife, attractive, gentle and retiring. But back in private life their roles began to change. Alice joined various Democratic committees, while Dean became more and more withdrawn, finally taking refuge in writing books in a graceful and precise style. But it was not until he was persuaded to write his memoirs, *Present at the Creation*—fifteen years after he left office —that he scored on the best-seller list.

During a discussion of his books one evening at the house of Francis and Katherine Biddle, the patricians from Philadelphia—he had been at one time FDR's attorney general, she was a fine poet—I ventured to say quietly how sorry I was, now knowing what a fine writer Acheson was, that he had not written his own speeches while in office. Biddle gently knocked on the table to get Acheson's attention and asked whether he had heard what I had said, to goad Dean into an argument with fiendish anticipation. I expected the worst to happen when Acheson began by saying slowly and deliberately, "Francis, you know of course what I think of the press . . ." He paused for effect, looking at me with a basilisk stare, his mustache twitching. Then he added: "But I can't help agreeing with Henry. The reason was that I did not have enough time to write my own speeches." Without my having indulged in the Château Haut-Brion earlier I would not have bravely interjected that Churchill, although he too had very little time, wrote his own speeches. Acheson on the defensive was a rare sight, and everybody waited for the counterblow. But Dean only reached for his brandy glass and said quietly: "I wish I had paid more attention to composing my speeches."

Some time later, in June 1957, Acheson asked me back to the farm for lunch. It was a beautiful sunny day and we began by clearing the leaves out of the swimming pool. Then we had a swim and after the usual two martinis, sat down to lunch. The conversation drifted to the question whether the time had come for an armistice in the cold war, and with grave weariness he replied: "No, not yet. The time to take our winnings has not yet come. If the West waited, it would not have to make equal concessions but could compel the Russians to take less. We can afford to lose propaganda battles, they don't matter." The telephone rang: it was a newspaper reporter. When at the State Department, Acheson had had to fire a foreign service officer, John Service (one of McCarthy's targets because he had predicted that communism would prevail in China), after a Loyalty Review Board had found "reasonable doubt as to his loyalty." The reporter informed him that the decision had just been reversed by a Supreme Court ruling and Service had been reinstated. Did Acheson have any comment? He did not. Then putting the telephone down, he said: "Well, I did not feel like a hero when I fired Service, but I couldn't go against the findings of the Loyalty Review Board. It is the kind of repudiation that will not trouble me."

It was proof that even a governmental board created by the president had been so intimidated by the McCarthy witch-hunt that justice had indeed been hard to come by. I suggested that it seemed as if a century had passed since those distressing times, and he nodded silently. He had withstood the McCarthy onslaught, but it was a wrenching memory. Acheson was a proud man and he had good reason to expect to be vindicated by history, but at that moment he did not feel exuberant about himself. It was Felix Frankfurter, his best friend, sitting in the court that exonerated Service, who helped to correct an injustice that Acheson could not.

Not until President Kennedy came to power was Acheson again called on to perform a public duty. He was asked to develop options about what to do after Khrushchev at the summit meeting in Vienna in June 1961 had threatened to oust the allies from West Berlin. Acheson was back in his element and convinced the president that he must stand up to the Soviet challenge and send additional troops to Europe. He rebuked those who favored firm military measures to be accompanied by words of willingness to negotiate, but it was their advice that Kennedy, after a long controversy, finally accepted. Acheson won in the sense that his main recommendation for sending military reinforcements to Europe became policy, but, as Arthur M. Schlesinger, Jr., put it in *A Thousand Days,* "Acheson's star began to wane when the President heard about some of his cutting criticisms of the conciliatory passages in the President's speech."

Nonetheless, Kennedy called again on Acheson's advice during the Cuban missile crisis, and used him as an envoy extraordinary to inform de Gaulle about the reasons for his deep concern. General de Gaulle had tried earlier to get the American and the British to agree to a triumvirate to be put in charge of directing global political and military strategy, but it was turned down. It was not an unreasonable request, in my view, even though he may have proposed it in the expectation that it would be turned down. General Al Gruenther, chief of staff to General Eisenhower, wittily summed up the reason at a staff meeting: "The trouble is that the French think three countries is the maximum to control global strategy, the British believe that two is enough, and the United States that one is ample."

Acheson, as a consultant to the State Department, anxious to preserve the house he had built, from then on worked hard to keep NATO alive after de Gaulle had brusquely pulled France out of it and advocated an incomprehensible entente with the Russians "from the Atlantic to the Urals." The idea of a multinational fleet, an artificial, unrealistic idea aimed at tying Germany to the West and giving it a semblance of participation in the NATO military command and an imaginery finger on the trigger, promoted fervently by George Ball and Henry Owen in the State Department, caused a hysterical controversy in the Kennedy administration and hard feelings when it was given the deserved coup de grace by President Johnson. McGeorge Bundy, who had sent Professor Richard Neustadt to London on an independent fact-finding mission, wrote the briefing paper for the president on the eve of a visit by Prime Minister Harold Wilson, and summed up the British and German reactions to the idea with devastating clarity.

Acheson, in the eyes even of some of his best friends, began to show evidence of a hardening of his political arteries. He continued to view any negotiations with the Russians with a jaundiced eye, he advocated all-out American intervention in Vietnam, he became the last defender of President Salazar and the Portuguese empire. At a dinner party at Luke Battle's he was still such a committed supporter of the pursuit of the war in Vietnam that he tore into Senator Stu Symington (Democrat from Missouri), who had just turned dove on the war, telling him to his face that he now regretted having backed him for the presidency in 1960. But about three weeks later, after the shock of the Tet offensive, which on the basis of first reports looked like a disastrous defeat for the American forces, he obtained President Johnson's permission to consult experts of his own choice and not, as in the past, only the Joint Chiefs of Staff, Walt Rostow, the deeply committed National Security adviser, and CIA people. As a result he then told the president that he was being led down the garden path and that he should get out of Vietnam rather than send additional troops. His volte-face created some shock waves within the administration.

There was another, almost more astonishing change in Acheson's attitude. It happened at the Gridiron dinner in 1969, a unique annual occasion when the press and the politicians, from the president down, square off against each other in fun and good sportsmanship. Richard Helms had offered Dean Acheson a ride home and the former secretary of state begged him to wait a few minutes because he wanted to talk to President Nixon. Acheson went over to the man who had been part of the McCarthy torture chamber and shook hands with him. "I'm Dean Acheson," he said to Nixon, who looked utterly surprised. "I know," replied Nixon. And that was the end of the encounter, as Acheson later reported to Helms. I can only assume that Acheson's respect for the office of the president asserted itself, for that was how he had been brought up.

NATO, Acheson's brainchild, went through many crises, yet it still stands strong, with its deterrent power enhanced, a monument, above all, to his stewardship. He may have pressed for German rearmament too soon and too purposefully, but it has proved to be the right policy. He was wrong in agreeing to the crossing of the 38th parallel, but he was up against MacArthur's bravura performance at the Inchon landing and it was therefore hard to deny the general anything. He was correct in his withering remark that the British had "lost an empire and had not yet found a role," and it led to some healthy soul-searching in Whitehall after Prime Minister Macmillan had defensively criticized him for it in the House of Commons.

Acheson's quizzical arrogance was at times irritating, but also endearing, all part of his panache. He was, without a doubt, a statesman in the grand manner, a leader with a strong will and a sharp mind. He stood on the bridge, next to the president, at the right time when, due to the cold war, most of the East-West issues were painted darkly in black and white and not, as they are today, full of confusing and distracting shades. It needed a man of his strong convictions to build the kind of firm, lasting structure to protect Western civilization about which his friend Oliver Franks had spoken so eloquently. The Western world owes him a tremendous debt.

Dean Acheson survived Secretary of State John Foster Dulles, who died in office, by a few years. He went to Dulles's funeral, as did almost all of official Washington. Later he called his former private secretary and friend, Luke Battle, by now an ambassador, to tell him what a huge and endless ceremony it had been. "Some big shot got up and read all the Old Testament, and then another one got up and read all the New Testament and then the eulogies began," he recounted. Then, laughingly, he added: "The greatest mistake I made was not to die in office."

6

Eisenhower and the Power of the Dulles Brothers

I HAD high hopes for Eisenhower's presidency. His election saved the United States and the Western alliance from the isolationist outlook of his Republican rival Senator Robert Taft, and he arrived at the White House with more experience as a leader, and a world leader at that, than any of his predecessors. He was thus something rare in American history. The American political system is not the training ground that the British parliamentary system is, in which politicians are forced gradually to climb the ladder toward a leadership position. Eisenhower had the advantage that as a military commander he had sharpened his wits in his dealings with men like Winston Churchill, Charles de Gaulle, and many another difficult foreigner. His talent for statesmanship had been tested more than his generalship, in the wartime alliance. He had learned how to maintain a consensus.

To me, as to most people, Ike was a decent, moderate, intelligent, affable, somewhat reserved man. He projected the best American qualities. He exuded confidence and optimism, qualities that also helped make Kennedy and Reagan popular. With his pro-British instincts and his experience as wartime Allied leader and later supreme commander at NATO, I expected him further to consolidate the Western alliance and Anglo-American relations. In 1957, true, I credited him with having created "a national atmosphere of calm, contentment, and a general spirit of accommodation in domestic and international affairs and an extraordinary absence of political partisanship." And yet his White House years gave me my worst days in thirty-six years of reporting from Washington, for two reasons: his failure to use his power to stifle Senator Joseph McCarthy, whose moral darkness and political venality became a serious menace to the health of the American body politic and to the sanity of the nation; second, the Suez crisis, which became a serious threat to the Western alliance.

With his heroic aura, his remarkable popularity, and his reputation for integrity and fair-mindedness, it was hard to understand why Ike was loath to take advantage of his great assets and exercise strong leadership—unless one remembers that he had always been a consensus maker, anxious to avoid controversies and conflicts. It was one reason why, in order to avoid show-downs with his field commanders, he decided to advance across Europe on a broad front, it was also one reason why, in order to avoid a confrontation with Roosevelt and Churchill, he communicated directly with Stalin without first consulting the two. Most likely, he also hoped to establish some working relationship with the Soviet leader. I doubt whether his refusal to conquer Berlin made much of a difference, since its political fate had already been decided, but the liberation of Prague would have been a psychological triumph. I discussed these wartime decisions with his friend and confidant General Andrew Goodpaster—I am afraid I lacked the courage to confront Ike himself with the issue in his retirement. Goodpaster said that Eisenhower put saving human lives ahead of political considerations. He added, though, that had Ike been ordered to proceed, he would have done so. And, as I saw with my own eyes, the liberation of Prague, at least, would have been a walkover.

I had known Eisenhower from my time as a war correspondent, but only from a distance. I had no occasion to talk to him as NATO's supreme commander and I rarely joined his campaign travels after he was nominated for the presidency. When a new administration takes the helm, one of the problems a Washington correspondent faces is to establish ties to the new cast of characters and to adjust to a changing battleground of politics. It is very different from the situation under a parliamentary system. There if the opposition comes to power it is not much more than a rotation of the political turntable. And since the leader of the opposition and most shadow cabinet ministers simply step out of the shadow and into the limelight, there is no need to start from scratch as in the American political system, under which a horde of new men few people have heard of before are drawn into a new administration.

Eisenhower was correct and impersonal in his dealings with the press, not chummy like Truman or flattering like Kennedy or ingratiating like Johnson. He thought it was more profitable to be in touch with the high command; he invited publishers for cookouts and broiled steaks for them. But he was mistaken; it was the reporters who set the tone of his presidency. Unlike any of his successors, he held press conferences every week with almost military regularity and kept his press secretary, Jim Hagerty, up-to-date on his doings.

Hagerty was his shield and very effective at that. A very willing and loyal tool, Hagerty nevertheless once complained to Ike that he hurt all over having had to defend him concerning some controversy. The president, he told us, smiling put an arm around his shoulder and said to him comfortingly: "But, Jim, better you than me!" Still, life for a White House press secretary was a bed of roses compared to what it is today. The pressures for news, for information, for ferreting out official dirt were not what they are today. It was a much more leisurely job except when the occasional lightning struck. Outside the cramped press room there was a large lobby where the "regulars" lounged around in soft, bottle-green leather chairs, playing cards, reading, or snoozing off a boozy lunch. They were there to keep watch on the president's visitors coming out of the Oval Office and into the lobby. Their task was to buttonhole the callers and take note of some sort of soporific, self-serving comment; those who preferred silence or anonymity left by the back door. Hagerty's twice-a-day press briefings were a clubbish, almost intimate affair, not the inquisition they have become in the presence of the television cameras. It did not mean that the adversary relationship between press and government was not alive—after all, it goes back in history to the Founding Fathers—but it was fought most of the time by the Queensberry rules.

Ike fulfilled his two functions, head of state and head of government, better than any other president I have known. He had of course learned changing hats without changing uniforms during the war when he played field marshal and statesman rolled into one. If we reporters underrated him, it was because as a public man he cherished his privacy and because he was self-confident enough not to be excessively worried about what the press thought of him. We were misled, above all, by the accounts from members of Congress, especially Lyndon Johnson's, then the majority leader in the Senate, who after their regular meetings with the president reported that he was relying more on his charm than on his knowledge of legislation. Stories about his attaching greater importance to his paintings than state papers, about the regularity with which he practiced on the putting green behind the Oval Office or about engaging in such pursuits as reading up on the origins of the Jewish people in the *Encyclopaedia Britannica,* all however true, created a misleading picture of the man. Now that I have read some of the official reports on the debates and decisions in the National Security Council and the letters to his close friends, I have also come to realize that he was much more engaged in the business of the presidency and that he was a far deeper thinker than I had assumed.

Curiously enough, though a consensus man, he did not particularly bother to reconcile his own views about dealing with the Russians with those of his secretary of state. Dulles believed that any accommodation with the Russians would undermine what he considered to be a fragile Western consensus in support of containment. Ike, in contrast, firmly believed that in the nuclear age the West had to exhaust every possibility for coming somehow to terms with the Russians. It was the cautious, distrustful lawyer against the self-confident leader who had seen the horror of war at close range. At any rate, this difference in outlook did not trouble Ike. He knew he could overrule Dulles whenever he wanted to and did so several times. Dulles, for instance, had major reservations about one of the president's most effective speeches, his address to the American Society of Newspaper Editors on April 16, 1953, in which he offered an arms limitation agreement and international control of atomic energy, hedged by a number of demands, which he knew would be unacceptable to the Kremlin. C. D. Jackson, the president's chief adviser on psychological strategy, Paul Nitze, and Emmet Hughes strongly favored the thrust of the speech, Dulles had major reservations. But Ike, I was told later, wanted to make the speech to establish who was in charge. And Dulles had to go along. Naturally, it troubled Dulles, made him feel uncomfortable and wondering at times about the good sense of Eisenhower's judgment.

The two outstanding men of the Eisenhower administration were the Dulles brothers. It was then unique to have two brothers, very different in character, in such influential positions as secretary of state and director of the Central Intelligence Agency. In addition, the brothers' grandfather and uncle had been secretary of state. John Foster accumulated a substantial reputation as a foreign policy expert and as a corporation lawyer, and, reflecting the power of a president who rarely disagreed with him publicly, he became a towering figure on the foreign affairs horizon. Eager to prove his individuality, he made it clear in his first foreign policy pronouncements that rather than continuity, he would stress the differences from the Truman policies. He gave them a belligerent, nationalistic tone, with a new emphasis on American interests in Asia. There was the announcement of new military pressures at all sensitive points in the Far East—Korea, Formosa, Indochina. There was the threat of the "agonizing reappraisal" if the French government did not ratify the European Defense Community. There was the rollback of the Iron Curtain in Eastern Europe—an embarrassment when the Hungarians in revolt asked for American help. There was the new military strategy of "massive retaliation" that was to allow the United States to withdraw its troops from abroad and to contribute only air and sea power to the defense of Europe—this smacked of a new isolationism, and French Foreign Minister Georges Bidault characterized it as a policy of "Americans flying and Frenchmen dying." These were all memorable phrases with a haunting afterlife. Especially the last one brought back to my mind a written exchange I had had with Eisenhower when he was president of Columbia University.

I had written questioning the meaning of a speech in which, it seemed to me, Eisenhower favored the withdrawal of American troops from abroad and the creation of a central reserve based in the United States. In reply I received a letter dated November 4, 1950, on stationery that was very English in style. In the center at the top was a small ring of five stars in red and beneath just the three initials D D E. "Dear Mr. Brandon" and "Sincerely" were written in longhand, the rest typewritten. In this one page, single-spaced reply, he argued that my reading of his speech would give his statement "a very restrictive meaning" and that he was "not laboring under the delusion that American forces are not needed in such a critical spot as the western area of Europe." He then added what seemed to be central to his thinking, that "no nation, however strong, can provide cordon defenses throughout the world. Any such attempt would tie down, irrevocably, all the available forces and make the entire structure a brittle defense that could be broken easily." In my view Eisenhower was stating the obvious and taking cover by a "worst case" prospect. Six weeks later President Truman named Eisenhower supreme commander of NATO, as good a choice as there was. In his new position, of course, he had to adhere to official policy. Acheson certainly would not have wanted him even to breathe about troop withdrawals or a central reserve: the entire buildup of American troops in Europe was to enable the West to negotiate with the Russians "from strength."

One of Eisenhower's early presidential achievements was that he brought the war in Korea to an end. What brought the Chinese to the conference table was not a specific threat Eisenhower conveyed via India or otherwise that he would use atomic weapons, if necessary, to finish the war, as has been generally said, but most probably nothing more than the lingering fear that he might. Nobody, not even the president, knew at the time that the United States had enough plutonium for only eight A-bombs, and that it would take several months to produce even those. General Chester "Ted" Clifton, then General Omar Bradley's public relations adviser, told me much later of Bradley's embarrassment and concern when he had to tell this to the president.

As soon as the Korean truce had been agreed on, Eisenhower asked the new Joint Chiefs of Staff to review overall American strategy. Admiral Arthur Radford, their chairman, later declared that military planning was to be given a "new look," whose object was to reduce the costly commitments of overseas garrisons inherent in the Acheson "situation of strength" policy, and to discourage future aggression by the threat of reprisals from a highly mobile striking force largely based in the United States, equipped with aircraft and atomic weapons. It was no other than the concept of the central reserve which Eisenhower had "fudged" in the letter to me. Actually Eisenhower was never able to put the new look fully into practice. Foreign affairs experts, according to General Goodpaster, talked him out of it with the help of the continuing Soviet threat.

John Foster Dulles's verbal militancy—he critized "the foot-dragging" of the Europeans, he boasted to a group of diplomatic correspondents that the United States' power advantage would be greatest in the next two years, and he made it clear publicly and privately that this was a time when the United States could take risks—gave an added chill to the cold war.

Unsurprisingly, none of this augured well for Dulles's first visit to London in October 1953. Britain's ambassador in Washington, Sir Roger Makins, therefore sent a "priority confidential" telegram to London, telling the Foreign Office that he hoped it would be possible to make Mr. Dulles feel that he really was welcome. "I do not mean officially of course," he wrote, "but through the handling of the press and radio. I have indisputable evidence, apart from my own conviction, that Mr. Dulles is sincerely trying to make cooperation with us the keystone of his policy." Sir Roger went on to offer an apologia for the Dulles lip, in sterling diplomatic style: "Mr. Dulles is handicapped by his poor performance in public relations, on which he is badly advised by his old friend Mr. McCardle. He is unpopular with the press, who never gave him a chance or seem to understand the immense political difficulties in which he has to operate. But I am sure that he is sincerely and patiently working on a settlement both in the Far East and Europe and that his objectives are the same as your own, even if he has sometimes to take rather labyrinthine roads towards them. I know he feels very keenly the constant attacks which are made on him from British sources and anything that can be done to make him feel at home would be helpful."

The head of the News Department of the Foreign Office, a diminutive, foxy old hand in press relations, William Ridsdale, replied that "unfortunately Mr. Dulles is a much maligned character, due largely, as we all know, to his clumsy public performances particularly where press correspondents are concerned. It is uphill work in the face of these to persuade correspondents that Mr. Dulles is sweetly reasonable when he is talking privately . . ." The telegram ended with Ridsdale saying that "it is doubtful that eulogies in the British press would do Mr. Dulles much good with many of the more recalcitrant Republican senators . . ." This reply, though, was relatively more forthcoming than an earlier one to a somewhat similar plea by Sir Roger. The influential columnist Joseph Alsop had proposed to him that the *Times* of London should be induced to publish an editorial welcoming Mr. Dulles's appointment as secretary of state. "News Department have done their best," the reply ran, "and the suggestion has been carried to the top, but *The Times* are unwilling to comply. They say they honestly don't share the view that Mr. Dulles' appointment is a good thing, and they do not wish to tie their hands by giving him an endorsement at this stage. They are however quite willing not to be beastly about him." In a short footnote the undersecretary added: "I can't help sharing the view of *The Times.*" So much for the efforts of the Foreign Office to influence the British press, and so much for Mr. Dulles's standing with both.

Dulles, as secretary of state, was a different man from his former self as a Republican adviser to the Truman administration. He now saw himself as the great foreign policy maker of the West, and in private conversation tried to impress on me that it was he and not the president who made foreign policy. It was also his habit to imply offhandedly in such situations that he was telling me something he had not told anybody else, even if this was not so. He was convinced that he knew how to manipulate the press and once, as the defeat of the French at Dien Bien Phu began to look almost inevitable, used me to influence the British government's policy. On Thursday, April 8, 1954, I got a phone call from Mr. Dulles's office to come and see him the next morning at eleven; he was scheduled to leave for London the next day, Saturday. My story was to be published on Sunday. He had a slight tic in his face, as he usually did, when he spoke about a delicate problem. He repeated to me first what he had said already publicly, that he would consult with the British and French about creating a "united front" to resist Communist aggression in Southeast Asia. But then he told me that the United States was prepared to intervene with air and naval power to save Dien Bien Phu if necessary and that in case of open Chinese military intervention it would broaden the intervention beyond Indochina against Communist China. The use of nuclear weapons, he said, was not excluded. It was quite obvious to me that he wanted to use *The Sunday Times* to put public pressure on the British government to reinforce his private pressures. It was also clear to me that Foster had handed me quite a sensational and exclusive story. Naturally, I reported what I had been told, attributing it to "the highest authority," but also convinced that the secretary was indulging in a favorite pastime, brinkmanship. I therefore sent a service message to the editor not to lead the front page with my story. It was the only time that I downplayed one of my own stories. According to the seventeen-volume official history of the Vietnam war, Admiral Radford, the chairman of the Joint Chiefs of Staff, who generally favored the use of nuclear weapons, argued in the Dien Bien Phu case that such an intervention would be "altogether disproportionate to the liability it would incur." But there is also evidence that he approved a carrier-based air strike to aid the French garrison at Dien Bien Phu and that it was Eisenhower who insisted on needing congressional approval for such an intervention, knowing full well that such approval was out of the question. Mr. Dulles soon found out that the British reaction was very similar to that of the congressional leaders—cagey. One's own instincts in those days were a better guide to policy than high-level leaks.

Allen Dulles was a quite different person. He did not have the intellectual force and assertive personality of Foster or even of their redoubtable sister, Eleanor, who once at a birthday party at her house got on the table and danced for the guests. Allen was not quite as freewheeling but he was much more relaxed and at ease with himself than Foster. From the soft manner of speech, his avuncular, professional manner, his old-fashioned courtesy, one would never have guessed that this man was the American master spy. These attributes were misleading. They cloaked a toughness of spirit, a shrewdness and guile which his steady piercing gaze through his rimless spectacles ultimately betrayed. He was obsessed by the spy business and much less interested in analytical intelligence. And he was more open-minded than his brother, much less the austere Presbyterian. He had a sense of humor, enjoyed telling stories, and was a strong Anglophile, which could not be said about Foster. Nor did he share Foster's prejudices against neutralism, especially Indian neutralism, his anticolonialism, or his early idealistic beliefs in the UN's becoming the world's "town meeting." Allen, slumped in his armchair, chin on chest and his long legs stretched out, had the air of a practiced listener, and with good cause. He could never forgive himself for having refused to see a man whom another member of the American Embassy in Bern described as "bearded fellow whose name was Lenin . . . he got some theory." But Dulles was all set for his morning tennis game and sent him a message that he was too busy to see him. That was three days before that bearded fellow left in a sealed car for Russia. He admitted that because of this experience he had listened to many more crackpots than he cared to remember.

Winston Churchill's dream, and his solution to many of the world's problems, was the creation of the closest possible link between Britain, the Commonwealth, and the United States. He wanted to forge bonds that were so interlinked that even in adversity they could not be broken. He did not succeed either with Truman, when he tried the idea first on him in Potsdam, or with Eisenhower. Misled perhaps by his wartime experiences, he misjudged American presidential thinking: in peacetime presidents must become more conscious of the fact that they preside over a vast pluralistic society, one difficult to govern, and not just over the eastern seaboard. After the war both Truman and Eisenhower felt forced to view American interests in a much wider focus than the Anglo-American relationship.

The most important component of the original Anglo-American intelligence relationship, authorized informally by Churchill and Roosevelt, was that between the US National Security Agency and the Government Communications Headquarters (GCHQ) operation in England at Bletchley Park in Buckinghamshire. For a while, Americans in the know told me, the British were slow to cooperate because they wanted to see whether the Americans could keep secrets. After the war the NSA-GCHQ relationship was formalized, and a brief, general agreement signed in black and white; it was twice revised at the time and never needed to be revised again. Here, perhaps, Churchill's wishes came true: this relationship continues to exist, and, in fact, in some exceptional cases British officials even became section or branch chiefs in the NSA's offices in Washington, something few are aware of. Sometimes, too, as a well-informed American put it, the British have skills that "are more finely honed than ours. We particularly appreciate certain of their special qualities: they are better in retrospective analysis—they have a historic perspective which they add to their perceptions which we do not have. Second, they have a grasp of the English language and a sense of logic which we do not have. Third, they have more experience because they were more active than we before World War II when the UK effort was much broader than ours. Fourth, they are better than we are in summarizing a situation and that is why we sometimes ask them to do it. But when it comes to the design and development of modern equipment, we are better, for our education puts greater emphasis on it than the British."

The NSA-GCHQ intelligence relationship was never seriously questioned and has rarely been written about. NSA controls an enormously costly satellite system the British on their own could not afford, but, as one former NSA employee put it: "The British put in stuff which we would not have been able to get otherwise. The whole is greater than its parts. There were of course Anglophobes in the organization who were and are against this collaboration, but the majority believes that it is to our advantage. That is why it has survived all administrations and all British governments irrespective of their politics. It has of course helped that NSA and GCHQ have remained above politics and independent of political hazing."

The Anglo-American intelligence relationship came under strain however after Kim Philby, Donald Maclean, and Guy Burgess, all of whom had been assigned to the British Embassy in Washington in the late forties and early fifties, came gradually under suspicion of being Soviet spies. Of the three I knew only Burgess from the days when he was an aide to Minister of State Hector McNeil. He was posted to Washington in October 1950 and shortly after his arrival in Washington I drove into the British Embassy courtyard. As I parked my car I recognized Burgess sitting in a huge twelve-cylinder Lincoln convertible. Surprised at seeing him here and knowing what an unstable character he was, I could not help exclaiming with obvious disapproval in my voice: "Guy, who on earth sent you to Washington?" Burgess, not quite sure whether to be flattered or offended by my incredulity, replied that he had just joined the embassy staff as a second secretary concerned with Far Eastern Affairs. When I inquired in the embassy whose idea it had been to send Burgess over, I got nothing but expressions of despair and annoyance with those in charge in London, since his antics and excesses and weaknesses were known to everybody. Burgess had never disguised his drinking habits, his homosexuality, or his eccentricities; he was proud of them. Guy Francis de Moncy Burgess, as flamboyant a name as he was, made common cause with Donald Maclean and Kim Philby as an undergraduate at Cambridge. Their allegiance to the Communist Party was an open secret. They combined an outrageous joie de vivre with their radical objective of revolutionizing British society with the help of Marxist teaching. What was not known was that they had become tools of the Comintern as early as 1933 and that they had become active spies for the Soviet Union. In Washington I did my best to ignore Burgess, though inevitably I ran into him here and there in the corridors of the British Embassy or at private dinner parties.

To invite Burgess to a party entailed risks that he would embarrass his host or insult a guest, but he could also be the life of a party. His dark suits were always unpressed, covered with ash from cigarettes—he was a chain-smoker—his shirt cuffs and collar were frayed, his face flushed, his fingers tobacco stained. But people forgave him for his scruffiness because he was oh, so

British, and full of good provocative stories. After he had been in Washington for about three months, I got a letter from Hector saying that Guy was feeling "lonely" there and could I ask him to some parties of mine? So, to please Hector, I asked Burgess for drinks to my apartment and to one or two dinner parties. He was always surprisingly civil. Several times on leaving my apartment he said to me in a quasi-confidential tone of voice that he was going to spend the evening with Sumner Welles, a very rich man who used to be undersecretary of state under Cordell Hull and a traveling "presidential agent" in the Upton Sinclair fashion for President Roosevelt. With a twinkle he suggested that he was a fine man to have an affair with. Since Burgess was a congenital name-dropper, I did not pay any attention to this; I only remember that he claimed that Hector's last bit of advice to him on leaving London was: "For God's sake, Guy, don't flirt with Paul Robeson!" Welles, at any rate, was a highly respected personality who lived withdrawn, shying away from any publicity.

Burgess was outspokenly anti-American, considered the American intervention in Korea a "scandal," and viciously attacked Truman for "dragging the world into a third world war." He hated the ambassador, Sir Oliver Franks, who gradually demoted him from one job to another until he was left with administering the George Marshall scholarships. His great passion was the Lincoln convertible, which he had bought secondhand and which he drove every weekend into the Virginia countryside at such pace that his accumulation of speeding tickets became intolerable to the embassy. Whether his blunt and outspoken anti-Americanism and his ostentatious efforts to break the driving laws were designed to get him out of the country which he obviously loathed or whether it was simply part of his normal perverted sense of fun, I don't know, but he often said how much he longed to be back in London.

Though by 1951 Philby and Burgess had come under loose American surveillance, British counterintelligence was extraordinarily slow doing at least the same. James Jesus Angleton, the CIA's crafty American head of counterespionage, put pressure on the British to withdraw Philby, who had been fingered by a Russian double agent as a Soviet spy. Although Maclean and Burgess frequently traveled to New York to deliver their stolen wares to their Soviet handlers and the code-breakers had established that highly sensitive top secret documents were being transmitted from there to Moscow, neither the British security people nor the FBI discovered the reasons for these sinister excursions. But the evidence that Maclean and Burgess worked for Soviet intelligence began to accumulate until the two sensed that they were in danger of being exposed and left in the dead of night for the Continent. Whether Burgess had been ordered by Philby to rescue Maclean and himself or whether he was under orders to make sure that Maclean would not have second thoughts about his escape and refuse to go to the Soviet Union is uncertain. In any case, he decided to rescue himself as well. The scandal not only shook the British government, but it also had a devastating effect on the Anglo-American intelligence relationship. Above all, it heightened bitterness and suspicion among various individuals who resented the casual manner with which the British went about cleaning their Augean intelligence stables, especially after the defection by Philby, who by then had taken refuge in the Middle East on assignment by the *Sunday Observer* of London. Overall, though, the usefulness of British intelligence assets asserted itself again and much of the former cooperation was gradually restored.

One reason for my relatively easy access to Allen Dulles was that we had met several times at the Walter Lippmann's, another that he was an avid reader of James Bond thrillers. Intrigued by Ian Fleming, the creator of James Bond, he could not hear enough about my boss's idiosyncrasies and his life-style. When I finally persuaded Fleming to swallow his raging prejudice against Washington and to come for a visit by promising to bring him and Allen Dulles together, that very weekend Dulles happened to be out of town. Ian therefore had to content himself with seeing at dinner an old friend of his, one of the most attractive and amusing among Washington blue bloods, Oatsie Leiter, whose husband figured in at least one of Fleming's books, along with Senator John F. Kennedy, Joseph Alsop, and CIA Division Chief (covert) John Bross. Asked over brandy what Bond would do to get rid of Castro, Fleming's sense of vivid fantasy sparkled, producing such ideas as using itching powder that would force Castroites to shave their beards and thus lose the symbol of their virility, dropping faked dollar notes from the air to destabilize the economic situation in Cuba, and several others. I was surprised when Allen Dulles—a man who had made his reputation in intelligence when in 1944, as an operator for OSS, he got advance notice of the July 20 plot against Hitler— called me the following Monday wanting to know where he could reach Fleming. He had heard that Ian had developed some "interesting ideas of how to deal with Castro," and wanted to hear them from Fleming personally. But by then Fleming had left town. He would have had a good, if contemptuous, laugh, had he been still alive to read about the CIA's plan in 1960 to "destroy Castro's image as 'The Beard' " by dusting his shoes with a strong depilatory that would cause his beard to fall out. It was to have been administered during a trip to Chile when Castro would leave his shoes outside the door of his hotel room to be shined. But the scheme was never carried out because Castro canceled his trip, according to a report of the Select Senate Committee on *Alleged Assassination Plots Involving Foreign Leaders,* published in 1975.

Allen Dulles enjoyed an extraordinary amount of freedom from presidential supervision, much more than his brother, for whenever Foster came close to translating his pretensions to brinkmanship from words to actions, he was stopped short by Eisenhower. Allen most probably enjoyed such a free hand because of the successes he had scored: the overthrow of Iran's tiresome Prime Minister Mossadegh, the ouster of the Communist government of President Arbenz in Guatemala, the development of the U-2 spy plane, and landing the most valuable Soviet spy ever caught. Actually Penkovsky first approached the

British and, when they hesitated, then the Americans, to offer his services. It was such a major operation that handling him became a joint American-British transaction, with the British bringing businessman Greville Wynne as Penkovsky's contact in Moscow. Incidentally, according to Richard Helms the story told in considerable detail by Greville Wynne in his book *The Man from Odessa*—and adopted in *The Agency* by John Ranelagh—that Penkovsky was flown specially to Washington to meet President Kennedy was a total fabrication on Wynne's part.

Dulles's skein of triumphs unraveled at the Bay of Pigs in 1961, when a poorly planned invasion of Cuba by an inadequately supported group of anti-Castro Cubans ended in a shattering debacle. Other, lesser operations in Indonesia, Cambodia, and Laos also misfired. The organization clearly suffered from flaws on the covert operational side, but its overuse as an instrument of foreign policy in the aftermath of the Korean War and the new emphasis by President Eisenhower on reductions of defense expenditures piled too many responsibilities on the CIA. Its various setbacks had broken the derring-do spirit that had inspired the "Clandestine Service," its bureaucracy had lost some of its independence, and Congress insisted on exercising stricter controls.

Among CIA professionals I got to know Richard Helms best. We lunched together from time to time at the old Occidental Restaurant, whose walls used to be covered with the signed photographs of famous visitors from presidents to members of Congress to such ancient film stars as Tom Mix. Helms was always punctual to the minute, always sat with his back to everybody else, and was never accompanied by a security officer. It would draw the kind of attention to him, he explained, he wanted to avoid and thus make life unsafe. I valued his interpretations of the world scene, especially his assessments of Soviet intentions and capabilities. He was a sober, rational, down-to-earth kind of man, an experienced professional who did not shirk whatever instructions he was given. His aim was to prove that the CIA was a "can-do" organization. He started his career as a reporter for United Press, which must have contributed to his understanding of what newsmen needed for analytical reporting. If it helped at the same time to improve their views of the CIA and aid the understanding of its role in the interest of national security, all the better.

Helms, in looks, reminded me of George Sanders, with his charm overlaying a toughness that a lifetime in the CIA breeds. He was not a man who wanted to create mysteries about CIA activities or deny that there was a dirty side to CIA's activities, but he insisted that it had not engaged in activities for which it did not have the green light from higher authority.

Among the CIA's achievements that he could discuss, he was proudest of the spotting of the Russian missiles after President Kennedy, very reluctantly, authorized a U-2 flight over Cuba (many Soviet experts had insisted that the Russians would never risk such a venture so close to the American mainland). The aerial photographs not only confirmed the presence of those missiles, they also showed the presence of a soccer field which gave the clue to the Russian technicians' nationality. Later flights enabled the military experts to determine exactly how long it would take these Russians to finish the missile sites, so that the president knew how much time he had to force Khrushchev to withdraw the missiles. Another little invisible ribbon he wore in his buttonhole was the CIA's estimate that, first, Israel did not need American help (as it claimed) to defeat the Egyptians in 1967 but could secure victory with its own means and, second, that if attacked it could win within two weeks at the most. The conflict, when it came, went down in history as the Six-Day War. What worried Helms at the time, though, was how badly Russian intelligence had miscalculated in assessing Egyptian military capabilities. The best explanation as to why Moscow gave the Egyptians the go-ahead, for they could not have moved without Soviet approval, was that Russian intelligence simply believed what the Egyptian generals told them about their own and allied armies. "Never trust generals," Helms added without sarcasm, "they tend not to have a perspective." It was his experience that whenever he carried bad tidings to President Johnson, it upset his personal relations with him and made it difficult to communicate with him. When he, for instance, had to tell Johnson some bad news or report on differences with the military about Vietnam, Johnson asked him: "Are you guys on the team?" Or, when LBJ, after the overthrow of Khrushchev, challenged Richard Helms on why he had failed to predict such an important event, Helms had a quick answer: "Not even Khrushchev knew in advance what was going to happen to him, Mr. President."

Of all my meetings with Helms one stands out in my memory because I only later realized the full significance of what he told me, as, by the way, did he. It was a lovely, sunny Sunday morning—June 18, 1972; my wife and I had been invited to play tennis with Helms and his wife, Cynthia, and afterwards stay for lunch. During lunch he told us, obviously still puzzled, that he had had a strange telephone call the night before from the CIA's chief security officer, Howard Osborn; Osborn informed him that a former CIA operative, James McCord, had been arrested with four other men after they had been caught red-handed installing wiretaps on the telephones at the headquarters of the Democratic National Committee in the Watergate block. He was also told that another CIA veteran, E. Howard Hunt, was an accomplice in the burglary.

Helms was clearly annoyed that some old CIA men got themselves in-volved in such a "caper," as he called it, that no one had asked him about employing these two men, and he wondered aloud what it all meant, what it signified for the CIA, and how to handle the situation. His inclination was to ridicule the situation, but at the same time he also wondered whether there was not a rat buried somewhere. In the following days he realized, as the story unfolded, that someone was trying to use the CIA as a convenient cover—what a paradox—and that he had to do all he could to distance the CIA from what came to be known as Watergate. He kept his struggle to protect the Agency against all insinuation by the White House under wraps to avoid an open clash, pretending that business-as-usual prevailed. He was later taken to task for not having come forward with a full account of what the White House tried to do to him and the Agency. For refusing to provide the cover they had originally demanded, President Nixon and his entourage never forgave him. In November 1972 Nixon asked Helms to come to Camp David and in the course of the conversation said that he wanted "new blood" in the CIA, that he wished to replace Helms and offer him the ambassadorship to the Soviet Union. Helms replied, as he remembers it, that he did not want to become an ambassador and that anyway to go to the Soviet Union would not be proper. Nixon, ignoring his lack of interest in an ambassadorship, pressed on, asking him what country he would like to be an ambassador to if he were to change his mind. Helms then said he would opt for Iran.

The issue of the sanctity of CIA secrets came to a head during Helms's confirmation hearings for the ambassadorship. When asked about the CIA's role in Chile, Helms testified that the CIA had not tried to overthrow the Chilean government and had not given money directly to opposition leaders and so on . . . but he obviously held to such a thin line between truth and lie in order to live up to his oath as CIA director to protect the secrets that he was ultimately accused of perjury. Should he be indicted? The question exploded into a passionate debate within the administration and in public among those who defended Helms for putting the security interests of the nation first; those, like Senator Frank Church, who argued: "I thought there was to be an end to the double standard of justice for the big shots"; and those, like Senator Joseph Biden, who feared an arrangement that avoided a criminal trial could set a precedent for making intelligence officials immune to accountability before Congress or the courts.

Over lunch in September 1977, when the possible indictment for perjury was hanging over his head, Helms was boiling mad about being treated as if he had committed a crime when all he was doing was protecting the national interest. I had never seen him so convulsed with anger. How could he be true to two oaths, one to his office and the other to Congress, when it came to divulging highly sensitive information? If it came to a trial, he would have to reveal things that would be highly embarrassing to the government, because he would explain how various presidents had instructed him and how things are stacked. What troubled him most was that former colleagues of his would be called to testify, which would be bad for the morale of the Agency. All his commitments to the government would suddenly be suspended and he would feel free to tell all. Then with an ominous undertone he added: "That will be quite a staggering event." He went on to say that the decision was up to President Carter, but, unfortunately, he and those around him did not really know what was involved in their decision and what it could bring on. He concluded by saying that his defense would be based on the conflicting oaths, on the duplicity of standards, and on how today's yardstick cannot be applied to past decisions taken under different circumstances. It was quite a mouthful, but it was not surprising that a public servant whose loyalty and integrity were being questioned under highly dubious circumstances was bitter and utterly disillusioned.

In the end President Carter authorized Attorney General Griffin Bell to propose a deal to Helms under which he could plead *nolo contendere* to two misdemeanor counts, with the promise that he would be given neither jail nor a fine. However Judge Barrington D. Parker did impose two years in jail and a $2,000 fine, both suspended, to make it clear that intelligence officials have no license to operate freely outside the dictates of the law. Both the *New York Times* and the Washington *Post* gave editorial support to what they saw as a difficult judicial decision. Public officials, however loyal and meritorious, are often treated with bland disregard for their contributions to the national interest in the United States, and that applies to the courts, to Congress, and to the news media.

I mentioned at the outset my critical view of Eisenhower's failure to deal with Joe McCarthy. The Dulles brothers, pillars of the Eastern Establishment, their anticommunism unassailable, were no help: both acted as if they were in awe and fear of the senator. I had assumed that the president, after his impressive electoral victory, would use the new power the nation had conferred on him and his old standing as a man of integrity to rid the nation of this scourge, who in the final Truman days had built himself up into a real threat to the American system of government. But Ike dismayed many Americans, people abroad, and certainly me by letting the witch-hunting senator continue his wild accusations against totally innocent people in the State Department, the Pentagon, CIA, wherever he could trump up a charge. John Foster Dulles, from the first day as secretary of state, by demanding "positive loyalty" from his staff—which the members of the foreign service considered an insult—signaled that he was making a bow to McCarthy. He made an even deeper one by appointing Scott McLeod as his controller of security. Apart from his carefree character assassinations, McCarthy showed the world how easy it is to pervert the investigative powers of Congress. Under the American Constitution "all legislative power" is vested in the Congress. From this it was always assumed that the Congress had the right to inquire into the administration of existing laws and the need for new laws. By exploiting these assumed rights as giving unlimited scope for investigation, however remote the legislative connection, McCarthy went farther than anybody had done before him. His maniacal crusade satisfied the long-standing yearnings of the most extreme Republican right for an onslaught against the old-established liberalism—Democratic and Republican—of freedom and diversity, an attack against the influence of intellectuals on American society.

I will never forget how utterly shaken Mary Bundy looked when one mid-July evening in 1953 I arrived at her house for dinner and she apologized for Bill's absence. He had had to go out of town suddenly, on instructions from

Allen Dulles, to prevent having a subpoena by McCarthy served on him. Bill Bundy must have looked to McCarthy a perfect target: contributor of $400 to the Alger Hiss defense fund, Dean Acheson's son-in-law, a Democrat, and an obvious member of the Eastern Establishment. I was shocked that even an Allen Dulles—Bill then worked in the intelligence assessment branch of CIA —would blink in this situation. The same shocked astonishment was expressed that same evening at the house of Frank Wisner, who was in charge of CIA's covert operations. The bitterness, however, dissipated when it became known that Allen had not exactly knuckled down to McCarthy but was trying to gain time to mobilize the help of Attorney General Herbert Brownell and Vice President Richard Nixon, both friends of McCarthy, to prevent, in a noncon-frontational manner, an attack on CIA. Dulles succeeded, and kept Bundy in his job while he was investigated.

It took a year to clear Bundy, a paragon of integrity, loyalty, and devotion to public service. Sharing the shock the family suffered, seeing the finest among Americans humiliated by the sensation-seeking senator, their self-respect shaken, their faith in justice undermined, was an experience no one can appreciate who has not lived through it. McCarthyism had some similarities with the waves of persecution that despoiled European history. McCarthy could not send people to the gas chamber, but he destroyed many of those at whom he hurled the thunderbolts of his trumped-up charges. So jittery was Washington that it was considered something of a heroic act when the Wisners had Chip Bohlen or Charles Thayer, both outstanding foreign service officers, staying with them while they were under attack by McCarthy, or when Paul Nitze helped John Paton Davies, another fine member of the foreign service, to start a new career in Peru after he was forced to resign under pressure from John Foster Dulles. That McCarthy succeeded in staying on the rampage for almost four years must be blamed in great measure also on the naiveté, poor judgment, and headline journalism of the news media which, in the honorable but often mistaken tradition of keeping news and comment separate, for too long reported his allegations as straight news just as if this faker had offered convincing proof for his claims. If the news media from the beginning had put emphasis on the fact that his allegations lacked factual proof, he probably would not have gained his momentum. If they had followed that other honored journalistic course, independent investigation, and exposed the McCarthy methods, it too would have helped to defuse him. It was not until Ed Murrow summoned enough courage and elicited enough support from his bosses to take the lead, and the Scripps-Howard newspapers ran a courageous exposé, that the tide turned.

McCarthy had started by attacking the State Department, then tried to investigate the CIA and, finally, the Army. But in taking on the Army he came up against Joseph Welch, the shrewd Army counsel who exuded the best of the traditional American values and on top of that was a clever lawyer who exposed McCarthy's weaknesses effectively with remarkable patience, sense of humor, and common sense. He also won the support of President Eisenhower, who, by denying the Committee access to people and records, contributed to the hearings' fizzling out.

It was during the Army-McCarthy hearings, which were carried live on television, that I managed to get an interview with the country's then richest oil man, H. L. Hunt of Dallas, Texas, who normally refused to see the press. My talk with him gave me an idea of the mind-set of an ardent McCarthy enthusiast. Before I was allowed to see him, one of his directors took me to a sumptuous lunch at the Petroleum Club. I soon realized that his mission was to determine my politics and therefore switched our conversation to depletion allowances and other technical small talk of the oil world. When I was finally taken into Hunt's inner sanctum, he got up to greet me from a chair in front of his television set. He had been watching the hearings and, full of hate, said: "They are trying to destroy McCarthy. But they won't!" He then went back to his desk and sat down behind it. He wore a white smock and with his thick nose, tiny, piggish eyes, and bald head needed only a gray top hat to be taken for W. C. Fields. But that was where the comparison stopped, for this rough-hewn oil prospector had no sense of humor, took himself very seriously, and felt obviously uncomfortable in my presence since, presumably to relieve his tension, he began our conversation with a dirty story. Next he told me how during and after World War II he sent one of his directors several times to England to persuade two English spinsters who owned some land bordering on his ranch in West Texas to sell it to him. They refused each time, contending that the money would go into taxes. In 1948 they finally accepted his offer, which by then had tripled to $200,000. When I asked him whether he had found oil on their land, which I presumed was the reason for his wanting to acquire it, he replied that he did drill nine holes, but they came up all dry, or as the experts say, "dusters." Not accustomed to the ways of an oil wildcatter's thinking, I said that he could have saved himself a lot of money had he left the spinsters alone. To which he replied: "But imagine how much money we would have made if we had found oil!"

Then he shifted the conversation to politics by attacking me for the British government's recognition of Communist China and the carrying of goods there in British ships. He said he had agreed to see me only to warn me that the West was in imminent danger of being conquered or taken over by the Communists. When I said that I had confidence in the military leadership under Admiral Radford, Hunt replied: "I wouldn't trust him too far!" I then expressed my faith in President Eisenhower's leadership; he mumbled: "What, that Communist!" At that point I lost my patience and said: "Mr. Hunt, I have more confidence in the American Constitution and the good sense of the president than you have!" He looked at me, his little eyes getting littler and full of hate, then grabbed all the papers he had on his desk and, holding them high, walked out of his office, leaving me alone with his embarrassed director, who had given me lunch. I felt sorry for this man, but he, most apologetically, accompanied me to the elevators, shaking his head and saying: "This has never happened before."

In January 1954 I wrote in my diary: "There is a strange gulf between the men of the Eisenhower administration and the country. This is a managerial government which allows little room for human factors. Economics are dominating their thinking, actions are carefully charted by publicity consultants, and too many agencies are coming under the direct control of big business, which in the end may not be good for capitalism. While the British still view their relationship with the United States as a continuation of the wartime relationship, American policymakers see Britain as a spent force, desperately hanging onto the idea of being a great power. Meanwhile the alliance is languishing. The State Department is paralyzed, intimidated by Senator McCarthy, avoiding initiatives that could be twisted into accusing the State Department of appeasing communism." But Eisenhower had a point when, according to his biographer Stephen Ambrose, he complained: "We have here a figure who owes his entire prominence and influence in today's life to the publicity media of the nation and now these same media are looking around for someone to knock off the creature of their own making." Some credit, though, must go to the senator's own Goebbelsian sense of propaganda, some to the unpopularity of the State Department, an institution often considered to be looking after foreign rather than American interests, and some to McCarthy's sense of theater. He spoke with the slow voice of the prophet, full of weighty foreboding, the man who carried all the responsibility for the security of the United States on his own shoulders, the lonely patriot trying to stem a tide.

A Republican was the first to dare rise on the Senate floor to give McCarthy the coup de grâce—although it was not grace that he deserved. But only after the Democrats had won a majority in the Senate in the 1954 elections did the opposition forces gather enough strength. I remember sitting in the press gallery when the gray-haired and dark-suited Senator Ralph E. Flanders of Vermont, embodying the name of the "granite state," rose on the Senate floor, his ascetic face exuding dignity and uprightness and his hand playing calmly with the golden chain across his vest. It was a moment full of suspense and quiet drama. The parliamentary instrument Flanders used for his coup was a resolution censuring McCarthy for abusing members of the election subcommittee investigating his finances. It was the kind of accusation on senatorial home ground that senators could rally to without getting involved in the political arguments McCarthy had been so skillful in fending off. Still, it needed courage to give the signal for the attack. Two equally courageous senators came to Flanders' support, J. William Fulbright of Arkansas and Wayne Morse of Oregon. But it needed the help of conservative Democrats to pass the resolution of condemnation—a weaker word than censure. The historic date was December 2, 1954. Like gangster Al Capone, McCarthy was not sentenced for his real crimes.

One night at dinner in July 1965, Ed Williams, who had been McCarthy's defense counsel, told a remarkable story I have never seen in print. Eight months before McCarthy died he had been persuaded by his notorious so-called gumshoe, Roy Cohn, to invest in a mining stock that was selling at one dollar. As soon as the rumor spread around Wall Street that McCarthy was playing this flyer, it was assumed that he had had a hot tip from some oil man and the stock quickly rose to fourteen dollars. At that point McCarthy went with Jean, his wife, on a holiday, promising to give up drinking. When he returned to Washington a few days later, the stock had dropped to two dollars. McCarthy, according to Williams, tried to call Roy Cohn, but he never came to the telephone. Cohn meanwhile had made about half a million dollars by selling the stock at the right time. McCarthy after that went back to drink and two months later was dead, dissipated by alcohol and psychologically devastated by having become a has-been. His crusade, of course, had been more than a personal affair. He succeeded so demonically well and kept himself in the headlines for such a relatively long period because he touched a sensitive nerve in many Americans—their fear of communism. It is a nerve that can, at the right time, be exploited by clever demagogues and for that reason remains a latent threat to the balance of the American cast of mind. Fortunately there are usually strong enough countervailing forces that gradually assert themselves in a country that is essentially centrist in outlook. Extreme deviations from American centrism (which is, however paradoxical it may sound, movable), such as McCarthyism, do not lead to specific organizational forms.

McCarthy, like a comet, streaked across the American horizon, lighting up dark corners of suspicion in many Americans. They easily believed clandestine cells were secretly manipulating the country, that the New Deal was too sympathetic to communism and the Soviet Union, and that European socialism was only some sort of euphemism for communism. I remember how virtually every member of the British Labour Party who visited this country, when interviewed over television, was asked whether there was a difference between socialism and communism. Hugh Gaitskell, the party leader, for instance, was appalled at how little Americans knew about the origins and the conflicts of the two doctrines, at what political ignorance this question reflected.

Americans have used violence to subdue those unwilling or unable to blend into a consensus society. They used it against Indians, blacks, and trade unions, and of course to subdue the South. Now and then Americans get frustrated by the limited political choice they have under the American party system, the limited nature of their political options, and either the Republican right or the Democratic left tries to break through the constraints. McCarthy used star-chamber methods in an attempt to capture the Republican Party. In

Europe he would have tried to start a new opposition party—which, of course, can grow into a threat to the entire nation, as did Nazism and Fascism.

McCarthyism, for all its assault on communism, did not prevent a thaw on the cold war fronts. With Stalin's death and the Malenkov peace feelers, followed up by the signing of the peace treaty for Austria, one could almost hear the ice breaking. It looked as if a new chapter in world diplomatic history had begun. There was a new recognition in Washington that the Communist regime in China was firmly established and that the vacillation by the Eisenhower administration between preventive war against China and coexistence with it had come to an end. The Geneva summit meeting by the Big Four in July 1955, at least superficially, contributed to an improved climate.

Eisenhower and Dulles approached the conference as a cautious prospector approaches an area rumored to bear oil, determined to take time and care to test the quality and consistency of the oil. But the probes did not produce a gusher. "It's poetry which counts at this conference, not policy," a French diplomat said to me at the end; what mattered were soft words and good-humored relations, not the great issues which divided the world. Nobody really assumed that a four-power agreement for the unification of Germany was a real possibility. But Adlai Stevenson, once again seeking the Democratic nomination against Eisenhower, blamed his administration for having misled the American people about the so-called Spirit of Geneva. Stevenson still could inspire and excite people, with his words and his vision and civility. But he was also up against the fact that 1955 had been one of the most prosperous years in American history. The only question mark on the horizon was whether Eisenhower's health, after a heart attack, would permit him to run again.

The year 1955 was also when I got to know one of the most charming, most polite, most modest men I have ever met. In his lowly station he exercised no power whatsoever, the greatest failing known to Washingtonians, but nevertheless a man I will always remember. Charlie Brown was in his early eighties when I first encountered him. By then he had been for sixty-eight years in His or Her Majesty's service as a valet, mail clerk, messenger, and man-of-all-work, and there was not a British visitor of note to the British Embassy to whom he had not been introduced. When he met the then Princess Elizabeth his usually imperturbable poise was shaken—so was that of the ambassador when Charlie, whose dark skin had a wonderful shine, in his dignified Victorian English said to him: "I don't think, sir, that the embassy has had such a splendid and distinguished gathering and given such pleasure to so many prominent people since the Infanta Eulalia and Prince Antoine of Spain were entertained by Lord Pauncefote upon Queen Victoria's birthday in May 1893."

Charlie had joined what was the British Legation at Connecticut Avenue and N Street, N.W.—in those days, a rather remote section of the city—under the reign of Queen Victoria. Horse cars, he told me, then ran on Connecticut

Avenue as far as Dupont Circle, at that date the city's boundary, where thickly wooded fields, rushing creeks, and precipitous ravines made for ideal hunting country.

On Sunday mornings some of the young, attractive attachés would drop in on the Russian Legation at Connecticut and K Street, where the energetic wife of the Russian minister liked to entertain for breakfast and fencing, a sport then in vogue. Charlie also remembered how, under Lord Pauncefote, the British caused a stir when they sent to the State Department the first typewritten diplomatic note and how on February 6, 1925, the British Embassy moved to Massachusetts Avenue and he climbed up on the steep roof of the new building to raise the Union Jack on the new mast. He had a law degree, presented to him by President McKinley, but he was so mesmerized by the international world that he decided to stay in the embassy's service for the rest of his life, which ended abruptly when at the age of eighty-eight he was hit by a taxi. At his funeral his coffin bore a special symbol of Britain. On one of Winston Churchill's visits, the prime minister had been presented by a group of admiring ladies with a hand-knitted Union Jack, which they had framed. The ladies never learned that Churchill on his departure omitted it from his baggage, and abandoned it to the care of the embassy. It was handed to Charlie, who treasured it so much that he asked in his will that it should accompany him to his grave; it was buried with him. I had spent many fascinating hours with him, listening to his life story and his description of the British ambassadors as he watched them from his lowly perspective. I could not get him to confess which one he admired most—they all did a fine job in his view; he was the diplomat par excellence. Like so many Washington figures, he, too, could not resist writing his memoirs, and when he could not find a publisher to print them, he had them published under his own imprint. He then wrote to every British diplomat who had ever served at the British Embassy in Washington and virtually all those still alive sent their five dollars to obtain a copy. One quote from his memoirs would have made the perfect epitaph for him: "I have had experiences and contacts that come only to a few. Kings and queens and prime ministers don't often come into people's lives. People love to read history, but few see it and live it at such close quarters as I did."

Today, it has become the raison d'être for most Washingtonians.

7

Eisenhower and a Turning Point in British History

IN THE first few months of 1955 President Eisenhower took an unusual number of historic decisions. He quietly abandoned the idea of seeking a nuclear-free world and replaced it with the more limited aim of promoting arms control agreements. He told a news conference that he would scale down the defense program to ensure a healthy American economy. He wondered how to prevent an arms race with the Soviet Union and gave serious thought to a four-power summit meeting if the Russians agreed to sign the Austrian State Treaty (which they did). John Foster Dulles was opposed to a summit, fearing that it would undermine the consolidation of NATO and arouse the ire of the Republican Old Guard. But he was more impressed by a plea from Anthony Eden, who had succeeded Churchill and was facing an election. Eden urged he needed a popular issue, such as a summit meeting, for the campaign, and since Ike was appalled by the thought he might have to deal with a Labour government if the Tories were defeated, it further reinforced his hankering for a meeting with the Russians. The Spirit of Geneva did not last very long. Whether its dissipation had anything to do with Eisenhower's heart attack, which left the conduct of foreign policy in Dulles's hands, is hard to know. A contributing factor certainly was Egypt's shift of its arms purchases from the United States to Czechoslovakia which could not have acted without Soviet approval.

The British considered the Suez Canal the military-strategic link to their interests east of Suez and the economic lifeline for Western Europe's oil supplies. To protect it, they maintained a military base and a garrison of 80,000 in the Canal Zone. In 1954 they agreed to withdraw those troops within twenty months (the last British soldiers left a month before Nasser seized the Canal) and readily agreed to join the Baghdad Pact, an idea Dulles had thought up as a barrier to communism. It was to include the United States, Britain, Egypt, Iraq, Turkey, and Pakistan. Then Dulles got cold feet, and Colonel Nasser refused to join so as to preserve a more neutral position between Washington and Moscow. Dulles, incensed by Nasser's shift and his joining what were then called the nonaligned nations, decided abruptly to cancel an earlier American promise to finance the construction of the Aswan dam. "Dulles' clumsy handling of the final stages of the cancellation played into Nasser's hands," as Harold Macmillan put it in his memoirs *Riding the Storm 1956–1959* (Harper & Row), and gave him an excuse to nationalize the Canal, which he did triumphantly in a boastful speech on July 26, 1956. The British could not put all the blame on Dulles, for they had advance knowledge of Dulles's decision, transmitted forty-eight hours earlier by the British ambassador, Sir Roger Makins, and did not object to it. By seizing also the international company administering the Canal, Nasser gained income which helped with the financing of the construction of the Aswan dam. Anthony Eden, determined to prevent the Egyptian leader, as he put it, from having "his thumb on our windpipe," vowed that he would use force as a last resort to teach Nasser a lesson.

On the weekend of July 27, with tension in the air, I risked leaving Washington well ahead of my deadline for filing to London and flew with Senator Kennedy to Newport, Rhode Island, for the wedding of a friend of ours, Robert Blake (from the State Department), to Sylvia Whitehouse. In those days, to get from Providence to Newport one chartered a Piper Cub plane and as we boarded ours, a two-seater, I wondered who would be paying Jack's fare —whenever he invited me to lunch I picked up the tab because he never had any money on him. To my great surprise it was Kennedy who insisted on paying—he had a charge account with the company. His wife, Jackie, was waiting for us at the little local airport, from where she drove us directly to Bailey's Beach Club—the social center of Newport—so that we could refresh ourselves with a quick swim before all the wedding festivities.

One of the first people we ran into there was Winthrop Aldrich, American ambassador to the Court of St. James's. He said that he had just arrived from London—he was an uncle of the bride—and had been looking forward to staying in Newport for a week, but he had just had a call from Dulles to say that he would be going to London for talks on Wednesday. That meant, Aldrich added, that he had to fly back on Monday to be prepared for the secretary's arrival.

I pricked up my ears, and as we moved to the Kennedy cabin, I checked with Jack whether he had heard what I had heard, that Dulles would be in London unexpectedly on Wednesday. Kennedy confirmed that this was exactly what he had understood. To me it meant that Dulles suspected that the British were preparing to use force against Nasser and that Dulles was trying to prevent a serious crisis from developing between London and Washington, which could present the United States with awkward dilemmas. So instead of going to the cabin, I rushed to the public telephone in the club and rang my friend Ed Dale, who then covered the State Department for the *New York Times,* to ask him whether there had been any official announcement that Dulles would be leaving for London next week. Ed said that there was nothing on the ticker about such a visit; nor had he himself heard anything of the sort unofficially. I told him how I got wind of the information, and that I would call my office in London from Newport to file the story. The ambassador surely could not have invented such a proposal. Ed asked whether he could himself use the story for Sunday and I said, "Yes; but, please, not before."

I actually filed over Friday night and Saturday went to the wedding. That evening the Kennedys gave a splendid dinner party at Hammersmith Farm, one of Newport's stately homes, which belonged to Mrs. Kennedy's stepfather, Hugh Auchincloss. Parties at the Kennedys were always great fun. What sticks in my mind about that occasion—apart from my forgetting all about my exclusive story—is Jack sitting next to a pretty but flat-chested girl and loudly paying tribute to another at the other end of the table for her handsome and very evident breasts. The first girl blanched, the second blushed.

Curiosity and suspense of a different kind got me up early next morning to look for the *New York Times* and Ed's story, which was front-paged. In the afternoon Ed called me, sounding a little crestfallen, to say that the State Department had officially denied that Dulles would fly to London. I began to wonder whether Winthrop Aldrich, who was admittedly showing his age, could have misunderstood Dulles after all. On Sunday, at the Beach Club, I asked him if he still planned to return to London on Monday. Yes, he said, he did. I called Ed back and told him of this confirmation, which raised our hopes that we would still be proved right. Two days later, on Tuesday, the State Department, ignoring its denial of Sunday, simply announced that Dulles would be in London on Wednesday for talks with the British and French.

During that fateful weekend the military plans for the invasion of Egypt were set in motion, and Eden and Macmillan, in separate messages, informed Eisenhower that the government had taken "the firm and irrevocable decision to break Nasser." The readiness of the British to use force shocked Eisenhower. The Joint Chiefs of Staff recommended that unless the Egyptians could be made to turn over the Canal into friendly hands "the US should consider the desirability of taking military action in support of the UK, France and others as appropriate." But Ike, not for the first time, rejected their advice. He was adamantly opposed to the use of force and was determined to prevent it. In one of his more philosophical letters to his friend Sweet Hazlett he wrote at the time: "In this kind of world that we are trying to establish, we frequently find ourselves victims of the tyrannies of the weak." This was not the attitude of an empire builder or empire preserver. He thought in terms of what would help or hurt the prestige of the Western powers.

Also during that weekend in Newport Kennedy, out of the bluest of blue skies, suddenly asked me whether he should attempt to compete for the vice-presidential nomination at the Democratic convention the following month. To myself I said that this man was not yet ready for the job, but all the same I could hardly let him think that I doubted his ability to fill it. I can still remember hearing myself saying: "Jack, you certainly have the capabilities, but you are so young, you have so much time and so many opportunities ahead of you." Kennedy then switched the subject. What I did not know was that his minions had already begun "to test the wind," as Arthur Schlesinger, Jr., put it in his *A Thousand Days*. When Stevenson allowed Kennedy's name to be put in nomination at Chicago and he almost defeated Senator Estes Kefauver of Tennessee, I reflected somewhat ruefully on my talents as a personal political adviser. Kennedy, to his credit and my relief, was kind enough never to remind me of this exchange.

The next week in London Dulles did succeed in persuading Eden to delay whatever action he was planning until there had been a meeting of the signatories of the Canal convention of 1888. Eden also agreed to the idea of a board under the United Nations to run the Canal, which he correctly assumed would be unacceptable to Nasser, in the hope that this would ensure American support for his ultimate plans, which by then had become quite firm in his mind. These plans were based on a cabinet memorandum of July 28, 1952— four years earlier—when for the first time, he outlined British policy toward Egypt: ". . . steps must be taken to safeguard the free transit of the Suez Canal irrespective of whether or not the current bilateral discussions with Egypt made headway and irrespective of the decision taken in respect to a Middle Eastern Defense organization . . ." This was a kind of political sheet lightning: it foreshadowed British determination to prevent any "precipitate action" by the Egyptian government.

Also in the background was a memorandum from Sir Roger Makins giving on February 15, 1954 his diplomatic and carefully balanced interpretation of the question that was crucial for the British government: were the Americans consciously trying to substitute their influence in the Middle East for Britain's? His answer was "No . . . but." "If this is not their conscious policy now," he wrote, "much will depend on whether it will become the inevitable conclusion of the present trend of events and how we adjust ourselves to this new American factor in Middle East politics." He went on to say that the Americans were not "deliberately" pushing Britain out because that would involve the extension of American military commitments. But he also criticized British Middle East policy because "it asks the Americans to accept limitations on their

activities which the British Government is unwilling to accept for itself . . .
We want to have the American cooperation on our own terms and do not fully
recognize their own interests there," he concluded with remarkable candor.

Indeed, it was not American policy either consciously or unconsciously to
push Britain out of the Middle East, for Eisenhower was cautious about
extending global US commitments. But at the same time successive American
governments believed that the longer the colonial powers lingered on their
overseas territories the more the discontent they created could be exploited by
the Soviet Union. Americans, because of their own experience, had great faith
in the idea that independence would sooner rather than later bring about a
regime sympathetic to American ideals.

At first both the British and American governments were in agreement that
Nasser was a dangerous man, because he wanted to lead a Pan-Arab movement
and was playing the West against the Soviet Union. They also agreed to deny
him funds for the construction of the Aswan high dam. Both Dulles and Eden,
however, miscalculated when they supposed that the Russians would not use
the opportunity to walk through the door Mr. Dulles had conveniently opened
for them into Egypt and help to construct the Aswan dam.

Many Arab leaders, opponents of Nasser, advised the British and American governments not to use the issue of the Canal to get rid of Nasser, because
of the degree to which Suez was seen in the Arab world as a symbol of
colonialism. King Ibn Saud of Saudi Arabia, in spite of wanting Nasser
removed, nevertheless was one of them. However, it took Eden less than
forty-eight hours after Nasser's seizure of the Canal to cable Eisenhower
proposing joint military action to bring Nasser "to his sense if necessary
by force," the proposition he had first contemplated in his 1952 cabinet
memorandum.

The Americans were ambivalent. They wanted to "weaken" Nasser, as
Eisenhower put it, and in that sense sympathized with the British, but they
recoiled from the idea of the use of force, fearing that it would provide an
excuse for the Russians to expand their influence in the region. Dulles had
returned from London believing that he had succeeded in restraining any
precipitate action by the British and French, but as in the following weeks he
threw one proposal after another on the negotiating table, hoping to gain time
until tempers had cooled, pressure for action had lowered, and Nasser had
become more willing to compromise, mistrust of his maneuvers rose to new
heights in London. What made it so difficult for the Europeans to trust Dulles
was his many-faceted character. It was hard to predict whether at any given
moment, the blunt politician, the Christian moralist, the bluffing psychological
warrior, the clever lawyer, the nationalistic patriot, the scheming Machiavelli,
or the mature statesman would dominate his words and actions.

A shadow-boxing game began, with Eden giving strong hints that he was
disenchanted with the lame ideas thrown out by Dulles and pressing his
conviction that unless the Nasser problem was resolved, Britain would go

down to defeat, which he would not permit to happen without a fight. To this Eisenhower, in various written and telephonic exchanges, replied by asking Eden what were his goals after the overthrow of Nasser, what kind of relationship did he foresee for the United States and Britain with Egypt and the Arab world generally? According to General Goodpaster, Eden never answered these questions categorically, and Eisenhower himself felt that it was never clear just what end Eden had in mind.

But it was not only the Americans who were kept in the dark about the plot hatched between London and Paris, and Paris and Jerusalem. None of the key British ambassadors, in Washington, Paris, Cairo, or at the United Nations, was kept informed. Nor was the Foreign Office. In the case of Sir Humphrey Trevelyan, the British ambassador to Egypt, it was not until British bombers appeared in the skies over Cairo on October 31 that he realized what was afoot. Sir Roger Makins suggested to me years later that had this influential group of ambassadors been aware of the conspiratorial plans, they would have banded together and opposed as sheer madness what their government was trying to do to avenge Suez.

It was an indication of how low the whole affair rated in American electoral politics that at neither the Democratic nor the Republican convention was Suez ever mentioned. Senator Kefauver came closest, saying that Britain and France should be given "very positive backing" in their insistence on effective international agreements to preserve freedom of navigation. What I found most encouraging at the conventions was that both parties and Eisenhower and Stevenson agreed on the broad fundamentals of American world responsibilities. Any differences were matters of style more than principle. Eisenhower tended to follow rather than guide developments, but during much of the Suez crisis he was in command, something Eden did not realize.

I have always enjoyed attending party conventions. They offer one a chance to see and hear the American nation in microcosm. All one has to do is go on the floor where the delegations from each state sit, and talk to them, ask about the problems in their state, in the nation, and in the world, and one gets a good idea of the state of public opinion. The Democrats used their convention in 1956 as a stage for a bitter inner party struggle; the Republicans, who had gone through that kind of ordeal in 1952, used theirs (at San Francisco) as a demonstration of power and a public demonstration of President Eisenhower's recovery from illness. The phenomenal reception he received surpassed the acclaim any Democrat got in Chicago. It made Republicans supremely confident. When Charles Wilson, the secretary of defense and former chairman of General Motors, and renowned for his intrepid faith in that corporation, was asked whether in his view the Republicans or the Democrats had produced the better policy platform, he simply replied, "When at General Motors we sold Cadillacs, we never mentioned the other guy's goods." Republicans, though, were convinced that they had the better goods to offer.

"Every tomorrow has two handles," Eisenhower told his convention in a classic example of speechwriter's metaphor. "We can take hold of it with the handle of anxiety or the handle of faith." Stevenson's intuitive reaction to the problem of leadership was to reach for the anxiety handle, not from fear or uncertainty but out of modesty and a habit of contemplation. Eisenhower grasped the handle of faith: he was an optimist. He believed in his capacity to serve another term. He also had little reason to worry about the outcome of the elections. Faith, optimism, self-assurance are what appeal to the instincts and mores of the self-made American aristocracy and the middle classes. They believe that humanity is perfectable. Britain's equivalents are much less enterprising. Theirs is a pessimistic outlook, the belief that since mankind is inherently flawed, it must be better to keep things as they more or less are than go for dramatic social and political change.

A few days after the conventions I spent a week at the Walter Lippmanns' summer retreat at Northwest Harbor in Maine. Walter referred to it as a camp, but like Camp David, it was a very comfortable place with three houses and a tennis court. I enjoyed those visits for good conversation, for the long walks and tennis, but Maine water to swim in was only for the very hardy. Adlai Stevenson came for a short stay, once again the presidential candidate, to solicit advice, as he put it, but I surmised that what he really hoped for was Lippmann's support. His charm and his wit were as beguiling as ever. But in discussing his aims with the leading columnist of the United States he was surprisingly unconvincing. Once upon a time he excited and inspired people because in words and manner and wit he was so convincingly a civilized man. But now, instead of inner dynamism, he projected sedateness, fatigue, and a dearth of new ideas.

He was too civilized a man, too burdened by qualities of moderation and balance, qualities that appealed more to Europeans than Americans. He was too judicious, an analyst rather than an action man, for the cruel game of politics. He did not have much faith in himself anymore or in his prospects of winning, and if there had ever been any real fire in his belly, it seemed to have gone out. After he left, Helen Lippmann confided that Walter had offered to help him with advice. But, as later emerged, Lippmann also decided to tilt his writing more in favor of Stevenson's candidacy. He probably was swayed by the feeling that Stevenson was a prudent man in the best eighteenth-century Voltairian fashion, a man who represented Western civilization at its most beguiling. Furthermore, Eisenhower had become a deep disappointment to him.

But Stevenson failed to project himself as a leader. He seemed to be running for office out of some sense of duty rather than conviction. Despite his disarming, self-deprecatory sense of humor, there was something sad about him. His speeches were thoughtful and well-crafted, knowledgeable and intelligent, full of awareness of the problems of the exercise of responsibilities in the nuclear age, but he did not convey willpower or a sharp enough political bite. Twice a presidential loser, he was respected as a politician by neither Kennedy nor Johnson. They tolerated him, because he remained an influence among liberals and enjoyed great respect abroad.

The last time I met Adlai was in 1965, the day before he was to make a speech at the twentieth anniversary of the founding of the United Nations in San Francisco. Instead of keeping the appointment we had at his delegation office in New York, he asked me to ride with him to the airport that morning to enable him to put the finishing touches to the speech he was to deliver in Chicago on his way to San Francisco. As we drove out he confessed that he still did not know whether President Johnson would come to San Francisco to deliver the keynote address or whether he would have to stand in for him. He seemed deeply discouraged. "I'm a very lonely man," he said. "Nobody pays any attention to me in Washington." Shortly after the UN anniversary session (which Johnson did come to address), Stevenson flew to England. London had always been congenial to him, a place where respect for him had remained high. He died while passing the American Embassy. It was almost as if he had willed it that way.

Britain's Suez campaign was not helpful to Stevenson, even if it did embarrass Eisenhower, for in a military crisis voters tend to stick with a president who they believe knows all about wars. But Eisenhower nevertheless was outraged at not having been consulted by his closest ally when British forces attacked Egypt without forewarning him. The order out of the White House was to keep a distance from British officials, to avoid inciting Arab suspicions over secret contacts. The British Embassy was treated like a leper colony. Whenever I went there to check what London was likely to do next, there were no answers, only embarrassment and despair. Even among British correspondents only very few of us still had access to American officials and only on a personal basis and to be told how outraged they were by it all. It was on Eisenhower's decision that the administration began using every lever at its disposal to bring the conflict to an end. A combination of a welling up of deep-seated anticolonialism mixed with blind rage at the deception, suspected collusion, even betrayal gripped Dulles and, above all, Eisenhower. It was Eisenhower who authorized the United States to join the Soviet Union in forcing Britain's hand (egged on by Henry Cabot Lodge, the US representative at the United Nations) to accept a cease-fire, it was Eisenhower who had earlier authorized the move from the Security Council to the General Assembly to circumvent the ability of the British and French to use their veto, and it was Eisenhower who stalled when Britain sought to exercise her legal rights to withdraw funds from the International Monetary Fund to stop the gold-letting Britain's reserves suffered and who held back his approval for the major oil companies to reroute Europe's oil supplies around South Africa to relieve the shortage of oil, one of the many problems the British government was facing.

Only Lord Harcourt, financial adviser to the ambassador, had confidential access to Treasury Secretary George Humphrey, because of their long-standing personal friendship, but, when I went to see one of Humphrey's aides, I soon realized that the man whom the British considered their lifeline to the White House was actually Eisenhower's willing instrument in compelling Britain to accept the cease-fire ordered by the United Nations' resolution. He achieved this by withholding the $1.5 billion loan Britain urgently needed to stop the run on sterling and by refusing to help Britain with measures to ensure its oil supplies. Harold Macmillan must bear some of the blame, for as chancellor of the exchequer, while encouraging Eden to resort to military action against Nasser, he failed to take measures to protect sterling of the kind that governments usually take before they decide to go to war until Britain had become a supplicant. This serious oversight made it easier for the United States government to force Britain to bow to its demands and thus lose the war when, at least on the field of battle, it had almost been won.

The Sunday Times, staunchly conservative, firmly supported Eden's policy in editorials written by H. V. Hodson, the editor, an intellectual of high caliber and a high Tory. I was the only one allowed to introduce a mild critical note: "I more than doubt the British assumption that the Presidential elections influenced Mr. Eisenhower in his decisions. It was his and Mr. Dulles' honest and considered conviction that military action would alienate Asia and Africa from the West and do far more harm than anything that could flow from the Suez dispute."

By coincidence it was on the eve of Britain's attempt to recapture control of the Suez Canal that Harry Hodson and his wife, Margaret, arrived in Washington. The war clouds had been thickening, but at that point nobody in Washington still really believed that the British would actually go to war. Dean Acheson was therefore somewhat surprised when he sat next to Margaret Hodson at dinner and heard from her that she would take any bet that an invasion was about to happen, since she had seen warships, in full panoply, pull out of Southampton. After dinner, over the brandy and cigars, Acheson argued with some force that going to war over Suez looked foolish to him. Hodson disagreed. Acheson suggested that he should imagine himself sitting at a National Security Council meeting and having to present the case in favor of the use of force. Hodson, thus challenged, presented a persuasive enough argument for the former secretary of state to admit: "You have made a good case. If you succeed I'll back you, if you fail I'll be against you." Next day the Hodsons flew to California, but having ignored their own hunches, were forced a day later to return posthaste to London. They broke their journey in Washington to gauge American reactions. Over lunch with Walter Lippmann, Hodson had another opportunity to defend Eden's decision. Lippmann did not disagree. He too was worried about Nasser's Pan-Arab designs. All he said in reply to Hodson was that this kind of operation "can only be justified by success."

The *New York Times* editorially sided with Eden in early September and so did some of the leading American commentators, such as Lippmann, James

Reston, and Joseph Harsch, because, as the *Times* put it: "Prime Minister Eden was right in arguing that there must not be a repetition of the appeasement of the nineteen thirties." Lippmann wrote: "We cannot now wish that they [the British and French] should fail." But they all turned against Eden once it became clear that he favored the use of force.

Eden had miscalculated. He became obsessed by a false historic parallel when he compared Nasser to Hitler, for the Egyptian, though a dictator, lacked the military means to do in the Middle East what Hitler did in Europe. He assumed that the Suez Canel was still important to Britain, though India, the "jewel in the crown," had become independent and that crown was disintegrating. Eden did not calculate the military risks carefully enough, nor did the chiefs of staff. With the military punch too slow in coming, foreign disapprobation was bound to overtake it. And as to the "special relationship," he and Eisenhower, as General Goodpaster said in 1985, "were not communicating. Eisenhower thought in terms of the need of a relationship with Egypt and the Arabs that could be sustained over a long period and that, he was convinced, could not be achieved through the use of force." Eden relied on the afterglow of the special relationship, but international relations, friendships, and national interests don't always mix. In this case there was a fundamental clash of purposes. "Had the British and French been able to clinch the objectives of their military operations quickly and effectively," Goodpaster speculated, "I think this would have made a difference. We had of course a problem with the Russian invasion of Hungary after the uprising there and, I remember, we argued among ourselves whether, if we were denouncing the use of force in Hungary, we had to do the same at Suez." In the end Eden's miscalculation exposed Britain's military weakness, the limits of the special relationship, and the inability of Britain's leadership to weigh the country's true national interests. Suez was the outward symbol of a crisis to which Britain's leaders had closed their eyes ever since the end of the war. It put an end to the forlorn hope that the fading of Britain's prestige and authority was only temporary. The Suez debacle put an end to the illusions of those American officials who wanted someone to share their newly acquired world responsibilities. The harshness with which Eisenhower reacted weakened American power in the world.

It is hard to determine how Eden's illnesses affected his judgment over Suez. Two mishandled bile-duct operations in London and the corrective one at the Lahey Clinic in Boston must have weakened him appallingly. Sir Roger Makins flew up from Washington in June 1953 to ask the doctors about the prospects of Eden's recovery and they were anything but encouraging. They estimated the prospects for survival after the operation at fifty-fifty, the chances that he would never be able to lead a normal life again at 80 percent, and the prospects of carrying on as before at 10 percent.

Eden lasted much longer than the doctors expected. After the cabinet reluctantly conceded a cease-fire on November 6, Eden was forced to surrender by the party elders, who were about to force him out. He resigned on

January 9. A few weeks earlier Eisenhower, Dulles, and George Humphrey had begun to worry about the possibility of a Conservative government being replaced by the Labour Party and hoped to discourage this by making enough concessions to keep Britain solvent and to provide it with needed oil. But they failed to attain one of their main objectives, which was to prevent the Soviet Union from gaining a "political and psychological foothold in the Middle East." The Soviets became a major influence in Egypt for the next fifteen years. Nasser retained the Suez Canal company and the income it provided.

Shortly before John Foster Dulles died, the British foreign secretary, Selwyn Lloyd, visited him in hospital. According to Lloyd, Dulles asked him, "Why did you stop?" Lloyd, startled, replied, "Why didn't you give us a wink?" To which Dulles said: "Oh, I couldn't do that!" Sir Harold Caccia, the then British ambassador, who was present, confirmed this reply to me. Burke Wilkinson, a deputy assistant secretary to Dulles, later reconfirmed the Jesuitic postscript to Dulles's career, as reported by Lloyd and Caccia (many thought that the two had invented the story in defense of the British case). He was present during an interview Dulles gave to Sir William Haley, the editor of the *Times* of London, at a time the wrought-up feeling about Suez had begun to simmer down. As Wilkinson described it, Dulles sat down on the sofa, legs outthrust and keys jingling in his pocket, and asked: "There is one question I wanted to ask you: Why did the British stop the invasion when they did?" Sir William was flabbergasted. In effect his answer was that it was surely the US which had stopped it by bringing pressure to bear in many forms. Mr. Dulles then explained that the US could not condone aggression, particularly, he reminded his guest, at the exact moment in time when the Soviets were brutally suppressing the Hungarian revolt. Dulles laid great stress on the role of Eisenhower in this decision. But he made it quite clear, too, that what he had said and done in condemning the aggression was very much at odds with what Eisenhower and he wanted for the allies. It sounded to me like a Jesuitic postscript because the two pursued their efforts to bring the Suez invasion to an end with unnecessary tenacity.

After Foster Dulles's death I wrote in *The Sunday Times*: "It is very difficult for the President to face the possibility of being without his 'Prime Minister,' for in many ways that is what Mr. Dulles really has been to him." I came to realize only after Eisenhower's papers became available that it was a mistaken conclusion, for Eisenhower proved that he did better in foreign affairs without Dulles, trusting his own judgment.

The basic postwar assumption had been that in the event of another conflict, Britain would hold the Middle East while the United States would take on the Soviet Union. That division of responsibility, after Suez, was upset. US policy from then on was perforce to include the Middle East as one of its own responsibilities, to persuade Britain to shed the vestiges of imperialism, dismantling its Commonwealth preferential trading area, and instead to fashion and join a new federated Europe based on the American experience. But no

British government could or would shed the symbols of past greatness except under pressure of events. Suez was an event that unhinged Britain's greatness.

A few months before his death I had a last and fascinating encounter with Anthony Eden. It was at the villa of Averell and Pamela Harriman in Hobe Sound, Florida, where, thanks to their matchless hospitality, Eden together with his caring wife, Clarissa, spent the last months of his life in the most agreeable surroundings possible.

The first thing Pamela (who had once been married to Randolph Churchill —Clarissa had also been a Churchill) said to me on my arrival was: "Please, Henry, don't mention Suez!" There was a quiet, cheerful elegance about the house and an unobtrusive hospitality. The Edens did not make an appearance on either Friday evening or on Saturday, but on Sunday morning they joined us at the swimming pool. Eden, suntanned and dressed in a bottle-green terry-cloth robe with a broad-brimmed straw hat that he wore at a rakish angle, looked almost as handsome and dashing as ever. His stride was springy like that of a young man, and his smile and casual talk were as if there was nothing wrong with him.

His smile however disappeared for a moment when he said: "Henry, I have a bad case of cancer. But I am taking a new drug, which has not yet been approved for public use. It has done wonders for me. I want you to be in the picture, but I don't want you to write about it." This little soliloquy reminded me of the casual introductions to his briefings as foreign secretary when he often said: "I have just had a telegram from Molotov and I would like to tell you more about it, but you must not write it . . ." The new drug, he said, had all sorts of side effects which forced him to go to bed after taking it, therefore he would not come to either tea or dinner.

Carefully following Pamela's instructions, I steered as far away from Suez as I could and began discussing an interesting review by John le Carré of *A Man Called Intrepid,* about Sir William Stephenson, who had acted as liaison man between American and British intelligence during the war. Then the conversation strayed to Henry Kissinger: Eden considered him and Acheson the two greatest American state secretaries. He praised Kissinger for his inventive approach to the SALT negotiations and for the "great job" he had done in the Middle East. That reference suddenly triggered him into bringing up the Suez crisis. It soon became clear to me that Eden was using my presence to plead once more for justice before history, presenting his case as he saw it, offering new and dispassionate afterthoughts. He recognized his mistakes, but to him they were excusable, because Eisenhower and Dulles had misunderstood him. *They* had failed to see the consequences of their own strategic narrow-mindedness.

"My biggest mistake," Eden began, "was that I was firmly convinced that the Americans would let us, the French, and the Israelis do our business at Suez with Nasser, while they would look after their business of taking care of the bear." (He liked to refer to the Russians as "the bear.") "I also misjudged

Ike. I considered him the kind of friend of Britain who would do everything in support of our cause, which, after all, was also the American cause. I would never have expected him to turn with such vengeance against us. I have been told that he got frightfully angry with us because I did not tell him when we decided to launch our offensive. But I purposely did not tell him because I thought it would be an advantage to him if he could claim ignorance and thus argue that he had no way of preventing our using military force."

He then admitted a second mistake, which was his belief that Dulles all the time was acting on his own and that he was the man to blame, while Ike was keeping his powder dry. "I still believe that one reason that Dulles did not want to give us the time to finish the operation was that he still resented my having refused to back his proposal for giving a joint assurance of support to the French in their war in Indochina. He wanted to encourage the French to keep on fighting and he also wanted to lay the basis for a Southeast Asia pact." This explanation was new to me, a seeming afterthought in his attempt to find as many excuses for his own miscalculations as possible. Indeed, Eden's suspicion was not unfounded. Dulles resented what he considered Eden's shiftiness, because he had been under the impression that Eden had made such a commitment.

When I suggested to Eden that either he had asked the military to undertake an operation beyond their means or they had badly misjudged the pitfalls they were facing, he became slightly agitated. He replied that when he approved the plan it seemed to him sound under the assumption, of course, that the Americans would be patient enough and let him proceed with it. He did not expect that it would prove to be politically and diplomatically intolerable to them. Unfortunately, the naval convoys had to proceed at the speed determined by the cumbersome landing craft, which slowed everything down. To have relied on surprise and the effectiveness of a few parachutists to recapture the Canal, as the French advocated at one point, he said seemed to him too risky. "I wanted to avoid all loss of life if possible," he said. To my question as to whether he had a firm plan of what to do once Nasser was overthrown and Cairo had surrendered, he first made a gesture with his hand as if he wanted to wave away a fly. Then, after some hesitation, he said: "We probably would have installed a military government for a very brief period and then gone for some sort of trusteeship or a government of friendly Egyptians." It was obvious that this was not something he had given much thought to. It was to him a minor matter to be solved on the basis of the prevailing circumstances.

The ghost of Suez was still stalking Eden as he was getting ready for the end and wondering about the verdict of history. In his mind his whole proud career had been fatally scarred by a decision which misfired for lack of American cooperation. He spoke not with bitterness, only with regret and sorrow. After about two hours he ended what had been most of the time a monologue with a conclusion which proved that common sense had triumphed over passion and statesmanship over deep resentment: "Don't get me wrong," he said very quietly, looking suddenly straight into my eyes after having stared most of the time into the clear sky, "the Anglo-American alliance nevertheless remains the key to the preservation of our and Western security." He then got out of his deck chair and walked into the swimming pool. He gave no hint of pain or physical discouragement. He was grateful for any day he remained alive in the warm sunshine and the lovely surroundings of the Harriman estate. He did not seek to arouse pity or to pillory anybody. But he was consumed deep down by the sorrowful knowledge that history would not treat him with kindness.

There have been British prime ministers who had an instinctive feel for Americans, among them Churchill, Macmillan, Alec Douglas-Home, James Callaghan, and Margaret Thatcher. Eden was not one of them. He understood Europeans and felt comfortable in European capitals, but not in Washington. He did not realize that Americans want to be trusted, want to be sure that you are on their side. They like to play it straight and expect the same from others. Eden treated Americans with distrust. At least that was how Eisenhower interpreted the stealth and deception Eden indulged in with his Suez plans.

Eden failed to realize that for Britain to undertake that kind of military operation at such a distance needed American approval. It can be argued that Mrs. Thatcher did not consult the United States before engaging in the defense of the Falkland Islands. But there Britain reacted to military aggression; Britain did not initiate the war. The Reagan administration was also much more willing to consider the consequences were there to be a British defeat by the Argentinian tin soldiers, particularly the effect this would have on NATO. Though Mrs. Thatcher, by nature, welcomed an opportunity to prove that Britain still had muscle, she hardly had an alternative to accepting the Argentinian challenge. Still, she would not have succeeded without the supplies she obtained from a strongly Anglophile secretary of defense, Caspar Weinberger, who, when I asked him what the US would do if a British aircraft carrier were sunk, replied without hesitation, "I would lend Britain an American carrier."

It was not immediately evident, but gradually it seemed to me that Eisenhower also began to think more about his likely place in history and so—not having made up to then much of an impact, except for bringing the war in Korea to an end—in his second term he began to take the affairs of state into his own hands, became more his own spokesman, and set the compass on a more conciliatory policy toward the Soviet Union.

Anglo-American relations in the wake of Suez remained strained. There was little the new British ambassador, Sir Harold Caccia, could do beyond proving that having been a rugger player was a better toughening-up for the galling treatment he got from the Eisenhower administration than his training as a diplomat. In talks during the first few months of 1957, he made no bones about the decline of the Anglo-American relationship and how difficult it had become to do anything about it, especially in the Middle East, where Dulles was determined to pursue his own goals. At an open congressional hearing Dulles went so far as to say that he would not fight in the Middle East, flanked by a French soldier on the left and a Britisher on the right. When the British minister of defense visited Washington, he asked Dulles about this remark, and Dulles apologized, blaming the television klieg lights for having "brain-washed" him.

On the eve of the Bermuda conference I wrote in *The Sunday Times*: ". . . people in England are now franker about the faults of their own Government in the Suez affair, but they feel still deeply aggrieved about the American attitude last autumn. They remember the brusque and threatening language used against them and compare it with the gentle rebukes administered to Egypt now. There are ways of assuaging those feelings and building a new partnership. It will have to be based on realism rather than sentiment, though the fact that the two countries fundamentally want to see the same kind of world remains their strongest bond. The feelings of the American people toward Britain, it seems to me, have been astonishingly little affected by the Suez incident. But the British people, for their part, need to be made to feel again that the United States is 'on their side . . . ' "

By July of 1958, in the absence of the British, Eisenhower had to deal with the growing fears that a pro-Nasser coup in Iraq could become the opening shot for similar upheavals in Saudi Arabia, Jordan, and Lebanon. When he called Prime Minister Macmillan, telling him that he had received calls for help from King Hussein and President Chamoun of Lebanon, and that American Marines were on their way to Lebanon, Macmillan laughed and, more than pleased, suggested, "You're doing a Suez on me." Eisenhower (who could not help joining in the joke) asked him whether he would be prepared to send British paratroopers into Jordan. Eisenhower turned down Macmillan's suggestion for joint action, but promised not to leave him in the lurch later. Macmillan did what he had been asked to do, because, as he put it, "we must keep the bear from the honey, and we will try to keep order among the bees."

Ｈow unsatisfactory—at least to the British—Anglo-American relations remained was brought home to me during a private interview I had with Macmillan. To him this relationship was vital not only to Britain's future but also to that of Europe. Just as it was crucial to keep the West Germans anchored to the West, so it was essential to keep the United States anchored to Europe. Our meeting took place on July 12, 1957, during a stay in London. It was my first interview with a British prime minister, and so a kind of milestone in my life as a reporter. Not even a bleeding ulcer, which forced me to spend three days at the London clinic, prevented me keeping this appointment.

Just as any newcomer to the White House is surprised by its beauty and modesty, so I was surprised at how much 10 Downing Street felt like a private home rather than the prime minister's offices. In this country of magnificent stately homes, it was not more than another charming small row house. There was nothing stately inside either. A small, unassuming, rather dark front hall, a very small waiting room with no great paintings on the walls to add some grandeur to the slightly faded interior. Macmillan received me in his study, which had a chintzy, comfortable feel. He sat in a big armchair from which he lifted himself up slowly as I entered. He began by making a flattering remark about my dispatches from Washington and on that soothing and reassuring note moved immediately to the subject that obviously was most on his mind: President Eisenhower.

"I knew Ike as a military commander," he began. "We spent a lot of time together in Algiers during the war, but now he is not acting like a commander nor like a president, but like a king." He paused to give me a chance to reply. I then suggested that he should not expect Truman-like leadership from Ike because, by inclination, he was more a mediator and conciliator, but that, because of this cast of mind, he might gradually move to restore Anglo-American relations. It seemed to me that since Ike was a man inclined to be honest with himself, he might by then have second thoughts about the treatment he had meted out to the British during Suez. (His memoirs however disprove my assumption.) I then told Macmillan how Emmet Hughes, Eisenhower's former speech writer, once explained the president to me: Ike does not appear to be a strong leader, but it does not mean that he is a weak person, basically unwilling to lead. His military experience made him assume that when he took a position and then issued an order it would be carried out. It was enough for him to take a stand for everybody to know what to do. Second, Ike did not believe in cracking the whip with party politicians who disagreed with him, because he believed things could be done by persuasion and persistence. His cunning political instincts told him that what mattered was not the words he spoke but the atmosphere he created.

Then, taking my courage in my hands, I said that since Eisenhower was unlikely to take bold initiatives, this was an opportunity for Britain to take the initiative and if it did—I put it impersonally—Eisenhower was likely to back it. I then asked Macmillan whether he planned to lead Britain into the European Community, for, after all, he had been eager to do so for some time. A sheepish smile enlivened his droopy face suddenly and he said: "You know, when I was foreign secretary I soon realized I could not do it from the Foreign Office because the civil service was staunchly against it. Then I moved to the Treasury and I thought it would be easier to accomplish it on economic grounds. But I stayed at the Treasury only nine months. And now I am prime minister and from here it seems politically almost impossible . . ." He paused again, pleased with his confession of impotence. Then he went on: "Still, I will either lead Britain into Europe or fight Europe. So much depends on the French and whether they will make concessions on agricultural products." I suggested that he try to get American support before going into negotiations with the Europeans, for it would strengthen his position. Macmillan liked the idea and said he would follow it up.

He then asked whether Ike would succeed in his effort to amend the McMahon Act, which cut the British off from the exchange of nuclear information. I thought he could, to which Macmillan replied that he would then go to Washington to sign a new agreement. Britain, he explained, had to go ahead with her H-bomb tests as a protection against the United States going isolationist again. To which I replied that British testing had engendered a good deal of resentment in Washington, just as it was resented in 1949 when the UK produced its own atomic weapons. Macmillan slightly lowered his voice, as if to indicate the confidentiality of his answer, and said: "The H-bomb is not important in the defense of Britain. We would never use it first. It is important that in case of a Russian attack we can trigger the American nuclear deterrent in our defense."

Macmillan did well in blowing new life into Anglo-American relations when he arrived in Washington for another meeting with the president. He was probably helped by the shock the launching of the first Russian satellite, Sputnik, had on American public opinion, for it made Americans realize that they had been too complacent, that they had to speed up their space program, and that they needed more support from the allies. The meeting laid the basis for Eisenhower's quest to restore the sharing of nuclear information with the British although the Atomic Energy Commission and the Pentagon were opposed to it. Eisenhower, who knew how much the British shared their secrets with the Americans during World War II, insisted, perhaps as a token of the resumption of the alliance in a new post-Suez mood.

When Eisenhower suffered a mild stroke on November 25, 1957, Vice President Nixon began to cast himself in a new leadership role, ostensibly to meet the rising public complaints about the decline of American military power in the face of Sputnik. It gave him a chance to step out boldly where Eisenhower had tiptoed. Nixon bluntly confronted the country with the meaning of Russia's dangerous head start in space shortly after Eisenhower had declared it did not worry him "one iota." Then, in this case taking a leaf out of Eisenhower's book, he cautioned Americans against concentrating too much on meeting the military threat and overlooking the importance of the economic one. Nixon's political instincts told him that to gain a reputation for statesmanship he had to assume responsibility also for some unpopular issues, so he took the question of foreign aid by the horns. The tactics he had used to catapult himself on his meteoric career, I wrote at the time, seemed to me those of "a flighty girl who had married and settled down and wanted to become a pillar of society . . . that he was a man with a promising future who will be around for a long time." He was setting the scene for his own run for the presidency.

A year later, the vice president asked a group of British correspondents to dinner at his house in Wesley Heights. We found ourselves in an upper-middle-class home, tastefully furnished in the *Better Homes & Gardens* style. The sitting room was in light green, the furniture in subdued matching colors. There was a fire in the open fireplace, though it had been the first warm spring day. Fine trophies such as Chinese scrolls (from Taiwan, he pointed out), lacquer paintings, jade pieces, and a vast collection of ivory pieces were scattered throughout. As he gave us a little tour he pointed at the bookshelves lined with Churchill's works. Other titles proclaimed the range of Nixon's interests: *Brave New World Revisited, The Human Use of Human Beings, The FBI, The Theodore Roosevelt Treasury, The Ugly American,* and so on.

Asked whether it would be a mistake to invite Khrushchev to the United States, he replied that such an invitation would enhance the Russian's prestige too much and would be interpreted behind the Iron Curtain as the United States having given up on Eastern Europe. But less than a year later, a more flexible president invited the Russian leader to come to the United States. Nixon proved to be well-informed about British politics. Talking about Aneurin Bevan, for instance, then leader of the Labour Party's left wing, he said that he considered Bevan's formal declaration at the party conference as responsible, in contrast to what he said at political rallies. Then he added, and it sounded like a guideline for his own behavior: "A politician ought to be permitted a bit of leeway between a certain amount of demagoguery and a certain amount of appeal to the galleries, as long as he acts responsibly when it comes to actual policy decisions."

The reason for our invitation soon became evident when he was asked about the birth of the "New Nixon." It was not surprising, he replied, that he had changed: "After all one changes with experience, time, and events. I made my name as an extremist and was called an isolationist. Both are false. Firstly, because I made my name in the McCarthy period, because I brought the issue of Communist infiltration to a head with the pursuit of the Alger Hiss case, and because other men associated with this period were extremists. Yet I voted for the Truman Doctrine, the Marshall Plan, the Reciprocal Trade Act, all proof that I am an internationalist. One of the disadvantages I will have to live with for the rest of my political career is the idea that I am an extremist." Little did any of us suspect that much worse was to come that he would have to live with for the rest of his life.

He was somewhat pained when I asked him about a statement he had made after the Suez crisis to the effect that the American action in the United Nations against Britain and France meant a declaration of independence from the two. He confirmed that he still believed what he then meant, because, even if the operation had succeeded, it would have been a Pyrrhic victory. It would have gone counter to a trend toward independence among the colonial territories that had become inevitable and would have spoiled everything Britain had ever achieved whether in India or Pakistan, Libya or Ghana.

"He certainly is a man who, if he became president, would act like one," I wrote in my diary afterwards. To us British correspondents he wanted to indicate that if he came to power foreign governments need not worry because he would act like an internationalist, ideologically as a centrist, and toward the Western alliance as its strong supporter.

Nixon might have had a good chance of succeeding Ike in 1956 had the president not made such a remarkable recovery from his heart attack and had the Republican Party not been determined to renominate Eisenhower. He had hardly got back on his feet when Len Hall, the Republican Party's chief organizer, flew to Denver to convince him that he had to stay on. I remember sitting with a few White House correspondents in the lobby of the Brown Palace hotel in Denver when Hall strode in, sat down with the group, ordered a drink, and reported that the president looked fine and would run again. The reporters still had their doubts about it, and to twist his arm to give a more convincing answer, asked him what he would do if the president died. Hall, a politician's politician, replied without flinching: "We would run him anyway. There is nothing in the Constitution that says that the president must be alive." He reflected the utter distaste among the Republican power brokers for a Nixon presidency.

In 1959, when Nixon was determined to seek the presidency, Eisenhower first ignored his campaign, then in the absence of anybody better, agreed to support him. He distrusted Nixon, actually (and prophetically) tape-recording their conversations in the Oval Office. Nixon was never invited to the president's private quarters. At one press conference Ike was needled with questions designed to establish the truth of Nixon's claim that he had participated in some of the administration's most important decisions. Angered by the insinuation that he could not make up his own mind, Eisenhower went so far as to say, "If you give me a week I might think of one." Although everybody talked rather haughtily about his syntax being not quite up to scratch, Eisenhower conscientiously maintained his regular weekly press conferences. He became most articulate and informative about his own thinking when asked a broad question, one that might start with "Could you, Mr. President, tell us about your philosophy . . . on this or that . . ." Blunt, hard-hitting questions brought either a refusal to answer or severe irritation. Whenever his neck suddenly reddened, it was a sign that he was speaking in anger—which was what happened over Nixon's share in decision making. Ike later apologized to him, but of course the damage was done. If Eisenhower had been supportive of Nixon's candidacy from the beginning, Nixon, most likely, would have defeated Kennedy. Eisenhower's treatment of him was among Nixon's many trying experiences, but he seemed invulnerable to hurt and insults. Nothing could defeat his drive and ambition. I can think of no one else in modern American history who so managed to triumph over humbling setbacks of the kind that Nixon experienced.

By 1957 I credited Eisenhower with having given the nation time to take a deep breath and to regain a certain inner calm after the tensions of the cold war under Truman and the threat to American democracy caused by McCarthyism. A certain sense of well-being, contentment, even complacency descended on Americans. This state of mind was reflected, though, with a difference on the university campuses. At a dinner party given by the Canadian ambassador, Norman Robertson, Elizabeth Bowen, the Irish novelist, who for three months had been teaching at the University of Wisconsin, spoke of a new kind of alienation among the students: rejection of the placid image of life that the churches, schools, and American media were trying to imbue them with. They were seeking adventures in love instead but when they got home in the morning, they still felt very lonely. This was the so-called Beat Generation. Their prevailing mood was one of protest by inertia, a kind of studied passive resistance. Zen Buddhism became their doctrine.

In June 1958 I attended a gathering of the Renaissance Group in San Francisco's North Beach, the center of the Beat Generation cult. Some five hundred "faithfuls" and a sprinkling of "pagans" had gathered in a big barn. Had it been in the basement rather than at street level, the ceiling low instead of high, the curtains tattered burlap instead of tattered red velvet, it might have generated a genuine Left Bank atmosphere. But this was not Paris. It was the great annual jamboree of the "Poets' Follies," with all the Beat stars on the program: Kenneth Rexroth, Lawrence Ferlinghetti, Kenneth Patchen, and others. The audience was the oddest collection I had yet seen in the United States: girls in tight-fitting cotton slacks and loose blouses over bra-less breasts, their hair cropped short, and the men chiefly sporting goatee beards—the rest did not matter. All the poems were insufferably long, especially one that was not accompanied by jazz but by nihilist contortions from a dancer. One poem, although it offended my tender feelings for San Francisco, made an impression on me because of its brutal analysis of the dark soul of a city where alcoholic consumption and the suicide rate were the highest in the country. I left in the first interval—that is, after almost three hours of poetry readings—and not until I found a pub installed in an old spaghetti factory, where among faded Victorian furniture a color photograph of Adlai Stevenson with a white ruff stylishly encircling his neck looked down from the red walls, was my mental balance restored. I thought at first that the Beat Generation could become harbingers of a new spiritual sense of purpose, but after this experience I concluded they were not much more than the unemployed from a mass educational system. In the end they proved to be just part of an aimless protest movement against American conformity, one that tried to drop tragedy into the opium of optimism that Eisenhower dispensed.

A few weeks later I went to Huntsville, Alabama, where big road signs, something you just could not fail to see, proclaimed SPACE CAPITAL OF THE UNIVERSE. There was humor in the American desire for the ultimate. On the tree-shaded main square people sat lazily around on benches and gazed into the sky as if comatose. Alcohol could be bought only at the local state-

controlled liquor store and there were no open bars. There was also no industry
to speak of. This was cotton country, at least until the Army and its Missile
Command base inflated the town from 16,000 inhabitants to 50,000 in less than
eight years. Staff and faculty of the command center amounted to 1,400,
including 100 German scientists brought over by Wernher von Braun, who
during the war built the notorious V-rocket bombs, but since the end of the
war had been working in the United States. There was a beat here too, the beat
of the guidance systems of the new intermediate range missiles.

Meanwhile President Eisenhower, seeing time running out on his greatest
goal, to make for himself a niche in history through some form of accommodation between the two mightiest nuclear powers, decided to invite Nikita
Khrushchev, the combative, provocative, and daring Soviet leader, to the
United States. What made it easier for him to issue an invitation was that John
Foster Dulles, who did not believe in summitry, had died. Eisenhower thought
the uncertainties surrounding the Berlin situation and the obstacles to coalition
diplomacy by Chancellor Adenauer and General de Gaulle were opportunities
to test his skills as a negotiator. When John Foster was buried in the stillness
of the Arlington Cemetery, it also meant the burial of an era of dominant
American leadership, of the cold war in its classical simple black-and-white
form.

There were some indications that the Russians would welcome a face-to-
face meeting with Eisenhower. I went to Moscow for six weeks in the summer
of 1959, and a high Russian official commented to me that Khrushchev felt he
could work things out with Eisenhower but for his being too much a prisoner
of his own administration. In a personal encounter this could be overcome. The
same official suggested also that any new president brought to power in 1960
would need at least two years before he had acquired the confidence of the
American people "to allow him to do what Eisenhower can do today." To
reassure the allies that he was not planning to make a deal with Khrushchev
behind their backs, Eisenhower decided to visit Bonn, Paris, and London. In
London he discussed with Prime Minister Macmillan the Anglo-American
proposal for a partial ban on nuclear tests, a ban on atmospheric tests, and a
British idea of a limited number of veto-free inspections. Afterwards we were
told so little about their discussions that an American colleague quipped that
we had a choice between "being skillfully deceived" by Peter Hope, the British
spokesman, or "inadvertently misled" by James Hagerty, the White House
spokesman.

My visit to Moscow was my second since 1947 and the changes were
striking. Eisenhower's overtures had indeed inspired new hopes. I found a new,
however hesitant, willingness to strike up conversations with foreigners, at
least among those Soviet citizens who had in them a few grains of adventurous-
ness. They were driven by a thirst for information about the outer world. And

just as it was a coup for me to have found an interesting Russian to talk to, so to them, as one confessed, I was something of a "catch."

The easiest way to meet a Russian and to get to know him better was to go to a restaurant at which Intourist coupons were not accepted and to share a table with somebody else. It is an established custom because there are not enough restaurants or cafes or tables. Sometimes this recipe worked, sometimes it did not, depending on the willingness of an individual to start a conversation. This, at any rate, was the way I met an extraordinarily intelligent, articulate Russian, who became a real friend. He was not a dissident and was far too bound to Russian soil to want to emigrate. But he did not like the Russian ruling system. We spent endless hours walking, as one does in Moscow to escape the microphones. Sometimes I got back to my hotel absolutely tired out. But our talks were worth it, for he could be searchingly serious and delightfully amusing. I don't want to say more about him lest it give away his identity.

Sometimes he brought friends along, of whom some were more, some less open-minded. One evening I was asked to explain what I meant by the rights of the individual. I replied in the simplest terms: the right to read what I want, to travel where I want to go, to listen to what radio station I choose. The more liberal Russian would say that he completely agreed with me, the more conservative would argue that the rights of the individual "must remain subordinated to the common ideal as long as we are trying to catch up with the United States." I explained that one of the basic worries in the West was that Soviet policy depended on one man and that the people had no influence on him. They admitted the problem, but argued that there was the question whether the British and American governments always followed the will of the people. In the Soviet Union, they confessed, not enough people were sufficiently educated and therefore did not know what was good for them. "We know there is something missing in our political system, but we don't quite know what it is. The trouble is the Russian people have never known what freedom is."

Khrushchev had become the "great white hope" of many Russians—a leading Soviet scientist said to me that we in the West should back him because he had courage and the drive and imagination to bring about better relations —but he lacked the respect of many because he remained too much the crude peasant. The last time I had seen him was two years earlier in Berlin. He looked tense and grim then. The Hungarian uprising was obviously still in his bones. When I saw him this time at a reception in the Kremlin for Emperor Haile Selassie of Ethiopia, Khrushchev seemed relaxed and confident, and smiled most of the time. As so often, during the toasts he could not resist one of his famed allegorical tales. He said he often remembered how as a boy he worked on a farm behind a plow pulled by an ox. "The ox is a very stubborn animal," he said, a shy smile in his eyes, "and nothing you can do will make him go faster. I had to be terribly patient. In a way it is the same in big power diplomacy," he added, now smiling broadly. "I can't make it go faster, so I have to be terribly patient." But thanks to Eisenhower "the ox" began to walk remarkably fast and Khrushchev's visit to the United States, which he had been eager to accept, came sooner than he had expected.

When he stepped off his plane in Washington on September 15, 1959, the Western press gave him a treatment neither presidents nor kings had ever received. The whole visit was more like an epic tourist adventure. His own behavior was like that of a smoldering volcano, at times inactive, at times boiling under the surface, at times erupting with elemental force, spouting words instead of lava. He set the tone by dropping first his visiting card not at the White House, but on the moon, in the form of a launch of a moon rocket and then by threatening to "bury" American capitalism by emphasizing Soviet military, economic, and scientific might. Still, there was also an ever-present deep-seated inferiority complex that made him act like a Texas millionaire in *vieux riche* society. When the needle was applied to him he reacted defensively and insisted on his prerogatives. Heckled at an Economic Club dinner, he rose in anger shouting: "I have come here as the representative of a great people who made the great October Revolution and no cries can do away with the great achievements of our people." In a more jovial mood he said he had come to prove that he had no horns—"and I certainly have no hair to disguise them." When the chairman of the Economic Club remarked about the unusually large turnout, Khrushchev quipped: "There are areas in our country where people have never seen a camel. And if a camel appears many people show great interest in him, and some even want to pull him by his tail."

I followed him on his tour of the United States and for me one of the most unforgettable moments was when, after watching the shooting of a scene from *Can-Can,* a film with Frank Sinatra and Shirley Maclaine—Marilyn Monroe was in the audience—Khrushchev stepped out into one of those long corridors between studios and suddenly noticed Marilyn walking off wiggling her behind cheekily and rhythmically (as someone said, like "two babies fighting under a blanket"). He stopped and watched her for about a minute; he obviously had never seen any women moving like her.

A few members of the press, about three at a time, were allowed to enter Khrushchev's Pullman car as our train moved north from Los Angeles toward San Francisco. I happened to be led in for a closer glimpse of the leader by Yuri Zhukov, the Pravda correspondent whom I had met in Moscow and at the United Nations, just at the moment the train pulled into the sunny, serene, sleepy railroad station of ultra-capitalistic-minded, pleasure-loving Santa Barbara. Seeing some five hundred people smiling and waving to greet him, this wayward Russian tourist could hardly wait to clamber off his well-guarded carriage and, for the first time in the United States, shake hands with ordinary people. And he did it like an electioneering American politician.

With him, as a kind of literary exhibit, was Mikhail Sholokhov, author of *And Quiet Flows the Don.* It was about eleven in the morning, but it was obvious that the writer had already had quite a quota of vodka. When I mentioned Boris Pasternak and *Dr. Zhivago,* which had been suppressed by the Russian censor, he denounced the novel as "misinterpreting the thinking of the Russian intellectual," and denied that his own novel *Virgin Soil Upturned* had been delayed because of objections by the censor. But he agreed that Russian literature was stagnating, and argued that it took many years after the Napoleonic wars before Tolstoy wrote *War and Peace.* "We can send rockets to the moon, but we still lack a cure for cancer," he said. "Nor have we yet produced the great postwar novel." As we parted, he remarked: "Talking about literature bores me. If I spent so much time in discussing it with you, it is because I have a great admiration for your Queen." That was an unexpected end of my conversation with Sholokhov, whom I nonetheless found a thoroughly unpleasant man.

As the Khrushchev circus moved around the country, people flocked to see him. Here was a man who could go through the scale of all human emotions in a few minutes. He had an obvious instinct for the jugular, yet he knew also how to coax tears or to jerk at one's heartstrings. He was, in short, a master politician. Only a man of his boundless self-confidence would have dared to embark on this adventure and stand up to its early vicissitudes. His harsh candor, his cruel humor, his violence, and his perversity were theatrical attractions and in that sense some Americans either took to him as a unique character or they were repelled by him as one more proof of how dangerous an adversary the Soviet Union was. "He may be a damn butcher," said a man in Pittsburgh, "but we have to get along with him somehow."

Eisenhower's instructions to Ambassador Henry Cabot Lodge, Khrushchev's tour guide, and Llewellyn Thompson, the American ambassador to the Soviet Union, were to show Khrushchev how strong and healthy the American nation was and to bring him back in good humor for their Camp David talks. Those talks turned out to be a disappointment to Eisenhower. The crucial issue was the Russian threat unilaterally to turn Berlin over to the East Germans. In the end Khrushchev backed down, and the two agreed to meet for a four-power summit in Paris the following May. In view of Eisenhower's receptivity to a more cooperative relationship, Khrushchev missed a crucial opportunity when he failed to open a broad discussion about new ways of accommodation. General Goodpaster, who was closest to those talks, says that Khrushchev made a vague offer for a rapprochement which, as he put it, "was veiled in a kind of double-negative in the sense that there was no reason to threaten each other and to maintain the kind of hostility that now prevailed. Admittedly, this was a very veiled hint, but we had a sense that he wanted to shift away from mutual hostility." Khrushchev also emphasized the huge cost of the arms race and the need for disarmament. Eisenhower tried to induce Khrushchev to say something about the future of Sino-Soviet relations, but he refused, hinting that it was too delicate an issue. What Eisenhower, and maybe even Khrushchev, did not realize at the time was that his visit to the United

States would contribute to the split between the two nations. Chairman Mao accused him of selling out to the West.

The answer to the question why the Camp David talks led nowhere can be found in Khrushchev's own memoirs. "I was convinced that as long as the U.S. held a big advantage over us, we couldn't submit to international disarmament controls. That was my point of view, and I think, at the time it was correct," was how the Soviet leader candidly explained it. He also said how much he admired Eisenhower "for his modesty, his common sense, and his many years of experience," and how disappointed he was when "we had failed to remove the major obstacles between us . . . I could tell Eisenhower was deflated. He looked like a man who had fallen through a hole in the ice and been dragged from the river with freezing water still dripping off him . . . I knew how he felt, but there wasn't anything I could do to help him." Here was Khrushchev's own testimony—and I believe that Khrushchev's comments were authentic—on why the timing for an agreement had not yet come.

What finally destroyed all prospects of an improvement in relations built on those Camp David talks was the U-2, the spy plane which had been flying for months over the Soviet Union without the Russians' being able to bring it to book. When they did, it was almost as much embarrassment to Khrushchev as it was to Eisenhower. The plane was born of the need to photograph important Soviet military installations secretly. In 1952 the United States heard about a new Soviet missile center at Kaputsin Yar on the Volga. The CIA then asked the US Air Force to overfly the spot and provide photographs. General Nathan Twining, who commanded the USAF, said it could not be done. The British, when asked, sent a Canberra bomber all the way from Germany to the Volga and down into Iran and despite the risks involved, it brought back some fair pictures. The Americans were grateful and asked for more, but the British replied that they would never want to undertake such a mission again, because they knew that the whole Soviet Union had been alerted to the exploit; it had almost created an international incident. With the US Air Force still continuing to refuse, the CIA decided to develop its own spy plane, the U-2, in 1956. Everybody was well aware that it would have a life of only limited duration, because the Russian radar was bound to improve and so would the interceptors and the accuracy of surface-to-air missiles. For some time, though, the Russians, well aware of the U-2 intrusions, preferred to keep quiet about them since they could not do anything about them. When at last they succeeded in shooting one down, however, they had no alternative but to raise hell about this cocky, clever high-flying spy machine. The crock had gone once too often to the well. The Russians captured not only the broken-up plane, but the film and the pilot, whose name, Gary Powers, became famous when his release caused endless and acrimonious negotiations.

According to a memorandum by General Goodpaster, the CIA was authorized one last U-2 flight to check on any new Soviet missile sites, and the order was that the flight had to be undertaken before May 1—that is, before the summit. The president wanted to avoid any risk of provocation on the eve of the Paris meeting. But because of bad weather the fatal U-2 takeoff was delayed until May 1. Eisenhower was horrified, and Khrushchev's unorthodox "I like Ike" stand had been compromised. He had insisted, in defense of a policy which defied all Communist dogma, that Eisenhower was different from the rest of the American "ruling class." Now it was suddenly obvious that he was not. Worse, when Khrushchev announced the U-2 incident before the Supreme Soviet, he still tried to dissociate the president from responsibility, expecting the president to follow tradition and deny he had known about the operation. But Eisenhower, after the Russians produced Powers and his plane, and thus disproved the CIA's cover story that the plane had been on a weather mission, instead of denying that he had sanctioned the U-2 mission, defended the policy of overflights over Soviet territory. Khrushchev squirmed with embarrassment. According to Goodpaster, Ike's advisers were unanimous that what he said in explanation had to be true in order to preserve his credibility before the American nation. They also feared that if the president denied that he had approved of the operation or known about it, Khrushchev could charge him with irresponsibility or failure to control the CIA.

When I got to Paris to cover the summit I found the American delegation more nervous and uncertain than I had ever seen one before. Khrushchev came to Paris, but only to administer a shriveling rebuke and to spit into the face of the other three leaders. Macmillan made a faint effort to rescue the conference, but in vain. The world was aghast at Eisenhower's attempt to make aerial espionage respectable, but it was even more upset by Khrushchev's torpedoing the summit. As Mr. Nehru put it, "No good can result from angry approaches to difficult problems, even though the anger may be justified."

I was never as critical of Eisenhower as I was later of Presidents Johnson, Nixon, or Carter, but he disappointed me because I had geared my expectations too high from the start. I did not mind his spending time on the golf course; on the contrary, I thought it was good for his clarity of thinking. Nor did I care about the weak syntax of his answers at press conferences; there was, quite often, between the lines enough that revealed his thinking. I sympathized with his method of using others as lightning rods to keep his own reserve powers intact, but I expected him to deploy them more often. General Goodpaster said that Ike frequently exhorted his aides not to "hold a pistol to his head," meaning not to press him to take decisions at short notice. I also expected a golden age of Anglo-American cooperation, an expectation that was badly shattered, at least until Eisenhower in the course of a meeting with Macmillan in March 1960—a meeting that above all dealt with the prime minister's pet issue, a nuclear test ban—exchanged notes with him letting the British, when necessary, have either the Skybolt or Polaris missile vehicles (by sale or gift) to ensure the preservation of Britain's independent nuclear deterrent. The deal included a quid pro quo, a lease to the US Navy of Holy Loch, which was to serve as a supply base for Polaris submarines. If for some reason

Skybolt, a missile to be launched from a bomber that was to extend its range by 1,500 miles, proved unsatisfactory, the British, according to Eisenhower's undertaking, could count on obtaining the Polaris vehicle, providing the nuclear warhead themselves. Macmillan at the time opted for Skybolt because it was much cheaper. It proved a miscalculation because of the crisis in Anglo-American relations that Skybolt caused two years later in the Kennedy administration. Had Macmillan chosen Polaris, he would have saved himself grave political troubles and, in the end, it would have cost the British government less.

In recent years I have begun to feel more charitable about Eisenhower's contribution to affairs, for when a president leaves overall a positive imprint on history—and that Ike certainly did—his weaknesses tend to fade into the background and his positive achievements dominate people's memories. The gradual lifting of secrecy on the documents of that period has also thrown a new light on his accomplishments. Almost everybody remembers his attack on the "military-industrial complex" in his swan song speech; the phrase passed into the language. It seemed greatly out of character for a member of the military caste to point such an accusatory finger at the military, and the explanation was given at the time that a liberal-minded speech writer had slipped that phrase into the speech. Since then, however, we have learned from his private papers that this whole question worried him throughout his stay in the White House. As a soldier himself he was an insider who knew what the Pentagon was up to. And the battles he fought against it, as we found out only later, were almost epic. He resisted the demands for a crash program to catch up with the Russians and he rejected several demands by the Joint Chiefs of Staff for the use of nuclear weapons against China in the defense of the offshore islands, against North Korea—a special request by General MacArthur—against the North Vietnamese, in defense of the French at Dien Bien Phu, and in the Middle East. Even though he agreed to an American strategic plan that provided for the use of nuclear weapons in support of ground forces, he did so assuming that he would never have to deploy them. He had no choice but to acquiesce in this strategy in order to get the military to agree to the defense cuts he insisted on in aid of a balanced budget. He took the risk because he was convinced that no large-scale war was likely to occur. He quietly scrapped the "liberation doctrine" for Eastern Europe, which was nothing but a political gimmick; he rejected the CIA's request for dropping arms and supplies over Budapest during the uprising; he put down Secretary of Defense Neil McElroy for hinting at the possibility of the United States launching a first strike; and although he authorized the preparations for an invasion of Cuba by Cuban exiles, he allowed himself some elbow room by asking that a Cuban government-in-exile in the United States be first established, something the CIA had difficulty in setting up.

It thus became clear from his own papers that he had exerted firm leadership whenever he had no more room to procrastinate or whenever his judgment told him that he had to exert himself in defense of his own principles. Especially in military affairs he felt strongly that he had thought these problems through in their totality and understood them better than anybody else. He must therefore get credit for having steered a steady course and for the courage with which he overcame a serious heart attack and other ailments.

Why did Eisenhower allow the world to underrate him so badly in his first term? Even as close a friend as General Goodpaster says that it is hard to find an answer. One probable reason is that he felt so secure in himself, so sure of his instinctive judgment that he did not care what other people thought. In a curiously English way he preferred to understate his role. He probably felt that he had already an assured place of honor in history as the man who commanded the victorious Allied armies, but in his second term he began to think harder about the contribution to peace he could make. He was as strongly anti-Communist as Dulles, but the latter's confrontational style came to grate on him. His knowledge of the dangers of nuclear war also made him anxious to pay more attention to mitigating Soviet-American hostilities.

Ironically, as fate would have it, Eisenhower's own efforts to usher in a less tense world failed. It was left to the man he disdained, Richard Nixon, to do the most active testing of the negotiating track, the Eisenhower legacy. He went about it with much more realism than did Eisenhower, but he had learned valuable lessons from him.

Eisenhower out of office became less ambiguous and more direct in the advice he offered Presidents Kennedy and Johnson when they solicited it. Although he had carefully avoided getting engaged on the Asian mainland, he advised Kennedy strongly to make sure that Laos did not fall into Communist hands. He was afraid that it could become the first domino to cause others to fall. He also advised Johnson to slug it out in Vietnam because by then the United States was too deeply committed there, and a retreat, he cautioned, would hurt American prestige in the world.

Alfred Duff Cooper, a friend of Churchill's whose last public position was British ambassador to France, wrote a charming autobiography which he called *Old Men Forget,* a title quoting from Shakespeare's *Henry V.* Eisenhower, too, especially when out of office, showed that he had a short memory. When President Kennedy, for instance, stumbled into the Skybolt crisis after his Secretary of Defense Robert McNamara had decided to scrap the missile's development, I received an indignant letter from the ex-president: "I was astonished when I read in the newspapers that our government had abandoned the effort of producing weapons of this kind and was, of course, concerned as to the possible effect on our British friends . . ." Had he given enough thought to "the possible effect on our British friends" of his attitude toward Suez? Alas, old men forget.

8

Kennedy's Triumphs and Tragedy

THE KENNEDY PRESIDENCY held a very special meaning for me, one that still remains. For the first time I had a personal friend in the White House. I had known Kennedy for about ten years and Jacqueline Bouvier Kennedy a little longer. We had met professionally and socially, discussing politics, playing charades after dinner, or judging point-to-point races in Virginia. Suddenly the two had become the most exalted couple in the United States, perhaps in the world; two people with whom I had a very informal relationship had been lifted onto a unique formal pedestal. They were bright and intelligent without taking themselves too seriously and shared an enormous curiosity about people and the world. They were certain to give the presidency a new flair, a new élan, a new direction. As I went to see the new president for the first time I found myself wondering how it would be, switching from "Jack" to "Mr. President." But it was a silly question. Once in his presence the "Mr. President" came instinctively and naturally. As I faced him, slightly awed, he said: "Things have changed a little since we last met." Then with a twinkle, he added: "What you can still do [I was still a bachelor] I won't be able to do anymore . . ." There was the old Jack, helping me to relax, easing me through this new-style encounter.

When I first met Jack (everybody called him Jack in those days), he was a member of the House of Representatives. Most of his friends assumed then that his ambitions were more a reflection of his father's than his own, and that in lieu of anything better, politics was as good an occupation as any for a playboyish Irishman from Boston. He was rich, well traveled, at ease with public affairs, but it was not until he got into the Senate that he began to feel politically committed. The outward image became misleading as underneath his own ambitions began churning. As yet they lacked clear directions and were focused mainly on domestic matters, but he was a good listener and the more he came into touch with problems, people, and the world, the more questions he began to ask. A sense of purpose and duty gradually grew in him and people began talking about him as a man with a political future. When in 1956 he almost won the vice-presidential nomination, his appetite for the highest office in the land was more than whetted, it became an obsession.

One evening in my house in the early fifties I realized for the first time how intense was his interest in domestic politics. Although after dinner quite a fascinating debate developed, Kennedy, much to my annoyance, spent an endless time on the telephone trying to find out details about the outcome of the congressional elections in Massachusetts, and with the votes coming in slowly, went back to the instrument time and again. What also sticks in my mind from that evening is that later, during a lively debate about foreign policy, he dissociated himself from the fray, saying, "Foreign policy is for the experts."

Several years later, over dinner at the Kennedys' house on P Street in June of 1957 he mentioned that he was planning to make his first foreign policy speech, advocating that France proceed without further delay to give Algeria its independence. He pulled a draft from his pocket and, asking for comment, began to read excerpts from it. It was obvious that he saw this speech as an important first in his political life. He made no bones about wanting to hit the French hard. "How will the British react to it? And the French? And the Europeans?" He was eager to find out. He asked questions about other aspects of the speech, wanting to be absolutely certain that he ran no risk of embarrassment over any detail. We discussed the speech further the next day, and again after he had delivered it. The fury it aroused in France delighted him. The publicity it got in the United States and abroad went far beyond his expectations and, most probably, made him aware that to wax about foreign affairs was much more worthwhile from a publicity point of view than to do so about domestic politics. As president he became fascinated by foreign policy problems and by foreign statesmen. After that first speech, although his voice in foreign afairs had no echo, it suddenly became one to be reckoned with, even though much of the American press, especially the *New York Times,* severely criticized him for stirring the pot of a brew he knew nothing about.

Dean Acheson later mentioned the Algeria speech in a book about Congress as an example of the wrong way for a member of Congress to intervene in the making of foreign policy. After publication, he found himself by chance sitting next to Jackie Kennedy on a train that had to slow down because of a snowstorm. Jackie, as the loyal wife she was, took Acheson to task for his criticism. This amused him, he later told me, but since, as he put it, he did not want to argue with a beautiful woman about foreign policy, he suggested to her that in view of the fact that they were condemned by fate to have to keep each other company, she had a choice of spending the time fighting or being pleasant. Jackie, disarmed, said that she preferred pleasantness. During the 1960 election campaign Acheson wrote Kennedy two letters of advice. In the first he suggested that the candidate "will find no lack of advisers on foreign policy, but that he will need all his good judgment to disregard most of their advice." In the second he counseled him that the president cannot "lighten his burden, he must carry it." It was sound advice, but hard for Kennedy to accept then. Since the American political system allows men untrained in governing to compete for the presidency, it takes quite a long time before American presidents learn the most basic task, the management of power. Certain men are born to lead and I think Kennedy was one of them, but it took him at least two years in the White House before he had fully grasped what this meant for him.

When Kennedy first began to think about reaching for the presidency, his attitude reflected both the flippant and the serious side in him. The playboy coexisted with the earnest student of politics and history. I found it difficult to judge how deeply he was driven by convictions and how much by ambition. But there was a purposefulness about him which permeated everything and everybody from the start. What appealed to those eager to work for him was that here was a man not only interested in creating an effective political machine, but also attracted to the realm of ideas. He combined a casual, almost aristocratic manner with the recognition that he needed to learn a lot, and so he was never shy of asking questions. He was at ease with reporters and knew instinctively, it seemed, how to exploit the techniques of modern mass media to his advantage. During the election campaign, he often asked me, for instance, about the significance of events abroad, about the impression he was creating overseas, and how I rated the other candidates. (He continued the habit later, on one occasion, at Hammersmith Farm in Newport—he had already become president by then—getting me to rate the influence of various American columnists at home and abroad.)

When a leak flowed the candidate's way about an opinion poll the United States Information Agency had commissioned in Europe, showing that American prestige under Eisenhower had declined, he checked with me and other foreign correspondents as to the accuracy of the conclusion and then moved fast to make an effective and successful campaign issue out of it. His interest in the press and in foreign affairs, of course, appealed to us foreign correspondents, as did—after the provincial Truman and the remote Eisenhower—Kennedy's youth, charm, wit, irreverence toward pomposity and cliché, and his affection for style and language. Intellectuals were impressed by his interest in them and their ideas, the young felt that for the first time they had their own man in the White House, the politicians appreciated his instinctive sense for their business. The conservatives were reassured that his overriding foreign policy issue during the campaign had been "who can best stand up to the Russians" and the liberals, though they found his silence about Senator McCarthy disturbing, drew comfort and hope from his political sophistication and in the new tough-minded progressive attitude of the men surrounding him. However, he was a difficult man to pin down politically, for he was in many ways like an English Wykehamist, detached, cerebral, self-contained, pragmatic, a man of reason, not of passion.

Early in the election campaign I got what I considered an embarrassing request from my editor. He asked me to get myself photographed separately with the two candidates, the photos to be used to promote my election coverage in *The Sunday Times.* I first called Kennedy, apologized for such a ridiculous request, and then explained its purpose. Kennedy only laughed. "Of course, I'll do it any time," he replied. "After all, Henry, promotion is our bread and butter!" A few days later I took George Thames, a *New York Times* photographer, to Kennedy's Georgetown house. It was different with Nixon. After prolonged negotiations with his people, and my pointing out that Kennedy had already acceded to my request, it was finally agreed that a photograph could be taken in the studio after a television appearance.

Two things in particular made Kennedy a controversial candidate: his Catholicism and his "failure to speak out" against McCarthy. I assumed that Kennedy preferred not to discuss either of them and hence I had never broached them with him in private. But when I interviewed him on the record at the start of the election campaign I raised both issues. He willingly admitted that his Catholicism made him controversial, but he did not think that this was necessarily disadvantageous. He readily admitted that the fight for religious freedom, the struggle for the Reformation, and the whole character of the United States made the prospect of a Catholic president a matter of serious concern to many Americans. But he also believed that once certain questions were answered responsibly, the Catholic issue would fall by the wayside and other, more serious questions would assert themselves. He gave his own answer in a brilliant speech in which he laid down his own law: "I am not a Catholic candidate for president. I am the Democratic Party's candidate for president, who happens to be a Catholic. I do not speak for my church on public matters —and the Church does not speak for me . . . But if the time should ever come . . . when my office would require me to either violate my conscience, or violate the national interest, then I would resign the office . . ." It was one of those speeches that made history: it defused the Catholic issue during the campaign and after Kennedy's election eliminated it not only as a roadblock to the presidency but also as a divisive element in society.

In McCarthy's heyday Kennedy had never criticized or dissociated himself from his fellow senator, and I knew that raising the issue could embarrass

Kennedy. I therefore approached it by recalling that Arthur Miller, the playwright, had suggested to me that in a sufficiently serious international crisis McCarthyism would recur. What did Kennedy think? He replied that he was not sure whether any historical period repeated itself in the exact same form. He did not think that the words "appease" and "soft on communism" and all the rest that had been thrown around with some vigor would influence the elections. He agreed that there were those in the United States who would be glad to take the ax off the wall if political pressures sufficiently disturbed them and go back to the old techniques. But when I pressed him further as to whether he would, if it arose again, take a much stronger position on McCarthyism, he would only say: "I don't agree with the technique, nor did I ever." Such were his political parameters on the right.

I do not think they related particularly to the views his father had held as American ambassador in London in the 1930s. When, at some point during the 1960 elections I asked Kennedy to introduce me to his father, he replied defensively: "We have many disagreements on policy and have for a great many years. He has a wholly different view of what role the United States ought to play in the world than I have had in the fourteen years I have been in Congress. And on many domestic matters his opinions differ substantially from mine. But it's not a matter of discussion between us. We do disagree and therefore I'm not going to attempt to convert him, and he does not attempt to convert me. So it's outside our personal relationship which, as such, is very satisfactory. And as to introducing you to him, Henry," he added laughingly, "I'd better not because if I did, you'd never speak to me again." He was much more trenchant about his father than about McCarthy.

At any rate, I never really got to know Papa Kennedy. I did not regret it; I already felt a loathing for the man and his appeasement attitude toward Hitler, and Jack's remarks only confirmed my feelings. When I finally met the father at the Kennedy villa in Palm Beach immediately after the elections, it was by chance. Jack Kennedy had invited a group of correspondents to hot dogs and a swim, and it was just as I entered the house that our paths crossed. I introduced myself, not immediately recognizing who he was. When he heard that I represented a British newspaper, he started giving me a lecture on how socialist Britain's Conservative Party was. What was more interesting about the occasion was how utterly disconcerted Jack Kennedy was by his margin of victory, the narrowest in American history. He won by 49.7 percent of the popular vote against Nixon's 49.5 percent, a plurality of a mere 118,550. Everybody, including myself, had expected him to do much better. After all, he had the better political machine, he had defused the Catholic issue with such skill, and he had won the support of the distrustful liberals, thanks to Arthur Schlesinger's yeoman work in persuasion, in spite of having chosen Lyndon B. Johnson as his running mate.

More surprising still, a majority of the women's vote went to Nixon, which puzzled those who had been convinced that Kennedy's youth and charm, his reputation as a womanizer, would surely make him popular among women. Frank Holeman, the then Washington bureau chief of the New York *Daily News,* told me that during the campaign he told Kenney O'Donnell, Kennedy's close campaign aide, that if it became known that Kennedy had a girl in almost every town, it would have a devastating political effect. O'Donnell replied that if that story broke, they would not deny it, because he was convinced it would only help. His outlook was not unique. In Florida, also during the campaign, Bill Haddad told me that he had proof that Nixon had a "love nest," as he called it, somewhere in the Bahamas. I expressed great skepticism about the story, and, asked what he would do with it, he said, without hesitation, "Nothing, because it would only help Nixon. Womanizing may be frowned upon publicly, but secretly Americans admire and envy a swordsman." As long as it is done with a certain amount of discretion—not the Gary Hart style—for then, to paraphrase Mort Sahl, the satirist, "there is no use writing about what you can't document."

Between swims and drinks at Palm Beach, Kennedy went over the detailed results with us. Why did he lose Ohio and why was Illinois that close, after Mayor Daley of Chicago, that master manipulator of political wards, had promised a satisfactory majority? At least briefly, Kennedy did worry about rumors about irregularities in the vote count in infamous Cook County, Illinois, because of the uncertainty over whether Nixon would ask for a recount (to the surprise of many, he did not do so). Those were uncomfortable hours in the Kennedy camp. Years later, at a mayors' conference in Boston, I asked Daley how he managed to have a balanced budget when most big cities were reeling under debts. Daley, mayor of a notoriously corrupt city, looked me in the eyes for a few seconds, then raised his forefinger like a preacher and with a meaningful smile gave me his recipe for success: "You must have friends." He obviously knew how to make and keep friends.

Shortly after Kennedy's election I saw Prime Minister Harold Macmillan in London at 10 Downing Street. He wanted to know all I knew about Kennedy. "I'm asking you all these questions," he explained, "because I don't know how I'm going to be able to establish the kind of close relationship with Kennedy I used to have with Eisenhower. I got to know Eisenhower in Algiers during the war, we belonged to the same generation, and we had more or less the same outlook on the world. Now there is a president in the White House who belongs to a much younger generation, whose outlook on the world I am not familiar with, and whom I have never met before. How am I going to be able to create a close relationship with a cocky young Irishman?" The prime minister sounded truly worried and at a loss. Close relations with the United States were as crucial to his thinking as to Churchill's.

I tried to reassure him that Kennedy was quite different from his father, and, in fact, had done many things to compensate for his father's past political sins. I reminded Macmillan that Kennedy had written *Why England Slept,* an analysis of Britain's unpreparedness at the outset of World War II. Kennedy, I told him, was an unsentimental Anglophile who felt comfortable in British high society, had kept a deep respect for British traditions, a love of the English language, an admiration for the way Britain had launched her colonies into independence, and a political outlook that bore a resemblance to that of his own enlightened conservatism. Anglo-American understanding was not automatic. Every British government, every American administration had to make a special effort to create its own new climate, and in Kennedy's case it should be particularly easy. I suggested that Macmillan initiate a correspondence with the new president in advance of their meeting in person. He did so, as he told me later, though he feared the brisk young president would have little patience with one so Edwardian in style and in outward appearance—and a friend of Eisenhower, a Republican, to boot. In December 1960 Macmillan sent an outline of his ideas about disarmament and the nuclear test ban, and in January on East-West relations, though by then he had not yet received an answer to his first letter. Macmillan's basic theme was that the Kennedy presidency would be a time when much could be done to make the world safer and to work for an East-West détente. President Kennedy, when he did reply, encouraged these exchanges.

In truth, in spite of his informality, Kennedy was not an easy man to know or to strike up a relationship with. But it probably helped that President Eisenhower in briefing Kennedy initially had said to him, "You'll find Macmillan a good friend whose counsel you should listen to."

What I had in mind when in early February I went to see Robert Kennedy, the new attorney general, was to find out how he planned to run such an important job. What I came away with was something of very different significance. I knew Bobby, but not well. As a rule it was possible to have a close relationship with only one Kennedy. Each had his own circle of friends. I had hardly sat down in his office when he said to me with characteristic directness: "I hope you know we want David Ormsby-Gore as British ambassador here. You'd better tell your prime minister and your readers."

Sir David, who was minister of state at the Foreign Office for disarmament problems and United Nations affairs, had become a friend. He was related by marriage to the Kennedys, but he and Jack had met in London as enterprising bachelors and become friends before World War II. Having watched Ormsby-Gore at the United Nations, I was much impressed by his meticulous understanding of complex arms control problems, by his political savvy and his sensitivity to American problems, marrying them skillfully to British interests.

David, in the circumstances, had good reason for wanting to become ambassador to the United States. But even by the beginning of 1961 he had no firm commitment from the prime minister (to whom he was also related). I thought that he and John Wyndham (later Lord Egremont), a kind of political secretary and court jester to the prime minister, should know about Bobby

Kennedy's candid *demandeur* remark, and I wrote to both of them. I knew that John Wyndham, whose sense of humor was as infectious as Petworth, his Sussex home, was stately, was most sympathetic to David's going to Washington. A correspondence then developed between David and me in which he wrote about the controversies his appointment generated in the British press and Parliament. It gave me an insight into the complications facing even a man with David's connections. In early April 1961, for instance, he wrote: ". . . the Beaverbrook press have mounted a rather ludicrous contrived campaign against my appointment. Nepotism is of course the charge. The next is that the professionals in the F.O. will view it with a jaundiced eye. In fact, the reverse is true and the most senior officials have been strongly supporting my candidature. Finally, it is suggested that the powers that be in Washington, including the President, might prefer a professional diplomat to a politician. It is here that I thought you might be able to help . . . it might be valuable for Anglo-American relations in the future if some authoritative voice was heard indicating that my appointment would not be all that unwelcome to the Kennedy administration . . . the fractious critics would be considerably disheartened if they knew that the decision would meet with a happy response where it mattered most. This is particularly true at a time when Kennedy is regarded almost as infallible . . ."

By the Beaverbrook press, David meant the *Daily Express,* which went to bat for Sir Hartley Shawcross, the former Labour attorney general, with a brilliant, steely mind, who, at the United Nations, had taken on the Soviet Union's wily and stubborn Vishinsky and carried the day. But he was, in my view, too haughty, too formal and legalistic to suit Kennedy's Washington. Others were mentioned, but nobody with better credentials than David, and since I considered him the best possible choice for Washington, I made a point of reporting that he was Kennedy's own favorite, even though David had suggested that I should not bring the president himself into the controversy. In his next letter, apart from thanking me for my little contribution, he mentioned that Professor Arthur Schlesinger, Jr., on Kennedy's instructions, had come to see him to tell him the unvarnished details of the Cuban Bay of Pigs fiasco (which I shall discuss later in this chapter). "I got the strong impression," he wrote, "that if one of his top advisers had come out firmly against the operation, the President would have been most happy to cancel it, but all the advice, and particularly the intelligence reports, were stacked heavily in favor of going ahead. The truth is that as a result of mistaken policies over many years, Kennedy has in a number of areas been dealt a very bad hand. A period of regroupment and reorientation is badly needed if we are to see better results in two or three years' time. Quick, ad hoc, decisions cannot reverse the tide in the near future."

David's appointment as ambassador heralded the zenith in Anglo-American relations, though not an unblemished one. His close relationship to President Kennedy trumped Sir Oliver Franks's to Dean Acheson, simply because

he was a friend of the president. It was unique in the annals of British ambassadors in Washington. But even such an intimate relationship, as we will see, is
not protection against serious pitfalls, for the American government is a jungle
with hundreds of trails to which there are no safe guides.

Under the British political system the development of foreign policy moves
down well-defined lines through the cabinet, the prime minister, and through
the hierarchy of the Foreign Office. In the United States, because there is no
cabinet system and because the president is able and, indeed, frequently inclined to carry out his own foreign policy, there are two founts from which
foreign policy should conventionally flow—the president and the secretary of
state. It means that the chain of command is much less clearly defined, which
makes the evolution of foreign policy much more difficult to follow. Furthermore, the legislature has a greater impact on the development of foreign policy
than it does in Britain. The congressional committee system gives the Foreign
Relations Committee of the Senate considerable influence on foreign affairs.
Under the British system there is nothing comparable to it. Debates in the
House of Commons are usually fought on straight party lines. There is no body
within the legislature divorced from the executive which has views of its own
that need to be taken into account by the policymakers. For all these reasons
the significance of the State Department in the development of foreign policy
is not as clearly defined as it is in the case of the Foreign Office in London.

The first meeting between Kennedy and Macmillan, at Key West, was a fairly
impromptu diversion on the prime minister's part from a holiday trip to the
Bahamas. Kennedy wanted Macmillan to help him with the situation in Laos
which, Eisenhower had warned him, was the key to all Southeast Asia. But
Macmillan pleaded the need to consult with his cabinet before he could make
any commitments. In fact, the Foreign Office was highly critical of American
policy in Laos and the destruction of Souvanna Phouma, whom it considered
the best man to keep this tiny land non-Communist. And so instead of a firm
commitment on a participation of British forces, Kennedy got only a contingent one.

Early in April Macmillan came to Washington for his first formal meeting
with Kennedy, which again turned out to be only a limited success. As one
of the American participants put it to me: "The prime minister floated on too
many clouds of fuzzy eloquence," which led to confusion as to just how far
he had committed himself to a policy of leading Britain into the Common
Market. The prime minister had prepared himself for this debut with Kennedy
as an actor might study his entrance to an opening scene because he was unsure
of how to pitch his own personality to the young president. In the exchanges
he became a shade too longwinded, too pedantic, too often belaboring the
obvious for Kennedy's taste; still Kennedy was intrigued by the man, his
manner, and his sense of history.

Macmillan later told me with an amused smile that when he entered the

Oval Office for his first meeting with the president, Kennedy had nothing on his vast desk but one book. And when he picked it up to see what the president was reading, he found to his great surprise that it was a book called *As We Are,* my collection of interviews with famous Americans from all walks of life which had just been published. Quite clearly, Kennedy wanted to do me a favor. He wrote to me a few days later thanking me for the book (which also contained an interview with him), saying that Macmillan "was probably somewhat perplexed to find me in the company of Norbert Wiener, Peter Ustinov and Mrs. Arthur Miller (or is it Mrs. Joe di Maggio?), but it does not appear to have impaired Anglo-American relations. I was also somewhat surprised to find that quite a number of the themes we discussed over poached eggs last June [a reference to my interview with him] are still subjects of conversation at the White House breakfast table. I am afraid that my days as an author will be interrupted for a few years now, but I am glad that I was able to make this small contribution while still a politician-at-large. With every best wish . . ."

Kennedy later remembered that Macmillan's reaction on seeing my book was: "Oh, a book by Henry Brandon . . . haven't seen it yet . . . good man, Henry, good man . . ." Kennedy clearly was amused by having surprised the prime minister and thus started the conversation off on a most informal and lighthearted way. It was part of the Kennedy style.

Outwardly the contrast between Kennedy, the political prodigy, and Macmillan, the "old hand," was striking. One needed only to watch Kennedy's forceful stride and Macmillan's quivering one, Kennedy's determined manner and Macmillan's tremulous hesitancies. Some fifteen years later, when I called on Macmillan at his country place at Birch Grove, he came out on my arrival to greet me, leaning heavily on his cane. But later, when he had to leave the room for a moment, he walked quite well and quite fast and without it! Harold Wilson once said of him that he was "a great actor-manager whose greatest role was pretending to be a poseur." It was his way of camouflaging his inner strength and determination. He never aged. He was an old man from the first time I saw him, and remained one to become the oldest old man. He remained remarkably consistent in his manner, his thinking, and his speech.

At any rate, there was Macmillan in the president's Oval Office, with his crofter ancestry creeping out occasionally from his deeply ingrained intellectualism, visiting Kennedy, the masterful Boston-Irish politician with his anti-intellectual family background who became a determined Harvard man. Both were conservatives who, either by expediency or by growing conviction or pragmatism, had become liberals of their own particular hue. Both were cool and unemotional. Macmillan, though, could easily turn sentimental; Kennedy shrank from such an indulgence. Where Macmillan expected an obstreperous Irishman, he found instead rationality, mastery of the facts, and above all, an unexpected appreciation of the value of Anglo-American relations. Both had their own characteristic charm, dry and wry humor, self-assurance, inborn dignity and a devotion to history. It was not surprising therefore that the two struck up a relationship that went well beyond the national interest and developed into a kind of personal interdependence. Invariably whenever I saw Kennedy, his first question would be: "How is Macmillan?" as if I kept more in touch with him than he did. I believe his question was mainly to indicate how much he cared about him.

After a tense summer over the Berlin Wall crisis and Khrushchev's threats to the West's access routes to Berlin, the two decided to meet in Bermuda. Their discussions there took place in an intimate country-house atmosphere and the interest they developed then and there in the test-ban issue ultimately became the most important positive result of their relationship. By the time they met again in Washington late in April 1962 they were old friends. Yet despite the growing informality between the two, Kennedy still began his letters "Dear Mr. Prime Minister," while Macmillan chose to say "Dear friend." At about that time, though, the PM for the first time received a letter from the president which in turn addressed him as "Dear friend." A well-kept secret can now be told. This new salutation did not indicate a significant change on the part of the president, as Macmillan probably assumed, but was due to an accident. The White House duty officer, as he prepared to dispatch the letter by telegraph, found the salutation missing. Looking at Macmillan's last letter he saw that he addressed the president as "Dear friend" and, reasoning that this was the customary style, inserted "Dear friend" and so it remained from then on.

Kennedy became used to working with men considerably older than himself. The president began to like the rational Hugh Gaitskell, the leader of the Labour Party, whom Macmillan had described to him as easy to work with "though a bit reactionary," and the ebullient George Brown, but he found Harold Wilson too cold and withdrawn. He was fascinated by de Gaulle, but relations with him quickly soured after his Paris visit, and he never warmed to Adenauer. But, as he once put it to me, "I feel at home with Macmillan because I can share my loneliness with him. The others are all foreigners to me."

Yet there was a strong tendency within the Kennedy administration, abetted by Kennedy at least for the first two years, to subordinate the Anglo-American alliance to Britain's entry into the European Common Market and to absorbing the "independent" nuclear deterrent into a multinational arrangement under NATO, a Rube Goldberg construction, that came to be called the MLF (Multilateral Force). The plan called for a fleet of surface vessels equipped with missiles and manned by sailors of various nationalities. The British blamed a so-called cabal in the State Department for trying to overcome deep-seated and complex issues such as nationalism, nuclear jealousies, fears of nuclear ambitions and nuclear proliferation with a public relations stunt, well-meant but naively conceived, considering the sophistication of the officials involved. George Ball, Robert Schaetzel, Henry Owen, and others thought of themselves as farsighted men, wishing the best for Britain's future and European unity, but they failed to understand that they pursued their idea with too much passion and not enough diplomatic subtlety. On reading a still secret National Security Council directive, drafted by Schaetzel and sent to Secretary of Defense McNamara under the signature of Secretary of State Dean Rusk, who was not a true believer, one can understand why the British government resented the ideas of the "theologians," as they were also called. The directive advised that "over the long run it would be desirable if the British decided to phase out of the nuclear deterrent business, that the United States should not prolong the life of the British deterrent, except for the Skybolt missile promised by President Eisenhower, and after the British negotiations with the European Economic Community, the special Anglo-American relationshp be re-examined; to expand the relationship . . . could seriously . . . prejudice . . . sound multilateral arrangements." The theologians, I must admit, were correct in believing that Britain belonged into the European Community, but they overrated American power to force the British hand and underrated the resistance the application of that power created.

When McNamara, for reasons of cost-effectiveness and doubts about its technical feasibility, decided to cancel the Skybolt missile without consulting anybody, the theologians saw this as a God-given opportunity to advance their own dogmas. To the British, however, this unilateral decision represented a devastating blow because Skybolt was to prolong the life of the British V-bomber force, the badge of Britain's independent deterrent whose effective life was expected to expire within another five to seven years. The expression "cost-effectiveness" had not yet become common currency in London or even entered "Whitehallese." Therefore when members of the British defense staff came to Washington, John Thompson, a counselor at the British embassy, the British answer to McNamara's whiz kids, had some difficulty making them understand its meaning. At a dinner he gave for them he therefore served three different red wines and asked them to tell him how, according to their taste, they rated each. After they had done that he told them how much each cost and then he asked them which, taking the cost into consideration, they would buy. The wine samples did what wine does not always do, it cleared their minds, and thus "cost-effectiveness" entered the English vocabulary.

McNamara, who was good with statistics but not with politics, ignored the political consequences of his decision for the British. David Ormsby-Gore on his part was slow in following up the cancellation rumors that had begun to seep out of the Pentagon or in explaining the consequences a cancellation would have for Britain until after McNamara had taken the decision. He went to see McNamara on November 9, 1962, assuming that nothing was final. A day later McNamara phoned his opposite number in London, Peter Thorneycroft, a pugnacious right-wing Tory with little patience for Americans, who argued that if Skybolt was canceled, he expected to get Polaris as a substitute.

George Brown, the then shadow minister of defense in the Labour Party, had a standing invitation to stay with me, dating from the early fifties, the first time he had come to the United States. He had wanted to stay beyond the time that some official organization had paid for, and asked me whether I could put him up for a few extra days. I was delighted because George was entertaining company. So when in July 1962 he wrote that he would be "footloose" from the fifth to the eighth, that he hoped to see McNamara and, beyond, that he would be "glad to see some mutual friends" (which meant could you have a party for me and invite them), I of course invited him and arranged for a dinner party at home. A party for George was always a risk because he was not only one of the most uninhibited and provocative among politicians I knew but he did not hold his alcohol well. Even two gin-and-tonics could have an inflammatory effect and make him lose control over his language. He once offended Frank Wisner, a suprisingly vulnerable man in one of CIA's toughest jobs, so mercilessly that he left my dinner party in a huff and would not be soothed, even though Bill Bundy followed him into the garden to try to persuade him to return. The most sensitive reader of character, my sixty-year-old housekeeper, adored him and was charmed by his calling her "ducky." Though his normal approach to a conversation was to force his own views on somebody else or to compel others to give him their own, sometimes teasingly, sometimes with grim earnestness, everybody forgave him for his transgressions.

When in October 1963 he came to stay again and I called McGeorge Bundy to invite him to dinner with George, he said he would be delighted to have me bring him to his house for dinner. Senator Hubert Humphrey, Undersecretary George Ball, Arthur Schlesinger, Jr., the historian and White House aide, Walter Heller, chairman of the president's Council of Economic Advisers, and Bill Bundy all came to listen to George expounding what the Labour Party would do about Europe if it came to power. He left no one in doubt that the Multilateral Force was the wrong vehicle because it brought Germany too close to the nuclear trigger and declared that West Germany's Socialist leader Willy Brandt was equally opposed. At one point Brown even threatened that if the United States tried to push something like the MLF too hard, it could destroy the alliance. Furthermore, he argued, why worry about the Germans, they had nowhere else to go. Worry more about us (the British) and the French!

To all of which he was told that, first, de Gaulle would not change his mind about Britain's entry into the Common Market and, second, wasn't it also true that the British and French had nowhere else to go? And what made him so sure that the Germans had altogether excluded from their minds another Rapallo treaty (with the Russians), for there were such dangerous nationalists around as Franz Josef Strauss. Brown was also told that President Kennedy did not really trust Harold Wilson, because, among other things, he had equated Adenauer with East Germany's Ulbricht by saying on a recent visit to Moscow that both were equally dangerous. Brown was a fountain of candor, but so were the Americans because they trusted Brown as a friend, which he was.

Actually, as Professor Richard Neustadt learned during an investigation (assigned to him by President Kennedy) to find out in retrospect how such close allies could have misunderstood each other so badly, that "a latent sentiment existed in the British Cabinet against sustaining the independent nuclear deterrent"—"Rab" Butler and Reginald Maudling for reasons of costs, Ted Heath because he thought Britain's entry into the Common Market would be made easier, Iain McLeod and Edward Boyle because they were impressed by McNamara's arguments—expressed in a commencement address—criticizing the national deterrents of other governments as strategically irrelevant, destabilizing, wasteful, and likely to invite an attack rather than to deter it. When McNamara found himself accused of denigrating the British deterrent, he issued a meek disclaimer. However, for Macmillan the independent deterrent was an essential aspect of the special relationship, and a proud ornament of his own place in history. He was not going to be the leader to deprive Britain of this symbol of power or, as he called it, membership card to the club of the Great Powers. What made matters worse at this particular vulnerable moment in British history was a speech at the US Military Academy at West Point by Dean Acheson saying that "Britain has lost an empire and has not yet found a role." Those words struck like lightning over 10 Downing Street. Macmillan, with his back to the wall, gave a stinging rebuke. Suspicions that an officially inspired attack had been launched were heightened when McNamara repeated the theme in his own Ann Arbor speech.

The atmosphere between London and Washington had become electric, even explosive. Realizing that they had to think of an alternative, Kennedy, Rusk, McNamara, and McGeorge Bundy met, and the secretary of defense proposed giving the British Polaris missiles as a more up-to-date weapon, but only if the British were to place them under the command of NATO—in other words make them a multilateral weapon. Rusk preferred the idea of letting Britain finish the development of Skybolt. Kennedy expressed a preference for McNamara's proposal. Immediately afterwards McNamara flew to London. On arrival he poured more oil onto the already inflamed situation by announcing that all five Skybolt tests so far had failed. The writing was on the wall for everybody to read. It was McNamara's way of cutting the Gordian knot. But the British government, after having refused to believe in a cancellation, did not want to accept the inevitable. After all, it saw itself in a good bargaining position. It did have a firm promise for Skybolt and, if necessary, for a substitute. Above all, it could threaten to cancel the American privileges to use the Holy Loch base in Scotland for the servicing of American nuclear submarines.

McNamara and Thorneycroft did not mince words when they faced each other across the conference table: the two disliked each other intensely. McNamara put forward his alternative, Polaris under NATO command, and

Thorneycroft, objecting to the multilateralization of the British deterrent, threatened to edge out of the Holy Loch commitment. But as Paul Nitze later put it, McNamara took this threat "like a tank being spattered by eggs."

The controversy in the American camp meanwhile heated up too. Rusk was accused by the "cabal" under his own roof of putting British wants ahead of European needs when he opposed depriving Britain of the independent deterrent in order to force Britain into a multilateral arrangement. "We have to have somebody to talk to in the world," he insisted. The special relationship still meant something special for him. Kennedy too felt that the United States under the agreement with Eisenhower was committed to provide a replacement for Skybolt.

En route to a Nassau rendezvous with Kennedy, Macmillan met with de Gaulle at Rambouillet. It was a cold and drizzly day, de Gaulle was his more-than-haughty self, and Macmillan was at his most conciliatory, trying to convince the French leader that first of all he would do everything to preserve Britain's independent deterrent with Kennedy, and, secondly, that this issue should not prevent Britain from being admitted to the European Common Market. De Gaulle remained convinced that Britain would seek to maintain its special relationship with the Americans and hence be only a halfhearted member of the EEC, and so hardly reacted when Macmillan confided to him that he would ask Kennedy for Polaris. Macmillan was still hoping that de Gaulle would not veto Britain's entry into the Common Market, but at this point what mattered to him most was the preservation of the British nuclear deterrent.

He could not afford politically to come to grief over it. It was with this thought uppermost in his mind that he arrived in Nassau. Knowing how the British and the Americans felt, it was not difficult for me to predict in *The Sunday Times* that "in an extraordinarily precipitous fashion, the Kennedy-Macmillan talks in Nassau next week have suddenly developed into a crisis meeting—so much so, in fact, that it may turn out to be one of the most crucial 'tests' for the Anglo-American 'special relationship' since the war." At a colloquium offered by Macmillan's sensitive biographer Alistair Horne at the Woodrow Wilson Institute in Washington in 1983, McGeorge Bundy said that it was this dispatch that made the American side for the first time aware of the angry mood that prevailed on the British side. In fact, to my mind, the British arrived in Nassau in the angriest frame of mind of any delegation at an Anglo-American summit since the war. The only parallel was the British feeling after the Suez crisis, but then there was no actual confrontation between the two heads of state. In contrast to previous meetings, there had not been an advance exchange of position papers; in fact David Ormsby-Gore left Washington on Kennedy's plane unaware that the British cabinet had, at the last minute, decided to opt for Polaris.

The compromise he and Kennedy worked out provided for the British to continue to develop Skybolt with the United States, splitting the costs fifty-fifty to counter any charges of bad faith and to keep the British nuclear deterrent alive. But on arrival in Nassau Thorneycroft told him that it was Polaris or nothing.

Macmillan opened the conference like a Mark Anthony giving the funeral oration—I come to bury Skybolt, not to praise it—and launched into a moving review of the history of Anglo-American relations. He spoke about the proud days when it was chiefly due to British scientists that the atomic bomb was developed, when later their work was shifted from beleaguered Britain to the United States, and that in the light of all this the two countries in a sense owned an equal share in this nuclear equity. He then, according to the British record, approached what was to him the central concern: the hurt Anglo-American relations would suffer if the United States came under suspicion in England of wanting to deprive Britain of her nuclear capacity. He said Britain would not welsh on any of the past agreements with the United States, the Polaris depot could remain in Holy Loch, the advanced radar station would be allowed to operate from Fylingdales, the bomber bases would remain at the disposal of the United States, but—but having said all this—he felt obliged to add that the United Kingdom had run and was still running risks by harboring these bases. Would the president really want Britain to take these risks yet exercise none of the powers? If this seemed to be so, it would inevitably shatter US-UK relations, and public opinion, fickle as it is, could get out of control.

Kennedy was moved, but not yet fully convinced. He brought up how long the British had known about the cancellation of Skybolt, the alternatives he had offered, and that Britain could still proceed with Skybolt. But Macmillan made it clear in the midst of all his grief that Skybolt was gone, with the somewhat Victorian observation that "the girl has been violated in a public place." Kennedy laughed and realized that his option now was between offering Polaris or having Macmillan return home in a huff, blaming him for having deprived Britain of its badge of power. He also calculated that the American public would be sympathetic to such British accusations. Overnight he decided to ignore the desperate efforts of the "Europeanists" to protect their cause, depriving Britain of its privileged position with the United States. The compromise that satisfied him, and was acceptable to Macmillan, was to proceed with Polaris, on financial terms favorable to the British government, with the provision that it would be at the disposal of NATO, though to the British alone in case of a national emergency. The compromise paved the way for a graceful transition from independence to interdependence. It did not please the cabal or General de Gaulle. To the latter the Nassau agreement was a good excuse, if he needed one, to keep Britain out of Europe. The American offer to give the French Polaris under "similar" conditions was a non-starter. De Gaulle was convinced that France had to have its own independent *force de frappe*. It was as important to him politically as it was for Macmillan.

As seen from Nassau, Macmillan had scored a remarkable personal triumph, as Kennedy readily admitted. But on arrival in London the British press gave the prime minister a monstrously unfavorable reception. It called Nassau a defeat. Once on the wobble, it is not easy, even for such a master of political balance as Macmillan was, to stay steady on the tightrope.

Kennedy, tired but content, flew from Nassau directly to Palm Beach for a rest. However, when early Saturday morning a Pentagon announcement, totally out of the blue, reported a successful flight test of Skybolt, he hit the roof. McNamara was equally incensed. It was, however, nothing but the final twitching of the tail of a dead lizard.

Rethinking Nassau, it was obvious to Kennedy that something had gone wrong in communications between Washington and London. It troubled him how close it came to a serious break in the special relationship. From my own findings and those of Richard Neustadt and access to various still secret documents, it is clear that no single person deserves all the blame. McNamara set it all in train by being too cautious about admitting that he had made an irrevocable decision, then by not being frank about it with the British. Rusk, since it was more a political than technical problem, should have taken the lead in initiating negotiations. He was too permissive in allowing the "Europeanists" to exploit this opportunity to deprive Britain of its independent deterrent. David Ormsby-Gore, when he saw Kennedy after Thanksgiving, did not give the president due warning of the consequences of McNamara's decision. David Bruce, the American ambassador in London, was told to stay out of an issue which was to be resolved between two secretaries of defense. McGeorge Bundy, who often thought he was walking on water when he was in fact skating on thin ice, underrated this crisis and was himself of two minds about what the president should do. He had several crises to focus on at the time, especially the Cuban missile crisis in October and November 1962. As Neustadt said at the time, "One wonders whether Bundy might not need a Bundy of his own." De Gaulle's reaction to Nassau was much like that of the British press: that Macmillan had forfeited "independence," lost his fight, and returned home without a national deterrent which he had claimed at Rambouillet he would preserve. And so what to those present at Nassau looked like one of the most brilliant and muscular negotiating performances, was seen in London as a disguised Macmillan defeat.

The whole Skybolt crisis was indicative of the thin thread on which Britain's nuclear power position hung, how dependent it was on the United States, how delicate the Anglo-American special relationship had become, and how difficult it was for Britain to keep a foot in the American and European camps.

History, though, vindicated Macmillan. For it was thanks to his foresight and stubbornness that Britain, when President Reagan and General Secretary Gorbachev agreed to proceed with the zero option for intermediate-range nuclear missiles, had its own nuclear deterrent to fall back on.

In later years whenever I met Macmillan alone or at social occasions the first thing he wanted to reminisce about was the golden days of Anglo-American relations under Kennedy, a president who appreciated his political wisdom and who, especially regarding the nuclear test ban negotiations, not only shared his views but allowed himself to be influenced by them. He considered the treaty, as he put it in his memoirs *At the End of the Day,* "the greatest of my parliamentary successes." But his admiration for Kennedy went much beyond the Polaris and test ban treaty. He was exhilarated by his intellectual exuberance, by his receptiveness to ideas, by his political acumen, by "the boy on holiday with the dignity of a President," as he put it so aptly. Thus we had something in common which created a bond I deeply appreciated.

Kennedy's presidential training in crisis management began uncomfortably early when the attempt to invade Cuba and overthrow the Castro regime, the so-called Bay of Pigs fiasco, exploded in his face in the third month after he had assumed the presidency. That it happened at all was due to inexperience and a too-ready acceptance of a scheme fathered by the CIA under the Eisenhower administration. A group of specially trained Cuban exiles landed after Kennedy had canceled a pre-invasion air strike against Castro's airfields and, badly hit by Castro's air force, tanks, and infantry, found itself within two days of fighting in deep trouble. If there was a positive side to it, it was that it brought some intellectual sobriety to Kennedy and his equally inexperienced staff. None of them was then attuned to the pitfalls of the exercise of power. I happened to have a long prearranged lunch at the Hay-Adams Hotel with Bill Bundy, who was then working for the CIA, on the day he got the first indications of the effect of the failure of the invasion force on anti-Castro Cubans. Bill was obviously shattered by the news. Afterwards I ran into his brother McGeorge, Kennedy's National Security adviser, as he rushed from the Executive Building across the narrow parking alley into the White House. He was even more distraught than his brother, his eyes looking haggard and his face white as chalk. "I'm guilty," he exclaimed hurrying past me. He told me later that shortly thereafter he wrote a letter to the president offering his resignation, including a sentence that, in case it was not accepted, the president should keep on file for possible future use.

The CIA blamed the president for the fiasco because he refused to let the US Navy and Air Force rescue the operation from the jaws of failure, but in retrospect it was the CIA's underrating of the risks, its ramshackle operation and management, the poor choice of a landing strip, and false intelligence expectations of the landing's reception inside Cuba that were mainly to blame. An air strike would not have been enough, a rescue would have required bringing in ground troops.

On Kennedy's part there was too much trust in the personalities involved and a failure to examine the attendant risks carefully. He was impressed by Allen Dulles's judgment, as he put it to him, that he had much more confidence in this operation than in the CIA's engineered overthrow of the Guatemalan government in 1952, and he relied too much on the widely admired brilliance of Richard Bissell, the man in charge of the operation.

I knew Bissell from his more innocent days with the Marshall Plan and was impressed by his intellectual competence, his managerial assertiveness, and his dedication to his work. Sometimes, though, I had a feeling that there was a gap between his training as an economist and his intellectual spinning of grandiose ideas. In the Agency and beyond he had scored with the development of the U-2 spy plane, which, even though it crashed at the wrong moment in world diplomacy, had given the CIA and its intelligence gathering an enormous boost. Kennedy considered him the CIA's best man, and the Bundy brothers looked up to him as one of the most brilliant they knew. In fact, he was once Bill's economics instructor at Yale. A major factor in Kennedy's decision to proceed with the operation was the so-called disposal problem, which meant what to do with the Cubans who were panting to throw themselves into this operation, the liberation of their Cuba. Allen Dulles warned him that if the invasion, so long in preparation, was canceled, the story could not be kept secret and the desperate Cubans would accuse him publicly of having stopped Eisenhower's plan for the liberation of Cuba.

Trusting Allen Dulles's experience in the business and having almost limitless confidence in Bissell's judgment, Kennedy and his advisers never asked whether the CIA had the means to carry out and support a paramilitary operation. Nor did they try to find out what the Agency's view of the operation was. They would then have found out that there was strong opposition to the Bissell plan. One who blamed himself was Dean Rusk, for having taken too narrow a view of his portfolio and consequently not taken the interest in the affair he should have. Bissell not only was relatively new to the job of chief of covert operations, but, ambitious as he was, he wanted to score with a spectacular operation. Much is also overlooked, old CIA hands explained to me, because of the tunnel vision that imposes itself on a man who becomes intensely, even passionately, involved in as complex, dangerous, and deeply absorbing an operation as the Bay of Pigs invasion was. Finally, once such an operation was in progress, it became hard to stop or reverse. Too many people had acquired too many important stakes in it. Perhaps the most powerful factor was the hatred Bissell and others had developed of Fidel Castro, who had the temerity to set up a Communist regime almost in sight of the American coast, in a strategically critical area, and in a position to infect the rest of Latin America with communism. It was not surprising that the desire to get rid of Castro became a crucial objective for CIA. It has remained so ever since.

At a press conference shortly before the Bay of Pigs invasion Kennedy had promised unequivocally that there would be no direct American military involvement, and he held to that promise. He decided instead to cut his losses, despite pressures by the military to send the US Navy and Air Force to the rescue, and to face a political setback of major proportions. His readiness to assume responsibility for the disaster created a kind of pride in fortitude and a rallying of the public to a seriously weakened president, so that he rose in the public opinion polls to 83 percent—the highest rating, by the way, of his entire presidency. The only public figure who urged him openly to communicate with Khrushchev about the event was Richard Nixon, but when the two world leaders met in Vienna, Khrushchev's approach was to try to take advantage of a young and "wounded" president.

Their encounter left a deep impression on Kennedy. I will never forget his frozen face as he stepped out of the Soviet Embassy after the first meeting. I was standing close to the entrance of the embassy and he happened to look straight at me. But I had a feeling that so dazed was he after the treatment he got from the Soviet leader that he did not recognize me. He had expected this summit to open the way to the relaxation of tension that he had promised in his inaugural, and instead it had turned into a bewildering showdown for which he had not been prepared. It was, he said afterwards, a "somber affair." His meeting in Paris did not provide him with a success either. De Gaulle, it became clear to him, aimed at a revived, powerful Europe that could fulfill an historic, independent role between the two giants.

President Kennedy, used to a life of unfailing fortune and success, now had to adjust to the hard realities of governing and they did not allow the miracles that he had seemed to promise and people had come to expect. When he called the American presidency "awesome," he had not actually quite believed it. He did now. He also recognized that it deserved more humility than he had thought. Now, too, he sought greater diversity among his advisers, for the minds around him were too much like his own. His recipe—combining the muscular intellect of a McGeorge Bundy with Robert McNamara's sharp technocratic mind and Dean Rusk's tentative personality—was not producing the expected results. Too much had gone wrong too soon. It was unnerving at first, however much sympathy I felt for him, to watch his costly education. General de Gaulle's parting words to the President: *N'écoutez que vous même!* ("Listen only to yourself!") reverberated in his ears. Whether the general had meant to compliment him on his mature views or simply to flatter him, he did not know, but he had reason to think that his own political instincts were sounder than much of the advice he was getting.

Cuba was and still is a thorn in the American side—indeed, the whole of Latin America is a nightmare for American governments, because of its chronic instability. The Cuban revolution, for instance, was not a reflection of the strength of communism, but of the new economic and social forces let loose in the hemisphere. It had seemed to me therefore important to learn something about the goings-on in this region and so I had used the interval between Kennedy's election and his inauguration to visit nine countries in Central and

South America. I had returned with the conclusion that Castro had touched deep-seated sympathies among the lower classes, but that the Cuban revolution had passed the peak of its popularity.

One of the greatest fallacies, I learned, was to see Latin America as if it were a homogeneous continent. Pan-Americanism had very little meaning as a slogan. The problems of these differing countries are similar but the necessary solutions differ from country to country. As I flew, for instance, from Buenos Aires to La Paz, first over the unrelieved flatness of the pampas with its lack of usable roads and poorly cultivated land, then over the arid chains of the Andes with only an occasional pockmark habitation, to land finally between the snowcapped Cordilleras at 13,000 feet in Bolivia's capital, I felt as though I had spanned civilizations several centuries apart. The question I asked myself later was whether the changes due to growing instability and insecurity, to the lack of social consciousness of the rich, to the growing restlessness of the poor, and to the mistakes of American policies would lead to evolution or revolution and, in the latter case, whether it would be the Mexican or the Cuban model. Since then both have lost much of their attraction. Perceptions change fast. What has not changed is the hatred the International Monetary Fund aroused then and now. When in Brazil I asked President Kubitschek's economic adviser what would have happened to the United States if the IMF had existed one hundred years earlier. He replied: "The United States would still be an underdeveloped country."

It was not until October 1962 that I visited Cuba for the first time. I had of course no idea on arrival that the Soviets had begun building missile bases there and that the most serious crisis of the thermonuclear age between the United States and the Soviet Union was only weeks away. Only by an extraordinary fluke of good luck did I find out about the Soviet-inspired threat to the United States. It began with an unusual interview with Che Guevara, which I owed to an Argentinian friend who lived in Washington, married to an American. When she heard that I was off to Cuba, she volunteered a letter of introduction to "Che," who, she said, had been a teenage friend of hers in Buenos Aires. My problem on arrival in Cuba was how to get the letter to Che without going through official channels. So I decided to go directly and personally to his Ministry of Industry after the official hours. There I asked to see his own private secretary, who duly came to meet me in the entrance hall after I had told him over the house telephone that I had a private letter for his boss from an old friend and gave him her name. The next morning I got a telephone call from the same private secretary at my hotel asking me where he would be able to reach me during the day because Che was anxious to meet me, but could not give me a definite time as yet.

It was not until nine P.M. that I got another phone call asking me to be at the ministry at 10 P.M. Che Guevara received me in his drab khaki-green uniform with the front buttons open exposing his hairy chest almost to the navel. He exuded an aggressive charm that might have made even Charles

Boyer envious. The conversation began with his questioning me about his former girl friend; he had not known that she now lived in Washington. What did she look like, to whom was she married, how many children did she have? After about twenty minutes of this he broke off to say that, after all, I had not come just to tell him about her, and he invited me to ask him questions.

Was he concerned, I asked, that one of these days the United States might move decisively against Cuba. "Direct aggression against Cuba," he replied flatly, "would mean nuclear war." Turning his charm suddenly into a mean grimace, he added: "The Americans speak about such aggression as if they did not know or did not want to accept that fact." He said he disagreed with a statement Ahmed Ben Bella, the Algerian president, had just made on arrival in Havana: "The situation in Cuba is as dangerous as that in Berlin." Then Che continued: "Of course, we won't be so stupid as to furnish the Americans with a pretext to attack us by, say, contesting the Guantanamo naval base or by sending arms to Latin American countries. We're following a cautious policy, we are not imbeciles." When I raised the question of the fishing port which Castro had said the Russians were going to build, an announcement that had aroused suspicions in Washington, he replied with a broad smile and a casual wave of the hand: "Of course it will be a fishing port, and it will be right here in Havana Harbor. And even if this harbor should be suitable for submarines," he asked rhetorically, "what right has the United States to object to it? This is our harbor, where we can do as we please." His cocksureness was obviously based on promises Castro had received from the Russians. But when I asked what sort of arms the Russians were supplying to Cuba, I drew a curt, slightly amused blank. Finally, after three hours of talk, including a good deal of self-serving praise for Cuba's industrial progress, he got up, thanked me for bringing the letter, and added: "Tell my dear old friend that if she ever wants to visit me in Cuba, she will be most welcome and will be treated like a queen." A few months later Che Guevara, unhappy with the sedentary life of an unsuccessful minister, left for Bolivia in the hope of organizing a Castro-like revolution there. Instead the saga of this glamorous adventurer and hero to many young people ended in violent death.

At a small cocktail party I met one of those bearded veterans of the Castro revolution. He wore his green khaki uniform with obvious pride and carried an automatic gun in his trouser pocket. He was blond with a very white skin and his manner was austere, serious, and intense. He had been a student in France and one reason for his interest in me was that I spoke French. We met again the next evening in one of the small taverns in the old city of Havana, an occasion full of fascination and apprehension that I will never forget. He told me at great length about the history of the Castro revolution, about the months in the mountains when American correspondents came to see Fidel and how he told them that he was reading Montesquieu, while to his followers he spoke about reading Lenin and Marx. Gradually he came to tell me about Cuba as it had become. However, when I suggested that close alliance with the Soviet Union could lead to American intervention, especially if Castro disregarded the conditions President Kennedy had laid down for the security of the United States, he suddenly jumped up, gritting his teeth, and shouted at me angrily, "Cuba is not as defenseless as you may think. We now have missiles on Cuban territory whose range is good enough to hit the United States and not only Florida!" Then he added with a certain sense of triumph: "And they are manned by Russians!" I could hardly believe my ears. But he repeated the last sentence to make me realize the importance I should attach to what he was saying. He went on: "We will not use them for aggressive purposes, of course. Why after all would little Cuba want to attack the giant United States? But we need them to be able to hit an attacker's territory as a means to deter such an attack."

What a revelation! What a story! I said to myself. We went on talking and talking. All the other customers had long left, but he did not seem to be aware of how late it was. Finally, at about two A.M., he suggested that we leave. Across from the restaurant was a small parking lot with one solitary car left, his Saab. But as we approached it, he stopped in the middle of the parking lot and began to harangue me with a fervent lecture about Marxism, what it meant to him, to Cuba, to the world. It was a wierd, almost surrealistic scene. There was I in romantic Havana standing under a beautifully starlit sky, forced to listen to a lecture on Castroism. It seemed to me as if we were the only people still awake, and the longer this towering figure, silhouetted against the sky, lectured me, the more uneasy I felt, wondering how this would end. All this had gone on in elegant French. Suddenly he broke off, lowered his voice—and motioned me to get into his car. He was his calm self again and said that he would now drive me back to my hotel, the Riviera. I felt a little silly about having been a bit frightened on that parking lot. My next thought was how to get confirmation of that intriguing missile story.

The next day, therefore, I went to see the British ambassador, Bill Marchant, whom I had met before on his way through Washington. I knew him to be an experienced professional whom I could take into my confidence. When I told him what had happened to me and asked whether he had any inkling about these medium-range Soviet missiles, he shook his head and suggested that I discount what I had heard. There had been plenty of rumors about such missiles having arrived in Cuba, he said, but he did not believe them. He did not think the Russians would be so foolish as to bring them into Cuba. I left, uncertain what to do next, because there was nobody else in whom I could confide without arousing all sorts of suspicions or giving the story away. Somehow, though, I still believed my bearded Cuban companion.

At a loss about my next move, I decided first to apply for my exit visa, to be sure I could let the world know about this sensational development, then to seek him out once again to see whether he would be willing to repeat his statement in the light of day. I rang him at the number he had given me, his office, but it took two days before he returned my call. He seemed delighted that I had got in touch again, and suggested that we meet that evening early at his apartment. He warned me though that he had a rendezvous with his girl friend later and therefore could only have a brief dinner with me. We met at his small apartment where he introduced me to his pretty, young wife, who was busy looking after their newborn baby. Then we drove to the hospital where his girl friend worked as a nurse. She was even better-looking than his wife. At a nearby restaurant I then got my chance to bring up the question of the missiles again, and to my great relief he had no hesitation in confirming what he had already told me. He even added that a high Soviet official—I assumed he referred to Deputy Premier Anastas Mikoyan, who had visited Cuba recently—had reassured Castro that Russia would not push the Berlin crisis, which had flared up after the Vienna summit, to a point where it might lead to American retaliatory action against Cuba! This was an interesting strategic wrinkle that had not occurred to me before, but which I now realized was of cardinal importance to Castro.

On my two-day trip through the countryside, sponsored by the Cuban Foreign Ministry, we visited at my request the Bay of Pigs, scene of that abortive invasion. Most of the villages we passed seemed out of a picture album of the American Wild West. The cowboys still had their lassos, though most of them rode ponies. The hideous crocodiles which once infested the swampland we crossed were now neatly gathered in artificially built basins at what was called Treasure Island, which was Castro's idea of a vacation spot. It was a boy's dream of an Indian village among well-groomed flower beds that even the gardeners at Versailles would have been proud of. The restaurant, the log cabins around the lake, all looked like a Hollywood fantasy. Cuban sightseers jammed it because, as we found out gradually, they could get not only beer here, which was virtually unobtainable in Havana, but also a nice chunk of either beef or pork and a heap of rice with black beans for lunch. The Bay of Pigs was a few miles on from Treasure Island. We drove all the way to the entrance of the bay and looked at the various landing places, which were still marked by charred, chopped trees and a few bomb craters. On a little airstrip we could still see the debris of a crashed B-26. Strategically, it seemed to me outrageously badly chosen because swampland and the narrow bridge were bound to slow down any advance. It was also too far from the mountains for invaders to escape, hide, and organize a guerrilla operation—all this quite apart from their having had insufficient guns and ammunition and no proper backup supplies.

Back in Havana I took a stroll along the coastal road to look at those brand-new dark-green Russian-built trucks that rolled along all day, carrying wooden crates marked "handle with care" in Russian, but nothing more to indicate the contents. The dozens of cement mixers that also passed by were unlikely to be needed in those numbers for the prefabricated houses the government was erecting everywhere. All the men on the trucks had distinctly Russian features; the Soviets obviously did not trust the Cubans with what they were doing.

Thanks to my early application, I managed to get off the island just before all exit visas were canceled. A Swedish colleague, for instance, who applied for his exit visa one day later had to spend the entire time of the confrontation between the United States and the Soviet Union under house arrest in Havana. My plane was due to leave in the early morning of Saturday, October 20, for Miami, but because of the endless search the luggage of Cubans who had emigration papers to go to the United States was subject to, its departure was delayed by several hours. Consequently I arrived late in the afternoon in Miami, from where I called my editor to tell him about my findings. It was almost midnight in London by then and since there had been no developments concerning Cuba, we agreed that instead of filing a short story about the Soviet missile rumors, I would tell the entire story in great detail the following week. Events were thus conspiring—in ways that I could not guess—to deprive me of a major world scoop. It is one of the hazards of working for a Sunday-only newspaper.

When I arrived in Washington I found an invitation to a wedding anniversary party for the Alfred Friendlys. Alfred was then the managing editor of the Washington *Post,* and since both were dear friends of mine, I decided to join the celebration however tired I felt after this nerve-wracking but exhilarating Cuban experience. Even at the merriest of Washington weddings, the business of politics will not go away. After dinner, as the dancing began, guests began telling one another that the president was preparing a very important speech, though no one seemed to know what its drift was to be. I noticed that Al Friendly suddenly left; so too did Arthur Schlesinger. There was suspense in the air.

Next morning I got a call from McGeorge Bundy, who had heard that I had just returned from Cuba, saying that the president would like to see me to hear about my trip, but since he had reasons to avoid my being seen to enter the White House, in view of the fact that several of my colleagues knew about my visit to Cuba, would it be convenient if instead of my seeing the president, I would see Bundy's deputy, Carl Kaysen, at my house. Of course, I replied and Kaysen arrived shortly thereafter. I told him how I had discovered the presence of the Soviet missiles and that I would be writing about it in next Sunday's *Sunday Times.* Then an awful thought began to dawn on me and I asked him whether the president's speech, scheduled for Monday, would deal with Cuba. Kaysen, keeping a straight face, then indicated that I was on the right track without actually answering my question. That morning the President asked Ormsby-Gore to come to the White House, but, please, not in an ostentatious embassy car! He then gave him advance notice of the content of the announcement he would be making the next day. Later, in the afternoon, he spoke to Scotty Reston, then head of the *New York Times* Washington bureau, who had called him on Bundy's suggestion to ask whether in view of all the various military moves that had come to the notice of his newspaper, he was about to impose a blockade on Cuba. Kennedy confirmed that he would, but also expressed the hope that the *New York Times* would not break the news before he had announced it, since premature disclosure could lead the Russians to giving the United States an ultimatum. Reston replied that the decision was up to the publisher, but before recommending against publication could the president assure him that there would be no bloodshed. Kennedy replied that Reston could have his word of honor that there would not be bloodshed or violence before the announcement.

What I did not know was that on Tuesday morning, October 16, 1962, the CIA's U-2 reconnaissance plane had brought back convincing evidence of what I had observed on the ground and learned from my Cuban contact, that the Russians had been moving medium-range ballistic missiles that could carry nuclear warheads into Cuba. President Kennedy, in a way, scooped me, when he disclosed the presence of Soviet missiles on Cuba and that he was imposing a naval blockade to prevent further missiles from reaching Cuba. I consoled myself when *The Sunday Times* the following weekend gave a full page for what was still the only eyewitness account of what had meanwhile become a beleaguered Cuba.

The atmosphere in Washington—in fact, throughout the world—became tense. A sparring match between the two superpowers had begun, the most serious confrontation since the end of World War II and the first in the nuclear age. It was deeply disturbing, with everybody's fate at stake. Did they have the wit to find a way out? Did they know what was at stake? Would Khrushchev, that firebrand of a leader, accept defeat? President Kennedy, by then, had assembled a group of men who were so conversant with the facts that it was unnecessary to bring in departmental experts, and paperwork was reduced to a minimum. The debate was conducted directly by men of high intelligence who sharpened their wits on one another. This was probably the only viable approach to crisis management in the nuclear age. The members of the Ex-Com, as this Executive Committee was called, disagreed among themselves, often quite sharply, but it would be wrong simply to divide them into hawks and doves. The former, at least in the early discussions, favored an air strike against the Soviet missile bases in Cuba—a surgical strike, as they called it. They felt confident that the Soviets would not retaliate, say, against Berlin, because they knew that the United States had nuclear superiority and could then retaliate against Soviet targets.

By coincidence, and in a most unprecedented way, the Anglo-American relationship came into play when on Tuesday, after the president had delivered the speech imposing the blockade, David Ormsby-Gore, during a private dinner with the Kennedys, suggested, first, that the aerial photographs the United States had taken of the missile sites be given publicity, and, secondly, that the distance at which Soviet ships were to be intercepted be reduced from the original 800 to 500 miles in order to give the Kremlin more time for ordering its ships back. Regarding the photographs, David told me later, he pointed out that in Britain, for instance, a good many people were not convinced that these medium-range missiles had been put into Cuba. The president agreed and they selected a few which uncontestably proved the American claims. Later, during the evening, Bobby Kennedy joined them after he had seen the Soviet ambassador, Anatoly Dobrynin, in the hope of discovering whether the Russian ships had received instructions to turn back. He reported that Dobrynin knew of no such instructions. The possibility grew that next day, Wednesday, when the blockade was to come into effect, a confrontation would occur. It was at that point that David argued that the Soviets had some difficult decisions to take, that they had to climb down as gracefully as they could, and that every additional hour that could be given to them might be helpful. He therefore suggested, as he put it to me, "that for the US Navy to go far out into the Atlantic to seek a ship in order to intercept it, perhaps would not be wise." Impressed with the argument, Kennedy then instructed McNamara to set the distance at which Soviet ships were to be intercepted at 500 miles. Then David, as an afterthought about the advantage of having been such a close friend of the president, said to me: "It was fortuitous that I happened to be having a very private dinner with the president that night." Rome and Athens were on the same wavelength . . .

To ensure that not only Macmillan but also de Gaulle and Adenauer had a full appreciation of what had made him move so resolutely against the Soviet Union and Cuba, Kennedy sent Dean Acheson first to Paris, then Bonn and London with the aerial photographs that revealed the missile emplacements. Acheson's account of his meeting with the French leader was so superbly characteristic of the general's style and behavior that I am reproducing extracts as told to Luke Battle, with the latter's permission from the Acheson file at the Kennedy Library in Boston.

De Gaulle was obviously pleased with Acheson's visit: "Your president has done me a great honor by sending so distinguished an emissary," he said as they shook hands. Acheson commented that there was no possible reply to this wonderful phrase, except to bow. Then, after reading the letter from the president, de Gaulle started right off in a businesslike manner: "In order to get our roles clear, do I understand that you have come from the president to inform me of some decisions—or have you come to consult me about a decision which he should take?" To this Acheson said: "I have come to inform you of a decision which he has taken and which will not materialize unless and until Russian ships attempt to violate the blockade."

"That was a wise step," de Gaulle remarked. Then Acheson continued: "I have outside the photographs of these missiles. I think you might want to see them." The general waved this suggestion aside and said, "Not now—these will only be evidence—a great nation like yours would not act if there were any doubts about the evidence and, therefore, I accept what you tell me as a fact without any proof of any sort needed . . . but let's get the significance of the situation before we look at the details of it." (This was directly the opposite of Macmillan's attitude, as I learned later, who said, "We must publish these right away—we must get these in the papers—no one will believe this unless they see these." General de Gaulle didn't care whether anyone believed it or not—he did, this was enough for him. There was no need to bother about anybody else.)

De Gaulle then asked Acheson whether he thought the Russians would attempt to force this blockade and whether they would have reacted if President Kennedy had taken even sharper action. Acheson replied no to both his questions. Then he showed him the photographs with every detail of these missiles. De Gaulle was impressed and asked from what height they had been taken. Sixty-five thousand feet, Acheson replied. The general started to say that France did not possess such advanced aerial photography, but caught himself and simply admitted that it seemed a remarkable achievement to him. Then the soldier in him took over and he studied every one of the photographs. The IL-28s were first photographed on the deck of a ship; then, the same crates with the same markings on them were seen on an airfield. One of these had been broken open and here was an IL-28 with one wing on—the other had not been put on yet—but the photograph of that and a photograph of an IL-28 were put side by side. They were 500-mile-range atomic jet bombers. Concluding, de Gaulle said, "You may tell your president that France will support him in every way in this crisis." Acheson, in finishing his account then said: "De Gaulle didn't say I will—or the French government will—or anything. He was France. He then spoke the only words in English: 'It would be a pleasure to me if these things were all done through you.' " To Acheson, as he said later, this last sentence sounded as if Louis XIV had said a nice word to an ambassador from the Sultan of Turkey.

Throughout that week the Ex-Com struggled in vain to overcome the clashing viewpoints of its members and to reach a consensus. There were the worriers (as Professor Neustadt phrased it) or doves: Robert McNamara, Dean Rusk, Adlai Stevenson, Vice President Lyndon B. Johnson, and George Ball, the undersecretary of state. They favored trading missiles in Cuba against the American Jupiter missiles in Turkey. The nonworriers or hawks—Dean Acheson; Douglas Dillon; Paul Nitze, then an assistant secretary for international affairs in the Pentagon; General Maxwell Taylor, chairman of the Joint Chiefs of Staff; John McCone, director of the Central Intelligence Agency—still favored an air strike against the Cuban missile bases and an invasion by American troops if necessary. In between the hawks and the doves hovered the "owls"—pragmatic hawks—McGeorge Bundy, Robert Kennedy, and Llewellyn Thompson, the American ambassador to the Soviet Union. As the two superpowers seemed to head toward a confrontation that could ignite a nuclear catastrophe, Walter Lippmann wrote a bitter column about the absence of any diplomatic initiatives, not knowing that Robert Kennedy had assumed the role of the secret interlocutor who transmitted, through Ambassador Dobrynin, the compromise proposal that defused the crisis. That proposal was in reply to the earlier of two letters Nikita Khrushchev had sent on October 26, indicating that he would be prepared to dismantle the missiles; the second, harder in tone, raising the swap of Cuban against Turkish missiles, the president decided to ignore.

Twenty-five years later, most appropriately at Harvard's Kennedy School of Government, three of President Kennedy's chief lieutenants, McGeorge Bundy, Robert McNamara, and Ted Sorensen, met with two remarkably candid and well-informed Soviet representatives: Fedor Burlatsky, a speech writer for Khrushchev and Brezhnev; and Sergey Mikoyan, who flew to Cuba with his father, Deputy Primier Anastas Mikoyan, the great survivor from the Stalin days, when Fidel Castro had a fit over the withdrawal of the Soviet missiles. The result was an archaeological dig deep into the crevices of their combined memories. Both sides were aghast at how much they had failed to grasp each other's anxieties, motivations, and aims before and during the crisis. McGeorge Bundy called it the "battle of blunders." What the Russians found hardest to believe was that the Americans had no intention of invading Cuba. The Americans were startled when told that Khrushchev's main reason for sending those missiles to Cuba was to deter such an American invasion. Khrushchev, the two Russians told us, decided to smuggle those missiles into Cuba only after the military had assured him that it could be done covertly and expeditiously and after he had convinced himself that the Americans would neither try to force their withdrawal nor take retaliatory actions. He was also influenced by his assessment of Kennedy, Mr. Burlatsky said, as an intelligent but weak man "who would crumble when tested"—a memorable illustration of the importance of not giving the Kremlin the impression of weakness. Perhaps Khrushchev's worst mistake, Mr. Burlatsky said, was that he did not ask himself what he would have to do if the Americans resisted the emplacement of the missiles in Cuba. He went on to say that one of the problems under Mr. Khrushchev was that in the discussions in the Presidium of the Central Committee, as the Politbureau was then called, he purposefully spoke first, which kept everybody else from stating his own position. It was the "wise" thing to do, as he delicately put it with a sardonic smile scurrying over his face. It is true that policies in the Soviet Union as well as in the United States are made by one man, the general secretary and the president, but there was a vast difference between the searching, rational discussion in the Ex-Com that gave Kennedy an understanding of all the alternatives, and the very personal and emotional one by Khrushchev.

Kennedy, in the end, reached the conclusion that those outdated Jupiter missiles in Turkey were not worth fighting a war over and was willing if necessary to propose a straight deal, their removal in exchange for the withdrawal of the missiles in Cuba. He confided such a move to no one else but Dean Rusk. However much Kennedy and others worried about the threat of

American credibility with the NATO allies implicit in the withdrawal of the Jupiters from Turkey, when it came to avoiding the risk of war, the president was willing to pay that price. Khrushchev, according to Mr. Burlatsky, got a case of angst, and was much relieved when he was offered the semblance of a face-saving device. We were told that Dobrynin first advised against the withdrawal of the missiles, but then supported the compromise offer, a guarantee not to invade Cuba and a promise to withdraw the missiles from Turkey. Mr. Gromyko, the foreign minister, was the author of the second, uncompromising letter that caused so much confusion in the Ex-Com.

Zbigniew Brzezinski, twenty-five years later, suggested to me that while the Cuban missile crisis was a tactical success for the United States, because Khrushchev agreed to remove the missiles from Cuba, it was a strategic success for the Russians, because Fidel Castro is still in control of Cuba. Should Kennedy have adopted a tougher stance? Bundy's reply to this is that the overthrow of Castro would have necessitated an invasion of Cuba by American forces, an alternative that was never under serious consideration. In fact, I was surprised that American nuclear superiority (five thousand warheads against three hundred) played virtually no role in the Ex-Com discussions. In the twilight chorus among historians criticism comes easily— Kennedy wanted nothing else but the removal of the missiles from Cuba.

Listening to both, the Americans and the Russians, makes it clear how difficult it is to know one's enemy, and, above all, how important it is to keep open channels of communication that will continue to function in all crisis situations. The Russians used not only Ambassador Dobrynin, but also the embassy's top KGB agent, who transmitted a conciliatory message through John Scali, the ABC network's well-connected diplomatic correspondent. President Kennedy deployed Robert Kennedy as an *interlocuteur valable*. Interestingly enough Walter Lippmann's column, suggesting the Cuban-Turkish missile deal, which greatly irritated the president, did not influence Mr. Khrushchev's thinking; in Russian eyes a columnist is not *valable* enough . . . Another important lesson to be drawn from this crisis is how easily the competition over control of a third world country can lead to a superpower confrontation, and of how little use are the stockpiles of nuclear weapons in such a crisis. As Mr. Burlatsky summed it up: "It was a bad crisis but a good ending."

The transcript of the October 27 Ex-Com debate should be read by every American and Soviet leader and their aides, even though the United States has since lost its nuclear superiority. What accounted for the prolonged suspense were the human factors at play on each side, the contest between "strength of will" and "the power of restraint." These are crucial ingredients of leadership, and Kennedy proved to have both. (Khrushchev, too, proved to be much saner than had been assumed.) Both offered the world the first example of the art of nuclear-age statecraft. It was not the Dulles kind of brinkmanship, but the judicious use of presidential powers and the careful calculation of the odds by balancing the military threat and the parameters of political accommodation. He did not stage a victory parade, even though when the Russians hastily took their missiles out of Cuba and allowed their ships to be inspected, the world knew that they were witnessing the first victory in the thermonuclear age without a poisonous fallout.

When on Sunday (October 28) McGeorge Bundy's secretary called me to say that our regular early morning tennis game, which included Bundy, Walt Rostow, and John McNaughton—like Paul Nitze, an assistant secretary for international affairs at the Pentagon—would be resumed on Monday, I knew the crisis was virtually over.

At a small private dance at the White House on November 9, Kennedy took me aside and made it clear that Cuba to him was only a carbuncle compared to Berlin, which he considered a cancer. Cuba, though, was still on his mind then, for he said that he had read my report of October 28 on my Cuban visit and, quoting from it, began to ask me questions about whether I had concluded that Castro had been a Communist from the start and how committed I thought he now was to the Soviets. I replied that he seemed to me a convinced Communist, but an admirer of neither Soviet nor Chinese communisn, though he depended on the Soviets for his survival. Kennedy then switched the subject to tell me how pleased he was with the outcome of the congressional off-year elections, for he had come close to achieving what only the Roosevelts, Theodore and Franklin, had been able to accomplish—gain political strength rather than lose it, as was the tradition for the party in power. From his electioneering, he said, he had learned that the peace issue was politically more effective than the economic one, and he would keep this very much in mind for the presidential campaign in 1964. The president did not dance much, he preferred either to watch the pretty women in their tantalizing evening gowns—and Jackie always made sure there were enough—or to chat with them in a corner. But in between he could not resist, even at his own dance, talking politics. Jackie came to interrupt our conversation, and, dancing, began to reminisce about a much smaller private affair she had given the previous September at Hammersmith Farm in Newport for a few friends, including Gianni Agnelli, the racy, shrewd, and well-informed Fiat tycoon, and his beautiful wife, Marella, as if to indicate to me that she did not find the ambience at the White House as congenial as that in a small private home.

Nevertheless, the glamour and elegance and the emphasis on promoting the arts Jacqueline Kennedy injected into White House entertainment were unprecedented. It gave the Kennedys an aura of sophistication which perhaps went beyond what they deserved. But, sensing the political and cultural values, they helped to change Washington from what Kennedy called the cultural wasteland to a city that developed a cultural taste and built him his most enduring monument, the Kennedy Center for the Performing Arts. The refined taste of White House entertaining not only inspired Washington hostesses to put their best dance foot forward, it even enthralled blasé New York society and spurred Truman Capote, the writer, to prove that he and New York could do even better. One day he told Katherine Graham, who had recently assumed control of the Washington *Post* after her husband, Philip, had committed suicide, that she needed cheering up. "I'll give you a party at my beloved ballroom at the Plaza Hotel," he told her. "I want everybody to dress in black and white as Cecil Beaton staged the ball scene in *My Fair Lady*. You'll be the guest of honor!" Kay did not believe he was serious until she got word from him that she could bring twenty of her friends from Washington to the party. At the time she did not think that she needed this kind of extravagant cheering up, but in fact, she had hardly recovered from a period of extreme mental torture when Phil, once a very handsome, smart, go-ahead young man, began to suffer increasingly from bouts of mental depression during which he threatened not only to divorce Kay but to take the Washington *Post* from her. He would have been able to do that because Kay's father, Eugene Meyer, had given him more shares than he had his daughter, maintaining that a man should not work for his wife. Phil, with ruffian cruelty, made Kay a foil of embarrassing jokes in front of her friends which outraged them. She, nevertheless, remained utterly supportive, continuing to tell everybody how marvelous he was and had been.

The *Post* began to recover from a serious crisis when she took command, and one of her first moves was to bring in a new, younger editor, Benjamin Bradlee, who, after an inconclusive discussion with Kay, began to push her like a terrier who had smelled prime beef, asking her to make up her mind. The brasher he became, the more impressed she was by him as a man of energy and daring. Together they transformed the *Post* from a good local newspaper with an outstanding editorial page into a newspaper of world renown.

By the time Truman Capote landed her as his guest of honor, she had begun to enjoy the power of being in command of the second most important newspaper in the land. The bal masque gave Capote all the publicity he had ever dreamed of, and for Kay it was like setting off a Roman candle against the New York sky, and an infusion of pride and confidence. Truman indeed helped her to banish the last shreds of the shadow left from the tragic death of her husband. Kay gradually acquired the reputation of being one of the most powerful women in the United States; for Truman Capote, however, it was downhill from then on. When one evening some nine years later Kay recalled his celebration of multinational "chic," there was general agreement about how unthinkable such a party had become by then. In retrospect it seemed a kind of gaudy memorial to the joie de vivre of the Kennedy days, a last hurrah to its social pretensions as well as to voguish ribaldry and to the foolishness of a fine writer.

With a spacious house and huge garden in Georgetown, Kay gradually established herself as a political hostess. She did not entertain for entertainment's sake as some ladies did; to her it was an adjunct to what she was doing as a publisher. On Sundays, for the enjoyment of good conversation, she used to give small lunches at one of which (we were about eight), she playfully suggested that we each declare what other person we would like to be if we were to get another chance of life on earth. When her turn came, to my great surprise and amusement, she said Antonia Fraser, the English author, because she was one of the most beautiful among women she knew, the mother of six children, and yet had enough time to write interesting and successful books and to lead quite an adventurous life outside them.

Before one of those Sunday lunches, I remember, I found Kay sitting with her chief police reporter of the *Post*. He had brought the unexpected news that her oldest son, Donald, who had been a Marine in Vietnam, on his return had quietly, without telling her, applied to join the Washington police force. No picnic even for a former Marine, he said, and made it clear that if Mrs. Graham wanted, the application could be turned down. Kay thanked the reporter for his help, but, without hesitation, replied that she would not be able to live at peace with her conscience if she interfered with her son's wishes. He served for eighteen months.

One of the most elegant hostesses in Georgetown was Lorraine Cooper, the wife of the Republican senator from Kentucky, John Sherman Cooper, a man highly respected in both parties. One week, for instance, Kay Graham felt rather lonely and did what she confessed she would not have had the courage to do earlier. She called Lorraine to ask if she could come for dinner during that week. When she arrived on the agreed evening, there were a dozen friends and as her "extra man" she found to her total surprise President Kennedy. Mrs. Cooper, despite her delicate face and figure, had a commanding appearance and, however much magnolia scented, she belonged among the political rather than social wives. She proved it when her husband, after he had lost his Senate seat, became ambassador to India and later East Germany. She took her job seriously—and not only the entertainment side—to assist her husband. She and others in her tradition like Mrs. David Bruce or Mrs. Frank Wisner (their husbands served in London and elsewhere, or Mrs. Chip Bohlen, whose husband became ambassador to the Soviet Union and France) were no pioneers of the women's liberation movement but worked hard at making diplomacy and politics an art as well as a profession. They are a dying breed. Gone also is the classic Washington hostess of the Mrs. Arthur Woods Bliss variety, who reigned in the 1950s and 1960s. She had the dainty ethereal look of a Dresden porcelain figurine, beautifully polished, with a high-pitched yet soft voice, usually dressed in frilly clothes and decked with fine jewelry. She spoke fluent French and sprinkled her English with appropriate French words to emphasize, I assumed, her high breeding. It reminded me of a telephone conversation I once overheard between my editor W. W. Hadley and *The Sunday Times*'s famous drama critic, James Agate, with the former asking him pleadingly not to use so many French words in his reviews! Mrs. Bliss owned the stately pile of Dumbarton Oaks in Georgetown, with its large, terraced formal garden, an enchanting place to linger, especially in spring, when everything was in bloom. After she had given the building to Harvard University for Byzantine studies, she asked Philip Johnson, the architect, to create a museum for her pre-Columbian collection and he responded by designing a jewel as lighthearted as the diminutive treasures on exhibit. At Dumbarton Oaks she organized for the Friends of Music concert recitals that included such artists as Joan Sutherland, Renata Tebaldi, the Vienna Octet, even entire operas. She commissioned Igor Stravinsky to write a concerto which immortalized the name "Dumbarton Oaks" in musicology; it became a forerunner of the current trend of chamber orchestra music. Washington has since become a much less social and a much more political sweatshop. So many Washington women are now busily engaged in their own professions that they are too tired to entertain when they come home or they cannot afford elegant entertaining, with the possible exception of Kay Graham or Pamela Harriman. Gone is the leisure of the earlier, serener days.

Still, enough wit and tolerance on the social circuit continued to linger on to inspire Alexander "Sandy" Trowbridge, the head of the Washington office of the National Association of Manufacturers (which seeks to defend the interests of industry), to offer his friends at a more recent party at the Georgetown Club, one of the newer social gathering places, the following witty summary of the capital's almost limitless activities:

> Some negotiate
>> some advocate
>> some activate
> Some litigate
>> some investigate
>> some pontificate
>> some aggravate
> Some legislate
>> some prognosticate
>> some arbitrate
>> some articulate
> Some prevaricate
>> some correlate
>> some obfuscate
>> some contemplate

He ended: And luckily for our society, all tolerate.

For President Kennedy good conversation at small dinner parties or having a tête-à-tête in a corner with a beautiful or/and amusing woman were his way of relaxing, though even he could never quite toss off the world he carried on his shoulders. Still, as he liked to say, "there are only three things in life that are real—God, human folly, and laughter. And since the first two are beyond our comprehension, we must do the best we can with the third."

Increasingly preoccupied with the question of how to promote some sort of modus vivendi with the Soviets, he now began to think more about the desirability of negotiating a nuclear test ban treaty with the Russians, especially since he had ordered a resumption of testing a few months earlier. The issue was close to Macmillan's heart, and he relentlessly kept it alive in a voluminous correspondence with the president. Then on June 10 Kennedy gave the peace issue new momentum with his commencement address at American University, the central theme of which was a moratorium on atmospheric testing. It marked a watershed in the thinking that used to underlie the Pax Americana as conceived by Dean Acheson and Paul Nitze. "By peace," the president said, "I do not mean a Pax Americana enforced on the world by weapons." The conciliatory quality of the speech obviously impressed Khrushchev, who badly needed a success after the debacle in Cuba, and after a relatively short time, with skillful handling by Averell Harriman, a limited test ban treaty was signed. Some Sovietologists believe that this was one of those rare opportunities when more could have been achieved had Harriman pressed harder for a comprehensive ban, but, according to Harriman, it was Khrushchev who insisted that he could not go beyond a limited test ban.

Meanwhile Kennedy's "Grand Design" for Europe was sputtering. On New Year's Day, 1962, he had given vent to his impatience with the allies at his annual background briefing for the press. He indicated then that he expected "to get more done even though it may cause friction," a remark which was blown out of proportion; two news agencies' stories said the "highest authority" planned to "whiplash" the allies, and a third predicted another round of tough talk. Naturally, the foreign press did not take kindly to such threatening language. Both the White House and the State Department, reviewing what Kennedy had actually said, felt that his message had been grossly exaggerated and were eager to correct the impression created. When I was shown the transcript I agreed that the president's words had been overplayed. I suggested that since I would be writing about the president's European policy anyway for Sunday, I could in that context correct the misleading impression created, but that in order to prove that the earlier interpretations had not been accurate I would need to quote from the transcript verbatim. My reasoning was accepted and so I went ahead using a direct quote in the body of my interpretative dispatch. But by doing this I violated the so-called background rule which prohibits direct quotes. Alistair Cooke in the *Guardian* called my action "a betrayal," one he bore with consummate equipoise since he was the only foreign correspondent present at the briefing and had obeyed the rule of referring only to the "highest authority"—actually a hollow not a hallowed rule because everybody of course could figure out that there was only one "highest authority." Tom Wicker, then the chief of the *New York Times* Washington bureau, for instance, wrote that the American-British press furor was approaching "the status of an international incident" and Ben Haig Bagdikian, the media critic, entered the incident in the annals of journalistic history by mentioning it in one of his books. To Kennedy, however, it was more important for his words to be published verbatim than for the background rule to be kept inviolate. Twelve days after my story had appeared, I received a private letter from the president on White House stationery giving the incident a humorous shrug. He wrote: "Dear Henry, As crises go these days this was a small one. It raced Pierre Salinger's [his press secretary] adrenals for a few hours, however, and that is a good thing. Very best regards . . ." McGeorge Bundy wrote to me in a similar vein in longhand, two days after the president's note, saying that he could not see what harm the incident had done—"if there had been a tea-potier tempest, I don't recall it." Pierre Salinger was left in ignorance about my behind-the-scenes discussions, but the incident annoyed him because the White House reporters assumed otherwise, and bitterly protested that it was unfair to have allowed me to quote the president directly. Even twenty years later when I mentioned the president's letter to him for the first time, he did not smile. The story in the journalistic teapot, however, was soon relegated to its proper place as a footnote of journalistic history. The "backgrounder" survived this crisis—even Ben Bradlee's prolonged efforts to get it abolished—and is alive and well as ever. Yet I continue to wonder with the *Arizona Star,* which at the time said editorially, "After reading it [the transcript], one wonders why direct quotations were not allowed, because it reflected the President at his best."

Walter Lippmann once wrote that a long life had convinced him "many presidents ago" that there should be a larger air space between a journalist and a head of state. "Put not your trust in princes. Only the very rarest of princes can endure even a little criticism, and few men can put up with even a pause of adulation." As we now know, Lippmann himself did not follow his own advice too consistently: he was at various times very close to a number of statesmen and even wrote speeches for them. It did not necessarily mean that he "trusted in princes," but he trusted himself not to be seduced or blinded by being close to a leading statesman. One must guard against seduction and, at times, in my relationship with Kennedy that was not easy. One way I dealt with this problem was to keep my private and professional relations separate. I never asked the president a professional question at private occasions. Or, whenever I criticized Kennedy or his administration, I never asked myself whether this might end my relationship with him. At that dinner party in Newport, for instance, he suddenly asked me about two articles of mine that seemed to have interested him but whose thrust he thought was unsympathetic. One was about his enemies, the other about the dynastic problems Teddy Kennedy's candidacy for the Senate had stirred up. He did not deny that the dynasty issue existed; in fact, he thought that it offered more advantages than disadvantages. Several years later—in 1967, if I remember correctly —the same issue came up in conversation with Vice President Hubert Humphrey, who was then preparing himself to contest the presidency against Robert Kennedy. Did he think that belonging to a dynasty, as Bobby did, was an advantage or disadvantage? I asked. Without hesitation he replied that he considered it an advantage. When I expressed my surprise, because I had thought that Americans mistrusted, even resented, anything even resembling hereditary power, he countered by saying that I was utterly wrong. Americans, he said, secretly admired dynasties! At any rate, Kennedy gently complained about my treatment of the two subjects. I, in turn, explained to him that people would consider me a hack if I reported only favorably about him and that anything positive I were to say would then lose credibility. It nevertheless took time to sink in. All presidents, I decided, dislike being criticized, however fairly.

One time, though, I expected a frown or a howl from the White House. It was after *The Sunday Times* printed an interview of mine with that amusing iconoclast Jonathan Miller (and now opera producer and polymath pundit), who had come to Washington with the cabaret *Beyond the Fringe,* a smash hit that tempted the Kennedys to see it. Jonathan, who hardly ever sees things the way ordinary people do—he is a true original in the best sense of the word —began by characterizing the Kennedy administration as follows: ". . . sex is the cement of the New Frontier. A special sort of girl has turned out for it. They are sort of neat and cool, and they have a nice dry wit . . . and they create a sort of elusive cool atmosphere about themselves." When I suggested to him that, maybe, they were only decorations to make the setting more attractive, he replied: "It seems to me a lot more than just a setting. They seem to be actually an intrinsic part of the whole philosophy. They are quite organically part of the setup . . . what's interesting is that one attractive president has attracted to him more girls than a president can use, so the system has become permeated by it . . ." Merriman Smith, the United Press White House veteran, picked up some of these quotes and made a story out of them. He expressed wonder at the White House's taking these suggestions so passively, clearly hoping to start a little brawl. But the president had far too good a sense of humor to react in that way; he probably thought, in accordance with the earlier cited rules of political behavior, that Miller's sallies would only add to his sex appeal.

In the 1980s when politicians were asked the most indiscreet questions about their sex life, the press was accused of having protected Kennedy's escapades. But those were still times when reporters made a distinction between professional and private life. There was a feeling in the press corps that a president who had to live under constant tension deserved some relaxation and that it was up to him whether he preferred to play golf or have a fling with a woman. It was not until Teddy Kennedy abused the tacit discretion of the media at Chappaquiddick that their attitude changed and that excessive womanizing became a target of "investigative journalism." Looking back to the Truman days, relations then with the press were almost collegial. I remember how the entire White House press corps used to go with Truman to Key West, his favorite haven out of Washington. The Navy in those days provided us with yachts—with a captain and a hand and fishing tackle—for deep-sea fishing, and neither the Navy nor the press thought there was anything wrong with it. It certainly did not influence any of the reporters in the way they treated the president. Today the Navy could neither afford to offer such facilities nor the reporters to accept them. The informal camaraderie that existed then is gone. It would be frowned upon today; the relationship has become so confrontational that it has made governing under the American constitutional system even more difficult than it already was. If Chappaquiddick made the intimacies of life fair game, or rather unfair game, then the lies about Watergate perpetrated by the Nixon White House made the media act like bloodhounds.

What made my special relationship with Kennedy and my reporting about his administration relatively easy was that I found myself in sympathy with his policies most of the time. It never really complicated my professional life. I can say the same thing of another relationship, which did not exactly involve me directly. That was when my wife became social secretary to the White House under the Reagan administration. It came to both of us as a great surprise, for my wife made no bones about having once worked in Bobby Kennedy's election campaign. It did not mean that I gained a special entrée to the president; on the contrary, I was particularly careful not to take advantage of my wife's privileged position. In fact, I had a much more distant relationship with President Reagan than I had with most other presidents. At the same time, no one in the White House complained either to my wife or directly to me about my frequent critical commentaries. For three years my wife and I had a compact not to discuss life in the White House. And we lived happier ever after.

The only time I saw Kennedy really angry was in May 1962, during an interview in his office immediately after he had seen André Malraux, de Gaulle's emissary, together with French Ambassador Hervé Alfand in the cabinet room. The French visit delayed my appointment by about half an hour, which I spent sitting in the office of Ms. Evelyn Lincoln, the president's personal secretary, watching the traffic with fascination and amazement. There was Ted Sorensen, who waited impatiently, not surprisingly thinking that it was more important for the president to see him than me; there was Mike Forrestal, poking his head round the door, nervous about the latest news from Laos; there was Ken O'Donnell, the president's cool political manipulator, darting in and out; and Senator Henry "Scoop" Jackson, who had brought some local politician from his state to get him photographed with the president. The latter took two minutes, which was enough time for the president to ask Scoop teasingly whether he had read Richard Rovere's piece in *The New Yorker,* mentioning him as an honorable man, but one who could not overlook the dependence of his state on Boeing Aircraft. It earned Scoop Jackson the nickname "the senator from Boeing." Scoop was not amused, even though Kennedy had put his arm comfortingly around his shoulders.

Once we were alone in the Oval Office, Kennedy, tipping back in his famous rocking chair, began without any introduction to denounce de Gaulle's and Adenauer's efforts to defy his policies. This was a different Kennedy from the one the public was shown. What annoyed him about Adenauer was the chancellor's constant suspicion that any dialogue with the Russians would be to Germany's disadvantage. "I have made a great effort to show the Germans and Russians since my Vienna meeting with Khrushchev that I mean to defend Berlin," he said with exasperation. "I have increased military spending by five billions, increased the military forces by a hundred fifty thousand, while the Germans haven't done a damn thing . . ." A reported remark by the chancellor, that he felt nostalgic for the Dulles times, only further incensed him.

Four months later in Newport, Rhode Island, I watched the America's Cup races from the president's destroyer. It was a lovely day, the sea was calm, and only mad optimists gave the British, who had tried fifteen times to win and always failed, an outsider's chance. Newport was home for the Kennedys, especially Jackie, whose stepfather built a weird mansion with a strange plenitude of turrets, close to the sea. It has since become a museum of Kennedy memorabilia, a tourist mecca like many of Newport's old stately mansions. Among the earliest settlers were Quakers and Jews (who built the first synagogue of North America here, a perfect example of caring preservation). After the southern planters, who used to summer here, the barons of business's knaves, villains, and fun-loving rascals moved in on the city, and built the Palladian, Gothic, Greek, cinquecento, Colonial, or fantasy villas that gave it its grand and monstrous style. In the late nineteenth century, some of the nation's richest men lived here and created their own type of gold-leaf Disneyland. It is still a very special symbol of the dawning of the American Century, but it predates Henry Luce's by almost two centuries and it is holding on desperately to the current one.

Going out to sea and watching the Cup race from the height of a destroyer was a holiday outing, a day of relaxation, for the president. For me it provided an opportunity to see not only Kennedy the president, but also the father. As usual, our conversation began with a remark, quite unsolicited, about Macmillan, who, he thought, not unlike Truman was likely to look much better in the perspective of history than he did then. Soon however we were interrupted when his little daughter Caroline hopped by; he grabbed her lovingly and sat her on his lap. She, delighted at having a chance to be so near him, asked him to tell her a story. Kennedy immediately obliged and became completely absorbed in her, spinning a story about how the fishes were trying to follow the race. It was, she said, a "scary" story, but she loved it and looked, riveted, into her father's face. It was a different Kennedy I suddenly saw, an adoring father watching his child's delight in having his attention and slipping into his playfulness. Jackie joined this idyll, sitting down next to the president and putting her arm around his neck in quiet affection. Having finished his story, he teasingly asked Jackie why she did not wear a hat instead of the kind of mantilla she had tied around her face, because if she wore a hat it would please the milliners. She then got up mimicking one of Newport's leading matrons going to church in a big pompous hat. We laughed, and Jackie had won her case against hats. Meanwhile one of the secret service men had teased Caroline away and they began chasing each other about the deck. Jackie moved on too and the president began to complain to me about Henry Luce, whose *Time* and *Life* magazines had been criticizing him for not doing enough about Cuba. But, he said, when he asked Luce what he should do, Luce had nothing concrete to suggest. What irritated him, he said, was that *Time* pretended to be unbiased and few people abroad knew how biased it really was.

Later that evening at dinner at Hammersmith Farm, the president again complained about Chancellor Adenauer's refusal to talk to the East Germans. He thought it was shortsighted of him, for some time earlier he could have got quite a lot for East Germany's recognition; very soon, however, it would not be worth very much. He then switched to complaining about the attempt by the British to weaken the dollar in order to improve their own condition, saying it could lead to a curtailment of American business investments in Britain and the Common Market, and that he could not afford the outflow of two billion in investments a year plus one billion in tourism abroad, which included, he said, switching from being serious to flippant, his wife's spending on foreign travel. When I replied that the United States must act as behooved a Great Power and not curtail the export of dollars because it weakened the dollar, he insisted that the United States could no longer afford such largesse. Later, Jackie spoke with great admiration—though not in the president's hearing—about General de Gaulle as a great man in history in spite of the fact that he made Jack's life difficult. She quoted Harold Macmillan, who had told her that when he asked the French leader whom he expected to succeed him, was given the reply: *Après moi le délice de déluge* ("After me the deliciousness of a deluge").

Of course, gossip too abounded around the Kennedy dinner table, but there was always a great deal of serious talk. Jackie that evening, for instance, wanted to know the difference between the presidential and the parliamentary system, not exactly the subject to keep a soufflé airborne. But she was endlessly inquisitive about people and ideas.

Somehow Prime Minister Nehru's name came up. That reminded the president about a conversation he had with him during which Nehru recounted, still with some heat, how Churchill had sent him to prison during World War II. Then shortly thereafter Churchill sent a message to the Viceroy of India, asking him to inquire of Nehru whether he was comfortable and needed anything. Kennedy, reacting to Nehru's lingering anger, had said: "But don't you think it was something special of Churchill, who had so much to worry about during the war, to send such a message?" Nehru looked into the distance for quite a while without saying anything. Then he suddenly replied: "It was only because we both had gone to Harrow." Kennedy was clearly amused by this instance of the old school tie at work, however perversely.

Eight months after my formal interview with the president in which he made it clear that he had convinced himself that the stubborn de Gaulle would not make any concessions to American policies, the French leader vetoed Britain's entry into the European Common Market. After that black day, January 29, 1963, a deep soul-searching began about the future of the Western alliance. It was a brutal body blow to Britain above all, but also to Kennedy's European policy. Jean Monnet, the apostle of a United Europe, told the president that de Gaulle would eventually accept what he could not change, but Kennedy disagreed with him. He thought that there was no way other than to await de Gaulle's demise.

With the "Grand Design" in jeopardy and his handling of the Cuban missile crisis seen as too lenient, especially by Republicans in Congress, Kennedy was thrown on the defensive. It was not the avoidance of war and the quiet withdrawal of Soviet missiles that were uppermost in many people's minds, but the realization that Castro might now be able to maintain himself in power much longer than anybody had reckoned. As this chapter is written, he is still in power, and though no threat to American security, he remains a great nuisance.

Public opinion polls showed that abroad Kennedy scored higher than any other foreign statesman with the exception of de Gaulle. But at home his approval rating had dropped from 64 percent to 56. He had thrown in the towel on a bill to cut taxes after having campaigned for it ceaselessly. (The fact that an American president could not get a tax cut when he wanted one seemed utterly to baffle Macmillan during one conversation I had with him at 10 Downing Street—which was something no less baffling to me in a man with his knowledge of American politics and history.) But it was not only the tax bill that troubled Kennedy. Enjoying the company of reporters more than any other president, it puzzled him why they had become so critical of him, so somewhat naively the White House arranged for a conference with the heads of various news media in a quiet villa in Virginia in a vain attempt to defuse the criticism.

When Kennedy introduced the on-the-record televised press conference and moved it to the big State Department auditorium, it significantly changed the role of the news media. They began to occupy a much more important position. Reporters were no longer part of the scenery, they became actors on center stage. It mattered to reporters to be recognized at a presidential press conference (one publisher fired a reporter because he never caught the president's eye), it mattered to editors to see their representative ask a question (often one they had suggested to him), and so reporters who had relied on their bylines to achieve fame now had to become personalities to make it on the television screen. Gradually it was not so much the substance of the question that mattered but the reporter's performance, because it led to bigger and bigger salaries. James Rowe, who had been a political counselor to several presidents, advised Kennedy against televised press conferences as too risky an exposure. But Kennedy rejected his cautionary words by saying that he could not afford to give up his live press conferences because sooner rather than later the press would turn against him, and he had to make sure he could get his side of the story over to the public. One reason that he performed better than any other president was that he was well informed, that he seemed to enjoy the occasions and hardly ever lost his sense of humor. Reporters looked forward to these occasions not only for their news value but because they were good theater, they provided a new stage for them and gave them a new notoriety. Some resented the instantaneity and the importance presidents began to attach to television reporters. If Kennedy has one serious competitor in the handling of the television medium, it is President Reagan, who had the advantage of being a professional actor, but to compare Kennedy's performance to Reagan's would be to put "Brideshead Revisited" against "Dynasty," and I am not overlooking that the latter has a much wider audience. For Presidents Johnson, Nixon, Ford, and Carter the televised press conference was an ordeal. They did not have Kennedy's quick wit, his cool, his presence or Reagan's easygoing charm and his imperturbable, detached attitude of almost fathomless placidity toward any crisis situation, at least until he had to confront the arms-for-hostages deal with Iran.

The inevitable presence of television cameras at presidential press conferences has robbed them of a certain intimacy and has given them a new importance because of the visual impact they have on the viewer. It led me to watch the president's performance on the television screen at home or at the office. In the older days it mattered to me, as a print reporter, to be able to describe how the president handled himself and what impression he had made on me. But once television carried the press conferences into the living room, what mattered to me was to be able to report how the *nation* saw the president perform, what impression they were left with. The image began to matter as much or more than the words. Close-ups through the television lens, I learned, were more revealing than seeing the president in the flesh. Sometimes quickly suppressed anger or a pearl of perspiration were more revealing than the content of an answer. And so the presidential press conference became showbiz.

On April 30, 1961, at a dinner party at General Maxwell Taylor's house, I began to understand why the Kennedy administration got so confused about the strategic importance of Vietnam. The dinner was a kind of send-off to Taylor and Walt Rostow, who were leaving the next day for Vietnam to determine at firsthand whether their recommendation for sending two or more regimental combat teams to reinforce the hard-pressed South Vietnamese would be a sound move.

After the men had separated from the ladies and were having their cigars and brandy, Walt Rostow, full of ebullience and intellectual self-confidence, explained why he believed that such a move made sense, even though the South Vietnamese had not yet asked for it. He was convinced that the sending of American troops would psychologically bolster their fighting spirit, would help dampen Communist cockiness, and because of the consequence of a Chinese intervention, might lead the Soviets to slow down their appetite for "wars of liberation." Taylor was relatively taciturn but he agreed with Rostow that if the situation continued to deteriorate, serious thought should be given to the deploying of American troops on a larger scale, since an American setback in Vietnam would make the Russians even more hardheaded in the negotiations over the future of Berlin. My suggestion that the presence of American troops would lead the South Vietnamese into thinking that they might be able to shift the responsibility for the war to the Americans was given short shrift. Taylor felt confident that the United States had enough influence in Saigon to prevent that. Asked why the mission did not include a member of the State Department, Taylor explained that the mission's task was to resolve a military question. The political aspects of a military involvement simply were not on their agenda. This seminal two-man mission, in retrospect, was not a true reconnaissance mission because it was obvious that they went in search of support for their belief that American combat teams should forthwith be dispatched to help the South Vietnamese.

My own first encounter with that huge booby trap called Vietnam occurred in 1952 on my very first visit to the Far East, when the French were desperately trying to stave off the Communist Vietminh and when it was only too obvious that this war was much more a political than a military problem. The secretary of defense of Pakistan, a robust, outspoken Sandhurst graduate, argued that the American containment theory, applied to Asia, was based on a fallacy because the situation in Indochina would be decided not by military power but the power of nationalism, whose aspirations needed to be satisfied. Prime Minister Nehru of India wondered whether, like the French Revolution, communism would gradually lose its violence and have a healthy influence, and also whether the differences between Chinese and Soviet communism would not surface soon and rip apart that ideological front. The French I talked to in Indochina believed, as did Presidents Johnson and Nixon years later, that if they could enlist Soviet or Chinese support in the peacemaking, Ho Chi Minh would become more amenable to ending the war. They were all wrong. It also became obvious to me that the Eisenhower administration was mistaken in thinking that the French could be persuaded to fight for total victory. American officials in Saigon did not believe it and said so in their reports, but, as one of them said, "What's the use of sending reports to Washington if policy is made on the basis of what Congress wants and not on the basis of the facts as they exist out here on the spot."

Kennedy, even though that banana skin report drawn up by Taylor and Rostow was only partially followed, nevertheless accepted the idea that American military help could turn the political tide. He therefore must bear a good deal of the blame for having initiated one of the great blunders in American history. He did not observe a remark de Gaulle had made to him in 1961, and which Kennedy himself repeated to me at that time: "There is no military solution to Vietnam." Unfortunately, Americans considered any advice from the French as too tainted by their own experience. When I wrote in a retrospective piece about President Johnson in *The Sunday Times* in December 1968 that Kennedy had committed what may have been "the crucial mistake" leading to the greater involvement in Vietnam, I received a letter from Averell Harriman, who was then in Paris trying to negotiate with the North Vietnamese to end the war. He wrote: "The only satisfaction I can see of being in Paris these days is to be able to read your dispatches on Sundays. I was aghast, however, that you said, 'Maybe the crucial mistake was committed by President Kennedy when he escalated the number of American military advisers from 700 to 18,000.' To me the awful blunder was Dulles's decision to step into French shoes in 1954 and take over responsibility for South Vietnam which was politically and militarily unviable. The JFK expansion flowed from that blunder. LBJ's in '65 was an expansion of the Kennedy decision. We can discuss this at greater length after my return January 20." Harriman was intensely loyal to the Democratic Party and to the Kennedys and at the time of writing this letter was working for President Johnson. It was not surprising to me that he should have wanted to shift the blame for what turned out to be a catastrophic involvement altogether to a Republican administration, though it too can't escape blame.

If I learned something from my first acquaintance with the Far East, it was that the Communist threat was not seen there as we see it in the West. Some feared a veiled threat of Chinese imperialism, others, especially the Japanese, the old Russian threat in a new form. But to none was it a concerted plot for world domination. Vietminh communism was not of the Russian or Chinese or the "stomach" kind, but thrived because it was able to exploit the mistakes of past French colonial policies, and when France offered independence for Indochina, the presence of French troops muffled the political impact of this promise.

Europeans do not generally understand why Americans feel so insecure and exposed on their Pacific flank. But Pearl Harbor has the same ominous ring in American ears as Dunkirk has in British and Sedan in French. They also remember having had to fight in World War II in the Pacific virtually alone, and later in Korea they had to shoulder "nineteen-twentieths" of the burden. Communist China to them was a hostile power that had to be contained, and Japan, Formosa, the Philippines, South Korea, and Vietnam were to be made into the pillars of that simplistic cordon.

The shock of having "lost" China, which once had been a romantic playground for commerce, clipper ships, missionaries, a kind of American protectorate, to communism; the Korean War; accusations of "softness" on communism; rhetoric deployed to obtain congressional support for aid; fear of another "Munich"—all these conspired to drag the United States into the Vietnam morass. The idea that a variation of the application of a "graduated response," born in the Cuban missile crisis, could also succeed in Vietnam was another serious miscalculation.

One of the leading members of the Kennedy administration who invoked the Munich analogy was Dean Rusk, the secretary of state, and he did it at times with a vengeance. Once over lunch at his private dining room at the State Department he argued with some passion that I as a European must understand the Munich parallel and that therefore he would expect me to agree that the United States was doing the right thing in Vietnam. He even suggested that I persuade my editor to write an editorial advocating Britain's participation in the war. I had no success in convincing him that there was a great difference between Ho Chi Minh and Hitler and between the Vietminh and the Nazis. Walt Rostow shared Rusk's historic outlook. Kennedy, in private conversation, was skeptical about a major American commitment in Vietnam, but somehow felt sucked into a situation from which he, for domestic political reasons, found it difficult to extricate himself. He was constantly buying time, first with President Diem, then without him, then by the "can-do" esprit of most of the Kennedy advisers, who were not discouraged by their own unfamiliarity with Asia. McGeorge Bundy, who continued as national security adviser in the Johnson White House until February 1966, remained convinced that the United States was pursuing the right policy, and so did Walt Rostow, General Maxwell Taylor, Robert McNamara, and Bobby Kennedy. Americans are not alone in having difficulty understanding Asians. Often even Asians have. The wise and charming Sir Benegal Rau, India's ambassador to the United Nations, once told me about one of his shooting expeditions in the Indian jungle and how after proceeding for three days, the carriers suddenly refused to go any farther. Nothing could persuade them to move. They insisted on pausing for twenty-four hours "until their soul caught up with their body . . ."

McGeorge Bundy and Robert McNamara were convinced that if you approached people rationally and the war rationally, it would lead to a rational solution. They thought they were dealing with rational people, who after being bloodied would come to the conference table. Just before Kennedy's assassination the American commitment in Vietnam was still negligible, about 16,000 troops, but considering the advice he was getting, he was on a slippery slope, and hence there remains the tantalizing question whether he would have skidded into the Vietnam maze the way Johnson did and have escalated the direct American involvement or cut his losses in time. From random private remarks one could sense that by the autumn of 1963 Kennedy had begun to get impatient with the war and asked here and there how he could get out of it. He even offered Mike Forrestal, his aide on Asian affairs, odds of a hundred-to-one that the United States could not win in Vietnam, though McNamara, returning from Saigon that October, reported "great progress" . . . giving "promise of ultimate victory." His report was discussed in an NSC meeting with the president, and in a public statement afterwards considerable emphasis was given to the possibility that by the end of the year 1,000 of the American military personnel could be withdrawn. McNamara drew my attention to this announcement recently as an indication of the way the wind had begun to blow —that talk about withdrawing American troops altogether by 1965 had set a new direction. Whether or not a present-minded sense of history tends to exaggerate the significance of that statement which, according to the Pentagon Papers, was designed "to influence both North and South Vietnamese to set the stage for bringing the insurgency to an end," the talk actually was about ending the training program and withdrawing "the bulk of the U.S. personnel by 1965." McGeorge Bundy doubts the significance McNamara now attaches to this announcement.

Even if Kennedy had augmented the American commitment, I am convinced that he would have kept it more limited than did Johnson and, with his sensitivity to public opinion and his caution, found ways to cut short the American involvement. Wanting to see the coonskin of victory pinned to the wall was the Johnson psychological state of mind. Kennedy, at least during the Bay of Pigs fiasco, showed that he was capable of avoiding becoming more deeply enmeshed in a losing military gambit and that he had the inner self-confidence to swallow defeat and cut his losses. Johnson lacked that inner security.

Originally, I did not plan to accompany Kennedy in November 1963 on his first political foray into Texas. But when it was announced that Jackie would be accompanying him and, possibly, even make a campaign speech or two, I was tempted. Jackie hated politics. She was a free spirit; she did not mind embarrassing the president by taking off in a helicopter in her riding clothes while Jack was having breakfast with members of Congress; she loathed crowds, shaking hands and being on display. Her affections were with the arts. In a student competition for *Vogue* magazine while at Vassar she wrote that she would like to become "a sort of overall art director of the twentieth century," and apply to her time the theories of art of three men whom she wished she had known: Baudelaire, Wilde, and Diaghilev—the first two because as poets and idealists they "could paint sinfulness with honesty and still believe in something higher," and the third "because he brought about the interaction of the cultures of the East and the West." Her piece won first prize among 1,280 entries.

What finally decided me to go was a remark by Fred Holburn, a charmingly unpredictable and donnish White House aide, that there had been warnings of possible trouble. That was all he said. (I learned later that these warnings were based on trouble Adlai Stevenson had encountered in Dallas, where he had spoken at a United Nations Day, troubles fanned by General Edwin R. Walker, an extreme right-winger.)

The presidential visit began promisingly at San Antonio, where Jackie made quite a hit speaking in Spanish to a Hispanic audience, and the president's speech in Houston too was a huge success. Then we flew to Fort Worth, where the next morning I exchanged what were to be my last words with the president after he had spoken in the early morning to quite a crowd on the parking lot opposite our hotel. "Things are going much better than I had expected," he said on the fly to get ready for another speech before a big audience which had foregathered at our hotel for breakfast. Prompted partly by the president's remark I went to the press room to begin what I thought would be my story for Sunday: "I crossed the American border by jet yesterday into hostile Texas with a small guerrilla band of White House officials, led by President Kennedy . . . We entered enemy territory by landing near that relatively safe base—San Antonio—which with its 60 percent Mexican and Negro population had voted for Kennedy the last time."

We all knew Dallas was anti-Kennedy territory. As the presidential cavalcade drove into town the sun was shining, but the crowds were thin. I noticed one hostile poster dipped in humor: "Let's Barry King John," supposedly a pun on both Goldwater and the Kennedy dynasty. In the old days moderate Democrats, with the help of the rich and the votes of the poor, had been in control in Texas. Yet by now oil and cattle were no longer true symbols of its prosperity, but rather the enormous industrial complex that the original oil wealth had created. This profound change engendered an emotional confusion and violent antagonisms. Kennedy sounded like a radical, but acted like a gradualist, which added to the confusion.

I sat in the press bus as our column of cars approached the School Book Depository. We heard a shot, or maybe two, but it was hard to hear anything from the old rattling school bus the press found itself in. It was only when we arrived at the Trade Mart where the president was to have addressed a luncheon that we got a one-sentence message from the police: "President was shot." It sounded totally unbelievable. In some sort of a trance we boarded the bus again to get to the hospital. A few minutes later Senator Ralph Yarborough, with tears in his eyes, told us that what he had seen driving behind the president's car was "too horrible to describe" and that the injuries were very grave. He actually knew that the president was dead, but did not want to be the messenger of death.

Feeling icy numbness, deep shock, and utter despair, I said to myself that I had to keep my mind on the story, the biggest and most shattering I had ever covered. I could not believe that anyone could be capable of such an act of bestiality. A president, a world leader, a friend had been brutally assassinated. I watched Tom Wicker of the *New York Times* in front of the hospital going about calmly trying to piece the story together. It helped me to pull myself together. Most of the White House correspondents stayed on in Dallas to cover the almost instant succession of Vice President Lyndon B. Johnson; what mattered to me was to write the best piece I could about Kennedy. And so I flew back to Washington on the half-empty press plane to start work on it right away. I had heard Kennedy talk seriously about the possibility of his being assassinated, but I could never make myself listen to such ghoulish talk.

When a personal telegram arrived, signed by Robert Kennedy, inviting me to the White House where THE PRESIDENT'S BODY WILL LIE IN REPOSE IN THE EAST ROOM before lying in state under the dome of the Capitol, I was staggered that such personal attention was still possible even in the face of this terrible event. At eleven A.M. on the twenty-third, a Saturday—I had been working on my *Sunday Times* dispatch until six in the morning—I went to the White House where Sargent Shriver, the president's brother-in-law, greeted me with a wan welcoming smile. The blinds had been lowered, the curtains and the white marble fireplaces were covered with black crêpe, four candles were flickering, and a guard of honor was standing in attendance. I suddenly saw the president laugh and joke in my mind's eye as I took my farewell.

At noon the cortege left the White House, Jackie looking bravely into the air, her face taut, her eyes clear. She walked behind the caisson and the riderless horse with one boot in the stirrup in reverse. It had been Jackie's wish to walk to the church. She was flanked by Bobby and Teddy. Both seemed collected. The children followed in a black Cadillac, not really aware what had happened. Among the crowd of foreign dignitaries the towering figure of General de Gaulle in uniform stood out, his head high and swiveling in his characteristic way. Somehow his presence meant more than anybody else's. Prime Minister Alec Douglas-Home in an old dark winter coat looked frail against the powerful figure of the general. Sir David Ormsby-Gore was immaculate, top hat in hand.

My editor, Denis Hamilton, sent me a cable that day saying: ALL OF US HERE VERY CONSCIOUS YOUR LOSS OF PERSONAL FRIEND AND ADMIRE VERY MUCH THE WAY YOU HONORED HIS MEMORY ON SUNDAY IN DESCRIBING THE INCREDIBLE LAST HOURS. Reminiscing about his own last meeting with Kennedy a year earlier, Hamilton described him in an editorial page article with great perspicacity: ". . . the spirit of adventure was still there, but harnessed by events to statesmanship on a world scale . . . a leader so intelligently

aware of the importance of close relations with today's mass media . . .
endowed with a subtle system of intellectual checks and balances."

To me Kennedy had become a man born to lead, ruled by reason in search
of what was essential, not merely politically feasible. He was a leader after my
own taste because he had a profound understanding of the awesome dangers
and human necessities of our age, and weighed with enormous intellectual care
the deployment of American destructive and healing powers. His personal
detachment did not prevent him from being kind and considerate, or from
being ruthless with those whose loyalty he questioned. He was not, nor was
his brother Robert, a man who easily forgot or forgave. He was helped by men
of intellect whom he respected, though they did not prevent him from committing some serious errors. Every encounter with them, though, was a cerebral
challenge which added to the pleasures of reporting from Washington.

In Kennedy's thousand days there was real growth in the understanding
of superpower statesmanship. Truman launched the building of "positions of
strength"; Eisenhower, who had a remarkably coherent view of the world,
added the recognition of a need for negotiations with the Soviet Union;
Kennedy broadened the foundation for superpower diplomacy together with
the biggest American military buildup in peacetime, but equally he laid the first
cornerstone of détente. Pax Americana, as he proclaimed it, was a popular
notion then.

When Denis Hamilton called shortly after the funeral asking me whether
I would like to go to Moscow on a six-week assignment, sensing that what I
probably needed was to bury myself in the problems of a very different country,
I gratefully accepted. To my great surprise mourning for Kennedy was almost
more intense in Moscow than in Washington. What did not surprise me was
that everybody asked me who was behind the killing of JFK. Every Russian
had convinced himself that Lee Harvey Oswald had been the instrument of
some right-wing conspiracy. Russians have conspiratorial minds and my own
insistence that the assassination was the lone act of a deranged individual was
usually shrugged off with some sort of a remark about my naiveté. There was
also much speculation—Russians love to speculate and gossip—whether
Jackie would marry again. One Russian newspaperman whom I knew from
previous visits and whose uncanny understanding of the United States never
ceased to astonish me because it was entirely based on his regular reading of
the Paris *Herald* and *Life* and *Time* magazines, said to me: "Do tell Jackie
that she should marry a foreigner, she would be much happier than with an
American!"

Soviet affection for Kennedy was based on the feeling that the man who
administered an embarrassing defeat to the Soviet Union had not rubbed
Khrushchev's nose in the dirt, but instead opened the door to an accommodation over nuclear testing and a big and controversial sale of wheat. Khrushchev, in his memoirs, claimed that he had tried to put the missiles into Cuba

because he feared a follow-up to the Bay of Pigs invasion which, if not prevented, would have meant the loss of a valuable socialist outpost and a blow
to Soviet prestige, especially in Latin America. His excuse for removing the
missiles was that they had served their purpose once the United States had
pledged not to attack Cuba. But he also wrote that he would "always remember the late president with deep respect because, in the final analysis, he showed
himself sober-minded and determined to avoid war . . . I believe that if
Kennedy had lived, relations between the Soviet Union and the United States
would be much better than they are. Why do I say that? Because Kennedy
would have never let his country get bogged down in Vietnam." Glenn Seaborg, in his book *Kennedy, Khrushchev and the Test Ban,* put it even more
strongly: "That brush with calamity seemed to forge a bond between them.
They appeared to understand each other better, to buttress each other's efforts,
to avoid making the other look bad. They began to consult each other more
frequently, to work together on problems of common interest." This feeling
was also widespread when I went to Moscow and has lingered on ever since.

Shortly before David Ormsby-Gore left the embassy to return home for good,
we spent a long time reminiscing about the Kennedy days. He looked drawn,
his eyes tired and sad. The high point in his life had come to an abrupt and
deeply wounding end. It was for him like walking into the sunset with the sun
already gone. His own father had died; and he could not bear a Washington
without Kennedy. I tried to convince him that he should throw himself into
British politics; after all, he now had stature, experience, and a honed judgment. But he was determined to assume his father's title which made him a
baron and prevented him from seeking a seat in the House of Commons.

Ruminating about the past, he called his relationship with Kennedy a
"historic freak" because he had happened to know him for more than twenty-
five years before he was elected president. He said that being on personal terms
with the president had been a substantial advantage "because the American
system is so unlike ours, the presidential system so unlike a cabinet government, because you only really know what the United States administration, as
it is called, is going to do if you know the president's mind. Under the
American cabinet system, which meets only irregularly, there isn't a consolidated opinion in an administration such as you have in the United Kingdom and this makes it particularly important to know how the president's own
thinking is developing. During the negotiations over the Test Ban Treaty, for
instance, there were a good many people in the American government who
didn't see much advantage in continuing the exchanges with the Soviet Union.
The fact that all through that period I knew very well that the president
himself was very anxious to maintain contact with Moscow, in spite of disappointing replies from Khrushchev and so on, did make the exchange of view
between Harold Macmillan in London and President Kennedy here much
more fruitful."

I was very tempted to ask David how he viewed his role during the Skybolt crisis, the one time he did not in timely fashion take full advantage of his closeness to the president, but I did not have the heart to remind him at a sad enough moment for him of an issue he probably felt too sensitive. Instead I asked him about his last conversation with Kennedy. It was at a private dinner à quatre. The most significant part of that conversation, he remembered, was the way Kennedy made it clear that he was determined to maintain the momentum after the signing of the Test Ban Treaty, which he felt at last meant that a start had been made toward reaching a better understanding between East and West; it was necessary to nurture this rather tender plant. He also told David on that occasion that he had made up his mind to visit the Soviet Union at the first suitable moment. He thought that a world in which people threatened each other with nuclear weapons and didn't try to find some modus vivendi was crazy, and even during the Berlin crisis and during the Cuban missile crisis, he had always hoped that as a result of their solution he would be able to get back onto the high road toward some means of living together on this planet with the Soviet bloc.

Nobody expressed quite as graphically as Ilya Ehrenburg, the Soviet novelist, the difference between Kennedy and Lyndon Johnson, between the civilized American and the super-prototype of a Texan, as it was seen abroad. In his apartment, where he lived surrounded by paintings and drawings given to him by his friends Picasso and Chagall and others, he first talked about his admiration for the Soviet poet Mayakovsky, who lived and died tragically young in the 1930s, and about his detestation for the contemporary poet Yevtushenko. Suddenly he raised his voice, stretched out his arms above his head for emphasis, and shouted: "Kennedy, to me, is like Mayakovsky and Johnson like Yevtushenko!"

Kennedy will always remain a question mark in history because we will always wonder what would have happened had he lived and had he won a second term. It had been his rule that in order to win the presidency one had to be a cold warrior, but in order to win a second term, one had to be seen in search of peace. The rule worked for Nixon and would have continued to work had he not been such a sinister character. It did not work for Carter because he confused the two issues. Reagan did not confuse the issues but the public. The balance Kennedy developed between his military buildup and his drive for accommodation with the Russians appealed to the Europeans, and his outburst about being a "Berliner" reserves him a warm place in German hearts. No other president spoke for Europe, and with such understanding, as he did, and, I dare say, none ever will. De Gaulle, although he clashed with Kennedy time and again, in a private conversation said *C'est un Européen* ("He is a European"), which in his vocabulary meant a civilized man. In fact, one reason why Kennedy enjoyed such popularity in Europe was the impression he had created of being a living fusion of the American and European cultures.

The brutal cutting short of a man so attractive, so intelligent, so able, so much at ease with himself, and so full of puckish fun transformed admiration and respect into a legend and made it blossom. If the blossoms are gone by now, some twenty years later, it is not surprising, for one main reason: the new generation entering adult life did not experience the yeasty nature of the Kennedy days. My own impressions of the Kennedy administration may therefore be among the last written by an eyewitness under the influence of the Kennedy magic and nostalgia for some of the most delightful years of my own life.

Not long after my return from Moscow, on a visit to New York, I met Jackie for the first time since the funeral. I found her preoccupied with President Kennedy's likely place in history, but what seemed to matter even more to her was for her children, John and Caroline, to be living not in the shadow of their father but in his reflected light. I had called her on the spur of the moment and she immediately asked me to come to see her in her new home on Fifth Avenue. The apartment had an unfinished look. Packing cases were still there, with curtains not yet hung and furniture standing around that obviously had not yet found its proper place. The maid led me into the library, which at least looked fully furnished and with the shelves filled with books. There was the elegant black-edged stationery on the desk and a Boudin painting still to be hung, half-unpacked, under the table. And there was a magnificent view over Central Park.

Jackie looked pale and ethereal, but she seemed very much herself. We had hardly sat down when she asked me whether I had heard that Mary Meyer, a mutual friend, had been murdered by a laborer on the towpath along the Washington Canal. I had not and was shocked, just as was Jackie. It was not only the loss of a friend for her, but it must have roughed up deep wounds, still bleeding. "Why is there so much violence in this world?" she asked in her muffled, tremulous, troubled voice. "The worst in life is losing someone one loves . . ." She paused and then went on: "I wonder whether it is chance or destiny?" She paused again, to collect herself, then she continued quietly as if in a trance: "I often wake up at night suddenly, and then I look for Jack next to me . . . and he is not there . . . I wonder whether I am going to see him after death?" No doubt she was still very much under the spell of her shattering loss.

There was agitation deep within her, but also serenity and a colossal sense of responsibility for the children's future. She looked beautiful in an austere way, like a fine crystal glass, fragile, delicate, and vulnerable. Her big dark eyes exuded apprehension and a great uncertainty about her own future. What she wanted to talk about was whether history would do justice to Jack, for there was so much he had wanted to do and could not. "Bobby," she said, "tried to console me by suggesting that if Jack had been shot after the Bay of Pigs, he would have looked like the worst president . . ." It did not seem to me a particularly sensitive way of consoling her and so I spoke instead of the great moments of his presidency and what would make an indelible imprint on history as I saw it, and about Ilya Ehrenburg's remark, a great compliment, no doubt, in Russian terms. She had also heard about an article by William Rees-Mogg in *The Sunday Times,* in which he referred to the new dynamism that Kennedy conveyed and that Britain badly needed. She was eager to read it: "Europe understood Jack," she said. "He knew that Europeans understood him better than Americans. It was one reason why he liked Europe so much!"

She then wanted to know about the election campaign. She was appalled how awful people were in thinking that Bobby had taken her son, John, to their old house in Georgetown for publicity reasons. Then, half-questioning, half-pensively, she added in a forlorn way that she might make an appeal in support of President Johnson's reelection on the last day before the balloting.

Then she returned to the murder of Mary Meyer. "Mary is all right now, it's the children who suffer," she said, expressing the awareness that was the special spur for her devotion to her children. Jackie inspired in them the kind of esprit and approach to life Jack would have heartily and gratefully approved of. She can be proud of the way she husbanded this precious legacy.

9

How Greatness Passed Johnson By

LYNDON B. JOHNSON assumed the presidency with impressive dignity and restraint, suppressing both the shock and his elation with remarkable self-control. Without disrespect or seeming to be unfeeling to the Kennedy tragedy, he had to establish his own authority as swiftly as was decently possible. But the ghost of Kennedy was to haunt him virtually throughout his time in the White House. He remained aware that he could not match Kennedy's easy charm, intelligence, sophistication, quick wit, knowledge in foreign affairs, and consummate skill at press conferences. And then there was Bobby. LBJ believed, and not without reason, that Robert Kennedy connived to regain the presidency for the Kennedy dynasty from the day his brother was murdered—first by trying to force Johnson's hand to make him vice president, and later by contesting his second term in 1968. When Bobby went to Europe, calling in at Berlin, Warsaw, and Paris, hitting the headlines everywhere, it was not exactly done to take a bow for the United States, but to advance his own popularity at home and to prove that the dynasty was very much a reality. On his return President Johnson gave him what came close to a dressing-down because he had strongly implied at a press conference that the United States had no European policy. LBJ also resented his having advocated peace feelers to Hanoi: "You'll be guilty of tying the hands of our boys behind their backs, of being guilty of having killed many," he told him with undisguised hatred.

Johnson never seriously thought of making Bobby his vice president. He did not want to find himself sandwiched in history between two Kennedys. But he did offer to help Bobby if he sought high office through the electoral process. Bobby had no doubt of his own ability for leadership; he had served his brother through many crises with advice that had usually proved to be sound, as well as a trenchant report card on other people. Whenever I visited him in his office in those days, he looked more like a harried news editor before edition time than the august protector of the law. There are few offices in Washington as vast and dignified as that of the attorney general. It was therefore something of a shock to see this wiry, electric figure behind a mammoth desk, in rolled-up sleeves, collar carelessly loose, tie drooping, his blond hair flapping down his forehead and on the wall the latest doodles of his many children. When Bobby wanted something he acted like a terrier. People feared his quick temper and his adherence to one of the less attractive Kennedy traits: "If you are not for us, you are against us." His steely blue eyes could look very cold indeed. I can imagine how they must have fanned the embers in Johnson when he asked point blank for the vice presidency.

For a long time Johnson remained wary of some sort of conspiracy of the Kennedy faithfuls, especially before the 1964 Democratic Convention. He was well aware, for instance, of McNamara's loyalty to the Kennedy clan, but was anxious to hold on to him, partly to see if he could convert into a Johnson admirer a man he admired for his quickness of mind, his brilliance with statistics, his mastery of concepts. He never quite succeeded. McGeorge Bundy, who remained his national security adviser, was a different case. He was the optimum civil servant in the British sense and as such could serve any president, whether Republican or Democrat. Johnson did not consider him exactly a soul mate, because, as he once explained privately, "he is an easterner, a snob, unpleasant but indispensable." William McChesney Martin, then chairman of the Federal Reserve Board, on a flight from Atlanta to Washington gave me what he considered to be Johnson's true perspective on an easterner and on England: "First of all you have to know that he does not consider easterners, those I mostly associate with, as real Americans. To him they look too much to Europe. Secondly, the line of Texas, Missouri, Minnesota to him is the real America. Those Texans who have gone to live in California are in his mind Texans who weren't able to make a go of it in Texas. In this picture, England figures about as large as North Dakota."

Johnson actively resented the Eastern Establishment, though as a politician he recognized, however reluctantly, that he had to tolerate it. The Washington "branch" consisted of those easterners who moved to the capital to ensure that government policies took a course that would help to preserve their values and outlook. They were able to exert maximum influence in the Truman and Kennedy days, but lost much of it under President Johnson because he did not feel comfortable with them. What appealed to him, though, was their self-confidence and their willingness to indulge in the game of power poker. Alas, like the president, they too were tempted to assume that they held a royal flush and that the enemy was bluffing—as, for instance, in Vietnam. Johnson, like Nixon and Carter, actively resented those who lived in Georgetown, which he saw as a conspiratorial power center, controlled by the Eastern Establishment. Eisenhower was secure enough in himself not to care. Kennedy, who owned a house in Georgetown, considered it his playground. Ford took it in his stride. The Reagans were socially so self-assured with anyone that they did not at all mind going to a dinner party at Katherine Graham's house in Georgetown, this Democratic lion's den.

I got a taste of Johnson's anti-Georgetown prejudices when during an interview he said to me with his nostrils flaring that I probably belonged to those who lived there and agreed with them that that was where power resides. Pointing emphatically at the floor, between his legs, he said: "Power resides here!" In order not to spoil the rest of the interview, I waited until the end to tell him that I did not, as he had assumed, live in Georgetown, but in Cleveland Park, and almost next door to one of his best friends, James Rowe. And so the interview ended with his smiling benevolently.

My very first interview with President Johnson, in June 1965, began in the most unorthodox manner. Marvin Watson, his appointments secretary, instead of taking me to the Oval Office, led me into the cabinet room where the president was speaking to several American ambassadors before they were leaving for their posts in Morocco, Ivory Coast, Poland, and Liberia. I was motioned to sit down to listen to the president, instructing them to tell the people in the countries they had been accredited to the story of American progress in civil rights, economic growth, space exploration, and how the government looked after the people's needs. His homily completed, he introduced me to the ambassadors, who diplomatically concealed their embarrassment at being treated like undergraduates, and said to me: "You see I have seen so far one hundred fourteen foreign ambassadors and only sixty-four American." He meant to impress on me the importance he attached to foreign relations and to keeping in touch with ambassadors. When I later ran into one of the ambassadors, who had been lectured to by the president, he said to me: "We're meteorologists, but Johnson wants us to be rainmakers . . ."

As soon as McNamara and Rusk entered the cabinet room to add their own briefings, the president asked me to follow him to his office. He immediately settled down in his rocking chair next to the sofa I sat on, ordered a cup of soup for himself and some coffee, as I had suggested, for me. He then leaned over as close as he could into my face as if he wanted to hypnotize me, and said: "Shoot." He was anxious to answer every question as forthcomingly as he could until I asked about whether he would agree to a bombing halt in Vietnam while a Commonwealth mission, an idea Prime Minister Harold Wilson had thought up, was trying to find out in Hanoi whether there was any way of getting a negotiated peace. He promised to be "helpful" and "reasonable" without exactly answering my question; it had clearly irritated him. He then picked up the latest report on the situation in Vietnam, which his secretary had just brought in, and began to read it to me. He stopped though as soon as it referred to new pressures by the Vietcong and a retreat by the South Vietnamese. He then gave me a lecture on his Vietnam aims. Suddenly he put his hand on my knee, reinforcing his words with physical contact. Slightly uncomfortably, I remembered a favorite Johnson phrase: "If you can get him by the balls, the hearts and minds will follow."

We discussed other matters. I asked whether he would be prepared to help Britain again if the pound got into further trouble and he replied with a twist of irony in his voice: "We won't let the British Empire go down the drain." He then confided that he would not press the prime minister anymore about the Multilateral Force because he did not think anything would come of it, which was interesting news. Almost every minute the president's mood, face, position changed. He would walk over restlessly to the news tickers he kept in his office to give me the latest on some vote in Congress, then to a table to show me action photos taken during cabinet meetings, giving me a few, then he sat down again and suddenly asked: "Do I look reckless? Do I look like someone not giving enough thought to a problem?" Of course, I reassured him that he did not.

He switched to talking about the American press and Scotty Reston, who sounded so misinformed, he said, because he had not been to see him since January. "Big Walter [Lippmann] and little Scotty" had become thorns in his side: less than a year earlier he and Lippmann had been on the best of terms. I remembered how in September he had come to Lippmann's birthday party with two gifts, a leatherbound visitors' book and a tie, and had arranged for Walter to be awarded the Medal of Freedom. But since then the influential columnist had become disenchanted with Johnson's conduct of the Vietnam war and by an abortive episode in which LBJ showed him in advance the text of a major address about policy in Southeast Asia and solicited his advice. Lippmann told me later that the draft he had been given contained the phrase "unconditional negotiations." After he had read the text Johnson talked to him for about an hour, and though he didn't actually ask if he approved it, he gave him the impression that it was the final draft. When the speech was delivered the phrase was changed to "unconditional discussions." Lippmann felt deceived, and angered by what seemed a blatant attempt to "co-opt" him. For Lippmann the initial hint at the president's willingness to enter into negotiations was not enough; to support his position he wanted to see it publicly confirmed in the speech.

I knew that Johnson had become mesmerized by Vietnam war statistics, such as the body count, but he surprised me with such details as that three or four British newspapers were for him and about the same number against, that the ratio in West Germany was about eight to six in his favor—he personalized everything. Yet he pretended that he did not particularly care what foreign public opinion thought of him since most people, because of the attitude of the news media and particularly the BBC, were misinformed about what was going on in Vietnam. His confidence in being able to win the war, and he meant win, was based on the simple concept that since neither the Russians nor the Chinese wanted war with the United States, then the United States, with infinitely greater firepower than the French had commanded, should be able to defeat the Vietcong.

I left President Johnson that day feeling that he certainly had a more winning personality than he projected on television. People underrated him because he was so different from any other American politician, even different from any Texan. It was hard to come to terms with a man so compassionate and yet so crude, so overpowering yet so lacking in self-confidence, so warm and friendly and yet so vindictive, so hard to predict and so determined to lead. Even James Rowe, who had known him longer than most, found it hard to deal with him. Rowe had been his election campaign adviser in 1960 and after that felt compelled to write him a letter suggesting that he treat his staff with more forbearance. Johnson never replied and broke off all contact with his old friend—until he became president. On that first morning he telephoned him and asked him to be his first visitor in the Oval Office. Nobody could have been more surprised than Rowe was, and more pleased. Johnson, when Rowe came to see him in the Oval Office, greeted him as one would a long-lost friend and tried to overwhelm him with apologies. He blamed himself for having ignored Jim for three years, asked forgiveness, and finally begged him for his support and counsel now that he carried the country on his shoulders. Rowe, with tears in his eyes, began to apologize that it had been his not the president's fault that they had not seen each other, when LBJ interrupted him and said, smiling impatiently: "Goddamn, Jim, can't you be content with being the first person the thirty-sixth president of the United States apologized to!?"

One of LBJ's great problems was that he had a universal heart and a Texan head. He wore his universal heart on his sleeve. As he once put it: "I want to leave this world behind as a place where man no longer destroys his brother and where every child born into it can have a healthy body and a prepared mind." He thought in sweeping, idealistic terms about doing away with poverty and racial hatred; he wanted to go down in history as the builder of the Great Society. He did not just want to turn clichés into glitter, but to become a real savior. Yet he couldn't live down Texas. "When I became majority leader," he once told a small group of reporters, "the press woke up to the fact that I was born in Texas. I have prayed that my dear mother come back from the dead and conceive me all over again, so I could be born in some state like New Jersey or New York. You people just can't get away from the fact that I am a southerner and a Texan to boot." In June 1965, well before he thought of denying himself a second full term, he said to Hugh Sidey, *Time* magazine's connoisseur of presidents: "I'm not sure that I can lead this country and keep it together with my background."

When the Washington *Post* called him the "antithesis of John F. Kennedy
. . . the cowboy who had rented the Taj Mahal with a rebel yell . . . a caricature
out of an American Western, with an uncultivated accent and an often unintel-
ligent turn of phrase . . . ," it was not just with a rebel yell that he replied;
it turned him into an enraged gored bull and confirmed those deep-seated
insecurities that he often hid with his overbearing manners. Later, when a *Post*
reporter wrote that in reply to a question as to whether General Earle
Wheeler's remark about a change of policy in Vietnam was correct, the president had said: "Bullshit" (the *Post* used only "bull . . ."), Johnson complained
sardonically: "Since I was from Texas I couldn't use that sort of language, and,
you know, it's funny that whenever I say it, it comes out crap. But whenever
a Georgetown boy [and the Kennedys were in his mind Georgetown boys too]
says it, it comes out smelling Chanel No. 5."

Jim Rowe contended that he was two men, the consensus man and the
tough guy who wanted to show off his "pride of power," as Walter Lippmann
called it. He was a consensus man when he could see two objectives between
which to seek a compromise and the power man when he couldn't see both.
He then thought to impose his will. "The danger then is," Rowe added, "that
if he gets a bloody nose, he will even get more stubborn and hit back even
harder." Johnson was by no means a dictator, but the presidency suddenly sat
on an isolated pinnacle, its power virtually unchallengeable, at least in the
president's own eyes, and he assumed a terrifying presence. He strode through
the White House, he took us reporters on a walk around the south lawn the
way you take dogs out round the block and gave them a tongue-lashing.

Some presidents come to power at the right time. I believe Johnson did not,
and that was his tragedy. He was a master politician on the home front, but
he was condemned to deal with the worst foreign problem any American
president had to deal with in peacetime—the undeclared war in Vietnam. For
a while, though, it looked as if he would go far toward becoming a great
president. "I have much hope in the healing arts of Lyndon Johnson," Lippmann wrote in 1964. "We can turn to him with confidence. For his great gift
is in finding the consensus without which the American system of government
with its states and regions, its checks and balances, is unworkable." After a
visit to California he wrote that the "calming effect of the nuclear détente,
which was, it may well be, the crowning achievement of President Kennedy,
has coalesced with the feeling of confidence that Lyndon Johnson is a prudent,
old-fashioned American who has no taste for gambling and foreign adventure." Scotty Reston too took an optimistic line, predicting that Johnson would
get what he wanted from Congress and would be nominated and reelected in
1964.

Johnson's original plan was to continue détente with the Soviet Union, put
a "hold" on Vietnam, and warn the Cubans not to interfere with the U-2 flights
over Cuba. When Deputy Prime Minister Mikoyan came to see him on
Khrushchev's orders to convince him that Lee Harvey Oswald was not, as

some rumors had it, a Russian agent, and had not acted on orders from Moscow, Johnson in turn reassured him that he would continue Kennedy's policy toward the Soviet Union. I held reservations about Johnson and foreign affairs because, unlike Kennedy, he had been a long-standing member of the Senate Armed Services Committee, but had never served on the Senate Foreign Relations Committee. Still, I believed that what he lacked in knowledge and experience in foreign affairs would be made up by the old Kennedy team, Bundy, Rusk, and McNamara. Moreover, Jack Valenti, the president's long-time handyman and fellow Texan, told me that Johnson planned to build up his home base first, and anyway not having a vice president made it difficult for him to indulge in trips abroad. He wanted to wait until he had been elected president in his own right. Valenti advised me to forget about Johnson's style, which he well realized repelled the Europeans, and keep my eyes on substance. Valenti had acquired the reputation of a fawning sycophant and yes-man, but he struck me as a much more intelligent person than most people gave him credit for. He had a way of speaking and dressing that created the impression of a provincial dandy who was too impressed with his entry into the new social scene, but in fact he had a shrewd judgment of people and politics and, above all, he was a very personable chap. And how could anyone be only a flunky who knew as much about the British historian Macaulay as he did!

Under the Johnson presidency the Churchillian legacy of the Anglo-American relationship began to suffer from serious anemia. Johnson lacked the empathy that Eisenhower and, particularly, Kennedy felt for it. In fact, dealing with foreign statesmen was a nuisance to him. As he himself admitted: "The trouble with foreigners is that I did not grow up with them." And Britain's prime minister, Harold Wilson, however much he wanted to preserve a closer Anglo-American relationship, did not understand Johnson or the Democrats. Like other Labour leaders, he was under the mistaken impression that there was little difference between a New Dealer and a British socialist. To him the Great Society was another way of talking about Labour's kind of socialism when in effect Johnson's approach to the welfare state did not prevent his being closer to business than to the labor unions. As soon as Johnson realized that Wilson was trying to manipulate him for his own political ends, he resented him. Political manipulators rarely get along; they know too much about how it's done. What annoyed Johnson above all were Wilson's attempts to inject himself as a mediator between the White House and the Kremlin. Furthermore, Johnson resented the devaluation of sterling, which weakened this convenient first-line defense of the dollar, the pullback of British forces from east of Suez, and the refusal to send at least a token military force to Vietnam. But Wilson was in the unhappy situation of having the weakest bargaining hand of any prime minister since the end of World War II; he had to govern with a very small majority in Parliament, and public opinion was in such a mood that he could not afford to give Johnson even a token force. And so not long after Dean Acheson shot his well-aimed poison arrow across the Atlantic about Britain's having lost an empire and not yet found a role, and after Whitehall recognized that Britain could no longer aspire to stay in the global race, the special relationship had lost several of its moorings. Johnson, after one of Wilson's visits to the White House, told one of his aides that spending two days with a British prime minister was overdoing it because Britain was not that important anymore. (This verdict was almost as discouraging as a letter I received at that time from Peal & Co., the shoemakers in London, saying that due to "the ever-increasing difficulty experienced over the last few years in obtaining skilled labour to replace long-serving staff who have left due to retirement and death," they were closing their bespoke workshop.) When, after the Vietcong attack against Pleiku, LBJ ordered the first retaliatory bombing raid against North Vietnam, Wilson tried to rush to Washington in the Attlee manner. True, the bombing was a turning point in the war, but Johnson had to say no four times, emphasizing that this was Vietnam not Korea, where there had been British military fighting units, before Wilson gave up badgering him. David Bruce, the American ambassador to the Court of St. James's, later told me that after that incident he managed to convince Wilson that it was better to communicate with the president by teletype, because a man like Johnson to whom reaching for the telephone was second nature and principally an instrument to pressure people, did not like others using it to put him on the spot.

I also dabbled at fishing in those troubled waters of Vietnam when I accompanied Lord Thomson, the then owner of *The Sunday Times,* to Moscow to assist him in an interview with Soviet Prime Minister Alexei Kosygin. For a variety of reasons, this interview remained indelibly etched in my mind. Denis Hamilton had called me from Washington for this special assignment because of my experience in reporting from the Soviet Union. I found Lord Thomson easy and delightful company, a thorough contrast in his modesty and informality with his predecessor, Viscount Kemsley. Roy Thomson was a very unusual press lord, an unassuming man who never forgot that his father had been a barber and that he himself had become a millionaire only at the age of sixty. He insisted on grabbing my portable typewriter whenever I had too much to carry, he said he collected newspapers the way other people collect ties, and he could rattle off the names of most of the ninety newspapers he then owned. He was a man without secrets. He told me, for instance, what he had put into his will and he was free in telling me exactly what he thought of people whether in the office or outside it. His comments were usually laced with humor and never malicious. When Lady Egremont once asked him during a weekend at Petworth whether he would like a book of poetry to read himself into sleep, he replied that he never read poetry, but that he read his balance sheets in bed and they, to him, read like poetry. The night before the Moscow interview Lord Thomson confided that he planned to give the Russian leader a present as a souvenir and that he had brought several pairs of cuff links with him:

would I select the one I liked best? With this he threw five little boxes on the table. I opened them all and found that none of them was in gold or silver. All were just silver-plated. A little hesitantly, I wondered whether he was aware of that and whether therefore they were suitable as a gift to the Soviet prime minister. But Lord Thomson had no doubt: "These cuff links were all given as presents to me, and if they are good enough for me, they are also good enough for Kosygin!" That settled that.

I was surprised that once we had entered the Kremlin grounds—our personal guide was the son of Foreign Minister Gromyko—nobody asked us again for any identification. Nobody even examined my Rolleiflex camera which I had brought along in case there was no official photographer at hand. I suspected that Lord Thomson would be keen on having his picture taken with his host.

If de Gaulle impressed with his cold, erect grandeur and Johnson with the eagle's-wing sweep of his long arms over everybody else, Kosygin, a totally colorless Russian, was the epitome of the éminence grise behind Party Secretary Leonid Brezhnev. In dealing with foreigners the Russians like to be, as they put it, businesslike, and Kosygin was certainly that. He welcomed us stiffly, bending from the hips during his handshake. At the long conference table, covered with green baize, it soon became clear that the message he wanted to convey was his disapproval of current British foreign policy. In reply to our question whether he could exert his influence in Hanoi to help get the United States out of the morass of Vietnam, all we got was irony smothered in sarcasm. The United States, he replied, had its own ships to take its own troops away and if that was the American aim, he could arrange for those ships not to be shelled while withdrawing. That was all he wanted to say on that score. He insisted that North Vietnam had a strong independent government and the South did not, and it was the United States that ran the show there.

Kosygin remained his cool, dignified impersonal self throughout, except when Lord Thomson asked whether some recent reforms might herald changes in the Communist doctrine. Suddenly the Soviet leader became agitated and reassured us with some heat that whatever the changes they would not affect "scientific communism." In economics it was not management that should play the main role, but profits. Lord Thomson pricked up his ears, but Kosygin quickly added, "Because they increase the national income. You think that if we talk about profits, we have entered the capitalist path. That is wrong. Sometimes I am sorry we do not use another word. But, mind you, profits in our society are different because we do not have private ownership or shareholders. Profits enable us to judge the efficiency of the enterprise . . ."

When the interview came to an end and we got up, Lord Thomson presented Mr. Kosygin with the pair of cuff links he had selected. Kosygin, surprised, lost his composure for a second, then opened the box, and from his full height, without bending, looked into it. Then without saying a word or examining them more closely, he put them almost furtively into his coat pocket.

If there was any political lesson to be drawn from the interview, it was Kosygin's conviction that Hanoi would ultimately win in Vietnam and that all he was interested in was to end the war through negotiations to accelerate the American total withdrawal. This conclusion of course carried no conviction in Washington.

The most blatant attempt by the British government to inject itself as a messenger between Washington and Moscow occurred during a dinner party I gave at home for George Brown, the foreign secretary, on Saturday, October 15, 1966. It turned into the most turbulent dinner party I have ever given. Fortunately, the ebullient, irrepressible, extraverted Brown had some of the same quality as Lord Thomson, in that he could go far in offending people without their taking offense. Lord Thomson, however, never went as far as Brown, who used words that simply were not in his lordship's vocabulary. My other guests were Vice President Hubert Humphrey, British Ambassador Sir Patrick Dean, Robert McNamara, Senator Stuart Symington, Bill Bundy, and Bromley Smith of the National Security Council.

Almost from the start Brown tried to wheedle out of McNamara conditions for a reasonable basis for negotiations with Hanoi which he could put in his pocket to take to Moscow. What are your minimum terms, he repeated time and again, with McNamara and Bill Bundy, by then the assistant secretary for Far Eastern affairs in the State Department, answering with generalities. Brown—and I had restricted him to one vodka and tonic before dinner —began to get hotter and hotter under his collar, finally exclaiming: "You, Bob, you don't speak with the same voice as the president [whom he had seen that morning]. Your president said quite different things to me. You sound as if you didn't want to get into negotiations! The president does! Bob, you're protecting your ass when nobody is trying to bugger you!"

At that point McNamara, smarting with indignation, lost his temper. He was fuming, his eyes were rolling, and he jumped up and said: "The president is now in the White House. I'll take you there right away and we'll see who is right!" I had never seen McNamara so enraged. Brown too jumped up, obviously only too glad to have another go at the president. It was close to nine P.M. and dinner had not yet started; as the two headed for the door, Bromley Smith and I jumped up too. First of all, I did not think this was the best way to approach Johnson and, secondly, I did not want to have my dinner party blown ceiling high. Helpfully, Bromley Smith piped up, saying: "I believe the president is making a speech somewhere in Maryland." That stopped the two, who were already on the steps outside my front door. I suggested that they wait until Brom, as we called him, checked by phone whether the president was at home, and whispered to him as he headed for the telephone in the next room to say that, whatever the situation, he should report that the president was not at the White House. Indeed, after another minute, he returned with the truth, namely that the president was making a speech outside Washington. What he did not tell us was that he had asked that the chopper bringing the president back from Philadelphia be delayed by a few minutes before landing at the White House to make sure that the presidential log did not contradict his report to us.

McNamara and Brown returned, calmed down, at least for a moment. However, as soon as we had sat down at the dinner table Brown began to needle McNamara again. He accused him of being inflexible to such an extent that he, Brown, was losing faith in the genuineness of the American readiness to negotiate, and he shouted Bill Bundy down as not being in McNamara's league and that he'd therefore better shut up. At that point McNamara, with an envelope next to his plate, began to write something, and in no time offered Brown a set of conditions acceptable to the United States to get negotiations started: halting all infiltration from the North, slowing down the pace of the war in the South, preventing infiltration into the neutral zone with some sort of international supervision, indications that they were going to leave the South independent. Brown was now satisfied, almost triumphant, having got some words he could take to Moscow. He then asked how soon he could go there. McNamara encouraged him to do so before the pressures for further escalation became necessary. Brown pleaded that the bombing was not achieving its objectives, except perhaps in keeping up the spirit of the troops in the South and that, if a further escalation happened, he would turn against the United States. McNamara did not contradict him, but emphasized how important it was to have Britain's assistance. He wanted to make Brown feel appreciated.

What struck me as funny was that both McNamara and the British ambassador were taking notes—I, as the host, could not. There was general agreement that the Russians were now actively interested in bringing the war to a close. The vice president throughout had been strikingly nonpartisan in this transatlantic altercation and left after the discussion trailed off into less controversial problems. Brown too left soon after him. McNamara, although no one in the American government would dare treat him the way Brown did, still seemed to feel kindly toward Brown, even though he said he thought he had worked rather hard for his dinner. Still, he said, he enjoyed it, and I thanked him for his patience and the sense of humor with which he tolerated Brown's insults. It did not seem to me as though Brown had got terms Hanoi would accept; still, he left contented.

Mrs. McNamara said to me the next day, "You must have had a real cockfight on your hands. I only hope Brown is not organizing his own undoing. He is like a pistol, but Bob enjoyed him. You can't help forgiving him in the end." And that's how most of his friends felt, but not his enemies.

Brown came in a very different mood, rather disheartened, to cushion the shock in Washington after I had reported that in April 1967 the British government would decide to withdraw from east of Suez. My report had caused such embarrassment in Whitehall that Harold Wilson felt compelled to order one of those fruitless investigations to discover the source of this indiscretion. What complicated the investigation was the fact that I had just spent a few days in London, and at 10 Downing Street they did not know whether I got my information in London or from the Washington embassy. To mislead any possible investigator I also protected my source by giving the impression that the story could equally well have come from American contacts.

The reason for the consternation in Whitehall was that the Americans were bitterly opposed to such a withdrawal and were still hoping that their warning not to take such a drastic step was being taken seriously, especially since the prime minister had promised the president to stay put east of Suez. Francis Bator, a Harvard economist, and a special presidential assistant, defined the point well to me. It was essential, he said, for Britain to remain the protector of the ramparts east of Suez because it represented an important ingredient in Anglo-American relations. Withdrawal would greatly diminish Britain's value as an ally, would make it less tempting for the Europeans to let Britain, as a truncated world power, into Europe, and—God forbid—mean that the United States would be on her own making policy in an area about which it knew very little. He also thought that Britain's annual cost east of Suez of about $140 million could be halved without seriously jeopardizing the security of the British forces out there. Actually, the costs were higher, about $800 million.

Unfortunately, however anxious the United States was for Britain to stay out there, it had not thought about any possible alternatives. Worse, various departments were at cross-purposes. McNamara wanted Britain to stay at least while the American forces were tied up in Vietnam, and preferred some troop withdrawals from Germany rather than from Singapore. At the same time the so-called theologians at the State Department did not want the slightest troop withdrawals from Germany because, they argued, it would undermine European confidence in Britain's intentions. No financial inducements were offered for the British to stay. In order to take advantage of my first disclosure, I went to see McNamara to ask him whether he might be prepared to subsidize the costs of keeping British troops in the Far East, but he said categorically "no." He could not add to the costs of the Vietnam war, which was already making deep inroads into his defense budget. It was a shortsighted decision, for ways could have been found to avoid creating the strategic vacuum that has come to haunt Western interests around the Persian Gulf.

And so Brown came to mitigate the likely explosive effect the withdrawal would have on Anglo-American relations—no mean task. He came under the guise of having to attend a SEATO meeting which, earlier, he had decided to give a miss. It was at a SEATO reception that Dean Rusk asked me, rather solicitously, where I got my story—whether in London or Washington—to which I answered only that I was sure he would not want me to give away my sources. Later, when Chalmers Roberts of the Washington *Post* challenged George Brown with the same question—a most unusual one for a reporter to ask in this situation—Brown, probably to make sure nobody suspected him as my source (he was not), replied impatiently: "Don't you know, Henry gets his information from the Defense Department," a hint at my special relationship with McNamara. Brown later complained to me, with some irritation, that I had embarrassed him and the British government. He was careful to say publicly that he had come to get the American reaction and that nothing had yet been decided. But even with his skill as a debater and the fund of sympathy he enjoyed, he left behind a grave suspicion that the Labour government was in fact contemplating more than a "major withdrawal" from the Far East. The confrontation with Rusk, normally an even-tempered fellow, was bruising. He and McNamara made a last ditch effort to convince Brown of the catastrophic damage the abandonment of Singapore, the sheet anchor of Britain's military presence, would cause. But when Brown asked the question I had already put to McNamara—would the United States be prepared to mitigate the costs of staying (he suggested heavier arms purchases from Britain)?—he got only vague answers. But it would not have been an acceptable alternative even for the British. In cabinet Harold Lever, the shrewd financial adviser to the prime minister, asked Denis Healey why he did not get the Gulf states to pay for the continued British presence there—something they were prepared to do—to which Healey replied that British soldiers were not mercenaries. Lever countered that mercenaries were soldiers who fought other people's wars, but in this case they would be protecting British interests. But Healey would not hear of it. When I asked Conservative Prime Minister Sir Alec Douglas-Home in 1971 whether he would accept an American or Gulf state subsidy to prevent a total withdrawal from east of Suez and reverse the Labour government's decision, he too said with finality: "British soldiers will not be used like Hessian soldiers." I was disappointed. But I will always remember him with warm feelings because when he once came to our garden in Washington for a few moments and our three-year-old daughter, Fiona, greeted him with a little pile of earth and some worms on her trowel, he sat down with her and suggested that she put those worms into a glass jar with some leaves and watch how they behaved. Fiona dashed into the kitchen and within seconds returned with a jar, and he and she filled the jar with leaves and the worms. He was delighted to have inspired her so instantly, and for her it has remained an unforgettable occasion.

And so the United States, which in the fifties tried to accelerate the dismantling of the British Empire and gravely weakened it in the wake of the Suez crisis in 1956, in the late sixties was pleading fervently but in vain with the British government to preserve its last remnants. McNamara argued that 5,000 British soldiers east of Suez meant more than 10,000 in Europe; President Johnson feared that Britain's pullback would encourage the North Vietnamese to continue the war. But Wilson was facing a revolt in his own party: the only major concession he was able to make was to spin out the withdrawal over five years.

Five days before Wilson announced the British withdrawal from the Far East and the Persian Gulf, Dean Rusk, according to a memorandum whose declassification I recently obtained, had reported to President Johnson that he had expressed his "dismay" to George Brown over the pending actions by the British government, and had explained to him that "they would have profound repercussions on the future of the free world, on US public opinion, and on the American political will to maintain an American presence." He had also told Brown that "the US would not and could not fill the vacuum left by the British and urged the British government and people to consider most carefully alternatives to this path of action on which they seem to be setting their feet." Tom Hughes, the assistant secretary for intelligence and research, on January 16, the day Wilson announced his measures, interpreted them for Mr. Rusk, according to another recently declassified dispatch, as follows: "They represent the most dreaded combination of all the possible economies that had been rumored. They show that none of the attempts to dissuade the UK—by the US, Singapore, Malaysia, Australia, and New Zealand—was successful. They indicate that, in the protracted cabinet struggles over which programs to slash (six agonizing meetings in ten days), Wilson and [Roy] Jenkins, who apparently favored economy above all else, won out over Brown, Healey, and Thomson, who were understood to have argued that defense and foreign policy considerations should prevail over all-out cuts."

In another declassified secret dispatch from the American Embassy in London the minister, Ronald Spiers, reported that "it was ironic that the January 16th decisions were not the result of any strategic reappraisal or of a coherent review of Britain's international politics and objectives, but the result of three weeks of intensive horse-trading between different spending ministries . . . a series of Pavlovian reactions to conflicting economic stimuli and political pressures." He asked, "Were these decisions a historical watershed or were they inevitable consequences of a path that Britain began to tread after World War II? Is Britain finally finding the inevitable right role for itself or is it the case of a weak Government being buffeted by economic exigencies, groggy like a prizefighter about to drop on the canvas?" He did not offer his own answers to these questions.

Ever since Britain had given India its independence and had lost control over the Suez Canal, British governments debated and increasingly doubted the validity of the east-of-Suez strategic concept. But they never came to grips with the issue because, in the final analysis, the decision meant the end of Britain's big-power role outside Europe. Successive economic crises had forced Britain to give up its efforts to remain a world power. "We have come to terms with our role in the world," Wilson told the House of Commons, ". . . no amount of economic revival over the next few years is likely to lead Britain to reverse this fundamental turn in its outlook and interest in Europe."

Also inevitable was the decision to throw Britain's weight into Europe and not into the Far East, as McNamara and Rusk, rather selfishly, advocated. For the first time in three centuries a weak western Europe was not in Britain's interest, because it would only make her weaker. If a choice had to be made, Wilson made the right one, but he remained unwilling to commit himself fully to a genuine participation in the new Europe, still waiting for the demise of the supreme spoiler, General de Gaulle. Whether it would have been possible politically to get Congress to provide funds or the Pentagon to make more arms purchases from Britain is hard to judge in retrospect, especially since it was not a Communist threat—as when Britain relinquished the protection of Greece and Turkey to the United States—that forced the withdrawal from east of Suez. But I wonder whether it would not have been worthwhile for the United States to assume the costs for the maintenance of Singapore, just as it is now paying all the costs for the building up of a British possession, Diego Garcia island, as a military base in the Indian Ocean.

Johnson's ambitions for domestic expansion were almost limitless, and yet, with the costs of the Vietnam war escalating and inflation biting into American prosperity, he insisted that the United States could afford "guns and butter." His reluctance to raise taxes weakened the dollar, the domestic economy, the international monetary system, and the Pax Americana. But on June 6, 1965, he told the nation that "America shall not be deterred from doing what must be done to preserve this last peace man shall ever have to win or lose . . ." and in his January 1966 State of the Union message he proclaimed that "Time will require further sacrifices . . . But we will not heed those who will wring it from the hopes of the unfortunate in a land of plenty. I believe the Great Society can continue while we fight in Vietnam."

Just as the Vietnam crisis preoccupied President Johnson, so the preservation of the pound became Prime Minister Harold Wilson's menacing shadow, which, in turn, became in its own peculiar way, my own crisis and that of *The Sunday Times.* It all started rather innocently with Denis Hamilton asking me whether I would be prepared to brave the barriers of Whitehall and do a historic reconstruction of the crisis that led to the devaluation of sterling. I knew that Whitehall became obsessed with secrecy whenever a reporter tried to penetrate its intricate web of policymaking, but I never imagined that this assignment would get me and my newspaper directly involved in the heat of a national election campaign. I was aware that Anthony Howard, whom Hamilton had specially appointed "Whitehall correspondent" to apply his exceptional bird-dog sense for political news and to investigate the mysterious and not so mysterious operations of Whitehall, had to give up after the powers there lowered an iron curtain when *The Sunday Times* made the mistake of ostentatiously and challengingly publishing the purpose of his mission. I would have suffered the same fate had I not been able to claim that I already had (as I did) half the story from a source in Washington. This argument impressed the prime minister, who was anxious for me to write my report on the basis of the views held in Whitehall and not just in Washington. Yet vaulting the Whitehall barriers proved far harder than I had expected. Everybody involved knew about my assignment because they had all been warned in advance, and they nervously awaited what in the end I would come up with. To avoid any major boners I proposed to show the final typescript to Sir William Armstrong, permanent secretary of the treasury and head of the civil service, and Derek Mitchell, the principal private secretary to the prime minister, for factual matters only. They accepted and pointed out some flaws, which I duly and gratefully corrected. But to my small discomfiture they also hinted that they would leave some in, in order to be able to prove that the help they provided was limited.

The date of publication for the three-part series had been set for March 6, 1966, weeks in advance, when nobody had an inkling that the prime minister would call a snap election, causing the campaign virtually to coincide with my first article. The editor was pleased with this coincidence because it would heighten interest in what was to be called "How Sterling Came In from the Cold." Then on the Friday before Sunday publication was to start (with the pages all ready to go to press), the chancellor of the exchequer, James Callaghan, after consultations with the prime minister, called Lord Thomson and asked him to come to his private quarters at 11 Downing Street because he wanted to talk to him about my serial. Thomson replied that he did not know anything about my articles and that he would see him only in the presence of Denis Hamilton, the editor, and then only at eight thirty A.M. because he had to see his doctor later about his lumbago.

When they met (I was not present), Callaghan began by saying that he had heard about my articles and in view of their content was now asking them to postpone publication until after the election because they could hurt sterling in the world. (Callaghan, on whom I paid a call during my research, had then refused to answer any questions unless I first told him whom else I had seen, which I declined to do. That ended that interview.) Lord Thomson now made it clear that he would leave all decisions in the editor's hands. Denis, annoyed by this interference, first argued that what could really hurt sterling was the government's policy of promising more welfare-state measures, as foreshadowed in the chancellor's own speech in the House of Commons. Then he asked whether he could direct a question at Sir William Armstrong, who sat at Callaghan's elbow. Callaghan said yes, whereupon Denis asked whether Armstrong agreed that my articles could hurt sterling. Sir William hesitated for a moment, then he said: "Not really, but they would not help it either"—quite a courageous answer in view of what the chancellor had just said. Callaghan ignored this diplomatic disavowal and appealed to the proprietor "on patriotic grounds" for postponement of my articles. Denis, answering for Roy Thomson, said he was sorry, but he saw no good reason for holding back.

At this point the chancellor raised his voice and said that if we did publish he would have to initiate an investigation of all the officials who had helped me, by appointing a royal commission—he would invoke the Official Secrets Act. Roy, not exactly succeeding in lowering the temperature, then said: "Jim, you made a foolish mistake, because once you threaten my editor, I know there is nothing I can do. You made a great mistake." Denis, accepting the challenge, then said: "Fleet Street needs a martyr! All I can say now is that we have to proceed with publication and as to the threat to those civil servants who are in danger of being prosecuted I can only say that *The Sunday Times,* if their careers are in any way affected, will look after their livelihood." Hamilton was never a man who could be intimidated or deviate from his principles, and for that and other reasons, was an ideal editor. However, he was also a man who preferred compromise to confrontation. Therefore when Callaghan, realizing he had gone too far, suggested that Denis might want to go over my report with Sir William who would "identify" any possible errors of fact, he agreed, since it did not commit him to anything. Then they all got up and when they reached the door, Roy, who had that rare quality of being able to be candid without ever causing offense, turned around, grabbed the chancellor by his lapels, and said, smiling: "Jim, you're not really worried about sterling, you're worried that these articles may lose you the election." The meeting between Armstrong and Hamilton did not happen. Callaghan called Denis to say that he had talked about it to the prime minister, who had said no, because it would create a precedent. The chancellor was suddenly full of pleasantries, having obviously realized that this ill-conceived attempt at intimidation could have a more explosive political effect on the elections than the articles.

That evening Lord Cromer, chairman of the Bank of England, invited me to his apartment, worried about "some of the fly-on-the-wall stuff" I had got from him, but I reassured him that it would not "break the bank." Early on Saturday morning however Cromer arrived in person, unusually agitated, at Denis Hamilton's office, worried about the rumor he had picked up about a royal commission. Denis assured him that he did not need to worry. A little later Sir Eric Roll, another of my sources, called asking for a minor deletion; he too had heard about a possible investigation. I am mentioning this episode mainly to illustrate the havoc Britain's Official Secrets Act can cause even among the highest government servants. The series led to some searching questions at some press conferences given by the chancellor—especially he was asked whether it was true that he had tried to suppress the second installment, which he denied—but it hurt neither sterling nor the Labour Party, which scored a resounding victory.

Many years later James Margach, the political commentator on *The Sunday Times,* and one of the best in the business, published a book called *The*

Abuse of Power, about the war between prime ministers and the media from Lloyd George to James Callaghan. In it he published two secret memos from Sir William Armstrong and Sir Derek Mitchell to the prime minister, both reporting to him about my efforts. They showed how much more tightly knit Whitehall is than Washington and how much more sensitive the British government is to "investigative journalism" than the American. Armstrong reported to the PM that my treatment of some of the technical issues was "at times naive," but that I made a serious attempt to be balanced. He explained that my style of reporting was "purporting to take the reader behind the scenes, very much like his celebrated articles on the Skybolt affair." He also reported that to my question whether the article as a whole could do damage to sterling, he had "found it very difficult to say." He concluded: "I did not feel myself however that the article was so damaging that I must plead with him not to publish it." Mitchell's memo was even more fascinating, because it mentioned that he had heard from the Treasury that the chancellor's conclusion was to ask *The Sunday Times* to defer publication until after the election, and because his own recommendation was opposed to the chancellor's inclination to seek the suppression of the articles. "It would be highly damaging if it became known that the chancellor had got the articles suppressed. Although it could be said that this had been done in the interest of sterling, it would be assumed that it had been done in the interest of the Labour Party during an election campaign. And, if the chancellor were rebuffed by Lord Thomson, *The Sunday Times* . . . might well blow the whole thing up . . . This is an awkward situation, but in retrospect I do not think that there is anything that could have been done by HMG [Her Majesty's Government] to avoid it apart from strangling the project at birth, which would have been extremely difficult." I was very much impressed by the fairness and integrity of these two civil service "mandarins," who made no attempt to disparage or undercut my efforts, and by the candor with which they advised the prime minister.

Though Britain's overall influence had shrunk badly when it failed to provide military power, it began, in the mid-sixties, quite unexpectedly to provide cultural power. Nothing had had quite as electrifying an effect on the young in America since the Beatles went out of fashion as the Mods and Rockers, who wafted on beat music across the Atlantic. Dukes and duchesses had had their day; now it was the boys in the leather boots and their uncut manes, and the girls with long-flowing hair in lace stockings and soft culottes, who became the social drawing cards in the best of drawing rooms. The "English look" tailored in Carnaby Street, I concluded, had a healthy influence. The girls discovered femininity. It was not beauty that mattered, but personality. Jean Shrimpton became New York's leading fashion model. What appealed to me about her was that despite her sudden fame, she remained a beguiling little English girl with a slight cockney accent. When I asked her to dinner in New

York, she invited me instead to her little basement flat for a plate of spaghetti. She was not swept off her feet by fame and modeling fees, but was determined to go back to England, get married, and have kids. Thus quite unexpectedly, good old England brought the cult of youth to the United States.

The rage against the Vietnam war among the students, however, became a much more powerful movement. It began to gather momentum when draftees and reservists were getting their call-up orders and when teachers and professors, whose ranks in the age of mass education had swelled to over 400,000, began to establish themselves as an important political lobby. Fifteen hundred of them came to Washington to participate in what used to be called a teach-in, including such stars as Arthur Schlesinger, Stanley Hoffmann, Zbigniew Brzezinski, and Hans Morgenthau. Even McGeorge Bundy decided to step into the ring, because, he said, feeling the pull of his academic ties, "these are my own people, I had to do it."

The general public was still remarkably steady in the face of the specter of a deeper American involvement. But a global disquiet began to set in. Johnson was still an unknown quantity in foreign affairs and his lack of sensitivity to world opinion, his impersonal treatment of allies, his untiring effort to look twenty feet tall, were disturbing, as was the broad question, what would the current strains do to the coexistence policy with the Soviet Union? The Democratic Convention in 1964 had given Johnson a resounding mandate, though one somewhat diluted, at least for him, by the sixteen-minute ovation for Robert Kennedy, who stood in a sea of applause, his head bowed under the halo of his mourned brother. (A film album of the Kennedy years had been part of the program.) The Kennedy name still evoked a more spontaneous reaction than Johnson's.

On the eve of the Republican Convention in San Francisco in 1964 I sat next to Clare Boothe Luce at a dinner party at Senator Sherman Cooper's house. She was still a beautiful woman, an interesting mixture of mature femininity and masculine assertiveness, who knew how to take command of a conversation by dipping into her political past or her reservoir of witty stories of her encounters with the great. Her views never lacked originality or candor. Talking about Vietnam, she spoke with the self-assurance of an experienced politician: "The United States has two alternatives—getting out or clobbering the Chinese mainland completely and since we don't want the latter, we must prepare to negotiate." And as to the prospects of the Republicans with a candidate like Goldwater, she said despairingly: "The trouble is that there are too many haters and too many prejudiced people to let us moderates prevent his nomination. Unfortunately, Eisenhower is gaga, Scranton [governor of Pennsylvania] has no guts, Rockefeller only ran with his left hand, holding his new wife with his right one—and who wants Dick Nixon?" At that point her husband, Henry Luce, the *Time* and *Life* empire builder, weighed in to bring the discussion down to earth: "Our problem is that the two-party system gives the extremists no chance because each party extends over the entire political spectrum and therefore provides no real choice for the Know-Nothings."

The Republican Convention was a disappointing affair and to cheer myself up I decided to go on a wine tour, my second in twelve years, through the Napa Valley. Scotty Reston of the *New York Times,* who did not consider himself a wine connoisseur but was always willing to learn something, joined me. Among others we visited the Beaulieu vineyards, to which I had first gone in 1952, when the manager, somewhat embarrassed that he could not find a good bottle of red wine, apologized for the shortcomings of his *réserve privée.* But this time I had good reason for congratulating the old marquis, who was married to a granddaughter of one of the first California vintners, the de Latours, on the fine selection we had with lunch. But the old Frenchman, a caricature of a French aristocrat, leaned over to me and whispered in French: "You're not an American, so I can be frank with you. These California wines are like Algerian wines," which is about the worst that can be said about wine. The old French patriot obviously could not bear that anybody could think that a California wine, even grown on his own vineyard, could be as good as the French. I would bet that even though the Beaulieu wines have greatly improved in the intervening years, he would say the same thing today he said then.

Listening to Senator Barry Goldwater before the convention platform committee had been quite a disturbing experience. He was in a self-confident, belligerent mood and visibly impressed the delegates, who at Republican conventions tend to have a strong right-wing core, much more than Governor William Scranton, who sounded weak and indecisive. However, when a black delegate asked Goldwater how, as president, he would carry out a law (the Civil Rights Act) that he had voted against and declared unconstitutional, he shouted at him: "You're questioning my honesty." Gone was his senatorial diffidence and aloofness, the demagogue in him was exposed. In later years, though, he mellowed like good wine. It happens quite often, especially in democratic societies, that once an extremist, whether of the right or left, ceases to offer a political threat, he can gain popularity for having become a wiser man.

Every morning I had breakfast in the coffee shop of the Mark Hopkins Hotel with Norman Mailer, whose bulldozer of a mind seemed curiously narrow, imprisoned by his own world, and Murray Kempton, one of the subtlest and funniest among domestic political commentators; and every morning we contemplated afresh the dangers of the Goldwater candidacy. Both, but especially Mailer, were scared that he would move closer to the center and that George Wallace's candidacy could enable him to do to Johnson what the southerner J. Strom Thurmond once tried to do to President Truman. Goldwater's nomination was a setback for the United States almost anywhere in the world, because to many it proved that it was not a country one could rely on indefinitely for commonsensical leadership.

Americans too wondered about the significance of Goldwater's nomination. At a dinner party at Clinton Rossiter's house, President James Perkins of Cornell University, Professor Richard Neustadt of Columbia University, Professor Arthur Mizener, and one or two others were all convinced that Johnson would win the election, but what puzzled them was whether Goldwater represented a political aberration or whether the people behind him would permanently influence American politics. The conservative right certainly suffered a whopping setback. Despite the outward appearance of disorder and confusion, bordering on turmoil and chaos, in reality the political shifts as usual were only minor. It was another example of the remarkable stability of the American political scene.

With Johnson triumphantly confirmed as president in his own right, most of my friends continued as before. My early tennis games continued as in the Kennedy days. McGeorge Bundy continued to deliver his sliced forehand with careful intellectual analysis of the opponent's weakest point; Walt Rostow, who usually teamed up with him, threw the full weight of his hefty but extraordinarily mobile body into his forehand in the belief that physical power was the key to success; and John McNaughton, who was usually my partner, relied mainly on his hard service and his dexterous net game; I was the weakest among the four, playing a defensive game hoping to hold my ground until my opponents came to grief. At eight fifteen we dispersed, with Bundy, Rostow, and McNaughton rushing to their cars, waiting for the shower and change of clothes until they reached their offices. Policies were never discussed, the early morning hour was devoted entirely to recreation.

Of the three I saw Bundy most frequently. He had a feel for foreign affairs, a pithy way of expressing himself, and a clarity of mind that made each visit to his basement office a treasure trove for a commentator. He was also closest to the seat of power, and more of a policymaker than he had been under Kennedy; he established the precedent for a strong national security adviser. His views therefore were among the most authoritative in the government. I believed that he had a great sense for friendship, even though he told me years later that one reason he used to see me relatively frequently was because he knew that I saw President Kennedy from time to time privately and that I had similar access to British prime ministers. This, he felt, gave me an unusual perspective on Anglo-American relations and on the differences of viewpoints. With Johnson he developed a kind of Becket relationship, though there was never any doubt that he was only the chancellor and not the archbishop. He epitomized the qualities of the Eastern Establishment and some of its weaknesses. He was a man of great personal and political integrity, always aware that he had to live up to an ancestry that went back to the Lowells and other first colonial families, an intellectual who enjoyed the exercise of power to a point where his utter self-confidence and his trust in American power made him more a man of action than of careful analysis, when it was the latter he was responsible for.

A fine example of Bundy's clarity of mind and his own ruthlessness as a critic was a top secret memo from him to the secretary of defense in reply to one from the Joint Chiefs of Staff, dated June 30, 1965, proposing an increase of 200,000 men in troop commitments for Vietnam: "This memo is designed to raise questions and not to answer them," he began, "and I am afraid it may sound unhelpful." Then he talked about the "grave limitations" of the Joint Chiefs' memo; he complained that it proposed new land commitments "at a time when our troops are entirely untested in the kind of warfare projected, proposes greatly extended air action when the value of the air action we have taken is sharply disputed, proposes naval quarantine by mining at a time when nearly everyone agrees the real question is not in Hanoi, but in South Vietnam." Without mincing words, he concluded: "My first reaction is that this program is rash to the point of folly . . . this is a slippery slope toward total U.S. responsibility and corresponding fecklessness on the Vietnamese side . . . If we need 200,000 men now for these quite limited missions, may we not need 400,000 later? Is this a rational course of action?" Still more brutally, he asked: "Do we want to invest 200,000 men to cover an eventual retreat?" He also criticized the paper for omitting certain "additional possibilities that should be considered before a specific program of pressure is adopted." For instance: "It is within our power to give much more drastic warnings to Hanoi than any we have yet given. If General Eisenhower is right in his belief that it was the prospect of nuclear attack which brought an armistice in Korea, we should at least consider what realistic threat of larger action is available to us for communication to Hanoi . . ."

I am mentioning this memo to illustrate the occasional awareness of the "folly" of the escalation of the American commitment in Vietnam and the failure to avoid it when the chips were laid on the table. Bundy's top secret critique provided a perfect model for the role the national security adviser is supposed to perform. I found it therefore hard to understand that Bundy, in an article "The End of Either/Or" in *Foreign Affairs* magazine in 1967, when he had become president of the Ford Foundation, not only approved of the "slippery slope" but advised that "we should be ready to do our full share to help prevent the Communists from taking South Vietnam by force and terror." When I tried to solicit an explanation from him in January 1986 of how he had shown such clairvoyance in June 1965 yet expressed such firm commitment to the prosecution of the war in 1967, he said that he did not want to discuss the matter and cut me off with such brusqueness that it made me realize how sensitive the nerve I had touched still was. I could only guess that being the loyal civil servant he was, he did not want to undercut an official policy he had helped to frame.

It has been suggested that if Johnson had not kept the "best and the brightest" of the Kennedy crew and chosen his own men, he would not have fallen into that deep well of Vietnam. I doubt that very much. Clark Clifford, who was one of LBJ's closest counselors, would certainly have become either secretary of state or secretary of defense, and it was he who had accompanied President-elect Kennedy to a last briefing by President Eisenhower. In contrast to his own policy as president, Ike warned Kennedy that the tide of communism must be stemmed in Southeast Asia. As he put it: "Our country should do all that it can to persuade our allies to assist us in the conflict in Southeast Asia." He counseled, "But if we are unable to persuade them to cooperate with us, then we must go it alone." Clifford told me later that Kennedy took this warning seriously and began to act on it. When LBJ took over, the policy he inherited from Kennedy had a profound impact on him. Clifford also said that he too was impressed by Eisenhower's stern advice.

Well into 1965 I got a telephone call from Clifford, whose friendship with LBJ had made him into an éminence grise, inviting me to have lunch with him in his private office. He was one of those superlawyers who was held in great esteem as a brilliant attorney and as a shrewd political wizard. I had known him since his days as chief of staff to President Truman. The first thing he told me, even before we sat down, was that he had his office swept for "bugs" once a week and that I could therefore be certain that whatever I said would remain between those four walls. I was quite startled that even a man of his standing and his power could not be sure whether the president or J. Edgar Hoover or somebody else was not wiretapping his office. I said that I had no great secrets worth bugging, but Clifford became very serious when he confided to me that the president had asked him to find out what was wrong with the State Department and that he had asked me to lunch to solicit my candid view of how it looked from the outside, to a foreigner. Virtually every president distrusts the State Department and complains about its being more concerned about the interests of foreign governments than its own, but LBJ, I had firmly believed, had the utmost trust and confidence in Dean Rusk, a fellow southerner from the plains of Georgia (who he once said "did not go to poolrooms and cocktail parties in Georgetown"). LBJ was always ready to climb on any soapbox to praise Rusk as the "best secretary of state in this century." I defended the State Department, much to Clifford's surprise, because I thought that the average quality of the foreign service officers was high, but I was critical of Rusk, whose integrity and decency I admired, but whose leadership qualities and services as a presidential adviser I considered left a lot to be desired. His premises for the American involvement in Vietnam were misconceived, and they were so deeply rooted that in contrast to Bundy and McNamara, for instance, he held on to them even in retirement. His conduct of alliance policies and East-West relations, too, showed a certain lack of vision; he was a man outstanding as a civil servant but not as a policymaker.

Clifford, a handsome man with carefully coiffed white wavy hair who never wore anything but double-breasted suits, looked more like an ageless matinee idol than a tough attorney. He relied on persuasion and the towering authority he exuded at all times. With our discussion of the State Department and the simple sandwich and iced tea lunch at an end, I turned the tables and asked whether Harold Wilson had shown a lack of courage by failing to entice LBJ into a deal that would have made the withdrawal from east of Suez unnecessary. Clifford leaned far back in his leather swivel chair and replied with the utter confidence of a man who knows what he is talking about: "Henry, believe me, LBJ is a hard man to bargain with. The shivers go down your spine when he gives you that cold and hard look, or just stares at you in silence. It probably kept Wilson from even asking."

In the middle of our conversation we were interrupted by a telephone call from Lady Bird Johnson. She wanted to know whether her and her daughter Lucy's thank-you letters for wedding presents could go out at government expense. He told her that hers could but not Lucy's. But Lady Bird persisted: there were, after all, nine thousand letters that had to be sent! Presidential advisers, I thought, get the oddest questions, but Lady Bird at least asked before making a mistake. Clifford, unimpressed by the cost insisted no, and she finally accepted his advice. Clifford smiled as he put the receiver down; he had, as usual, prevailed.

We then briefly discussed Vietnam where, he felt, the United States had to press the enemy relentlessly. "Too bad," he said, "that the North Vietnamese do not have the same grace as Kennedy had when he made it possible during the Cuban missile crisis for Khrushchev not to lose face." He still held the conventional view about forcing Hanoi to the conference table, but he already suspected that in the process the United States might suffer a loss of face. In departing Clifford assured me that all the rumors that he would succeed either Rusk or Ball were wrong. Four days later I heard Johnson say at an off-the-record briefing that Rusk was "a man of overall wisdom and a mother's tolerance."

The Vietnam war has been endlessly chronicled, analyzed, refought, and rethought. But living in political Washington, close to those deeply involved in its conduct, I can't help remembering the emotional turmoil and the mental strains it caused among those to whom I felt close. McGeorge Bundy had a hard-edged mind and was a pragmatist on most issues, except the war in Vietnam. But Bob McNamara, despite his confident, assertive manner, became more and more overwrought by his own humanitarian conscience, the pressures from his family, and the growing realization that his confidence in the statistics of military power was ill-founded. McNamara, for instance, the most creative among secretaries of defense, would have become a much more tragic figure had he not, after presiding over the most extensive buildup of American nuclear power, used his technological proficiency for pointing the way in new directions. After having convinced NATO to abandon the massive retaliation strategy and adopt his flexible response strategy (which served it well for the next twenty years), he has now become that strategy's severest critic and an advocate of replacing nuclear weapons in Europe with conventional ones. But where this leaves NATO's future strategy he fails to tell. It is a question that will loom large in the 1990s and beyond.

In February 1964, at a small dinner party for Denis Hamilton, McNamara sounded surprisingly defensive. He complained that the Saigon government had no political organization, no proper administration, no well-trained troops. He sounded almost despondent about the absence of American experts who were familiar with Vietnamese traditions, languages, or psychology. But if you drew from this the conclusion that he was ready to throw in the sponge, you were quite wrong, for in May 1965, for instance, he was gung ho about the need to reinforce American troops faster than before to prevent the North Vietnamese from catching the United States unprepared for the tasks it had taken on. Shortly thereafter he even went so far as to doubt whether the United States could win this war decisively enough to be able to leave Vietnam because there would never be the right conditions for it to do so.

Just before Christmas 1965 I joined his family skiing in Aspen, Colorado, as for a good many winters before. He was an enthusiastic, fast, and secure skier, but not a stylish one. What mattered to him was the exercise. One day during lunch at the restaurant at the top of Ajax Mountain a woman suddenly approached our table and, leaning forward to McNamara, spewed out a few words, soaked in venom: "Doesn't the blood of the dead and wounded spoil your appetite?" Momentarily he looked startled. But before he could say anything in reply, she had disappeared, almost like some devilish apparition. For a few seconds her words had upset and shaken him. Then he turned to us, conscious how his official life had suddenly impinged on his private one, and said how much he sympathized with her but that, alas, his job was being secretary of defense. I had just returned from London where I had addressed the Labour Party's Foreign Affairs Committee in the House of Commons, and mentioned to him that most of the questions I had been asked related to the prospects of a pause in the bombing. McNamara listened intently and then agreed that it would be a good thing to try for one, not because of the effect it would have on Hanoi—he doubted it would have any—but on world opinion.

What I did not know at the time was that the repeated telephone messages he got at the top of Ajax and the telephone calls he made from public telephones were about persuading the president to accept a bombing halt. When the president did indeed announce a bombing pause on December 24, McNamara was quietly relieved and triumphant. But after thirty-seven days the North Vietnamese still had made no move to come to the conference table. By the following July, at a background briefing disguised as a dinner party at Stewart Alsop's house, McNamara sounded again gung ho, convinced that the North Vietnamese could not sustain the punishment they were getting. He restated his confidence in the effectiveness of American air power and reported with satisfaction a kill ratio of one hundred Americans to three hundred Vietcong a week. We were all stunned by his strange misreading of the writings on the wall.

The only high official who persistently opposed the war was Undersecretary of State George Ball. He was tolerated, but since his own secretary of state violently disagreed with him, and since he was concerned not with Asian but with European policy matters, he provided only a footnote to a tragic miscalculation. It took more than three months before his dissenting memorandum, of which he was justly proud, reached the president, but when it did, LBJ did the unusual: he called an NSC meeting to give Ball a chance to present his case. To the president he had made a good case, but Johnson also criticized Ball for not having proposed any alternatives. Ball admits the correctness of this dismissal. No one else was prepared to join in Ball's dissent. Walt Rostow, who succeeded McGeorge Bundy as national security adviser (Mac becoming head of the Ford Foundation), was a "rooter and advocate" where a careful analyst and judge was needed. President Johnson himself acted like a donkey: at first it was difficult to get him across the bridge and into the war, because he feared that it would badly interfere with his Great Society, then once he had crossed it, he dug in stubbornly and refused to give up.

Just before Christmas we were again skiing at Aspen. Every effort to end the war by negotiations had petered out and the burden of the fighting was now on the shoulders of American troops whose commander, General Westmoreland, took to war in the jungles of Vietnam like a horse to swimming. Once again we were having lunch at the top of Ajax Mountain and once again a young woman stopped at our table. This one, almost with a whisper, said: "I don't want to spoil your holiday, but I want you to know that there is a great groundswell in the country against the war in Vietnam." McNamara nodded —didn't he know, he seemed to say. Then he asked her what she did professionally and she replied that she was a teacher. "I don't envy you," Bob replied with a slight flutter in his voice. The woman looked at him surprised, then left, for he seemed at a loss for words to say anything more. He looked utterly fatigued and disheartened. Indeed, two of his own children were hardly on speaking terms with him. His son had gone to the Galapagos Islands as a farmhand to be as far away from it all as possible. His mother, Margie, went to visit him there. It took quite a few years until father and son became reconciled.

Almost a year later, in November 1967, I was asked to dinner at the McNamaras'. I had not been told in advance that this was to be a special occasion with President Johnson and Lady Bird as the guests of honor. The party was very small: Undersecretary of State Nick Katzenbach and his wife; Ellsworth Bunker, ambassador to South Vietnam and his wife, Carol Laise, ambassador to Nepal; William Roth, the president's trade representative and an old friend of the McNamaras' from San Francisco, and his wife; Cy Vance, the deputy secretary of defense, and his wife; Katherine Graham and myself.

During drinks I sat next to the president, who praised, for everybody to hear, an interview I had done with Lady Bird for the *New York Times* Sunday magazine. In his usual flamboyant way he said that he did not remember having seen as good an interview the whole time he had been in Washington, and that he had read it at two thirty in the morning. "Usually Lady Bird does not go to sleep before I do," he said. "She has difficulty sleeping. But that night she had fallen asleep. However I thought that this was such a great interview that I woke her up to tell her." A few days earlier, after a press conference, the president had come over to me before leaving and thanked me for the interview. "We have not had such good publicity for months," he then said, and putting his hand around my shoulders in a sort of fatherly way, added: "Henry, come and see me any time, just call Marvin Watson!"

During dinner LBJ was at his loquacious best, relaxed, jovial, informative, and amusing. One story followed another in rapid sequence. He acted out how Japanese Prime Minister Sato had presented him with an educational network for Vietnam, with $200 million more to help the balance of payments and with $100 million for the Asian Bank, and how he himself, like a grocery clerk with his pencil behind his ear, looked quite "common and quite unpresidential" as he helped to add it all up and write the communiqué. He asked me whether I thought that George Brown, whom he liked, could survive politically. I said that I doubted it because of his self-destructive nature. He warned me that the pound might have to be devalued and that the dollar could also lose in value if the franc followed the pound. Several times he overflowed with flattery in talking about Bob, going at one point so far as to say that if he could only finish the war quickly, he would make him welfare czar of the United States. Bob beamed; it was a task he hardly dared to dream about.

Two weeks later the president announced that McNamara had resigned as secretary of defense and would become head of the World Bank. That same evening I saw Bob at a dinner party at the Averell Harrimans' and asked him whether he had known about this shift at the time of the dinner party with the president. He said he had not, that it came as a total surprise, for he had assumed that he would stay on until the 1969 budget was completed. It was quite true that George Woods, then head of the World Bank, had visited him in April and had asked him whether he would be interested in succeeding him, to which McNamara had replied vaguely no more than that he would be interested. He did not realize that LBJ had decided that he could not work with a secretary of defense who no longer believed in the prosecution of the war. (In 1973 a leading member of the Pentagon hierarchy told me that Paul Nitze, who was a deputy undersecretary of defense under McNamara, found out about his superior's change of jobs only from a wiretap intercept of a foreign embassy . . .) On December 4, at a news conference, the president was asked whether he had urged McNamara to stay or whether he had just acceded to his wishes. The president pointedly ignored the substance of the question and referred to his earlier statement in the most matter-of-fact way. That was all. "Johnson is a very complex character," McNamara went on to say to me. "He is first a politician and as such he has higher loyalties." He did not know whether he should feel hurt by the president's implied rebuff or grateful to have been given a new, constructive task that suited his current state of mind better than the destructive one of fighting a war. He wanted nothing more than to forget the past, did not care what to make of Johnson's attitude toward him. His mind was already concentrating on the new challenge before him.

The most fascinating interview I have ever had with LBJ occurred on February 5, 1968, five days after the start of the infamous Tet offensive. This was at first reported as a crucial setback for the American forces and more than any other event turned American public opinion against the war. It may have been due to "crisis journalism," as Peter Braestrup claimed in his book *Big Story,* but the call-up of the reservists also had a devastating impact. Judging by my World War II experiences as a reporter, it is often hard to assess the overall consequences of a major battle without reliable information on enemy losses. We learned only much later, thanks to Stanley Karnow's reportorial enterprise, recorded in his *Vietnam, A History,* that the North Vietnamese not only suffered much more serious losses than the United States but that General Giap, far from considering the outcome of the battle a "deadlock," had been forced to throw in all his reserves. Not surprisingly therefore I waited with pent-up expectations as I sat in the Roosevelt room, wondering whether my interview set for 12:30 would even come off. After more than an hour's wait, I was still without word whether the president would keep the appointment. Finally, at 1:55 P.M. I was ushered into the Oval Office.

The president greeted me with a "Hello, Henry." Then we sat down, he in his rocking chair, I on the sofa next to him. We were almost touching elbows. After checking with Tom Johnson, his alert deputy press secretary, whether the entire interview was off-the-record (which he confirmed, and I did too), LBJ gave me a letter to read which he had just dictated and signed, addressed to General Westmoreland. In it he reassured the general that he had every confidence in him, that the stories in the European press about his recall had no foundation in truth. He wanted me to have proof that the reports about Westmoreland being out of favor were totally untrue.

He then unleashed a torrent of almost uncontrollable abuse about the unfairness of the reporting in the American press, cursing above all the *New York Times* for not giving him credit he thought he deserved. He said that Westmoreland had told him that in a month's time "we would be much further toward military success than we are now." He said it with as much confidence as if the promise had come from God. (When I had talked to Westmoreland in Saigon four months earlier he had given me the impression of a man who was fighting a war according to the textbooks he had used while at West Point and lacked the imagination to adjust the old rules of battle to the jungle war in Vietnam.)

Then switching to domestic politics, Johnson derided a poll showing that Robert Kennedy could win against a Republican, and bemoaned the existence of such "fuzzy and idealistic" thinkers as Eugene McCarthy, whose presidential ambitions interfered with the conduct of the war. Then he picked up opinion polls from his desk to prove how high he still stood in the public mind.

When I brought up Britain's withdrawal from east of Suez, he said that it made him "sad and sorry." Then he added: "Nevertheless we will always remain friends. But, of course," he cautioned me, "when our common interests shrink, the flow of communications and common business shrinks too. What Britain did was unnecessary, unwise and not in the British interest." There was a sudden edge to his voice. Then, speaking more in sorrow than in anger, he said: "But the British government did what it thought it had to do, and even if you think it was unwise, it must know better than I what is good for the country." As if he felt he had not yet put enough balm on his harsh earlier words, he added: "I'd be a slave today without the British and Churchill if they had not done what they did in the first two years of World War II. They did it for America too. I will not forget when Churchill came over here in 1941, barefoot and his fly open [his way of saying Churchill was vulnerable], just before the clock struck twelve. I admire the character of the British, it is difficult to beat them in the clinches." After insisting that Britain had no alternative but to go into the Common Market, he changed the subject to prove to me that he was spending more for education and welfare than Eisenhower and Kennedy had, that he could not get any American newspaper to print the statistics because they believed he had "finagled" them. The lament became a long and bitter accusation about the constant fight he had with the press, and the "Georgetown set," and the Kennedys, who were all trying to hurt him. It was 3:10 when Marvin Watson appeared in the door to bring the interview to an end. I felt exhausted, but Johnson, in a last disarming gesture, pulled from his pocket the memo which I had submitted a few days earlier, listing the subjects I planned to raise to reassure himself that we had covered them all. He could have gone on for another hour, forgetting in his fervent plea for a fairer deal from a foreign correspondent than he was getting from the American press, that he had more important matters to deal with than talking to me.

There was indeed an overwhelming desire in the man, when giving, to give his all. But giving meant making a total effort to convince the other party that he was right and everybody else was wrong. I have never found any statesman more difficult to argue with. He was not interested in debating or listening. When I first entered the Oval Office, he stood there like a confident, proud matador ready to take on a tame bull; when I left he did not seem certain whether he had won my "ear," but he was convinced that he had done his best.

He did not realize that by being constantly on the offensive, he made it difficult for himself to establish a personal relationship or an empathy with a visitor. He spent more time with the press than any other president, but instead of giving the impression of wanting to inform, he created the impression of wanting to persuade, to impress, to cajole, to dominate. Reporters, however amused or repulsed by—or in awe of—his performance, were suspicious that they were getting a highly one-sided account, even when he gave an honest accounting. And as to discussing personalities, he was far too honest or too savage or too effusive or too volatile to be credible. It was unfortunate that he did not realize how counterproductive his private encounters with the press were, or how crude his behavior looked to us when he walked a few reporters around the south lawn and Lady Bird, every five minutes, called in vain from the balcony that lunch was waiting. He never minded being, in Jack Valenti's words, the "mean bully" or making people feel that he was reaching for their jugular, because his Texan heart told him that he had given the blacks their voting rights and the elderly and the poor Medicare and Medicaid. Those were indeed epochal achievements which gave him hope that history would vindicate him and credit him with greatness and with having been a good man.

A month later, on March 11, I went to see the president again, with Denis Hamilton, who was once more visiting Washington. Earlier in the morning we had seen Bobby Kennedy in his office. It was obvious that he was mentally ready to challenge the president. "Almost anything could make me run for the presidency," he said to us, "especially if Johnson decides to escalate the war by sending more men to Vietnam." Bobby at one point was so eager to involve himself in the war that he wanted to go as ambassador to Saigon before he decided to run for the Senate. But this now was a different war. His brother had resisted the Americanization of the war; under Johnson American combat units and American bombers had come to dominate the battlefield. To Bobby it was a new war and he turned violently against it. It was clear that he believed that the crucial moment had come to keep Senator Eugene McCarthy, who had scored a surprise near-victory in the New Hampshire primary, from snatching the great prize himself.

When at the age of twenty-seven Bobby began managing Jack's 1952 campaign for the Senate, he was inspired by a certain hero worship of a brother eight years his senior. Gradually a genuinely mature working relationship developed, with each anxious to reinforce the other. The formalities and vanities of power between the two shriveled into nonexistence. Jack was the wiser and more mature, the graceful, the subtle and the cool. His comments were primarily intellectual, not emotional. Bobby was the more compassionate, the more instinctive in his involvement in the causes he espoused. Basic to their relationship was the special spell that the paternal leadership of Joseph P. Kennedy cast over the family.

Now Bobby was the scion of the family, his inner engines were turning over fast, driven by his hatred for Johnson, his disdain for McCarthy, his dynastic sense, and his own ambition. The Kennedy shock troops rose to the occasion, but they failed in Oregon, which was too middle class, too taken by McCarthy's sophisticated veneer. California, with all its minorities, was different, but even there Bobby soon realized that it would not be a walk-over. When I came to have breakfast with him in his hotel suite in Los Angeles as the campaign was moving toward its climax, I found him having a shower and his talking to me from under it. He sounded worried and unsure, he wanted to know how he was doing, what the reporters were saying. He won narrowly, but he lost his life to a madman. I will never forget that strange cortege on rails, the special train that carried friends and members of the press and the body from the heart-stirring service at St. Patrick's Cathedral in New York to Arlington Cemetery, with the oldest son, Joe, walking through the train, playing the charming host and thanking everybody for joining in the last farewell to his father.

But to come back to my editor's visit: In contrast to the rosy-cheeked, bright-eyed, confident Kennedy, the LBJ we met on March 11 looked dispirited, doleful, and broken-hearted, a shattered man. I was aghast at the change written all over the president's face—ashen white, his eyes haggard and surrounded by deep shadows, his wrinkles as if drawn in thick india ink. He seemed so utterly tired he could hardly get up to greet us. For a while I feared the interview would not get off the ground at all. The president reacted as if he were too tired to think, too tired to look at us, too tired to do anything. There was a twitch in his cheek and instead of sitting down in the rocking chair, he stretched himself out on the sofa. Denis, sensitive as he was to the president's flagging spirit, tried hard to resuscitate it, to relax and to comfort him. Gradually, Johnson began to get interested in Denis. "Do you know where I have just been?" he asked rhetorically. "I went to see Ike to ask him what would happen if I sacked General Westmoreland. Would it have an effect on morale? Would it make a difference?" Ike had told him that there was a great difference between the American army fighting at a distance of 12,000 miles and seeing the Germans across the cliffs of Dover getting ready to invade England. Also Westmoreland's task, he said, was more difficult than his own in World War II because he had always known where the enemy was, while Westmoreland did not. As to Johnson's question about sacking Westmoreland, however, Ike said he could not help him make up his mind. Ike had said to him that the two men he admired most were General Marshall and Churchill, the latter for his tenacity. Then switching back to his own problems, the president said: "I hope to be equally tenacious," for he was still convinced that if he persisted he would succeed in Vietnam. Then, as if searching for a lifeline, he said to Denis: "Tell me everything you know about Churchill, especially everything you remember about Dunkirk and that famous speech of Churchill's that gave such courage and inspiration to you British. What was it he said? 'Fighting on land and on the beaches . . .' " Johnson now sat up. His guest had captured his interest. "I want to make a speech along those Churchillian lines he made after Dunkirk." Denis still knew those lines by heart: ". . . we shall go on to the end, we shall fight in France, we shall fight on the seas and oceans, we shall fight with growing confidence . . . whatever the costs may be . . . we shall fight on the beaches, we shall fight on the landing grounds . . ." Johnson's eyes now sparkled. Churchill's words were an inspiration to him. Still sounding tired, but much more himself, he began to give us the litany of his achievements, about his priorities, about Vietnam, about the Middle East, about Cyprus, about gold, about the problems of the cities. But he sounded as if all these problems had become agonies to him, as if he had lost the stamina to run for another presidential term. I asked whether he thought of serving another four years out of a sense of duty or pleasure. "I don't think of the next four years," he said with a sigh. "I only think of the next four days."

I have always been suspicious when American statesmen referred to Churchill, asking myself if this was not just their way of flattering a British editor or correspondent. But I am as sure now as I was then that Johnson was sincere. I have never been admitted to the presence of any leader in so disconsolate a state as that in which he began our interview. He was looking for strength and sympathy. Like so many other presidents he hoped that he would get from me as a British correspondent a more objective treatment than he might from an American. Indeed, I tried to see myself as an objective student of affairs rather than someone representing a "constituency." When I asked questions, it was not solely from a narrow British point of view (though of course I had the needs and interests of my editor and my readers at home very much in mind), but from a global one.

Clark Clifford meanwhile had succeeded McNamara, but he did not remain for long the convinced supporter of the war that he had been. He spent all his time investigating the prospects of the war. In October 1967 during a visit to Vietnam I reported that "a tiger like the United States has never allowed itself to be locked into such a confining cage, and I am convinced if America had known what she was letting herself in for in Vietnam, she would never have committed herself to that extent . . . however much one sees, however much one talks to the best informed, there is in effect, no agreed assessment of the state of the war . . . the American military position is secure . . . to prove that the US forces can turn the tide of this seesaw struggle decisively in the present crisis is much more difficult . . . there is no military solution to this war . . . there is some bitter truth in the image of the tiger being unable to catch the mosquito; it can be done only by homemade Vietnamese flypaper."

Clifford examined the disarray after the Tet offensive, took aim at a high-level study into a new request from General Westmoreland for more troops and much more equipment, and traveled to Saigon. At the same time a majority of the so-called wise men who also had been consistently supporting the war—led by Dean Acheson, of all people—turned against it. During March the president delivered two very emotional speeches in which he summoned the shadow of Chamberlain to warn Americans against appeasement (an argument often stressed by Rusk) and in Churchillian terms that peace could be won only on the battlefield. But by the end of March the president, who first had asked suspiciously: "Who poisoned the well?" began to have second thoughts, however reluctantly. A new draft for a speech set for March 28 was brimming with Churchillian cadences of tenacity. But when Harry McPherson took over the drafting from Rusk and Rostow, it took on a conciliatory rather than defiant tone. Instead of opening with the wish to discuss the war in Southeast Asia, it spoke of wishing to discuss peace in Vietnam. And that ended a bitter argument that had been raging that entire month. However, what nobody foresaw was that this speech would end with the president's abdication. There were both heroic and tragic overtones in his announcement that he would not seek reelection. It was an admission of failure of leadership clothed in an act of statesmanship. Here was a man ruined by the faults of his own virtues. Proud, vain, self-centered, stubborn, and imperious, as he was, he was also a realist. He had come to recognize that even if he won the election after a savage internecine fight, he would not have the power to heal those wounds, reunite the nation, and prevent political paralysis in Congress, for the country was in a state of rebellion.

As if to underscore the extent to which Johnson's presidency was haunted by tragedy, in April 1968, shortly after his painful abdication, the man who had done so much to advance the cause of the blacks found himself engulfed in a whirlwind of racial rioting that broke out after the heinous assassination of Martin Luther King, Jr. April 4 was a night of arson and plundering unprecedented in the history of the capital. Washington was indeed burning. I happened to be—of all places—in the press plane that was to accompany President Johnson on a trip to Hawaii for a meeting with American officials in from Saigon. We were waiting for the takeoff signal on Andrews Air Force base when we were given the laconic message that our departure had been delayed for some unstated reason. Fifty high-priced White House correspondents, locked in their plane, from then on clustered around one little transistor radio, full of suspense, waiting for an explanation until the news of the murder of Martin Luther King was announced. We were shaken, staggered and shocked, wondering what sort of a tempest this would trigger. A few minutes later the president's trip was canceled. We scrambled out of the plane to the military buses that had brought us to Andrews and were driven back to the White House. There was an eerie, frightening stillness around Pennsylvania Avenue, the stillness that usually precedes a hurricane. Then the glow of homes on fire lit the sky and clouds of smoke rose above the city. There was hardly a vehicle on the street. I never felt scared during World War II, but I was scared that evening. I wondered how I would get home—it was close to ten in the evening. I decided to stay close to the White House and its police detail, hoping to find a taxi eventually. It took about an hour of anxious waiting before one passed by and stopped in response to my frantic signals. Behind the wheel was an older black man who explained the dearth of taxis in the streets because most black taxi drivers had gone on a protest strike. "I'm an old man," he explained. "I don't care about what goes on, I just mind my own business." And so I got home safely. It had started to rain, which was a godsend. It would cool the anger and make it easier to keep the fires under control, I hoped, but rioting, I thought, even though President Johnson had gone on television with a tribute to King and to calm the nation, seemed inevitable.

Once again a single gun was playing havoc with this nation. It had played such an important role in obtaining American independence and in opening the West, and hence it remains—in the mind of too many Americans—part of the furniture. In Washington high schools, for instance, children in the tenth grade were being taught how to shoot. The idea was that knowing how to use a gun is just as important in life as knowing how to drive a car. Of course, for kids who have learned how to shoot, the temptation is great to prove that they have learned their lessons well and know how to use it.

I wrote in my diary that day: "Most of the morning I worked on my leader-page article for *The Sunday Times,* but I very soon realized that I could not sit still at my typewriter as the news of rioting spread. People had hoped that riots could not happen in Washington because the blacks here are moderate, unemployment is minimal, and most of them in one way or the other are employed by the government. I wondered, if this capital city had to be kept under control by a 4 P.M. curfew, what would have to be done if something more serious happened to the United States. This country has not experienced war on its own soil in this century. It has no real measure of what real danger to its own order and security means. It tends to overreact therefore in such situations. People get panicky, they flee to the countryside, they buy up food as if war were imminent." The enforced curfew lamed this capital city in no time. To get a feel for the public mood, I decided to venture into the black quarters. I drove in my own car slowly along 14th Street, the main artery, which divides the city, to see the devastation this Walpurgisnacht had wrought. At one point I stopped, got out of my car to interview a few people, but a middle-aged black woman I approached said in a whisper: "Don't walk here, go home, it's dangerous." I took her advice and got back into my car. Meanwhile the city was emptying to obey the curfew. Cars were bumper to bumper on all the roads out of Washington. The government was virtually at a standstill. This country was terribly vulnerable, it occurred to me. It possessed all those missiles, but it lacked the kind of self-control that makes life go on in an emergency. People talked about fear for their properties and lives. I asked myself whether the sight of the charred timber lying around on 14th Street would make the division between white and black worse or turn out to be the beginning of a reconciliation. My black housekeeper said: "We're all right but sorry in between." Many blacks were ashamed of what their brethren had done, just as many whites were ashamed, quite apart from the guilty feeling about the murder of Dr. King, of having let blacks suffer such a state of deprivation.

By midafternoon the ghettos began to heat up again and President Johnson decided to send more federal troops into Washington—12,000 it was announced—to put a damper on the widespread rioting and plundering. Johnson was suddenly fighting two wars, at home and in Vietnam.

The first time I met Martin Luther King was on the campus of Howard University. He had come to speak to the students and the faculty, and I went for the experience of listening to him to find out what mysterious powers he had at his command. He did not sound to me like a revolutionary nor did he look or act like a charismatic leader. I was surprised. There was something curiously tranquil, rational, almost stolid about him, but, gradually, I realized that these qualities were a reflection of his inner confidence, which in turn created trust in his powers and hope in the future he talked about. His magnetism was in the rhythm of his eloquence and in his warm, sonorous voice. He stirred the emotions of his audience, but he did not try to incite them. He came across as a preacher and persuader and a prophet, not as a fanatic. He was confrontational but with the emphasis on nonviolence, he tried to break the segregationalist barriers but he never stopped talking about the brotherhood of man. I was startled by his use of quotations from Shakespeare, Whitman, Carlyle, Mills, Niebuhr, Hegel, and others, most of whose names were, no doubt, unknown to most of his listeners. But it was their ideas that mattered, not their names.

After that speech I had my first talk with him. Outwardly he gave me the impression of being pleased with his reception—though many of the students advocated a more radical approach. He looked searchingly into my eyes to gauge my own reaction, then he invited me to drive back with him to his hotel. He spoke about the way he interpreted Gandhi, how he translated his teachings to the American civil rights scene, and how difficult it was to hold the balance between radicalism and nonviolence, between mobilizing black consciousness and controlling militancy in view of the snail's pace set by the white civil rights movement. The time had come, he said with deep conviction, for blacks to fight for their own cause. "Why we can't wait" was the title of his manifesto.

It was a long track from the desegregation of buses in the South to being jailed in Birmingham, Alabama; from the Freedom rides to the March on Washington on August 28, 1963—the most massive civil rights demonstration, with about 250,000 people, black and white, participating. At the end of that day he made his most moving and most effective public speech from the Lincoln Monument. That day he launched millions of new hopes when he exclaimed: "I have a dream." By then the American dream (of a different kind) had begun to fade, but among blacks it was a growing inspiration.

Illustrative of the searing contradictions that were burning in the hearts of blacks was a conversation I had with Roger Wilkins at a party of the Walter Ridders', copublisher of the Ridder Newspapers, whose house was a popular gathering place of the Democratic Party faithful. Wilkins, who circulated with the greatest ease in white society, bitterly denounced the moderate policies of the National Association for the Advancement of Colored People, which, for years, had been led by his uncle Roy. "Roy believes in seeking change by legal means," he said. "I support the force of rage. He disapproves of the Black Panthers, I approve of them. I think Malcolm X was a great figure, he does not." The contrast reflected the generational change and a growing impatience with those leaders who believed that gradualism would open the doors faster than radicalism. But he also admitted progress when he pointed out that the phrase "black power," which had been the watchword during the last three years, had disappeared from the vocabulary and been replaced by words like "black consciousness" or "black pride," which meant to him that black confidence was beginning to grow, that middle-class blacks who up to now had only looked up were now beginning to look down, trying to help the poor. When I asked whether this new sense of faith in the future would translate itself into a mood of reconciliation, he first said yes. Then he corrected himself by suggesting that this would be too optimistic an expectation. Then, thinking aloud, he wondered whether a deep division would not remain, with both sides trying to look after their own security, their own destiny. Fifty percent of the blacks today, he said, are under thirty, and they are imbued, above all, by a drive for self-assertion. When I wondered whether he was not, in fact, talking about a new black nationalism, he objected because to him this phrase meant separatism and raised the problem of how to reconcile it with American national unity, which, after all, was fundamental. The dilemmas for blacks were infinite.

But separatism was still a way of life. One of the strangest things about Washington living was and still is that a white person need hardly be aware that this city is deeply divided into two cities, white and black. Whites avoid going into black areas and blacks prefer to keep to themselves. Over the years I rarely met a black at a white party, nor do I remember, with one exception, being invited to the home of a black. In the mid-fifties, after meeting at one of my neighbors' a young black lawyer, Alan Barth, who wrote about judicial problems for the Washington *Post*—an intensely warm and caring person— I rang him up to invite him to lunch at a well-known restaurant. After a long pause he asked me whether I knew that I could not take him to that restaurant, for blacks were barred from all the better restaurants, hotels, movie theaters, and the National Theater. I replied that as an ignorant foreigner I was willing to take the risk of inviting him to the Vendome restaurant, owned by a

Frenchman. But he declined nevertheless, saying that he did not want to create an incident. He did though accept my invitation to my house for lunch.

Even in the mid-sixties it was still an unusual event for a black woman entertainer to perform for a president. After Sarah Vaughan, for instance, had sung for President Johnson and Japanese Premier Eisaku Sato at the White House, Bess Abell, who was then White House social secretary, went to her dressing room and found her in tears. Asked why she was crying she said, still sobbing: "Do you realize I sang for the president of the United States and the prime minister of Japan?! I danced with the president of the United States in the White House and when I first came to Washington I couldn't even get a hotel room . . . !"

When I recently described to my teenage daughter the discrimination that used to pervade the nation's capital, in fact the whole country, she could not believe that blacks in those days were barred from most hotels, restaurants, movie theaters, and that they were so cowed that many had their curly hair flattened out with an iron and took potions to lighten their skin in the belief that "assimilation" was the password to success in what used to be considered a white society. Nor could she imagine Washington as a white citadel that was denied home rule by Congress; she knows only the Washington that is administered by a city government with more than half of the jobs held by blacks and presided over by a black mayor.

The estimated median income of blacks in Washington in 1985 was $24,400, which was thousands more than among blacks in any other urban area. For comparison's sake, in New York it was $16,000, in San Francisco $20,000, in Houston $20,000, in Boston $17,000, in Chicago $18,000. Washington also outranks other leading metropolitan areas in the number of black households. Proportionately, there are 26 percent in Washington, 18 in Chicago, 12 in Los Angeles, 12 in Dallas, 19 in Detroit, 6 in Boston. One of the touchiest among racial issues has been interracial dating or marriage. According to a Gallup poll the acceptance level for interracial dating was 44 percent in 1983; in Washington 63 percent of both blacks and whites said they felt comfortable with interracial dating. Although by day blacks and whites share offices and schools and all other facilities, by nightfall blacks and whites return home to still largely segregated neighborhoods. But the progress made in interracial coexistence in the capital is impressive. It has much to do with the fact that on average the black population in Washington has a higher educational level than in any other urban area and that the federal government is the most sought-after employer among blacks.

No other country in the world, I believe, has mastered a major internal racial as well as social upheaval with relatively so little turbulence and bloodshed as the United States. In fact, integration has produced less violence and bloodshed than was caused by segregation and race hatred. When, backed by the radicals of the New Left, the younger generation of black militants, impatient for the implementation of equal rights and equal opportunity, threatened

to mount the barricades, and the segregationist George Wallace movement
rose defiantly to fight back, the federal government—which both groups considered a barrier to their demands—stood its ground effectively. There were
tense moments when, for instance, "Ole Miss," the University of Mississippi,
was forcibly integrated under the threat of drawn bayonets. I watched the shy,
pale, and obviously scared black student, James Meredith, being led, protected
by a considerable number of federal marshals, into the university building with
a cluster of white students shouting obscenities with their fists raised, and only
two students, courageous enough, welcoming him inside an empty classroom
where he sat down on a bench, a lonely, embattled symbol. But he fulfilled his
mission, and once the supremacy of the federal government had thus been
asserted by President Kennedy the aches and pains of one hundred years of
American history passed and the United States moved on to a new chapter.
The shot that killed Martin Luther King also was a warning shot that American society had reached a crucial moment in its history, and that a growing
minority could either give this country greater moral and economic strength
or seriously jeopardize its inner peace.

The election campaign of 1968 was the most tumultuous, the most disturbing
I had ever covered. It strained American democratic institutions almost to the
breaking point—it was police power that saved the Democratic Convention in
Chicago—but it did not break them. The antiwar protesters, reinforced by
young blacks, impatient with the slowness, as they saw it, with which Americans conceded to them not the principle, but the practice of equal opportunity,
used the convention setting and the concentration of the news media to demonstrate their outrage with President Johnson, the Democratic Party, and the
outlook for the future. At some point we reporters were virtual prisoners in
the Conrad Hilton Hotel and had difficulty getting through the police cordons
to the convention hall, where the reactionaries, the George Wallace movement
on the right, were trying to score against those under the influence of the New
Left who were making common cause with the black militants. Both wanted
to destroy the power centers, whether they were called federal government,
city hall, school board, university administration, or more mystically, the
establishment. The antiwar movement, of course, wanted to force an end to
the war; President Johnson wanted his policies to be vindicated; Humphrey's
supporters, the warriors of Franklin Roosevelt's welfare liberalism, wanted to
protect the party's political center, which had given this country its broad
political stability. Hubert Humphrey, as an authentic exponent of the New
Deal, faced with all this disarray, had a hard time making himself heard over
the cacophonic rebellious voices. One of his great handicaps during the election campaign was that Greek chorus from the Vietnamese front that accompanied his campaign speeches on television. It was the first war brought live
and "in living color" into every American home. It was a devastating experience for those at home, comfortably ensconced in their easy chairs, to be

exposed to the horrors of war. Eric Sevareid, the most literate and thoughtful among television commentators, told me at the time that "the trouble with television is that it has no managerial editorial direction and control. A TV picture is like a flash in the darkness, everything else is lost, only one point is lit up to the exclusion of everything else." When Eric retired in December 1977 there was an outpouring of eulogies in terms usually reserved for obituaries. He admitted that his narcissism was still fully functioning and that he therefore enjoyed it all, but it troubled him professionally that the media personalities are today the most talked about people. Why? Most likely, I believe, because the once-upon-a-time glitter of Hollywood stars had faded, the fascination with "café society" of the Walter Winchell days is as dead as its courtier, and New York's "liberal chic" has been suffocated by "fashionable chic" and gone the way of all fads. Political power now has the "sex appeal," and that is why Washington and the media personalities who report on its power struggles are the stars of today.

Johnson's "abdication" had brought the North Vietnamese to the conference table. But as the election drew near, the peace negotiations in Paris had reached a stalemate because the feline and wily South Vietnamese President Nguyen Van Thieu was hoping that a Nixon victory would prolong the war. Averell Harriman, the man for all missions at all seasons and presidential agent par excellence, led the American team in Paris. He invited me to lunch when I passed through Paris at the time, and I was pleasantly surprised that I would be getting a briefing and a gourmet lunch. While waiting in the anteroom to his office at the American Embassy, wondering which would turn out to be his favorite Paris restaurant, he appeared and, taking me by my arm, said: "Henry, let's go to the embassy canteen, they have the best value for the money in Paris." However, an invitation from the then American ambassador in France, Sargent Shriver, to celebrate Averell's seventy-fifth birthday the following day made up for everything. Sarge had done an inspiring job in creating the Peace Corps, one of the most lasting and most memorable among Kennedy's achievements. Later, when Johnson made him head of the antipoverty program, I asked him why he attained greater fame with the former than the latter, to which he replied: "It's easier to play God than brother." He was a man who exuded—or better, gushed—eternal fun and enjoyment of life, and for this occasion he had asked André Vrinat, the patron of Taillevant, an exceptional three-star restaurant, to search his cellar for the best seventy-five-year-old wine, and M. Vrinat, as the owner of one of those cellars worth his gourmet standards, came up with a seventy-five-year-old Château Lafitte. I had never tasted a fine wine as old as this one; in fact, I had never tasted a wine that old at all. It still had an extraordinarily mellow bouquet.

LBJ hoped to end his presidency with a bang, a dramatic summit meeting with the Russians, with him stepping like an emperor from an American cruiser onto Russian soil at Leningrad. In fact, the Russians had already given him the green light for the voyage and the landing. But the tragic mishaps that haunted his foreign policy and the United States throughout 1968 shattered that event too. Deeply upset that he had no spectacular gain on his foreign policy ledger, he had to give up his last chance to make his contribution to arms control when the Soviets invaded Czechoslovakia. The invasion delayed the start of the strategic arms limitation talks (SALT), which, if they had been initiated at that time, might have come to fruition earlier and a treaty been ratified by Congress.

Humphrey made some headway when he began to distance himself from the president on Vietnam and, persuaded by George Ball, who by then had left the State Department, made a speech in Salt Lake City that came close to suggesting that the United States must find a way out of the war. The deviation enraged LBJ and, as Clifford told me later, the president and Humphrey had "quite a frank and spirited conversation," with the president advising Humphrey that his administration had a policy with respect to Vietnam and he expected everybody in the administration to conform to it. Humphrey advanced in the polls while Nixon had reached a plateau. What seems to have played in Nixon's favor was well summed up by a man I talked to in Wisconsin who said: "Wallace wants to end violence with violence, Humphrey thinks he'll end it by giving in to the blacks. Nixon is somewhere in between the two. He'll end the rioting fairly but firmly." Perhaps, had Humphrey been permitted to pursue the theme he adopted at Salt Lake City—alas he feared that Johnson might come out extolling Nixon's position on the war—it could have made the difference between electoral victory and defeat. That was also Clark Clifford's belief, whose estrangement from the president by then had grown worse, for Humphrey won 42.73 percent of the popular vote as against Nixon's 43.16 percent. Several opinion pollsters thought that had the campaign lasted another week, Humphrey might have overtaken Nixon. Thus not only Johnson's policies but also the primitive mixture of pride and defiance that made him force Humphrey to toe the line may have cost the Democratic Party the presidency.

Looking back to the turbulent Johnson days, they were strong medicine but without a healing effect. Divisive policies deeply undermined some of the best qualities in the American character: optimism, can-do-ism, self-confidence. They caused disillusionment with traditional institutions, with military prowess, with the hallowed American way of life, with the qualities of the establishment. The president's advisers cornered themselves through a misreading of historic precedents, the power at their command, the extent to which they could defy public opinion, and American willingness to practice a form of imperialism. Not even an appeal to such an ingrained feeling as anticommunism succeeded. British imperialism, while it lasted, was based on national self-interest: trade. The war in Vietnam became unpalatable to Americans when they began to weigh the national interest against the costs in American lives and money. There was a limit to the radius of American globalism that fear of communism could inspire.

Americans—and how un-American this was—had grown tired of new challenges, new responsibilities, new sacrifices in men and money. Yet, in his gang-busterish way, LBJ when he acceded to the presidency was confident that he, the master of political rodeo, could lasso in all his objectives. He was convinced that he could subdue a primitive Asian country with superior weapons, could make American cities habitable, lift the poor above the poverty line, resolve racial injustices, create a neo-Rooseveltian world, the Great Society, as his monument to history, and climb the summit with his Russian counterparts for humanity's sake rather than to extol his own achievements. But it was part of the tragic destiny of Johnson that even his acts of greatness and vision either turned sour or became suspect as self-aggrandizement. He was, I think, defeated by a combination of circumstances and his own flaws of character. There was real greatness in the man and the knowledge of it came to haunt him. He desperately wanted to carve out for himself more than a niche in history. In the Senate he proved to be a connoisseur of the art of the possible, but not as president. He was too much a provincial. I do not mean a Texan provincial, as so many assumed and he suspected them of assuming, but a Washington provincial. The world that mattered to him was the world between the two ends of Pennsylvania Avenue, the world between the White House and Capitol Hill. That was the world he knew better than perhaps anyone among his predecessors and it misled him into believing that what mattered most was whether the government functioned, not whether the nation was in tune with it or with him. The nation to him was like a mule that had to be dragged along, if necessary flogged. Too often he whipped it too hard by overdramatizing the problems and overstating the effectiveness of his solutions.

He might not have had to whip the mule quite so hard had he had the gift of communicating with the American people nationally. He was a superb persuader on a one-to-one basis but not over television or at press conferences, both of which he hated. He was, moreover, in Marshall McLuhan's jargon, a "hot" type at a time when the country was anxious to catch its breath and yearned for cool, reassuring, and less demanding leadership. The national fatigue and the costs and preoccupation with the war in Vietnam notwithstanding, his legislative record was remarkable. The advances he scored in Medicare, education, housing, racial reforms were unique, the results of deep inner yearnings to improve the lot of the common man and of the boundless ambitions of an overachiever. But however skillful he was in "pressing the flesh" of members of Congress, his legislative triumphs were, above all, a reflection of the forty extra seats in the House of Representatives the Democrats gained in the 1964 elections. For the first time since 1938 a reform president had a working progressive majority in the House. Yet his miscalculations in handling the war have determined his place in history. The war forced him to look reality in the face, to withdraw from the presidential race; it led to his party's defeat in the elections. It not only divided the nation as it has not been divided since the Civil War, it also caused the disruptive student rebellion and aggravated racial tensions. It also soured the American outlook on the world, on itself, and on its role as a world leader. To the students of government his mishandling of the economy was an even graver error of judgment because it was entirely within his own powers to raise the taxes to pay for the war and for his Great Society; failure to do so was an error that destabilized the solvency of the United States for more than a decade.

If the "spirit of the Alamo" dominated Johnson's mind to the end, he shared this weakness with other strong leaders who overestimated their power and influence at the sunset of their political lives, such as Churchill, Franklin D. Roosevelt, and General de Gaulle. To abandon contesting the presidency for a second term was bad enough for him to swallow, but not getting recognition for his Great Society was worse. Since then his megalomaniacal ambition to go down in history as the great social reformer has induced a backlash against the welfare state that was partially responsible for bringing Ronald Reagan to power.

LBJ, aware by then of his public repudiation, seemed to drag a burden of anguish in his wake when he spoke his own epitaph during a flight to visit President Truman in Independence, Missouri, aboard Air Force One: "The only difference between Kennedy's assassination and mine is that mine was a live one, which makes it all a little more torturing."

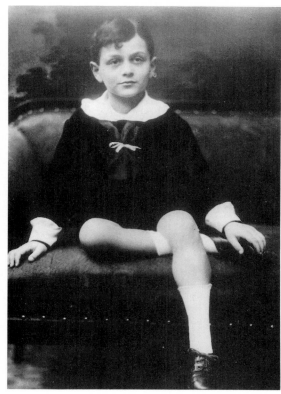

The earliest photograph of myself
that I have, taken in Prague when
I was about six years old.

When I was eight years old my
parents took me to Venice and we
posed on the Piazza San Marco;
more than five decades later, my
daughter Fiona and I returned to
the same place.

Headquarters Berlin District Command
SHAEF PUblic Relations Party

SUBJECT: Discipline.

TO   : All War Correspondents.

    1. The following named War Correspondents have been suspended for
violation of a security order idued verbally on the first
correspondent's meeting, 3 July 1945:

        Kathryn Cravens   Mutual Broadcasting System
        Henry Brandon   London Sunday Times

    2. These Correspondents entered a forbidden area in violation
of the aforementioned security order.

    3. These correspondents are suspended for 72 hours from 1000
hours 7 July 1945 and may not leave the area of the Berlin District
Command until further notice.

    4. Ignorance of an order is not an excuse for failure to comply.
However any correspondent who may have arrived in this area subsequent
to the War Correspondents conference referred to in Paragraph 1 above
and who may be ignorant of the circumstances surrounding the issuance
of this order, are requested to see Lt Col J.M. Redding, PRO, or Lt
Col G.W. Gilchrist, Deputy PRO, for clarification.

                          /s/ JOHN M. REDDING
                              Lt Col AC
                              Commanding

Memories of my career as a war
correspondent: my identification
card, issued by the French after
the liberation of Paris; a reprimand given to me and Kathryn
Cravens; and a snapshot of myself
in my British army uniform. Cravens autographed the reprimand
after it had been displayed on the
bulletin board in the press room at
SHAEF Public Relations Headquarters. Against orders we had
driven to Potsdam in the Russian
zone on the eve of the Potsdam
conference, discovered that it
would be held in the Cecilianhof
Palace, and managed to persuade
a Russian interpreter to give us a
tour of the conference rooms. The
tour came to an abrupt end after
Cravens doffed her raincoat and
the Russian saw the words "war
correspondent" on her shoulder
patches.

President Eduard Beneš and Winston Churchill reviewing Czechoslovak troops training in England in 1940.

The joint press conference with Franklin Roosevelt and Winston Churchill in the Oval Office on December 23, 1941; moments after this photograph was taken, Churchill climbed atop the president's desk to speak to reporters.

This photo of my buttonholing Gromyko after he walked out of the UN Security Council on March 28, 1946, hit virtually every front page of every newspaper in the world. My efforts, however, to find out whether he was walking out of the UN forever were in vain. The "grim and stony-faced young Andrei Gromyko," as the New York Times described him, remained not only stony-faced but silent too. (UPI/BETTMANN NEWS PHOTOS)

An article in London Illustrated about the British correspondents covering the United States, including me with Secretary of State Dean Acheson.

O. H. BRANDON, VOYAGER FOR SUNDAY TIMES

DEAN ACHESON, U.S. Secretary of State, is interviewed by O. H. Brandon, permanent representative in Washington of London's Sunday Times. Proficient in five languages, thirty-three year old Brandon eased into diplomatic reporting through friendship with statesmen like Jan Masaryk and leaders of refugee Allied governments in London during war. His diplomatic contacts were invaluable after war and wherever statesmen met from Lake Success to London, Paris to Moscow, Brandon was shifted about to cover their doings with bewildering rapidity of bishop in a chess game. He has made thirteen Atlantic crossings since the war ended.

Truman giving an impromptu press conference on the airport tarmac before taking off for a Key West, Florida, holiday in 1949.

A snapshot I took of Walter Lippmann at his Maine summer home in 1955.

Acheson with Foreign Minister Ernest Bevin in a 1949 meeting to address British monetary difficulties. (AP/WIDE WORLD)

Supreme Court Justice Felix Frankfurter. (AP/WIDE WORLD)

Sir Oliver Franks, British ambassador to the US, in 1950. (AP/WIDE WORLD)

*With Field Marshall
Bernard Law Mont-
gomery in 1960 dur-
ing a weekend at the
country house of
Denis Hamilton,
my editor.*

*Interviewing Secre-
tary of State John
Foster Dulles.*

*John Foster Dulles
with President
Eisenhower, report-
ing to the American
people on the 1956
Suez Crisis.*
(AP/WIDE WORLD)

*CIA Director Allen
Dulles.* (AP/WIDE
WORLD)

The Times *commissioned photographs of me with both Richard Nixon and John Kennedy to promote its coverage of the 1960 presidential campaign.*

David Ormsby-Gore, British ambassador to Washington, who became a close friend of President Kennedy's. (AP/WIDE WORLD)

President Kennedy with Prime Minister Harold Macmillan on the occasion of the latter's first visit to the White House, April 5, 1961. (AP/WIDE WORLD)

Aboard President Kennedy's destroyer during the America's Cup off Newport in September 1962. President Kennedy is speaking to his daughter Caroline and an unidentified boy; Mrs. Kennedy, talking to painter William Walton, is at the left in the photograph, holding her sunglasses; Gianni Agnelli, the owner of Fiat, his arms folded, catches a nap in the background; I'm leaning back over my chair talking to an aide and at the same time trying to listen in to the president's conversation with the children.

An exclusive—my investigation in depth into the Skybolt crisis.

THE SUNDAY TIMES

WEEKLY REVIEW

An exclusive three-page report by Henry Brando

8 1963

SKYBOLT
THE FULL INSIDE STORY OF HOW A MISSILE NEARLY SPLIT THE WEST

nearly two years tish and American licies on our dependent deterrent orked at astonishing ross-purposes...

LITTLE did President Eisenhower suspect how premonitory was his gesture when he presented Harold Macmillan with a table model of a Polaris submarine at Camp David in 1960. It was at that meeting that the United States promised to supply Britain with the ill-fated Skybolt missile, a promise which less than two years later led to the most perilous crisis between these Allies since the Suez affair.

How two such men as President Kennedy and the Prime Minister, who kept their special telephone line between London and Washington fairly "hot," could so miscalculate each other's reactions—especially with Sir David Ormsby Gore, close friend of Mr Kennedy, as British Ambassador in Washington; how the top levels, cushion and Allies in constant touch at so many levels, could fail out so badly and misjudge each other's intentions and psychology so glaringly is still a mystery.

It perturbed and puzzled President Kennedy so much that he asked Professor Richard E. Neustadt, of Columbia University, to conduct an inquest to try to determine what went wrong; that secret: But after weeks of extensive study, which is secret: But after weeks of extensive study in Whitehall and in Washington I have been able to piece together the story of this failure in trans-Atlantic communications. It is an intriguing story, full of the political stakes forebodings and uncertainties, of a chain of errors ... ependent on technological progress, of a chain of errors ... incident carefully kept from the public gaze and, ... at Nassau, one of the great confrontations in the ... Anglo-American relations.
... as it should be:
... Anglo-

report prepared by a committee of ca
of Mr Kennedy serious doubts we
continuing the development of Sk
McNamara, the new Secretary of D
the recommendation of this report
on defence had been written by Pa
his Assistant Secretary for Interna
worried by the "missile gap" wh
and the United States which Mr
played up during the election ca
take out an insurance, so to say
be serious. He therefore deci
which Gates had withdrawn an
somewhat. Whitehall took a de
Through various techniques an
group captain at the Pentag
to follow the tantalising pro
Government was as well
ment. There was always
noises in the Pentagon, w
competing weapons system
Air Force which said, in e
the end force the necessa
the British Government,
ington. And London ra
Command in London.
Nobody in London
McNamara, once in ind
be intimidated by wha
well address called t
He perceived Skybolt time
which fights with the
on. Having introduc
system to establish c
to cut out, he had s
In the autumn w
Brown, Director of
Professor Jerome
Adviser, and Dan W

It began at Camp David, March, 1960. For Britain's V-bombers, Skybolt; for America, the Holy Loch base for Polaris submarines

Secretary of State Dean Rusk, Secretary of Defense Robert McNamara, and President Johnson during a meeting to discuss Vietnam.

Interview with President Johnson in the White House, June 1965.

My visit to Vietnam in October 1967: trying to protect our broken-down jeep in guerrilla-infested territory.

With Elliot Richardson, retired US ambassador to the Court of St. James's, and Sir Peter Ramsbotham, British ambassador to the US.

Prime Minister Edward Heath signing my caricature of him before a performance on "Meet the Press," December 1970.

FBI Director J. Edgar Hoover, who ordered the wiretap on my telephone. (AP/WIDE WORLD)

With Secretary of State Henry Kissinger.

My wife, Muffie, with President Nixon in the garden of his villa at San Clemente, California, following an afternoon spent with him and Kissinger on the day Nixon announced his first visit to China. The president was trying to pick a specially beautiful Peace rosebud for her.

My job and travels put me in touch with many world leaders, among them Israeli Defense Minister Moshe Dayan, Soviet Prime Minister Alexei Kosygin, Chinese Foreign Minister Qiao Guanhua, and Japanese Minister of Foreign Affairs Miki Takeo.

A series on cultural figures led me to meet and write about, among others, (top) Ben Shahn, Edmund Wilson, (center) Frank Lloyd Wright (POPPER PHOTOS), James Thurber, (bottom) Henry Moore, and Marilyn Monroe.

With Prime Minister Margaret Thatcher at 10 Downing Street, spring 1988.
(FRANK HERMANN)

At the White House, President Gerald Ford meets with a small group of reporters, myself included, on May 23, 1975. Back again on October 2, 1979, when President Jimmy Carter invited a half-dozen reporters to breakfast.

President Reagan shaking hands before a breakfast meeting with the so-called Sperling group, of which I am a member, on February 16, 1984.

● Henry Brandon worked with The Sunday Times for more than 40 years, until his retirement at the end of last month. He arrived in Britain just before the Second World War, a refugee from Nazi rule in Czechoslovakia, and began to freelance for Fleet Street newspapers. One of his earliest assignments was to visit the United States where he was eventually to spend most of his long and distinguished career as The Sunday Times Washington correspondent, and where he will continue to live. In this last article, Brandon looks back at the enormous changes he has witnessed in his 34 Washington years – the crucial years of the "American Century".

Brandon with Senator – soon to be President – Kennedy in 1960 (right); and with Marilyn Monroe on the set of Let's Make Love

MY LOVE AFFAIR WITH AMERICA

MY LOVE affair with the ed States began in the mid-atic in November 1941, I d myself on a Norwegian er in a convoy of some 50 s flying the British, Norwe-Swedish, and Dutch flags. had reached the mid-Atlantic ct where the British escort , in our case two destroyers four corvettes, usually turned

will never forget the sight of an rican cruiser and eight de-ers lining up that soft sunny ing on the horizon next to the -looking British escort ships. two leading ships exchanged s of greeting. And then the h ships disengaged and ed back, while we, powerfully cted under the American , headed toward New York. one was exultant. We all felt ad witnessed the symbolic nstration of a new beginning nglo-American cooperation, ur hopes that the US would ne a full ally soared.

and so I arrived in New York an exclusive report on the ship rendezvous to which Sunday Times gave a two-n headline: "America takes in mid-ocean". A two-an headline in those days was aximum. It was a lucky start first foreign assignment.

ning from Europe, I was at utterly shocked by the lacent remoteness of the can mood. The man-in-the-seemed far removed from aked realities of war. Even on Sunday of Pearl Harbor, e did not seem to be able to n what it all meant.

was a treacherous act by the ese. But I could not help ing at the time, as I still do, without it, and without 's declaration of war against S, President Roosevelt would ave been allowed to bring the of the US to the defence of rn civilization.

watch the American giant s muscles – to see the men in rm and overalls getting ised – was an exciting ience.

besides that process of ening two events stand out in ind: the joint press confer-Roosevelt and Churchill held ecember 22, 1941, and my anch at the White House.

presidential press conference ose days was an intimate compared to the televised it is today. My American ues, on hearing that it was est, hospitably allowed me to forward and stand smack st the president's desk in the Office, facing the man I had red for so long from a ce. His was a surprisingly n face despite the familiar jaw, Winston Churchill sat d and to one side of him, g earnest, more the bulldog the cherub, dressed in a black and striped trousers.

er a few domestic announce-, Roosevelt explained that d proposed to Churchill that uit himself to a statement and ut spared questioning by the ican press, "who are wolves ared to the British lambs". Churchill demurred. He

jnsisted on taking his chances, And when he rose to speak, the corps broke out in spontaneous cheers and applause.

Some embarrassing questions followed. One, no doubt, was prompted by proverbial American optimism: "How soon, Mr Prime Minister, do you expect we will win the war?" Churchill, instead of getting impatient, blithely replied: "If we manage ..."

half as long as if we manage the war badly".

Lunch at the White House some eight months later began with an embarrassment. It was one of those blisteringly hot and humid summer seasons, and being short of dollars, officially and person-ally, I had decided not to invest in a white suit. Friends told me the only alternative was to go in a dark one, which I...

would like to become correspon-dent in Washington. It was my best ever Christmas present.

When I returned to Washington the following April, I found that not much had changed in the previous five years. It was still a truly southern, provincial town. A black could not go to a restaurant with a white, or to the No...

dents like Johnson, Nixon and Carter avoid it; the Reagans, however, are sufficiently self-as-sured to feel at home wherever they are.

The real attraction of George-town, though, is not its reputation as a centre of power, but its quiet tree-lined ...

One of the supreme examples of discretion, albeit in wartime Washington, was told to me by Frankfurter at one of our regular lunches in his chambers, which were a very special treat because he was, as someone once called him, a journalist by nature and a jurist by perversity. He was not only one of the best informed men in Washington, with close ties to Roosevelt and Truman, he was also an avid reader of British publications and an emotionally committed Anglophile, a man of spontaneous enthusiasms and lifelong hates.

It was in 1944, he recalled, just before the American elections, at a dinner party given by Lord Halifax for Winston Churchill. There were seven Britons and seven Ameri-cans, including Eugene Meyer, the publisher of the Washington Post, and a Republican senator. Chur-chill, for everybody to hear, said that he counted on Roosevelt being re-elected. When some expressed doubts, he was obvi-ously taken aback. Suddenly he got up and made an impassioned little speech, saying "if that hap-pened I would have to get up in the House of Commons and tell it that this is a calamity of the gravest sort". If that little peror-ation had leaked out, it could have swung the elections against Roose-velt – but it did not.

Much later, sitting next to General Eisenhower at a dinner party at the Danish embassy, just after the General had accepted the presidency of Columbia Univer-sity, and before he was drawn into politics, Frankfurter turned to him, saying he felt the urge to tell him to his face what he had been saying behind his back. Then sheepishly, he told Ike: "I have been saying that it speaks for you to have accepted the presidency of Columbia in spite of the many more lucrative positions you had been offered, and it speaks against the trustees to have offered it to you", Ike heartily agreed.

Americans, even of the Acheson class, are unsure of how to deal with British royalty. But when he had an audience with Queen Elizabeth in 1952 he remembered how much King George VI had praised Winston Churchill for keeping him fully informed about everything. Therefore when Queen Elizabeth started off by saying that she hoped all had gone well between him and Eden, Acheson, a little mischievously, shook his head to indicate that in fact not everything had gone as he had hoped. Suddenly the Queen got very interested and so did Prince Philip. While both continued to ask questions, Eden began to finger his tie nervously. The audience lasted well beyond the appointed hour. Later, Eden sounded annoyed that Acheson offered the Queen too much information. Acheson, however, took a puckish delight in having done so.

Ernest Bevin, in Acheson's view, was one of...

feel at ease with the world. Occasionally, as we sat around the fireplace on Saturday evenings, he took a slightly sadistic pleasure in leaning over to such other guests as Justice of the Supreme Court Felix Frankfurter...

GOOD WISHES HENRY, FROM ALL YOUR FRIENDS AT THE SUNDAY TIMES.
— PLUS, CERTAIN OTHERS ....

A farewell article to my time as American correspondent for The Sunday Times *on the occasion of my retirement in 1983 and a farewell card from my colleagues by a* Sunday Times *cartoonist.*

With my daughter Fiona and wife Muffie after receiving the CBE from Queen Eliza-
beth in 1986 in the court of Buckingham Palace.

IO

"Nothing Is Forever Here, Not Even the End"

—MEG GREENFIELD

PRESIDENT-ELECT RICHARD NIXON announced that Henry Kissinger would be his national security adviser shortly after the 1968 election. When I visited Kissinger in his temporary headquarters at the Pierre Hotel in New York during the transition period, I found him almost childishly exhilarated by the challenge and utter surprise that he, a well-known Rockefeller loyalist, a critic of Nixon, an intellectual with Harvard credentials, should have been chosen to help the president become a world leader. I was impressed and so was he that Nixon, for the sake of enlisting a man who had written several learned books about foreign affairs, had thrown all his prejudices overboard and appointed a German-born Jew to such a critical position. I was also surprised that Nixon was confident enough to opt for a man who might well make him feel intellectually insecure.

I had met Henry earlier at Harvard, on my periodic visits to learn from him and others, such as Professors Richard Neustadt, Tom Shelling, Patrick Moynihan, Stanley Hoffmann, and John Kenneth Galbraith, what the world looked like from this august mountaintop of higher learning. With Henry I used to discuss American and British politics, his own ideas on current affairs —nothing particularly personal.

I liked his tough-mindedness toward the Russians, his understanding of the relationship of forces in the world, his recognition that reliance on military security needed to rest on more than deterrence, that there was a need to bring great-power diplomacy into play. The United States had to grapple with problems similar to those the British faced in the eighteenth and nineteenth centuries. Then they played the balance-of-power game with great skill to preserve their own power position, and when they could no longer play it in 1917 and 1941, they enjoyed the advantage of calling on the United States to redress the balance of forces. The United States now lacked a similar advantage. It required the development of an entirely new world system, and I felt that Kissinger, with his Bismarckian ideas on world diplomacy, had the attributes and the conceptual perspectives to develop an updated one for the United States.

My direct empathy for the man was based, above all, on my admiration for a foreign-born who in time attained a position of the highest order in government, unsurpassed in American history. It was an achievement inconceivable within Britain's closed society. I found persuasive the skepticism about President Nixon's character that Kissinger expressed to me and was in sympathy with many of his ideas on world affairs—perhaps because so many had a European pedigree. He shared with Nixon the basic principle that had animated American foreign policy since the end of World War II, that the survival of Western Europe depended on an absolutely firm commitment of American power. Each also recognized that rough military equality now existed between the two superpowers, so that they should test the possibilities of reaching agreements with the Soviet Union rather than perpetuating a sterile confrontation policy.

Our friendship developed naturally from these earlier professional encounters. I saw a good deal of Henry in 1969, when I was still a bachelor, but when I got married in 1970 our well-run household on Whitehaven Street became a kind of haven for him where he could relax, let his hair down, bring his girl friends, take a swim in our pool, and come for a meal when the spirit moved him at short notice. After Nancy Maginnis became his steady girl friend, he usually brought her for lunch on Saturday or Sunday and they usually stayed for the rest of the day.

We enjoyed their company. Talking about his day and his depressions or his amusing encounters with famous and infamous people was his way of relaxing. He mixed history with the gossip, the encouraging with the ominous, the self-deprecatory with pride in his own achievements. He had a knack of bringing personalities to life in our living room and occasionally gave us a snapshot of his personal relationship with the president, lifting the veil ever so slightly from an enigma that intrigued us and the world, and at times left even Henry still puzzled. When our daughter, Fiona, was born, he participated in the event like a member of the family; when I had to undergo an operation he was the first to call the hospital. With all his cares about the world, I could not help but be enchanted by Henry's thoughtfulness.

Nixon's most innovative and politically most daring move was his decision to unlock the door to Communist China after he had been one of the faithful supporters of Generalissimo Chiang Kai-shek. For him to order Kissinger as early as February 1969 to develop a new policy toward China showed that he was a far more practical politician, unhindered by ideology, than anyone had assumed. Nixon and Kissinger have been accused, often rightly, of a penchant for secret diplomacy, but if Kissinger had not used stealth to approach Beijing, the domestic uproar could well have choked these overtures before they could lead anywhere at all. It was one way of freeing old foreign policy moorings, deeply embedded, especially in Congress, which tends to respond too readily to the corrupting special interest groups rather than the national interest.

Nixon's initiative made eminent sense, but it required courage not to allow himself to be weighed down by past Republican policies. It was tragic that the previous American presidents had felt unable to face up to the domestic political challenge and recognize Communist China sooner. It is my belief that had John Foster Dulles had more foresight, the Eisenhower administration could have risked making contact with Beijing. Most likely it would have kept the United States from intervening in Vietnam, a policy based on fear of China's expansionist aims in Southeast Asia. One could even argue that if the Truman administration had recognized China when the British government did in 1949, the United States would have had better communications with Beijing and the Chinese intervention in the Korean War could have been prevented. President Kennedy avoided coming to grips with the issue because Eisenhower is said to have threatened to turn publicly against him if he recognized Communist China. In the Johnson administration the State Department's legal adviser, Abram Chayes, and Robert Barnett, the assistant secretary for Asian affairs, made faint efforts to get the top policymakers interested in a new approach to Beijing, but stood no chance of success: Lyndon Johnson did not want to grasp this nettle either. The argument one often hears, that Nixon's move did not require much courage because the time had come and any other president would have done the same, is in my ears a lame one. Only after the fact did it become evident that the traffic light on the road to Beijing had switched to amber.

Nixon and Kissinger also agreed that the Vietnam war must be brought to an end as soon as possible but without too much loss of face—"honorable" was the key word. Eisenhower, according to General Goodpaster, who acted as liaison between the former president and LBJ, told Johnson that he should act in Vietnam as behooved a great power and deploy overwhelming force to bring the war to a rapid and decisive end. But Johnson shied away from this, and so succeeded in telling Hanoi more what he was *not* willing to do, enabling the North Vietnamese to see that the war would be won not by military but by political means.

In 1968, soon after Nixon became president, Kissinger brought up the possibility of a "savage blow," but only in a halfhearted way because he knew that neither he nor Nixon had the stomach to take such a drastic decision at that time. He did not press it because he did not want to alienate his intellectual friends, especially those at Harvard. In retrospect, though, he mused that had they done in 1969 what they did in 1972, what came to be called the Christmas bombing, plus a blockade of North Vietnamese harbors, they would not have paid a significantly higher price and would have brought the war to an earlier end. "It was a mistake. I was ambivalent," said Henry.

The two might have given the idea more thought, perhaps, had they listened to Averell Harriman, who had just returned from Paris empty-handed. He said the North Vietnamese were quite different from the Koreans: "They don't shout, they preserve all the niceties, and they serve tea. Yet no one should have any doubt that they are determined to get what they want and that they are convinced that having made progress over the years, they will in the end prevail." One of the negotiators once very quietly but bluntly told him: "Look, we are winning the war because we are willing to take your bombing. We expected the destruction of Hanoi and we were willing to abandon it and live in holes in the ground. Furthermore, you have half a million troops in Vietnam and yet, if we want to, we can attack any of the cities and cause havoc behind your lines."

Harriman accordingly told the new administration that the war was un-winnable. It was the last among innumerable public services Harriman had rendered American presidents ever since Franklin Roosevelt had sent him as "defense expediter" to London in February 1941 with as his main task oiling the wheels of lend-lease to Britain and bolstering Churchill's and the British people's will to fight. He established a close relationship with Churchill in the process and acquitted himself of his task in such an impressive way that Roosevelt later sent him as ambassador to Moscow and Truman sent him as ambassador to London. It was on his first mission as expediter that he also met Pamela Churchill, then married to Churchill's son, Randolph, whom he married more than thirty years later after both had become widowed. He had a magisterial presence, the look and the understated self-confidence of a Brahmin and an ability to express complicated problems in simple matter-of-fact sentences. He never acted like a messenger, always like a born presidential agent. He was not an intellectual or a brains truster, but he was a man of good sense, reason, and moderation. When asked how he came to acquire such good judgment, he replied that it was based on his experiences. Then, with a straight face, he asked rhetorically, "And do you know what I base my experiences on?" He smiled and continued: "On my bad judgments."

His basic guiding thought in relation to the Soviet Union, he said time and again, was that he did not like the Russians any more than anybody else, but since next to the United States they were the world's strongest country, the United States had to find ways of getting along with them and that that was the most important thing for any American president to understand. "There are many ways of disagreeing with them, but the issue is to find ways of collaborating with them." He also insisted that over the fifty years since he had first gone there, he had learned that the Soviet Union is not a monolithic structure of Communist dogma, that it is affected by changes of personalities, even if all their leaders, past and present, remained convinced since they had the truth by which man was destined to live, that communism would ultimately sweep the world.

Harriman's dealings with the Soviets go back to 1926, when he negotiated with Leon Trotsky, who was then chairman of the Supreme Economic Council, the sale of a manganese mine the Harriman bank owned in Georgia. To visit the mine he rented, in the manner of a railway tycoon, a Russian railroad car. It took a year for the deal to be consummated, but he succeeded in getting all the Harriman investment plus a small profit out before all foreign-owned properties were confiscated. In 1963 I accompanied Harriman on a visit to a car factory near Moscow that he had come to view not as a railway tycoon, but as the man who was instrumental in arranging for lend-lease aid to the Soviets during World War II. The acclaim he got from the factory workers as he walked through the plant was extraordinarily touching and visibly moved him. It took him back to what he considered his heroic period. Only his negotiations for a partial nuclear test ban agreement assumed an almost equal importance in his mind and led to the problems of arms control becoming the passion of the rest of his life. Not exactly a passion, but a delight were his own birthday parties. The most memorable was a bal masque when he turned sixty-five: Robert Kennedy was the host and Vice President Hubert Humphrey came, although LBJ by then detested Bobby, whose presidential ambitions had begun to sprout. Politics were more fun in those days than they are today, and Humphrey joked about hoping that nobody would give away the fact that he had gone into the lion's den. Gradually his birthday parties became less of a public and more of an intimate occasion, attended only by friends he had known for a long time. The only time I remember Averell's being less formal and more personal was at his ninety-third birthday party, when he explained the presence of Kay Graham. It was in her house, he said with obvious gratitude, that he met Pam again after not having seen her since their friendship blossomed in London twenty-five years earlier. A year later, at his ninety-fourth, Pam told a story that illustrated his unquenchable drive to win—a drive in which he did not always succeed. Pam had bought a racehorse and informed him that she planned to call it Governor—even friends still referred to him as Governor long after he had ceased to be governor of New York State. "Governor?" he had asked, "and what if the horse loses?" He belonged to a nobility of public men of whom he was one of the last survivors.

However, Harriman's warnings that the war in Vietnam was unwinnable were discounted. Kissinger believed that the right mix of diplomacy and military force would lead to an acceptable compromise solution. He tried to convince the North Vietnamese that they had a choice between endless warfare with heavy casualties and little prospect of winning control of South Vietnam, or a foreshortened war with more than a fair chance that they would gain control gradually by political means rather than by force of arms. But the American strategy of gradual withdrawal only reinforced the Harriman thesis —the belief in Hanoi that with a little more patience and perseverance victory would be theirs. Kissinger and Nixon committed a grave error in misjudging not only the Vietnamese fighting spirit, but also American tolerance in support of an unwinnable war. For a rational man such as Kissinger, it was hard to believe that men could be so irrational as the North Vietnamese—but this was the first time that he had found himself dealing with an Asian mentality.

Henry seemed to have a fascinating time organizing his National Security Council and all its various specialist panels, drafting contingency plans, setting up his own miniature State Department, and trying to apply the Wagnerian dictum of seeking to become master of events, rather than being at their mercy. He also enjoyed his budding fame and the exercise of power and not only because it affected him like an aphrodisiac. He himself was puzzled and surprised by his change in personality from the shy, ivory-tower intellectual to the witty, self-assured man of the world.

But in early November 1969, during lunch at his office—the Soviet ambassador, Anatoly Dobrynin, had passed me as I entered Henry's sanctum—I was taken aback by the sudden disenchantment and pessimism that seemed to weigh heavily on his mind. He looked dejected and in what I learned to recognize as one of his dark moods about the future. He sounded like a man chained to the mast. He had had a personal relationship with Nelson Rockefeller, he said, but he did not have one with Nixon. He felt detached, unable to establish the kind of mental contact with the president he thought was essential. He also indicated that he did not agree with everything Nixon had said in his speech setting out Vietnam strategy. The intellectual community of which he used to be part had shunned him, and this also upset him. Henry looked numb, and whatever wit he displayed was forced. Nixon had just given a speech about Vietnam, which I interpreted as an attempt to build up a strong front behind which he could slowly disengage, but Henry insisted that this was the wrong interpretation: Nixon did not mean to pursue some devious tactic but considered the honorable outcome so important that he placed it above his own political survival—if necessary, he would be the third president to stake his fate on obtaining a reasonable settlement. I was quite shaken by this new emphasis, which sounded to me more like a fight to win than to get out.

Nixon, unfortunately, took the advice of Sir Robert Thompson, the British guerrilla expert. Thompson convinced him that he could succeed in Vietnam, just as the British did in Malaya against the Chinese insurgents (hated by the Malayans and hence easier to combat). On the other hand, de Gaulle had warned that this was an unwinnable war and advised Nixon to disengage from it as soon as he could without too much damage to American prestige. Nixon also failed to understand the disintegration of public support that destroyed President Johnson, and erroneously assumed that in the interest of improving Soviet-American relations the Russians would force Hanoi into a compromise. Not only did Moscow not have that kind of power over the fanatical North Vietnamese, the Russians looked constantly over their shoulders, worried that Hanoi might try to play off the Soviet Union against China. Like Rusk and McNamara, Nixon underrated Vietnamese hostility to the Chinese—stemming from their thousand years of dependence—that was bound to keep China out of the war.

Another problem was that in Vietnam the United States pursued the wrong kind of military strategy: "Search and destroy." The military believed that putting green berets on the heads of their soldiers would transform them into guerrilla fighters. I saw American troops in combat in Vietnam in 1967 and was impressed by their spirit and their courage. But after a talk with General Westmoreland, I did not think that they had been given the commander they needed. This was, by the way, also a view held by Ambassador Ellsworth Bunker, who gave General Abrams, his deputy and then his successor, a much higher rating.

Nixon had the rough-and-ready foreign policy design, but it was Kissinger who provided the diplomatic tactics, the methods and the options. Nixon still did not actually like Kissinger (in fact Kissinger suspected him of being a closet anti-Semite), but he considered him a skilled executor of his policies. Patrick Buchanan, who was more impressed by Kissinger's weaknesses than his strength, once told me that Henry talking to Nixon sounded like James Burnham, the right-wing political philosopher, and talking to his Georgetown friends like the liberal columnist Joseph Kraft. Buchanan, who was well to the right of Kissinger, was of course not an unbiased observer. Nixon, however, readily admitted how much Kissinger had contributed to putting flesh on the bones of his foreign policy concepts. Helmut Sonnenfeldt, who was a member of Dr. Kissinger's national security council staff and born in Germany, once compared Kissinger's role with Nixon to that of the European psychiatrists whom middle-Americans were visiting to learn how to cope with their anxieties. The analogy does not encompass Henry's role in its entirety, but it was certainly part of it.

Sir Isaiah Berlin, the most respected philosophy professor at Oxford, and Henry Kissinger had never met, and I wondered what these two brilliant intellectuals would have to say to each other. Isaiah was born in Lithuania, spoke a fearfully fast Oxford English with a slight Slavic intonation, and could hold an audience spellbound with his fund of knowledge on almost any subject. He was an expert not only on the Soviet Union, but also on the United States, since he had served at the British Embassy in Washington during World War

II, reporting on American domestic affairs. His dispatches became such a political and literary event that Churchill read them regularly and so did most important figures in the British government. In those old emotional days of the birth of the special Anglo-American relationship, Isaiah made many lasting friendships in Washington and whenever he returned for a visit, his friends hotly competed for the honor of entertaining him. I knew him from those early days at the British Embassy and, faithful as he was, he came to us to lunch in March 1971, on a Saturday, with Henry Kissinger, the British ambassador and Lady Cromer, Mrs. Alice Longworth, and Kay Graham.

Henry as usual took command of the conversation, telling us how the president had ticked him off and how J. Edgar Hoover had given him a separate half-hour dressing-down for having spent one and a half hours with some Harvard professors, who had come to make it clear that his alma mater was dissociating itself from his misguided policies in Vietnam and Cambodia. He made light of it all, but I knew that his old colleagues' visit had upset him deeply.

Isaiah did not comment on the professors' visit, but began talking about Machiavelli, who we all knew was considered to be one of Henry's intellectual mentors. Machiavelli, Isaiah told us, had been required reading for Charles V, Lenin, and Stalin and the onetime Soviet foreign minister Vishinsky (who quoted him as the symbol of the immoral policies of capitalists). It was unfortunate, said Isaiah, that it was he who had become such an inspiration to so many statesmen and political leaders, and not Erasmus of Rotterdam, the great humanist of the Renaissance, whose teachings about the moral conscience offered spiritual inspiration. He attributed Erasmus's relative obscurity as compared to Machiavelli's immortal fame—despite the fact that he had such an onerous reputation—to the fact that world leaders wanted pragmatism rather than spiritualism. The reason for this, Isaiah suggested, was that Machiavelli was so much closer to the truth of political life than Erasmus. As if to take the edge off his remarks, in view of Henry's presence, he added that he did not consider Nixon Machiavellian, and that he agreed with many of the things he was doing, especially his efforts to keep the United States from going isolationist. What troubled him about Americans, though, was that they had lost confidence in themselves, lost too some of the nerve they formerly had; there was a smell of the Weimar-type of decay around—a thought that was never far from Henry's mind either. I ventured to disagree, since there was no inflation raging, nor were people rallying to extremist parties such as the Nazis and Communists. Isaiah allowed the truth of this, and so our discussion ended on a reassuring note.

Another lunch that I enjoy recalling was when Slava (Mstislav) Rostropovitch came to our house for the first time, without his cello but with his little dog on a long leash. He is like a volcano filled with love which easily spills out. He is even more demonstratively affectionate than Leonard Bernstein. His passion for people, for music, for freedom, for love of life and for giving enjoyment are almost boundless. He quoted the French politician and humanitarian Simone Weil as having said that "all great art is to describe God," to explain why he was a believer. "Every good deed," he said, "is a description of God." He spoke with sadness about his old friend Solzhenitsyn, who had stayed in Slava's dacha outside Moscow while he remained an excommunicated writer, because now they were hardly on speaking terms. His own admiration for the United States and Western culture and Solzhenitsyn's aversion to it ended their friendship. As one who had done so much to enhance Washington's artistic life, Slava was upset that when he was invited to the White House for the Bicentennial celebration program, his wife and daughters had not been included. When he inquired, he said, whether the president knew that his wife too was a famous artist (the singer Galina Vishnevskaya), the answer still remained no. Not surprisingly, he declined the invitation.

But what mattered to him more was to get to see the president in order to ask for help with some friends who wanted to leave the Soviet Union and could not get their exit visas. I promised to tell Henry, but I also suggested that he might want to talk to Senator Henry Jackson, whose so-called Jackson-Vanik amendment, instead of facilitating Jewish emigration, had brought it to a halt. It made the "most favored nation" status in trade between the Soviet Union and the United States dependent on increased Jewish emigration. Slava said that this amendment was a big mistake and that he did not want to talk to him because, he explained, it could lead to political controversy. Talking about Khrushchev, he said that Soviet history should give him credit, first, for having denounced Stalin, second, for letting thousands of prisoners out of the gulags and, third, for having opened Russia to the West. But, he added: "My countrymen, in their foxiness, are very dangerous; don't ever believe them, because they want to be the strongest."

However much social Washington was nauseated by the idea that Nixon had made it to the White House, Mrs. Alice Longworth, who was the reigning social dowager, had a special liking for him, because he treated her with reverence, paid his respects on her birthdays, and came to see her quietly even after he had become president. Perhaps he paid her so much attention because she was President Teddy Roosevelt's daughter, perhaps because this grand old lady carried a kind of golden seal of social approval which still meant something in this quasi-egalitarian society and particularly to a kind of social outcast such as Richard Nixon had been; perhaps it was because Mrs. L., as her friends were allowed to call her, had met his mother in his early congressional days and then told him how impressed she was with her as a simple but good woman. After Kennedy defeated Nixon, Mrs. L. invited his whole family to dinner to her musty townhouse of faded but warm and comfortable elegance. Julie, the daughter, Mrs. L. told me later, passionately defended her mother when her father offered as one reason for his defeat Jackie Kennedy's beauty. "But Mommy is prettier than Mrs. Kennedy!" she exclaimed. Mrs. L. concluded that Nixon had a tendency to blame others for his defeats, that he lacked a feel for the meaning of loyalty and generosity, and that he had little respect for Pat, who, according to Mrs. L., had "a very limited vocabulary which, she assumed, was one reason why she said so little in public."

Mrs. L.'s supreme charm was that she was amusing and provocative, rare commodities in a generally earnest, self-conscious town where words are too often passed through a mental filter before being spoken. She was serious about literature and, thanks to a phenomenal memory, was able to recite, even at the age of ninety, Lord Dunsany's ballads, which she had adored all her life. Another of her favorites was Kipling, whom she met as a child and remembered as "curious-looking with tremendous, intimidating eyebrows." She was irreverent about politics and malicious about people. "My middle name," she used to say, "is malevolence." Nobody aroused her malevolence more than FDR, except possibly his wife, Eleanor. "I don't think anyone has ever properly diagnosed the distress an Oyster Bay or Sagamore Roosevelt felt about the Hyde Park Roosevelts. The latter were fifth cousins and they got into the White House! Can you think of anything more distressing?! And on top of it FDR was elected four successive times. No Greek has ever had a tougher time with hubris and nemesis!" At the slightest provocation she was ready to impersonate Eleanor with her eyes signaling mischief, loathing, and amusement. Averell Harriman, she remembered, was first treated dreadfully by his father, and then was so intimidated by "that man Peabody at Groton School" that from fright he began to stammer. He was never frightened, however, she added of ladies, who found him extremely handsome. "He had eternal youth and Pam made it even more eternal." (Pamela gradually created her own political salon, comingling the old and the new generation Democrats, building up a fund-raising organization and a political counseling team. Her dinner parties resounded with Democratic Party strategy talks and often resembled a paddock where the best horses for the electoral races were paraded before the so-called fat cats and tested for their ability to jump political hurdles.) Mrs. L. liked Jack Kennedy and had no taste for Bobby Kennedy, but she was fascinated by Henry Kissinger. She admired his extraordinary ability to deal with people because he knew how to make them believe what he wanted them to believe, and because he was a more dedicated American than most because he was foreign-born. Another quality, she said, that differentiated him from the American-born was his sense of tragedy, based on his early experiences in Hitler's Germany.

To me she was rich territory for archaeological digs into politics and society. She talked about the days in the White House when Washington still had a postbellum atmosphere and K Street was where the people lived who later moved to Georgetown—Cabot Lodge, Henry Adams, John Hay, and their ilk. Her father invited adventurers, sheriffs, foreign potentates, and intellectuals to the White House, though "we didn't think of people in those days as intellectuals," she said, "but as men of learning, of scholarship and erudition. They were taken for granted. There wasn't that self-consciousness about them. I think the taste for intellectuals began with Franklin and his brains trust, they then went underground and came out again with a bang in Jack Kennedy's time."

Churchill once asked her why her father seemed prejudiced against him. Unfortunately, she replied, Teddy Roosevelt had picked up some gossip in South Africa that Churchill had been sitting in a tent behind netting while other people outside were being chewed up by tsetse flies. "He is a coward. He sat in his tent," was her father's verdict. If Winston and her father had been the same age, she said, there would have been a terrific confrontation or a great friendship between them, because to her both were Kiplingesque and both were—what has become an "anti" word—jingoists. She was proud of her father for many reasons, but particularly because when Owen Wister (author of *The Virginian*) exhorted him to do somthing about Alice, he replied that he had to choose between governing the country and governing her, and that he could not do both.

Even at the age of ninety-two she remained a mixture of austere beauty and unlovely plainness. Her light blue, challengingly flashing eyes were her dominant feature and her quizzical restlessness gave her a kind of eternal youthfulness. As she grew older and frailer, she spoke more and more about herself and with the same kind of sardonic cynicism she used to apply to other people. She would talk about her hypochondriac habits, how she was surrounded by sixteen pillboxes, and how she had come to worry about herself. When during a dinner I noticed that she looked pale and thin, she suddenly said: "You know, I'm dying. I've had a big cancer here," and she pointed to one side of her chest, "and a small one there," and she pointed at the other side. "I don't expect to go on much longer, but I don't want to go because, although everybody is so pontifical, so platitudinous and mean, I enjoy it all. I'm aging rapidly but I'm trying to do it languidly because I'm too interested to see the disintegration of our country before I depart." She remained full of malevolence to the very end.

Early in 1971 Henry Kissinger suggested to me that I write a history of the evolution of the foreign policy of the Nixon administration. It seemed to me an attractive idea, but premature. Still, he continued to insist that I would find it a worthwhile undertaking, since I would be writing about an entirely new phase in American foreign policymaking, and he whetted my appetite by promising that he would help as much as possible and instruct his aides to do likewise. I now realized that he was really serious about it, but I still wondered whether I could cope with two assignments, the book and my reporting for *The Sunday Times.* I also wondered whether I would have enough perspective at such close range. In the end the temptation became too great and I signed a contract with Doubleday, who had published an earlier book of mine, *As We Are.*

An early bonus was an interview with President Nixon on February 26, 1971. As I was waiting in the Roosevelt Room, I contemplated the extraordinary mental and physical resilience of the man who beat the odds when he won his seat in Congress in 1946, surmounted Eisenhower's readiness to dump him from his presidential ticket, overcame his defeat in the race for the presidency against Kennedy and for the governorship of California against Governor Brown, and how he returned east, exhumed himself politically, and finally made it to the White House despite his checkered past, his lack of charm, and his widespread unpopularity.

Nixon was not the first American president who wanted to cast himself in a Churchillian mold. He had studied, as a mechanic studies the engine of a car, the methods of leadership of the Roosevelts—Theodore and Franklin— Disraeli, Churchill, and de Gaulle to draw lessons for his own ways of leadership. What attracted him particularly to Churchill, he once told me, was the historic parallel he saw in his own defeats and spectacular recoveries and Churchill's sense of defying fate.

One has to be far more of a psychiatrist than I am to explain the strengths and weaknesses of Nixon's character; his weathering the ignominy of his ouster from the presidency and his resurrection as a superior statesman in foreign affairs are unique in political history.

The key to his outlook on life is perhaps best reflected in a sentence from his book *Six Crises,* which he wrote in 1968: "A man who has never lost himself in a cause bigger than himself, has missed one of life's mountaintop experiences. Only in losing himself does he find himself." His life is really a chain of finding and losing himself, of climbing mountaintops and falling off mountain cliffs. He made a political career out of being a strong anti-Communist, but became enough of a statesman to move from confrontation with the Soviet Union to negotiations, from keeping Communist China in isolation to building a bridge across that void.

Nixon came to power at a very difficult moment for any president. The unpopularity of the Vietnam war, the bitter antiwar protests, the explosive youth rebellion, the festering racial crisis, and the violent death of three popular leaders, President Kennedy, Robert Kennedy, and Martin Luther King, Jr., were seriously fraying the fabric of the American political and social system. Traveling across the country I found that one of the first things Americans were asking me with disarming frankness was whether I thought that American society was sick and what I thought had gone wrong. Everybody seemed to be searching his soul, everybody was wondering how to meet this crisis to which all realized there were no quick and obvious solutions. The majority of Americans were still middle-of-the-roaders, but on the fringes the right and the left were more polarized, more wrought up than perhaps ever before. Americans were upset at the impotence of the leaders of their society and of government. They began to doubt the validity of many of their long-cherished principles—and also to question some of the newer values that had debilitated what they considered the American faith and dogma. It was disturbing to see the most optimistic, the most powerful nation in the world going through a mental depression with nobody quite knowing where it was all leading.

Under these circumstances a visit to Mississippi with my newly wedded wife, Muffie, held out unexpected promise. I had not been in the deep South since Bull Connor sent his police dogs against civil rights protesters and "Ole Miss" University was forcibly desegregated, and I wanted to see how much progress desegregation had made since. Only five years earlier Joseph Rauh, a deeply committed civil rights lawyer, and Aaron Henry, the president of the National Association for the Advancement of Colored People, and owner of a drugstore, had desegregated the first restaurant in Clarksdale, Mississippi, with the local sheriff and his police dogs watching from the outside, hardly able to keep their distance. Since then, I was told, at least theoretically all schools had been desegregated. So was housing, and motels and restaurants. To visit Aaron Henry we drove to the other end of Clarksdale, where he had his small and cluttered drugstore. Henry was a modest, gentle, quiet-spoken man, battle-scarred but undaunted. In his shop window was a handwritten sign that said: "Attorney General Mitchell please don't make the Justice Department in Washington as meaningless as a town in Mississippi called 'Liberty.'" This was not the language of the northern black militants. This was definitely not Black Panther country. Their southern brethren had their own approach, more restrained, more pleading. "Down here black power simply means a risky lifelong fight for civil rights by whipping them with the white man's laws," Henry said in explanation of his window sign. "The Nixon administration hasn't got as good a rapport with the blacks as the Democrats had, but I sense changes when they occur. When I call Ehrlichman on the telephone [he was Nixon's adviser in charge of domestic affairs] I can get through to him." Then he pulled two letters from under the pile on his desk, one from President Nixon and another from Elliot Richardson, the secretary of health, education and welfare, both in support of his civil rights causes. He also mentioned with obvious satisfaction that George P. Shultz, another Nixon aide, who later became secretary of the treasury and President Reagan's secretary of state, had sent his daughter to Clarksdale to spend a week with the black parents of a fellow student. To Henry these were all signs of progress and he did not mind measuring it by inches.

At the other end of the town we looked at a long, flat steel building that looked like a tractor shed, which we soon came to realize was a symbol of desperation. "We may have to work twenty-four hours a day to get this private all-white school ready by September," the man in charge told us. "Last month a hundred twenty white Clarksdale citizens agreed to guarantee $5,000 each so that local banks would advance a $600,000 loan for this school. In the last few days the so-called cut-glass set—affluent whites—donated $108,000 toward the cost of the school." Semmes Luckett, the lawyer representing the school, said, to illustrate the prevailing desperation, "Some people may have to give up smoking or drinking to afford to send their children to this school—and they will. If people in Clarksdale are unwilling to maintain this school, then the whites will move away and this town will die." Then, raising his voice, he added: "Mississippi nationalism will prevail. Just as the South Africans are holding out successfully, although the whole world is against them, so will we, although most of the United States is against us." He was far too narrow-minded to see the difference between the situation in his South and in South Africa. He underrated the sense of survival among the business community and the power of the law. "Even though the traditions are deeply embedded here," Dr. Miller, the soft-spoken black principal of Coahoma Junior High School, told us, "and people are reluctant to change them, there is no open animosity here. On the contrary, I sense that there is change in the air. Fear too, and on both sides, of what may happen." Aaron Henry's last words, when we said good-bye to him, continued to ring in my ears: "I have a dream—and they have a nightmare, baby." Indeed there was change in the air, and far more than either blacks or whites expected then. It was fascinating to watch how American society, as it became more and more conscious of the injustices within it, was increasingly anxious to make up for lost time to avoid what it disliked most—turmoil.

A more immediate danger to the inner cohesion of American society was the discontent over the commitment to the Vietnam war among American youth. And it had a worldwide impact. For this new generation this unhappy war became a formative experience, blotting out almost everything that had happened before. They had no firsthand knowledge of American military successes in World War II, no understanding of the healing effect of the Marshall Plan, of how the Soviets subjugated Eastern Europe, or the origins of the attack against South Korea. Life began with the Kennedy era, which to them was the golden age of youth coming to power. Beyond that they saw only failure, humiliation, and tragedy. They saw nothing worth committing themselves to, so why not avoid work and military service and instead crusade for causes such as "making love not war," sublimate worldly concerns in mind-numbing drugs, decry American culture, education, and the profit motive? The "flower children," the hippies, the students' freedom movement expressed their rebellion and their egalitarian outlook by wearing the simplest clothes and long hair, by becoming dropouts of one sort or another, by turning against their parents, their teachers, their church, and the mores of their elders. Puritanism, which for so long had dominated American thinking and mores and had served as the last parental disciplinarian authority, had died out. Nobody quite knew what new values, if any, existed to replace it. Our household of four children remained, fortunately, almost untouched by those passing fads; at the time we did not quite know whether they were indeed passing. My stepson, John, could not resist the lesser temptations of rebellion and forms of experimentation, nor could my older stepdaughter, Elizabeth, then about twelve, resist such serious social trends as the new women's rights movement. Elizabeth, for instance, expressing her growing feminist oats, one Sunday evening commanded Bill Safire, who wrote speeches for President Nixon, and Helmut Sonnenfeldt and me to repair to the kitchen to wash the dishes, in what she considered the new spirit of liberation.

It was a depressing time to be young, to be a parent, teacher, or cultural leader. The young grew up watching the horrors of war and hearing and reading about the threat of nuclear bombs to their existence, parents did not know how to counter the rebellion in their own home, teachers were at a loss to maintain discipline and get the students' attention, and cultural leaders had a hard time preserving cultural values. Carter Brown, the outstanding director of the National Gallery in Washington, for instance, told me that he had been asked to make a speech about whether art still existed. He said he was embarrassed because he was not sure whether permanent values still existed: everything seemed transitory. He blamed the news media, and with reason, for giving exaggerated attention to the unusual, the trendy, the freaky, the extreme. He mentioned that the National Gallery was currently looking for a curator of twentieth-century art, but that he had great difficulty deciding who understood it and could winnow out the lasting values. It was not easy, for instance, to determine who had left a greater impact, the student radicals or Andy Warhol, and how enduring the impact would be. "The French invented the word 'chic,' " he said, "and that is what seems to matter these days. This faddishness extends not only to the arts but also to politics. The pace of change has thus enormously accelerated and the changes that have taken place in the last ten years are far greater than in any equivalent ten years."

When at last I was led into the Oval Room for my interview with Nixon, it was as quiet as the corridors I had just walked along, past two immobile secret servicemen who leaned listlessly against the wall. The president, as soon as I entered the inner sanctum, dismissed an aide he had been talking to and motioned me to walk over to the open fireplace at the other end of the room, and there pushed the two yellow-upholstered wing chairs into a position that would make us almost face each other. After we had settled down in our chairs, he asked me whether I wanted coffee or tea and when I replied tea, he said that he would join me since he had already had too much coffee to drink that morning during a National Security Council meeting. He then reminded me that the last time we had seen each other was when I taped my interview with him during the election campaign in 1959. I congratulated him on his unusual memory and recalled my embarrassment at the editor's request to have myself photographed with the two candidates for promotional purposes. At that moment, as if until then he had forgotten, he pressed a button under the table and a photographer entered immediately. The photo session was over in a few seconds. It was not the endless picture-taking feast that every interviewer experienced with President Johnson, whose photographer stayed on for most of the interview snapping pictures from every possible angle.

As if he wanted to describe the changes he personally had gone through since the Eisenhower days, Nixon said that an individual was now needed who could see the world as it was and keep an open mind. He should have a basic idealistic concept but not go overboard, as Americans sometimes foolishly did in times of peace, believing that everything could be solved at the conference table or by the United Nations. What was needed was a sense of history, an enormous capacity to keep up-to-date without getting bogged down by ir- relevancies, and a clear concept of priorities.

"Wilson was an idealist," he said, "but the world today needs more the idealism of a Teddy Roosevelt. When Kennedy spoke in his Inaugural about virtually unlimited American world involvement, it appealed to me. But that is no longer possible. Americans would no longer support it. We welcomed a world role, all we had to think about was how to keep stronger than our monolithic opponent. Today we are facing a new isolationism. Americans are getting disillusioned with their world role, they are more interested in their domestic problems. The Nixon doctrine I spoke about on Guam, which al- located American backing to those willing to defend themselves, was a method to stay in the world and play our part at a time when American power was in decline. There are no ideas today such as 'Manifest Destiny' or 'Self- determination,' which once upon a time aroused so much enthusiasm. Nothing has taken their place. The old isolationism was totally selfish, the new one is that we don't have any higher goals anymore, because we turn our isolationism inward."

Nixon looked remarkably relaxed, and at ease with himself as I had never seen him before. Although he made it clear that he believed he stood at a historic crossroad, he created the impression of feeling that he was, so to say, on top of the world, that he was in control of the situation. However reassuring his words, however acute his analysis (with which I agreed), his refusal to look one straight in the eye was disturbing to me. He either looked straight ahead of himself or at my lapel. Talking about the Russians and the Chinese, he suggested that they too might be turning inward, although their expansionism was still in evidence, and that even though Marxism was becoming more mature and less adventurous, it was essential to maintain areas of strength in the world into which revolutionary forces could not move with impunity.

Then he spoke of his two most anguished moments: the decision to deliver his November 3, 1969, speech on Vietnam, and the Cambodian invasion. He said that he had been given all the reasons for not doing it, and they were persuasive, but he concluded nevertheless that if the United States did not fight in Cambodia, it would be worse off than the public outcry that would follow the attack. "You listen to everybody's advice, but then comes the moment of truth when you have to make your own decisions. Then I sit alone with my yellow pad and write down on one side of it the reasons for doing and on the other for not doing it. I remained secluded at Camp David for two days, weighing the odds with very little sleep. President Johnson was basically a strong man, only too emotional, and the worst decisions are made in an emotional state of mind."

Then he outlined what he considered his own rules of behavior: "A president must be cool, unflappable, mature, and with a feeling for what the nation needs. Can the United States, after two frustrating wars in Korea and Vietnam, grow up and provide mature leadership? That is the real question."

There seemed to be indeed a "new" Nixon, more the statesman than the politician. His eyes, though, looked as cold as ever, often shooting cruel flashes. He had virtually no eyelashes and under his eyelids there was a redness that betrayed fatigue. I also had the feeling throughout the interview that here was a man who constantly tried to observe himself, how he was doing and how he sounded. At 5:10 P.M. his secretary came in to say that Secretary of State Rogers was waiting.

Nixon, as we got up, asked me about my book and what I conceived it to be. I replied that I planned it as an assessment of how he redesigned American foreign policy to fit the new balance of forces in the world. Then, using the opportunity, I asked whether he would give Dr. Kissinger a free hand in providing me with a good insight into the policymaking processes of the Nixon administration. He sat down again, pressed a button on a telephone that was attached to his chair, and I heard him say: "Henry, I promised the other Henry I have in my office now that we would fully cooperate in helping him with his book." I felt reassured that Henry now had the president's authorization to do what he had promised me. In the following months he did indeed live up to his promise and gave instructions to his staff to fill in the details. It was at times quite difficult to get the kind of detached perspective that I wanted to give my book because in so many cases there was nobody with whom to countercheck Henry's accounts. Henry, after all, kept so much to himself or to his innermost circle of advisers. I got up at four or five o'clock every morning to write, then breakfasted with Muffie, and during the day gathered material for *The Sunday Times* reports or for the book. It was an exhausting exercise, very much against the advice Walter Lippmann gave me, who said that one should never try to write a book and at the same time continue in one's regular job. (He spoke from experience, for after he wrote his *Public Philosophy,* while continuing his column, he suffered a nervous breakdown that confined him to the Lahey Clinic for about three weeks.) Muffie realized how much this book meant to me and was totally and affectionately sympathetic and supportive and so were my three stepchildren, John, Elizabeth, and Alexandra; Fiona, my own, was still a baby. It took me eighteen months to research and write the book and when I told Henry that I was considering calling it *The Retreat of American Power,* he thought it a very apt title.

Nixon's and Kissinger's star skyrocketed under what I called their "bombshell diplomacy." After the stunning surprise of the opening to Beijing, the president launched something even more spectacular—secret peace negotiations with the North Vietnamese, pulled out of his hat with the flourish of a magician's wand. Kissinger's eighteenth-century, very personal, very conspiratorial approach to diplomacy, combined with Nixon's dramatic, McLuhanesque, electronic style gave one a sort of surrealistic vision of twenty-first-century diplomacy. Only a man like Kissinger, willing to dispense with the collective wisdom of the bureaucracy and vested with extraordinary presidential authority, could have pulled off such a surprise. It all so brilliantly contradicted what British Ambassador Sir Oliver Wright once told me, that "the role of a journalist was to make boring things exciting, while the role of the diplomat was to make exciting things boring."

Kissinger with his National Security Council created a new power center not accountable to anyone but the president. It disturbed political Washington, the allies and foes, but to the broader-minded, who chose good theater over bureaucratic tradition, Kissinger became something of a Scarlet Pimpernel. For a long time he defied an old Washington dictum that you can have either visibility or influence, but you can't have both. Washington worships virtuosos but it strangles them with attention and blinds them with limelight. If the virtuoso is also powerful, he is as much admired as feared, as much lionized as berated. Kissinger mitigated his dramatic lurches into self-promotion by self-deprecation. When asked whether he was planning to resign, for instance, as he was at a Press Club dinner, he replied that he would not announce it before such a small audience, for, after all, there were twenty thousand people in the State Department alone who wanted to be there for that occasion.

Considering the continued opposition to the Vietnam war, Nixon and Kissinger did remarkably well in the public opinion polls and in January 1973 *Time* magazine chose the two as its Men of the Year. But the star that rose so rapidly did not take long to fall. The slowness with which Nixon at first developed his Vietnam policies, then the secret bombing, and later the invasion of Cambodia, stirred up the news media, the young, and members of Kissinger's own staff. I remember my horror watching federal marshals storming Howard University on May 8, 1969, when some thirty other university campuses were aflame with antiwar passions; then a year later the antiwar rebellion exploded anew and four students were killed in Ohio in a clash with national guardsmen who had fired live bullets. Kissinger's confrontations with the press became very unruly and he began to be steeped in gloom when several of his staff, in protest against the Cambodian "incursions," as they were officially called, threatened to resign, and their wives held vigil with candles in their hands in front of the White House. Nixon, rattled by the rising tide of protest, one day at dawn, accompanied only by his valet, drove to the Lincoln Memorial to give a group of young students a crude lecture about patriotism and to remind them of Chamberlain and Churchill and the difference between appeasement and resistance to it.

In the midst of all this Bert Neustadt, the kind and caring wife of Professor Richard Neustadt, had the idea of a triple birthday party. Bert herself, Pat Moynihan, and I had our birthday all in the same week. Pat by then had withdrawn after serving for almost two years as urban affairs adviser to Nixon. As a Democrat and a liberal, he exerted a remarkable influence on domestic policymaking. He authored the Family Assistance Plan, a new National Health Plan and more, but when Nixon lost interest in an innovative domestic program and concentrated on his passion, foreign policy, Moynihan returned to teaching at Harvard. About a year earlier I had had a most startling interview with him, just after he had been appointed counselor to the president, a title he knew had no meaning because his entire staff had been transferred to what became the Domestic Council, chaired by John Ehrlichman, who had no experience in this field. Moynihan had ripped his white telephone out of the wall. "Telephones are the symbol of power here," he told me in his slight charming stammer, his blue, watery eyes bulging and his red cheeks getting redder, "I traipsed into Ehrlichman's office this morning and presented him formally and ceremoniously with this f——— telephone. I did not have to say anything, he knew what I meant. And that was that."

The other birthday guests were William Bundy, who with his wife had moved to Harvard to recuperate from the draining years he had spent in Washington; Jerome Cohen, who headed Harvard's department of Asian Law, and his wife, Joan, who had been my neighbors in Washington when he worked as a clerk at the Supreme Court; Francis Bator, who was back teaching economics after five years in the Johnson White House; and Paul Doty, who specialized in arms control studies. Henry Kissinger, too, flew up to Cambridge from Washington for the occasion.

His presence engendered some good-natured teasing and discussion of some of the problems he had to grapple with at the White House, from the unpleasantnesses of dealing with Nixon's palace guard to the pressures from Zionist quarters, which he insisted would not affect his decisions, possibly even have the opposite effect. This gave way before a desire on everybody's part to make him feel at home among his old chums in his old academic surroundings and amid hints that bygones were bygones. Henry appreciated this reunion because he still cared what they were thinking in Cambridge about him. Still, I had a feeling that he did not feel at ease anymore in these academic surroundings; they were the past now. Life at Cambridge suddenly looked narrow and provincial and removed from reality. He was now steeped in the game of world politics.

When the debate began to get divisive, especially discussing arms for Israel

—we avoided talk about Vietnam—Bert, to keep the birthday party spirit alive, proposed a game of charades. Everybody heartily approved and we began making preparations and dividing into teams—except Henry, who said he was sorry but he never played charades. To help change his mind I recalled that I had read in a charming memoir of Paris high-society life how Prince Metternich arranged a charade party at the emperor's chateau near Paris. The memoir was written in the form of letters by an American-born wife of a French aristocrat to her mother in Philadelphia (*In the Court of Memory, 1858–1875* by L. De Hegerman-Lindencrone, Harper & Bros., 1912). In one of the letters she described how Metternich had equipped himself with such prerequisites as "an oil-can, a feather duster, a watchman's rattle and enough wax, paint and powder to have made up the features of the whole Comédie Française." But Metternich's penchant for charades was not Henry's style, and when we decided to go ahead, he decided to leave.

With the opening of China, the next equally important aim was the establishment of a new relationship with the Soviet Union, which was bound to take time and to engender a great deal of domestic political stress. Nixon's order went to Kissinger, because Secretary of State William P. Rogers, though an old friend of Nixon's and a decent, courteous, experienced lawyer, had no experience in foreign affairs. His task seemed to be to keep the State Department at bay, while the president and Henry went about making foreign policy.

What greatly aided Kissinger in developing the rapprochement with the Soviets was the presence of Anatoly Dobrynin, the Soviet ambassador, an impressive man, well above the usual standards of Soviet diplomats. He was intelligent, knowledgeable, and well-mannered, and he seemed to have a direct line to the Politburo. He also belonged to that team of Soviet officials who favored détente with the United States and hence was considered by Kissinger a man who would want to play a positive role in this rapprochement. And so he became what Kissinger called the "back-channel," which allowed both to bypass the State Department and carry on under direct control and firm instructions from the president.

The first time I met Dobrynin was when he was only a minister counselor at the embassy in 1952. It happened at the annual party of the October Revolution, a kind of catch-all for diplomats and the press. He approached me with a smile and a teasing question whether I would dare to have lunch with him. I hesitated. It was at the height of the McCarthy witch-hunt—not the most propitious time to be seen lunching with a Soviet diplomat. At the same time I did not want to admit to being afraid to be seen with him. Nobody who has not lived through that period will appreciate how difficult my decision was. In the end, I summoned enough courage and said yes, expecting to leave the actual meeting for the indefinite future. But Dobrynin lost no time in following up by asking when and where we should meet. Pinned down, I had no alternative but to commit myself. I suggested the Sheraton-Carlton Hotel, which in those days was the fashionable place to take high officials out to lunch, and Dobrynin readily agreed. Dobrynin proved a good conversationalist and, professionally, the occasion was not a total loss for he offered some hints about the Soviets' Berlin policy, which was then of considerable interest.

After three years in Washington, Dobrynin returned to Moscow and five years later, after a stint in the United Nations Secretariat, was appointed ambassador to the United States in 1962, a post he held for twenty-four years until March 1986, when he was named to the Central Committee Secretariat and shortly after that was made a kind of national security adviser to General Secretary Mikhail Gorbachev. He had the appearance of a benevolent professor, but in the clinches I was told he could be as tough as any of his predecessors. He was known, when put on the spot, to resort to what Elliot Richardson, the undersecretary of state under Kissinger called, the "squid trick," a protective retreat behind a cloud of impenetrable generalities of flanneled inconsequences.

The one time I got a glimpse of the human being behind those bland-looking eyes was in January 1970 at a dinner party for the ambassador at the Stewart Udalls' house (he had been secretary of the interior in the Kennedy administration). I had just come out of hospital after a hernia operation, but I did not want to miss the party and since I felt well enough, I went. The other guests were the Averell Harrimans and Scotty Reston of the *New York Times* and his wife, Sally. The presence of the Udall children gave the occasion a particularly informal ambience.

Perhaps to show that Russians and Americans shared problems that were not all geopolitical, Dobrynin talked with surprising candor about the trouble he had with his daughter because she refused to see the world as he saw it. His outlook had been formed by the experience of World War II, by the hardships he suffered when all he got was one pound of bread a month and hot water instead of tea. Therefore he could appreciate what had been achieved. However his daughter did not understand his reaction to the war; it was remote to her thinking because she had grown up in a society without serious hardships. Then Udall's son spoke up, saying that the society in which his parents grew up had its good side, but he and his generation could not but reject most of it; there was a need for new ideas to cope with what his generation rejected. However deep the ideological differences, there was clearly a similarity in attitudes of the new generation in both countries.

Time and again Dobrynin had asked the young what it was that their generation wanted from the older generation because it was so difficult to understand what they were aiming at and why they rejected so much of what they saw when it was so much better than what the older generation had to put up with. Nobody in Russia would want to fight another war, he argued, and if Russia tried to fight a war far away from her frontiers as the United States was doing in Vietnam, they would be against it too. This meant that the USSR would fight a war only if attacked. Nobody mentioned what had happened in Czechoslovakia two years earlier. The Afghanistan war was still ten years away.

Dobrynin looked a little uneasy when Tom Udall's girl friend suggested that the young in the United States no longer saw the world in terms of national boundaries—it had become too small for narrow nationalism; if nationalism died away, she said, the world would be much more peaceful. It was Mrs. Dobrynin who interjected at this point, and like a reproachful teacher—and her reproach seemed aimed at her husband—said that in Russia the young didn't want anything different from the older generation, except that they wanted it faster and better. Then I asked Dobrynin whether, looking at American youth, its rebellion against the established institutions and many of the old ingrained traditions of this country, and comparing it with the stolid, unchanging situation in the Soviet Union, would he agree that the United States was a more revolutionary country than the Soviet Union? He replied that whatever was going on in the United States, it was very hard to apply the word "revolution" to it: to a Russian, he said, the word "revolution" meant the complete overthrow of government and of the political system. The changes in America were merely on the surface, and temporary. In my view he was only half right.

Lee Udall, one of the daughters, asked why some of the great Soviet writers and artists were treated like outcasts in the Soviet Union. Instantly the tone of our conversation changed and the two Dobrynins reached for the party line like a life raft. Both argued that Solzhenitsyn had been built up by the Western press as a great writer when there were far better ones in the Soviet Union. Only in the West, Mrs. Dobrynin argued, were writers popular who concentrated on the negative aspects of life. The important thing was for writers to stress the positive and to give moral encouragement. Later, as we drove home —the Harrimans gave me a lift—Averell commented that there were subjects where even the Dobrynins could not deviate from the official line; nevertheless he was the most "civilized Bolshevik" he had ever known.

Dobrynin was independent enough to give me on one occasion an on-the-record interview—rare in those days for a Soviet diplomat. His most critical time in Washington was the Cuban missile crisis, he said. Robert Kennedy, in his book *Thirteen Days,* recalled how Dobrynin reassured him about a week before President Kennedy imposed the quarantine on Soviet ships to Cuba that Chairman Khrushchev would not want to embarrass the president, and that something like placing ground-to-ground missiles in Cuba "would never happen." This proved false, but it did not damage Dobrynin's standing with the Kennedys because they were convinced that he had not known in advance of the missile plot. But they were equally convinced that Gromyko had lied when he claimed ignorance.

Commenting to me on Robert Kennedy's book, Dobrynin's voice had a sarcastic edge: "The United States did not behave as bravely as the attorney general described it," he said. "Both sides were afraid that the other would do something dangerous, but both had enough nerve and courage to be just reasonable enough." Then, by implication, he admitted that the Soviets were somewhat more afraid: "We didn't boast that these qualities were evenly distributed between the two, but the Americans promised us something in return for the withdrawal of the missiles from Cuba." Kennedy wrote that Dobrynin had "raised the question of our removing the [United States] missiles from Turkey. I said that there could be no quid pro quo, or any arrangement made under this kind of threat and pressure. . . . However, I said, President Kennedy had been anxious to remove those missiles from Turkey and Italy for a long period of time . . . and that, within a short time after this crisis was over, those missiles would be gone." This was new to the Kremlin and hence, as Dobrynin said, considerably helped to influence Khrushchev's decisions. It was also true that the United States gave a pledge against a future military invasion of Cuba. Asked whether in retrospect he thought Soviet-American relations had been best under the Kennedy administration, Dobrynin said that Kennedy became very popular in the Soviet Union but only after his American University speech, charting the future of Soviet-American relations, in which "he was wise enough to accept the existing realities and pointed the way how these relations should develop. That speech from our point of view was a basic change in the American position, which used to be based on the principle of negotiating only from strength. Furthermore, his death evoked deep sympathies and a feeling of the loss of a man after he had made a good start on a new trail." Soviet-American relations, he concluded, were best under Nixon.

When I tried to give Robert McNamara some credit for having alerted the Soviets to the need for arms control at the Glassboro summit between Prime Minister Kosygin and President Johnson, he disagreed. "What played against McNamara," he said, "was that he was considered a military man who discussed a political subject." Since then of course there has been ample evidence that the Soviet military have played an important political role, although there are some indications under Gorbachev that their position in the Politburo has been downgraded.

The test of a good leader, Dobrynin said, was whether he knew the limits of his powers and when to impose them. He credited Kennedy, Johnson, Nixon with that sense. Talking about diplomacy, he regretted that he did not live in the sixteenth century when ambassadors might have to travel thousands of miles to get to their destination in horsedrawn carriages and thus, because of the distance and slowness of communications, themselves shaped policy. Today an ambassador was at the end of a telephone and had to "tell it as he is told." Then he added with a twinkle: "Of course, there are different ways of telling the same thing!"

This remark reminds me of a dinner a few reporters gave one evening for Henry Kissinger in Key Biscayne. Talking about diplomacy, he mentioned Prince Metternich's view that there had to be a strict relationship between negotiations and military moves—something he had to disregard in his negotiations with the North Vietnamese because he was seeking to attain a settlement while the United States was withdrawing its forces. Nor had it been easy in Metternich's own day, because the problems of communication made it necessary not only to give broad instructions, but to explain the reasons for them so as to allow for sufficient flexibility in the absence of further continuous instructions. Nowadays, Henry argued, one could restrict oneself to giving just instructions, without accompanying them with the reasons that inspired them. It didn't affect the negotiations, only the ability of modern historians to write history: "1870 was about the last time," he said, "that history could be written with a complete picture of all the reasoning behind each move." Perhaps with an early eye to his royalties, he added that only he and the president could write an accurate book. One of Henry's favorite remarks was that "every historian is exposed to the interpretations of different generations, and to his own prejudices."

I had already gone to bed on May 10, 1973, when, at about 10 P.M., the telephone rang. Larry Stern, one of the Washington *Post*'s star reporters, was on the other end of the line to tell me that he was writing for next morning's paper a story about a group of reporters and White House aides whose telephones had been wiretapped by J. Edgar Hoover from May 1969 to February 1971 on orders from the White House, and that I was among them, with William Beecher and Hendrick Smith of the *New York Times* and Marvin Kalb of the Columbia Broadcasting network. Did I want to comment? I replied, rather sleepily, that the story did not make much sense to me and that I preferred to wait with my comment until I had seen the story.

The *New York Times* carried a similar story the next morning and guessed that the taps followed so-called unauthorized disclosures about the SALT talks; when they called me to ask whether I had about the same time had a scoop about the SALT talks, it led me to assume that one of my SALT stories could have been the reason for my being included in this august company. The reason that some White House aides had been included, I assumed, was that they were under suspicion of having "leaked" the stuff.

Actually it was *Time* magazine that had the first report about the wiretaps authorized by John Mitchell, the attorney general, saying that they included telephones of White House staffers. The report was based on a tip Hays Gorey of *Time*'s Washington bureau got from a former White House aide, who in discussing Nixon said at one point that he was capable of doing anything. Then he added: "Any guy who can wiretap his own brother's telephones . . ."; then he broke off and clammed up. Gorey tried to prod him to tell him more, but he refused, saying that he had already said too much. He encouraged Gorey, though, to check it out. *Time* editors then sent Sandy Smith to follow the scent, as he had the best sources at the FBI. But they claimed ignorance. Then, at the 1972 Republican Convention in Miami Beach, Smith learned that there had indeed been a wiretap on Nixon's brother Donald, on some White House aides, and on a few reporters. From another source he then heard that a few men in the FBI, just below the Hoover level, were so disgusted with that operation that they had begun dropping hints to a few reporters, including the names of the wiretapped. Kissinger, reportedly, had ordered the wiretaps on his aides, allegedly to protect them against those who claimed they were security risks. Others gave the accusations a different spin. They suspected Henry of wanting to find out who among his aides was leaking. An Associated Press reporter suggested that since Kissinger himself was the biggest leaker among them all, he wanted to find out whether those independent leakers on his staff were disloyal to him. Another option among the many was that the Nixon palace guard and the Department of Justice were out to investigate Kissinger, whom they distrusted, to find reasons for incriminating him. It all sounded farfetched, more the stuff of farce than of anything else. And yet in a Nixon administration, anything was coming to seem possible.

As to the tap on my own telephone, Hoover must have known that Henry spent weekends at our house and that the president called him there two or three times during a day. When that happened, I was amused seeing him sitting at our telephone in the kitchen (out of earshot, I'd better add, and with no tapes running—except Hoover's) discussing high-wire diplomacy with the president. I could easily imagine J. Edgar hitting the ceiling when told about these discussions from an unprotected telephone—which on top of all belonged to a foreigner! And so I went on speculating until I read that Mort Halperin, a member of the National Security Council staff until September 1971 and an occasional luncheon companion of mine, was indeed one of those wiretapped. Had my calls into his private telephone aroused the FBI's interest in me? I was then working on a book about the Vietnam war and he was one of many who helped me in reconstructing its history.

William D. Ruckelshaus, the deputy attorney general and acting director of the FBI, was first to disclose publicly that Kissinger, at a meeting with FBI Director Hoover, had requested the wiretaps. Kissinger immediately denied that he had ordered the phones of the four newsmen tapped. The same day I had a call from an American columnist with especially good connections in the Department of Justice, warning me that Kissinger was lying.

The next morning on May 24 therefore I called Henry and asked to see him right away. He said that if I needed to see him for a review of foreign policy, he could not because he had a very full day, but if it was for personal reasons, he was "honor bound" to see me immediately. I said that it was for personal reasons and he gave me an appointment for half an hour later. When I arrived at his office in the White House his aide told me that a minute earlier Dr. Kissinger had been called to the president's office and that thereafter he would have to attend a cabinet meeting, but he would inquire whether I should wait.

Five minutes later Henry received me saying that, alas, he had only ten minutes, but he wanted to know what troubled me. He looked glum, his jowls were drooping more than usually, and his body was hunched heavily in his chair. I told him immediately that I had come to find out from him, personally, whether he had a hand in the tapping of my telephone since a colleague had hinted that he did have something to do with it. He assured me that he had not, and urged me to trust his assurances. He went on to say that it was his belief that it was more against him than against me, for, after all, it would not make sense for him to want to listen to my telephone when he saw me so frequently anyway. He said he trusted me completely and that whenever he showed me documents, it was with the permission of the president. I expressed my surprise that somebody mistrusted me in the administration and yet the president had been prepared to give me an interview—how could this be? Henry replied that by then the tap had been removed—which, on checking, I found was correct. When I asked him why, as a friend, he did not raise objections to my tap, he said that in those early days—four months after he became national security adviser—he did not have the power he acquired later, that he was then only an "option man." When we parted he said with a deep sigh, "I'm buffeted between the brutality of the conservatives and the perfectionism of the liberals."

Nancy, by then Henry's wife, was particularly upset by all the suspicions that swirled around his head and wanted him to resign because, she said to me, he had lost his power and influence, and his own people were trying to hurt him. She also reassured Muffie that she had asked him point-blank and Henry had sworn to her that he had nothing to do with the tap on our house.

I hated all the publicity and the calls from colleagues that followed. They gave me a taste of what it was like when investigative reporters went on the warpath. But there was comfort in the letters I received from fellow reporters and friends. Russell Baker, the witty *New York Times* columnist, wrote that to have been included among the seventeen tapped was "better than a Pulitzer Prize," Larry Stern of the Washington *Post* wrote: "Why do you get all the good breaks!?" David Anderson of the London *Sunday Telegraph* said he expected his editor to send him a query any moment saying: "Why your phone unbugged?" And so it went. Then on May 28, the *New York Times* carried a long story about the party Nelson Rockefeller had given Henry Kissinger for his fiftieth birthday at his spectacular country estate, Pocantico Hills, overlooking the Hudson River. It had been "attended by some eighty friends, including at least three couples whose telephones had been bugged." It mentioned me and quoted Muffie, in reply to a question from a reporter why we attended when Kissinger bugged our telephone, saying: "Henry had denied that he had anything to do with bugging our telephone. We've chosen to believe him . . ." We both had agreed, on discussing whether to attend, that if Henry as a friend assured us of having had nothing to do with the wiretap, we in turn were "honor bound" to believe him. Rockefeller, as the party reached its climax, made quite a moving toast, which ended with a line that brought the house down: "Henry worked with me in three election campaigns and it was he who ended up in the White House." Henry, in reply, made a serious speech about the anguish caused by the Vietnamese war, his hopes that its end would bring national reconciliation, a hope he now thought was dashed by Watergate. He ended with the prediction that the differences which now tormented Americans would pass and that "peace within ourselves, peace at home" would come soon. It took much longer, as we now know, than he had expected.

Question marks still hung over the wiretap affair. What were the reasons for this vile invasion of privacy? Was it legal? Was there anything I should do? I began to contact friends in the administration in the hope of separating truth from rumors and to satisfy myself whom to believe. It also underlined how important it was in my profession to have an absolutely clear conscience.

William D. Ruckelshaus, who was as independent-minded as anybody I knew in government and a man of high integrity, after he had resigned from government, said to me in answer to my questions: "Henry, you must take into consideration that the FBI reads its record literally: it says to itself that if it's on our record, it is the truth." Later, the former Attorney General Elliot Richardson, who proved that he could fill virtually any job in government, assured me that Kissinger had nothing to do with my wiretap, that I had been, in FBI parlance, an intercept. Because I called into the tapped telephone of Morton Halperin of the National Security Council, I became a suspect. Furthermore, he explained, I had been a kind of "mystery man" to Hoover. First of all, Hoover was suspicious of most foreigners. Next, I had been stationed in the United States an unusually long time, over twenty years. Then, as it was put in an FBI summary I saw later, I had "many high level and other sensitive contacts," and though British, had been born in Czechoslovakia. A Hoover memo specially mentioned some of my "sensitive contacts" with such *dangerous* men as Clark Clifford, Robert McNamara, Dean Rusk, Helmut Sonnenfeldt, etc. Hoover, said Richardson, was always able to convince himself of a notion even if he did not have the facts to back up his suspicions. He apparently suspected that I might be "a member of the intelligence service of a friendly nation, whose service may have been penetrated by an unfriendly nation." I never had, of course, any connection with British intelligence, a connection which in my book of principles is incompatible with the journalistic profession. If I can find some lame excuses for my background to have set Mr. Hoover's imagination spinning, it was even more surprising that he suspected Marvin Kalb, the well-known television reporter, of working for the Romanian Intelligence Service!

Richardson told me that Hoover's mentality appealed to Nixon because he, together with some of the men who surrounded him, believed that politics was like a four-ball billiard game: you can play against any edge, even with a warped table. I asked him whether Kissinger could have prevented the tap on my telephone. Richardson, who has a habit of speaking in slow cadences, weighing every word as it rolls off his tongue, thought for a while, then he said firmly: "No. Henry at the time was still testing his influence against that of Secretary of State Rogers and was well aware that neither Haldeman nor

Ehrlichman considered him someone they could trust. Moreover, he would have had to confront Hoover, who probably welcomed the opportunity of bugging the Brandon telephone. Since even presidents hesitated to take on Hoover, why should Kissinger have taken on the most feared nonelected official in Washington, who did not trust him either?" In 1973 testimony to the Senate Foreign Relations Committee, before he was confirmed as secretary of state, Henry, in discussing the thirteen wiretaps on members of his National Security Council and the four newspapermen, told the committee that of all the members of the press corps I was the one he knew best, that he was a personal friend of mine, had visited our house often, and that certainly any wiretap on my telephone would have included records of our frequent telephone conversations; yet, he said, the FBI never sent him a summary of those.

Kissinger's testimony, given partially in executive session, not only threw light on the weird and tortured minds of the men in the Nixon White House, but also on Hoover's. "The conversation I remember with Mr. Hoover," he testified, "involved his description of a hostile world that surrounded us and of his special qualities to save us from that hostility . . . I also fitted into some of those categories he considered invidious. In one letter he referred to a Kennedy-type Harvard professor." Then, referring to his own sense of insecurity, Kissinger went on: "Hoover was rather suspicious of me and therefore in my conversations with him, I might have had a tendency to show that I was alert to the dangers of security, particularly considering his political power in Washington." General Alexander Haig, whose telephone was tapped too, excused the tappers by admitting that he and Kissinger "were suspect because of the character of the staff we had put together. I feel quite frankly that part of Henry's own mental comfort with these proceedings [wiretappings] was an effort to vindicate those men and to assure those who had suspicions."

It was obviously an administration in which nobody trusted anybody. Nixon, because he insulated himself from what was going on in the White House and left its administration to Haldeman, not only remained remote but further aroused suspicions that were based on ignorance as to what the palace guard was up to. In the middle of it all was the supreme survivor, J. Edgar Hoover, who was the only one who thrived in a world of distrust. He managed to stay on so long in his job, as Clark Clifford once explained to me, by collecting the kind of information about politicians in his private files he could use for quiet blackmail—morsels about the hidden love lives of politicians, their visits to certain "fancy houses" whose madams were on his payroll and dutifully reported to him those tidbits that no politician ever wanted to see the light of day. Even a man as clean-living as Truman, Clifford recalled, kept him on to avoid a political storm by the Hoover claque, but he too gradually developed an appetite for Hoover's little alley-cat stories, as did earlier and later presidents. Among Hoover's private treasures were memos about the sexual exploits of men like John F. Kennedy as naval officer, senator, and president and Lyndon B. Johnson as senator and president, and when the two extended his term in office their informed assumption was that he possessed embarrassing private files about them. As Johnson once put it privately in his immortal phrase: "I'd rather have him inside the tent pissing out than outside pissing in."

I never met Hoover personally, but his aides told me that one of his great ambitions was to give the FBI the same sort of world fame Scotland Yard had established for itself. He succeeded in this, for his G-men became famous in the 1930s and 1940s for hunting down gangsters, Communists, and Communist spies. He carefully avoided taking on the Mafia, as later Robert Kennedy insisted he should do, because he was said to be afraid they would bribe his agents and thus corrupt the FBI.

According to Richard Helms, the former CIA director, Hoover played the power game better than anybody in Washington. He kept all the vital reins, contacts with the White House and individual departments, in his own hands. When Hoover, after having been taboo for so long, came under heavy fire from liberal and conservative critics, President Nixon defended him. It was not until William Ruckelshaus blamed Congress for permitting "too much unchecked power to accumulate in Hoover's hand" and Attorney General Edward Levi, under President Ford, explained the dangers of the Hoover dictatorship, that a law was passed limiting the tenure of the FBI director to ten years. And it was not until William Webster, who brought the experience of a judge to the job, that the FBI once again acquired a good name.

According to Kissinger's memoirs, it was Hoover who, when asked by Nixon and him how best to stop "press leaks of military operations that were needlessly jeopardizing American lives," recommended wiretaps as the best method for detecting the leakers. He added reassuringly that wiretaps had been widely used for these and other much less justified purposes by preceding administrations. "When the Attorney General Mitchell affirmed their legality," Kissinger wrote, "the President ordered them carried out . . . seventeen wiretaps were established by the FBI on thirteen officials and four newsmen, lasting in some cases only a few weeks and in others several months. (My office was not aware of all of them.) Contrary to malicious lore, senior officials did not spend time pruriently reading over lengthy transcripts of personal conversations. What was received were brief summaries (usually about a page in length) of what the FBI considered discussions of sensitive military and foreign policy matters . . ."

The first of the seventeen to be tapped was Morton Halperin. His tap was installed on May 12, 1969. On May 27, 1969, I telephoned into Halperin's home phone and asked him, as reported to the White House, whether he could track down for me a memo written in 1961 by Dean Rusk, the secretary of state, warning Kennedy of the possible consequences of stepping up the number of advisers in South Vietnam, a memo Rusk is rather proud of today. My interest in it was for my history of the Vietnam war.

Two days later I was caught in the spider web taps and our telephone became the toy of faceless eavesdroppers until February 1971. But it was not until May 1973 that I learned about it. The summaries of my telephone conversations included references to discussions with State Department officials, Democratic former cabinet officers, a CIA official, other newsmen, a Supreme Court justice, a telephone call from the press attaché of the Soviet embassy inviting me to meet with visiting Soviet editors, and so on.

The president must have felt comforted by an FBI summary of October 24, 1969—it was also sent to Kissinger—in which I am quoted as having said to Halperin after a visit to Europe that "in Europe people are beginning to feel sorry for the President and his Vietnam problem. They feel that he is trying to do the right thing, but that he won't be able to because of public pressure. Brandon said that the right thing to do was to get out of Vietnam at a certain pace but not too fast because if you cede under public pressure, you will lose control which is bad for the President's prestige . . . etc."

Kissinger underrated the gossipy inclinations of the eavesdroppers, when he stated that the summaries did not include personal matters, for a report sent to the president, for instance, "reflected on a conversation with a divorced woman in whom he [Brandon] had a romantic interest" and that I had made "arrangements to meet her in another State . . ." (This was Muffie, who later became my wife.) There were other mentions about such personal intimacies, but one should be enough to convey the intrusiveness into one's private life and the feeling of nakedness that I felt on reading these summaries. Courtland Jones, who edited the telephone logs that were sent to him by the men who actually listened in to our conversations by day and night, was not a political functionary. He claimed that he deleted some reports involving gossip by and about very personal political friends because, he said, he knew what people in the White House would do with such material; after all the White House had hired Tony Ulasewicz, the New York policeman, to dig up dirt on Senator Edward Kennedy. I was also told that his eavesdroppers were under instructions to take down verbatim any mention of Averell Harriman and Clark Clifford, both friends of mine, both among the best and most patriotic among American public servants. I then remembered that in the early sixties an FBI man had come to my house to ask me whether I considered Mr. Harriman a reliable enough man for the job he was about to be appointed to. I told him that the question was preposterous since Harriman was one of the greatest among living Americans who had already served his government in more sensitive jobs than most. The embarrassed FBI man apologized, explaining that his was simply a "routine check," yet he took down every word of my glowing view of a man I greatly admired.

The most ridiculous among wiretaps was that on William Safire, then one of Nixon's speech writers. He became an intercept because he was included in the "chain" after discussing with me, according to a memo of October 1969, a speech about welfare reform to be given by the president the following Saturday. Later Bill (by this time one of the most straight-shooting among newspaper columnists) told me that he had actually been under instructions from the president to give reporters some advance information about the speech to generate interest in it. But in the bureaucratic sewers he became an intercept's intercept.

I had always assumed that my telephone might be routinely tapped once or twice a year, but I was really outraged when I learned that mine lasted for twenty-one months. When I asked Attorney General Edward B. Levi in the Ford administration what might have caused the spigot on my tap to be kept open for that long, he reminded me that I should not underrate the lethargy of bureaucratic procedures. Nixon, he speculated, probably forgot about it and Hoover was not likely to remind him of it, especially since so many politically important people called in to us. The reason that it was taken off in February 1971, he suspected, was because March was the time when Hoover used to submit his budget request to Congress (Halperin's lasted the same length of time, although he had long become a private citizen) and Hoover liked to impress the legislators with the low number of wiretaps he was using.

When my editor asked me to tell our readers what it was like being wiretapped, I made light of it all and described the sort of sympathy we developed for those invisible eavesdroppers who learned about our fourteen-year-old's Latin homework, about insurrection music by James Taylor, his favored pop musician, the tragedies that befell the rabbit owned by our eight-year-old. I also wondered what they made of my wife's conversations about such highly suspect electronic devices as vacuum cleaners, ovens, etc. Code words? Little did we know at that time that my wife's fury and my indignation at being wiretapped were justified not only on ground of violation of our privacy, but also, as we learned much later from Seymour Hersh's book *The Price of Power,* because the FBI whetted official appetites for gossip by sending transcripts of her conversations with her friend Joan Kennedy, then Senator Edward Kennedy's wife, to the White House.

Kissinger did not in any way curtail our social or professional relationship and, as he later told me, maintained them as further testimony of his trust in me. The wiretap affair hurt Henry more than it did the seventeen of us who were its victims, for it was seen by many as proof of his alleged duplicity, personal insecurity, and callousness. In fact, at one point he was accused of having perjured himself and threatened to resign unless he was given a clean bill by the Senate Foreign Relations Committee. The threat of resignation was his ultimate weapon and, most of the time, was remarkably effective. In 1972, for instance, Nancy, his wife, called me in tears saying that Henry was in a dejected mood and had told her that he would resign on a specific date, January 27, and could I call him in San Clemente to talk him out of it. I promptly did, knowing of course full well that every word I was saying was bound to be recorded and, most likely, reported to the president. But I did not care if Henry wanted to send a message to Nixon through me, especially since I believed that Henry's presence in this administration was essential.

Two years later he told me why he had been seriously considering resignation that January 1972. It was over the so-called plumbers operation, which went beyond wiretapping to illicit break-ins and an investigation into a leak about a debate in the NSC concerning the Indo-Pakistan situation. Henry apparently had convinced himself that Ehrlichman, who was in charge of the "plumbers," was trying to use the investigation to get him. He told me that he was convinced his telephone was bugged, though he had no proof of it.

From my personal viewpoint the wiretapping was offensive; from an objective viewpoint it was ludicrous, since I considered it absolutely against my journalistic ethics to use my information for anything but my journalistic activities. What I found most offensive was that my tap was kept on for eleven months which could well have been because of the interest the White House had in gaining insights into the Kennedy household.

When General Haig, who was the one who carried the formal requests for the wiretaps to Hoover, became secretary of state in the Reagan administration, I asked him about the results of the wiretaps on my telephone since he had read many of the FBI wiretap reports. In reply he was at pains to confirm to me, and in writing, that he had no personal knowledge that I had ever been involved in any activity inconsistent with the American national interest; hence there was neither legal nor factual basis for the insulting procedure. An FBI memo in 1973 reached a similar conclusion. It stated that the surveillance did not indicate a violation of the federal law or any specific instance of information being leaked in a surreptitious and unauthorized manner. In his memoirs Richard Nixon indicated no regret about the wiretap operation on the seventeen carried out by the FBI or the one on columnist Joseph Kraft's home phone installed by the plumbers, but he admitted that they "unfortunately did not turn up any proof linking anyone in the government to a specific national security leak."

Looking back as a memoirist, it all seems to fit what the eighteenth-century playwright Reinhold Lenz understood by what is called today black comedy, as John Peter, the theater critic, reminded me the other day: comedy was a portrait of society and if society wore a grave aspect, the play couldn't be all hilarity. For the historian, the central issue still is what the wiretap affair reveals about the character and state of mind of the White House at the time those wiretaps were installed and maintained. For the journalist, one of the inevitable if happier aspects of his profession is that it never allows him to linger for too long over one event.

When my lawyer friend Lloyd N. Cutler asked the FBI in 1981 whether they would destroy the documents relating to my taps, FBI Director William Webster replied that an order entered in the lawsuit *Halperin* v. *Kissinger, Mitchell and Haldeman* precluded him from doing or saying anything about the Brandon "materials," and that was eleven years after the suit was filed! In December 1986 the Court of Appeals denied Hendrick Smith of the *New York Times*—one of the seventeen—(whose telephone was tapped for eighty-nine days) a trial on the ground that he himself admitted to having received classified information from "well-placed informants," as one of the judges put it. "In his case there is a compelling reason to subordinate the individual's interest to the national interest." What is disturbing about this ruling is that a report of the kind Smith wrote, detailing the government's secret strategy for negotiations with Japan on the conditions for returning Okinawa to Japanese control, can be used to install a warrantless wiretap to determine which official disclosed the information. If that is good enough reason for a wiretap for eighty-nine days, then I can only say with Talleyrand: "It is worse than a crime, it is an error."

I hesitated about whether to discuss my wiretap experience in this memoir at all. But it was such a bizarre and troubling experience that I felt it belonged in this book. Henry Kissinger advised against it. He considered it a can of worms for, as he put it, "one can never know what some fool might have put into one's file. There is a risk, once something is written down, people believe it, and anybody can be destroyed in this town if somebody wants to do something really nasty while in government. All he has to do is to put some memo of conversation with the victim into a computer and simply leave it there, say for five years, whether it took place or not, and then request it under the Freedom of Information Act five years later. The victim will never remember what was said—it's one's word against a document." And he recalled how years ago something of the kind happened to him. Henry's argument seems to me an added reason for including my version here.

From my own investigation into the origins of my wiretap I concluded that neither Henry nor Al Haig initiated it. I became an intercept after I had phoned into Mort Halperin's telephone and a victim of Hoover's state of mind. It made me more aware than ever of a dictum that "honor is a luxury for a politician but a necessity for journalists." I must also say that despite Hoover's suspicions, they never affected any of my special or not-so-special relationships in Washington and I shall be eternally grateful to the multitude who never wavered in trusting me.

Nixon, despite his hard-line past, believed that it was possible to make a deal with the Soviets and make it stick. He and Kissinger eagerly pursued such an agreement when they found the Russians willing to reciprocate. To them it meant a contribution to greater stability in the world. It was Kissinger who laid the groundwork for Nixon's dramatic visits to Moscow and Beijing in 1972, two firsts for an American president. The negotiations that led to this unique experience and Henry's tales about his meetings with the Soviet and Chinese leaders who were an enigma to the world were absolutely riveting. Henry considered Brezhnev a tough yet quite human individual, not an unreasonable negotiator, who gave him the impression of seeking steadiness and stability. "If Khrushchev had been in his place," Henry suggested, after the United States had bombed and mined the harbor of Haiphong, "he would have hit the ceiling, but Brezhnev remained cool and did not let it interfere with what he considered was most important to the Soviet national interest." A perfect example of how much in history depends on the personality of individuals.

The Russians, Henry said, never admitted a mistake to him and when they offered a concession implied that they were doing it to be nice to the United States. The Chinese, on the other hand, admitted mistakes and carefully hinted at concessions by saying: "Do we understand you correctly that you believe that . . ." etc. Henry and I made a bet after the bombing of Haiphong. He was convinced that it would lead to the cancellation of the US-Soviet summit, I believed that it would not. I chanced the bet on the basis of a conversation I had when I walked back after a White House press conference with the Tass correspondent, who said with reference to the announcement that "the most important Soviet policy decision was the decision in favor of détente with the United States."

On July 15, 1971, Henry invited me and Muffie, who had gone with me to San Clemente to get a taste of California sunshine, to lunch at the president's compound. In the middle of some frivolous talk about Henry's conquests among film stars, the telephone on our table rang. It was the president, and when toward the end of the conversation Henry was asked with whom he was lunching and said with the Brandons, the President asked him to take us over to his villa after lunch. That was at a time when I still had no inkling of the wiretap, which, Mr. Nixon most likely knew, had by then already been removed for some four months.

The private White House west, overlooking the Pacific, was a Moorish-style villa with a red-tile roof whose charm and beauty surprised me. It had color, airiness, and quiet seclusion. Outwardly, it was certainly a very different place from the house Nixon used to live in in Washington. Inside, however, the furniture, the pictures, carpets, and wallpapers betrayed the same *Better Homes & Gardens* magazine conventionality.

Nixon received us in his study, a comfortable light room with a smallish desk and a soft, modern black leather desk chair. The president, in a sky-blue linen blazer, gray flannels, and black alligator loafers with gold buckles, though smiling invitingly, seemed as usual ill at ease, and his features more gaunt than he looked on television. Still, he was anxious to make conversation and eager to please his impromptu guests. He enjoined us to gaze at the beautiful view through the wide picture window and told us, almost with the intonation of a tourist guide, about the history of the house and how he had acquired it. Kissinger, who had joined the little circle of chairs around the president, had become much more formal, more distant, more deferential, keeping out of the conversation.

Suddenly the president changed the informality of his tone of voice and gave it some presidential weight mixed in with an almost youthful excitement. "We shall have a very important announcement to make this evening." And as if he wanted to give me a hint, he added: "Just remember this room and this view when you hear it." He clearly wanted to whet my appetite for the exclusive story by playing charades, but he did not go further.

He then gave us a generous tour of the house, explaining how he spent the day, how his body clock awakened him in the West at six A.M. and how that gave him a welcome early start on his papers. From the way the president described every little trinket in the house, it was clear that he was very attached to these surroundings. Then before saying good-bye the president took my wife to the garden, leaving Kissinger and me behind, and heading for a rose bush tried to pick the most beautiful among the buds for her. Quite a struggle then ensued between him and the thorny white Peace rose and the more resistant the rose stem became, the more persistent the president was to break it. But he refused to give up, stubborn as he obviously was, and finally with a courteous gesture, and relieved that he had won, he presented it to Muffie, almost petalless. Kissinger by then was showing some impatience, for he had in his pocket, he told me later, a list of twenty ambassadors whom he wanted to telephone before the president made his triumphant announcement that he had accepted an invitation from the People's Republic of China to visit Beijing. It was a daring foray for which Henry had set the scene, but it was Nixon's own dramatic decision to meet with the Chinese leaders on their territory that gave the occasion its full meaning. Had Henry not gone through such elaborate efforts to make his own first contacts with Beijing in secret, the China lobby would probably have succeeded in quashing this historic initiative. Both Houdini and Machiavelli would have been proud had they been in Kissinger's place.

By making his "journey for peace" first to China, Nixon aroused the desired discomfiture in Moscow. It enabled him to exploit the Soviet-Chinese split, which finally led to the kind of decisive Soviet intervention in Hanoi that Kissinger had waited for from the very start of his efforts to bring the Vietnam war to an end. The Kremlin had decided that advancing the cause of détente meant more than the continuation of the war. Nixon had come to realize that the war could not be won by military means, nor could he win at the conference table what he had failed to achieve on the battlefield. This recognition led him to offer a "cease-fire in place" in South Vietnam which conceded to the North Vietnamese their presence in wide areas they had captured in the South. It did not represent a withdrawal with "honor" and President Thieu for that reason rejected the terms Kissinger had negotiated. It represented a major retreat

from the earlier proposal for a "mutual withdrawal," and the shrewd Mr.
Thieu, reading between the lines of the agreement, recognized that it was
nothing more than a way for an American unilateral withdrawal, giving the
South Vietnamese barely more than an outside chance to preserve their independence. But with the Russians telling Hanoi that they would cut down their
arms aid, the Chinese promising to pressure the North Vietnamese into accepting the American offer, and Saigon concluding that the American conditions
could lead only to their early defeat, Hanoi accepted.

The sight of Kissinger shuttling between Moscow and Beijing was a kind
of superpower diplomacy new to the allies, new to everybody. Some of the
allied leaders accused Kissinger of being too eager to reach agreements with
the Soviet Union, but to him détente was a key to international stability. He
hoped he could gradually shift Soviet emphasis from its "revolutionary" aims
to one giving priority to its national interests. He admitted that détente was
not "rooted in agreement on values," but insisted at the same time that to
preserve peace was "in itself an objective not without moral validity." Balance-
of-power politics went against the basic anti-Communist reflexes of many
Americans. To make his policies more acceptable politically, Henry insisted
that détente rested not only on arms control, trade, and credit agreements, but
that there had to be a linkage between virtually all the problems affecting
Soviet-American relations.

Peace to him was indivisible. It was this aspect of the Nixon-Kissinger
concept the Soviets never accepted and it gradually vitiated détente. A major
contributor to torpedoing détente on the American side was the skeptical
Senator Scoop Jackson, who gained many converts by questioning its reality
after the Soviets had threatened to intervene in the 1973 Arab-Israeli war. The
administration pointed in defense to the progress in arms control, to the
Kremlin's more helpful attitude in Hanoi, to the caution it ultimately showed
in the Arab-Israeli war, to the Berlin accord, which defused what used to be
a constant source of tension, and to the improvements in communications
between the White House and the Kremlin. Nixon asked Congress whether
it preferred confrontation and tension instead. But Senator Jackson with Senator Barry Goldwater, his principal supporter on the Republican side, argued
that détente played into Russian hands and provided them with American
technical know-how and trade credits that were ultimately going to strengthen
their competition with the United States.

By the time I traveled with Nixon and Kissinger to the second summit in
Moscow on June 27, 1974, the two had made a good deal of progress in building
a scaffolding for arms control. They had signed two bellwether agreements,
one placing limits on missile defenses, exposing each other's territories to the
threat of mutual destruction, and the other prohibiting the Russians from
increasing their total number of strategic missiles. The bargaining over submarine limits was so tough that final agreement remained in doubt until two

and a half hours before signing. President Nixon was able to decide on the spot how far he would go in making concessions; in contrast the Politburo took two meetings before Mr. Brezhnev could sign—an unusual juxtaposition of the power of the American presidency and that of the Soviet dictatorship.

For Kissinger and Nixon the experience of negotiating with their two great adversaries, the leaders of China and the Soviet Union on their home ground, was a test for American diplomacy unequaled in the country's history. All this superpower diplomacy left the allies looking on uncomfortably from the sidelines—quite different from the Eisenhower and Truman days, when they participated as equal partners in negotiations with the Russians. Yet it also comforted them that the world looked safer with the two superpowers in closer communication.

After the decades of Berlin blockade, Korean War, fighting in Greece and Iran, Hungarian revolt, Cuba, and Vietnam, Americans were in a general mood to welcome the Soviet-American rapprochement. It was a relief that after the tense, frustrating and, at times, frightening cold war period, a safer one had begun to dawn. Both the United States and the Soviet Union felt strong enough to enter into serious diplomatic discussions, both recognized that peace in the world could not rely simply on fears of nuclear war. Nixon from the start of his presidency, had been keen on following Churchill's dictum, "We arm to parley," and to translate it into practice. As Pamela Harriman has pointed out, Churchill in his famous Iron Curtain speech not only warned that the Russians would like to control Europe from the Atlantic to the Urals, but also spoke of the need to negotiate with them, a point which was lost in the controversy the speech precipitated.

When I boarded the press plane for the second Moscow summit, the tune that wafted through the aircraft was "There's No Business like Show Business." There seemed to me something symbolic about this musical warning, for President Nixon by then was virtually drowning in the flood of Watergate and tempted to look for successes abroad. Watergate also put him on the defensive and forced him to follow a narrow path between his commitment to détente and the growing skepticism in Congress about its value and meaning, for he did not want to antagonize the conservatives in the Senate on whose vote he might have to rely to protect him if the House of Representatives decided on impeachment.

Kissinger had proved to be a shrewd negotiator with the Russians, he had command over the technological intricacies of arms control, and it was he who advised Nixon what concessions he could afford to make. He knew, to use a Bismarckian phrase, how "to turn the scales with a feather." But in the secretary of defense, James Schlesinger, a tough, uncompromising, and self-confident man—who knew as much about arms control as did Kissinger, except that he took a somewhat different ideological tack—Henry had a formidable opponent. Schlesinger did not believe that the Russians would faithfully adhere to an agreement. His outlook was similar to that of those conservatives

who persuaded President Reagan to destroy SALT II in 1986. He favored the
kind of drastic arms reductions President Reagan proposed later but which
Kissinger claimed the Russians would not accept since they were still trying
to catch up with the Americans in the area of independently targeted warheads. And so the weapons race remained in full swing. If the Soviets had
moved to a more obvious reordering of their priorities, from an emphasis on
building weapons to improving the civilian economy, the Jackson-Schlesinger
approach would have been less influential, but that did not happen. The
1973 summit therefore struggled to keep détente alive rather than to move it
forward.

By the time we landed in Düsseldorf on our return flight from Moscow and
Kissinger transferred into a helicopter to fly to Essen for a World Cup soccer
game, he had forgotten the strains and disappointments of the summit. I flew
with him because I was the only one among White House correspondents
interested in soccer. I became what was known as the pool correspondent for
this unorthodox expedition, something I soon began to regret when we flew
into such an awful thunderstorm that on landing a dozen fire engines awaited
us ready for any emergencies. My pool report was of little interest to my
colleagues, who did not care who won the game. The only tidbit I could
contribute was that Henry, who watched the game from a center box of the
grandstand, found himself next to the box occupied by the world's most
famous soccer player, the Brazilian Pelé, who was besieged by autograph
hunters, while Henry, the famous diplomatist, usually the target of autograph
hunters, found himself passed by.

The most serious setback Kissinger suffered was the cunningly conceived
Jackson-Vanik legislation, which on the surface was to assist him in getting
the Kremlin to allow many thousands more Jews to leave the Soviet Union
in exchange for trade concessions. But it set back Jewish emigration for more
than ten years to come. The number of émigrés had reached 34,000 in 1974 and
would have gone up further but for Jackson's excessive demand for doubling
this number. When Nixon warned a group of Jewish leaders that Jackson had
put forward the legislation because he was against détente and not for humanitarian reasons, they left in a quandary, but later found themselves forced by
their own internal pressures and by their desire to back Jackson's presidential
ambitions, to reaffirm their support for the bill. It was another example of how
difficult it is for any president to conduct a coherent foreign policy under the
American political system. The Jewish leaders hurt their own cause rather
than Jackson's. They went along with him because he had been their staunch-
est friend in Congress. It undermined Kissinger's credibility, whose "super-
man" image had now been diluted to that of a mere human being.

By then, too, the most influential columnist and supporter of détente had
passed away. The last time I had seen Walter Lippmann was in January 1974

in his nursing home, a comfortable, old-fashioned sort of boardinghouse staffed with kind and helpful ladies at his call. Walter's looks had deteriorated to a point that shocked me. He mentioned that he had read Nigel Nicolson's book *Portrait of a Marriage* (about the author's parents, Harold Nicolson and Vita Sackville-West) and found it "disgusting." He referred to Elliott Roosevelt's book about his father which he considered even worse, but he had great hopes for the one Ronald Steel was writing about his own life because he was "a good writer, a scholar and a gentleman." He would not have been disappointed had he had the opportunity to read the finished opus. Steel used Walter's life as a fascinating personal guide through the American Century. Walter told me about a letter his wife, Helen, had discovered among her papers, written by him before their marriage, which went into great detail about their premarital relationship. He said that he and Helen had been debating whether to give it to Steel and that he favored doing so. Clearly, it was a major decision for as private a man as he was. (They gave it.) He then wanted me to tell him about Kissinger's continuing efforts to keep détente going and after hearing me out called him "an able and clever man who is accomplishing big things." They had a common bond: both believed in realpolitik.

Virtually all his life Lippmann had been engaged in the great issues of the times, analyzing them, defining them, promoting or criticizing them, developing his own theories about them. He was not a crusader, though there was at times deep if controlled passion under his academic detachment; he was a searcher for solutions. He was also a very good listener. Since I did much more legwork than he—he did quite a bit, though in a very discreet way, never showing off that he had seen the president or the secretary of state—he was interested in hearing about my own findings and helping me with advice on how much importance to attach to this or that source, an essential ingredient in the Washington maze of information.

Once in 1963 I received a letter from that grand old man of the publishing world and crusty gourmand of literature, Alfred Knopf, suggesting lunch in Washington to discuss my doing a book on the anatomy of the United States, inspired by Anthony Sampson's successful *Anatomy of Britain*. I was flattered by the offer, but felt overwhelmed by the size of the undertaking and, after consulting Lippmann, suggested that I would need at least two researchers for two or three years whose cost would most likely exceed $50,000. Knopf, full of enthusiasm about the idea and my being tempted by it, said that he would see whether he could obtain foundation money for the research. In one of my letters I mentioned that Arthur Schlesinger, Jr., the historian, had said to me that "it requires sixteen lawyers to find a way to circumvent the rules governing foundation grants" in such a case, and, indeed, after a few weeks Knopf reported that the foundations he had approached all said that under their rules they could not support a project that would be published commercially. When I mentioned Knopf's vain attempt to obtain foundation money to Lippmann, he shook his head and said: "The one thing you can always get in this country is money!" Knopf was taken aback on learning this and wrote to Lippmann asking what he meant. Lippmann replied with one sentence: "Exactly what I said." His advice led to some more inquiries, but without success, and the idea never came to fruition. When I told Lippmann that his advice did not prove to be correct, he laughed and said: "Well, maybe, I should have said: 'There is always *big* money available.'"

In 1970 Walter asked me to collaborate with him on his last book, which he hoped would be his legacy to the young generation. He was deeply preoccupied by the "ungovernability of mankind in our era": finding answers to the problem of political order after all had been one of his lifelong concerns. The provisional title for the book was *The Ungovernability of the World.* Much against his own habit and tradition—ordinarily he never asked for a contract, holding that it was not necessary among gentlemen—he asked for a contract to be drafted in this case, since my own rights were also involved, and, most generously, he wanted me to have my byline on the cover next to his. We met at irregular intervals in New York, where he was then living, and it was my task to get him to generate his ideas in what was half-interview, half-conversation. It was to have been his last effort to come to grips with some of the most basic problems plaguing Western civilization. He meant to apply all his accumulated vision as historian and philosopher, all the wisdom and experience he had garnered over a lifetime of thought and inquiry. He also hoped to provide some answers to such questions as, Why is it that in the advanced countries of the world so much progress has been made by the standards accepted twenty or more years ago, yet the world has never been more disorderly within the memory of living man? Why is it that people in these advanced countries are unhappy at the "progress" made during this century with more wealth, more widely distributed, and with standards of life having gone up so remarkably? And why has humanity, in spite of great wealth and great power and so little complacency, not been able to cope better with this disorderly world? "I think this is the most uncomplacent period I have lived in," he once said.

Walter contended that such inventions as the automobile, the pill, satellite communications, nuclear weapons, the disintegration of the family, religious beliefs, and mass education had broken down the pillars of society so that we now lived in a transitional period when the old order was dying and a new one being born—the pangs of dying and the pangs of being born were both here, and individual man hung uncomfortably between these two worlds. He defined that state as a revolution in the sense not of the Russian or the French revolution but of the Industrial Revolution. Since World War II not only our society but the world as a whole had become increasingly ungovernable. We discussed the decline of the ruling elites of the past and the rise of the new technological elite, the trained managers, the applied scientists, and the experts who run the big organizations, the big businesses. Our problem, he believed, was not with the military, but with the technocrats, even though they were not in charge of political decisions, because they were hard to control and hard to do without. They not only created a new Great Revolution, but they transformed revolution itself. In the old days, he argued, the obsolete order would be replaced by a new class, as were, for instance, the landed gentry by businessmen and they again by industrial workers. Modern technology, however, is so productive, affluence spread so far and wide, that what used to be an elite has become part of a broad establishment that is responsible for changing the world order, which knows no limits in space and time, and has become the aim of every class, every race, every community of men. It has its own momentum and seems to have no obvious limits. All this has made the tasks of representative government exceedingly difficult. Although inclined to being a pessimist, he was anxious to give his ideas a positive thrust to engender in the younger generation hope in the future. He argued therefore that since men so often achieved the impossible, there was no reason to assume that they could not achieve what to us currently seems impossible. But what distressed him (and also me, as I proceeded acting as the catalyst for his ideas) was the realization that the more we delved into the problems of how to make the world more governable, the more he became aware that despite his accumulated knowledge, experience, and intelligence, he had no great new positive and convincing answers to offer. With this realization, sadly, he lost the inner drive for the project.

Helen Lippmann, who now lived by herself in New York, came to see us in Washington and seemed in incomparably better health than Walter. We were flabbergasted therefore when three weeks after she had come to us for dinner, she suddenly died of heart failure. Walter survived her by eleven months. "The Gentle Thunderer," as *The Sunday Times* headlined the obituary I wrote, had been silent as a columnist since 1971 and nobody really was quite able to fill that space he used to occupy in the newspapers or exert his influence. He was unique in his profession and will remain so, because essentially he was a philosopher who had decided to communicate ideas and analyze those of others. Like most members of the Eastern Establishment in the thirties, he believed the British navy was the best way of protecting American security in the Atlantic. And when the Royal Navy lost its power to protect the sea lanes early in World War II, it was Lippmann who launched the idea —inspired by Lord Lothian, the British ambassador—of transferring fifty American destroyers to Britain in exchange for several British sea and air bases vital to the defense of the United States. His European origins led him to promote the importance of the Atlantic Community, an expression he coined. Like all of us, of course, Lippmann had his lapses of judgment. And if his critics remember those lapses so vividly even today, this only indicates the attention he aroused and the debates he sparked. His main aim was to educate men to be able to save themselves.

In June 1971 there was a dramatic display—unique in American history—of the power of the American press, illustrating the seeming inability of the American government to protect its top secret documents, and an extraordinary confrontation between press and government of a kind unthinkable in any other country. It followed the publication by the *New York Times* of what became known as the Pentagon Papers, a gigantic coup of a scoop, and an unprecedented breach of security. The papers were a secret study of the Vietnam war, ordered by Robert McNamara while still secretary of defense, in an attempt to retrace its history to determine how the United States could have made such a massive miscalculation. This was not the McNamara who pursued the war with a vengeance, but the tragic figure who, deeply depressed, wanted to make a clinical examination of the unwinnable war and the lessons to be drawn from this national catastrophe. The papers' discovery and unauthorized publication caused a sensation and had the Nixon administration fighting for the protection of government secrets, even though they were those of previous administrations. Kissinger, particularly, made no bones at dinner parties about how shocked he was by the precedent that the publication of this secret study amounted to and was one of those who pressed hardest for taking the case to the courts. The administration, already on hostile terms with the news media, thus risked something it should have known to avoid: trying to climb a legal wall that had never before been successfully scaled. "Prior restraint," which the government invoked—Chief Justice Charles Evans Hughes called it "the essence of censorship"—had never been effectively imposed on an American newspaper. Its second mistake was not taking into account the political astuteness of those who decided to create that massive breach in the dam of governmental secrecy in order to influence Congress to speed up the withdrawal from Vietnam.

The case gave rise to several far-reaching and historic precedents: as a breach of security, as a confrontation between the press and the government over the cherished principle of freedom of the press, as a court order restraining an American newspaper from publishing a specific article, as a battle between the two leading American newspapers, the *New York Times* and the Washington *Post*. Few legal battles have escalated with equal swiftness. Within twelve days the case had moved up to the US Supreme Court, which agreed to meet immediately on Saturday, June 26, though it was the last day of its term.

People began to queue up at six A.M. to get one of the 174 seats reserved for the public. I have always considered the Supreme Court chamber the most dignified of all secular halls in the United States. The red plush against the white marble walls, the dais high above the lectern where the attorneys apeak, the nine justices in their black robes—leaning forward or bobbing with a superior mien up and down and sideways in their black leather swivel chairs —give any hearing a solemn, almost awesome feeling and, no doubt, make it quite an intimidating experience for any attorney. And this time the stakes were momentous. A great legal match of vast repercussions, a confrontation between Professor Alexander Bickel of the Yale Law School, and the leading expert on the First Amendment, defending the *New York Times,* and the solicitor general, Erwin Nathaniel Griswold, a former law professor from Harvard. The justices, with their sharp questions, forced Bickel on the defensive, but the government, by resting its case on a misuse of the Espionage Act, led from a weak hand. The government lost the case, but it was not a clear victory for the freedom of the press because some of the justices laced their opinions with unpalatable reservations.

To Kissinger, who had seen the pillars of the government crumbling under the weight of the Pentagon Papers' indiscretion, the Supreme Court decision was a disaster. But disasters do not last long in Washington. There are usually others to redirect public attention. After the last American ground forces had been withdrawn from Vietnam Americans' self-confidence, optimism, and trust in the geopolitical judgment of their leaders had reached a very low ebb. Asked by the *New York Times* to comment on that disaster of another sort, I wrote: "Americans have a tendency, and Mr. Kissinger is no exception, to exaggerate their successes and their failures . . . there is little likelihood that the fall of Vietnam will affect the assessment of American power in Moscow or Peking . . . both have shown a steadier view of American deterrent and staying power than have many Americans . . . American influence, however, is not only based on being the strongest military and economic power in the world, but also on the policies that govern the uses of this power and these in turn depend on the relationship between the Executive and Congress. It is the deep differences in outlook on the United States' role in the world that exist between the two branches that is undermining American credibility. There is a good deal of questioning abroad whether, after the trauma of Indochina, the basic premises of American foreign policy will continue . . . More likely than not, they will remain solid, except that the era of American omnipotence, the willingness to exercise power alone, and the idea that the United States can control events, are passing into history." The experience of something that came close to defeat gave Americans that sense of tragedy the lack of which, Kissinger always maintained, deprived them of a true awareness of history. Beyond that, though, despite all the prediction of the domino effect, the nations of Southeast Asia not only survived the shock with remarkable resilience, but they are stronger today than they have ever been. Instead of a burden to the United States, Vietnam is a thorn in China's flank and a financial burden to the Soviet Union, as well as an irritant for both in their bilateral relations.

There was good reason for some of the complaints among allied leaders that Henry had a tendency to pay more attention to his adversaries than to his friends. Indeed, in his first three years as a policymaker he concentrated almost exclusively on the Soviet Union and China and neglected Western

Europe, which in his academic days used to be his main preoccupation. In so many ways, of course, it was much more challenging to him to cut through the diplomatic underbrush in still unexplored policy jungles than to pursue the well-trodden, rather stagnant path of power in Europe.

The European leaders admired Kissinger's intellectual brilliance, his negotiating skills, and his leadership qualities. What worried them was not so much that he was not paying enough attention to them as their underlying fear that he was constructing a three-cornered world balance-of-power system over their heads. In addition, the British had the uncomfortable feeling that he had no emotional commitment to the special relationship; the West Germans saw in him the image of Bismarck, a man willing to reverse alliance and to ignore legality if expedient; and the French distrusted his direct and secretive dealings with the Russians. By the spring of 1973 the rising criticism in the European press and along the diplomatic circuits had become so clamorous that he decided to declare that year the "Year of Europe." He wanted to make it clear that he would give the alliance first priority and concentrate on refurbishing NATO and, more generally, American relations with Europe. Unfortunately, the vehicle he drafted looked too much like an artificially conceived gimmick —a new Atlantic Charter. It was altogether badly conceived, badly timed, and badly handled diplomatically. The reaction of Sir Christopher Soames, then the equivalent of foreign minister to the European Economic Community, was typical: "To speak about a 'Year of Europe' is like a husband saying: this is going to be the year of the wife."

Kissinger was furious when the European allies talked his new charter to death by insisting that they first had to formulate an agreed position to it among themselves. Cooperation, he said, was a two-way street. This adversary procedure, he predicted, would produce fears about European unity in the American mind. Europe would not be able to play the role of military balancer, he warned, or mediator. Only by being attached to one or other superpower, he added, can one exert influence. He reminded me of Churchill's remark to de Gaulle that the British wanted to be always close to the Americans in order to be able to influence their thinking, to which de Gaulle replied that he believed it to be more effective to oppose the Americans. Then Henry growled that a change in the quality of relations between the United States and Europe could well be in the making. I thought that he was making a mistake by hinting at cuts in the number of American troops in Europe, for their presence, not the nuclear weapons, were the ultimate deterrent to a Soviet attack.

In retrospect Kissinger now agrees that the Year of Europe initiative was poorly timed, but for different reasons. The European leaders—Prime Minister Edward Heath, Chancellor Willy Brandt, Premier Georges Pompidou—and indeed Nixon, were either politically or physically ill and therefore preoccupied with other problems, and for the British it was a particularly difficult time to take the lead in getting acceptance of a new Atlantic Charter, for they had only just joined the European Economic Community. They still had to win the trust of the Europeans and the Europeans still had to adjust to Britain's presence. Anglo-American relations were brought to a particularly low point when Ted Heath refused to give American planes the right to use British bases for refueling on their way to supplying the Israelis in the war with Egypt because the United States could not come up with a secure cover story to protect Britain against this concession becoming public. Kissinger had to call the planes back in midair when he got Heath's no.

The allies vaguely closed ranks by producing an alternative to Henry's charter which only ruffled Henry's plumage even more and reinforced his doubts about future European unity. Unlike previous administrations, he did not want to get involved in promoting European unity, most likely because he himself was of two minds as to whether it would be to the advantage of the United States.

It was about that time that Kissinger, at a large reception, said to Robert McNamara: "I'm the highest ranking guest here and nobody seems to want to talk to me." Then he fell into his disarming self-deprecating mood and added smilingly: "Maybe I'm slipping, Bob, did this happen to you too?" McNamara looked him in the face and smiled back: "Yes, Henry, when I was slipping."

The man who really began slipping was Richard Nixon, after the famous five burglars were caught in Washington's Watergate office building in the head-quarters of the Democratic Party's National Committee at two A.M. on June 17, 1972. Dirty politics are nothing new in American history and if the White House had quickly said "Sorry" instead of stonewalling, who knows how differently history might have been written? (President Reagan made a similar error when he refused to admit that his secret dealings with Iran had been a mistake.) I was not alone in regarding the break-in at first as more a caper than a crime, and since my editor occasionally asked for some lighter fare than the usually serious Washington diet, I proposed writing a story on the incident as a spoof on Sherlock Holmes. To my delight I got an instant go-ahead, and when my piece appeared it was given the appropriate headline: ELEMENTARY, MY DEAR BRANDON. Editors with this kind of sense of humor were rare in Fleet Street, but Harold Evans had flair. Naturally, I met with Sherlock Holmes over a whiskey and soda in the exclusive Watergate bar, where I let an old hound dog lay out for me the evidence he had already assembled and ended with Holmes saying: "Between the moralists, who say that the Republicans are all bad, and the cynics who say that it's all happened before in American politics, between the innuendoes and the half-truth, I find it confusing to work here. American politics are dirtier and people more tolerant of dirt than I thought. You have said, my dear fellow, that this would be a great place for me to work because nothing ever remains secret in Washington. Well, that would tempt me to come back after the elections when the great unobservant public cares again about the finer shades of analysis, but on second thought,

I won't because in Washington, to paraphrase Gustave Flaubert's remark: *L'homme c'est rien—la politique c'est toute.* " Nobody could doubt that Holmes, indeed, had grasped instantly—even if he did not unravel the riddle of Watergate—what Washington was all about.

But it turned out to be politics of the most sordid kind, like nothing I had ever covered before. My dispatches on Watergate became longer and longer as the editor's and the readers' curiosity grew and as the cancer of mendacity spread through the administration's body politic. It was staggering. Almost every arm of government was used to ensure Nixon's reelection. An attempt was made to use the Central Intelligence Agency, as Richard Helms, the former director of CIA told the Ervin committee—whose official name was Senate Select Committee on Presidential Campaign Activities and as such came to investigate the Watergate break-in; the Internal Revenue Service was deployed to intimidate people; the FBI was forced into assignments it objected to; the State Department was dragged into an attempt to forge diplomatic cables to damage Senator Edward Kennedy should he become a candidate; the integrity of the Department of Justice was put into question by pressures to drop an antitrust action against ITT after handsome offers of political campaign contributions were conveyed; the Securities and Exchange Commission was enlisted to protect a heavy contributor to the party kitty; and so on. It was frightening testimony to how vulnerable democratic government is when those in charge lack a basic sense of morality and loyalty to the law. The brash, ambitious young men such as John Dean, Gordon Strachan, Jeb Stuart Magruder, and others had in common what Hannah Arendt called "the banality of evil." These men believed in "game plans" and their loyalty was their readiness to execute any order given to them. Chuck Colson had the phrase for it: if loyalty to the cause required it, "I would walk over my grandmother." When Patrick Gray's nomination to FBI chief was in trouble, Ehrlichman pronounced the immortal phrase: "Let him twist slowly, slowly in the wind."

The event inspired a burst of shaggy humor. Senator Robert Packwood, a highly sophisticated (and moderate) Republican senator from Oregon and his wife, Georgie, for instance, invited friends to a "first rate anniversary celebration of a 'third rate burglary attempt.' " The invitation went on to say that "as of this date, all previous invitations are inoperative" to request casual dress "surgical gloves optional," and to advise that the invitation should not see the light of day but be dropped in the nearest burn bag or shredder. It ended "please garble your response to . . ." Enclosed was a fake $100 note with a label: "Laundering instructions: for best results wash in warm Mexican cycle. Do not bleach or whitewash." All of these witticisms, of course, exploited the new Watergate currency.

Len Garment, a special assistant to the president and once his law partner, came to a dinner and gave us and William Rees-Mogg, then editor of the London *Times,* a vivid idea of the depressing confusion that overtook the

White House in the later stages. Some five hundred lawyers, he said, were engaged generally in the Watergate affair, but only four of them worked for the White House, and they had to deal not only with the legal issues, but also with speech writing, public opinion assessments, and stage-managing the presidency. He said he lived in constant uncertainty, because Nixon was a centipede of problems and Garment did not know what shoe would hit him tomorrow. It could be a document or a tape, and each could entail enough evidence to prove the president's direct involvement in Watergate. Even for presidential aides the masked life the president had been leading was a mystery. With disarming honesty, bordering on helplessness, Garment confessed that all were demoralized because the president himself had handled his case so badly—the great survivor's revolting misjudgments now finally threatened to destroy him. "The ultimate power of the individual," said Garment, "is the power to commit suicide. Watergate seems almost self-willed by the president. He acted like a man driving recklessly along a dangerous highway. With the men he chose as his senior advisers he created a powerful center, but as a group they were incompatible, with no one to act as a fail-safe mechanism. What he conceived as an aggressive, strong cadre in effect only reinforced his own vulnerabilities. Nixon is a psychological mystery and Watergate can only be explained as a puzzle of Chinese boxes, one inside the other, with only Nixon in possession of the key he seemed to have misplaced. I only hope the ending will be dignified."

It seemed to me as if the Age of Future-shock had finally arrived, yet on the outside, it was for long inconceivable that Nixon could be or should be impeached. Senator Mike Mansfield, the idiosyncratic Democrat from Montana, said publicly that impeachment would help no one politically and serve only to hurt the country. He reflected the majority view among Americans, and very much the prevailing opinion in Europe. Europeans, in particular, failed to grasp the determination in Congress to prosecute the president. Still British interest in Watergate was undiminished. My reports, on orders from the editor, went to unprecedented length. He had come to realize how much suspense, human interest, political machinations were involved. And looming behind it all was a supreme test of the American political system.

When Elliot Richardson, perhaps the most versatile public servant in recent history, was asked by Nixon at Camp David in May 1973 to leave the defense department and become attorney general, he felt for a brief moment that this was an unusual opportunity for him to say something useful to the president. Speaking quietly and very earnestly, he began to tell him what in his view had gone wrong with his presidency: that it continued to reflect the prejudices Nixon had accumulated in his earlier life—his mistrust of people and his suspicions of the bureaucracy, his self-inflicted persecution complex, and other fears. Did the president not appreciate the implications of his landslide victory? Was he not aware that even those who had voted against him now wanted him to succeed? He urged Nixon to realize that he was president of all the people and that this was also the way people saw him. They would not want to destroy him, therefore he should reciprocate and not consider them as enemies. He ended with an appeal, he told me, for magnanimity instead of even harsher partisanship.

Nixon looked at him unblinkingly, as if either Richardson was wasting his breath since the President could not do anything about the way he was, or even that Richardson's words had not penetrated his mind at all. Richardson then recalled the oddest but perhaps most indicative remark of Nixon's deeply ingrained distrust of people. It had occurred just after he had been made secretary of defense: "Watch Kissinger! Check on him!" (Shortly thereafter, on August 22, 1973, Nixon announced Kissinger's appointment to secretary of state!) It naturally startled Richardson because he had assumed that the two were political allies, sharing common concepts and interests. In unguarded moments, Elliot added, Nixon revealed flashes of cynicism and vindictiveness that made him wonder how deeply they reached into his subconscious. He compared those flashes to veins on rocks whose depth one cannot fathom from looking at them. When Richardson became exposed to Watergate, he realized how deep and wide those veins reached.

As Watergate progressed, Kissinger began to feel that it was weakening his negotiating hand. He spoke about the White House as "sick," about how Nixon's insecurities would be aggravated by Watergate and how he wished the president could be left alone so that he could begin to govern again. There was too much at stake in foreign affairs and it needed the president's full attention. He worried that the president was now permanently hurt, although he assumed there would not be enough evidence to corroborate the claims of John Dean to the Senate committee. Kissinger said also that the president never apologized to him about the tapes; and indeed he had not known anything about them. A month later, he called Nixon "a man who committed suicide after he had been declared dead." Henry grew increasingly depressed, lamenting America's misplaced sense of morality. Like him, most newspaper editors could not believe that Congress would go further in castrating the president's authority, or go as far as impeaching him. But the American political system lacks the device of the censure vote to force new elections. There are only two ways to get rid of a president: impeachment or resignation. Neither case leads to new elections. Instead the vice president steps into the vacant presidency. The four-year term is written almost in granite as the key to American political stability.

On October 20, 1973, Professor Archibald Cox, the special prosecutor, called a surprise press conference for eleven A.M. It was a Saturday, an unusual day for announcing anything newsworthy. Speaking quietly with the voice of detached professionalism, only occasionally betraying the passion for the law that had made him act, he disclosed that he would accuse the president of contempt of court for refusing to surrender the White House tapes he had subpoenaed. The White House reacted vehemently, claiming that Cox, an employee of the executive branch, could not "subpoena notes or memoranda of Presidential conversations." It was obvious that Cox was trying to force the president's hand either to surrender the tapes or to dismiss him. The spotlight was now on the so-called Nixon tapes.

After I had filed my story, I thought I had done my last deed for the day and in the late afternoon went to a concert in aid of the United Nations at the Kennedy Center. My wife was in bed with influenza, but she insisted that I go. The music had just about enveloped my mind and had made me forget the dramatic events of the day when I suddenly felt someone touching my shoulder and heard a voice whisper into my ear that my wife was waiting for me in the foyer and would I come out right away. I jumped out of my seat, worried about what had got her out of bed and brought her here, and rushed out through the dark concert hall. Outside I found Muffie, waving me hurriedly to follow her, saying that she would tell me everything in the waiting car. I noticed that her nightie was showing under her overcoat.

Once in the car she told me that she had heard rumors that Elliot Richardson was about to resign—it was now past seven P.M.—and that she had called Ann Richardson, Elliot's wife and a friend of hers, and got confirmation that the announcement was due in half an hour. At home I rushed to the telephone and dictated the news and its significance to *The Sunday Times,* still in time for a bannerline in the last two A.M. edition. Muffie took her 103-degree fever back to bed, happy to have helped her husband score a scoop.

Richardson, indeed, after a tense meeting with the president, resigned "in the public interest" when asked to fire Cox. Ruckelshaus, his deputy, and a sturdy fair-minded middle westerner from Indiana, also refused to fire the prosecutor, and followed with his resignation. The deed was finally done by the former solicitor general, Robert Bork, who became acting attorney general, though to the utter dismay of the White House he insisted on appointing a new special prosecutor with the same powers of investigation that had been vested in Cox.

The ferocity with which the public reacted to Cox's dismissal flabbergasted everybody in the White House. As Nixon put it in his memoirs: "For the first time I recognized the depth of the impact of Watergate . . . my actions were the result of serious miscalculation." To Garment, it only confirmed the "inward thinking" that occurs in crises. "The most dangerous thing in the world is to be totally absorbed in a problem, to be inside the belly of the whale. You wind up blind-siding yourself," he commented later. Nixon was paying now for the insulated and isolated life he led behind the White House walls.

Yet it is extraordinary to remember now how Nixon's support endured in the country. When *Time* magazine, breaking with tradition, published a two-page editorial calling, like others, for Nixon's resignation, 5,000 letters poured in;

4,500 resented the editorial. To the "little" men and women across the country, Nixon had made himself the leader of the backlash against the violent decade of permissiveness. Between the New Left and the New Right, the liberal forces which had been the source of orderly progress during the previous thirty-five years found themselves choked to at least temporary extinction. Nixon spoke for the "silent majority" but he lost the "vocal majority"—the educated young and their parents who opposed the Vietnam war.

Nixon's desperate attempts in the face of impending doom to follow a normal course—the State of the Union message had something unreal about it—dismayed even the patient, gentle Len Garment. "Everybody you know here now has a sense of the provisional and the temporary," he said to me late one afternoon. "I'm not dealing with Watergate anymore, it became too difficult for me to help the president. You can only help as lawyer if you are given all the facts, and I was never given them. No one here really knows the facts." He sighed and wondered whether the president would have the stamina to get through the crisis. "It's one thing to be tough at particular crucial moments, another to be resilient enough. This is a dance of the thousand veils, a performance during which everything is slowly peeled off."

To my utter amazement, when Nixon addressed the nation on the eve of the release of the tapes, he did not seem a man in despair, but one seemingly confident that he would escape the impeachment guillotine. Six months earlier he had looked drawn, tense, on the edge of collapse. What gave him this new tenacity, gameness, and relaxed confidence? Len Garment put it this way: "He recognized that this was the ultimate battle for his survival. He sorted out his options, he swallowed his fears and guilts, he resolved to fight it through."

I will never forget Friday, July 26, when the House Judiciary Committee was scheduled to vote on the question of impeachment. On Thursday I had a call from Harold Evans telling me how many pages he would be devoting to the verdict and asking me how many pages I wanted for Sunday, a question no editor had ever asked me before. What made Friday night so trying was that the vote was not taken until the early morning and my deadline for the first edition of *The Sunday Times* was ten A.M., Washington time, on Saturday. It meant that I had to write at the same time as I was watching the House Judiciary Committee hearings on the television set in my office. The final vote was 27 to 11, the first time in 106 years that an American president had been recommended for impeachment.

It is hard to describe the gamut of shocks that reverberated through Washington as Watergate moved toward a climax, just as it is hard to describe one's personal reactions during earth tremors. There were the gleeful partisans who jubilantly foresaw good riddance; there was the distress among Republicans who feared the repercussions on their party; there was a majority that was filled with anxiety for the future of the Republic; there were those who wondered whether the Russians might take advantage of the paralysis in the government; and there were those whose concerns went to what seemed to me extremes, such as Secretary of Defense Schlesinger's order, a few days before the impeachment procedures reached their climax, for the chairman of the Joint Chiefs of Staff, General George Brown, to let him know instantly in case any orders from the president to block the "constitutional process"—a formal way of saying that he wanted to prevent Nixon from using the military to defy Congress—were transmitted to him. When rumors about this precautionary move, spread by Schlesinger himself, appeared in the press, I considered them preposterous. It seemed to me inconceivable that Nixon would attempt to defy the Constitution so brazenly. However T. Clay Whitehead, who worked on the transition team together with Vice President Gerald Ford's legal counsel, Philip Buchen, told me later that he and Buchen discussed the possibility that Nixon might try to use the military or the Executive Protective Police to defy Congress and the Constitution. They were trying to think about the obvious and the irrational, Whitehead told me, such as Nixon claiming that neither the courts nor the Congress had the authority to force him out of office. But they never confided their thought to Schlesinger. I completely discounted such extremes because I was also convinced that the only ones still loyal to Nixon were his family, not a position of strength from which to trigger a coup d'état.

Years later an interviewer asked Nixon what he would have done differently about Watergate, knowing what he knew now. Nixon replied that he would have destroyed the White House tapes. Haig, who was then Nixon's chief of staff, told me that at the height of the Watergate crisis he advised the president to destroy the tapes, something Nixon did not mention in his own memoirs. Haig, however, remembered that he himself felt so strongly that he had asked Vice President Spiro T. Agnew to come to Nixon's bedside—the president was at Bethesda Naval Hospital with a slight case of pneumonia—to reinforce his recommendation. Len Garment, the president's legal counsel, was also at his bedside. He challenged General Haig's advice, insisting that the destruction of the tapes would constitute an obstruction of justice since it was already known that the Senate Watergate committee would subpoena them. This itself, Garment said, could set the impeachment process in motion. As Haig remembers it, he countered that since the subpoena had not yet reached the president, Nixon could still destroy the tapes. But Nixon decided against doing so because, as Haig recalls it, the tapes were the only true safeguard he had, since he did not know what he would be accused of. What was even more surprising, according to Haig, was that Nixon did not realize the extent of his culpability.

When I asked Washington's most famous criminal lawyer, Edward Bennett Williams, in 1985 how he viewed the tape issue in retrospect, he replied: "Nixon had no obligation to make or keep the tapes and could have argued that his motive in destroying them was to prevent secret exchanges with other heads of government from being compromised." Garment, in reply, simply cited chapter and verse of the 1956 decision *U.S.* v. *Martin Solow* (U.S. District Court, New York), in which the eminent Judge J. Weinfeld stated that "defendant by allegedly willfully destroying the correspondence to prevent their production interfered with the due administration of justice notwithstanding nonservice of a subpoena." Furthermore, Garment also pointed out to me that "the Senate's intention to serve a subpoena was the leading news item." In early 1988, though, when I again discussed the tape destruction issue with Garment, he admitted that after fifteen years' experience of the flow of news in Washington, Williams was probably right that Nixon could have got away with the destruction of the tapes, but for the wrong reasons. "If he had agreed to publish the Dean tapes, which were inconclusive, and destroyed the rest, and given Williams's rationale for it, he could never have been impeached. There would have been a huge public outcry, but at that time by relying on the strength of the American presidency Nixon probably would have survived. The 'killer tapes' would no longer have been available to do him in. His strategy of 'toughing out' the pounding by the political opposition and the news media proved to be a blunder."

The law is a many-splendored thing! To speculate whether Nixon could have escaped impeachment had he destroyed the tapes is a tantalizing question. It probably still haunts Nixon. Haig, perhaps longer than anybody else, believed that it was important for the country and the world to preserve Nixon's presidency and let him serve out his term, however amoral, even culpable he was. Haig, as Nixon's chief of staff, kept the ship of state from running aground in the waning days of the Nixon administration. (Because of his impressive performance then many, including myself, were taken aback when he did not behave with the same sangfroid and equanimity as secretary of state in the Reagan administration.) What we did not know at the time was that Nixon vacillated between quitting and toughing it out to the last and that Haig was the one who in the end talked him into resigning, by carefully analyzing for him what would happen if he did not, and making it clear to him that he had lied, had manufactured evidence, obstructed justice, authorized break-ins and illegal wiretaps and spying on antiwar movements in the cities and on campuses, and had bugged every one of his visitors and, in the end, himself.

What to me became most important was the relative orderliness with which the presidential revolving door was set in motion. After the greatest constitutional crisis in American history, the shock to the system was overcome with remarkable speed and skill. But there was a debit to be paid, especially in foreign affairs. However much Kissinger tried to preserve continuity, he did not have the political strength to carry on an active foreign policy without Nixon, especially after the disintegration of the consensus in support of détente and arms control.

I watched Nixon's final farewell on television because I had come to believe that it was more important to me to know how the nation saw him than merely what I myself saw. It was a long way from the days of Truman, when the eyewitness in journalism was most important; when getting a personal impression and transmitting it to the public was what mattered. Presidents look different in the flesh and on television, and what mattered to me was to take in the impression he made on the national audience, not the press. History will not forgive Nixon for the way he desecrated the presidency, but he made a true confession: "Others may hate you, but those who hate you don't win unless you hate them, and then you destroy yourself." Nixon's own extraordinarily lucid insight into his own character, uttered intuitively, in the final moment of his presidency—his hatred as a self-destructive process—was literally and figuratively the clearest and last word on the death of his presidency.

Four years later I got an invitation from the ex-president to one of his monthly dinner parties in his apartment in New York. Those dinners for about a dozen men were, I was told, his instrument for keeping in touch with the outside world and making his own views known to news media representatives. The invitation presented me with a dilemma. Did I want to shake hands with the man who had ordered the bugging of my telephone? My immediate reaction was to turn the invitation down. Then I called Harold Evans in London and asked what he would want me to do. Evans, without hesitation, replied that he, as an editor, naturally was always interested in a good story and this invitation might provide one. But in view of my reservations he would leave it to my judgment whether I wanted to attend or not. After discussing the situation with my wife (for it was *our* telephone that was bugged) I called Nixon's private secretary, who had issued the invitation orally, and said that I would be glad to attend the dinner party if the president could find some way of expressing regrets for the bugging of our telephone. Three days later the private secretary called back.

He said I should forget it.

II

The Triumph of the Ultimate Survivors

THAT MALIGNANT TUMOR, Nixon, had been forcibly removed and the former vice president, Gerald Ford, had succeeded to the presidency and restored the normal functioning of the administration. But there hung over the nation a big dark cloud still, the decision whether to prosecute private citizen Nixon. Suddenly, on the morning of Sunday, September 8, 1974, after praying at St. John's Episcopal Church across from the White House, President Ford announced that he had decided to grant Nixon "full, free and absolute pardon . . . for all offenses." I was glad that he had the courage and the statesmanship to take this decision and so soon. I also expected that most Americans would want the Nixon nightmare to be put behind them, and therefore support the president's action. But no —however much the country had already suffered, a majority of Americans, according to the opinion polls, were outraged enough to want to see "equal justice under the law" applied to the ex-president. Personally, I felt strongly that the president should pardon Nixon, not out of any sympathy for the man, but for the country's state of mind. It was important that this ordeal be brought to an end. The biggest scandal before Watergate, the Teapot Dome affair of the Harding era, had dragged through the courts for seven years. Postponement of any Nixon trial would mean its opening in the middle of the Bicentennial celebration of the founding of the Republic.

I was convinced that the widespread suspicion that Nixon, through Al

Haig, had made a "deal" with Ford—a pardon in exchange for his voluntary departure—was wrong as it was unseemly. Ford was a man of high integrity, but in the aftermath of Watergate distrust of government had become almost automatic among the news media. Even among White House staffers, suspecting the worst was the order of the day. Haig passionately denied to me later that he had arranged a deal between Nixon and Ford which led to that pardon. "He did it," Haig said, "because he knew he could not have successfully taken the reins of government while Nixon was in the dock facing prison." But Haig had nothing to do with Ford's decision. Those in the White House who spread rumors among the press that Haig had been acting as an intermediary did so most likely in order to get him out of the White House. Ford's hope that Nixon would confess some form of guilt, more than just the implied admission in his acceptance of a pardon, remained unfulfilled, and Ford was too charitable to force the former president's hand by making it a condition. It has been argued that the pardon decision linked in the public mind the Ford and Nixon presidencies and most likely led to Ford's defeat by Jimmy Carter in 1976. But I doubt it: defeat came, I believe, because Ford failed to establish himself as a leader. He remained the solid, decent, honest, average American doing his best to find answers to his problems, but he did not inspire; his best was simply too pedestrian.

I first met Congressman Ford in 1964 at the Republican Convention in San Francisco when I was asked to interview him for a radio broadcast. His answers then were in the conventional tone of a cold warrior, a firm supporter of NATO, and a conservative in domestic political terms. In the early sixties he joined the so-called Young Turks, led by Congressman Melvin Laird, Charles Goodell, and Donald Rumsfeld, and he became a moderate conservative. In their simplicity his views reminded me of Harry Truman's except that Ford did not have Truman's spunk for politics or knowledge of history. Both reflected a middle-western outlook, except that Ford changed, as he explained to me in an interview that I sought in April 1974, while he was still vice president, in the expectation that he would soon succeed to the presidency. He then said that he remained a "middle American" until he went to Yale University (situated in Connecticut), where he studied law. "It got me out of the middle-western provincial atmosphere . . . and broadened my horizons," he said.

In that interview he tried to defend President Nixon's record by balancing the involvement in Watergate with his achievements in foreign affairs, his overtures to China, détente with the Soviet Union, and his efforts to end the Vietnam war, and by arguing that these preoccupations led him to leave all responsibilities for running the election campaign to Attorney General John Mitchell. Then, after saying that had the president known all the things that were going on, he would have categorically cut them off, he added: ". . . but I think that despite the pressing burdens of foreign policy, you just cannot as a president let things be under the total responsibility of others without doing some monitoring." Ford thus walked a narrow path between charity and criticism. To reassure me as a foreign correspondent, he also underlined that he shared Dr. Kissinger's ideas on foreign policy, though warning that unless some sort of agreement for mutual force reduction could be negotiated with the Soviets (the allies were not very keen on the idea), Congress was likely to demand some troop withdrawals from Europe.

Certainly it was true that he had broadened his outlook, was more self-assured. His was a plodding rather than an intuitive mind, but his honesty, modesty, and directness offered a favorable contrast to Nixon's twisted personality. He also knew exactly who he was and what his limitations were, and did not pretend that he was some great conceptual thinker. In a curious way he reminded me of Britain's onetime prime minister Clement Attlee. Gerald Ford was the very antithesis of the neurotic Nixon and, reassuringly, looked and sounded like the type of man this country, with its jangled nerves, badly needed at this stage. The great question was whether he had it in him to be a leader. He had been a team player all his life and it was this quality that helped him ultimately to reach the White House.

Two days after the pardon Edward Heath, recently deposed as British prime minister by Harold Wilson, came to Washington and saw President Ford. That evening at the British Embassy Heath asked me whether Ford would be able to survive the uproar his pardon had aroused. Ford, it seemed to Heath, was thoroughly confident that he had made the right decision and seemed very much at peace with himself about it. I assured him that Ford was right, pointing out that he had chosen Nelson Rockefeller as his vice president, a man with leadership qualities who knew how to supplement his own limitations with men of high quality.

But the most interesting part of our conversation was about Heath's recent visit to China. He made no bones about his anti-Soviet and pro-Chinese feelings, and was made very welcome. He had a long talk with Chairman Mao, who introduced Wang Hung-wen, who, Mao explained, had come especially from Shanghai so that Heath could get to know and understand him. Wang was then thirty-eight years old and widely mentioned as a possible successor to Mao. But times change. As one of those "helicopters," as the Chinese now refer to those who rise up vertically to success, he crash-landed and is now languishing in prison. When Mao expressed surprise to Prime Minister Chou En-lai that on Heath's arrival at the airport (which he had watched on television) there was no guard of honor or band, Prime Minister Chou replied that such an honor was reserved for heads of government and he did not want to offend Prime Minister Wilson. Mao, in reply, with a wave of his hand from his wrist, said: "Who cares about Wilson!" It endeared Mao to Heath forever. When Heath left China, he told me with a sheepish smile, he was seen off by an honor guard and a band! It was amusing to hear what impression Henry Kissinger had made in Beijing. Chou said that Henry on his first visit had acted "frozen stiff," and on his second shy and scared, but on his third was at ease and at his best. Chou spoke with great admiration of Kissinger and his success in his Middle East peace negotiations.

For years I had been yearning to see China, but since I was no China expert and it was difficult to get a visa anyway, *The Sunday Times* never thought of sending me there. But when Denis Hamilton on his visit to China in 1973 presented Chou En-lai with my book *The Retreat of American Power*, which had just been published, I received, very soon afterwards, an invitation from the Chinese government to visit China. I was told that Prime Minister Chou En-lai had read my book and found my chapter on Sino-American relations well observed, "with only very few misinterpretations," and that he wanted me to see China. Later, in Beijing, I heard that it had been translated into Chinese for circulation among high government officials.

A few weeks later, in November 1973, I was informed that a visa was now available for me and my wife and that I should let the Chinese Embassy in London know when I would want to leave for China. The invitation at that moment presented me with an agonizing dilemma, for the Watergate scandal was unfolding and it did not seem to me the time to absent myself from Washington. I hesitated even to ask Harold Evans for permission to go to China, but when I did call him he said, diplomatically, that he would leave the decision to me. Some of my China expert friends advised that I should not miss this opportunity because, if I turned down the offer, it was very doubtful whether it would be repeated. In effect, though, I had no choice. How could I have let my newspaper down at this dramatic moment in American history? And so, with a heavy heart, I wrote the Chinese ambassador in London, Sung Chih-kuang, a very apologetic letter, explaining that at this crucial moment in American history I could not leave Washington, but that as soon as President Nixon's fate was decided I would be free to come. His reply was a charming example of Chinese diplomatic politesse. He wrote that he fully understood my predicament and that he would have done the same thing had he been in my shoes. Would I advise him as soon as I knew when I could leave for China?

Twenty-four hours after Nixon's resignation I cabled that I was now in a position to come to China whenever it would suit the Chinese government. In return I received the most cordial letter asking me to select November as the earliest date since all interpreters were very busy with state visits in October. And so Muffie and I packed our bags on October 30 to collect our visas in London and then fly to Beijing via Paris and Karachi. For Muffie it was a journey to recapture some of the romance of her father's tales when he went to China on a mission, appointed by President Taft, to explore the prospects for American railroads and those of her mother, who, with her first husband, an explorer on assignment for the Smithsonian, had lived in China for five years in the early twenties. For me it was an adventure rather than a reporter's assignment, an eye-opener to an innocent, and a somewhat awe-inspiring assignment because I had no idea what in the end I would be able to produce to make it all worthwhile for my editor.

At the end of 1974 Chairman Mao Zedong's personality still loomed all-pervasively over China, though most Chinese were well aware that he was now wearily hanging on at the edge of his life. By the time we reached Beijing, Chou En-lai, I was told, had become too ill to receive anybody but his closest aides. This was sad news because I had been looking forward to meeting the man whom Henry Kissinger considered the most impressive personality he had ever met. As a substitute I was offered an interview with Foreign Minister Qiao Guanhua, a man who, not unlike Chou, was intellectually something of a blend of Eastern and Western influences, for he had studied philosophy for five years at the University of Göttingen, in Germany.

The interview was one of those graceful Ping-Pong games the Chinese are masters at, with neither side hitting the ball inconsiderately too hard. It was therefore more of a discourse about the disorders in the world, the rise of economic competition, the struggle of the Arabs against Zionism (as he called it), the risks of nuclear war, and the Soviet threat to China and Europe.

In the wake of the just concluded Ford-Brezhnev summit in Vladivostok, he was particularly scathing about the two powers presuming to decide "the destiny of the world." Qiao was utterly charming, occasionally improved on the accuracy of his young and pretty interpreter, and never stopped smoking his cigarettes. He rejected with contempt my warning about this cancer-causing habit, saying that this was one of those American old wives' tales. (The tale however proved only too true: he died a few years later—of cancer.) Toward the end of our talk I touched on Mao's failing health and what might follow. Qiao, predictably, replied that "of course, people die in the natural course of things but our policy will continue to be carried out true to the letter as determined by the Communist Party." Little did he suspect that he would become a victim of the post-Mao housecleaning which downgraded uncompromising ideology in favor of a more practical approach to real problems.

From my tourist viewpoint the most impressive ancient site we visited was near Sian, the old capital of China under the Han and Tang dynasties: the tomb of the Empress Wu Kung Tsu, set on a hillside overlooking an endlessly rolling countryside. A broad avenue led up to the top of the hill, lined with life-sized funeral figures, crude stone sculptures of men and magnificent horses. With the mist rising from the valley there was something mysterious and magical about it all. In ancient times this used to be forbidden territory because it was considered holy, but as a landscape it had not changed, we were told, in some three thousand years.

I learned more about China than I had from books or lectures on our thirty-two-hour train journey from Sian to Shanghai, a panoramic view filled with contrasts. From the lush countryside of Sian we passed through the poorest, barren mountain region of Itsiung-Erh Shan where we saw people living in caves, fields being worked over by plows drawn by oxen, and gaunt-looking people still carrying their water supplies in buckets hanging over their shoulders. We passed mountains that had been cut sharply and vertically down, as if with a butter knife, to the level of the plain, broadening the arable land, but relatively few industrial developments until we came to the abundance of the Yangtse River basin and the overpowering city of Shanghai, with its Western facades along the harbor front and the indomitable aspirations of a world entrepôt.

We traveled pretty comfortably in an old-fashioned Pullman train with sleepers and a dining car and with the cook visiting our compartment before every meal to take our order for whatever Chinese dishes we chose. What remains etched in my mind is a sense of the vastness of the country, the stoicism and endurance and discipline of the people, and an impression of stability despite the instability of China's human affairs, of the power of the land over history, and a basic unity despite regional differences. I realized how difficult it was to govern this country, once ruled by warlords and landowners —and how difficult it was for a newcomer like myself to reach any safe conclusions. It was impossible to grasp the staggering social changes of the past twenty-five years, the destruction of an ancient rigid class structure sanctified by the ethical teachings of Confucius—who had now become enemy No. 1. At the same time I began to appreciate in the most elementary terms why the Russians, as I knew from my many discussions with them over the years, are so fearful of the Chinese. One would think that they must feel superior. After all, they have far more military power and a far more massive industrial machine. But China is so huge, its people possess such extraordinary discipline, diligence, and resilience, that it is beyond assimilation or conquest. Chinese hatred of the Russians surpassed everything that I had ever heard among Eastern Europeans. Khrushchev's decision to withdraw Soviet technicians and industrial blueprints left an enduring resentment. The lesson that China must not become dependent on anybody but herself had sunk deeply into the consciousness of every Chinese. That conviction goes so far that a factory manager in Shanghai said to me: "The South must be independent of the North because one of these days the Northeast may come under Russian occupation." Or as a general put it to me in reply to my question of what would happen if the Russians invaded Manchuria: "They may get in, but not out." It is quite significant though that despite the relative primitiveness of the Chinese military forces and their second-rate equipment, the successor generation of leaders put far greater emphasis on spending to improve the economy than on military might, quite the opposite from the Russians, who are convinced that superpowerism depends on military strength. Not one Chinese referred to his country as a superpower and most of them called it, simply and modestly, a developing country.

Most disappointing to Muffie was the refusal of the authorities to let her see the inside of the house where her mother used to live from 1919 to 1922. She had the old address—the Road of the Dry Well—but it was only thanks to an elderly taxi driver, familiar with the changed street names and street numbers that we succeeded in locating it. It was a charming one-story court-yarded house, built under the shadow of the astrological instruments, perched on the ancient walls surrounding the city. Once we had found the little street we had no difficulty identifying the house from the faded photographs Muffie's mother had taken and the French enamel blue and white house numbers which she had brought from Paris half a century ago. Ironically, these Western symbols were removed from the wall the day after we discovered the location of this ancestral home as if to wrap it further in the obscurity of a vanished China. My wife used to stand on the opposite corner at dusk for several days, watching the families enter and leave, but despite our official requests permission to enter was never given. Muffie estimated that eight families now lived in a house which was originally built for one Western couple and four servants.

Having failed in this case to see the inside of a private house, we were therefore particularly curious to visit Mr. and Mrs. Frank Coe, whose telephone number had been given to us by Lois Snow, widow of Edgar Snow, the writer and an old companion from our war correspondent days in Europe. Ed's book, *Red Star Over China,* was the first authentic report about the rise of Chinese communism and the Long March of Mao Zedong's forces. No Western reporter had previously been able to penetrate into the blockaded Red area, but he did and met the Chinese leader at a moment when he was willing to talk about himself and his movement. What added to Ed's fame was that his prophecies for the future of this then hardly known movement proved extraordinarily accurate. Ed's heart was in China, but with Franklin D. Roosevelt committed to Generalissimo Chiang Kai-shek Ed returned to Europe disheartened, just in time to cover the fall of Hitler and to liberate a German Ford which General J. M. "Iron Mike" O'Daniel of the Third Division had given him as a present. My interest in "Frau Lizzie," as the khaki-colored hardtop had been nicknamed, developed a few weeks later when Ed, back in Paris, was lured into a fast, high-stake poker game by Bob Capa, Morgan Beatty, Charles Collingwood, Jack O'Riley, and Jack Belden—all star war correspondents and star poker players. They relieved Ed of eight hundred dollars in one night. Since he had to leave the next day for the Soviet Union and I had been looking for a car, I paid Ed's debts and became Frau Lizzie's happy owner. Ed was much comforted when I told him later that Collingwood that week lost his liberated Duesenberg and his Mercedes—Charlie always traveled in style. O'Riley later claimed that thanks to those high-flying poker games at the Scribe Hotel he was able to buy a farm in Bucks County. Anyway, Ed was a much better reporter (for the *Saturday Evening Post*) than poker player.

The Coes were Americans who had taken refuge in China after Senator McCarthy took aim at them and they wanted to avoid pleading the Fifth Amendment if asked whether they had ever been members of the Communist Party. As the director of research of the U.S. Treasury, Coe in April 1945 wrote a confidential memorandum for Secretary of the Treasury Henry Morgenthau,

Jr., in advance of his meeting Chiang Kai-shek's confidant Dr. T. V. Soong about the misuse of American financial aid by the Nationalist Chinese government. And he described a complicated scheme of financial dummy operations by which Chiang Kai-shek and his friends managed to stash away some $200 million of American aid. When his position in the Treasury subsequently became untenable, Coe became deputy director of research for the International Monetary Fund under Eduard Bernstein in 1946. The then secretary of the treasury, John Snyder, in 1952 asked Bernstein to dismiss him as having been disloyal to the United States government. Bernstein resisted since Coe had worked well with him for six years and he had no reason to think that he had been disloyal. Indeed, when told about Snyder's letter, Coe had said he would answer any questions he might be asked. But instead he pleaded the Fifth Amendment and resigned from the IMF in 1952. Unable to find work in private business because of his refusal to say whether he had been a member of the Communist Party, he decided to move to Communist China, where his early opposition to Chiang Kai-shek's financial manipulations and his Communist sympathies assured him a ready welcome.

We were greeted by Mrs. Coe, a short, stocky, energetic American, dressed in baggy trousers, Mao jacket, Chinese black slippers with white soles, and short clipped hair. After entering through a brightly lit red door and stepping over the high threshold, designed to keep out the evil spirits as well as the dust from the street, we suddenly found ourselves in the different and very private world of an old-style Chinese house. The courtyard was surrounded by a high, beautiful wall, the windows were of the "summer palace" variety, and an octagonal white marble fountain with lions on each corner pedestal stood in the center. The main house was on the opposite side of the courtyard, painted bright red with latticed windows, China loggia style. The living room had the slightly disheveled air of a Cambridge professor's house.

Mr. Coe, who must have been in his late sixties, wore a normal Western suit, shirt, and tie, and after offering us Scotch, beer, or brandy and peanuts, told us how he was accused of disloyalty, how McCarthy hounded him because of his revelations about Chiang Kai-shek, and how he later went to China to escape a long-drawn-out investigation into his Communist past. He told us that they had lived in Beijing with their two daughters, seventeen and eleven, both American citizens, ever since. Both daughters spoke better Chinese than English; in fact, the younger one had never been to the United States. The Coes' lifelines to the United States and the West were the *International Herald Tribune,* which arrived only three days late, and BBC radio reports. There were some thirty-five Americans living in Beijing like the Coes. All of them were invited to meet with Chou En-lai on the eve of President Nixon's visit to prepare them for the first opening in the bamboo curtain.

Mrs. Coe worked for the Office of Foreign Trade and he did translating work and acted as an adviser. The family seemed thoroughly at home in their surroundings; no one had any intention of returning to the United States, which had become a sort of faraway offshore island. When the older daughter came to introduce herself—the younger proved too shy—and I asked her what she planned to do after graduation, she said without hesitation that it was up to Chairman Mao to decide that. It devastated me to hear this stereotype reply from the mouth of what to me was still an American child, but it did not seem at all surprising to her parents, for whom she seemed to be only technically an American citizen.

The only opportunity we had actually to dine in a genuine Chinese home occurred in a village near Sian during a visit to a farm commune, whose leader, the so-called brigade leader, invited us to his home. His wife, daughter, and son stayed in the kitchen preparing the meal over hot coals while we were discussing the brigade's life with the commander and his eighty-year-old mother, who was quietly but surely in command in this family. She wore a black silk jacket and a black-and-white turban in the old fashion. When Muffie asked her how she managed to raise such a fine and honored son, she replied: "It's not I but the party which is responsible." The old lady, though dressed the old traditional way, had learned her Maoist lessons well.

The only American we met apart from Frank Coe, but one who had completely blended into the Chinese landscape, was the remarkable Dr. George Hatem, born in Buffalo, New York, of Lebanese origin, who had been Mao's doctor for forty years. Together with Edgar Snow, he was smuggled into Communist-held territory, and became one of two doctors in the entire Red Army. According to Snow, he "knows more about Red China and its leaders than any foreigner alive." He helped to organize the so-called barefoot doctors, to whom he imparted enough knowledge to deliver emergency medical service on the spot.

Dr. Hatem was lunching with some friends in the restaurant of our Beijing hotel when he was pointed out to me by our interpreter. Using Snow's name I introduced myself and he immediately agreed to have lunch with me the following day. He looked typically Lebanese, with dark deep-set eyes and a round, deeply lined face which exuded toughness as well as kindness. His ready smile and firm handshake were very American.

We reminisced about our old friend Snow and I mentioned how upset he was in 1952 when he was denied a visa to visit "his" China about whose leaders and the dawn of Chinese communism he had written so intimately and authoritatively. Hatem, suddenly speaking with the mentality of a Chinese, explained that Snow had forgotten that he himself had become a historical personality and that he too was therefore subject to the flows of history; at that particular time history and his own position in it were at odds. Later, he went on, Snow came to understand that once his personality had again become compatible with history, he was again able to play a part in it, which, indeed, he fulfilled by conveying the message that an understanding with the United States was possible. "It was sad," he added, "that at that point in history he had to go." The last time Dr. Hatem saw him was in 1972, when Mao sent him with a medical team to Switzerland to look after Snow, who was suffering from acute cancer. But it was too late. It was a gesture of appreciation, though, that meant a great deal to Ed. When I met Dr. Hatem again in 1980 in Washington he had come for chemotherapy treatment for his own cancer of the kidneys. Chemotherapy, he explained to me, was still in its infancy in China. He left after six weeks to return to China, happy to be experiencing a remission.

To my American wife the visit to China brought back, as she put it in her diary, "the values of my Yankee ancestors on the sandy shores of the Plymouth Bay, and I feel a circle has in some mysterious way been completed. Now that I have seen China I understand, as never before, what my great-great-great ancestors went through in the early days of that little commune called the Plymouth Colony. For this, if nothing more, I owe China a debt beyond words, for she made me understand my roots in a way I never have from the American history books."

To me as a reporter China remained a mystery. I found it hard to "read" in Chinese faces or to take for granted that they really believed in the stereotypes Mao had taught them. Not speaking the language and unable to hear its nuances was another obvious drawback. But I was deeply touched by people's friendliness, simplicity, humor, and natural intelligence. I left hoping that being shrewed, curious, ambitious, and history-minded as they appeared to me, they would not continue to parrot whatever the authorities told them to say. And my hopes have been more than fulfilled. Indeed, the speed with which Maoism was swept aside was stunning. For anyone who has listened for hours, days to the teachings of Mao and to the fulfillments of his aims, to the recantations of those who had not seen the light of the Cultural Revolution in time and their condemnations by the Red Guards, the storm of change that has since blown across the vastness of China is hard to grasp. Deng Xiaoping's muscular leadership set the stage for the "second revolution" and helped to overcome the initial obstacles. More experiments, new collisions are bound to follow, and whether post-Mao China will successfully digest this extraordinary upheaval will depend on the political and technical skill of the leadership. By coincidence, the two great Communist powers are now competing in the race to make their systems economically viable. It injects an uncertainty into their future which China, in the long run, thanks to the more pragmatic Chinese mind, may win.

By coincidence Henry Kissinger was due to arrive in Beijing at the very end of our grand tour. He had been in Vladivostok with President Ford for the Brezhnev summit and came ostensibly to brief the Chinese leadership on this encounter. Naturally, I decided to stay on to cover the visit and called the Foreign Office for the necessary accreditation. But the Press Department turned me down politely, saying that the Kissinger visit was a bilateral affair and "third country correspondents" could not participate. When I checked with some of my colleagues who were permanently stationed in Beijing, I was told that this was indeed the rule and that there was not much I could do about it, except to rely on American correspondents, who would attend the briefings, for information. I then called John Holdridge, the American minister, whom I had known for some time, asking if he could possibly send a message to Henry asking him to intervene with the Chinese for my accreditation. On the day of Henry's arrival I got another telephone call from a member of the Press Department saying that, as I had been told before, I could not be accredited as a "third country correspondent" to cover the visit. Then, after a pause, he added that since I was a friend of Dr. Kissinger's, arrangements had been made for me to cover the visit and to be invited to the formal banquet in the Great Hall of the People.

The Great Hall of the People was a typical example of Sino-Soviet modern drab architecture, designed to impress with hugeness, not taste. After Muffie and I mounted the broad, red-carpeted staircase with the rest of the guests, we were asked to pose for a gigantic group photo on a bleacherlike platform at the top of the staircase, so broad that the picture had to be taken in several sections with several cameras.

We sat at table 18 in that cold, austere-looking hall, Kissinger at table No. 1 with his children, David and Elizabeth. Nancy, his wife, was missing; I could only assume sympathetically that her ulcer must have flared up badly for her to miss this special occasion. The dinner was an endless parade of delicious Chinese dishes, some of which I had never tasted before. The toasts supposedly reflected the mood in which the conversations were held and they sounded to me artificially cordial and purposely restrained. Only Kissinger's seemed to have real meaning, for he told his hosts that President Ford meant to continue the Nixon foreign policy and that he expected the friendly relations that already existed to grow. To the tune of "Home on the Range" we left this huge echo chamber of a hall at nine o'clock and stepped into the cold Beijing night.

I exchanged a few words with the then Vice Premier Deng Xiaoping, to whom Winston Lord, an aide to Kissinger (whom President Reagan appointed ambassador to China on Kissinger's recommendation), had introduced me. But otherwise this had not been an occasion for the press to mingle with members of the Chinese leadership group. Even for a Chinese Deng was unusually short and slight in build, but his body seemed bursting with barely controlled strength. In his black Mao suit with white socks protruding under his narrow-cut pants, he looked unassuming, but the hard gaze in his eyes, the self-assurance he exuded, gave me a sense of the power stored in this diminutive body. Once a victim of the Cultural Revolution, he was soon going to be its conqueror.

I could talk to Henry only briefly on our way out as he was the center of everybody's attention, but managed to thank him for his intervention and to ask him whether in view of the communiqué being timed for Saturday, which made it very difficult for me to make my deadline, he could see me on Friday night. He promised to think about it. Next day, after the first official briefing

I got a message from him to await a US delegation car which would pick me up at the hotel and take me to the off-limits guest house where he was staying and where the talks were being held. When the time came the car was indeed waiting for me, as promised, and carried me to the guest house compound that lay beyond the center of the city within a large garden surrounded by a high wall. The car whisked past all the Chinese police patrols without being stopped and delivered me to the villa where Henry had his guest suite. A member of the American delegation then took me into a pleasant sitting room, offered me a soft drink, and asked me to be patient, since it would take some time—he did not know how long—until Henry could see me.

I had arrived at eight P.M. but by nine no Henry had appeared. A dutiful member of the American delegation, obviously instructed to keep me company, arrived, but by ten we both realized that we had run out of things to talk about. Curious himself what was delaying Henry, he disappeared to return after about an hour with the message that the talks were still continuing and that it was impossible to estimate when they would end. In any case, it was now certain that they would last too long for Henry to see me and that I had better return to my hotel.

What I did not know was that while I had been cooling my heels, Henry was being subjected to the crudest, almost insulting treatment ever meted out to him in China. After a bitterly contentious debate about the communiqué the session had to be adjourned and was resumed at midnight. The Chinese were upset about the Vladivostok meeting, which demonstrated to them that American-Soviet relations were far better than they had assumed; Foreign Minister Qiao Guanhua, who led the Chinese delegation, let fly about what a weak-kneed policy détente with the Soviets was, expressing himself with a kind of venom that Henry had never before experienced from a Chinese. In discussing President Ford's visit to China the following year, they insisted that he prepare then and there to complete the normalization of relations with China or at least make sufficient concessions to make it clear that it would happen soon, something Henry could not agree to since he knew that the president, facing a presidential election, could not afford to go that far. They were also worried about Ford's "Saturday night massacre," the dismissal of Secretary of Defense James Schlesinger, whom they had lionized because of his opposition to the détente policy. Faced with such radical changes, as they saw them, in the policymaking elite, they panicked: it looked to them like Mao's own purge of Lin Piao. The arguments reached such nastiness on the part of the Chinese that Henry suggested that perhaps Ford's trip to China should be put off. At this point Qiao changed his tone. It then became clear that they needed the presidential visit for their own purposes and he assured Henry that they would receive him with all courtesy. Henry's threat to cancel the Ford visit exposed the Chinese commitment to the American relationship. It was also proof of the existence of the "enduring play between strategic triangles," a game that can be played by any of the three but more easily by the United States than by China.

Not knowing any of this, I was driven back to my hotel, my high expectations unfulfilled, but amused about the unpredictability of things, even for a man of Kissinger's skill and reputation. I did not see Henry before his hurried departure, which clearly indicated to me that there was nothing he could say to me beyond the laconic communiqué announcing that President Ford would visit the People's Republic of China in 1975, that talks had been "beneficial," and that the commitment to the Shanghai communiqué remained unchanged. Such are the ways of diplomacy, however, that the irritation on the American side was expressed by including the Philippines and Indonesia in the president's tour, thus downgrading it and cutting Ford's stay in China by two days. The Chinese, as interpreted by some Sinologists in the administration, reciprocated by using historical analogy to criticize Kissinger. In an article in one of their newspapers they dug up the name of a once-famous minister to a powerful emperor in 300 B.C., named Ts'ao Ts'ao. He was not the man in authority, with real power, as one of the administration's leading Sinologists explained to me, but the implementer of policy and its manipulator. This picture of Kissinger was reinforced in their mind by his dealings with the Israelis, the Arabs, and the Russians, which left them uncertain about his position. They knew where Nixon stood because they knew how much he hated the Russians. They did not see Kissinger as the American press saw him, an independent force, separate from Nixon; it was Nixon who had actually taken the decision to open up relations with China, not Henry, even though his pace-setting secret mission had made him into a diplomatic superstar and had aroused widespread admiration elsewhere. Success in China therefore mattered to Henry enormously, and it was hurtful being treated as only a functionary—Ts'ao Ts'ao—rather than as a statesman.

Still, there was no doubt that the Sino-American relationship remained fundamentally stable. It did not depend on diplomatic protocol but on considerations of global strategy. As such it had assumed dimensions that went well beyond such issues as the status of Taiwan, for, lacking a navy, China must rely for its security in the Pacific on the United States. This did not mean however, as suggested by Senator Scoop Jackson after his visit to China, that Beijing would enter into a defense arrangement with the United States, or any other foreign power. His suggestion only proved how difficult it is for an American politician, even of the intelligence of Jackson, to think himself into the Chinese mentality, the Chinese view of history. Frank Giles, the much traveled then *Sunday Times* foreign editor, tells a story that illustrates the point. When Deng Xiaoping asked the departing British ambassador, Sir John Addis, about the deteriorating economic situation in Britain, Sir John replied that he expected the situation to improve and that in ten years' time Britain would have turned the corner. On hearing this Deng threw up his hands and exclaimed: "But what is ten years in the history of a nation!"

Since Washington always thrives more on discussing personalities than policies, it was not surprising that one of the first questions to be debated over dinner tables and in the press, was how the well-known ego of Henry Kissinger would mesh with the modest ego of President Ford. Some in the Ford entourage wondered whether the new president, as he sought to establish himself as a man in command for the 1976 elections, would want to step out of the Kissinger shadow, others to what extent he would be better off politically wearing a popular secretary of state in his buttonhole. And in Kissinger's entourage they wondered how his penchant for secret diplomacy would coexist with Mr. Ford's "open" presidency.

The basic question about the future Ford-Kissinger relationship was answered by the selection of Nelson Rockefeller for the vice presidency. Obviously, Mr. Ford felt much more secure than anybody had expected. It did not seem to worry him to have big men around him. The reason for this, most likely, was that he never expected to become president and therefore never acquired that warping ego that avid presidential contenders develop in the heat of election campaigns. Rockefeller, on the other hand, had gone through two disappointing presidential campaigns and if one cared to think at all of a really badly warped ego, his would do. In spite of his self-confidence, his financial means, his ability to summon the best expert advice, his desire to do good, and his conviction that he was about as good a public servant as could be found —the presidency eluded him.

To be offered what under certain, if remote, circumstances, could provide him with a shortcut to the presidency, was for these reasons a very welcome fluke of fate. But for a man filled with optimism and high expectations the vice presidency became an unhappy experience from the start. Rockefeller's confirmation hearings were a humiliating example of the kind of indecent nosiness into private affairs that members of Congress can be capable of. The legendary fortune of the Rockefeller family of course was a special temptation because of the fear that his millions could give him power well beyond the vice presidency. At one point, when senators began to demand details about his brother's holdings, Rockefeller seriously considered withdrawal. After four months of testimony he was finally confirmed 90 to 7—with Senator Goldwater, unable to forget Rockefeller's challenging his nomination in 1964, voting against.

The ordeal Rocky went through, no doubt, was not lost on many able rich men with ambitions to go into public service. However useful the confirmation process may have been in the past, it has dampened the desires of worthy men to enter government. In Britain, as in most parliamentary democracies, men chosen for important positions in government go through the electoral process and are trusted without having to go through an inquisition. There is much greater trust in the honesty and rectitude of men seeking to serve their country than is the case in the United States.

Rockefeller, whenever I saw him, whether in his office or on the campaign trail, struck me as the epitome of the American who wanted to be loved by everybody. His zeal to prove that there was more to him than his inherited billions and his ardor to improve life in the United States and in the world, turned him into a man in constant motion. But his tendency to play the sidewalk politician, eager to befriend people, seeking to shake their hands, asking for their votes or their sympathies, and to wallow in clichés and the obvious, raised the question how much depth there was in him. He was a shameless flatterer, but he also enjoyed being flattered. He once invited me to his three-thousand-acre estate, Pocantico Hills, near Tarrytown, north of New York City, and told me, infinitely pleased, that when the Shah of Iran visited the fifty-room Georgian house, seeing the fine art collection and the beautiful gardens, which included a nine-hole golf course, he congratulated his host on "a place fit for a king." When the United Nations decided to move to New York in 1946, he offered Pocantico free of charge to the United Nations, but was turned down. "Wasn't it a stupid decision," he said to me, pointing at the beautiful view over the Hudson River and what he called the quiet and peaceful surroundings. "Instead they built in Manhattan, in the middle of all the noise and traffic, and got lost." He made it clear that it would have been an honor for him had his offer been accepted.

Unlike so many members of the great families of Europe, who don't mind living ostentatiously and don't care what people think of them, Rockefeller avoided ostentatious living, anxious to give people the impression of being treated as equals. One man he did not treat as an equal, but held in special esteem, was his old friend and adviser Kissinger, whom he admired for his intellectual toughness. "Every period has its Humphrey Bogart," he said, toasting Henry at a dinner party, "and the tough guy of his time is Henry Kissinger!"

Like the Roosevelts and the Kennedys, Rockefeller had at his beck and call outstanding intellects in business, in academia, and in the science community. They supplied him with ideas, analyses, and position papers. Now, he thought, he would be in a position to translate them into action. But his expectations were bitterly disappointed. President Ford originally promised to put him in charge of the Domestic Policy Council, with the same kind of authority over planning and coordination as the National Security Council's in foreign affairs. It did not take Rocky long to realize that his own role and that of the council had been drastically clipped rather than increased. When I saw him in February 1975 he sounded like a man who was badly chafing at the bit. He felt under-used, even ignored. As governor of New York State he had talked to me with great pride about his studies of "critical issues" as one of his most positive achievements, but now that he was in a position to use them, no one seemed to be interested. President Ford, he said, did not have the same kind of intellectual approach to the great problems of our time that he himself had, and since he had no function, he depended entirely on what the president asked him to do. Even worse, some of the presidential aides, such as Donald Rumsfeld, did everything they could to defuse the vice president's eagerness to do good and to do well. With the resources outside the government at his disposal, they were afraid that Rockefeller could overshadow the president, and they were determined to prevent that.

Rockefeller indeed was so used to acting as an independent force, so irrepressible and accustomed to being the center of things, that he lacked the kind of sensitivity that would have told him on special occasions to restrain himself. Henry Kissinger, for instance, told me about a visit to the pope to which he had invited then-Governor Rockefeller. Henry warned him before they entered the pope's inner sanctum not to allow himself to be carried away and to let the pope lead the conversation. Rockefeller solemnly promised just to listen, but it did not take long until he interrupted His Eminence by asking him what he thought of the Italian government's shift to the left, debated that, and then lectured the pope on the necessity for morality and practicality.

Some years later Henry suffered another embarrassment during a visit with the pope during Nixon's presidency. Defense Secretary Melvin Laird had been told to miss out on this audience because, since he was not exactly a herald of peace, his presence would cause problems. After the American party had entered the pope's chambers, Kissinger suddenly spotted Laird and demanded to know why he had come along. Laird, smiling and nonchalantly flipping the ash from his cigar, retorted that he had been under the impression he was a member of the delegation. Kissinger had no choice but to let him tag along, but asked him to get rid of his smelly cigar and to behave inconspicuously. Later, during the audience, Kissinger found himself suddenly distracted by Laird, standing in a corner, flapping his arms furiously, seemingly to subdue a plume of smoke that was rising from his pocket. Laird, as he later explained, in order to do away with his cigar, stepped on it and then slipped it into his pocket, thinking it was dead. But it was not and a slow burn developed.

Rockefeller, of course, was not the first vice president to feel himself, as he put it, "stand-by equipment." Lyndon Johnson as Kennedy's "Veep" felt like a chained tiger. Hubert Humphrey, as Johnson's, was willing to subject himself to endless humiliation in the hope of having LBJ's support if and when he got his chance at the presidency. George Bush humiliated himself for the same reason. President Carter, perhaps more than any other president, allowed Walter Mondale to play an important role. I remember once sitting in the office of Hamilton Jordan, Carter's right-hand man, as the vice president flung open the door and, red in the face, ordered him to call Secretary of Agriculture Bob Bergland to tell him to "shut up." (It was at a time that the farmers had come to Washington on their tractors to protest low agricultural prices and Bergland had made a remark which had further infuriated the protesters.) Seeing me sitting there, he turned to me, and with his forefinger stretched out, pointing at me, said, "Henry, this is off the record!" And then he stormed out. Jordan got up immediately and telephoned Bergland, who happened to be away from his office. It gave me the impression then of Mondale's authority being somewhat more exalted than I had assumed. But even he later confessed to suffering from the in-built weakness of being a crown prince or "man-in-waiting."

Rockefeller was given one important and highly delicate assignment, an investigation into Central Intelligence Agency activities, mainly to defuse one by the Senate Select Committee under the chairmanship of Senator Frank Church, which, the president feared, would dig too deeply into the recesses of the agency. Both were the kind of investigation no other government but the American would permit. The Rockefeller Commission report stirred up controversy, above all, because it did not pursue allegations of the agency's involvement in assassination plots, as did the Senate's investigation. Rockefeller claimed lack of time, but the real reason was that the evidence pointed an accusing finger at presidents, beginning with Eisenhower. CIA Director William Colby tried to force the commission's hand by accusing the Kennedy administration of gross violations, including assassinations, but the vice president refused to get involved in investigating the acts of presidents. He therefore trod gingerly and concluded that while CIA had not engaged in massive violations, improved supervision was desirable.

The morning of April 28, 1975, was sunny and fine, except that during a tennis game I felt a sudden sharp pain in my chest. I stopped playing and rested for a few minutes until I decided to go home, which was only a few steps from the British Embassy tennis court. In no time my wife drove me to the doctor, who sent me by ambulance to the nearest hospital after having diagnosed that I had suffered a mild heart attack. Was it due to playing tennis shortly after having had breakfast, or a delayed reaction to the strains of covering the Watergate affair? At any rate, it was a bit of a shock to someone who felt in excellent health. About three weeks after the attack—I had to stay in hospital for ten days—I was asked to represent the British press in a group television interview with President Ford for distribution in NATO countries. Wondering whether I would incur any risks of straining my heart unnecessarily, since television interviews were not routine for me, I went to see my doctor for advice. His verdict was encouraging and surprising. He said participating in such an interview might do me a lot of good. Then, with a twinkle in his eyes, he added: "Mind you, never before have I prescribed a television interview with an American president as a cure after a heart attack." In the interest of medical history I should add that the interview did indeed become part of the cure.

The two intellectual heavyweights in the Ford cabinet were Kissinger and James Schlesinger, whom Nixon had put in charge of the Defense Department, replacing Laird. Not surprisingly, the two, holding strong views of their own and a ferocity of purpose, became bitter antagonists. Kissinger was now the carefully groomed statesman, looking slightly overfed on official luxury dinners; Schlesinger continued to look the academic, dressing sloppily and giving himself the bearing of an intellectual John Wayne. His rugged face exuded a certain unshakable conviction that he was right and everybody else was wrong —and quite often with some justification. He was a man I had learned to respect.

I got to know him in the Nixon administration when he dealt with Defense Department matters in the Office of Management and Budget, and went to see him not because of what he had to said about the Pentagon, but to listen to his global assessments. He had the rigorous outlook of a mathematician who chafes over imponderables, seeks to avoid risks, and believes in calculating the future over the next ten years as accurately as the computers will permit. Kissinger, on the other hand, in assessing national and world affairs, made the historian's allowances for the passage of time, for evolution and experience. Schlesinger remained essentially an optimist, if in a complicated metaphysical way. Kissinger held a tragic view of history, troubled by the ghosts of decline that were stalking the West, with Marxism making increasing political inroads and a United States too ungovernable to meet the challenge. If Kissinger considered détente a vital tool of diplomacy that would help to make the world a little more secure, Schlesinger winced at the idea, viewed it as little more than a cosmetic device that gave the United States and its allies an illusory sense of security. Kissinger's tools were persuasion, accommodation, charm, wit, and the ability to skirt confrontations. Schlesinger was the bullying type, abrasive, didactic, imperious, unwittingly (sometimes wittingly) offensive, but brilliant in his own intellectual way. Both belonged to a rare breed; they were thinkers and men of action.

Kissinger resented Schlesinger's intellectual capacities and the difficulties he created over SALT II. When during an interview with Schlesinger I used one of Kissinger's arguments in favor of SALT, he replied in his "rolling thunder" voice: "You seem to have listened too much to a senior State Department official" (the code phrase for Kissinger whenever he spoke for background only). At the end of the one-and-a-half-hour interview, he moved his face, half jokingly, half intimidatingly, almost into mine and, looking me straight into the eyes, asked challengingly: "How did I stand up to this inquisition?" Nobody could have been more disbelieving, more stunned, when he got top-level advance notice of a story in *Newsweek* predicting his imminent dismissal. Ford, informed that his decision had leaked, called Schlesinger in on a Saturday to tell him before he read about it in the magazine.

If Schlesinger was unaware of his incompatibility with Ford, Kissinger for some months talked privately about the insecurities of his own relations with the new president. He and Nixon complemented each other. When Nixon participated in negotiations, he had all the facts at his fingertips. But with Ford, Henry was in charge, never a comfortable position to be in with a president, especially with one who he could never be sure fully understood the ins and outs of the negotiations. But he still treated the president with far greater deference and understanding than Schlesinger, knowing that Ford was honest enough with himself to realize that he could not do without Kissinger. Kissinger, under Ford, attained a leadership position people considered on a par with the president, as Richard Cheney, Ford's chief of staff put it to me, which left him exposed as a political target as soon as the 1976 presidential election campaign got underway. The man who zeroed in on his foreign policy with a vengeance was Ford's rival for the nomination, Ronald Reagan. His clamor that Kissinger had allowed the United States to become militarily inferior to the Soviet Union made "détente" a dirty word, so much so that to Kissinger's disgust Ford substituted "peace through strength" for it in his speeches. Reagan also took to task Helmut Sonnenfeldt, a Kissinger aide expert in Soviet affairs, for having said that realism and Soviet power imposed limits to change in Eastern Europe, and generally forced Kissinger so much on the defensive that Henry himself began to harden his anti-Soviet stance. Congress went even further. It tried to crucify him for involving the United States in covert operations in Chile and Angola, and he escaped being cited for contempt by the House Intelligence Committee only after the president had agreed to divulge all the State Department proposals for covert operations in the previous ten years, including those that were rejected.

With everybody else, I assumed that it was personal incompatibility rather than policy differences that led as charitable a man as Ford to fire Schlesinger, who was one of the ablest secretaries of defense. General Haig later told me that this assumption was wrong, that Ford from the start wanted to get rid of him because he still resented an order I mentioned earlier that Schlesinger had issued to prevent Nixon from using the military to defy his impeachment. In his memoir *A Time to Heal,* Ford confirmed that "for the Secretary of Defense to speculate to the press that our military commanders—men who are controlled by civilians under the Constitution—might take some unilateral action at a moment of grave national crisis, was to stab our armed services in the back. And that, in my opinion, was inexcusable. Now, fifteen months later, I concluded that I had been remiss in not getting rid of him . . ." But when I asked Ford in March 1988 what made him dismiss Schlesinger, he waved away Schlesinger's instructions to prevent some kind of a coup with the help of the military, just prior to Nixon's resignation, and put virtually all the emphasis on the sharp disagreements between Schlesinger and Kissinger over arms control and the timing of the final withdrawal from Vietnam, which, he said, had become intolerable. Schlesinger, when asked how he interpreted Ford's action, said that his disagreements with Kissinger were substantial, and those with the president over the cuts in the defense budget and the disengagement from Vietnam, bruising. At the time, for instance, he had concluded that the war in Vietnam was all over, the president gave him and others a pep talk in the National Security Council that all was not lost. To this, he now admits, a little shamefacedly, he told the president, not appropriately deferentially: bullshit.

The Vladivostok agreement, which Ford and Kissinger thought had been a major achievement because it set the framework for a SALT II agreement, ran into such opposition in Congress that when Ford asked Donald Rumsfeld, then secretary of defense, to testify in support of it, he replied, according to Kissinger, that he would do so only if ordered. Once Ford realized that defending the Vladivostok agreement could seriously jeopardize his winning the presidency, he decided to let it lie fallow until after the election. It was during those days of disillusionment for Kissinger that Frank Giles, on one of his regular visits to Washington, and I had lunch with him at the State Department. He made no bones about his distress and his forebodings of defeat and tragedy, and angrily denounced the rising criticism of his policies. "The attacks on détente would not be possible without détente," he said. "All my critics are living off détente. They would not sound as belligerent if there were a Berlin crisis or the Russians were to send troops into Syria." He was convinced that despite all the objections, a Democratic administration would also opt for détente, and regretted that Congress was so firmly opposed to giving the Soviets preferential tariffs and credits because, he argued, these concessions were part of his détente package as he had negotiated it with the Russians. To him, getting tough was part of a process of positive incentives and negative costs. When Giles asked him pointedly whether in view of the mounting criticism directed against him personally, his holding on to being secretary of state was not undermining support for American foreign policy, especially in Congress, Henry, letting his bitterness well up, replied: "The graveyard of history is full of indispensable men."

But it was not only Congress and the public that turned against Kissinger's policies or against him personally. The Ford loyalists in the White House also were gunning for him. They felt that in order to give the Ford presidency its own place in history, Nixon's last remaining symbol, Kissinger, needed to be removed. But, according to Cheney, Ford relied more on Kissinger than on any other aide—sometimes, he said, unhealthily so. Rumsfeld, who favored Kissinger's elimination, had his own ambitions. He was a strikingly clean-cut young man with a kind of West Point gloss who had made his way up from being a congressman from Illinois to two minor posts in the Nixon administration and then ambassador to NATO. He was a hard-driving organization man, tough, shrewd, with a searching mind. I was amused when this moderate-conservative Republican told me that a speech by Adlai Stevenson, delivered to the Princeton class of 1954, inspired him to enter politics. He later gave me a copy of that speech and, on reading it, I could understand why the elegant eloquence of this civilized mind swept him off his feet. To quote one of the best passages: "It is to you, to your enlightened attention, that the American Government must look for the sources of its power. You dare not, if I may say so, withhold your attention. For if you do, if those young Americans who have the advantage of education, perspective, and self-discipline do not participate to the fullest extent of their ability, America will stumble, and if America stumbles the world falls." Stevenson had engendered such yearnings in Rumsfeld that by the time he played first fiddle in the White House, he considered himself ready to become secretary of defense or state, and Kissinger sensed it. It was not surprising therefore that Scotty Reston, after a talk with Henry, complained that Henry was "being German"—lost in gloom, comparing today with 1914—and he too wondered whether in those circumstances it would not be better if he gave up being secretary of state.

In November 1975 Muffie and I went to a dinner party at Henry Kissinger's, which seemed to me like a gathering of the last loyalists. There were the Rockefellers, Kay Graham, and Bill Simon, the secretary of the treasury; Bill Paley, the power at CBS, and David Brinkley, the sardonic commentator of ABC; Joe Alsop, the columnist, and the Tom Bradens. Rockefeller, in conversation at our table, wondered what Henry would do after his resignation, and Bill Simon said that this was exactly what Henry had discussed with him driving in a limousine through Paris recently. Henry had sounded on one hand scared of being on the skids, on the other he could not believe it. Rocky then complained that nobody had yet come up with any good ideas as to what Henry should do next. There was so much talk about Henry's declining prestige that one of Henry's ablest aides in the State Department, on another occasion, talked about "Henry's fall." He concluded that one of the most admired and successful of secretaries of state had become one of the most embattled, most criticized, most suspect. Kissinger himself, talking about the disintegration of the American government, recalled that at school he had discussed the decline of Catholicism in the Middle Ages with a Jesuit, commenting how unique it was for such a disintegrating organization to pull itself up again into a position of considerable influence. The Jesuit offered a very simple explanation: the grace of God. Nick Katzenbach, the former undersecretary of state, at that point chimed in asking Henry teasingly whether he expected the same to happen for him.

Looking back I can understand why Henry resisted all the temptations of writing the third volume of his memoirs, his time in the Ford administration. It was not a happy experience—too many setbacks, too many hoped-for solutions unraveled, too many petty, personal attacks showered on him, too much struggle to prevent the loss of diplomatic terrain hardly won. Bristling, he said one day: "They are trying to emasculate me."

He was disheartened. The forces arrayed against him, he said, were the Jewish lobby, which feared his putting undue pressure on Israel; the Greek lobby, which succeeded in cutting off aid to Turkey; those who could not forget Vietnam, and they were legion; the old Nixon White House conspirators who resented his having escaped the Watergate holocaust; and the Democrats who saw him as the continuing symbol of the Nixon administration's foreign policy successes. Here again is another illustration of how difficult it is under the American political system to conduct a coherent and rational foreign policy and how much depends on the president's willingness to bring his powers to bear on Congress and his ability to influence public opinion. Surrounded by hostile forces and a president too timid to take political risks that could jeopardize his nomination, Kissinger felt more than ever before like a martyr. As he had put it to me before: "I'm buffeted between the brutality of the conservatives and the perfectionism of the liberals."

Kissinger nevertheless was asked to make some campaign speeches for the president, who continued to hold him in high regard. But ironically, Ford also needed him to refute the attacks on his foreign policy. Opinion polls proved that he enjoyed a good deal of respect in the country and that the managerial class, the dominant force in the Middle West, sympathized with his détente policy because of the new rising farm export trade to the Soviet Union and China. Kissinger was by no means a classical example of a melting pot product as many middle westerners were, for he was too intellectual, too cool. Nevertheless his accent marked him as a recent immigrant, and his success was comforting proof to the professional managers who could not rely on inherited wealth, but had to create it with the help of a good education and their own talents, that under the American system even the highest ambitions can be satisfied.

Ford himself did not prove to be a good campaigner. He bored his audiences and barely managed to defeat Reagan in the New Hampshire primary and fend off his bold challenge at the Republican Convention in Kansas City. At the party convention Reagan came closer than anyone in ninety-two years to dislodging an incumbent president, but at the finish possession of the ultimate power of the presidency, the power to offer awards for political favors, won out.

In May 1976 Ford's precarious electoral situation was the main subject of conversation at a dinner party for Sir Christopher Soames at the house of Ferdinand Spaak, the representative of the European Economic Community and a son of the former Belgian prime minister. After listening to all the gloomy predictions, Kissinger mused: "I seem to be destined to work for losers."

All politicians are at risk from ridicule, but it still can provide a telling index of political welfare. Ford's ridicule factor reached a new low when the press played up a photograph of a ski tumble during his Christmas holiday and savagely presented it as further evidence of his notorious clumsiness. Having accompanied him to Vail, the Colorado ski resort, with the White House press corps, I saw him ski almost every day and I was quite impressed by his stylishness, physical fitness, and better-than-average control of his skis. But some public figures are simply haunted by bad luck and the day that Ford permitted the photographers and television cameras to follow him down the ski slopes, he fell, catching an edge as he turned too fast—his only fall of the day. The sad thing was that he could not shrug off his stumble with a funny, offhanded remark. When he mispronounced a word or committed a malapropism, instead of laughing it off, he always looked embarrassed. At one press conference he even confessed with disarming honesty to his hurt feelings about being seen as "inept" and "bungling," an honesty which many at the time interpreted as politically inept in itself. More than inept was his frightful gaffe of saying during a debate with Jimmy Carter that there is "no Soviet domination of Eastern Europe."

The 1976 presidential campaign was the most boring I had ever covered, because the two contestants lacked eloquence and personal electricity. What was reassuring to me at the time was that Daniel J. Boorstin's prediction made (after the Kennedy-Nixon debates) in his book *The Image* that "if we test presidential candidates by their talents on TV quiz performances, we will of course choose presidents for precisely these qualifications," was mistaken. Neither Carter nor Ford, judging by their performances, was a showbiz figure, and the man who precisely fitted this description, Ronald Reagan, did not make it. Little did I realize then that this was only incubation time for the Reagan presidency.

An interesting angle on Kissinger is provided by the estimates of those diplomats posted to Washington who dealt with him, observed him at close quarters, socially and professionally—and reported on him to their governments back at home. Three British ambassadors served while Kissinger was in charge of foreign policy. All arrived with high expectations about that mysterious blessing of the Anglo-American special relationship and all of them left disappointed about the inspirational effect it had and the influence it afforded them. Actually, this blighted hope at the end of their terms affected all British ambassadors, as far as I can recall, with two exceptions: Sir Oliver Franks, who got an enormous human satisfaction out of his turn, because he served under the most pro-British secretary of state, Dean Acheson, and because Britain still counted in the global power equation; and Sir David Ormsby-Gore, who did have the strong feeling of having an influence on President Kennedy's thinking and whose personal relationship with him was the zenith of his career.

British ambassadors, of course, are not powers on their own; they are primarily experts in diplomatic communications and much therefore depends on the policies of the government of the day they represent and the relationship between the British prime minister and the American president. Oliver Franks had an independent power to influence his own government and to a lesser extent the American; Sir Roger Makins had the illusion of being able to influence John Foster Dulles, but that was too difficult a task; Sir Harold Caccia, although he won the annual diplomatic tennis tournament, found in the wake of the Suez crisis that the odds were against him. Sir Patrick Dean did not feel comfortable in Washington. David Ormsby-Gore not only had the advantage of being close to President Kennedy but also enjoyed an unusually intimate relationship with Prime Minister Macmillan. Peter Jay, in the Carter administration, had a similar advantage thanks to the fact that he was the son-in-law of Prime Minister Callaghan, who himself had established a remarkably informal relationship with President Carter.

For British ambassadors who served with or under Kissinger, their mission was a constant challenge. The first was John Freeman, the former editor of the political weekly the *New Statesman,* a onetime Labour minister who had won his diplomatic spurs as a very effective high commissioner in India. His appointment, made before Nixon won the elections against Hubert Humphrey, aroused opposition on both sides of the Atlantic. Stewart Alsop, for instance, the trenchant and very pro-British columnist, angrily said his appointment illuminated "the slow decay and virtual dissolution of the ancient Anglo-American alliance," because Freeman had written some cutting if insightful editorials about Nixon. Anyway, he was miscast, and when he asked me shortly after his appointment but well before his arrival in Washington whether to offer his resignation to the Foreign Office to clear the way for a politically more congenial personality, I told him to expect a difficult time in Washington.

Against all expectations, except those of Richard Crossman, the *Statesman*'s new editor, he did remarkably well. It began with President Nixon lancing the Freeman boil at a small dinner at 10 Downing Street on his first visit to London, immediately after his inauguration, by telling the prime minister and Freeman in his toast: "They say there is a new Nixon. And they wonder whether there is a new Freeman. Let me set aside all possibility of embarrassment, because our roles have changed. He is the new diplomat and I'm the new statesman." This elegant and witty, almost convivial play of words, suggested by that expert juggler of words, William Safire, Nixon's inspired and often daring speech writer, provided Freeman with an unusually promising welcome to his new post.

Freeman arrived in Washington with his old "left wing" *New Statesman* coattails still casting their shadow on the red carpet, but being endowed with a shrewd, calculating intellect, he knew how to rise above prejudices, whether those of others or his own. During a long weekend that Henry Kissinger and the Freemans spent at our summer cottage at Plymouth, Massachusetts, I realized from our discussions how depoliticized Freeman's views had become, how scrupulously he adhered to the canons of the Foreign Office. In Washington, British professional diplomats tried hard to cultivate the manners of the amateur; in Freeman's case it was the amateur (as he was viewed in Washington) who cultivated the traditions of the professionals. In his first few months his behavior reminded me of a remark Richard Crossman made to me about Freeman: "He will do well because he is like an officer who stands erect under enemy fire."

Some two years later, when the Freemans left by their own choice, we gave them a farewell dinner. The warmth of Kissinger's toast and the special farewell message from President Nixon he read—an unusual honor for an ambassador—were in sharp contrast to the official reserve with which he had been received on arrival. It was all due to the extraordinary intellectual relationship he had succeeded in establishing with Kissinger, who, following his toast, digressed into an interpretation of the times, saying: "The Freemans were in the United States during a very difficult time in our history when it became obvious that there were no easy solutions to our problems. Americans always assume that at the end of the road there is the millennium, and now they are learning that at the end of the road they do not find their shining castle but only themselves. Americans are in the process of coming of age and of reaching maturity. They are learning what we in Europe have known for centuries, that one has to get used to living with problems which defy solutions."

When I saw John Freeman shortly before he left to take charge of a British television company, he summed up his Washington experience by saying that what he had learned above all was the extent to which the special Anglo-American relationship had declined. He spoke with heavy irony about those British cabinet ministers and distinguished members of the Foreign Office who continued to hold a romantic view of it, refusing to accept how much this relationship had changed with Britain's own decline and to what extent Britain had lost influence with the American government. He thought that Britain still had a slightly better position than any other country with the American government, but that was all. "The idea that we can influence the United States is minimal," he concluded. He did not even pretend that his personal special relationship with Kissinger had made much of a difference in the amount of influence he could exert on behalf of his government, but it gave him, he said, a very special personal satisfaction to have enjoyed the respect, the confidence, and the personal intimacy of a man with Kissinger's intellectual qualities.

Roly Cromer, as the Earl of Cromer was called by his friends, succeeded Freeman, but he and Kissinger had intellectually very little in common. What made it worse was that Edward Heath's great aim as a leader was to make Britain part of Europe and Europe into an independent force allied to the United States. He was the first British prime minister who was emotionally indifferent to the United States. It affected Anglo-American relations, even though Britain's entry into Europe was dashed by the legacies of Gaullism.

Sir Peter Ramsbotham followed Lord Cromer, an experienced professional diplomat following two semi-amateurs, with enough of an intellectual bent to hold his own with Henry, without however developing more than a formal relationship. He saw Henry more a Talleyrand than a Metternich because of his pragmatism. Bernt von Staden, the West German ambassador, a man who belonged to the best of the German aristocracy, considered him more a Metternich—who thanks to his superinstinct for diplomacy managed to bargain from Austria's strength by covering up her and his weaknesses after he had lost the reflected power of the Kaiser, very much as Kissinger had after Nixon got embroiled in Watergate.

Von Staden gave Kissinger immense credit for opening the eyes of Americans to the reality that the world they used to see in black and white was not the real world. After twenty-five years of nuclear superiority a new approach to the Soviets was necessary, and Henry played the first really important moves in this new game of diplomacy—détente. It was a complex attempt to manage the ascending power curve of the Soviet Union. Kissinger's wariness toward West Germany's Chancellor Willy Brandt, von Staden attributed to Kissinger's belief that the Germans were not good enough diplomats to pursue a successful Ostpolitik (relations with the Soviet Union and the rest of Eastern Europe). He reckoned that Kissinger by redesigning American foreign policy would go down in history, despite some obvious failings and mistakes, as a major world figure, though not quite as a statesman, because he underrated the need for establishing a better understanding with Congress.

In Sir Peter's eyes Kissinger fell just short of being a statesman because he lacked humility and was too cocksure of his own judgment. Ramsbotham did not object to the secretary's penchant for secrecy, because there was not enough of it in Washington; his main complaint was that Kissinger viewed each event by the extent to which it would affect the world balance between the United States and the Soviet Union. Among his troubling idiosyncrasies was that during the day he was driven to take positive actions, while in the evening, at dinner parties, he sounded like a Cassandra for whom the world was rapidly disintegrating. Both Sir Peter and von Staden complained that Henry did not handle European-American as well as Soviet-American relations; because, according to Sir Peter, Kissinger himself was a European and therefore saw through all its old weaknesses, while von Staden believed that Henry still saw Europe as a loose collection of nation-states and hence could not grasp its struggle for a new identity. What made it worse was that, both believed, he was of two minds as to whether a new Europe would be in the American interest or not.

There is of course a great deal to these ambassadorial comments, whether positive or negative. Kissinger, at any rate, was a hard taskmaster who preferred to deal with heads of government rather than ambassadors. He was a man of action and hence looked for shortcuts. Many times he held a weak hand of cards which he did not want the other side to realize, so he manipulated in secrecy, giving the appearance of difficulties or of getting fed up, or offering assurances without knowing whether he could fulfill them, all of which was much easier to do in Bismarck's time when subterfuge was a normal form of diplomacy, and a foreign minister could deliver on the commitments he made for his government. Nor was it easy for Henry as an American secretary of state to let pragmatism rather than morality determine his style and his decisions.

It has been said that American foreign policy aims at pleasing Americans rather than solving problems—they prefer to pursue causes rather than difficulties. Henry wanted to solve problems. The two that engaged his mind above all others were the Soviet-American relationship and peace in the Middle East, the most intractable of them all. He and Nixon, in order to preserve public support for what they were trying to accomplish, had a tendency to exaggerate their successes as well as their failures. Kissinger, for instance, paid dearly when he said at his press conference on October 26, 1972, that "peace is at hand" in Vietnam. It was widely interpreted as a deliberate effort to mislead in order to influence the outcome of the elections. It damaged his credibility so much that he never quite recovered from it, although, as he explained in his memoirs, it was neither a carefully prepared statement nor had he discussed it with Nixon. He and Nixon also oversold détente: it did not mean "peace for a generation," as Nixon put it, nor was it the cornerstone to the "structure of peace." By overselling, both raised expectations and invited criticism. Kissinger should have known that the Russians would never accept the idea of linking détente to the American idea of global containment. It was in direct conflict with their ideological concept and their ambition to establish themselves as a world power, of taking advantage of any weakness in the ring of containment. Moreover détente and the balance-of-power concept entailed many contradictions. Both went against the American grain. Americans find it much easier to be positively either for or against Communists—mostly against—but Kissinger in manipulating détente sometimes sounded highly critical of the Russians, sometimes seemed to be solicitously defending them. Understanding these tactics required the kind of sophistication Americans could not or did not want to summon. Détente is a tough but civilized dialogue that calls for progressively more interaction between incompatible basic objectives, such as keeping the Soviet Union economically weak and increasing trade and credits. Almost from the start the Nixon, Ford, and Carter administrations moved into too many incompatible directions without thinking through the consequences. Americans could not make out where Kissinger stood; he confused them and this made him an easy target for his critics. His insistence on "peace with honor" in Vietnam came to sound more and more like an excuse for a failed policy. And, naturally, when the North Vietnamese did what everybody had expected them to do, once the bulk of the American forces had withdrawn—violated the Paris truce agreement and inundated the South with superior force—there was no "honor" left in what became a rout.

In the Middle East Kissinger from the start asked himself, "How do I as a Jew make the Arabs trust me so that I can influence them as well as the Israelis?" In the end he was kissed by President Sadat and applauded by the Israelis, quite a feat, and if the final attempt at a peace settlement foundered, it did lay the basis for President Carter's Camp David talks. General de Gaulle once put his finger on the crucial reason for the ultimate disappointment of these hopes when he told an Algerian diplomat: *Vous Sémites, Arabes et Juifs, vous ne savez pas comment mettre des limites à vos rêves* ("You Semites, Arabs and Jews, you don't know how to impose limits on your dreams").

In matters of arms control, Kissinger considered himself so conversant with their intricacies that he, unlike any other secretary of state before or after him, felt secure enough in his negotiations with the Soviets to determine on his own how far he could go in making concessions without involving the cantankerous bureaucracies. In fact, at times he kept the agreements under wraps until he had clinched them in such detail that no spanners could be thrown into them. That did not protect him against relentless attacks, especially from the Committee on the Present Danger, whose highly effective spokesman was Paul Nitze; Nitze, in the Reagan administration, recognizing the desirability of "good" arms control agreements, turned his expertise to an intense positive search for compromise solutions. Détente and arms control became such political undertows that President Ford, as I mentioned earlier, put the Vladivostok agreement on the shelf after Reagan turned it into a target in the presidential election campaign. With more courage, he might even have used it to win the elections against Carter.

Americans are fascinated by showmen, and Washington worships virtuosos until it gradually strangles them with attention and blinds them with limelight. If the virtuoso is also powerful, as Kissinger was, he is as much admired as he is feared, as much lionized as berated. His flair for publicity, his keeping the company of attractive and desirable women (despite his not being exactly an Adonis), made some people, especially in the White House, wrinkle their noses and purse their lips, but it helped him to add a human dimension to the gravity of his personality. There were times when Henry sounded desperate one day and combative the next, or complained of having many bright young men around him, but no wise old men like Ambassador David Bruce. When I mentioned Henry's remark to David Bruce since it flattered him, he smiled with obvious amusement: "Henry's greatest weakness is that he is a loner and does not confide in anybody. This is the real reason why he can't get scholars to help him. They don't want to serve as a facade for policies they had no say in." And as to Henry's missing a man like him, he said, amused, that whenever Henry solicited his advice, it was only about whether to resign. Then he paused, smiled again, and said with conviction: "But all that does not diminish my respect for Henry's intellect and accomplishments."

Henry had many weaknesses, and one of them was a gift for making enemies, even though he also had a gift of turning them around by applying his sense of humor as balm on hurt wounds. In his office at the State Department hung a big poster of a huge, threatening gorilla with the caption: "When I want your opinion I beat it out of you." And below in ink was the following comment added by his staff: "We are most grateful for your superb achievements."

Henry was a born survivor, beginning with his escape from Nazi Germany, and he practiced this art all his life, especially while in government. After all, he managed to overcome the political drawbacks of having once worked for Governor Nelson Rockefeller, he survived his association with Nixon, and he remained untainted by Watergate. If he managed to stay in the limelight longer than any other secretary of state, with the possible exception of Dean Acheson, it was partly due to a general recognition that he contributed an unusual measure of professionalism to American diplomacy, that he handled East-West tensions with skill, and that he had the ability to wrap his ideas into concepts whose basic architecture survives. Much more might have survived (or been accomplished) had he not been caught in a double jeopardy between two presidents, whose power had faded or evaporated, and a society that was more inclined to pull away from an accommodation with the Russians than toward one. It turned his policies into a legacy that went politically sour. Much of the blame for its turning sour must fall on the Soviets, who were either too insensitive or too shortsighted to spot and recognize historic opportunities.

Nixon too was a survivor, and that became an important bond between the two. But there was also a politician-to-intellectual, brother-to-brother, statesman-to-historian relationship. The two were drawn to each other by the qualities one had and the other lacked, by Kissinger's admiring Nixon's decisiveness and courage and Nixon's admiring Kissinger's intelligence, and a feeling in both that one could not have functioned without the other. And since they were both self-centered people, both large figures, there was also lurking behind it all a reciprocal love-hate relationship. Together they presided over a period of transition from the Pax Anti-Sovietica to détente and they broke new ground by making their diplomacy triangular—raising China's geopolitical importance and thus weakening the Soviet flank. They also skillfully weakened Soviet influence in the Middle East.

If Kissinger remained the sought-after foreign policy sage and even managed to turn himself into a lucrative dispenser of advice to the corporate world, it was because he was able, thanks to his old professorial talents, his visions as a historian, and his posing as a prophet, to explain the world to big business, which did not know how to navigate in international waters, especially in times when the Carter and Reagan administrations failed to provide any clear policy directions and when the future, more than ever, comes only one day at a time.

Kissinger's star remained high on the firmament for an unusually long time and he continues to have access to most political leaders in the world because they continue to think that he is worth listening to. Nixon, however, was the one to capture the headlines by making critical statements of Reagan's uncompromising anti-Soviet rhetoric and by getting himself invited first to China and then to Moscow by Mikhail Gorbachev, the Soviet leader. He became a lone but sane Republican voice in the sea of Reagan's foreign policy confusion. He positioned himself slightly to the left of Reagan, more or less where he used to be while president, in order to protect his own foreign policy achievements and to buttress his future place in history. He scored with the news media and the foreign policy establishment by sticking to his own last and not adjusting it to new realities. Internationally, he will be remembered as a statesman who beneficially influenced world history, but in American history, I believe, his debasing of the American presidency is likely to overshadow the role of the statesman.

Kissinger can take comfort from the fact that President Reagan, who once upon a time called him the "evil perpetrator of détente" in the election campaign in 1976, has hailed him as a "very distinguished American, virtually a legend in the field of diplomacy." Henry readily admitted to me that since President Nixon had the responsibility for the big decisions, he is entitled to being given full credit for them. But Henry also clearly believes that he too deserves a good share of the credit, since he translated Nixon's ideas skillfully into practice. After the bitter disillusionment he suffered during the Ford years, I wonder whether there was not a hint at how he hoped to survive in the annals of history in a book by Sir Gavin de Beer, called *Hannibal Challenging Rome's Supremacy,* he once gave me as a birthday present.

I never questioned Henry about the book's deeper meaning to him. I simply assumed on reading it that he meant to remind me, first, that at least on the surface, there is nothing new about the idea of spheres of influence, about the conduct of the cold war, about imposition of trade restrictions, about psychological warfare or terrorism; they were all already deployed in the days of Hannibal. Second, and more important, he may have wanted to remind me that although the Greeks beat the Trojans, now after three thousand years it is a greater compliment to be called a Trojan, that although the Romans beat the Carthaginians and Scipio defeated Hannibal, now after two thousand years it is the Carthaginians and Hannibal who command fame and sympathy. In spite of Kissinger's having served two presidential losers and suffered disappointments and defeats, I shall nevertheless not be surprised when, following Hannibal's example, history gives him fame and treats him with sympathy.

12

When Leadership Is Elusive

AFTER my first interview with Jimmy Carter on his campaign plane during the elections, I could find nothing in my long experience of politicians and reporting to tell me quite what to make of him. In answer to one of my questions he had said: "I ask God for guidance, I ask him for proper judgment, so that I might make the right decisions. I do that in the privacy of my own life and within the personal relationship I have with God." Sensing perhaps my unspoken bafflement, he then added, as if he wanted to reassure me that his intellectual approach to problems was quite normal, "Mind you, I don't sit back and wait for some blinding flash of light or some message to be spelt out on the wall. I approach problems using all the resources at my command." And he stressed "all." Then he went on explaining himself: "I don't feel that I have been anointed to be the leader of the country, but I do feel a reassurance in the process of prayer and in the principles on which my life has been based . . . I also feel constrained to do everything I can in a secular way to make the right decisions . . . I think I would feel secure as president. I would not be constantly fearful of making the wrong decisions." It all sounded a little weird and unclear; what sort of a leader, I wondered, might he prove to be after telling me: "We should treat others as we would want to be treated ourselves under the brotherhood of man"? Or when, answering the question, had he a romantic or emotional attachment to any country, he said, "Yes, to Britain and Israel." Britain because there "his sense of brotherhood" was by far greater with it than with anywhere else, Israel because the biblical interrelationship had always been important to him. It sounded like an ecumenical approach to foreign affairs, yet, at the same time, I found that he also had a fair knowledge of world affairs, that he was an intelligent man with a retentive brain, a certain naive self-assurance, and sensitive political instincts. But although we sat next to each other, he seemed distant and impersonal and left me with the impression that, although a humanitarian, he was not a man who had it in him to establish quick and easy human contact; although a populist, he spoke in abstract terms about people; and although a deeply religious man, he spoke about religion in a very detached way. Still, the interview continued reverberating in my mind. I asked myself whether Carter would be able to cope with the harsh realities of political life and reconcile it with his obligations toward God and brotherhood. What did he mean when he said that we should treat others as we would want to be treated ourselves under the brotherhood of man? How would he react to the godlessness of the other superpower? It was disturbing to imagine what *could* happen if our fate were to be entrusted to a man of his outlook. Of course, as soon as I scrambled out of the plane at the next campaign stop and listened to him addressing a crowd, I felt reassured that he did not live on a cloud.

Jimmy Carter, throughout the campaign, emphasized what he considered one of his greatest assets, his being an "outsider" who was assaulting the ramparts of that ingrown, self-regarding fortress, Washington. He was determined, he preached, to pull down barricades of politics and prejudice that were as old as the Republic. His campaign rolled merrily along on the widespread anti-Washington bias, the belief that it is the capital that is the source of all problems, the obstacle to progress. It is of course true that divided government as conceived by the Founding Fathers purposely prevents the American government from working expeditiously and decisively. But it is also true that most Americans prefer it that way. All the same, when the newly inaugurated President Jimmy Carter walked down a sunlit Pennsylvania Avenue in January 1977, hand in hand with his wife, Rosalyn, he seemed exactly what the American people had wanted: a confident, decent, modest, religious man, inspired by uncommonly high ethical standards, untainted by Washington cynicism or the temptations of the imperial presidency.

For a year he acted as if he and his aides knew how to go about governing. They guilelessly bombarded Congress with new legislation and set new priorities for various foreign policy issues. But within less than a year Carter began to recognize that while being an outsider had been an advantage during the presidential election campaign, once in power it was necessary to learn the ways of becoming an insider. He had tried rational persuasion, emphasizing the need for innovation, preaching moral virtues, resorting to political vindictiveness, but none were substitutes for experience in dealing with Congress or in bringing presidential power to bear without causing resentment, or for knowing how to tame and utilize the bureaucracies. Sobered and realizing that things were not functioning as he had expected, he turned to that old Washington hand and political wise man Clark Clifford for advice. Clifford recommended bringing into the administration people who had served under Kennedy and Johnson, and to invite two or three former senior advisers to presidents every two to three weeks for an informal talk—not lunch—to find out how they would deal with the problems that confounded him; he offered a few names. Clifford later heard, secondhand, that Hamilton Jordan, Carter's right-hand man, had poked fun at Clifford's advice, saying that what he had really meant was for the perennial insider to sit in a chair in front of the president's office and about every hour the president would open the door and whisper into Clifford's ear, who would then either nod or shake his head and Carter would act accordingly; then thanks to Clifford's advice, the president's image would change in no time. "The Georgians want to do it their own way," Clifford concluded. "They don't want any gray eminences around." He shrugged his shoulders in regret.

Hamilton Jordan was one of those presidential aides who owe their position to their shrewd judgment as election campaign advisers but then find themselves at a loss when dealing with the problems of governing. After my first talk with him I left the way I would feel leaving Carnegie Hall after a Beethoven concert conducted by Johnny Cash. We looked at each other as strange animals in a strange laboratory.

I once suggested to Clark Clifford that there was perhaps a similarity between Carter and Truman, who succeeded to the presidency without any real experience, making many initial mistakes he later regretted. Clifford agreed that there was a parallel, except that Truman had come to the presidency much more suddenly than Carter. He had no team whatsoever in readiness, except for a staff of about four and some secretaries, because the Roosevelt people started leaving precipitately, claiming that they could not endure the trauma of shifting from the great FDR to the mediocre Truman —so at least they thought at the time. Carter, said Clifford, was in much better shape since he had run for the presidency and had come into the White House with a team of about ten close associates and a second circle of about thirty who had been with him through the campaign. Carter started confidently, believing he had a good feel and knowledge for what the presidency was all about. It took him a long time to discover that he hadn't.

The Georgian who adjusted more quickly than the others was Jody Powell, the president's press spokesman, perhaps because he had a dry sense of humor, did not take himself too seriously, and was equipped with enough mental brawn to cope with the daily inquisitions by the press. He admitted much later, when we discussed the Carter legacy, that one of the major mistakes the Georgians made was not to realize how important it was to bring men of experience and men who belonged to the traditional center of the party into the administration. Consequently the Carter administration remained representing only a minority in the Democratic Party. Nor did they realize how difficult it was to staff an administration with good people, which resulted in many jobs remaining vacant for too long.

On first sight the appointments of Cy Vance to state and Zbigniew Brzezinski to direct foreign policy seemed promising. Vance had been deputy secretary of defense under Robert McNamara; he had also served in the Kennedy administration, and as deputy to Averell Harriman in the Vietnam peace talks he had acquired experience in international negotiations. Brzezinski had been a prolific writer on foreign affairs, a professor specializing in Soviet and Eastern European affairs at Columbia University, and a secretary to the Trilateral Commission, a David Rockefeller brainchild. Vance was a man with a legal mind, competence, common sense, charm, and above all, high integrity. What remained to be seen was whether he had not been for too long in positions of deputy and therefore lacked the strength of leadership. Brzezinski prided himself on being a conceptual thinker who focused on the Soviet Union and the Third World. Whether he had the balanced judgment needed for the job of national security adviser was an open question for most of those who had known "Zbig" for a long time. But as he had served as Carter's foreign policy adviser during the elections, it came as no surprise that he was given the job.

Shortly after Carter's inauguration I accompanied Zbig on his early daily morning walk to the White House from his digs in an annex to Averell Harriman's house. He was his old self-confident, all-knowing self, throbbing with excitement about his new job. What disturbed him were newspaper stories predicting that he and Vance would become antagonists and that he would end up doing to Vance what Kissinger had done to William Rogers. He insisted that Vance was a friend whom he respected highly, and he had no intention of engaging in this kind of intrigue. Among the points he confidently made was his favoring the continuation of Kissinger's détente policy, except that he would seek limited and specific agreements and that he would counter the Soviet attacks on American imperialism with a strong emphasis on the lack of human rights in the Soviet Union. He also said that he would not mind stirring things up in Eastern Europe to make the Russians uneasy, especially within the triangle of East Germany, Poland, and Czechoslovakia, but he also admitted, when pressed, that while a revolt in that triangle would be highly embarrassing to the Soviets, it would also present the United States with a dilemma and leave it red-faced because in the end the American government would do nothing.

Zbig may have meant what he said about not wanting to do a Kissinger on Vance, but somehow circumstances conspired toward it, even if history did not exactly repeat itself. Zbig and Henry were equally ambitious. They had similar academic training, they had analytical minds and prided themselves on being conceptual thinkers. Kissinger, though, sought to develop his concepts with greater depth and scholarship from history; Brzezinski's were shallower and built on the present. He liked to be referred to as a "futurist." Kissinger was the son of a Jewish schoolteacher, Brzezinski the son of a Catholic Polish diplomat who helped Jews to escape from Europe to Canada, where he was stationed until he sought asylum there and became an exile himself. Both were outstanding students at Harvard, but, unlike Kissinger, Brzezinski failed to get the all-important tenure as a professor and left for greener pastures at Columbia University. Kissinger at fifty-three was informal and relaxed, but despite his professional self-confidence and panache, also insecure. Brzezinski had a youthful, brisk air, a metallic voice, and absolute confidence in his judgment. He hoped to do as well as or better than Henry. The secret challenge was not Vance but Henry's legacy. Zbig thrived on confrontations, Vance wanted to avoid them. Zbig believed in the use of force, if ncessary; Cy, having been involved in the Vietnam war, was repelled even by the thought of it. When President Carter at the very start of cabinet making asked Vance whether he would mind if he appointed Brzezinski as national security adviser, he said no, he would not; Vance believed in the capacity of men for accommodation. But gradually he came to regret it, for he found that his own character, which was self-effacing, reserved, and uncomfortable at public appearances, whether at press conferences or on television, was almost the exact opposite of Brzezinski's assertive, self-promoting, and articulate persona.

Cy's success in government was based on his integrity, reliability, his lack of self-importance, and his competence in carrying out policy decisions. His lawyer's training gave him a sense of the importance of detail, but also a tendency to want to deal with each case separately. He was not a man of many words and hence had not much patience in listening to long-winded expertise from among his aides. If everybody liked him, it was because of his friendliness, sincerity, and directness. He was a good analyst but he did not have the intellectual and conceptual mind of a Kissinger or Brzezinski. His gentlemanliness, his distaste for controversy and conflict, and his desire to avoid both led me to speculate, as I put it in my diary, how effective he would be in the roughhouse of bureaucratic wars and how skillful a bargainer he would be with the Russians. He did not underrate the Russian danger, but he was perhaps too fair-minded himself to understand the unfair-mindedness of Soviet officialdom. The setback he suffered on his first attempt at negotiating with the Russians on arms control hurt him deeply (since he had opposed the policy of deep cuts in nuclear arsenals the president had decided on, prodded by Senator Scoop Jackson and Brzezinski), while Zbig, who took a much harder line in his public pronouncements, gained in prestige. The debates over policy toward the Soviets in the inner councils gradually became less debates and more wrestling contests, with the news media watching from the sidelines and waiting for who would hit the floor first. If Vance saw Soviet-American relations as something to be managed, Zbig considered them a contest, and if Vance considered Brzezinski too belligerent, Brzezinski viewed him as too much of an appeaser. More and more these deepening differences contributed to the impression that Carter was not in command. Their differences reached the absurd when Carter took two drafts for a speech—one prepared by Vance, the other by Brzezinski—and simply stitched them together and delivered it, slightly edited for length, as if he were oblivious to its inner contradictions. Meanwhile the allies were wondering where Carter stood, whether he favored détente or confrontation with the Soviet Union. Much of the confusion was due to the confusion in Carter's own mind. Emotionally and sentimentally he leaned toward Vance; cerebrally, and in terms of reason, he tended to side with Zbig. He agonized about Soviet intentions. One day, for instance, he called in Marshall Shulman (Vance's own Sovietologist), Vice President Mondale, Brzezinski, his wife, Rosalyn, and his daughter, Amy, then aged ten, and asked Shulman searching questions about the Soviet Union and Eastern Europe. He seemed anxious to be able to compare Shulman's and Brzezinski's ideas, knowing full well that the two differed sharply. Sometimes his Christian peacemaker role was in the ascendancy, which told him to set things right, sometimes it was the need to prove that there was steel under his velvet glove. Cy and Zbig personified the president's own vacillation and sharpened its public manifestation.

My first contact with Cy in his new role was by telephone. I was writing a profile of him and needed to know what priorities he expected to set in foreign policy. To my great surprise he said the Panama Canal treaty topped the agenda, followed by arms control and the Middle East. Vance essentially was an optimist who looked for the silver lining. I had known him from the Kennedy days, when he worked first as legal adviser then deputy to McNamara. When I saw him in March 1977 he was well informed, looser in discussing his own ideas and discerning "real possibilities" in establishing law and order in Lebanon, more restraint on the part of the Syrians, and a new open-mindedness in President Sadat. He predicted new conciliatory moves by the South African government but feared a protracted civil war in Zimbabwe (then Rhodesia). He was confident about progress in the SALT negotiations with the Russians and hoped for a Carter-Brezhnev encounter at the United Nations. When I asked him facetiously how he felt about other people saying that he needed more steel in his policies (a remark Brzezinski had made) he replied, smiling, "What they mean is that if you know how to handle the Russians then all is well." Since he took this question in such good humor I asked to what extent he believed the president agreed with him on policies. Ninety percent, was his answer. Then he explained the missing ten percent: Carter did not agree with his conciliatory approach to Cuba. Carter wanted to hit them with his fist, he said, but, he added, when you explained to him that there was really nothing the United States could effectively do and that it was therefore better not to threaten anything, he accepted the advice, resigned that indeed nothing could be done to swat that mosquito, Castro. Vance also thought that Carter by insisting on a more "effective" SALT II treaty overlooked that the Soviets had been the ones who had done most of the compromising. Carter and Vance were both eager, indeed anxious, to play the peacemaker, which created a psychological bond between the two. Vance's considerate style—the family lawyer and the reasonable gentleman, modest, decent, and reluctant to step into the limelight—also appealed to Carter.

Zbig's appeal for the president was his ability to formulate the strategic choices, to provide the broad perspective in a few sentences, and to show how various aspects of a problem fitted together. He was an able coordinator but too pugnacious an infighter, too much of an activist, too quick to advocate a show of force or even military intervention, to inspire confidence in his tactical judgment. Consequently several of his ideas that involved taking considerable calculated risks were turned down by the president. Among them was his contention that to preserve the American strategic position in Iran the president should not "preclude the use of power" to protect American interests. Later, in the hostage crisis, he proposed the combination of a generalized retaliatory strike against Iran and a rescue mission. He favored the deployment of an aircraft carrier task force in reply to the Soviets' deployment of Cuban soldiers in Ethiopia, which the president rejected on advice from Vance and Secretary of Defense Harold Brown, a decision which marked, in Zbig's view, when things began to go wrong in US-Soviet relations—in my view a conclusion hard to justify. He also believed in the constant need to remind the Russians of the American political will. His suggestion that toward the end of the Camp David negotiations with Begin and Sadat in 1978 the president confront Mr. Begin once more with a kind of ultimatum to force the withdrawal from the West Bank by threatening the cancellation of the Israeli-Egyptian settlement already agreed on, did not appeal to either Vance or the president. Carter by then was already too weak to withstand domestic pressures from the Jewish lobby and not strong enough to force Begin to give way. It was true that Carter's policies needed more backbone from time to time, but Zbig too often proposed posturing rather than posture.

On paper there was something to be said for having a conciliatory minded secretary of state and a national security adviser whose adrenaline made him think if not act in a confrontational manner, to provide the president with a choice between two different policy approaches. But too often the president could not make up his mind whose advice to adopt. It reinforced the impression that he was suffering "from a chaos of clear ideas" and nothing quite hurt him so much in his first two years as reversing his neutron bomb decision. Until June 7, 1977, it was just another bomb that the public paid no attention to. But on that June day the Washington *Post* published a report by Walter Pincus about the planned deployment of the "enhanced radiation" weapon (ERW) in Europe. It described the bomb as a weapon that "destroys people and not property" and sounded like the most inhuman battlefield weapon ever invented. It predated the Carter administration, having been included in Ford's military budget, and had been discussed at great length with the allies, who hesitated about committing themselves to it. Now, the more was written about its inhumanity, the more reluctant they became. Chancellor Helmut Schmidt of West Germany made it clear that it was for the United States to make the basic decision whether to manufacture the weapon. After long-drawn-out and highly divisive negotiations, American officials wore down the allies and elicited their agreement to a NATO Council meeting on March 28, 1978, to endorse the United States decision to proceed with the manufacture of the neutron bomb and to defer a decision on deployment for two years until it became clearer how successful the arms control negotiations with the Soviets would be. Then Vance and Brown routinely sent their memo on the subject and the communiqué that was to be issued to Sea Island, Georgia, where the president was vacationing; only Leslie Gelb, director of political military affairs in the state department, had premonitions that Carter might do what would be too embarrassing to contemplate: postpone his decision at the very last minute. What had been unthinkable to Vance, Brown, Brzezinski, and others thus happened. Carter's ambivalence as to whether he wanted to be a man of power or peace asserted itself, and despite the most urgent warnings by his three top advisers, he decided against building the neutron bomb. In harmony with its reputation, it badly damaged one human being—Carter and his credibility—while everything around him remained unchanged. What sort of a leader, what sort of a brooding character was this president, people began to ask.

Virtually from the start of his administration, Carter fretted within himself and in private conversation with one or two of his top aides about the circumstances that might force him to the brink of ordering the use of nuclear weapons. He seemed aware that there was talk about his being a weak president who would not have the guts to push the nuclear button, and in a sort of ruminating way assured his closest aides that he had thought this issue through—that, admittedly, it was the toughest issue he could think of, but that he was willing to face up to it and was not afraid to carry out his responsibilities.

Shortly after his inauguration Carter had received a letter of congratulations from Andrei Sakharov, the most famous among Russian human rights activists, whose fame was based on his achievements as a nuclear physicist, his Nobel Prize, and the courage with which he defied the Soviet authorities. It would have been quite normal for the administration publicly to express appreciation for the letter and use it to give Moscow a broadside for its crass disregard of human rights. Instead Carter replied in a personal letter sent via the American Embassy in Moscow. For the president to behave in this way —both the letter and the use of the embassy—was unprecedented, and bound to outrage the Kremlin. Brzezinski in his memoirs, *Power and Principle,* admitted that "one has to concede that this event did not help the relationship between the new Administration and the Soviet Union . . ." and, with false naiveté explained that Carter's "rather carefully crafted comments on human rights" were intended to be "reassuring." What presidential novice Carter did not realize was how powerful an instrument the voice of the American president was, how strongly it reverberated in the echo chamber of the world, and how carefully therefore he had to calibrate it.

Carter's human rights campaign was something Americans wholeheartedly approved of. Europeans tend to be more cynical about morality, especially when invoked as a tool of diplomacy. As Macmillan put it in an interview with me: "Human rights is all right to talk about, but what's he going to do about it? There is nothing you can do in getting the Russians to accept the idea. Talking about human rights, for instance, is not a substitute for letting them have the Horn of Africa. And if you look back over the effects of a moralistic diplomacy in history you will find that Woodrow Wilson's moral emphasis on self-determination after the First World War led to the balkanization of Europe and the destruction of the Austro-Hungarian monarchy, once the bulwark against Russia. American liberals tend to forget that the Civil War was fought to prevent self-determination!"

Brzezinski shared Carter's desire for a strong emphasis on human rights because he felt that it answered two needs; it created a contrast to Kissinger's realpolitik, which, he felt, ignored moral values Americans cared about, and furthermore, it had global appeal, beyond the issues of capitalism and ideology. Kissinger, in contrast, was less interested in the propaganda effect of the human rights appeal than in getting results, which, he believed, could be achieved only if the appeals to the Russians were handled quietly and privately in direct negotiations. He demonstrated the success of his method by substantially improving Jewish emigration from the Soviet Union to Israel. From October 1968 to the end of 1970 this totaled 4,235, then gradually, as Soviet-American relations and the prospects for a trade agreement improved, the total went up to 34,733. The controversial Jackson-Vanik amendment gave Kissinger some leverage while it remained a proposal, but once it was passed in 1975, it badly hurt the prospects of emigration, and the quota went down that year to 13,221. Once Carter promised to seek the cancellation of the amendment the total rose to a new peak in 1979, with 51,320 visas issued. During the Reagan administration it dropped as low as 896 in 1984. It is tragic that Jewish emigration from the Soviet Union should depend on the state of Soviet-American relations.

There were of course excellent reasons for challenging the Russians on their insensitivity to human rights, but the challenge chilled the climate for the arms control discussions between Vance and Brezhnev which opened in Moscow on March 28, 1977. When Vance, his aides, and a dozen or so reporters, including myself, took off for Moscow we were all full of hope, despite the angry Soviet reactions to the Sakharov letter. What further lowered expectations was Carter's advance disclosure of his opening gambit. He ignored the Vladivostok agreement and instead opted for a comprehensive arms reduction package. He clearly wanted to put on it his own rather than Kissinger's imprint. Thus he waved aside the pleas of Vance, who wanted first to tie the loose ends of the Vladivostok agreement, and instead listened to Senator Scoop Jackson, who favored the new comprehensive package which he knew would be hard for the Russians to swallow.

Vance had signed on to it reluctantly, reckoning that if the Russians turned it down, he could fall back to the Vladivostok negotiating track. But when he opened his written instructions on the plane to Moscow, he found an added limitation prohibiting him from putting his fallback position on the negotiating table without special permission from the president. This was a severe constraint, and one that was upsetting to him. Most of his aides were convinced that the Russians were bound to turn down the comprehensive proposal; what then were they to do? On our arrival in Moscow the Russians lost no time in impressing on us that the president's letter to Sakharov was considered an insult and an interference in the internal affairs of the Soviet Union. With their deep-seated insecurity and conspiratorial cast of mind, they had convinced themselves that Carter, instead of wanting to stabilize the arms race, wanted to destabilize the Soviet Union.

Brezhnev listened to Vance's presentation and then flatly rejected the comprehensive plan. Vance immediately called the president, but, instead, could reach only Zbig, who told him that the president refused to authorize his immediately shifting to the fallback position. Vance, when he briefed us reporters at Spaso House, the ambassador's residence, tried to put the best face on the last and abortive session. But the slight tremble in his voice, his flushed face, and his desire to cut the backgrounder short, betrayed the shock he had suffered. The Russians' brusque treatment and the rejection of his offer to stay for one or two days more upset him deeply. When he got up after our briefing, he passed by me, and, perhaps because he had known me from his days in the Kennedy-Johnson administrations, he put his arm briefly around my shoulders and, in a low voice, said: "Henry, we blew it."

Over the years I have been on about a dozen shortish assignments for *The Sunday Times* to the Soviet Union, beginning in 1947. What struck me most this time was that the Russian people were more worried about war than we in the West. Russians would stop foreigners in the street and ask worried questions about the uneasy truce between East and West. Somehow there was more faith in the art of coexistence in the West than in the East. When the talks between Vance and Brezhnev came to an abrupt end, it was fairly obvious that this was only another round in a long and tedious bout. Carter's refusal to use the Vladivostok agreement as a way station to a more promising accord, though, was a major mistake, and recognizing it, the American delegation left deeply troubled. It was not an irremediable position as the later signing of the SALT II at the Vienna summit meeting between Carter and Brezhnev proved. One could, of course, equally well argue that the Russians made a mistake in refusing to accept Vance's offer of continuing the negotiations for another two days, but the West has become used to blaming itself for any setbacks, always assuming that the Russians are too thickheaded. However, because of the precious time lost in the submission to Congress and, as a result of the so-called Cuban brigade crisis, SALT II was never ratified. Historically, President Ford deserves a share of the blame because SALT II could have been signed and sealed in 1976 had he not postponed the issue on the advice of his political aides, who feared that Ronald Reagan, in his fight for the nomination, would exploit it unmercifully.

When I flew to Vienna in June 1979 to cover the Vienna summit meeting between Carter and Brezhnev, it was on assignment for the Washington *Star,* for which I had been writing a column twice a week since the publication of *The Sunday Times* had been halted. On November 30, 1978, I had received the fateful telex message from the editor saying: "I regret to inform you that *The Sunday Times* has now officially suspended publication. I shall keep you informed. Best regards from all of us." Labor negotiations had been dragging on for weeks, with the editor never knowing whether the unions would allow the paper to appear or would sabotage publication after the first edition. It was an exasperating time, and finally the patience of the management was exhausted. The initial expectation was that the unions would become more amenable after six weeks of total suspension, but nobody expected the strike or the shutout to last for eleven months. The editorial staff, fortunately and generously, was kept on full pay and under instructions to use the time to produce a variety of books. I decided to begin research for a book about leadership. Fortunately also, Murray Gart, the editor of the Washington *Star,* a good quality evening newspaper owned by *Time* magazine, had been chief of *Time*'s London bureau. Within a few days of the stoppage he invited me to become a regular columnist for his newspaper, something I enjoyed enormously because I suddenly had an American audience. I often heard from the White House if I had written something that displeased them, and from members of Congress and of course general readers. It was an entirely new experience and one that I enjoyed so much that when *The Sunday Times* resumed publication I asked Harold Evans whether he would allow me to continue my *Star* column. He readily agreed as long as I did not neglect my duties with *The Sunday Times,* and the column continued until the *Star* ceased publishing in August 1981. In my final one I argued that it was regrettable that the capital of the United States should become a one-newspaper town, notwithstanding the fact that the Washington *Post* was a newspaper of outstanding quality. The *Star* was a worthy competitor. It provided diversity and gave some spice to the political dialogue. I shall always be grateful to Murray Gart for having given me this opportunity.

Curiously, the Vienna summit found both superpower leaders under stress —Carter because of his decline in popularity with the American public and his lack of support in Congress, Brezhnev because of his precarious health and the evidence of a power struggle for the succession in the Kremlin. More people still were asking themselves whether Carter understood the game of power politics, that is the ability to combine political skill and intuition with a shrewd and sound appreciation of American power. Directly, his weakness at home led to doubts about the ratification of the SALT II treaty and his ability to give the Russians what they badly wanted, most-favored-nation treatment in trading with the United States. There was a widespread feeling in the world about the president which a high French official characterized by quoting Georges Clemenceau's comment about the Treaty of Versailles: *Trop mou pour ce qu'il est dur et trop dur pour ce qu'il est mou* ("Too soft for what is hard and too hard for what is soft"). But by the time the two leaders parted Carter's cool, measured reasonableness had a reassuring effect on the European allies and there was a general "good feeling" for a calmer Soviet-American relationship.

From Vienna I flew to Moscow, where the winds of détente were blowing again. The Vienna summit and the signing of the SALT II treaty were seen as proof that the basic Nixon-Kissinger policy, derailed by the first Carter proposals for SALT II, was again the guiding impulse to American policy. One of the most interesting interviews I had on this trip was with Valentin Falin, then the international spokesman for the Central Committee. Falin, who had six telephones on his desk, was a handsome, tall, lean man in his early fifties with a shock of black hair falling casually down his high forehead. Having served as ambassador to West Germany, he was familiar with the inquisitiveness of Western correspondents, and when I asked whether he could explain to me the mysteries of the Soviet decision-making processes, he responded that compared to the American system the Soviet one is much more centralized, that all foreign and national policy decisions must be decided in the Politburo by consensus, and if consensus is missing the problem is sent back to the Central Committee for further study. Most of the decisions are taken in the Defense Council, the Council of Foreign Ministers, or in the Central Committee and its subcommittees. However cumbersome, the procedure seemed less authoritarian than I had expected.

My interview with nuclear scientist Anatoly P. Alexandrov, then the president of the Academy of Sciences and director of the Kuchatov Institute for Atomic Energy, has since acquired an unexpected topicality. Mr. Alexandrov impressed first by his powerful build, his big oval, clean-shaven cranium, the caricature of an egghead, and by his autocratic manner in discussion. He was joined by the director of the Institute of World Economics, Nicolai Inozemsev, to answer any questions about the economy. Alexandrov, in a display of sweeping arrogance, blamed loose controls in the United States for inadequate safety standards, incompetent supervisory personnel and the voice of doom (the news media) for the harm done to the development of nuclear power. "I can't imagine the kind of accident that occurred at the Three Mile Island power plant happening in the Soviet Union," he said with an air of superiority and confidence in Soviet technology. The consequences of the Chernobyl disaster, which were much worse than those at Three Mile Island, hopefully will make the Soviet scientific community less dogmatic about the safety standards applied to Soviet plants. I believe that Chernobyl, no less than Hiroshima and Nagasaki in 1945, is one of the most important events of our time since it gave humanity a stark and frightening reminder of the devastating power of a nuclear explosion.

In these ten days in Moscow the change in the Russian mood was most striking. There was a general feeling of relief that Carter and Brezhnev had paved the way for another round in the détente cycle, and now when people stopped me in the street it was to say how much they welcomed another East-West thaw. But at the official level, while there was the same relief, I was left under no illusions about the Soviet determination to take advantage, wherever opportunities beckoned, to hold on to gains already won. This determination dominated all Soviet policy considerations.

In Washington meanwhile an anti–SALT II tide began to gather to prevent the ratification of the treaty. Its principal spokesman, Paul Nitze, representing the Committee on the Present Danger, was an extremely able and knowledgeable opponent, and as the tide rose, Carter, recognizing that he needed an able advocate and an experienced insider, appointed Lloyd Cutler, one of the most astute among superlawyers, to be his legal counselor and to lead the troops in defense of SALT II. But Cutler found that it was easier to win a case before the Supreme Court than before Congress, where outside events that have nothing to do with the issue at stake can intrude. Carter was haunted by bad luck and his own flawed judgment. What undercut Cutler's strategy was one of those classic intelligence snafus, a failure of the intelligence community's "institutional memory," as he himself put it. A key Democratic member of the Senate Foreign Relations Committee, whose vote would be critical to treaty ratification, was Richard Stone of Florida, a state with a large Cuban-American anti-Castro population. Stone had inquired about reports of new Soviet combat forces in Cuba, and had been assured there were none. Later in August, a CIA report in the *National Intelligence Digest,* which circulates among some two hundred officials and has a high leak record, said that the Agency had discovered that a new Soviet combat brigade had been *introduced* into Cuba. The administration saw that as a provocation which could unleash forces ensuring the nonratification of SALT II. To offset these, Carter declared that the brigade's presence was not acceptable, in the expectation that Moscow might be prepared to withdraw it. The fact was, however—as was later discovered—that the presence of the same brigade had been on photographic record since 1963. President Kennedy and Secretary of Defense McNamara had referred publicly to the presence of the brigade during the missile crisis. But no one had bothered immediately to go back and check the files. To prevent an uproar in the Senate, the secretary of state authorized his undersecretary David Newsom to brief chairman Frank Church on the misleading nature of the "discovery." Church, up for reelection against a right-wing conservative challenger, was under attack for an earlier and politically damaging visit with Fidel Castro in Cuba. Instead of helping to play down the report, to save his political skin in Idaho, he chose instead to play it up, linking the ratification of SALT II (of which he was an ardent supporter) to the withdrawal of the Russian brigade. His son, F. Forrester Church, in his biography of his father calls it "the most lamentable episode of Frank Church's Senate career." Cutler explained to me later that after the Cuban missile crisis in 1963, intelligence surveillance had been shifted from Cuba to more important areas in Eastern Europe and the Middle East; its resumption over Cuba because of Senator Stone's inquiries led to the discovery which was no discovery. The intelligence people responsible had failed to compare the latest intelligence with the intelligence from the sixties, and thus created an unnecessary storm that delayed the passage of SALT II in the Senate Foreign Relations Committee for ten crucial weeks so that it did not reach the Senate floor until November. Before the floor debate could begin the Soviet invasion of Afghanistan hammered the final nail into the coffin of ratification. SALT II, though unratified, continued to haunt Ronald Reagan.

After Callaghan's attempt to suppress my articles on the British sterling crisis in 1966, I avoided him for several years until one Easter—he had by then become prime minister—he came to Washington for a brief holiday. I asked whether I could see him and he reciprocated by inviting me to the British Embassy for tea. We discussed American and British politics, even a secret new arrangement for the transfer of some American weapons secrets, but there was no mention of "our" sterling crisis. I had a feeling that, fair-minded as he basically was, he had come to regret it. It was an incident we both wanted to forget.

At least officially, the prime minister had come to visit his daughter, Margaret, and his son-in-law, Peter Jay, a writer on economic affairs for the *Times,* whom he had appointed ambassador to the US. Jay also encountered antagonism among some key members of the embassy who found it hard to have to deal with such a young and self-possessed ambassadorial "upstart." One in particular, a passionate believer in Britain's mission in the European Common Market, found Peter's highly skeptical attitude toward British membership distasteful to say the least. But Peter reflected not only his, but also Callaghan's private and instinctive feelings. I became aware of those in a conversation with Callaghan shortly after he had been appointed foreign minister in Harold Wilson's cabinet, and it startled me when he asked—and it was his first question—whether I thought that there was enough support in the United States for Britain and possibly Canada to form a tripartite common market. No one, especially Britain's new foreign secretary, could have such illusions unless he had some deep prejudices about joining the EEC. And as to Peter Jay's role as an ambassador, his diplomatic skills were not challenged by any major crisis in Anglo-American relations. He excelled as a public speaker, and, taking advantage of this talent and his knowledge in economic affairs, he saw his main role in trying to reassure American businessmen by telling them that the Labour government practiced, in effect, what had come to be called "monetarism." Although he reflected more his own economic convictions than the government's, the British press did not catch on, with one or two exceptions, because he avoided giving out the set texts of his speeches and so the thrust remained virtually unnoticed in London.

I will always be grateful to Peter for a special act of samaritanism. One evening my wife and I were out at a dinner party when my twelve-year-old stepdaughter, Alexandra—she had already gone to bed—was panic-stricken by the sound of steps which she attributed to an intruder. Realizing that it would take us some time to get home, she telephoned the British Embassy, whose garden bordered on ours, and asked for the ambassador. When Peter heard that she suspected that a burglar had broken into our house, he rushed over, alerting his security officer to follow him, and guided by Alexandra, searched the house from top to bottom. Fortunately, it turned out to be a false alarm, but realizing that the girl was still in shock and that it would take us a while to get home, he stayed on until we arrived. There are other than diplomatic feats that can attest to an ambassador's qualities.

One of the pleasures of my life has been the way in which my professional role brought me into contact with often eminent men and women who had no role themselves in the international power plays but still tracked roads that intersect in Washington. One such event was a family dinner for Henry Moore, the sculptor, who, thanks to a mutual friend, John Russell, the brilliant art critic, then of the London *Sunday Times,* now of the *New York Times,* had once entertained us at his enchanting estate at Much Hadham in Hertfordshire, England, where he set some of his finest works of art, like gleaming shrubs, in his spacious garden. Moore clearly enjoyed being in the bosom of our family rather than being given a formal party. Full of exuberance—having spent all day positioning one of his sculptures in front of the new wing to the Washington National Gallery of Art—he spoke about the pleasures and drudgeries of the life of an artist with relish, contentment, and an old man's wistfulness.

Some fifteen years earlier I had acquired an early Henry Moore drawing, a heavyset nude, a sculptural sketch. Moore suddenly noticed it on the wall and began to comment on it: "This is a real life drawing and the two heads sitting on one body were inspired by Picasso's ways. Michelangelo used to do it too. It's a good drawing. I exaggerated the bulk of her, size was an element in itself to me. I liked to exaggerate at that stage, make things look bigger and heavier and make them three-dimensional."

For John, my eighteen-year-old stepson, Moore's visit was an especially exciting event, for he then planned to become a sculptor. It did not take long for John to challenge our guest with the question that was foremost on his mind; that he lived unfortunately in a time when it was hard to be an artist with nuclear war hanging over one's head. John, tall, long-haired, and typical of his blue-jeaned generation, towered over the stocky, silver-haired, wizened artist. Moore, quite obviously, took John's challenge seriously. "It's no good for a young man like yourself wallowing in nuclear pessimism. Art goes on no matter what happens." He then told how he spent his time in the underground tube stations in London during the Blitz, where people slept hiding from German air raids, and how he sketched those scenes. (They became a famous series of drawings.) "Art must go on, war or no war," he repeated. But John was not easily silenced. "As an artist I must be profoundly affected by the threat of nuclear war," he persisted. Moore, a little schoolmasterish, countered, "Don't be so self-indulgent! You didn't live through the Blitz, but for us it was as cataclysmic as nuclear war."

Then Muffie shifted the conversation to another controversial subject. She asked Moore whether he liked the Beaubourg building in Paris, which, so to say, spills all its innards from pipes to airducts to staircases into the open. He said that he hated it. "Architecture should be honest," he replied, "and not expose the inside. You don't want to see the inside of a woman either, do you?" Then he went on: "The difference between an architect and a sculptor is that once you have finished a sculpture you can't change it. An architect on the other hand can't be his own bricklayer. Michelangelo had private assistants and they later claimed that they had done his work, but nobody remembers them. Rembrandt had a school for sculptors, it is natural to have help. But to begin with he had no help, one must do everything oneself. It's like learning a business, you can't delegate the beginning. The bronzes by Renoir, for instance, were not done by him, they were done by a traditional sculptor to his specifications. What mattered were not the models but how they made his mind shine." Then he recalled how he had come to New York for the first time in 1946 when Jackson Pollock "gave art and artists a head of steam. All of them were on a crusade, they did good work, they had integrity, and they had each other the way Picasso and Braque had each other. Now anything goes, everybody can paint and sculpt. But there is no head of steam, no breaker of new ground among the young. They all have exhibitions, though, and they can live by their art. I had no exhibition until I was forty and I could not live on sculpture, I had to teach until the war came. Now, if you have not had a retrospective exhibition by the time you're twenty-three, you're considered a failure. Brancusi never had an exhibit in Paris. He and Archipenko and Lipchitz and me were the champions of that period. Yet sculpture was considered a dead art. Now there are hundreds of young sculptors, it's too easy, it's like having a correspondence course."

Henry spoke without rancor, offering more a commentary in sorrow on how times change than a worldly complaint. This visit to Washington was a happy moment for him. One of his spectacular works of art would grace the

entrance of one of the finest galleries in the world, and the gallery had agreed
to a slight shift of the massive sculpture to ensure that the sunlight would
reflect on it in what he considered to be the most favorable angle. This was
of course very important to him. And now that he had had his will, he felt
he could leave Washington contented, ensured of a long afterlife in the history
of the arts.

It was a curious paradox that although neither Nixon, Ford, nor Carter was
a particular champion of the arts or gave much thought to the mediocrity of
the institutions of higher learning in the capital, it was under their presidencies
that the cultural waves that Kennedy had churned up began to have an impact
on cultural life in Washington. What had often been referred to as a one-horse
town with "northern efficiency and southern charm" when I arrived here,
gradually became a modern, bustling city with a growing consciousness that
the eyes of the world are on it, yet without altogether losing that southern
charm and innocence. The Kennedy Center for the Performing Arts with its
three theaters, a concert hall with outstanding acoustics, and the home of the
American Film Institute provided the inspiration and impetus for the bloom-
ing of Washington into a cultural center when it opened in 1971. Gone were
the days when Washington did not have a stage where ballet performances
could be given without endangering the ballerinas' ankles or a concert hall
without dead corners in the audience. Attendance records have proved that
the skeptics were wrong and that there was enough of an audience to fill all
three halls of the Kennedy Center and some of the smaller theaters. Thanks
to the Mellon family and its genius for philanthropy, founders of the imposing
and impressive National Gallery of Art, a variety of museums of the highest
quality and unusual interest have sprung up which have made Washington into
something of a museum capital of the world. For a good many years Washington was without a first-class hotel, luxury restaurants, and delicatessens where
French cheeses and good wines could be bought. Today there is a surfeit of
luxury hotels and superior restaurants, and even supermarkets carry a vast
choice of foreign delicacies on their shelves. Washingtonians, in a relatively
short time, have developed a taste for the finer things of life.

What endears Washington to me in particular is that unlike most other
American cities, it cares about the preservation of its human dimension. It not
only keeps its parks with flower beds in fine condition, but instead of expanding
its buildings upward, channels the inflow of people into satellite towns. Each
is a perfect example of how people who once thronged Main Street now flock
into shopping malls. This "mallation" of the United States has now reached
the capital. It may be one reason why Washington has failed to develop in its
center a shopping street of elegant showcases, comparable to Fifth Avenue or
Bond Street. This is why the heart of Washington has remained an unusually
pleasant place to live and work in.

If the new federal architecture is appalling, there is some consolation to be found in some of the extraordinarily successful efforts to conserve the old and the historic. Lafayette Square, with its enchanting samples of the best of the early American architecture, is a fine example. In a different way so is the restoration of the old-fashioned Willard Hotel. In political architecture, the Democrats continue to have a stranglehold on the city government, except that the white leadership has been replaced by black. But in national politics the city has become a politically and socially polarized battlefield, and its political beat has changed from a slow-paced minuet to heavy rock, from a habitat of wholesome tastes, conventional and cozy dinner parties, to a social whirl of ostentatious entertaining, mostly in the aid of political lobbying and political money raising. With the proliferation of problems, the massive expansion of the congressional and White House bureaucracies, lobbying has become a growth business. Television, too, has changed the political games from a handshaking exercise to a massive financial investment in television commercials. And so greed forced its way into Washington's old-fashioned innocence. Public service has become a prelude to making a fortune. Big-time lawyers flocked into the city where Covington & Burling used to have a monopoly on size and a dozen law firms have sprung into action, many with one to two hundred lawyers on their payroll, most of them engaged in disentangling the ever-growing complexities of government and the laws. In the old days Republicans, after a brief stint in government service, rushed back to making money, having satisfied their conscience in doing some service for the public good. But nowadays Washington is not only a fine city in which one can live comfortably, but also one in which one can make big money. It has today the highest average income of any American city—as well as the most PhDs.

Those PhDs used to come to gain some experience and expertise in government. But nowadays many come to do research and write at the so-called think tanks. No preeminent university existed to serve Washington the way Harvard serves Boston or Columbia, New York or the University of Chicago serves its city. All this ended in the late sixties and seventies when Washington broke the accepted pattern that intellectual life had to be organized around a university by creating several think tanks. Academia began to realize that Washington offered unusual advantages, especially for the study of the social and political sciences; here were not only scholarly resources such as the Library of Congress, the National Archives, and the Smithsonian, and a whole array of statistical data banks, but also the government itself.

It was to study and to assist the American political system that think tanks were born, from the Brookings Institution, the oldest and most scholarly, to the Woodrow Wilson Institute to the Center for Strategic and International Studies, the Carnegie Endowment, the Institute for Policy Studies, and the Heritage Foundation, each trying to provide ideas to different political interests or to the public interest in general. They are a whole new industry designed to help government. James Sundquist of the Brookings Institution calls them "research brokers." They also serve to bring foreign scholars to Washington for relatively short periods, which universities cannot normally do. Many of the resident scholars orbit around the world dispensing their knowledge and helping to inspire the creation of think tanks abroad, where intellectuals are much less interested in the game of politics or power. Think tanks have provided Washington with a unique concentration of intellectual talent and expertise. They have not really resulted in a better functioning of government, but perhaps in a better understanding of the problems it has to deal with, and created a talent pool from which governmental departments and institutions can and do draw.

All this has helped to make the capital the focus for television. Anchormen vie with presidents and politicians for the attention of the public and hence for influence. There is no capital in the world where the news media play a more important role than in Washington. Thanks to the framers of the Constitution there exists a competitive relationship between Congress and the Executive which allows the news media to play one off against the other; now television, which speaks to the entire nation, has been able to establish itself as a new and powerful influence on the making of American policy. Before Vietnam and Watergate reporters might have been a bit too cozy with the powers-in-being; now, feeling that they were lied to, they have little tolerance of human short-comings and fallibility. Trust in and respect for government have lamentably deteriorated, and this deterioration has made governance even more difficult than it already was. In Britain the media primarily report and comment on what happens in Parliament; in Washington they have become the arbiters between the presidency and Congress, an independent political force.

Washington has thus become a springboard from which great careers (not only in politics, though everything here in one way or the other is political) can now be made. Even Wall Street has come to recognize that it is in Washington where the future of the American and world economies is decided and, however grudgingly, concedes the need (through a bevy of experts) to keep in touch with government. When about ten years ago I was asked by a corporate leader to give his board a *tour d'horizon* of the Washington scene, he thanked me after I had finished, acknowledged that it had been interesting, but then added: "I have been in charge of this corporation for a good many years and I never gave a damn about what was going on in Washington and we have done pretty well nevertheless." Few, if any, corporate executives would say this today.

The capital remains an early-to-bed city because so many of its inhabitants are harnessed to government, which means rising early and working late. The early mornings therefore are the best time to buttonhole Washington shakers and makers, before the telephones begin to ring and the minds get cluttered by the drone of everyday business. Hence breakfast is the chosen hour. The best-known and most highly regarded breakfast fraternity is the so-called Sperling group, named after its founder and chairman, who is an old hand at writing about American politics and one of the stars of the *Christian Science*

Monitor. Some twenty reporters, most of them heads of Washington newspaper bureaus or columnists, foregather around a long oval table in a downtown hotel like wildcatters drilling for oil. At the same time they munch breakfast of the highest cholesterol and take notes. Godfrey Sperling presides over the ritual two or three times a week, mixing the serious with the sardonic, the indiscreet with the humorous, and giving the reporters the opportunity to dig for oil. I have enjoyed belonging to this club, which is not only a fount of information but also a cornerstone of special comradeship. It all serves the interests of the print media and, of course, of the so-called victim, for whom this group is a quick way of getting publicity for his or her views in a wide cross-section of newspapers throughout the country. The president sees the group about once a year, other newsworthy personalities more frequently. Courtesy is the watchword, though occasionally tempers can flare, as, for instance, when Donald Regan, then President Reagan's chief of staff, described the arms deal with Iran as trivial and one of the reporters wondered whether there existed something like "trivial hypocrisy" . . .

Rising early and working late also means that wives feel neglected and marriages break up. Mrs. John Tower, a lawyer and the former wife of Senator John Tower, once said to me: "John and I try to keep equally tired because it is the only way to keep a happy balanced life." However sensible a recipe for a Washington political marriage, it did not help to preserve this one. It is said that when you ask how are you, the answer in London is "Desperate"; in Paris, *J'ai un tout petit malheur* ("Not too good"); in New York, "Wonderful, come over"; and in Washington, "I'm in a rush, there is a crisis—so what's new." What is not new is that there is always something new. Washington therefore is a paradise for reporters.

My wife and I in the last few years have often debated whether we might not prefer to live somewhere else, in quieter surroundings where power is not quite as much part of friendship. We considered Boston or Princeton or a southern or northwestern city, but every time we ended by concluding that Washington offers the best of all worlds. We can be in the finest rolling Virginia countryside in our cottage fifty minutes from the capital; we have tennis courts and swimming pools within a ten-minute radius of our house; we have good theater, opera, and concerts to satisfy our cultural needs; we have the great Library of Congress for whatever writing we might want to do and think tanks to ruminate in. For good conversation hardly any other capital can compete. And so I shall keep up my special relationship with Washington and continue to watch the presidents come and go, as I have done ever since Harry Truman.

Over the years *The Sunday Times,* with one exception, a ten-day visit to Israel, never sent me on assignment to the Middle East. The main purpose of that visit in 1967 was to familiarize myself with Israel's problems and the lay of the land. I did relatively little reporting on my impressions and conclusions. It was not until November 1976 that I flew to the Middle East on a major

assignment, to interview Egypt's President Anwar al-Sadat. On arrival I was
asked to come to his rest house in Barrages on the Nile, where he liked to take
refuge from the daily chores of leadership. The entrance to the estate that we
drove through led over a short footbridge with a strange, overarching medieval
stone tower. There was only one guard at the tower, but I was told later that
the many gardeners, with their oversized aprons, who were busy planting
flowers were also security guards. Inside, the villa was only superficially furnished; there was obviously no desire for ostentation.

Sadat greeted me warmly, even effusively, and with a burst of enthusiasm
about his friend Henry Kissinger. Then, with no more ado, he asked me to fire
questions at him as he sat puffing at his pipe. Pipe smokers are usually calm
and relaxed as they draw on their pipes. Sadat puffed on his as if he were
constantly afraid that it would go out. He held his bald, tanned head very
upright as if he meant to defy someone all the time, which he probably did.
The idea of his acting on his own in search of peace with Israel was probably
then still remote or in its incubation phase. He did not see himself as the great
initiator; instead all his emphasis was on the need for the United States to act
as the "middleman." "We need someone whom Arabs and Israelis can trust
the way we trusted Henry." (Kissinger's exit from government by then was
imminent.) Sitting down with the Israelis, as Prime Minister Itzhak Rabin had
proposed, he brushed off as a "pretext for not wanting peace," and he reempha-
sized that the long heritage of conflict made an intermediary essential. When
I followed with the question as to whether he would be prepared to exchange
ambassadors with Israel, he practically jumped out of his seat, almost losing
his pipe. Of course he could not do that, he said, and reminded me of how long
it took the United States to recognize the Soviet Union or China. He got even
more agitated when I asked whether, if he could not agree to diplomatic
recognition, he could at least agree to trade across the frontier with Israel.
"How can you ask such a question!" he exclaimed, throwing up his arms in
quasi-despair: "After four wars and so much bitterness, no one could do that.
Even Muhammad and Jesus could not have persuaded the Arabs and Chris-
tians to do that. It ignores the whole psychological dimension of the problem.
Look at Rabin, he is mobilizing public opinion against my peace offensive by
telling people that I don't intend to have peace!" When I pressed on to find
out whether he saw Israel continuing permanently as a state, he did not give
me a direct answer, instead he said that one had to be practical. Israel's
existence had been recognized by the two superpowers and by the United
Nations—"That answers your question," he said diplomatically. That interview and all his arguments against a direct approach to Israel made me realize
even more forcefully how much courage his decision required, how he was
willing to gamble his entire political fortune, even his life, on breaking the
deadlock of mistrust that existed between Israel and the Arabs. He then earned
the accolade of statesmanship by his willingness to move where nobody else
was willing to tread. With his descent on Jerusalem and his appearance before

the Knesset, he broke a dam that allowed floods to break through that nobody since then has been able altogether to staunch. He was the kind of political freebooter who did not feel bound by outdated traditions, outdated policies, outdated attitudes, and he did not think what anybody else was thinking or telling. He was proud of going his own way, proud of being able to act forcefully and independently, and, being an optimist, usually oblivious to the likely outcome.

A year later, on December 4, 1977, I went to an unusual party, even for Washington. Barbara Walters, the television star, wanted to celebrate the disengagement agreement between Egypt and Israel, the most dramatic achievement so far of Kissinger's shuttle diplomacy. The Israeli ambassador, Simcha Dinitz, and the Egyptian ambassador, Ashraf Gorbal, were the guests of honor and for the first time shook hands. Gorbal recalled taking Kissinger, after a three-hour session with Sadat, to a Cairo nightclub that featured beautiful belly dancers, saying that it inspired Henry to return to step-by-step diplomacy. Dinitz, for the first time in his life, spoke in the name of Israel and Egypt when he evoked the spirit of the first day of Hanukkah, the festival of lights, by remembering the children in the streets not only of Jerusalem but also of Cairo. Art Buchwald, the humorist, pointed out that the evening had brought together people who had never spoken to each other: Henry Kissinger, Bill Safire, and "Tip" O'Neill, the Speaker of the House. It was only when he introduced Bill to Tip, said Buchwald, that the latter realized whom he was being introduced to and said: "You're Safire, you bastard!" and then they continued to speak to each other. It was an evening of reconciliation, Washington style.

By the time President Sadat and Prime Minister Begin came to Camp David on September 5, 1978, much of the momentum of reconciliation had petered out and Washington looked on skeptically as their talks with Carter began. The obstacles to an agreement looked formidable and the idea of engaging in confrontational diplomacy, the traditionalists were convinced, would expose Carter as the ultimate loser. Carter was aware of these ominous predictions, but they did not deter him. Whether it was his instinctive biblical attachment to the Middle East that tempted him or his belief that he could successfully mediate between two such stubborn personalities as Prime Minister Begin and President Sadat, or whether he wanted desperately to prove that he was a leader and diplomatic innovator, is hard to know, but he had clearly convinced himself that a door was ajar enough to risk convoking his tripartite summit. William Quandt's insightful and detailed history of the Camp David conference, published by the Brookings Institution, shows why this was not a Kissinger-type step-by-step diplomacy; it was diplomacy by immersion and confrontation.

Base camp for the press was in the foothills to Camp David, but for almost all the thirteen days the conference lasted there was nothing much of substance to report, partly because a news blackout had been imposed, partly because the outcome remained in doubt almost to the very last day. Ten days after the start of the talks the gap between Sadat and Begin was still discouragingly wide, and when Sadat threatened a premature walkout, Carter virtually threw his own political survival into the scales. "It would probably mean the end of my presidency because this whole effort will be discredited," he told Sadat. It gives one an idea how relieved Carter must have been when this unorthodox conclave ended in achieving some major successes. Quandt, who participated in the talks as a staff member of the National Security Council, gives Carter credit for having played the central role in bringing about the Camp David accords, but he faults him for injecting himself too directly and, often, too soon into the negotiations and for "not always recognizing the connection among the issues," a major drawback for a negotiator. Still, Camp David was a major success for the president as an intermediary who exerted pressure with some skill. If the Camp David accords did not fulfill the high expectations they engendered, it was because initially confusion boiled up about the duration of the freeze on Israeli settlements in the West Bank and the failure of the conferees to bring King Hussein into the negotiations.

In January 1981 I did what I had dreamed about for many years, I sailed down the Nile. For a week I felt as if living in ancient days under the Pharaohs, so timeless and so fascinatingly evocative did my surroundings seem. The eighty-year-old British steamer moved by day and anchored during the night to give us a good night's sleep, and although all the brass rails shone and the cabins were comfortable enough, it too reinforced my sense of living in the past, if only the colonial past. Before leaving Washington, Egyptian Ambassador Gorbal had reassured me that I would be able to see President Sadat once more. But when I reached Cairo nothing had been arranged. Back in Washington I complained to Mr. Gorbal, who was duly surprised and apologetic. He soon called to tell me that the president, sorry about the misunderstanding, would make a special point of giving me a special interview on his next visit to Washington, a promise which he kept in August 1981. He made no bones in our talk then about how much he missed Jimmy Carter, after having found President Reagan a man who did not understand the problems of the Middle East.

But Sadat also suffered from a grave weakness. He was blinded by the adulation he received internationally and paid too little attention to the growing opposition at home in Egypt, so that when the situation there afterwards came close to being uncontrollable, he was smitten by a paranoia that led him to impose extreme measures of security. The man who had shown such cocky courage suddenly lost his cunning and succumbed to fears. His massive purge of fundamentalist Muslims, Christian Copts, left- and right-wing politicians, journalists, lawyers, teachers took his friends aback: had he confused his situation with that of the Shah of Iran before his fall? There was, after all, a basic religious difference. Egypt is Sunni rather than Shi'ite Muslim, with the Sunnis not disposed to large-scale violence, nor is there an organized Islamic clergy. Sadat, when he was assassinated, was mourned as a great statesman, a man of courage in an area that is overpopulated by cowardly, self-indulgent, self-interested leaders.

I had several interviews with Carter, but none alone. On the first occasion we were a group of about twenty. We assembled in the Red Room and, as we were chatting among ourselves, the president entered so unobtrusively that we at first were not aware of his having joined us. He made no attempt to draw attention to himself, or to try to "act presidential"; he wanted to be seen as a modest, simple man. In fact, in his medium blue suit, blue shirt, blue tie, he looked more insurance salesman than president. He smiled at us gently, moving from reporter to reporter, shaking hands. Trying to be pleasant, I mentioned the favorable headlines in the morning papers over the reports of his previous night's speech, but my remark had the opposite effect. His smile disappeared and with a bemoaning undertone he said: "But the television commentators last night were not so favorable." Meg Greenfield of the Washington *Post* came tartly to the defense of the importance of newspapers and the president quickly and gallantly reassured her that he did not underrate them—but it underlined what we newspaper reporters were only too well aware of, the power of television and the decline of the influence of the print media. Carter, once we sat down for breakfast, fielded questions, including the most provocative ones, with studied calm, careful not to raise the temperature. At the end, before we said good-bye, a photographer came in. We shook hands with the president as we left, and afterwards a photograph, with greetings and signature, arrived in the mail—an odd ending to a background briefing.

The most newsworthy interview with President Carter came out of the blue when on January 11, 1980, on a Friday afternoon, I got a call from Jerry Schechter, who looked after, among many things, relations with foreign correspondents, asking me to come to see the president next morning at ten thirty. He had no further guidance for me. The timing, of course, was perfect for a Sunday newspaper. But all I could tell my editor was that I would have an interview with the president and that I had no idea whether I would be able to write about it. I only wanted to alert him to the possibility that the president wanted to make news, as indeed it turned out he did. We were a relatively small group, Hugh Sidey of *Time* magazine, Rick Smith of the *New York Times*, Haynes Johnson of the Washington *Post*, and Carl Rowen, an independent columnist. The place, which was quite unusual, was the president's private quarters, which made it all more informal, if anything in the White House can really be informal.

The president, dressed in slacks and pullover, seemed unusually serious and matter-of-fact. He began by saying that in view of the developments in Iran and the Soviet invasion of Afghanistan, he had decided to create a "regional security framework" for the protection of the all-important Persian Gulf area, and that he had already transmitted a warning to Moscow that he would order the "appropriate military response" if the Soviets engaged in further "warlike postures," a phrase that is strong yet vague enough to appeal to officialdom. He told us furthermore that he had ordered a naval buildup in the Indian Ocean and that he would not hesitate to take military action to protect Southwest Asia, as the region had come to be called. He spoke with firmness and conviction, anxious to impress us with this proof of his leadership and his determination to play it tough. This was a different Carter from the one who warmly embraced Brezhnev in Vienna. However, in reply to our questions he could add very little, which led me to believe that what became the "Carter doctrine" in his subsequent State of the Union message was still a vague idea and, for the time being, designed more as a move on the psychological war front than a calculated military strategy.

As the minutes ticked away with questions that had little to do with the president's central theme, I became worried about missing the first edition in London. It was 11:50 in Washington, late afternoon in London, when I called Harold Evans, who I knew was the only one on the paper to move fast and decisively in such a critical situation, and told him of the thrust of my story, attributable to "the highest authority." Only five minutes remained before copy deadline for the first edition, so Harold told me to dictate to him one paragraph as a lead to my dispatch that I had sent the night before. Harold was a truly working editor and as I dictated my new lead, I heard him type it on to his own machine. Then, before taking the copy himself to the composing room, he said that I had two hours to write the full story for the second edition.

Such was the launching of what became known as the Rapid Deployment Force, a brainchild of Brzezinski's which, like many of his ideas, was more of psychological than practical value. But it was a timely idea and, at least on paper, four divisions and a variety of warships were assigned to it. It had a salutary effect on friendly countries in the Persian Gulf and gradually also persuaded the British and French to lend a hand. The Carter doctrine did not make history and, fortunately, was never put to a test, but as a desperate move to prevent the catastrophe of the fall of the Shah from creating even greater instability than already existed in the area, it was effective. The hollowness of the concept gradually became evident, but it was nevertheless a useful deterrent move at the time and it may still have its uses in the very uncertain future. I had never been to Iran or the Persian Gulf area, but when the Shah's throne began to shake and the Gulf situation began to assume crisis proportions, I asked Harold Evans whether he would let me go there for three weeks to familiarize myself with an area of which I knew little but about which I would have to write increasingly from Washington. He immediately agreed.

I left for Tehran on April 2, 1978, and found myself seated next to an American geologist, who turned out to be fascinating company. He was on his way to participate in a very important decision—where to position Iran's first nuclear power plant. A nuclear power plant in a country as oil-rich as Iran should surely not have high priority, but it did. It was a very controversial issue because in an earthquake-prone country it is imperative to select the safest possible location. It also affected the costs, as he explained to me. The plant in question, for instance, if built where the government wanted it to be, not one of the safer places, would cost a billion dollars more than in a safe area. Already on my flight to Tehran, I was having the Shah's extravagance demonstrated to me.

When I drove from the Bandar Abbas airport into town, I marveled at the beautiful four-lane highway—a symbol of opulence—but with hardly any traffic on it, for only fifteen years earlier, Bandar Abbas, which sits on the northern side of the strategically vital Straits of Hormuz, was a tiny fishing village surrounded by bleak desert land, a place of banishment, a prison for the worst criminals. The Shah had made it the biggest base for the Iranian Navy to protect that narrow stretch of water which connects the Persian Gulf and the Arabian Sea and through which then passed 51 percent of all the oil consumed in the United States, 80 percent of Japan's, and 70 percent of Western Europe's.

The crassest extravagance of all and the one that made me most aware of the fading of the Shah's glory was the extraordinary tent city at Persepolis, which out of courtesy to my guide I could not refuse to visit. It was built by the Shah in 1971 to celebrate the two hundred fiftieth anniversary of the Iranian Empire. There he received the great conglomerate of presidents, kings, and princes who came to render homage almost in the way the ancient bas-relief showed the petty kings and governors honoring the king of kings, Darius I, who reigned 521–486 B.C. The clay-colored tents with their Bordeaux-boudoir-red interiors were still standing, the furniture and the chandeliers were still all in place, but, while I was there, the skies unloaded a sharp squall of rain, and water began sadly dripping into the tents through the leaky canvas roofs. It gave it all a faded, dying look only too symbolic of what was beginning to happen to the Shah's own empire.

Many of the problems of modernization and reform, I learned, had their reflection in Persian art. Persian artists were perfectionists but not innovators. True to Islam, they excelled by craftsmanship not originality, they specialized in form rather than ideas. Persian poets too did not dare to break the mold of centuries of tradition. In the walled city of Shiraz I was shown the palace garden, one of the most beautiful I had ever seen, and a much smaller private one, which the owner had given a unique, charming combination of flora and poetry, something that outside the Islamic world would risk seeming mere kitsch. On almost every tree was a plaque with a carefully chosen quotation from a famous poem, appealing to human kindness, the human heart, to nature. Writing about my visit in the *Atlantic Monthly* I wrote in conclusion, "The Shah is a man in a hurry. He has a dream and he wants to make it a reality . . . but he must know that things will be quite different once he is gone . . . A man in a hurry, however, is in danger of losing his sense of time

. . . in pursuit of minipower status for Iran, he is forcing the pace of progress beyond the resources and skills of his people and what they can mentally adjust to."

Conceptually, President Nixon's decision to turn Iran into the guardian of the Persian Gulf had a good deal of logic to it, for the region had been left unprotected ever since the British withdrawal—completed in 1971—from east of Suez. Nixon gave the Shah carte blanche to purchase any amount of military equipment short of nuclear weapons. This not only overstimulated his latent megalomania, it also led him to instigate the steep rise in the price of oil in 1973 to make it possible for him to finance his purchases. The United States thus abetted the Shah's worst vanities. I had a number of opportunities to talk to top military leaders and operational commanders, and to visit a number of military bases. After I had flown in an Iranian Air Force plane to Oman across the Straits of Hormuz and close to the border Oman shares with South Yemen, people said joshingly that I had a lot of courage to entrust myself to an Iranian-piloted plane. But I found their pilots well trained and sure of what they were doing. The same did not apply to the top brass, which was more concerned with its comforts, its rank, and its influence on the Shah than on strategy and the internal political situation. The base commanders, on the other hand, were mainly interested in having at their disposal the latest and most expensive military equipment and, I was told, the Shah did his very best to provide their toys—some $20 billion worth. But when I asked them whether the Shah could rely on them to deal if necessary with civil disobedience, like most military anywhere, they said they did not want to have anything to do with it, that anyway they were poorly equipped for coping with civilian unrest. They also indicated that they were not sure how the ranks would behave in such a situation. But the Shah was firmly opposed to using the military because he was convinced, as he put it to the British ambassador, that there was no military solution to this crisis, that a dictator can survive by killing people: a king cannot. I very much doubt therefore that there was a realistic and promising military option, as Zbig believed, especially since the Shah positioned the military so that they would not gang up on him. He once told Richard Helms, when he was the US ambassador, that "without me, they would be at each other's throats."

I was hesitant about my own observations and judgment as a first-time visitor, but there were so many public and semipublic manifestations of the fierce undertow of feeling that I became more and more disturbed by what I saw. At the university of Isfahan the students were on strike, and riot police in steel helmets wielding shields and batons were standing by ready to pounce against the strikers. I was told at the entrance that I could not walk in because my presence might provoke an incident and put me in danger.

Mrs. Afkhami, the minister for women's affairs, who had once been a professor at the University of Colorado, a handsome woman dressed in Paris-designed clothes and wearing expensive jewelry, told me on my visit to her office that the new middle class approved of her new role for women, but that the silent masses did not. She was convinced, though, that her efforts strengthened the Shah's political support in the country. (Instead, before I left the country, Mrs. Afkhami had her ministry virtually abolished as being too provocative.) Later, I met Noosh, a nineteen-year-old girl whose father had died of cancer and her mother of a heart attack. Consequently her brother, an electronics engineer, aged twenty-four, was now in charge of the family, whose youngest member was a five-year-old girl. Her brother, Noosh explained, hated her having a job, hated her taking French lessons, hated her hankering for independence and her desire to be a person in her own right. This alone might seem excessive male chauvinism as we know it in the West, but he had gone so far as to object to her riding a bicycle and to threaten to kill her if she did. I asked whether he meant it literally or just figuratively. She gave me a pitying look: "Of course, he meant it literally. But how else am I going to get to work except on my bike?" On the university campuses most of the girls wore hip-fitting blue jeans and T-shirts, only a few wrapped themselves into the drab chador. When I asked one who did wear a chador why she did so, she said it was to protest against the Shah's squandering oil revenues on the military, the cruelty shown by the police toward students, and against the Shah's efforts to westernize Iranian society. She assured me that she was a modern thinking woman who counted herself among the new middle class—the engineers, economists, and scientists—whose aim was to turn Iran into a modern state, but she did not believe that the Shah's methods would work and she therefore made common cause with the mullahs who wielded power based on the Islamic religion, the only power that could mobilize the forces that could overthrow the Shah. Her description of the hidden forces that were gathering, according to her, had about it an inevitability that sounded both credible and intimidating.

The American ambassador in Tehran, William Sullivan, told me with unusual candor that in Iran he felt "like a fish out of water," that he had never before served in this part of the world and that he was very confused by what was happening. He simply had no "feel" for the situation. Britain's Sir Anthony Parsons, on the other hand, was a lifelong expert on the Middle East. He was clearly impressed by the positive contribution the Shah had made to Iran's growth into a minipower, and, although he was well aware of the smoldering opposition groups—the clergy, the bazaar merchants, and the students—he thought that these three groups were so disparate that they were unlikely to form a common front; he sounded confident that the Shah could hold them in check. What did worry him more was the Shah's moodiness and the lack of politically shrewd advisers in his entourage. He flatly denied that he used his close relationship with the Shah to act like an old-fashioned viceroy. Because of the Shah's dependence on the United States, the American ambassador had the ear of the Shah much more than he had. In his extraordinary self-revealing memoir, *The Pride and the Fall,* Sir Anthony states that even had he been more perspicacious in assessing the confluence of the opposition forces, he did not think he would have recommended to the British government a different policy—which anyway it would not have adopted. He attributed the fall of the Shah to the "liberalization policy" at the end of 1976 which loosened his government's controls to such an extent that it consolidated all the disparate opposition forces and made them irresistible.

When Carter decided, quite sensibly, to impose his own supervision on arms sales to Iran, it, no doubt, reinforced the Shah's earlier fears that he would not have the kind of easy relationship with Carter he used to have with Nixon, and to improve his relationship he put more emphasis on liberalizing his policies. There is reason for blaming the American pressures for speedy liberalization for the growth of the opposition to the Shah's policies. The contradictions in Carter's public statements and the unorthodox machinations behind the scenes—which had included Brzezinski's backchannel contacts with Adeshir Zahedi, the flamboyant Iran ambassador to the US and the efforts by General Robert Huyser, deputy commander of NATO Forces—must also have confused the Shah, who by then had virtually become a mental depressive. The disintegration of his self-confidence and trust in whatever was left of his own political instincts accelerated. Americans are quick to blame themselves for such catastrophes as the fall of Iran, but the Shah himself should have known that the speed with which he tried to westernize a country steeped in traditions hundreds of years old was bound to play into the hands of the traditionalists. The Shah had it within his power to slow down the modernization of Iran until he had greater political support. But he offered too small returns on his vast oil revenues to the students and lower classes. Instead he wasted huge sums on a spending spree for military hardware. It was bound to provide the glue to unite disparate opposition groups. The absence of wise and better balanced counsel, the failure to understand that Iran was not part of Western civilization cut off by geography from its natural partners, and finally, the fact that the Shah was suffering from cancer—all these contributed to his doom. The whole episode, too, was a highly uncomfortable reminder for Britain of how its role in this part of the world had sunk virtually without a trace.

Nor had the United States been able to replace it, as became only too obvious later when an utterly frustrated Carter tried to free the Americans held hostage in Tehran with a James Bond-like rescue operation that required the kind of precision in planning and execution of which the American military seem congenitally incapable. Instead, they moved ahead, trusting their machines and their luck rather than thinking through every detail of what may happen should an operation misfire. The seventy-eight-page postmortem report by Admiral James L. Holloway, a former chief of naval operations, faulted the planners for assigning an inadequate number of helicopters to the operation, for a lack of "command and control" at lower levels during the mission, and for not utilizing an existing military command but creating a new one lacking in cohesion. When Carter, in retirement, was asked what he would do differently if he had to do it over again, he said, "More helicopters."

Usually American military operations are criticized for overkill, as was the one against Grenada. Americans feel more secure and comfortable with superior numbers. But in the case of the Iranian rescue mission the military chose underkill and paid for it. The Israelis, who made a name for their commando raids, such as the one at Entebbe, carefully studied the records of British commando operations carried out during World War II, and concluded that they always included more men and matériel than the minimum, to allow for some losses.

But even if the helicopters had reached their destination, extricating the hostages from the American Embassy would have been an extremely dicey enterprise that many experts in retrospect consider an act of folly. First of all, according to Gary Sick's expert report, *American Hostages in Iran,* the success of the operation depended almost entirely on surprise. The bet was that after six months of guard duty the students had settled into a comfortable and generally relaxed routine and could be ambushed. But it is hard to believe that at least one man would not have been alert enough to sound an alarm. Next, and this has not been discussed publicly, those familiar with the embassy grounds knew that those hostages who found themselves in the basement of the Mushroom, the safe room in a separate building, a warehouse, were almost certainly doomed because the door leading to that room was so narrow that it allowed only one man to enter or come out and there was no way of blasting it open without injuring people behind it. Therefore many of those directly involved in the operation, and the former hostages themselves, were relieved that the rescue operation had to be abandoned in its first phase.

The feeling of impotence in the face of extreme provocation, the inability of the US government to pry the hostages loose after a number of desperate behind-the-scenes negotiations, and the sight of American diplomats handcuffed and humiliated in Tehran made the nation's blood boil. It was one more example of Carter's bad luck. There was indeed nothing decisive Carter could have done to prevent the collapse of the Peacock throne. It was a melancholy situation. What was self-destructive was Carter's mistake of magnifying the problem unnecessarily from the start—first, when he vowed that he would not leave the White House to campaign for his reelection until the hostage issue had been resolved, and, second, when he reversed himself and began to threaten military action. He thereby allowed the news media to give the issue front-page billing day after day, turning it into a test of his presidential leadership, which was rapidly becoming a serious and highly damaging election issue. It also alerted the Iranian militants to what a powerful weapon they had in their hands. And so the hostages became pawns in a much bigger chess game. Suddenly, the credibility of his promises, his most precious political asset, was doubted, although it was quite obvious to any rational person that the United States was powerless in the face of irrational political behavior, just as the United States had been powerless facing the Communist takeover of China some thirty years earlier. The tension that gripped the White House was more unnerving than at any previous time in the Carter administration because of the mounting fears that the outcome could have far-reaching repercussions on Carter's political future. Americans had made him president because at the time they saw in him an anti-interventionist, anti-imperialist, a man who would not drag them into another Vietnam. They sensed that, being a populist, he abhorred the uses of power. But when the president did not live up to these expectations, Americans recognized that what they needed was a strong leader who could restore the United States' prestige and steer the American ship of state with greater confidence and firmness. Americans, lacking strong and stable cultural underpinnings, had always been carried forward by their confidence in the future. However in the past few years they had suffered so many shocks that their engine of optimism began to sputter. Ceasing to be the one and only superpower, Vietnam, Watergate, and the dollar's loss of its dominant position gravely undermined American self-confidence. Carter's unsteady hand at foreign affairs and his handling of economic and financial policies reinforced these feelings. Prime Minister James Callaghan in March 1978 told me that he himself felt compelled to tell Carter that while he had given the world leadership on a "grand scale," he had not matched it by economic leadership. "I then began to understand," he said, "that Carter did not realize that the dollar was more than a domestic currency. I was tempted to send him Harold Lever, who can think up five ways of how to cope with every problem, but Mike Blumenthal [US secretary of the treasury] probably would not have appreciated it." As Richard Fisher, one of the bright young men who had made his pilgrimage from Harriman Brothers to the Treasury, said to me: "Foreign exchange rates and financial markets were not part of Carter's stream of consciousness." It was no consolation that this had in fact been true of most presidents: most presidents didn't need the knowledge, but Carter did. Mike Blumenthal became so impatient with Carter's lack of interest in macroeconomic problems that he wrote him a special memo to explain the effect of a tight monetary policy, and Carter, impressed indeed, attached his "Good memo, J.C." to it (he was in the habit of grading the memos of his aides like a professor). In a later memo Blumenthal went much further and took the president to task: "Saying that rising interest rates are inflationary was not too different from saying that taking the bitter medicine makes you feel sick. It can indeed while you swallow it, but if it does its job, it ultimately helps to cure your illness. Occasionally public statements commenting on such matters as interest rate increases may sometimes be necessary. But they should not be off-the-cuff without consultation amongst responsible cabinet officers." It was unusually forceful language for a cabinet officer to use in communicating with the president.

Carter did indeed swallow the bitter medicine that was forced down his throat. Under intense pressure from several foreign governments, fearful of the downslide of the dollar, the growing threat of inflation, and the damaging effect it all had on the climate for investment and growth, the administration pulled itself together and agreed on a "rescue package" which Carter hurriedly approved over a weekend. Later in 1979, in the face of continuing rampant inflation, he appointed Paul Volker to the chairmanship of the Federal Reserve Board; he hoped Volker's reputation as an inflation fighter would rekindle confidence in the administration's policies. Whether he realized that he would have to pay a high political price for it—a recession that was to weaken his prospects for reelection—is anybody's guess. Most likely he hoped that facing the problem of inflation head-on would bring its political payoff in time for the election campaign.

If Carter admitted that he did not have the economic background to understand the world role of the dollar, he did believe that he knew a lot about foreign affairs, and yet he never succeeded in riding herd over Vance and Brzezinski. Through the sponsorship of David Rockefeller (Nelson Rockefeller did the same for Kissinger), Zbig became a protégé of the Eastern Establishment, but by the time he joined the Carter administration, he had come to believe that it was an institution whose time had passed. He took a certain satisfaction in wrestling down Cy Vance, one of the foremost representatives of that dying breed. During the preparations for the Iranian rescue operation Zbig was gung ho for it; Vance remained the lone opponent, arguing strongly against it as politically and militarily ill-conceived and an undertaking that was likely to cost more lives than it would save. Underlying his arguments was his abhorrence of the use of force. Even Harold Brown, though skeptical at first, allowed himself to be convinced by the military that the operation had a good chance of succeeding. When the president ignored Vance's advice, Vance resigned in protest. No doubt, it had been a traumatic and heartbreaking decision for a man who believed so strongly in presidential loyalty. He told me afterwards that he tried hard to convince the president that there was no way of getting the hostages out without at least fifteen of them getting killed. So why risk their lives when they were all in relatively good health? Furthermore, it could trigger a political explosion in the Middle East, Vance said he argued. "I think the president did not have a sufficiently clear idea," he went on, analyzing the president's decision, "what the mission would accomplish. I'm not sure that he understood the consequences of the use of military force and, therefore, whether he could define the need to do so in his own mind. In earlier cases, when we were discussing what to do about deploying military force in Ethiopia, for instance, or Somalia, I asked him whether he was actually prepared to drop bombs, and if he was not, what would he be prepared to do? And I warned him that he could be sucked into a situation without recognizing what the consequences were going to be." In all earlier situations when the use of force was seriously discussed, Jimmy Carter agonized and then accepted Vance's advice. But in the case of the Iranian rescue operation, frustration and the presidential elections led him to adopt a rash decision. Maybe it was also proof, judging by Cy's comments, that those early doubts about the president's ability to take such far-reaching decisions as the use of force were justified and that he had reached a point where he felt he had to prove he could take tough decisions. But tough decisions taken from a sense of weakness are of course dangerous.

Vance's resignation, even though Edmund Muskie's appointment was well received, did not help Carter politically. It was seen as further proof of his failure as a leader if a man of such high integrity and such commitment to public service stormed out of the coop. Americans, almost in unison (including Democrats), were blaming Carter for the impression he had created abroad that the United States was "buckling." And so the lack of leadership became a winged accusation. When West German Chancellor Helmut Schmidt was asked for the reasons he delayed imposing sanctions on Iran, he cited his lack of confidence in Carter's leadership.

Carter was and still is a political pariah (as this is written ten years later). Why did the outsider who became something of an insider find himself an outsider again, and in the most humiliating way? The simple answer is that he did not have a feel for the art of leadership or the uses of power. He confused leadership with imposing on himself too many policy and legislative demands and keeping everybody guessing whether the uses of power or his moralism would prevail in his mind when taking certain difficult decisions. He played the foreman rather than the manager, the preacher rather than the pope. I am not sure how best to define the reasons for Carter's failure to create confidence in himself as a leader. Acts of statesmanship or military victories are not necessarily the essential ingredients for strong leadership. Johnson had a powerful personality and exuded authority, but overdid both. Even Jerry Ford knew who he was. With Carter however I was never certain whether he really did. His facial expressions too often reflected an inner insecurity which he transmitted, especially on television, to his audiences. I sometimes wondered whether the presidency was not a moral self-flagellation for him. During the hostage crisis there was a kind of frozen apprehension in his eyes, a kind of lugubrious despair. It was disconcerting to watch. If he had sported on a serious occasion the kind of baseball cap Reagan donned laughingly after the confused and painful breakup of the Reykjavik summit, he would have been severely reprimanded by the news media for such untimely frivolity; but in Reagan's case it was interpreted as a sign of confidence in the future. Ronald Reagan had the actor's ability—certainly till then—to call defeat victory, and be believed.

Where knowledge and understanding of the issues mattered—say, at press conferences—Truman, Eisenhower, Johnson, Ford, and Reagan often stumbled; Kennedy, Nixon, and Carter excelled. Only Truman, Eisenhower, and Kennedy saw the press as regularly as Roosevelt did. FDR did it with enjoyment and utter self-confidence. Truman, as we used to say, liked to "shoot from the hip" and as a consequence presented a special temptation to the press corps to throw some juicy banana peels into the ring for the president to slip on. Eisenhower did not enjoy his weekly press conferences, but considered them a duty and was therefore remarkably conscientious about them. When confronted with a sharp, direct question he usually became evasive, anxious to keep his options open, but when asked what his "philosophy" was about this or that problem, he became expansive and articulate and informative about his own thinking. Kennedy took a certain pleasure in confronting the press and could be even quicker with his off-the-cuff repartee than Roosevelt. Having attended press conferences of nine presidents, I give Kennedy the highest marks, because Johnson and Nixon, in particular, hated these occasions, preferred to evade them, and considered them a drag on their image. Carter was always well briefed, but anxiety was written all over his face. There has been much sarcastic talk about President Reagan's gaffes at press conferences, but in fact most presidents suffered from "gaffitis," except perhaps that he succumbed to it more than others. As a trained actor he was good at reciting his prepared lines, but when the questioning strayed into the unexpected, the absence of a prompter became noticeable. Where the uses of power mattered, Truman, Eisenhower, Kennedy, and Nixon proved to have great flair. Not until very late did Carter learn that preaching human rights, human values, and morality were not enough to exert leadership. Churchill once said of Anthony Eden that he was "totally incapable of differentiating great points from small points." One could say the same of Carter, and that therefore he failed to get the kind of recognition for the great points he scored.

The one time I had a chance to ask Jimmy Carter about his own definition of leadership was when I saw him with my then-editor Denis Hamilton. At the start the president went out of his way to emphasize how impressed he was with Prime Minister Callaghan and that he considered him "a very great friend." Toward the end I asked him how he defined the problem of leadership to himself. "A major indication of leadership to me is the assessment of the highest common denominator people are willing to strive for to realize their highest expectations," he replied. He went on: "It requires some degree of inspiration, some degree of practical planning, and the implementation of the difficult practicalities of legislation. I have a good relationship with the American people, I have a good idea of what they can accept. However, I know that getting those aspirations realized is a measure of leadership I have not yet proved." It was an answer that told a great deal about Carter's character and priorities: his modesty, his populism, his sense of the practical and the intuitive. What was striking was the total absence of any reference to the uses of presidential powers. Denis, after listening to Carter, said that he had a simpler theory about leadership: "One-third ability, one-third luck, and one-third just plain hanging on." Carter laughed and said: "The third is the one I can almost guarantee." He certainly had ability, even if at times it was not matched by enough experience. Luck eluded him once he became president, and as to his persistence and endurance he could hardly be faulted, certainly not in his

efforts to resolve the Iranian hostage crisis, which "almost became an obsession," as he put it in his memoirs *Keeping Faith*. It certainly contributed to
his defeat in the elections because, he admits, he kept the issue "at the forefront
of world attention." He did, after protracted but on the whole aboveboard
negotiations and keeping within the American law, obtain their release.
Whether Reagan's threatening language contributed to the Iranians' finally
accepting Carter's terms is hard to judge even in retrospect. If Carter was left
with his hands bleeding, they were nevertheless clean, certainly cleaner than
Reagan's after his botched efforts at bribing Iran into a hostage deal.

By March of 1978 (when the interview took place), the issue of leadership
had already grown into a huge cloud that was to darken his four years in the
White House. The idea of leadership had been fascinating me for several years.
What is it that makes for great and wise leadership? What are the mysterious
ingredients? What attitudes of mind does it require, what qualities need to be
summoned? With elitism fading away, mass education spreading, political
parties losing their cohesion, permanent reformism creating constant fluidity,
and a world growing in complexity, is it surprising that one of the greatest
crises we experience is the crisis of leadership? Is it surprising that the American presidency, like almost all offices of head of state, has lost much of its
authority? A leader today is less believed, has less of a buffer, less of a cushion,
less of an automatic drawing fund of goodwill or trust to call on. One of the
most frequently used and abused among words is "charisma": in the old
Weberian sense it meant a perception of mystic quality for the governance of
events but, in fact, it is nothing else than a matter of style and image and all
that entails—plus, of course, concrete achievements, which have much more
to do with power or the perception of power. The changing role of the media
has also something to do with the decline of leadership, and I don't mean that
it has just something to do with Watergate and the Vietnam war. The press,
and especially television, are more powerful because they can reach far more
people almost instantly and they are much less awed by authority than they
used to be. They have become almost as influential in the development or the
destruction of official policy as the executive or the legislature. They have
become an arbiter of society, judge rather than commentator, advocate rather
than analyst.

Americans, perhaps, are more aware of the problem of leadership than, say,
the European democracies, for the divided American government, designed by
the Founding Fathers for the protection from tyranny, cannot act with the
speed, the effectiveness of a parliamentary democracy. The American system
requires much greater resilience on the part of the president than the British
does of a prime minister who is not the chief executive and hence does not need
a large staff. In 1978, when I visited Harold Macmillan at his country place,
Birch Grove, he said, comparing the American and British political systems,
"We aren't a democracy. We have a system of the Queen's ministers who in

order to stay in office have to have the support of the House of Commons, which, of course, is elected by a very wide democratic system. A prime minister therefore does not have to think constantly of how his policies will appeal to Congress and to the public, as an American president has to. Personality and popularity therefore are much more important to an American president than to a British prime minister." He admitted however that television has forced even prime ministers to pay more attention to their popularity with the public. Still, he does not need quite as much ability to dominate "center stage" as an American president. Gregory Peck, the film star, in discussing President Carter's flaws as a leader with me, put the emphasis on Carter's inability to take center stage. "Success depends on it. You have to live your role, and it must be a very conscious decision, because you have to be able to attract all the attention without trying." Or anyway, being seen to be trying.

To Prime Minister Jim Callaghan leadership was not really a mystery: "I like to take every problem as it comes, using my instinct and experience. I say to myself, now what do I have to do to get this particular issue through in whatever way I want it." As the tools of leadership, he said, he used persuasion and pressure. "If the people are bullyable," he said, "I bully them. If they are persuadable I persuade them. I use any technique that is appropriate. But I do not believe in using blackmail and fear to influence decisions. Strong leadership to me means the ability to stand firm when you believe that you are doing the right thing." Moral leadership, Callaghan agreed, was important: "It is a way of appealing to people's hearts and minds. If anybody can appeal to that, and call it out, he's got a strength that is greater than any appeal to self-interest; but rarely is a person capable of it." Callaghan agreed that television contributed to the crisis of leadership. "People see through us more quickly and more easily and realize that we're not supermen." And while historical precedent could be helpful, a leader should not allow himself to be overcome by it. He agreed that Carter did not project the personality of a leader as had Johnson or Nixon, who knew what a complex web of experience, judgment, action was involved in being at the helm. Harold Macmillan and Sir Alec Douglas-Home, he volunteered, he considered people who knew what leadership was about, Ted Heath not quite because he was too much a man of principle and not enough a politician. Eden did not at all. Of advice from intellectuals in government, Callaghan thought they could make a vital contribution, but that their common sense was frequently deficient. He also mentioned George Brown, who, he said, was a "natural intellectual who combined it with a vivid capacity to take decisions. If only he had had more self-discipline, he would have made a first-class politician . . ." (When I ran into George the next day in the street, he looked sad and shrunken, and to cheer him up I mentioned to him the prime minister's flattering remarks. Alas, deeply hurt as he was in the political wilderness, he immediately used my remark to write a letter to the prime minister asking to see him, although I had begged him to keep what I had told him to himself. A few days later he sent me a copy of his letter and of the negative reply he got. Naturally, I wrote an embarrassed apology to Callaghan, who tossed the incident aside.)

General de Gaulle was obsessed with the question of leadership, and as a young officer wrote a book, *Edge of the Sword,* in which he described a leader as a man who is aware of the risks, but does not "scorn the consequences, measures them in good faith and accepts them without evasion, embraces action with the pride of the master." When Bobby Kennedy began to contemplate in March 1967 whether to run for the presidency he asked de Gaulle what he would do about the war in Vietnam if he were in his place. De Gaulle replied: "I have been in politics for a very long time. I have lost many battles and won others, but what I would do in your place, and you have a long career ahead of you, is to stay out of the debate." But Bobby was too emotionally involved. He entered the debate by actively opposing the war; he could not do otherwise to be politically viable.

Henry Kissinger once defined leadership in an article in the magazine *Daedalus* (Spring 1966) by making a distinction between the statesman and the prophet. "The statesman manipulates reality," he wrote; "his first goal is survival; gradualism to him is the essence of stability; he represents an era of average performance, of gradual change and slow construction."

By contrast, "the prophet is less concerned with manipulating than with creating reality. What is possible interests him less than what is 'right.' He offers his vision as the test and his good faith as a guarantee. He believes in the perfectability of man. His approach is timeless and not dependent on circumstances. He objects to gradualism as an unnecessary concession to circumstance . . . Paradoxically, his more optimistic view of human nature makes him more tolerant than the statesman."

Harry McPherson, a onetime legal adviser and speech writer to President Johnson, attributed the absence of leadership in the United States to the fact that "today's intellectual tradition is predominantly critical, resistant to the essential pretensions of leadership, meaning that a leader is capable of guiding others more wisely than they are capable of guiding themselves and they are therefore full of suspicion of leadership." Perhaps the problem of leadership is a matter of education, for Americans are brought up to view government with suspicion if not outright disrespect, an upbringing that breeds a deep-seated prejudice against the seat of government. This prejudice is reinforced by the endlessly exasperating process of the executive and the legislature reaching agreements based on compromises that are unsatisfactory to a substantial minority. Few people realize what it means to govern this huge country, an entire continent, and to look after American interests abroad. Contributing to the dissatisfaction is the impression government here creates that the people and the lands under the control of the federal government are mere statistics and graphs and the idea, widespread among officialdom, that people can be fooled. We Europeans are taught to respect government. According to the opinion polls the British public is content with the performance of Parliament; only 8 percent in a 1977 poll thought that Parliament did a poor job. Parliament, unlike the US Congress, accepts that the cabinet is in a better position to run public affairs than members of Parliament or peers, and few people would hold that decisions in the conduct of war should be left to a democratic assembly.

If President Johnson was too "hot" a leader for his times, Carter was too cool, too detached, too mechanical. It prevented him from capturing the hearts and minds of the people. When I asked Brzezinski in April 1980 why it was that Carter at his last press conference knew all the details and facts, yet could not turn them into a coherent whole, he replied that "like an engineer he did know how to put certain nuts and bolts together, but not how to make it all work." I recalled that three weeks earlier Carter had threatened Iran with military retaliation and then Jody Powell, on instructions from the president, had toned down the wave of belligerence, explaining that the president did not want the situation to get out of hand. Then why did the president threaten military intervention at his press conference? I asked. To frighten the allies and to make them cooperate on sanctions, Zbig replied. When I suggested that this was not leadership but taking a leaf out of John Foster Dulles's book, Zbig said that it was a form of playing games but for an important purpose.

The Carter administration failed to inspire confidence in its leadership both at home and abroad. It remained too amateurish and, worst of all, Carter failed to make Americans feel proud of this president. His handling of the hostage crisis, his vacillations, his exaggerated rhetoric, his saying first that to free America from its "inordinate fear of communism" was a major goal of his, then describing the Soviet invasion of Afghanistan as having changed "his opinion of the Russians . . . more dramatically in the last week than over the previous two and a half years" linger on. And so do some curious weaknesses in his character which, for instance, made him, in a sort of backhanded vindictiveness, criticize Vance during an appearance at the Council on Foreign Relations in New York—in Cy's presence.

Nevertheless when one looks more closely at his actual achievements in foreign affairs, I believe he will be given more gratifying credit in the memory of history than he is now. His first priority was the Panama Canal Treaty, which at the time looked to me misplaced. But thanks to the skill of two exceedingly competent ambassadors, Ellsworth Bunker and Sol Linowitz, and a well-managed campaign for the hard-to-get sixty-seven votes needed for ratification, he succeeded in a strategic devolution without which the United States would be haunted by even greater chaos in Central America than exists now. The treaty was bitterly opposed by Ronald Reagan during the election campaign. Carter's decision to go for the normalization of relations with China, also bitterly opposed by Mr. Reagan during the election campaign, made it much easier for him to terminate the defense treaty with Taiwan, which otherwise would have seriously jeopardized Sino-American relations and let the Russians have the last laugh. The Camp David accords were in themselves a remarkable achievement, even if they have lost much of their earlier promise. They did, however, enable President Reagan to launch his own, if abortive, peace process. He completed negotiations for the SALT II treaty and, together with Brezhnev, put his signature to it, another issue Mr. Reagan bitterly censured during the election campaign. Yet, as president, Reagan continued to adhere to the unratified treaty, if only barely, until he abandoned it in December 1986. Since the assessments of success and failure of presidents have to wait until they can be measured against the performance of their successors, it is still too early to reach any serious conclusions about Carter's record.

When Jimmy Carter left Washington defeated, he looked more dispirited than any other departing president in the last thirty years, with the obvious exception of President Nixon. The best indication of the mood in which he left—a striking contrast to Mr. Truman's—was Carter's very quiet reply to a suggestion made in private conversation to him that he would be well advised not to return to the remoteness of his hometown, Plains, Georgia: "It's a good place to hide," he said very quietly. A few days before leaving, he saw the new president for the traditional final briefing on the issues on which Mr. Reagan would have to fasten his attention, some dealing with highly sensitive security matters such as the management of the nuclear forces in time of an attack or such top-secret agreements as the American commitment to assist Egypt in case of an attack by Libya. Noticing that Mr. Reagan made no notes to take down some of the more complex issues, he offered him a pencil and note pad, but Reagan assured him that he had a good memory. He listened politely and patiently. President Carter had taken the trouble to prepare himself well for this last briefing and, as was his habit, went into considerable detail, but Reagan did not ask a single question. The only remark that elicited a comment from Mr. Reagan was when he was told that Korean President Park Chung Hee had not only closed the university when students started a major demonstration, but that he had drafted the demonstrators into the army. Mr. Reagan said that he wished an American president had the same authority in dealing with students. President Carter afterwards said that, when they parted after an hour, he was not sure how much his successor had understood and taken in . . .

13

Discussions with American Intellectuals

I N ALMOST FORTY YEARS of writing about the conduct of
American politics and its interaction with Anglo-American and Soviet-
American relations I met not only most of the actors who played a part
in forging the Pax Americana (the theme of this book's final chapter),
but I met also many of those Americans who, as I saw it, made a major
contribution to the American cultural scene. It was mostly a pleasure, but it
was also necessary to my full understanding of my own role.

After importing European culture and European ideas for generations,
American culture has come to exert a worldwide influence, thanks to the
American sense for innovation, the powerful influences of the environment, the
acceptance of the arts as a vital ingredient to life, the talent for "marketing,"
and the vast impact of the news media. Much has happened since Thorstein
Veblen published his famous book *The Theory of the Leisure Class,* for leisure
is not anymore a luxury only the upper class can afford. In 1959 Walter
Reuther, the leader of the UAW (United Automobile Workers of America),
said to me that "having taken care of the outer man, we want to find a way
to facilitate the growth of the inner man, for this is what life is about. I think
we can all agree that culture is the product of leisure and having satisfied man's
material needs we can now give the great mass of the people access to culture
and learning and the opportunities to facilitate the growth of the inner man."
President Kennedy carried the growth of the inner man to the national level

when he said that "life of the arts, far from being a distraction in the life of the nation . . . is a test of the quality of a nation's civilization." In the meantime classless leisure has become a reality. What the masses still need to learn perhaps is to go after leisure leisurely, not as an effort. Anyway, the puritanical glorification of work and the apotheosis of success have undergone an extraordinary transformation. Americans now have broader aims in life than they could either think of or afford before. So powerful is the American cultural influence today that in many countries it has aroused resentment. For even in the countries with their own strong cultural traditions, such as France or Italy or China or the Soviet Union, it has exerted a tremendous impact on youth, on living habits, on ways of thinking and acting. It is not something Americans consciously schemed; it just happened because it was new and because Americans have the marketing experience of a large continent to apply worldwide the vigor and drive and inventiveness that make them economically the most powerful nation.

The popularity of blue jeans, Coca-Cola, hamburgers, hot dogs, rock music, although clearly part of the American cultural influence, has overshadowed the deeper ingredients of American civilization. I thought therefore that instead of being still another foreigner trying to interpret American culture, I would let some of the leading American personalities do it themselves, opening to them, so to speak, the platform of my newspaper. Frankly, I also wanted to leaven the political loaf. I presented the idea to my then editor, H. V. Hodson, as, rather appropriately, we sat on a bench in Lafayette Park, in front of the White House, one sunny morning in 1957. I remember vividly how I tried to convince him that interviews with American cultural leaders (which I intended to tape-record and print as spoken) would be an effective way to prove to the world that we in the print media could compete with the directness of television. I thought that by being baited in terms of competing with television, the idea would stand a better chance of acceptance. But Harry Hodson made it clear that he was utterly appalled by the idea. With something like detestation in his voice he said: "We practice the written word, we therefore cannot print the spoken word in *The Sunday Times.*" It was that simple, at least to the Bishop, as he was called in the office, because he looked and behaved like one. He was an academic who belonged to that exceptional breed of Fellows of All Souls College, Oxford, a former civil service mandarin in India, and an editor of a small, esoteric magazine. It flattered Lord Kemsley, the then publisher of *The Sunday Times,* to have a man of Harry's intellectual qualities as an editor—at least until the growing battle for circulation with the *Observer,* when it became clear that whatever Harry's intellectual powers in writing editorials, he was not the man to boost sales. He was then replaced by Denis Hamilton, who, as Lord Kemsley's right-hand man, and as a backseat driver at editorial conferences, had proved that he had new ideas to take on the *Observer,* which indeed he did by increasing the circulation of *The Sunday Times* well beyond the one million mark. He also created the *Color* magazine, which has since been imitated by almost every other Fleet Street Sunday paper. When Lord Thomson also bought, in addition to *The Sunday Times,* the *Times* (to wrap himself in the equivalent of the Union Jack, as he put it), Hamilton became editor in chief of both papers and appointed Harold Evans, as the most talented and inspired, in his place at *The Sunday Times.* Evans was at home in the editorial chair as much as on the printshop floor. After beginning by extending Hamilton's method, he soon found his own style and distinguished himself by the paper's daring campaigns and investigations into corruption and other malpractices.

But to return to that bench in Lafayette Park: after a long argument during which I refused to take no for an answer, the Bishop agreed finally to my compromise proposal that I would do one pilot project which, if successful, would then lead to letting me proceed with a series of a dozen interviews. It put of course a premium on that first interview, and for about a month I hesitated whom to select as my guinea pig. In the end I gambled on Frank Lloyd Wright, the architect, because of his original and provocative ideas. He was delighted with the idea of my interviewing him about his views on architecture. Even at eighty-eight he walked erect and securely, so that his silver-capped stick was more part of his dandyish style of dress than a physical support. He wore a silken tie tucked under a flaring wide collar and over his shoulders a sweeping wide cape. His broad-brimmed hat completed his flamboyant getup. But there was a deeper meaning to the old-fashioned style of his clothes and the modernity of his architectural structures. He strove to combine the new with the traditional. I found him an ideal person to interview because he delighted in pouring oil on a discussion and then setting a match to it. "Architecture is the enduring testimony of civilization," he intoned. "It is the frame of human existence. In the case of our civilization, when future generations excavate the remains of it, what will they find?" He paused, then he answered his own question: "Bathtubs and dishwashers." But below his mocking, sardonic outlook there was also a vision for the future, what he called "organic architecture," which would replace the concept of the city whose skyscrapers were the culprits of the ever-growing congestion. He expected the great freeways to become the pathways to horizontal expansion from ocean to ocean. What troubled him about Washington was that it was not the show window for American architecture it should be because it seeks to represent history but not art. "We have a vast civilization but no culture because we have no architecture of our own." To my question whether the skyscraper was not an outstanding American contribution to architecture, he had this to reply: "The skyscraper is responsible for the congestion, and is making the city of today impossible to use. The skyscraper piles the crowd up high, dumps it on the street, stuffs it in again, and the streets are not nearly wide enough. Paris is so beautiful today because it has that sense of space without the skyscraper. London has something of that, and if it's invaded by the skyscraper, it will lose what it has. I think they should not build up those bombed areas either. They

should plant them to greenery. The greenery of London is one of its beauties."
My gamble with Wright paid off. He was a success with Harry Hodson, and
so my series went ahead.

The most aggressive defender of American civilization was Dr. Margaret
Mead, the anthropologist. Before I went to see her, I was advised to arm myself
with a bulletproof vest, for she was described to me as a sharpshooter in any
discussion. To my surprise I found her warm, kind, and easy to deal with.
Standing she looked quite short, but seated the only way to look at her was
up. She spoke fast, self-assured and with determination when it came to an
argument. She did not mince words. From her perspective, she said, she saw
a similarity between the Soviet Union and the United States in the sense that
both have the job of continually having to remake the next generation. "The
Soviets at first made over the children of the peasants and the children of other
groups within their society," she said, "Americans, in a different way, had to
make over the people who came from other societies, which accounted for the
thinness of American culture and for an ambitious commitment to the future.
Europeans like to consider conformism as an outstanding characteristic of the
American scene because they are not used to a country of the size of ours which
inevitably leads to the need for mass production and hence the impression of
conformity. But American tastes, desires, and needs have been changing. The
age of the gray-flanneled organization man was once the vogue. To be successful he does not anymore have to conform to a specific style. Americans have
grown confident enough to dress according to their own individual tastes,
indeed they have acquired their own taste." Americans, she explained, had to
learn about life from books rather than rely on traditions. They learned from
books how to make friends, how to influence people, how to make marriage
a success, how to become an executive, how to have sex, how to bring up
children, how to enjoy life. In all of this she gave psychiatry great credit for
helping to create a new society in what was once called the New World.

Her prognosis, however, was not encouraging. She thought that there was
a serious danger that humanity would destroy itself because the readings of
history and anthropology in general offered no reason to believe that societies
have built-in self-preservative systems. "Man has never been sensible enough,"
she said, "not to destroy himself. As long as he lived in small groups he did
not destroy everybody, but now that nuclear weapons destroy virtually everybody the danger of self-destruction cannot be overemphasized." I hoped that
the existence of the nuclear stalemate would change her basic readings of
history and anthropology, a hope that was somewhat subdued by the recollection of my earliest interview with Dr. Edward Teller, the physicist and, as he
was called then, "father of the H-bomb" because he contributed the missing
link that transformed a thermonuclear explosion into a controllable and deliv-
erable hydrogen bomb. To meet Dr. Teller I drove from San Francisco to
Livermore, his scientific bastion, where at his suggestion we met at the Golden
Creamery Cafe, an ordinary little fast-food place near his office. Teller was a

big, heavyset, sloppy kind of a man whose bushy eyebrows overhung his penetrating, heavy-lidded blue eyes, dominated his face. In repose he had a brooding, somber look, but when he broke into laughter, as he occasionally did, it was broad, husky, and shook his entire body.

Most of our conversation was about nuclear weapons and whether such cataclysmic weapons might not prove to be the best safeguard against another world war. Teller's eyebrows drooped lower and he shook his head sadly, no. When I pressed him whether I was right in assuming that the H-bomb would be used only as a last resort in war, he again shook his head, but this time his voice became categorical: "No, I disagree with your emphasis on 'last.' " Then he added as an explanation that the talk about radioactivity after a hydrogen explosion had been overdramatized and overplayed. "Too much attention is being paid to scientists," he said, "when our destinies are in the hands of statesmen." When I countered that there was ample evidence that scientists were gaining control over our destinies, he replied with a hollow laugh. Teller had been born in Hungary, and I could not help remembering somebody's observation that a Hungarian scientist who went to elementary and high schools in Hungary, then studied at German universities, was one of the most brilliant and dangerous people in the world. There were several Hungarian scientists who more or less have had that background. Teller is undoubtedly the most formidable among them. He not only played his part in developing the H-bomb, but also had a key role in convincing President Reagan that a space defense system was a better safeguard against nuclear war than either nuclear deterrence or arms control. SDI—the strategic defense initiative— became an obsession of the president and the principal obstacle to strategic arms control negotiations with the Soviets.

When a few years later, just after the Russian launch of Sputnik had had such a traumatic effect on Americans, I interviewed Dr. Isidor I. Rabi, who won the Nobel Prize in 1944 in physics and became chairman of President Eisenhower's Scientific Advisory Committee, he warned that in order for the United States to keep up the scientific race with the Soviet Union, the general public must learn to appreciate better the importance of science as an element of culture. Schools would need to change their curriculum so that more time would be spent on mathematics and science. "We must teach them," he said with gentle emphasis, "as an intellectual pursuit rather than as a body of tricks."

Harry Hodson by this time had come to appreciate my interviews to such an extent that he gave them the front page, pride of place, in the Review section; they began to attract notice in the United States, and some time later the *New Republic* serialized them. When I called Arthur Miller in Connecticut to ask if he and his wife, Marilyn Monroe, would be willing to give me an interview, he knew exactly what I was referring to. He had already read a few in *The Sunday Times* and immediately said that he would be glad to talk to me, but he had doubts whether Marilyn would want to subject herself to such a discussion. I replied that I was very keen to have Marilyn participate to make it a threesome. To my surprise Miller called back within half an hour to say that she was delighted with the idea and to arrange a meeting at the Beverly Hills Hotel in Hollywood.

I approached the interview in great suspense. Would the experiment of a triangular interview succeed? How would I react to her and how best could I bring out the contrast between the "brain and the body"? We met at their apartment in one of the bungalows in the palm-shaded garden of the hotel. Arthur Miller was very much as I had expected him to be, an intense intellectual whose outward informality and nonchalance were deceptive. Underneath were hidden strong convictions, passion, and professional frustration. Thus far he had been unable to translate the new social and human problems that preoccupied him into a play with the theatrical and intellectual quality of *Death of a Salesman*. He and I settled around the empty, and most probably false, fireplace in the Millers' apartment, with him complaining bitterly about what a deadly place Hollywood was to a writer like himself. He confessed that the only place where he could work was in his house in Roxbury, Connecticut, but living for even a few weeks apart from Marilyn, who inevitably had to spend a good deal of time in Hollywood, made him worry about what she might be up to. And when these thoughts became unbearable, he then flew to Hollywood to be with her. Then after a few weeks he got frustrated again with his inability to concentrate on his own work in Hollywood and decided to fly back to Connecticut. He sounded as if he was talking about the death of a writer . . .

After about two hours Marilyn made her dramatic entrance. It was almost breathtaking. Dressed in a startling ankle-length, off-shoulder negligee in scarlet velvet with a slit on both sides to allow glimpses of her legs, her bright blond hair pinned up to emphasize her long bare neck, she looked (perhaps only in my imagination) as if she had just stepped out of her bath. If this dazzling entry was designed to dazzle me, she succeeded. In retrospect I think that she chose to stage such a stunning entrance not to impress me, but to overcome her own shyness, for it took quite a long time before she entered into our conversation.

Well, there she was, the sex goddess so many men in the world dream about, I said to myself. I don't quite remember what I expected, but once the surprise of her entry had passed I began to realize that she was, at least to me, much more a beguilingly pretty girl than a sex goddess. This was not a man-consuming vamp but a little kitten one wished to protect, not a seductress to jump into bed with but a little girl to tuck into bed. Her voice had a girlish high-pitched sound with an occasional uncertain tremolo. After she had settled down on the sofa next to her husband, she tilted her head against his shoulder cozily, eyed me for a moment, then the tape recorder on the table as if to say that she was ready for whatever was going to follow.

For the first half hour Miller answered all the questions, even some of those

I had specifically directed at her, until she broke into one of his answers to correct him and to give me her own view. Arthur's masculinity and quick intelligence seemed to give her a welcome sense of security, even pride, but sometimes his patronizing ways annoyed her and fired her desire to assert herself and to prove how bright and clever she was. I was pleasantly surprised at how easy it was for Miller and then for her to discuss the mysteries of her sexuality which, I am sure, will surprise those millions who didn't think there was anything mysterious about it. Miller, for instance, explained it by saying that "she responds to the most elemental part of the human being near her . . . Marilyn has made sex a part of her existence . . . ," he said almost sounding like a Hollywood publicity man. "Well, I hope so," she chimed in, "since it is so." And talking about nudity she said: "In Swedish films sexuality seems more natural because their code is quite different from ours. The eroticism of one nation differs in the imagination of another . . . if I appeared without clothes in an American movie, they would not show it here, yet Americans like it and accept it in foreign movies." Talking about foreign movies, I wondered why she had wanted to play next to Sir Laurence Olivier in *The Prince and the Showgirl.* "I thought that chemically it was good, if a little incongruous," she said, "but interesting and lifelike." Could it have been a sort of *Lady Chatterley's Lover* situation in reverse? "No," she replied, "I never like to play a part to see what it's like. In life you find out almost what everything is like." There she was, sailing on her own, cutting off Arthur as he tried to catch some of my questions, bubbling with ideas, some good, some incomprehensible, but anxious to prove that she could hold her own. After dinner we went on chatting until late at night, and when we parted Marilyn invited me to the studio to watch her in front of the cameras.

Arthur drove me there next morning and while Marilyn dressed and made up for hours, he gave me a tour of the lifeless outdoor studio sets, the tombstones of past films. When we got back Marilyn was in her full makeup, dressed in the costume of an acrobat, a convenient way of enabling the filmmakers to expose her voluptuous form under the skintight leotard in *Let's Make Love.*

I happened to be talking to Lee Strasberg, her drama coach, when Marilyn suddenly jumped off the stage and ran toward me, grabbed me by the hand, and pulled me on stage. There were two empty high stools in front of me. She sat down on one and motioned me to sit down on the other one, reserved for Yves Montand, who was late. I had hardly climbed onto my chair when without a warning she snapped her fingers and ordered the cameras and still photographers to start shooting. I didn't quite know what was going to happen to me when Marilyn touched my arm to make me turn in her direction instead of staring straight into the cameras. "Look at me," she whispered, and then her eyes became heavy-lidded and she began to move her face slowly and deliberately into mine to kiss me. Can anyone imagine my embarrassment as she staged this mock love scene in front of some fifty film technicians, Arthur Miller, Mrs. Strasberg, and all sort of other voyeurs. The coltish little girl had suddenly turned herself into a woman with a puckish sense of humor. She wanted me to have a little souvenir of the occasion, she later told me, delighted that she had caught me by surprise. I treasure the souvenir. Fortunately I never saw or met the distraught, disheartened, and unhappy Marilyn who finally despaired of life. I am glad I didn't.

It was shortly after I had met Marilyn that another onetime sex-goddess happened to come to Washington to appear in a nightclub, in an attempt to drain out the last drops of her fame—Mae West. Since I belong to a generation which learned the essence of the meaning of Mae West from those bulging, inflatable life jackets which used to hang around our necks whenever we flew over water during the war, I decided to pay my respects to the authentic sex symbol of a generation before mine.

"Goodness," someone quoted from a movie as she joined our table, "what beautiful diamonds you have," and he pointed at the magnificent rhinestones which bedecked her body. "Goodness," came the expected reply in that famous nasal whine, "had nothing to do with it." And as we moved closer to her, she rasped another famous line: "Don't crowd me, boys, there's enough for all." There was indeed, as I had no difficulty observing. If everything in the world had deteriorated since this American authentic genius had made our fathers blush, she was proof of an extraordinary durability. To those with a good memory her songs and jokes sounded familiar, but what in the world had made them sound so funny and her a sex goddess? There she stood on the floor of the Casino Royale (now a porno-movie theater) surrounded with nine muscle men, all of them scantily dressed, all of them, but above all, the inimitable Mae, spoofing sex. And she did it to perfection. What she did was to strip sex of its mystery and to reduce it to a laughing matter. What self-conscious girls Jane Russell and Marilyn Monroe were in comparison. To me the evening was like a visit to Mme Tussaud's, but to many it was, judging from the applause, a vivid link with a happier past. Marilyn Monroe, though—let's say—aroused the interest of Nikita Khrushchev and may have been a first glimmer of her own version of glasnost.

Four years after the Monroe-Miller interview Miller invited me to the final dress rehearsal of his play *After the Fall,* which turned out to be a sad attempt to prove that it was Marilyn, not Arthur, who destroyed their fairy-tale union. It was an embarrassing occasion, for Arthur was convinced that he had turned a wrenching human experience of his own—he insisted in claiming that the play was not autobiographical—into great drama. What made it all worse was that the girl who played Maggie was chosen for her likeness to Marilyn and not for her acting. Afterwards Miller and a few friends went back to Arthur's apartment at the Hotel Chelsea for a nightcap. We all, except for Miller, felt that we had gone through a painful experience, but we did not want to say so outright. The play, though, was an indication of how deeply hurt Arthur felt after the breakup of the marriage. It kept him from realizing how low he had sunk by writing such psychodrama. But when I suggested, for instance, that

Quentin, played by Jason Robards, did not seem to know what it meant to love, Arthur protested angrily that I had misunderstood his role. Maybe the reason that the play failed—it was torn to shreds by the critics—lay in something Arthur said to me during our triangular interview: "I have never been able to understand why one is considered to be insensitive when one looks beyond the individual to society for certain causations and certain hopes."

Two men I was particularly eager to interview were James Thurber, the inimitable humorist of *The New Yorker,* and Edmund Wilson, its most distinguished literary critic. Thurber described himself to me as an "unabashed Anglophile"; Wilson, as he in turn readily admitted, had anti-British prejudices. They were friends and *New Yorker* stablemates. Both had the reputation of being difficult men, stubbornly independent, combative, and demanding of themselves as of others. I approached each with trepidation but also great curiosity. What made me nervous about the interview with Thurber was a story called "The Interview" he had once written, because it ended with the interviewer's pencil and notebook being flung out the window. Indeed, if he did not actually throw my notebook out of the window, he came close to it, but I do not want to get ahead of this story.

Thurber had an amusing way of describing American humor. He said that American humor did not go "deep," that America was the country of "the gab, the hotfoot, the payoff, the belly laugh," but if it were more imaginative it could never have overemphasized "Americanism" the way it did. "No other country uses a word combination such as 'un-American,' which is just another word for unpatriotic. The French do not say 'un-French' or the British 'un-British.' " When he wrote a little scene at a bar taking off the word "un-American" in 1951 (during the McCarthy period), nobody, he said, wanted to print it.

One of the funniest stories he told me was the exchange he had with the crusty, prissy, and dictatorial editor of *The New Yorker,* Harold Ross, when Ross objected to one of his drawings he had called "The Lady on the Bookcase." It was a nude woman on all fours on top of a bookcase and a man saying to a lady visitor: "That's my first wife up there," and pointing to another one, "and this is the present Mrs. Harris." It upset Ross's puritanism; he called Thurber to find out whether the woman on the bookcase was dead or alive or stuffed or what. Thurber, amused, said he didn't know and would have to ask, which irritated Ross more. When Thurber called Ross back, he said that his doctor had told him that a dead woman couldn't support herself on all fours and that his taxidermist had told him that you can't stuff a woman, so that she therefore must be alive. Ross, annoyed, thundered into the telephone: "Then what is she doing in the house of her former husband with his wife, naked?" To which Thurber, keeping his voice level, replied, "You have me there, Ross. I'm not responsible for the behavior of my characters." Ross overcame his perturbation and printed the cartoon, which became famous.

Thurber, who had gone blind, in discussing the subject of voices, which clearly fascinated him, made the best of his inability to see. "There's something about a voice that is destroyed," he said, "if you're watching the expression on a face. Everybody looks at the eyes and expression, but I concentrate on inflection, intonation, and dropping and raising of the voice—and often surprise people by saying: 'What's happened?' Well, how do you know that sort of thing?—Well, I can tell . . . Although they're saying something that isn't sorrowful or serious or tragic, you can tell. A man asked me the other day if I could get my sight back for one day, who would I want to see? Marilyn Monroe? I said: 'No, I want to see some old friends of mine. I have a pretty good idea what Marilyn Miller must look like.' " I then mentioned a current joke to him, the definition of an "egghead"—someone who calls Marilyn Monroe "Mrs. Arthur Miller." To which he replied that Philippe Halsman, the photographer, had made a remark to him about how difficult it was to get different expressions on her face, though she was a great comic. To get a special look on her face, therefore, he said to her: "How old were you when you had your first affair with a man?" And she said: "Seven"—she knew exactly what he was up to—and didn't change at all.

Thurber was a tall, gaunt, somber figure with a flat, commanding voice. We talked in his suite at the venerable Hotel Algonquin, the old haunt of the literati, across from the offices of *The New Yorker.* He seemed to enjoy the give and take, expressed himself with great fluency and accuracy, and when I left I felt pleased with the result. However a few hours later I found a three-page, single-spaced letter under the door of my room at the Algonquin, in which he tried to withdraw the entire interview because, he wrote, "off-handed answers have little value or grace of expression and only contribute to the decline of the English language." (Shades of Harry Hodson.) He pointed out that anything he wrote for publication he rewrote from five to twenty times and that it was therefore hard for him to think of his conversational replies being used as his final considered opinions and judgments. He therefore would prefer my using the ideas he had put down in the enclosed letter.

My heart sank. It was an interview I cared about very much. As I reread the letter I found a little escape hatch in the last sentence. It said: "Maybe it will come out all right, but here are a few written thoughts . . ." I sat down immediately to listen to the tape again and then compared it to his written thoughts. The latter were infinitely inferior, too harsh, rigid, and self-conscious. I decided to fight for the tape. That evening Thurber asked me to a party in his suite. I had planned to go to the theater and said that I would come after the show. I wanted to avoid having to discuss the interview in front of other people and take the risk that he would lose his temper and force my hand then and there. But I could not refuse altogether. I had hardly entered the room when Thurber, noisily, asked me whether I had his letter with me. I also noticed that everybody had reached a mood of well-loaded gaiety and I feared the worst. Uneasily I admitted that I had the letter on me. And how did I like it, Thurber asked, raising his voice even higher. Summoning all my courage, I replied that if he wanted me to be honest I would have to say that I much preferred the taped interview. There was a long pause, everybody looked at me and then at Thurber. Then Thurber, taken aback, asked me to read the letter for all to hear. I looked around and saw Russell Nype, the actor. Cornered, I tried to parry the thrust by suggesting that with professional actors present one of them should read it, and handed the letter to Nype, hoping that the idea of reading the letter would sink under the weight of the consumed alcohol. I also feared that if the letter got the stamp of approval here, I had no chance to retrieve the taped version. My idea was not only accepted by Thurber and Nype, but applauded. Expectations suddenly skyrocketed. But as Nype read on the general gaiety gradually subsided, the fun and laughter everybody had hoped for was missing. It all sounded dry and humorless and a silence descended over the company. After Nype had finished, Thurber asked challengingly: "Well, how did you like it?" Nobody said a word for quite a while. Thurber—with the particularly sensitive antennae of the blind—realized that the letter had fallen flat. And before anybody could say anything, Thurber said: "Henry, you won!"

The preliminaries took much longer with Edmund Wilson than with Thurber. As his first reply he sent me a printed postcard listing the many types of requests he could possibly get, from giving interviews to lectures to autographs, etc. He rejected them all by simply ticking off the requested item on the postcard. But the enclosed postcard was more to show me how he conventionally treated requests like mine. In the accompanying letter he confessed that he had never given an interview before and that he had great hesitation therefore about breaking an oath to himself. But, he added, in my case he would make an exception and agree to a tape-recorded interview as long as he could correct his spoken English to make it read well in print. I thought that this was a reasonable request in exchange for an interview with a man of his standing in American letters, and once I had informed him of my concurrence, he invited me to come to his house outside Talcottville, in northern New York State.

Justice Frankfurter, who had known Wilson for a lifetime, described him to me in this way: "Bunny approaches every book critique with the judiciousness of a judge. It seems to me that before he writes about a man he studies his whole corpus. Theodore Roosevelt, for instance, was to him something of a Kiplingesque swashbuckler. But after he got through reading his collection of letters, he gave the cultural range of the man full recognition." This description and the trepidation with which I approached this interview made me read every book he had written before I went to see him. Nevertheless, the interview got off to a bad start. What happened was that after he had picked me up at the airport and driven me in an old jalopy to his house, we began drinking Scotch before lunch, then a bottle of wine with lunch, and when we adjourned to his desk to begin the interview, he poured himself another whiskey and five minutes into the interview a second. It suddenly dawned on me that he was even more nervous about the interview than I was. Within a few minutes his voice became blurry and his eyes began to roll in embarrassment about the difficulty he had in formulating not only his thoughts but his sentences.

His attentive wife, Elena, who had watched us from the next room, soon realized what had happened and gently but firmly proposed that he go to bed for a good nap, to which he meekly acceded. Elena, well aware of my disappointment, comforted me and predicted that I would find him "like new" next morning, as indeed I did. He woke me up early by knocking at my door and admonishing me to get ready to go to work. He was indeed "like new," and we went on for several hours discussing the world of literature. He was a connoisseur of literature, a critic who, thanks to his linguistic versatility in Russian, German, French, Italian, English and, yes, American, could summon comparisons from world literature, a fiendishly fast reader, and a man of an extraordinary literary appetite. He could be crude and harsh or sensitive and tender. Whenever he made his literary or historical comparisons he spoke with the authority of a man who is utterly confident of his judgment. It was only when he came to talk about his own fiction, plays, and poetry—and I went about it gingerly—that he sounded perplexed, annoyed, and puzzled that they had not been more successful. It hurt him particularly that none of his plays had scored on Broadway.

I started by quoting Stewart Hampshire, the British philosopher and literary critic who, in his review of Wilson's *The American Earthquake,* had said that Wilson's attitude to Europe alternated between moods of chauvinistic contempt and moods of reverence. Wilson agreed that Hampshire had made a good point and compared his own attitude to that of the old Russian intellectuals who, like Turgenev, wrote to their Russian friends from abroad how awful the Europeans were and when they were back home would brood about how awful Russia was. "You'll find it in all our literature, especially in Walt Whitman, that we felt that they'd had it in Europe; that they were in a decline, that the time had come for us to pick up and show the world something better, something new. And the reason was that the English revolution did not occur in the eighteenth century. So you had the peculiar situation of a national revolution occurring geographically in another part of the world. This is one reason why the British establishment remained intact, more or less, and why it had this impetus from having made a new start. The trouble in France was that when the Revolution came, they had the whole thing on the premises, they had the old order still there along with the new, and ever since the whole thing has been scrambled." Nowadays, he found, Europe and America were beginning to merge more all the time. Then, as if to correct his earlier remarks about the British establishment, he admitted that it offered considerable advantages. "In spite of the fact that the angry young men were trying to knock it around, it seems to me that they can't get out of it; I mean, every time John Osborne tells you that his mother kept a pub, he tells you that his grandfather went to Eton! Or take John Wain and Kingsley Amis. They went to Oxford . . ." He praised British contemporary novelists for their sense of form and style, but said they have not produced anything comparable to their nineteenth-century predecessors: "You have a lot of people who are quite good, who write rather small-scale novels. They are sent over, as my wife says, like a lot of little cakes that we eat." But he confessed that he read more contemporary English novels than he did American fiction "because the American stuff is likely to be badly written and extremely formless."

I tried to keep him off politics, but it was not easy. After all, I lived in Washington, that hateful city, to him the seat of the American government that was conducting the cold war and mistreating the American Indians. And as to American culture, he had little faith in one developing. "In America now it is not merely a question of our relation with Europe, which in my youth was the important thing, it's also our relations with Russia and Japan and other parts of the world." I was surprised, though, that he considered Malraux the greatest living European writer and his novels very good examples of a kind of "novel that is characteristic of this period." I had read only *The Voices of Silence,* which I enjoyed but in the end was left with a feeling of charlatanism in the arts. He explained that his novels and those produced by the Italian writer Moravia, John Steinbeck, and the Russian writer Leonov were so interesting and readable to him because they dealt with things that were happening now. That brought me back to a visit I once had with Leonov in his Moscow apartment. He was a charming, rather shy man, so modest that he wondered why I had chosen to see him. He was one of those Russian writers who occasionally dared to criticize the authorities without however stepping over the borders of permissible criticism. One of his novels, for instance, was written in defense of the preservation of the beautiful Russian forests that were being cut down arbitrarily. Did it make an impression on the Ministry of Forestry, I asked. "No," he said sadly, "it made no impression whatsoever. It only proved to me how little influence we writers have . . ."

But to come back to Wilson, he said that in the early nineteenth century and in the twenties, as well as in the thirties, "the thing we were always debating was how this or that could be Americanized. It was discussed in the hope of how to create an American culture. We talked about such American writers as Eliot, Hemingway, Dos Passos, O'Neill, who closely studied European literature, to adapt what they were reading to American life, to American culture. That was one of our main occupations." Then after a long pause he added: "The thing that's upsetting now, in politics and literature, is that from the moment we lose the idea that we are concentrating on this country, we don't know where we are anymore." He blamed mass education as making it more difficult for the able to excel. He was in favor of unequal schools for students of unequal abilities. Interestingly enough, he did not think that there existed an Establishment, as in England, in the United States, which may explain, he argued, the lack of stability in the United States.

The reason that Wilson doubted an American culture was in the making was unusual and very much the opinion of a man of letters with his international range of knowledge. "The European and American literatures are merging," he said, "and Soviet and American literatures are becoming more alike since Americans are reading Tolstoy, Dostoyevski and Chekhov, and Soviet writers are absorbing Hemingway, Steinbeck, and Dos Passos."

Throughout the interview I often wondered whether I was asking the right questions or missing some good ones, but when after four hours of taping I ran out of tape and Wilson went to the telephone eagerly inquiring where I could find some more, I finally left with the feeling that I had done relatively well, held my own, and that he had enjoyed the experience of his first-ever tape-recorded interview.

About a year later I saw him again at a dinner Arthur Schlesinger, the historian, gave in his own house in Washington for the recipients of the Medal of Freedom which President Kennedy had introduced to honor leading Americans who deserved something more dignified than an Oscar—it was a kind of equivalent to the Queen's Honors List. Wilson hesitated whether to accept something that had the imprint of the White House, Schlesinger told me, but finally came. During dinner Wilson said that after the dinner at the White House the night before, he told Malraux that his dinner speech was not what he had expected from him. (Malraux said in his speech that the Roman and Byzantine empires were built by conquest, but not the American, because it was thrust into the hands of the United States against her will.) To which Malraux abruptly replied: "It was only a courtesy speech." That evening Wilson also mentioned to me that he would be going to Hungary soon to attend the opening of a play of his and that he planned to stay in Budapest for at least six weeks. When I asked him why on earth he wanted to stay there for six weeks, he said in order to learn Hungarian to express his appreciation to the Hungarians for their having gone to great trouble in translating one of his plays into Hungarian. I warned him that Hungarian is notorious for its difficulty to learn—and also for its coarse swear words. This made him prick up his ears and wonder whether I could provide him with some samples. Next day I mobilized some of my Hungarian friends at the Library of Congress who quickly obliged and I sent them on to Wilson. In reply he said that he had used his dictionary but could not find English translations for all the words. He listed the Hungarian swear words on one side and his translation, as far as it went, on the other. My Hungarian friends at the Library again obliged.

About three months later I was sent on a short assignment to the Soviet Union and on my return flight I decided to stop in Budapest to see how it had changed since an earlier visit. I had forgotten about Wilson's Hungarian visit, but one morning there he was, absentminded or confused, standing in the lobby of the Hotel Gellert, which then was still the leading hotel. At lunch he eagerly told me about his baffling experiences in Budapest. He said that he was taking lessons in Hungarian for two hours a day and that he was making good progress. He had met most of the leading Hungarian writers, he reported, but all of them, somewhat to his surprise, were against the government. Then came the most surprising request: "Could you introduce me to someone who can give me the government's official political line?"

He also told me that he had written an article in interview form for *The New Yorker* in which he asked himself the questions I had failed to ask him. A few weeks later it did indeed appear in *The New Yorker*. Years later in his *Letters on Literature and Politics 1912–1972* I found a letter he had written to Thurber dated February 16, 1959, in which he said: "Brandon's interview with me I thought much the weakest of his series . . . Brandon's idea in his little introduction that he disrupted my serenity is absurd. He expected to find me something different from what I am like: that is, he expected to find me a cloistered and mellow old man of letters—and kept asking me questions about books—a kind of thing that bores me, especially when I haven't read the books . . ."

The most effortless, delightful, and stimulating interview turned out to be one with Leonard Bernstein, who is not only a gifted musician, but extraordinarily articulate in talking about music. We met at his elegant apartment opposite Carnegie Hall and although he had just come from an exhausting recording session, he put on no star allures, offered no demurrals. Instead he made me feel instantly at ease, welcomed me as a friend and lover of music, not as a nuisance who would put him through an arduous interview session. There was an electricity about him that was infectious. It made me understand how, as conductor, he managed to transfer his own excitement to the orchestra, inspiring it and getting the most out of the players. He is in many ways the quintessential American who drew the best from European traditions and translated them into something authentically American. *West Side Story,* of course, is the outstanding example. British musicals, he argued, usually dealt with trifling matters; the American in contrast was concerned with real everyday life: *West Side Story* is a *Romeo and Juliet* set against the background of urban violence.

He divided American music into two categories, the self-consciously nationalistic, which "hardly ever works, with Gershwin a shining exception," he said, "and the unconscious one influenced by jazz and other typically American influences." He talked about the history of music and he took issue with Stravinsky about his different lives as a composer, musician, and teacher. After three hours I felt that I had exhausted him and made a move to leave. But he insisted on my staying for a while longer, sat down at his piano, and began to play from *West Side Story,* not to impress or amuse me, but seemingly just for relaxation.

A few months later Bernstein was appointed director of the New York Philharmonic and though he invited me to his first performance I was able to be there only for the second, the following day. The reviews of his debut by then were out and they were lukewarm in evaluating him as a conductor. After the concert I asked him how he felt about the reviews. Without the slightest trace of rancor he replied: "I'm not surprised, for music critics are by nature cautious. You must not forget that I have three strikes against me: I'm only forty years old, I have written music for Broadway—a sin for anybody aspiring to be a conductor of serious music—and I'm the first American-born conductor in charge of the New York Philharmonic."

Clare Boothe Luce may not be regarded by everyone as a symbol of American culture, but she had been a successful playwright, congresswoman, ambassador to Italy, and a brilliant conversationalist. I could not resist including her. She never cared to be considered a liberated woman, but, in fact, she is one of the best examples of that peculiarly American breed. She wrote what may still be the best play about women—not liberated women at that—as early as 1936. The London National Theater thought *The Women* good enough to revive it fifty years later! But the very first time it was shown on a London stage in 1939, after a successful run on Broadway, she specially flew to London to see the premiere. The man she was then most eager to meet was George Bernard Shaw, and through her friend Lady Astor she arranged a meeting. When Clare arrived at Shaw's apartment, as she remembered it, she was all set to start with a gushing little speech about her gratitude to him as a playwright. But when his secretary ushered her into his study, she had to clear her throat several times before he took notice of her. He then threw himself around in his swivel chair, looked her up and down, and said: "Come, my child, sit down here and tell me why you are here." As Clare recalled: "I then said that if it were not for you I wouldn't be here at all. Suddenly he seemed to get interested in me and asked: 'Do tell me, what was your mother's name?' "

During the war she was elected to the House of Representatives and made a name for her glib if original phrasemaking and her pugnacious Republicanism. When then Representative William Fulbright asked her: "Would the Congresslady yield?" she replied: "Not easily." He never forgave her, she said. She called Sputnik "a raspberry to a decade of American pretensions when the American way of life was a gilt-edged guarantee of our national superiority." President Eisenhower appointed her ambassador to Italy during a difficult period, when communism was on the march. It was then that Winston Churchill asked her to visit him in Sicily where he was vacationing. She flew down, accompanied by her military attaché, a general, and knowing that he was a blabbermouth, she warned him to keep his big mouth shut when talking to Churchill. It did not take long before she noticed that this bluff military man got into an argument with Professor Lindeman (later Lord Cherwell), Churchill's scientific adviser, and his voice began to rise only too audibly at one end of the lunch table. Churchill at the other inquired what the controversy was all about. "I'm having an argument with your scientific adviser," the general replied, "about whether, if we drop the A-bomb somewhere, there would be a mutation of our species as a result." To which Churchill roared back: "If we do that with these forbidden toys, it is quite possible that your progeny will be born with two heads! Then, General, do think how well we have been doing with one!"

Clare's own judgment in those days left a good deal to be desired. I remember, for instance, when she argued that if only the Allies had allowed the king to stay in Italy and preserved the monarchy, we would not have all this trouble with the Communists. In her eighties she saw the world through more mature eyes with a political mind that had mellowed. Her politics were not as blinkered as they had been and her sense of humor was aimed not only at other people's weak points, but also at herself. Indicative of the fact that she was not always as revered as she became by friends and foes (because she was too ambitious and too self-centered) was a remark Noel Coward made about her: ". . . that charming little meat ax with a bow on top." Wilfrid Sheed wrote a sympathetically biased book about her, whose subtitle was *From Courtesan to Career Woman.* How Clare reacted to it at the time of publication I don't know but she said later that she would have preferred if it had read *From Career Woman to Courtesan.* Even at the age of eighty-two and after a difficult colon operation neither her esprit nor her joie de vivre weakened. She still managed to take center stage at any party as one of the most amusing and interesting conversationalists. At her eighty-third birthday party, given by her biographer Sylvia Morris, when asked what a woman should do to be successful, she answered with a straight face: "Get herself elected to Congress, become an ambassador, and marry a rich man—all of this." Then, as an aside, she added: "It would have been awful if I had fallen in love with a man who had no money."

The man who, perhaps more than anyone else, made me understand the roots of American thinking and reacting to an ill-ordered world was Reinhold Niebuhr, the theologian, whom I got to know thanks to a mutual friend of ours, Dorothy Fosdick, the daughter of another well-known preacher, Harry Emerson Fosdick. Sunday lunches at the Niebuhrs' apartment in an old brownstone house not far from the main center of his activities, the Union Theological Seminary, were always thought-provoking. One reason why I enjoyed our discussions was that I completely forgot being in the presence of a preacher or even a teacher. This did not mean that I was not always aware of being in the presence of a man with strong, clearly developed views and an extraordinary range of interests. He was a tall, imposing figure, with strong facial features, a Franz Liszt kind of nose, a very high forehead, and a Churchillian cheekbone. Yet he never seemed to me overpowering or intimidating. What made it relatively easy to cope with his intellectuality was the ease with which he could explain complicated ideas and his willingness to listen patiently and understandingly to other people's points of view. I felt differently when I watched him preaching from the pulpit. He was suddenly a different person.

Then he seemed ten feet tall with a dramatic intonation that transfixed his audiences.

Curiously enough, it was his social gospel rather than his religious philosophy that made him one of the most influential theologians in the United States. Unlike so many other theologians, he preferred to live deeply engaged in the current streams of politico-social developments. He refused to stand detached on the banks of these streams, and was not only willing but eager to wade into them with both feet. As a liberal Democrat his influence was at a peak during the New Deal period, but it continued well into the Truman years, and in fact, Jimmy Carter was one of his great admirers.

There were two sources in the American experiment, he used to say. There was the Virginia source, Thomas Jefferson, and the New England one, the Puritans. They were both idealistic but also materialistic, because what the Puritans said was: "If we're virtuous, we'll be prosperous." And what Jefferson said was (and this is a vulgar interpretation of Jefferson): "We can be virtuous only if we're prosperous in a moderate sense." Materialism since then has won the upper hand, but the combination of the two still shines through American thinking at crucial moments.

When I once quoted the Jewish social philosopher Will Herberg that "never had so much been said about religion and so little meant by it as today" and wondered how Niebuhr reacted, he replied that this was true in a way because there is in America a great deal of religiosity, faith in faith. "President Eisenhower," he said, "never tired of saying, 'You must have faith.' But he didn't say faith in what. Just have faith. That's religiosity. It does not bother too much about the ultimate problems of human existence; this type of faith is not effective in changing the course of a nation's policy." He spoke about revivalism as basing itself on irrelevant expressions of the religious faith and defined Billy Graham's faith as relevant to some tortured souls who want some kind of simple, ultimate meaning for their existence. He agreed that in our age there were growing doubts about religion, the concept of God, and something of a crisis for Christianity, "but," he argued, "the ultimate religious problem is not whether we can justify belief in God, however defined rationally, but whether we can bear witness to a faith that in some sense has an idea of responsibility for its civilization and in some sense transcends it in the way that Lincoln transcended the Civil War struggle. That is, I think, the ultimate test." It was his darting into political comparisons that made his ideas more easily comprehensible and more interesting to listen to.

It was at our last meeting, after Dr. Niebuhr had recovered from a stroke, that the question came up whether there was enough vitality and imagination for the church to contribute to the almost insoluble problems of the nuclear age where, on one hand we face a resolute and powerful foe and on the other the problem of nuclear war. "If you ask me whether there is a Christian solution to this, I will say that there is a Christian approach, a religious approach which is valid. But if you say, Is there a Christian solution to this, it always turns out to be unilateral disarmament," he said with derision. "It's an old ethic of irresponsibility. The problem is how do we protect ourselves so that we are not overwhelmed by this great power and at the same time how can we come to terms with it. It is my view that however much we may hate the foe or fear the foe, there ought to be some residual imagination, whether it is derived from intellectual or religious imagination, that at least recognizes that we're involved in a common fate, and the common fate or dilemma is so great that it ought to bridge some gap. Our ability to do this, I think, is the price of our survival. The only chance that I see of survival is a gradual growth of community across the chasm of this international enmity under the umbrella of nuclear fear—rather than any provisional disarmament setup."

Niebuhr was a Christian realist who tried to come to grips with all the contemporary problems, but he never pretended to be a prophet. We miss today his relentless search into the relationship between the Christian church and the world, which helped to stimulate the mind of modern America in a unique way. Instead there is too much pretentious, simplistic religiosity spread by television evangelists and not enough searching for a balance between virtue and materialism.

If Reinhold Niebuhr made his reputation by emphasizing his social gospel, Ben Shahn, the painter, made it by injecting social criticism into his paintings and drawings. In his book *The Shape of Content* he rejected the assumption among contemporary American painters that art cannot have a social meaning and still be art. Shahn belonged to a different generation. He formed his political and social convictions in the years of the Depression in the thirties when he barely managed to eke out a living as an artist working under the WPA program Franklin Roosevelt initiated in support of starving artists.

When I asked Shahn for an interview in March 1958, he invited me without any ifs and buts, and even came to pick me up at the Princeton Junction railway station. On first sight Shahn, broad-set, round-faced, with a grayish, drooping mustache, looked more like a Russian muzhik than a painter. It took us about half an hour to reach his house, just outside the small town of Roosevelt, New Jersey. Instead of me trying to make him relax, it was he who put me at my ease, telling me of his recent trip to Europe, his experiences in London, and his secluded life in the town of Roosevelt.

Life as a painter in the United States, he explained, had dramatically changed since the days when he went to a bank to ask for a loan of $2,000 and was told that he had to get a decent job first. It took him twenty years, he said, of carefully paying his bills on time before he was accepted in the little community he lived in. "You English by and large are responsible for it," he said half in earnest, half in jest. "For generations you've written novels which we've read and devoured, in which the artist is turned into a character that may have existed but I have never met, the kind in Somerset Maugham's *The Moon and Sixpence* or in Joyce Cary's *The Horse's Mouth*. Absolutely incredible characters. I cannot conceive of a character just out of jail walking along the embankment and thinking what colors he would use for a sunset. We in America who became artists understood this. But those who did not, who were, you know, out in real life—they were terrified of these characters and that's part of it. So I'm blaming you partly for it."

He was inclined to think that it was patronage rather than any artistic movement—abstract art, for example—that had focused the art world's attention on America. Every artist, he said, wanted sponsorship and patronage if not in dollars then in adjectives. It took a very strong individual to resist that kind of wave in the way that, say, Paul Klee had resisted the endless waves of isms that flowed over European art during his lifetime. The American artist, Shahn declared, went after a patron whether it be the Museum of Modern Art or an individual like Jock Whitney.

Picasso, he thought, had had the greatest influence on art in contemporary America. A friend of his, he said, once divided the whole thing into three broad categories: the Maze—as represented by Pollock; the Order—as represented by Mondrian; and the Monster—as represented by Picasso. He confessed that a meeting had once been arranged for him with Picasso, but that shyness kept him from keeping it. The same happened to him just before he was to meet Frank Lloyd Wright. "They are both considered masters and I can't take that," he explained. Shahn attributed the great change in the public attitude toward painters in the United States to the fact that colleges and universities have become sponsors and patrons of the arts, with some having as many as twenty teachers in their arts departments. They offer economic security, something he has been terrified of. "I don't object to security," he said, "but I do find the peculiar removal from the outside world that the university always offers a doubtful advantage. I get nightmares when I think that Goya might have gotten a Guggenheim fellowship." What he feared was that art schools were teaching their students within six weeks how to turn out a creditable abstraction, distributing what sold, not what belonged to the spirit. When I asked him about other artists' criticism of him for doing a cover of Freud for *Time* magazine, he replied that it did not trouble him one bit, that he would do a portrait of anyone whom he found sympathetic. He had done another one for *Time,* he said—of Malraux—but had turned down one of Edward Teller. "You had to harden yourself to criticism," he said, "but every artist—no matter what direction his work takes—is stating his own beliefs. If the world around him is too much, he can withdraw within himself, but that in itself would be a statement of what he believes. It is, in a sense, the content of his work. Even lack of content is content."

About himself he said that what inspired him as an artist were the hopes and dreams, fears and tragedies of other people, his social consciousness and his driving need to comment on human nature against the background of the contemporary scene. It made him resist the tide of abstractionism that had come to dominate American painters and had placed him in a somewhat lonely position, reminiscent of Hogarth and Daumier, whose great satirical tradition he had tried to follow.

I quoted Bernard Berenson, who once had wondered whether we were passing through some abyss of despair about human nature and its destiny without having the fear of hell or the hope of heaven of early medieval man, and asked whether the nonrepresentational artist, by ignoring shape and substance, failed to make us long for the realms not only of actuality but of aspiration. Shahn, by way of reply, recalled a painting he had done some fifteen years earlier, called *The Red Staircase*, which showed a crippled man walking up an endless stair, who when he came to the top of it went down again. The whole thing was in a ruin of rubble and burned-out buildings. "To me this is both the hope and the fate of man," he said. "He seems to recover from the most frightful wars, the most frightful plagues, and goes right on again when he knows full well that he is going into another one; but that's that eternal hope in the human being."

I got to know Arthur M. Schlesinger, Jr., well during the Kennedy years. Unusual for a historian, he combined the experience of studying and writing history with watching it at close range, being almost part of it. Kennedy, not unlike Franklin D. Roosevelt, assembled an impressive collection of talent and brain power in the hope of using this engine to inject rationality into his policies. In all this he was also concerned about the reflections of his own administration in the mirrors of history and for that reason installed his own in-house historian in the White House, Arthur Schlesinger. His task, though, went beyond being a note taker of history. He became the contact point for intellectuals and a source for providing the insight of the historian into current events. It was not always an easy task, especially when things went wrong. One of the most difficult problems for the analysts among journalists, the problem of perspective, Arthur argued was much exaggerated, for the popular assumption that the more distant the event, the more detached the historian will be, and the more penetrating his judgment, was mistaken. "Any historical problem which engages emotion," he said, "and that may be something as remote as the trial of Socrates or the decline and fall of the Roman Empire, is one in which the debate may be as animated and intense as about the age of Kennedy or Macmillan." Even though this book is, above all, a personal memoir set against the broad-brush canvas of history, it is of course of considerable comfort to hear from a professional historian that history based on documents is not necessarily better history than history based on one's own experience, that it is only different history. His own account of the Kennedy administration, *A Thousand Days*, if not as critical of JFK's conduct in office as he might perhaps be today, is still the best so far.

From my experience in writing this book I came to share Arthur's view that "a historian can never recapture the totality of a situation; all he can do is give his own best understanding of the sequence and color of events and what the major determining factors were. The sense of what the major determining factors were is likely to vary from one period to another . . . Once an event has happened it disappears into the mists of the past and can never be replayed . . . the problems of motivation are mysterious when they happen; and after they have happened, they're gone, and the mystery is, I believe, permanent and irreducible. Then the trauma of choice is the problem for the historian." In the case of an attempt at a memoir such as mine, the selection is easier because the emphasis is on my own participation in events and my own vistas from the sidelines.

My key question to Arthur was an almost inevitable one, since "Munich," which has become the code word for political appeasement, had a great influence on Truman and Acheson when they decided to defend South Korea against the North Koreans and Chinese, on Eden and Macmillan when they decided to go to war against Nasser, and on Dean Rusk, Walt Rostow, possibly Kennedy, when they decided to intervene in Vietnam. Does knowing something about history help a statesman's judgment? Arthur's reply was this: "What knowledge of history does is to encourage in the statesman a sense of human frailty and a certain humility about the future. This should lead statesmen not to make drastic and terrible decisions—like picking a war with Communist China on the theory that if we don't, China ten years from now may be doing something we don't like. This does not mean that the statesman cannot and must not have some vision of the broad direction in which the world is moving and have his policies derive from that vision. That longer perspective, which history offers, is indispensable."

Isaiah Berlin took a more skeptical approach to the question of what history teaches. In his view it certainly taught that weakness was bad and that resolution helped: "The case is really not for the lessons of history, I think, the case is for general education, one enabling one to make an appreciation of what works and what does not work in specific situations."

Knowledge of history certainly helps one in dealing with the conflicts of life—so do affection, faith, and humor. That is why I have included encounters with some of the shining lights of American culture. They are only a few examples of an endless road of interviews and conversations. They are the lifeblood of journalism, which, unlike most professions, is not simply an obligation but an exercise in gratifying one's own curiosity. What could be more enjoyable?

14

Reagan Rides the Tides of History

HOW Americans in general—and President Reagan in particular —still truly felt about the Anglo-American special relationship was subjected to the most demanding test since Suez by the Falklands crisis. When the Argentinian military junta invaded the South Atlantic islands in 1982, Prime Minister Margaret Thatcher decided to prove that Britain still had enough imperial muscle left to defend that barren, distant outpost and to punish armed aggression. President Reagan did not want to prove anything. He wanted to prevent war, prevent getting drawn into a war, or having to take sides. The initial American public reaction, though, was amused disbelief: the idea of going to war over the Falklands seemed some sort of Gilbert and Sullivan comedy until it became clear that the lady was in deadly earnest—she is never anything else. The broad cooperation in global intelligence, nuclear exchanges of information, nuclear targeting —the bare bones of the special relationship—did not mean automatic American support for Britain. The prime minister remained in doubt for some weeks about American intentions and the ghosts of Suez began to haunt Whitehall. As Sir Nicholas Henderson, the British ambassador, put it later, he "never stopped sweating blood through the seventy-four days of the crisis." The sweating for him began on March 30 when he called on Haig to confront him with British intelligence reports signaling that the Argentine fleet was moving into a position from which an invasion could be launched within forty-eight hours. Congressional opinion and the news media, from the start, were more sympathetic to the British case than was the administration, which remained divided between those who sided with Britain, the ally, and those who were more concerned about relations with Latin America. President Reagan, after an attempt to impress upon President Galtieri that the British would resist an invasion and the crisis would jeopardize relations with the United States, remained a passive observer. On April 2, the Argentinian forces made the fateful move. To Al Haig this was a moment to prove his statesmanship. Taking a leaf out of the Kissinger textbook of diplomacy, he decided to try his hand at "shuttle diplomacy." When he imposed a black-out on his negotiations, I joined the press plane that accompanied President Reagan on a "working vacation" to a former British possession, Barbados. Shortly after our arrival on that serene, sun-drenched island, I sought out Bill Clark, the president's national security adviser, and one of those whose priority was relations with Latin America. We had known each other for some time and shared a special fondness for opera. (His went so far that once, during a performance of *Der Rosenkavalier,* when his office called to alert him to the arrival of a telegram that needed an immediate reply, he asked that it be delivered by messenger to the presidential box at the Kennedy Center. Ten minutes later he drafted the requested reply in the adjoining little salon and within twenty minutes he was back in the box listening to the third act.) I found Clark—Admiral John Poindexter, his deputy, was with him—unusually tense and edgy. He told me that Haig less than an hour ago, as he flew over the Caribbean on his way from London to Buenos Aires, had been in radio communications with the president, but had nothing encouraging to report. He then confided that Mr. Reagan had only reluctantly agreed to Haig's mediation effort and that the president would have preferred, as he initially proposed, to send Vice President Bush on a low-key mission to Buenos Aires. But when Haig insisted, he let him go ahead but came to resent his turning it all into a dramatic American diplomatic tour de force. Then, somewhat ominously, Clark added: "If he fails it will finish him." This startling remark made me realize how much Haig was out on a limb and how strained were his relations with the White House. Haig, by then, was very much aware of what was at stake for him and it made him the more frantic and anxious for success. His efforts ran from April 7 until June 14, when the junta surrendered, far too long, after it had become only too obvious that there was no prospect of Argentinian compromise. So confident of victory was the junta that it actually accused Haig of being a British spy whose mission was to rob it of certain victory.

The problem Sir Nicholas Henderson, the British ambassador, had, at least at the start, was to persuade the prime minister to show some flexibility in negotiations with Haig in order not to lose American sympathies and support. Mrs. Thatcher, fearing that those smooth foreign office types would lead her down a slippery slope of unacceptable concessions, resisted at first, but when Haig descended for the second time, she agreed, after tough exchanges, to a plan that kept his mission alive. However abortive, it did help to gain time for the British fleet to move into position. Haig insisted in preserving American neutrality, but the special relationship functioned nevertheless in its own peculiarly intimate and shadowy ways, thanks above all, to the deep-seated pro-British sentiments of Caspar Weinberger, the secretary of defense. I don't remember any other member of an American cabinet who was as convinced an Anglophile as was Weinberger. He acted under a broad policy guidance that the British must not be allowed to lose this war and early on made it clear that the United States would make available whatever supplies the British needed. He dropped what he called the "in-basket" procedures and established direct lines of communications from his office to the British military mission at the Washington embassy and to the military in London. The Americans helped with staging and communications facilities, airstrip matting, ammunition, aircraft fuel, and an array of spare parts. The military at the Pentagon, I sensed from my inquiries, had grave doubts whether the British, with the means at their disposal and the 7,000 miles the fleet had to travel, could pull off the complicated operation. When, at one time, rumors spread that a British aircraft carrier had been torpedoed by the Argentinians, I asked Weinberger at a social occasion what the United States would do if the rumor proved true. Without a moment's hesitation he replied: "Lease one of ours to the British." Then he added that this was of course only a personal reaction, not official policy. Fortunately, the rumors proved to be untrue. Haig, who was worried that the British might end up with a bloody nose, did not object to Weinberger's supply efforts—in fact, he thought they might aid his mission—and Weinberger did not object to Haig's diplomatic extravaganza because it helped the British gain time. The prime minister recommended Weinberger to the Queen for a knighthood in appreciation of the stalwart assistance he had provided. Clark's prediction that Haig would lose his job if he failed in his mediation efforts, of course, proved true. More recently Clark told me that it was less his failed mission than differences of temperament that destroyed his relationship with the president.

Sir Nicholas Henderson demonstrated how important an ambassador's role can be in a crisis. "One of the most challenging tasks under the system of deliberate diffusion of power," he said later, "is to understand the various conflicting forces that influence American policy, decipher American intentions at each critical moment during the crisis, and keep in touch with all the influential forces without crossing wires or offending anybody. Even when I thought I had found out where the pulse beat strongest at any given moment, there was then the problem of how to get at it. There is no simple prescription of how to exert influence in Washington—it is too complicated to define." This was a perfect description of the problems facing not only foreign statesmen, ambassadors or correspondents, but also American officials. There are not many rules, not many precedents that can be followed, for virtually every case is different. The value of embassy entertaining should not be underrated, for at crucial moments, such as in the Falklands crisis, IOUs can be cashed in with greater success than perhaps in any other capital. The complaints I received time-to-time from some members of Congress that they had not been invited to the British embassy proved that such invitations still affect some egos. Henderson also soon realized that his appearances on American television were at least as important as his almost daily interventions at the State Department. He therefore accepted every opportunity offered to him to explain and to defend British policy. Initially, he had to deal with the contradictory claims to sovereignty, the easily aroused anticolonial feelings, and the question of whether it was so-to-say a just war. In seventy-four days he gave seventy-three televised interviews; the ambassador became the message. His cause was aided by Argentinian intransigence, by Haig's growing recognition of the potential long-range repercussions of American neutrality on the NATO alliance as he shuttled between London and Buenos Aires, and by the material support provided by Weinberger without which the outcome of this gamble would have been in doubt. If the Falklands war helped the prime minister to win the next elections and to establish dominance over her party, it also gave her style of leadership an aura that made a deep impression on the president and on Americans generally, for however much they cherish the diffusion of power, they also yearn for strong leadership.

Although I have since enjoyed interviews with her at Downing Street, I met Mrs. Thatcher on her very first visit to Washington, at a little cocktail party given for her by a first secretary of the British Embassy. She still lived in the political shadows as secretary of state for education and science. She asked a lot of serious questions, she was obviously eager to listen and to learn and to extend her knowledge of the US political system. She was still the innocent traveler abroad. When asked about the women's lib movement, which had hit this country like a tidal wave, she spoke with some bewilderment about the ferocious passions the movement had engendered among American women. She did not see herself as holding up the flag for a minority, only as another politician doing her job like any man. In the United States the advancement of women in politics is often seen more as a need to pay homage to their "minority status" than as due to true merit. American women can be ambitious and hard-driving, but they somehow seem to be much more self-conscious about it than, say, Mrs. Thatcher or Mme Simone Weil, the highly respected French politician. Mrs. Thatcher, for instance, when asked at a press conference—she was prime minister by then—whether she minded being called "an iron maiden," expressed pride rather than embarrassment. Americans, and not only women, are much impressed by her fearlessness in taking command in a man's world. She reminds them as much of a handsome edition of Britannia as Winston Churchill did of a daunting British bulldog.

President Reagan governs by making people feel contented and intellectually unchallenged, Mrs. Thatcher by the force of her character and her convictions. He seeks to soothe people's worries, she tries to eradicate them by sheer force of argument. It is common knowledge that she and President Reagan have had a kind of political love affair. They not only share a deep ideological commitment to conservatism and anticommunism, but they also share a genuine liking for each other. Shrewdly aware of how important it was to her own power position to have a close relationship with the American president, she skillfully developed an understanding of trust and respect with Mr. Reagan which gradually permitted her to speak candidly, without guile and ambivalence, to him as an ideological soul mate. In matters of common Anglo-American and European interests, she had more influence on him than some of his own advisers. When the British and the Germans, for instance, proposed that the West abandon its insistence on reaching prior agreement with the Russians on the number of forces both sides kept in Europe, a condition that had led to a complete deadlock in the discussions about reducing conventional forces, and the issue came up in the National Security Council, President Reagan, reading from a letter Mrs. Thatcher had sent him, overruled the objections of the Department of Defense, the National Security Council, and the Joint Chiefs of Staff in her favor. The American official who told me this as an example of Mrs. Thatcher's influence on the president also commented: "Where Secretary of State George Shultz would have failed, the prime minister succeeded."

Earlier in her career as prime minister, when I saw her at 10 Downing Street and asked her why she had not yet made a speech on her views of the world, she replied with surprising candor that she did not yet feel secure enough in foreign affairs to give such a speech. She wanted first, she said, to develop her ideas on what kind of Britain she wanted, and next what kind of policies she wanted President Reagan to pursue that she could wholeheartedly support. Increasingly aware of how little the president knew about foreign affairs, she used her visits to explain to him Western European interests and to seek his support, as she did on her visits in December 1984 and October 1985. On the first she began a diplomatic campaign to make the president realize the far-reaching consequences of his "strategic defense initiative," the so-called Star Wars policy.

The idea of creating a nuclear umbrella in space to protect the United States from an enemy missile rain had clearly captured the President's imagination. It proved to be a brilliant coup de main by the opponents of arms control, who had been smarting as outsiders and victims of what they considered the condescension of the Eastern Establishment and its operational arm, the Council on Foreign Relations. They used it to keep the arms control bureaucracy and the Joint Chiefs of Staff at bay; they insulated the president and took advantage of his dream of a nonnuclear world, advertising it as proof that this president was not a warmonger but a man of peace. This unilateral initiative also seriously upset the NATO allies who had not been consulted. It struck them like lightening. They saw it as a dangerous attempt to shift

NATO strategy from deterrence to defense, with hidden isolationist under-
tones and implicit retreat from a commitment to use nuclear weapons against
a Soviet attack on Western Europe. It disturbed the Soviets, who even suspected that SDI was designed to give the United States a first strike capability
and superiority in space. The British and French wondered how adversely it
would affect their own limited nuclear deterrents.

To make sure that Mr. Reagan did not stray too far into fantasy land and
undermine the basic system of nuclear deterrence that had served Europe's
security admirably for so many years, Mrs. Thatcher flew to Washington on
December 22, 1984, for a private meeting at Camp David. Well briefed, as she
always is when the stakes are high, she gave the president some of the medicine
she sometimes administers to recalcitrant members of her cabinet. She made
no bones about SDI's strategic drawbacks, extolled nuclear deterrence and the
value of the ABM Treaty. She then surfaced what looked like a carefully
drafted statement, written in London without consultation with the British
ambassador. Secretary of State Shultz and Robert McFarlane, the national
security adviser, looked at each other in amazement at what seemed to them
an attempt to waylay the president and to get a quick endorsement of her
views. Still, after minor adjustments, the prime minister got the "clarification"
she wanted: that the overall aim of the United States was to enhance nuclear
deterrence, not to undermine it; that any SDI deployment was to be negotiated;
and that SDI was not aimed at achieving nuclear superiority, as the Russians
suspected. What mattered most to her was the commitment to negotiations for
reduced levels of offensive weapons *before* SDI deployment. To prove that she
was not altogether against Mr. Reagan's new fixation, Mrs. Thatcher said that
she favored research. To this the president said soothingly that research is
what this was all about and who knows how long it will take to find out
whether the SDI concept was feasible. The rest of the discussion was about her
recent encounter with Mr. Gorbachev with whom she had said publicly "she
could do business," a remark White House briefers, at the time, tried to
disparage. More recently, after the Moscow summit, the president in his
Guildhall speech recalled her remark and gave her credit for foresight.

Nevertheless, the implications of SDI remained a constant worry to her.
But when she brought it up again over lunch in the family dining room at the
White House in February 1985, the president, though always considerate in his
dealing with the prime minister, became unusually testy: "Yes, Margaret," he
said, "I understand why you are against a nonnuclear world, but that is what
I have in mind. We simply have to go in the direction of fewer nuclear missiles
and ultimately to eliminate them." He made it clear that he knew that what
he advocated implied a change in NATO strategy, even though he did not put
it in those words, but that it would not deflect him from going ahead with SDI.
To those present it was obvious that while he grasped the military implications,
he did not understand the impact it would have on the political cohesion of
the alliance or on the political capital invested in the nuclear deterrent.

Reagan's obsession with SDI, some of his former aides believe, goes back to a briefing he was given at NORAD, the strategic air command in Colorado Springs, while still a presidential candidate. NORAD's commander then told him that, based on the kind of hypothetical exchanges planners go through, nuclear deterrence depended on whether the United States was able to detect Soviet launchers and confident enough of the survival of its retaliatory systems. At that point Reagan is said to have asked whether this meant that the US had no way of preventing missiles from reaching this country. He was then told that this was indeed the case because the US had never had an air defense system worthy of that name and had adopted the "assured destruction" strategy, which relied on the enemy's awareness that in case of a first strike enough American missiles would survive to ensure a devastating retaliation.

Then in 1981 Dr. Edward Teller, the nuclear physicist who is credited with the development of the H-bomb, was invited to the White House by two presidential aides, Edwin Meese and Richard Allen, to brief the president on the state of the technology of defensive systems. Reagan was very much taken by what he heard, but at that time not even Secretary of Defense Caspar Weinberger thought that the state of the art was as advanced as Teller had claimed, and so nothing was done. It was only later that Robert McFarlane and others, fearful that the new Soviet mobile missiles, especially if fitted with multiple warheads, would cause a fundamental shift in the strategic balance, told the president to warn the Russians that these missiles presented the United States with a very serious problem, and that he would have to resort to defensive measures to prevent them from giving a decisive advantage to the Soviet Union. McFarlane believed that if the president were to put the Kremlin on notice that the US would make a major effort in the field of high technology, the Russians, well aware of American superiority in this field, would want to forestall them. But he miscalculated, because his aim was to achieve a political rather than a military advantage. The president, however, was much more captivated by the military aspects of the SDI idea. He saw it as enabling him to tell Americans that SDI would protect them from incoming missiles and that they would not have to rely on nuclear retaliation. To proceed with SDI thus became a moral imperative for him and proof that he was not the warmonger he was accused of being. McFarlane's expectations were confirmed when the Russians returned to the conference table in Geneva and committed themselves in principle to a 50 percent reduction in ICBMs if the United States would abandon SDI. It was a substantial concession, but Reagan was so hooked on SDI that he insisted on building it. He refused to be deterred by the enormous costs or the risks of failure, of distressing the NATO alliance, or of giving the Russians the impression that the US was seeking a first-strike capability. Neither Shultz nor McFarlane, using these arguments, succeeded in changing the president's mind. "It is no good to say something has worked for forty years, if that something is nuclear weapons," the president insisted. "They are losing ground. Look at the antinuclear movements in the United

States and in Europe! We have a moral responsibility to get rid of these weapons." Who would have expected the often bellicose-sounding Reagan to have such a powerful romantic streak in him! It troubled Americans as well as allies, for when it occurs with a simpleminded man, there is the risk that he will reach for too simpleminded solutions. In our complicated world, this can lead to dangerous misconceptions and irreparable pitfalls.

Apart from Mikhail Gorbachev, a well-educated, determined leader representing the younger generation, who had the courage to define what was wrong in the Soviet Union, other potent tides of history played their part in initiating Détente Mark II. One was the realization that economic growth and technology would in future matter more in promoting superpowerism than military power. As Ed A. Hewett of the Brookings Institution put it in his *Reforming the Soviet Economy* (1988): "So far the Soviets have managed to keep pace with, some would say outpace, the United States in the arms race. Until recently that race involved conventional arms and strategic weapons embodying technology that the Soviets could manage. Now much greater emphasis is on the state-of-the-art technologies, a shift symbolized by President Reagan's Strategic Defense Initiative. For the United States this is a shift toward a strength of its economic system; but for the Soviet Union this is a shift toward its greatest weakness." Another realization was the stultifying impact the Communist system had on economic growth. That is also why the Soviets and the Chinese began to look unashamedly over their shoulders to the West to find answers to their own economic problems. Disenchantment with communism had already spread to Europe—even Euro-communism turned out to be a short-lived fad—and now the Soviet leadership has had to admit the need for a drastic overhaul of the entire economy. Gorbachev concluded that in the interest of the Soviet Union's position in the world economy, to ensure Soviet national security and the hegemony of the Communist Party, far-reaching reforms had to be enacted. He mobilized the cultural and technocratic elite (which shapes public attitudes more than its counterparts in the United States) and the news media and took on the deeply entrenched opposition, the governmental bureaucracy. He injected a new flexibility into Soviet foreign policy that took the Reagan administration totally by surprise. He was not the kind of person who would make Khrushchev's mistake with his (to American ears) threatening forecast, "We will bury you!" Instead he talked of a new cooperative relationship, which, no doubt, he hoped will lead to more technical help from America and a broader participation in world economic affairs. He presented the West with a new problem, a Soviet leader who knew how to compete with Western leaders on their home ground and in the world at large.

Whether it was Reagan's proverbial Irish luck or the tides of history that brought Mikhail Gorbachev to his rescue, is anybody's guess. But it was the Soviet leader who effectively decided that even a badly weakened president could still play a powerful role on the world scene. He was shrewd enough to realize that in an age when power and politics are overpersonalized and overemphasized, it is often overlooked that American power is more significant than the state of the American presidency. American and foreign news media, for instance, consigned President Reagan to political oblivion after he had lost majority control in Congress, the attempt to strike an arms-for-hostages deal with the Iranians had misfired, and the budget and trade deficits caused a financial crisis. Soviet leadership, however, was much less influenced by public opinion polls and much more by the appurtenances of American power. Adding up the advantages of reaching arms control agreements with the most ideological, most anti-Communist, most conservative post–World War II administration, with a president so weakened that he would probably welcome a positive achievement in foreign relations and a Congress that was more arms control–minded than perhaps any previous one, the Politburo concluded that this was an opportunity not to be missed.

What the Politburo did not know—in fact, hardly anybody knew—was that Vice President Bush and Robert McFarlane had spent a great deal of time urging the president to take advantage of his enormous investment in military hardware and translate it into a lasting achievement in statesmanship. The idea that he could restore stability by using American superiority in high technology as leverage in the arms reduction negotiations was lost on him. He did not believe that this was the central argument. He insisted that the central issue was protecting Americans from nuclear explosions.

But when the vice president countered that the president would want to accomplish more than being able to say that he kept peace in his time, that he had an obligation also to future generations, that he might want to aim at codifying agreements that would last beyond his tenure, and form a coherent framework that could be carried forward by his successor, the president began to pay increased attention to the problem of how to do business with the Russians, how to find a formula somewhere between the two extremes, the cold war and the détente approach. At that point he had apparently no agenda or negotiating strategy and the leadership in the Kremlin was still moving from one funeral procession to another. When finally the next generation, with Gorbachev in the lead, assumed control, signs began to accumulate that the pendulum of history might begin to swing again and Secretary of State George Shultz started to press the president to engage the Soviets in negotiations. This led to a split within the administration with the vice president, Shultz, Mike Deaver, the special assistant to the president, and Robert McFarlane, the national security adviser, on one side, and Caspar Weinberger, William Clark, and William Casey on the other—with Nancy Reagan, not so quietly, siding with the first group. Such bitterness began to set in that at one point Clark handed Reagan's secretary a handwritten note for the president which was one long withering criticism of Shultz. However much fun is made of the vice presidential Soviet funeral duties, attending three in relatively rapid succession gave him enough of a sense of the new stirrings in Moscow to encourage the president to take advantage of these changes and translate them into a new mood in Soviet-American relations. Mr. Bush was not alone in fueling the ethics of a new look, but etiquette and modesty prevented him from claiming credit. In all my occasional meetings with him he refused to say whether he was able to exert any influence on the president. The president, willing to deemphasise ideology to satisfy his virtuous, almost naive, ambitions was soon buoyed up by the Kremlin's readiness to offer major concessions in arms control negotiations, began to see himself as a heroic figure destined to advance the cause of peace. He even convinced himself that with his gift of persuasion, he would be able to impress on the Soviet leader to act if necessary, outside the party system, just as he made SDI his historic cause, bypassing the regular policy-making procedures. That is how some of the men close to the president described the mood that overcame him. His naiveté startled and disturbed them, but it did not take long until limits imposed themselves on his hopes. Being able to credit his military build-up policy for inducing a change of policy in the Kremlin made it easier for him to drop the "evil empire" idea, a phrase speechwriter Tom Dolan put in his mouth. Mr. Gorbachev's own vision for economic reforms to preserve the Soviet Union's superpower status, of course, provided a great deal of the momentum of change in Soviet-American relations. Politics in the 1990s will be more about economic than military power.

The tides of history seemed to be plying their mysterious influence in the United States as well. Reaganomics, as it used to be called when Mr. Reagan came into office, ignited the longest growth period in American peacetime history. But it resulted in unprecedented budget and trade deficits that turned the United States from the biggest creditor nation to the biggest debtor nation in the world. Suddenly the US has lost control over its own economic destiny, and President Reagan's financial profligacy is being blamed for it. The next generation may well accuse him of having mortgaged its future. It may find itself saying with Bismarck that a leader who does not think of the next generation is not a statesman.

Nor did the Reagan era lead to a conservative revolution, as so many had predicted it would. The reason is that the political mainstream, even if it has shifted to the right of center, remains more powerful than the radical tributaries that flow into it, proving once again that America's pluralistic society has its own instinctive ways of cushioning and absorbing stress. What has changed though is that the United States cannot afford the kind of generosity, wastefulness, blunders, and mismanagement it once could. The world's well-being still largely depends on how the United States manages its economy and on the dollar's remaining the lubricant of world trade.

For a while Ronald Reagan's bounding self-confidence, his infectious optimism, his unsophisticated charm, the ease with which he carried the burden of governance, gave him a popularity unmatched since President Eisenhower. He inspired Americans with a new sense of pride and confidence after years of retreat and feeling on the defensive. He reminded them of the golden age when Hollywood mirrored on the screen a world with more silver linings than clouds. He had a primitive appreciation of the tactical uses of power. What mattered to him most was to revive the Pax Americana based on superior military power. He gave it a more nationalistic, militaristic, ideological, unilateral, and confrontational thrust. He gave new emphasis to the Soviet naval threat in the Pacific to justify the buildup to a six-hundred-ship navy and to the economic strangling of the Soviet Union. Even though some influential members of the so-called foreign policy establishment, such as Henry Kissinger and Zbigniew Brzezinski, began advocating a partial withdrawal of American troops from Europe, he showed no intention of wanting to weaken the NATO central front. He did, however, introduce his tentative but dramatic attempt to shift American strategy from deterrence, which had kept the peace for the last forty years, to a strategy of defense in space. He hoped that it would be his enduring gift to history. To sustain the psychological impact of power, especially on his adversaries, and to prove his readiness to use it, he ordered the shooting down of two Libyan warplanes in the Gulf of Sidra, he tried to assassinate Colonel Qaddafi by bombing his residential quarters, he ordered the interception of terrorists in flight over the Mediterranean, and he sent his forces into Grenada to teach Fidel Castro a lesson. However minute these demonstrations of hubris were, they were meant to be demonstrations of resolve and they had their salutory as well as their disturbing consequences. In many ways he fitted the description of American presidents Lord Bryce offered in 1888 in his much-quoted book *The American Commonwealth*: ". . . the American voter does not object to mediocrity . . . He likes his candidate to be sensible, vigorous and, above all, what he calls 'magnetic,' and does not value, because he sees no need for originality or profundity, a fine culture or wide knowledge . . ." In his own appealingly unpretentious way Reagan described himself in one simple, and all-too-true, sentence: "What you see is what you get." He made his decisions more by relying on his instincts than on the study of substance, more on his professional ability to learn his lines by heart than on the grasp of the issues. He acted like an accomplished actor playing the part of president, who relied on able directors, producers, and scriptwriters. As one of his advisers put it, he tended to ask not what he should do but what he should say. And he said it all with an appealing charm, and an unblushing intellectual emptiness.

I got an inkling of the magic of the Reagan charm, his skill as an entertainer, his use of anecdotes as a protective shield at a farewell party for a young White House aide, Morgan Mason, the son of the late film star James Mason, who was about the first among aides who decided on his own volition to return to private life. The host, Mike Deaver, a special assistant to President and Mrs. Reagan, did not forewarn us that the Reagans would join the party. They came, although they had only just returned from an exhausting political campaign trip, because Morgan's own charm and sense of fun had obviously won their affection. Like all other guests—we were about fifteen—the president and

Nancy stood in line at the buffet dinner table, plate in hand, to help themselves as everybody else did. Then, plate in lap, I found myself sitting in one group with the president; Frank Reynolds, the late television anchorman; Dave Fisher, a presidential aide; and Morgan's girl friend, Debbie. The president had hardly sat down when, in his informal, good-natured, enigmatic way, he began to regale us with his stories. Some had a pointed political meaning, such as the one about a woman who had written to him that at the age of forty-two she was wheelchair-bound, was married, had two children, but was not worried about social security because there were always ways to help oneself. Or another dating back to a visit to Taiwan where above a restaurant handicapped people worked, looking after themselves in the face of the absence of a governmental social security safety net. Clearly, this president had real doubts about a protective social security system.

After Frank Reynolds remarked on his extraordinary ability to communicate with people, the president began to reminisce about Franklin Roosevelt, who had managed to do so even in the age of radio. He spoke about Roosevelt's performance the way one actor speaks about another actor's gifts. When I weighed in with my recollection of the press conference with the two great communicators, Roosevelt and Churchill, I had attended in 1941, he took up my lead by telling us three Churchill stories, all illustrating his admiration for the man's ability to generate the kind of hope, confidence, and determination that hardened the British into resisting Hitler. "To steel an entire nation when there was so little hope . . . what a unique feat!" he exclaimed. To be able to communicate courage was clearly high on his talent scale. It led him to recall an incident from his high school days of a little scrawny Jewish boy—he even remembered his name, Harold Marx—who found himself suddenly threatened in the school yard by a big muscular bully who towered over him and was getting into position to hit him. "Okay, hit me," the little boy replied. "I'll hit you back if you do," and he assumed a fighting stance. The tough-looking bully, surprised by so much unexpected courage, looked him up and down for a while and then walked away in silence. It obviously was an incident that had made a deep impression on Mr. Reagan: "One must not allow oneself to be intimidated by bullies," was the moral of his story, making it clear that this was one of those experiences that he now carried into his presidential book of rules. Debbie's mention of having recently seen the film *The Santa Fe Trail*, with Errol Flynn, on television led to a flooding back of happy memories of his Hollywood days, and how he, as a lifeguard, had competed in 100- and 200-yard races, including the crossing of a 200-meter-wide river, which he remembered he managed in 2:07 minutes. All these sporting activities had kept him in excellent form, and so did his current exercises on the Nautilus stretch machine, he said. Having returned to the present, he suddenly remembered that it was time to leave. He got up, turned to everybody in the room, and said jovially: "Now you'll have a good time, this is when the teacher leaves . . ." What an engaging man, I said to myself. Comfortable with himself, anxious to make everybody else feel relaxed, and yet I was left with the feeling that it was a performance, a fine performance at that, but a studied act, of a man who preferred to walk on clouds rather than on terra firma. Then it occurred to me that, maybe, he did not quite know what terra firma was or, maybe, did not want us to know that he did not know what it was . . .

The last time I saw President Reagan officially and on a one-to-one basis was in February 1983, shortly before I retired from my job as the American correspondent of *The Sunday Times.* He was his confident self—he felt at ease with almost everybody, including foreign correspondents, just as did Presidents Kennedy and Ford—he looked one straight into the eyes unlike Nixon, who avoided eye contact most probably because he did not want the interviewer to look into his soul. Reagan did not seem to have anything to hide, or at least, he was not aware of it. He was at one with the principles he lived by. He was a worshiper of life. And yet despite his consummate effortlessness and adroitness, his cold, blue eyes, whether smiling or serious, reflected a kind of precarious innocence and a wonderment why everybody did not agree with him— after all it was so obvious that his policies were good for the country and good for humanity. Not until I quoted from his recent speech in Orlando, Florida, and his characterization of the confrontation between the United States and the Soviet Union as one between "good and evil" and "light and darkness," did the twinkle in his eyes disappear. To provoke a clear-cut answer, I asked him whether in the circumstances he was not implying the inevitability of war between two irreconcilable enemies. "No," he replied, "what I meant to point out was the need to face up to the basic differences between the United States and the Soviet Union and to remind everybody to be realistic about them. That was also the reason why I criticized détente, for I considered it simply an attempt to sweep those differences under the rug." He spoke with what sounded like deep-seated conviction. "At the same time," he continued, "I have expressed my determination and my belief that peace is achievable. I am very concerned with those people who somehow seem to think—without their realizing that they are thinking it—that war is inevitable. I can't subscribe to that at all." He made a similar point four years later on the eve of the Washington summit meeting in a television interview when he referred to "some conservatives . . . who in their deepest thought have accepted that war is inevitable." Then, talking about his proposal for the total elimination of nuclear missiles, he added: "We're ready to negotiate in good faith any reasonable proposal or suggestion on the way to the ultimate goal."

But what did he mean by "reasonable proposals," I asked myself later, taking into consideration that this president found it easier to give vent to his instincts than to articulate his thoughts. Did he indeed follow up on President Carter's rearmament program by drastically raising military spending on the Churchillian principle "We arm to parley" or simply because he wanted to see the United States "taller" than the Soviet Union? Some of his closest aides told me that they were convinced that he was not guided by a carefully conceived concept, that his master plan was nothing more than to restore American superiority over the Soviet Union. Like most Americans he concentrated on the present; he had no intellectually thought-out vision for the future. Like all presidents he had the ambition to advance the cause of peace, as he told the editors of the Washington *Post* in June 1980; he also considered himself ideally suited to negotiate with the Russians, for, as he likes to recall, he proved his mettle in dealing with Communists as president of the Screen Actors' Guild. He certainly never expected the Russians to take him up on a proposal for the total elimination of missiles, thought up by Richard Perle, the then assistant secretary for international affairs at the Pentagon, to counter and pacify the peace movements in West Germany, which had by then gained a momentum that the West German government feared could get out of control. On a visit to Bonn in October 1981 I watched the largest peace demonstration yet. It was orderly and nonthreatening, but some of the placards, such as one saying "Reagan go into a home for the aged so that we can get as old as you are!" made it clear whom they were directed against.

Five years later the Western world almost suffered a heart attack when, at the Reykjavik summit meeting, the Soviets challenged the United States to accept the Perle proposal as a serious basis for negotiations. The president and Mr. Gorbachev came close to agreeing in principle not only to eliminate all ballistic missiles, but even discussed abolishing nuclear weapons altogether.

Mrs. Thatcher, deeply disturbed by the eagle turning into a dove, hurried to Washington soon afterwards, in November 1986. She knew by then that she would not be able to banish the president's vision of making nuclear weapons "impotent and obsolete" by developing a protective screen in space nor his dream of a nonnuclear world. She had also learned that one should never simply dismiss Ronald Reagan, however tempting the circumstances may be. She therefore asked him only to agree to a statement (this time a draft of it had been sent to the White House in advance of her arrival) emphasizing the importance of nuclear deterrence and the need to eliminate the disparities in conventional weapons, and limiting SDI research to what is permitted by the Anti-Ballistic Missile Treaty. The president did indeed approve the statement. It sounded reassuring to the allies, possibly even to the Russians, though it was deceptively open to different interpretations. Still, it proved once again that she was NATO's most effective envoy to the Reagan court. Influencing policy from the outside, of course, is one thing, having the power actually to execute policy from the inside is another. It is not surprising therefore that a high-flyer such as Mrs. Thatcher wished she had the powers of an American president, for on boarding her plane at Andrews airfield, she was heard to say, "I wish I could run this country!"

Mrs. Thatcher is not the first woman who could cast a spell over Ronald Reagan. His strong mother was the first, Hollywood columnist Louella Parsons was another one, and his first wife, Jane Wyman, like Nancy, his First

Lady, were in the same category. Yet another, a strong woman with a more spiritual aura, was Mother Teresa, the saintly guardian of the poor. They met shortly after his lucky escape from an assassin's bullet in the White House. The President and Nancy Reagan were still suffering from the aftershock of that experience, but convinced that God had allowed a miracle to happen. Therefore when Mother Teresa put her hand gently on his shoulder and said, "God spared you for a mission to bring peace to the world," he nodded, awed by her words and the thought and with undisguised solemnity muttered: "I know." What we cannot know, of course, is how crucial this encounter was to Ronald Reagan's outlook on his presidency and his aim to denuclearize the world.

A few weeks after my Reagan interview *The Sunday Times* published my valedictory to my thirty-four years as Washington correspondent under the headline: MY LOVE AFFAIR WITH AMERICA. It virtually coincided with a splendid farewell party offered by the then editor of *The Sunday Times,* Frank Giles, which I approached feeling, like Chesterton, that "the fear of sentimentality is the meanest of all modern terrors." Surrounded by my British friends and colleagues, I remembered that Britain had given me a safe haven, a new national and cultural awareness, and a new sense of belonging and an anchor for life. *The Sunday Times* provided me not only with a superb springboard to a fascinating career, but with what is without doubt the best journalistic assignment in the world. Thanks to its reputation as one of the most respected newspapers in the world and its inspired editors, who appreciated the importance of reporting from the United States, I was able to get to know well the men at the levers of political, economic, and cultural power, win their confidence and occasionally their friendship. This gave to my commentaries an authenticity which was perhaps the main reason why I was allowed to stay in Washington for almost a lifetime. I was also greatly aided first by watching during World War II how such American star reporters as Ned Russell of the New York *Herald Tribune,* Drew Middleton of the *New York Times,* Helen Kirkpatrick of the Chicago *Daily News,* and other Americans went about covering the war and how they gained the confidence of those in power in the British government. Later in Washington, it was Scotty Reston, Walter Lippmann, Joseph Kraft, Joseph C. Harsch and Richard Strout of the *Christian Science Monitor,* and many others who made themselves available for advice. There existed a camaraderie among the Washington press corps and a readiness to help one other, despite the fierce competition in this business, that was unique.

I remember still the trepidation I felt when browsing in one of the *Times* bookstores in London on the eve of my original departure for the United States, and hearing someone comment on a display of Denis Brogan's book *The American Political System*: "I didn't know they had one." Since then I have spent more than thirty-four years in the United States, my greenness has

faded over those years, and I acquired enough gray hair to be invited by Lloyd
Cutler, the lawyer and student of constitutional history, to join a committee
he, Senator Nancy Kassebaum, and Douglas Dillon, the former secretary of
the treasury, had set up with the aim of developing reforms of the American
Constitution in preparation for its two hundredth anniversary. I accepted full
of curiosity, for I had come to believe that this eighteenth-century document,
drafted at a time when the United States stood on the sidelines of world affairs,
seriously required adaptation to the needs of a nation that was now a world
leader. The American presidency still resembles today much more the office
held by General Washington than that of Queen Elizabeth II. So little had
changed. It seemed to me that the division of power between the executive and
the legislature, especially when it came to the budgetary process and the
conduct of foreign affairs, now clearly required greater efficiency and dispatch.
I did not belong to those who favored a shift to a parliamentary system on
Westminster lines. Those who did represented only a small but forceful and
eloquent minority led by Professor James McGregor Burns of the Massachusetts Institute of Technology. I sympathized with Lloyd Cutler's formula-
tion that "the most one can hope for is a set of modest changes that would
make our structure work somewhat more in the manner of a parliamentary
system . . ." The parliamentary system, I believed, was too autocratic for the
kind of pluralistic society the American is, with all its contrasting regional,
economic, political, geographical, and climatic interests, and would gravely
strain the loose unity of this federal union.

Constitutional reform, however, is like the labors of Sisyphus. President
Lyndon B. Johnson, for instance, proposed a constitutional amendment to
extend the two-year term for members of the House of Representatives to four
years, but after he rolled the rock up the legislative hill in his State of the Union
message in 1966, he did not try again when no one stopped it from rolling
down. According to a poll by the magazine *Newsweek,* taken in May 1987, 44
percent favored some basic changes in the Constitution. Yet 72 percent replied
that a convention called to make basic changes would make things worse.
There is no sizable vocal majority that actively presses for constitutional
changes, though most Americans are well aware of the proneness to stalemate
of the American political processes and the difficulties this creates for those
charged with governing. They are still afraid of the dangers of the exploitation
of the arbitrary power a president can exercise, or they treasure political
stability more than the promise of improvements through reform.

After almost three years of careful studies and lively discussions the committee, which was composed of former members of Congress, cabinet officials,
academics, and experts in a variety of political fields, produced a number of
recommendations. First, we agreed there was much to be said for reducing the
requirements for treaty ratification from a two-thirds majority of the Senate
to 60 percent. It would be reassuring to foreign governments that have signed
a treaty with the United States to know that it will actually come into force.

In almost any other country but the United States this is a foregone conclusion. The obstacles and delays Congress initiated to make the conduct of foreign affairs even more difficult than it already was can be exasperating to all concerned. There was also much to be said for a "team ticket," which would list each party's candidates for president, vice president, the Senate, and the House, with four-year and eight-year terms for members of the House and Senate respectively, and with voting on the list as a unit. It would strengthen the political party structures whose inner disarray has contributed so much to the problem of governing and to the growth in power of single interest groups. The idea of permitting members of Congress to serve in cabinet posts without losing their seat in Congress also has considerable merit. We spent much time debating the equivalent of a parliamentary censure motion which would give either the president or Congress the right to call for special elections and tested it against major relevant events in modern American history. The threat of such special elections would certainly strengthen the president's hands in dealing with Congress and provide an alternative to the ultimate and cumbersome method of impeachment of a president by Congress. We found that in a good many cases a special election would not have been practical. Nevertheless there ought to be an alternative to impeachment.

The recommendations of the Committee on the Constitutional System stimulated discussions on television, in the press, on the campuses, and among the political elite, but Congress, which tends to be interested only in what happens today and in the next elections, showed little interest. Americans do not like to tamper with their Constitution, which they hold in awe. It is what holds this disparate, pluralistic, and adversarial-minded nation together. As James Sundquist put it in his *Constitutional Reform and Effective Government,* "issues pertaining to the structure of government do not stir mass excitement, in the absence of outright governmental collapse." It never occurred to the Founding Fathers to design a Constitution that would lend itself to the conduct of a Pax Americana. On the contrary, they fashioned it to prevent the United States from turning into an imperial republic. What the founders of the American world order accomplished, therefore, deserves the utmost admiration. For me, the exchange of ideas in our deliberations, their testing against historic precedents and against the safeguards erected by the authors of the Constitution, was a fascinating exercise and an invaluable education; above all, it gave me still further insights into the restless American mind.

Compared to 1961 the United States now finds itself in a situation which is a far cry from what my expectations were in those days. Walter Lippmann then chided me in a sort of fatherly way for wishing or even expecting the United States in the twentieth century to fill the role that Britain filled in the nineteenth. "After the Napoleonic wars there was a theory that a Pax Britannica ruled the world," he said. "But then after World War II, Britain having exhausted itself, more so than in World War I, and the United States having become very strong, the theory was propagated, foremost of all by Winston Churchill, that the United States should step into Britain's shoes. Now, that proved to be an illusion. We're living in the aftermath of that. There is no such thing as a Pax Americana. There won't be a Pax Sovietica either, or anything like it, because the world is too big to be governed by anybody."

A few years later I raised the same subject with Averell Harriman, and he sounded a similar note: "We decided on the Marshall Plan to promote political and military stability in the face of the Communist threat. We believed that the destruction of Europe wrought by the war would be so damaging as to make Russia the dominant force on the European continent. We wanted to help Europe back on its feet, but we also wanted to prevent Soviet expansionism. But there has never been a desire on the part of any president to build an empire, to dominate or control countries, to create a Pax Americana. What the United States wanted to do was to spread its influence."

Paul Nitze, the dedicated engineer of "positions of strength," who contributed a great deal to building some of the foundations of the Pax Americana, was even more outspoken. "I resent the term 'Pax Americana,' " he said with unusual vehemence. "It is the last thing we're psychologically equipped to manage, the last thing we want to be committed to. Moreover, it's a pejorative word, it's distasteful to me, for it suggests an American desire for control over the world, which is quite wrong."

No doubt, this is a very different world from the one in which the British had mastery of the seas. No doubt, the world is now too big to be governed by anybody: the fact that the United States in 1988 has more than 750,000 troops abroad—something few Americans are aware of—is significant and impressive, but it is not, Paul Nitze insisted, very "meaningful." No doubt, the idea of a Pax Americana goes against the American grain and, psychologically, Americans are not equipped to manage it. But ever since I had seen that confident, determined, and sovereign figure of Franklin D. Roosevelt at his press conference in 1941 and watched the American colossus flex its muscles, I had been convinced that the United States would have to assume long-term responsibility for the security of the West and keep its troops in Europe indefinitely once Stalin decided that he wanted to keep tight control over its Eastern lands. But American influence in the world was neither by doctrine nor by political or commercial ambition; it spread so rapidly because it promoted the idea of the freedom of the individual and improved living standards through economic growth. American marketing skills spread US products and all forms of American culture to the farthest corners of the world, even to such closed societies as those of the Soviet Union and China. The Pax Americana to me does not imply, as did the Pax Britannica, formal control over a great number of countries around the globe or easy access to raw materials or great international trading advantages—not even the satisfaction of being able to exert a civilizing influence. Still, despite the absence of structure or definition or a vision of universal order, the lack of an acquisitive instinct territorially or the desire and ability to bring American intellectual and national interests into a coherent concept, an American order—some will say disorder—does exist as an almost all-pervasive presence.

Few people will disagree with the assertion that the United States, considering the broader appurtenances of power, is still No. 1 in the world. The question many people, especially foreigners, are asking is whether Americans will have the stamina, competence, craftiness, managerial and planning skills to stay the course of world leadership with all the costs, the responsibilities, and the foresight this involves. I saw the United States rise to a military and industrial powerhouse, to the defense of Western civilization, to the restoration of Western Europe's economic and political health. I watched it providing the world with new ideas and new dreams and I also saw it tarring itself with the imperial brush in Vietnam. I lived through the painful sixties of the youth rebellion, the disillusionment with itself, the tottering of such hallowed institutions as the universities and the churches. I experienced the shocks created by the loss of nuclear superiority, the passing of the affluent society as portrayed by John Kenneth Galbraith, the defeat in Vietnam and, most recently, the realization that Americans are not anymore in sole control of their destiny.

Looking ahead, the rivalry between the United States and the Soviet Union will continue, détente or not, but, I assume, it will be less hostile, less fanatical, based on realpolitik not gullibility. And so the pendulum continues to swing; it swings faster in the United States than in most other countries, but for a nation that grew up with a deep-seated aversion to foreign entanglements, looking back over the last forty years, it has grasped the sinews of power and leadership in a remarkably short time and held on to them with surprising steadfastness.

The question now is how steadfast it will continue to be, for the end of these memoirs coincides with the United States's entering a critical period when the quality of men aspiring to leadership is declining, the terms of competition with the rest of the world are increasingly less favorable and the distribution of power in the world is cutting down American dominance. It is also a time when the new Soviet leadership is groping for a new image and new approaches to East-West relations, the once docile Japan is feeling its economic oats, and the European Economic Community and the developing world are eager to play a more influential role in the world. In this new constellation the United States will have to rely less on military power, as it did in the past, to assert itself and more on a nimbler application of diplomacy. It will require a good deal of rethinking in terms of presidential leadership and congressional attitudes, which can be remarkably generous when the country feels rich and narrow-minded and xenophobic when the American economy is under strain. If American moral authority is not what it used to be, it is because some presidents of recent vintage and leading men in Wall Street, the citadel of capitalism, violated some basic principles of moral conduct. Having been used to believing that the sky is the limit, Americans find it hard to husband their less abundant resources wisely and to focus on the essential economic and social underpinnings of power and society.

Troubled by the question whether a parallel was developing between Britain's decline and that of the United States, I asked Paul Volker shortly before he retired from the chairmanship of the Federal Reserve Board, having labored in the financial vineyards since his days as an assistant secretary of state for international affairs in the Treasury of the Kennedy administration, whether, indeed, he saw such a parallel. He said that, in his view, when the British government in the fifties could not bring itself to give up the pretense of being a world power, it was intellectually wrong, but mentally it simply could not change fast enough to do anything else. In contrast, the United States today, he said, could maintain its influence as a military, economic, and financial power in the world if it did what was intellectually right and chose those policies—and they are only too obvious—that would sustain her strength rather than weaken it. To develop these policies need not present any insurmountable mental or political problems.

The chairman of the Federal Reserve Board has come to be considered the second most powerful man in the United States because of the extent to which he and his board can influence the state of the economy. But it is still up to the president to devise policies to balance the budget or the trade deficit.

Americans and the world at large will look back to the Reagan years wondering what was real and what was make-believe, uncertain what was conjured up by his news and image managers and by Mr. Reagan's own magical appeal to a predominantly middle-class public.

Economists are likely to give the Reagan legacy poor marks. Among political scientists he may fare better, unless after all his subordinates have written their kick-and-tell books they decide that this was a phantom presidency. To political scientists, as Professor Neustadt wrote in his much quoted book, *Presidential Power,* what matters in a president is whether he brings to his job "a sense of purpose, a feel for power, and a source of confidence. . . ." And this Reagan did. In quite an uncanny way he succeeded in creating the impression, reinforced by his unpretentious self-assurance and his almost lighthearted enjoyment of being president, that he understood, whether by instinct or calculation, the uses of presidential power. In a good many ways, whether in dealing with Congress or the Soviets, he proved that he actually did possess that understanding.

At the same time his visible self-confidence was part of a performance; in reality he needed a great deal of ego-boosting. His wife Nancy, well aware of this, would say to him before he went to the Hill to deliver his State of the Union address: "Honey, remember, you're good, very good!" and afterwards she would usually ask friends such as Senator Laxalt or Ed Meese, to call the president to tell him what a success he had been. He apparently needed even more plucking up before press conferences. Mike Deaver, for example, just before the president stepped into the lions' den, would slip a piece of paper to the president's military aide to hand to the president as he braced himself for the confrontation. It was usually a last reminder of the subjects he needed to treat with the greatest circumspection. Once Deaver even called from Hong Kong, to instruct the president's secretary to hand him a note listing fifteen ways of saying "no" to any questions dealing with Ed Meese's troubles. Such care and attention, even beyond its practical value, apparently gave the president the reassurance he needed. All this does not mean that Reagan did not work hard after office hours in his private quarters or that he was not a quick study, an indispensable gift to any actor. It does indicate, however, his well-concealed insecurity and his need to lean heavily on his subordinates. One of Don Regan's biggest mistakes was to use the president's own words: "Let Reagan be Reagan."

But why was it that a man as charming, easy-going, oversupportive of his friends as Reagan, did not instill greater loyalty among his aides, who published more kiss-and-tell books while their president was still in office than had been the case under any previous administration? I put this question to quite a few of them. Explanations extended to his lack of interest in what went on in the White House beyond the Oval office, his lack of curiosity about issues beyond those few that fixedly engaged him, and his leaving the management of the presidency to others. All this added to the enormous strain on his entourage, especially on Nancy. They had to cope not only with most of his problems but also with decisions he preferred to avoid. The air controllers' strike was one of the few occasions that aroused his own passionate interest and engaged his full attention. He rarely displayed the kind of emotional dedication that would have fired their own commitment to his goals. Nor did he care about establishing a close and warm relationship with anybody but his wife. He was not inclined, for instance, to shoot the breeze with his aides over a drink, putting his feet up after office hours. He rarely let his hair down. Not surprisingly, he was even more reserved, more guarded, with people outside that circle. On the two or three occasions when I had an opportunity to talk with him, any truly searching questions brought down an invisible curtain and a glazing-over of his eyes. I could almost hear the turning of the key as it locked that inner door behind which he hides away. Another reason for the unusual crop of "insider" books, it was suggested to me, was the stoic and unruffled way in which the president took them on the chin—except for Regan's, whose poisoned arrows were aimed at Nancy. And of course, there was the no-less-than-usual eagerness of men who wanted to exploit their privileged position while it could still turn a buck.

The historians will probably agree that the "Reagan revolution," as his program was called, was more a psychological happening than a historic turning-point. Nevertheless, he forced the Democrats into curtailing their demands for welfare spending by brandishing his budget deficit, thus depriving them of their role as the party of social progress; and he gave the judiciary, including the Supreme Court, a more conservative direction. But he did not radicalize the Republican party as its hard-Right had hoped he would. And he surprised it by seeking a rapprochement with the Soviet Union. His reckless, almost childish belief in the uses of covert operations as an instrument of policy, passionately encouraged by his even more reckless director of the Central Intelligence Agency, William Casey, led to pitfalls in Central America and Iran, but if his concrete achievements in arms control and in improving Soviet-American relations progress beyond his presidential stewardship, they will ensure him a significant place in history. It is an unexpected irony for a man who came into office with a deep-seated indifference to foreign policy born of his lack of knowledge and experience; for one who, at times, looked not simply like an emperor without clothes, but like clothes without an emperor. Still, he proved that you can become a popular president if you offer the nation simply stated macro-goals, such as making the country or the world a better place to live (with low unemployment, low inflation, lower taxes, no involvement in war), and if you also have an intuitive sense for the uses of power, an instinctive feel for the mystique of a monarch, an actor's training in the use of television. And if you also possess a shrewdness for using "the policies of Washington to change the politics of Washington," as Professor Charles Jones of the University of Virginia put it, to overcome an extraordinary number of political setbacks and a surfeit of managerial and idiosyncratic flaws.

But if Americans want to reverse the current decline and keep ahead in this technological age, Reagan's successor, whoever he may be, will have to shift education, research, and efficient management into higher gear. With their strategies changed by arms control agreements, the military will have to revise their plans, adopt a more discriminating deterrence policy, and pay more attention to the dangers of Third World countries acquiring advanced weaponry. I would also advise the president not to underrate the mutual usefulness of the presence of American troops in Europe to the special relationship with the NATO allies, for without them the United States would soon lose its superpower status. The kind of unilateralism President Reagan sometimes engaged in—the Reykjavik summit was perhaps the worst example—could have a devastating effect. So also might such passionate insistence as his on building castles in space, which could only weaken the credibility of the American commitment to the defense of Western Europe. Still, even with the American Century in relative decline, I have every sympathy with my seventeen-year-old daughter Fiona's belief that her future lies with the opportunities offered in the United States.

When Britain joined the Common Market, I wondered for a while whether this would lead my editor's interests to shift away from what was happening in the United States. But they never flagged. Too much depended on American politics, policies, and events. In addition, the political, economic, religious, ecological, philosophical, even psychological interests of Americans are in constant flux. Social changes provoked in many ways an even greater fascination around the world than political ones. The impact of technological progress on our lives, the speed of communications, explorations in space, consumerism, the drug crisis, student revolts, rock culture, the rise of feminism, the decline of welfarism, the eclipse of the Eastern Establishment, the failure of liberalism to offer answers to new problems, the credit-card currency, supermarkets, fast foods—all these manifestations of the perpetual turmoil of US society became also part of the American cultural stampede that galloped around the world. One of the problems I faced virtually every week was to decide what not to write about; there was too much good copy around. To watch presidents struggling to create some sort of a consensus out of this pluralistic society under the divisive rules of the American Constitution was an unending and suspenseful drama. And time brought changes to the national psyche: increased sensitivity to the ironies and tragedies of life, the discovery that a compulsion to succeed and to win was not of itself a guarantee of success, the shrinkage of preeminence, the growing self-absorption, the decline in the quality of those seeking public office, the growing lack of a sense of responsibility leading to abuse of public trust for self-interest. But the bottom line of reporting from Washington remained the same: How was it affecting the rest of the world? Anybody reading this memoir will understand why I do not regret a single day I spent in the Washington ringside seat. There to rub shoulders with "princes," to use Walter Lippmann's expression, was easy by comparison to other major capitals—indeed, it was virtually unavoidable. But in a government of so many voices, to do so was essential for a reporter who wanted to do his own research and not simply rely on reports by the American news media. What mattered under those circumstances was not the lack of "air space" between the "princes" and the reporter, but the reporter's resolve to maintain his independence and integrity, and to criticize when necessary without regard to whether or not "special relationships" will be at stake.

Reliving the past for these memoirs, I realized anew how enjoyable, rewarding, often tantalizing were my special relationships and what an absorbing and exhilarating experience it was to live through the triumphs and tragedies of the Pax Americana.

BIBLIOGRAPHY

Acheson, Dean. *Present at the Creation.* New York: W. W. Norton & Company, 1969.

Ambrose, Stephen E., *Eisenhower: President and Elder Statesman 1952–1969.* New York: Simon and Schuster, 1984.

Ball, George W. *The Past Has Another Pattern.* New York: W. W. Norton & Company, 1982.

Bells, Richard K. *Nuclear Blackmail and Nuclear Balance.* Washington, D.C.: The Brookings Institution, 1987.

Berlin, Isaiah. *Personal Impressions.* London: The Hogarth Press, 1980.

Boorstin, Daniel J. *The Image.* New York: Atheneum, 1961.

Brandon, Henry. *As We Are.* New York: Doubleday & Company, 1961.

———. *In the Red: The Struggle for Sterling.* London: Andre Deutsch, 1966.

———. *The Retreat of American Power.* New York: Doubleday & Company, 1973.

Bryce, James. *The American Commonwealth.* 2 vols. New York G. P. Putnam's Sons, 1959.

Brzezinski, Zbigniew. *Power and Principle.* New York: Farrar, Straus & Giroux, 1983.

Burns, James McGregor. *Leadership.* New York: Harper & Row, 1978.

Calleo, David P. *The Imperious Economy.* Cambridge, Mass.: Harvard University Press, 1982.

Carter, Jimmy. *Keeping Faith.* New York: Bantam Books, 1982.

Caute, David. *The Great Fear.* New York: Simon and Schuster, 1978.

Chubb, John E., and Paul E. Peterson. *The New Direction in American Politics.* Washington, D.C.: The Brookings Institution, 1985.

Church, F. Forrester. *Father & Son.* New York: Harper & Row, 1985.

Clark, William. *Less Than Kin.* London: Hamish Hamilton, 1957.

Colville, John. *The Fringes of Power: Downing Street Diaries 1939–1955.* London: Hodder & Stoughton Ltd, 1985.

Cyr, Arthur. *British Foreign Policy and the Atlantic Area.* London: Macmillan, 1979.

Donovan, Robert J. *Tumultuous Years.* New York: W. W. Norton & Company, 1967.

Eden, Anthony. *The Memoirs of Anthony Eden: Full Circle,* Boston: Houghton Mifflin Company, 1960.

Ehrlichman, John. *Witness to Power.* New York: Simon and Schuster, 1982.

Eisenhower, David. *Eisenhower: At War 1943–1945.* New York: Vintage Books, 1987.

Ford, Gerald. *A Time to Heal.* New York: Harper & Row, 1979.

Foreign Relations of the United States, 1952–1954, Korea, Part One. Department of State, Washington, D.C., 1984.

Fox, Richard. *Reinhold Niebuhr: A Biography.* New York: Pantheon, 1955.

Garthoff, Raymond L. *Détente and Confrontation.* Washington, D.C.: The Brookings Institution, 1985.

———. *Intelligence Assessment and Policy Making: A Decision Point in the Kennedy Administration.* Washington, D.C.: The Brookings Institution, 1984.

Gati, Toby Trister. *The United States, the United Nations and the Management of Global Change.* New York: New York University Press, 1983.

Greenstein, Fred I. *The Hidden Hand Presidency.* New York: Basic Books, 1982.

Haig, Alexander M., Jr. *Caveat.* New York: Macmillan, 1984.

Halberstam, David. *The Best and the Brightest.* New York: Random House, 1969.

Harriman, W. Averell, and Eli Abel. *Special Envoy to Churchill and Stalin 1941–1946.* New York: Random House, 1975.

Harris, Kenneth. *Attlee.* New York: Weidenfeld & Nicolson, 1982.

Henderson, Nicholas. *The Birth of NATO.* Boulder, CO: Westview Press, 1983.

———. *The Private Office.* New York: Weidenfeld & Nicolson, 1984.

Hersh, Seymour. *The Price of Power.* New York: Summit Books, 1983.

Hewitt, Ed A. *Reforming the Soviet Economy.* Washington, D.C.: The Brookings Institution, 1987.

Hodgson, Godfrey. *America in Our Time: From World War II to Nixon.* New York: Vintage Books, 1976.

Hoffmann, Stanley. *Primacy or World Order.* New York: McGraw-Hill Book Co, 1978.

Hoopes, Townsend. *The Devil and John Foster Dulles.* Boston: Little, Brown & Company, 1973.

Jenkins, Roy. *Afternoon on the Potomac?.* New Haven, CT: Yale University Press, 1972.

Johnson, Lyndon Baines. *The Vantage Point.* New York: Holt, Rinehart & Winston, 1971.

Karnow, Stanley. *Vietnam.* New York: The Viking Press, 1983.

Kennan, George F. *American Diplomacy 1900–1950.* Chicago: The University of Chicago Press, 1951.

———. *Memoirs 1925–1950* (Vol. I). Boston: Little, Brown & Company, 1967.

Kennedy, Robert. *Thirteen Days.* New York: W.W. Norton, 1969.

Kissinger, Henry. *The White House Years.* Boston: Little, Brown & Company, 1979.

———. *Years of Upheaval.* Boston: Little, Brown & Company, 1982.

Link, Arthur S. *American Epoch.* New York: Alfred A. Knopf, 1955.

Lippmann, Walter. *Public Philosopher, Selected Letters of Walter Lippmann,* New York: Ticknor & Fields, 1985.

Lloyd, Selwyn. *Suez 1956.* New York: Mayflower Books, Inc, 1978.

Longford, Frank. *Eleven at No. 10.* London: Harrap Ltd., 1984.

McLellan, David S. *Dean Acheson: The State Department Years.* New York: Dodd, Mead & Company, 1976.

McLellan, David S. and David C. Acheson. *Among Friends: Personal Letters of Dean Acheson.* New York: Dodd, Mead & Company, 1980.

Macmillan, Harold. *Riding the Storm 1956–1959.* New York: Harper & Row, 1971.

Margach, James. *The Abuse of Power.* London: W. H. Allen, 1978.

Martin, John Barlow. *Adlai Stevenson and the World.* New York: Doubleday & Company, 1977.

Mee, Charles L., Jr. *Meetings at Potsdam.* New York: M. Evans & Company, Inc., 1975.

Miller, Merle. *Lyndon: An Oral Biography.* New York: G. P. Putnam's Sons, 1980.

Neff, Donald. *Warriors at Suez.* New York: The Linden Press, 1981.

Neustadt, Richard E. *Alliance Politics.* New York: Columbia University Press, 1970.

———. *Thinking in Time.* New York: Free Press, 1986.

Nicolson, Harold. *Harold Nicolson Diaries and Letters 1930–1974.* London: Hodder & Stoughton Ltd, 1985.

Nixon, Richard. *The Memoirs of Richard Nixon.* New York: Grosset & Dunlap, 1978.

Parsons, Anthony. *The Pride and the Fall, Iran 1974–1979.* New York: Jonathan Cape, 1984.

Powers, Thomas. *The Man Who Kept the Secrets.* New York: Alfred A. Knopf, 1979.

Quandt, William B. *Camp David, Peacemaking and Politics.* Washington, D.C.: The Brookings Institution, 1986.

Ranelagh, John. *The Agency: The Rise and Decline of the CIA.* New York: Simon and Schuster, 1986.

Reedy, George E. *The Presidency in Flux.* New York: Columbia University Press, 1973.

Reichley, A. James. *Conservatives in an Age of Change.* Washington, D.C.: The Brookings Institution, 1981.

Rivlin, Alice M. *Economic Choices 1984.* Washington, D.C.: The Brookings Institution, 1984.

Rothwell, Victor. *Britain and the Cold War 1941–1947.* London: Jonathan Cape, 1982.

Safire, William. *Before the Fall.* New York: Doubleday & Company, 1975.

Schlesinger, Arthur J., Jr. *A Thousand Days.* Boston: Houghton Mifflin Company, 1965.

Seaborg, Glenn. *Kennedy, Khrushchev, and the Test Ban.* Berkeley: University of California Press, 1981.

Senate Foreign Relations Committee, "Dr. Kissinger's Role in Wiretapping," Senate Hearings on Foreign Relations, 93rd Congress, 2nd Session, Washington, D.C.: US Government Printing Office, 1974.

Snow, Edgar. *Journey to the Beginning.* New York: Random House, 1958.

Spender, Stephen. *Stephen Spender: Journals 1939–1983,* London: Faber and Faber, 1985.

Steel, Ronald S. *Walter Lippmann and the American Century.* Boston: Little, Brown & Company, 1980.

Sundquist, James L. *Constitutional Reform and Effective Government.* Washington, D.C.: The Brookings Institution, 1986.

Talbot, Strobe. *Deadly Gambits.* New York: Alfred A. Knopf, 1984.

Trevelyan, Humphrey. *The Middle East in Revolution.* Boston: Gambit Incorporated, 1970.

Vance, Cyrus. *Hard Choices.* New York: Simon and Schuster, 1983.

West, Nigel. *The Circus: MI5 Operations 1945–1972.* Briarcliff Manor, NY: Stein & Day, 1982.

Weyden, Peter. *Bay of Pigs.* New York: Simon and Schuster, 1979.

Wilson, Edmund. *Letters on Literature and Politics 1912–1972.* New York: Farrar, Straus & Giroux, 1957.

Wilson, Harold. *The Labour Government 1964–1970.* New York: Weidenfeld & Nicolson, 1956.

INDEX